KAUAI
HANDBOOK
INCLUDING THE ISLAND OF NIIHAU

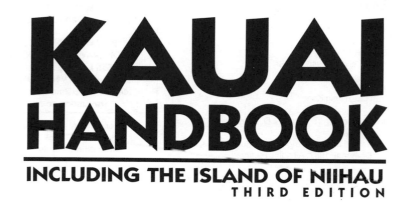

KAUAI
HANDBOOK

INCLUDING THE ISLAND OF NIIHAU
THIRD EDITION

J.D. BISIGNANI

MOON
PUBLICATIONS INC.

KAUAI HANDBOOK
INCLUDING THE ISLAND OF NIIHAU
THIRD EDITION

Published by
Moon Publications, Inc.
5855 Beaudry Street
Emeryville, California 94608, USA

Printed by
Colorcraft Ltd., Hong Kong

© Text and photographs copyright J.D. Bisignani, 1997.
All rights reserved.
© Illustrations and maps copyright Moon Publications, Inc.
and J.D. Bisignani, 1997. All rights reserved.

Some photographs and illustrations are used by permission
and are the property of the original copyright owners.

ISBN: 1-56691-091-9
ISSN: 1091-3335

Editing: Pauli Galin
Editorial Assistance: Matt Orendorff
Copyediting: Gregor Krause
Production & Design: Carey Wilson
Cartography: Chris Folks, Mike Morgenfeld
Indexing: Pauli Galin

Front cover painting: "Tropical Dawn," by Christian Riese Lassen, courtesy of Lassen International,
        Las Vegas, Nevada
All photos by J.D. Bisignani unless otherwise noted.

Distributed in the US and Canada by Publishers Group West
Printed in China

Please send all comments,
corrections, additions,
amendments, and critiques to:

**KAUAI HANDBOOK
MOON TRAVEL HANDBOOKS
5855 Beaudry Street
Emeryville, CA 94608, USA
e-mail: travel@moon.com
www.moon.com**

Printing History
1st edition — 1989
3rd edition — July 1997
5 4 3

In memory of Isabella Raco,
who led the way with love

CONTENTS

MAPS

MAP SYMBOLS

════════	Main Road	○	Town or Village	▲	Mountain
════════	Other Road	▪	Sight	∆	Campground
=========	Unpaved Road	•	Accommodation	🪨	Heiau
....	Trail	✈	Primary Airport		Water
◯	Highway Shield	✗	Secondary Airport	⚓	Swamp

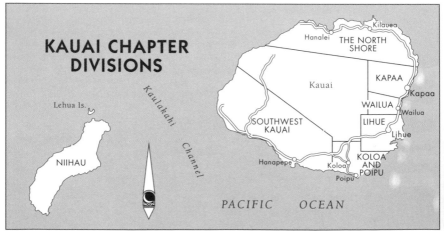

KAUAI CHAPTER DIVISIONS

CHARTS AND SPECIAL TOPICS

ABBREVIATIONS

AFB—Air Force Base
B&B—bed and breakfast
BYO—bring your own
4WD—four-wheel drive
HVB—Hawaii Visitors Bureau
NWR—National Wildlife
   Refuge

OHA—Office of Hawaiian
   Affairs
PADI—Professional
   Association of Dive
   Instructors
P.O.—post office
Rt.—route

SASE—self-addressed,
   stamped envelope
SRA—State Recreation Area
YH—Youth Hostel

IS THIS BOOK OUT OF DATE?

In today's world, things change so rapidly that it's impossible for one person to keep up with everything happening in any one place. This is particularly true in Hawaii, where situations are always in flux. Travel books are like automobiles: they require fine tuning and frequent overhauls to keep in shape. Help us keep this book in shape! We require input from our readers so that we can continue to provide the best, most current information available. Please write to let us know about any inaccuracies, new information, or misleading suggestions. Although we try to make our maps as accurate as possible, errors do occur. If you have any suggestions for improvement or places that should be included, please let us know about them.

We especially appreciate letters from female travelers, visiting expatriates, local residents, and hikers and outdoor enthusiasts. We also like hearing from experts in the field as well as from local hotel owners and individuals wishing to accommodate visitors from abroad.

As you travel through the islands, keep notes in the margins of this book. Notes written on the spot are always more accurate than those put down on paper later. If you take a photograph during your trip that you think should be included in future editions, please send it to us. Send only good slide duplicates or glossy black-and-white prints. Drawings and other artwork are also appreciated. If we use your photo or drawing, you'll be mentioned in the credits and receive a free copy of the book. Keep in mind, however, that the publisher cannot return any materials unless you include a self-addressed, stamped envelope. Moon Publications will own the rights on all material submitted. Address your letter to:

> *Kauai Handbook*
> Moon Publications
> P.O. Box 3040
> Chico, CA 95927-3040 USA
> e-mail: travel@moon.com

ACKNOWLEDGMENTS

Writing the acknowledgments for a book is supercharged with energy. It's a time when you look forward, hopefully, to a bright future for your work and reflect on all that has gone into producing it. Mostly it's a time to say thank you. Thank you for the grace necessary to carry out the task, and thank you to all the wonderful people whose efforts have helped so much along the way. To the following people, I offer my most sincere thank-you.

Firstly, to the Moon staff, professionals every one. As time has passed, and one book has followed another, they've become amazingly adept at their work, to the point where their mastery is a marvel to watch.

I would also like to thank the following people for their special help and consideration: Dr. Greg Leo, an adventurer and environmentalist who has done remarkable field research and provided me with invaluable information about the unique flora and fauna of Hawaii; Roger Rose of the Bishop Museum; Lee Wild, Hawaiian Mission Houses Museum; Marilyn Nicholson, State Foundation on Culture and the Arts; the Hawaii Visitors Bureau; Donna Jung, Donna Jung and Associates, who has shown confidence in me since day one; Haunani Vieira, Dollar Rent A Car; Keoni Wagner, Hawaiian Airlines; Jim and John Costello; Dr. Terry and Nancy Carolan; Aubrey Hawk, Bozelle Advertising; Constance Wright, Molokai Visitors Association; Barbara Schonley, of Molokai; Elisa Josephsohn, Public Relations; Faith Ogawa, for helping me keep the faith; Joyce Matsumoto, Halekulani Hotel; Bernie Caalim-Polanzi, Hilton Hotels; Nancy Daniels, Outrigger Hotels; Donn Takahashi, Regional Manager, Prince Hotels; Alvin Wong, Hawaii Prince Hotel Waikiki; Martin Kahn, Kahn Galleries; Allison Kneubuhl, Kahala Mandarin Oriental; Matt Bailey, Manele Bay Hotel; Kurt Matsumoto, Lodge at Koele; Stephanie Reid, Princeville Hotel; Margy Parker, Poipu Beach Resort Association; Yvonne Landavazo, Ritz-Carlton Kapalua; Catherine Sharpe, Stryker Weiner; Adi Kohler, Percy Higashi, and Jon Fukuda, Mauna Kea Beach Hotel and Hapuna Prince Hotel; Donna Kimura, Orchid at Mauna Lani; Denise Anderson, Hawaiian Regent; Dennis Costa, Maui Hill; Kim Marshall, Grand Wailea Resort; Sheila Donnelly, of Sheila Donnelly and Associates; Sandi Kato-Klutke, Aston Kauai Beach Villa; Barbara Sheehan, Sheraton Moana Surfrider; Aston Hotels; Norm Manzione, Suntrips; Renee Cochran and Will Titus, Colony Resorts; Linda Darling-Mann, a helpful Kauai friend; Sonia Franzel, Public Relations; Alexander Doyle, Aston Wailea Resort. To all of you, my deepest *aloha*.

BOB RACE

INTRODUCTION

Kauai is the oldest of the main Hawaiian Islands, and nature has had ample time to work sculpting Kauai into a beauty among beauties. Flowers and fruits burst from its fertile soil, but the "Garden Island" is much more than greenery and flora—it's the poetry of land itself! Its mountains have become rounded and smooth, and its streams tumbling to the sea have cut deep and wide, giving Kauai the only navigable river in Hawaii. The interior is a dramatic series of mountains, valleys, and primordial swamp. The great gouge of Waimea Canyon, called the "Grand Canyon of the Pacific," is an enchanting layer of pastels where uncountable rainbows form prismatic necklaces from which waterfalls hang like silvery pendants. The northwest is the seacliffs of Na Pali, mightiest in all of Oceania, looming 4,000 feet above the pounding surf.

After only 27 minutes by air from Honolulu (100 miles), you land just about the time you're finishing your in-flight cocktail. Everything seems quieter here, rural but upbeat, with the main town being just that, a town. The pursuit of carefree relaxation is unavoidable at five-star hotels, where you're treated like a visiting *ali'i;* or camp deep in interior valleys or along secluded beaches where reality *is* the fantasy of paradise.

Kauai is where Hollywood comes when the script calls for "paradise." The island has a dozen major films to its credit, everything from idyllic scenes in *South Pacific* to the lurking horror of Asian villages in *Uncommon Valor. King Kong* tore up this countryside in search of love, and Tattoo spotted "de plane, boss" in *Fantasy Island.* In *Blue Hawaii,* Elvis's hips mimicked the swaying palms in a famous island grove, while torrid love scenes from *The Thorn Birds* were steamier than the jungle in the background. Perhaps its greatest compliment is that Kauai is where other islanders come to look at the scenery.

AN OVERVIEW

Kauai is the most regularly shaped of all the major islands—more or less round, like a partially deflated beach ball. The puckered skin around the coast forms bays, beaches, and inlets, while the center is a no-man's-land of mountains, canyon, and swamp. Almost every-

KAUAI

Kuaehu Point
Anahola Bay
Kahala Point
Pohakuloa Point

Moloaa Bay
Kumukumu
Kealia

KAPAA BEACH
COUNTY PARK
Waipouli

LYDGATE STATE PARK

Kepuhi Point
Mokolea Point
Kilauea Point
Kilauea

HWY

Anahola

LIHUE AIRPORT
BEACH PARK

Kapaa

Kalapaki Beach
Nawiliwili
Bay
Kawai Point

KUHIO

ANINI BEACH
COUNTY PARK
Kalihiwai
Princeville
PRINCEVILLE
AIRPORT

56

581

Wailua
Hanamaulu

Niumalu

Lihue

HWY

Anahola Mountains

KEALIA
FOREST
RESERVE

Kapaia

583

580

Alakoko
Pond

Makaleha Mountains

Mt. Kualapa
(2,129 ft)

WAILUA RIVER
STATE PARK

Puhi

O'Kipu

Waita
Reservoir

LAST ERUPTION
ON KAUAI
Poipu

Hanalei
Hanalei Valley

Hanalei
River

Haena Point

Kealia Ridge

Lawai

Stream

Haenanahu
Reservoir

Omao

520

520

POIPU BEACH
COUNTY PARK

Hanalei Bay

HAENA
STATE
PARK

Lumahai
Beach

Lumahai

Wainiha

Haena
Hoena

Mt. Waialeale
(5,148 ft)

WORLD'S
WETTEST
SPOT
Mt. Kawaikini
(5,243 ft)

Alakai Swamp

LIHUE KOLOA
FOREST RESERVE

Koloa

Kukuiula

MAMALAHOA HALELEA
FOREST RESERVE

Kee Beach
Hanakapiai
Beach

NA PALI COAST STATE PARK
KALALAU STATE PARK

NUALOLO KAI STATE PARK
MILOLII STATE PARK

Makaha Point

POLIHALE
STATE PARK

Nohili Point

BARKING SANDS
PACIFIC
MISSILE RANGE

KALALAU VALLEY
LOOKOUT

NA PALI
KONA FOREST
RESERVE

KOKEE
STATE
PARK

550

Makaha Ridge

Kolo Ridge

PUU KA PELE
FOREST
RESERVE

WAIMEA
CANYON
STATE PARK

550

Mana

KAUMUALII

50

Kekaha

Kalaheo

Kauai

NA PALIKONA
FOREST
RESERVE

Kawaikoi Stream

Waialae Stream

Waimea Canyon

Kawaikoi River

Waialae River

Makaweli River

Olokele River

WAIMEA CANYON RD

RUSSIAN FORT
Pakala
(Makaweli)

Waimea

Olokele

Eleele
Hanapepe

SALT POND BEACH
COUNTY PARK

Kaumakani

Port Allen

Numile
Lawai

Koloheo

KAUMUALII HWY

50

Pu'u Ka Pele

Kaulakahi Channel

Ni'ihau

Kauai

Nihau
Oahu
Molokai
Lanai
Kahoolawe
Maui
Hawaii

Na Pali Coast

Kauai Channel

5 mi

5 km

© MOON PUBLICATIONS, INC.

one arrives at the major airport in **Lihue,** although another small strip in Princeville has limited service by commuter aircraft. Lihue is the county seat and major town with government agencies, full amenities, and a wide array of restaurants and shopping. Lihue also boasts some of the least expensive accommodations on the island, in small family-operated hotels; however, most visitors head north for Wailua/Kapa'a or Princeville, or west to the fabulous Poipu Beach area. Lihue's **Kauai Museum** is a must stop, where you'll learn the geological and social history of the island, immensely enriching your visit.

On the outskirts of town is the oldest Lutheran church in the islands and the remarkably preserved **Grove Farm Homestead,** a classic Hawaiian plantation that is so intact that all that seems to be missing are the workers. At Nawiliwili Bay you can see firsthand the Menehunes' handiwork at the **Menehune (Alakoko) Fish Pond,** still in use. Just north are the two suburbs of **Kapaia** and **Hanamaulu.** Here too you'll find shops and restaurants and the junction of Rt. 583 leading inland through miles of sugarcane fields and terminating at a breathtaking panorama of **Wailua Falls.**

East Coast
Heading northeast from Lihue along Rt. 56 takes you to **Wailua** and **Kapa'a.** En route, you pass Wailua Municipal Golf Course, beautiful, cheap, and open to the public. Wailua town is built along the Wailua River, the only navigable stream in Hawaii. At the mouth of the river are two enchanting beach parks and a temple of refuge, while upstream are more *heiau,* petroglyphs, royal birth stones, the heavily touristed yet beautiful Fern Grotto, and the Kamokila Hawaiian folk village, all within the **Wailua River State Park.** Here too are remarkable views of the river below and the cascading **Opaeka'a Waterfalls.** Heavily damaged by Hurricane Iniki, but making a comeback, Wailua's **The Coco Palms Resort** was an island institution set in the heart of the most outstanding coconut grove on Kauai. Its evening torch-lighting ceremony was the best authentic fake-Hawaii on the island.

Along Rt. 56 toward Kapa'a you pass **The Market Place,** an extensive mall that'll satisfy your every shopping need and then some. In the vicinity, a clutch of first-rate yet affordable hotels and condos line the beach. Kapa'a is a workers' town with more downhome shopping and good, inexpensive restaurants. Heading north toward Hanalei, you pass **Pohakuloa Point,** an excellent surfers' beach; **Anahola Beach Park,** where the water and camping are fine; and **Moloa'a Bay,** a secluded beach that you can have mostly to yourself.

North Coast
Before you enter **Kilauea,** the first town in the Hanalei District, unmarked side roads can lead you to secret beaches and unofficial camp spots. A small coastal road leads you to **Kilauea Lighthouse,** a beacon of safety for passing ships and for a remarkable array of birds that come to this wildlife sanctuary. **Princeville** is next, the largest planned resort in Hawaii, featuring its own airstrip. Here an entire modern village is built around superb golf courses and an exclusive deluxe resort.

Down the narrowing lane and over a single-lane, steel-strut bridge is **Hanalei.** Inland is a terraced valley planted in taro just like in the old days. Oceanside is Hanalei Bay, a safe anchorage and haven to seagoing yachts that have made it a port of call ever since Westerners began coming to Hawaii. On the outskirts is **Waioli Mission House,** a preserved home and museum dating from 1837. Then comes a string of beaches, uncrowded and safe for swimming and snorkeling. You pass through the tiny village of **Wainiha,** and then **Haena,** with the island's "last resort." In quick succession come **Haena Beach County Park,** the **wet and dry caves,** and the end of the road at **Ke'e Beach** in **Haena State Park.** Here are beach houses for those who want to get away from it all, *Kaulu Paoa Heiau* dedicated to hula, and the location where the beach scenes from *The Thorn Birds* were filmed. From here only your feet and love of adventure take you down the **Kalalau Trail** to back-to-nature camping. You pass along a narrow foot trail down the **Na Pali Coast,** skirting emerald valleys cut off from the world by impassable 4,000-foot seacliffs. All along here are *heiau,* ancient village sites, caves, lava tubes, and the romantic yet true **Valley of the Lost Tribe** just beyond trail's end.

South Coast

From Lihue west is a different story. Route 50 takes you past the **Kukui Grove Center** and then through **Puhi,** home of Kauai Community College. As the coastal **Hoary Head Mountains** slip past your window, **Queen Victoria's Profile** squints down at you. **Maluhia Road,** famous for its tunnel-like line of eucalyptus, branches off toward **Koloa,** a sugar town now rejuvenated with shops, boutiques, and restaurants. At the coast is **Poipu Beach,** the best on Kauai with its bevy of beautiful hotels and resorts.

Westward is a string of sugar towns. First is **Kalaheo,** where an island philanthropist, Walter McBride, gave the munificent land gift that has become **Kukui O Lono Park.** Here you'll find a picture-perfect Japanese garden surrounded by an excellent yet little-played golf course. West on Rt. 50 is **Hanapepe,** a good supply stop famous for its art shops and inexpensive restaurants. The road skirts the shore, passing **Olokele,** a perfect caricature of a sugar town with its neatly trimmed cottages, and **Pakala,**

an excellent surfing beach. Quickly comes **Waimea,** where Captain Cook first came ashore, and on the outskirts is the **Russian Fort,** dating from 1817, when all the world powers were present in Hawaii, jockeying to influence this Pacific gem.

In Waimea and farther westward in **Kekaha,** the road branches inland, leading along the rim of **Waimea Canyon.** This is what everyone comes to see, and none are disappointed. The wonderfully winding road serves up lookout after lookout and trail after trail. You end up at **Koke'e State Park** and the **Kalalau Valley Lookout,** where you're king of the mountain, and 4,000 feet below is your vast domain of Na Pali. Past Kekaha back on Rt. 50 is a flat stretch of desert vast enough that the military has installed **Barking Sands Pacific Missile Range.** The pavement ends and a good tourist-intimidating "cane road" takes over, leading you to the seclusion of **Polihale State Park,** where you can swim, camp, and luxuriate in privacy. If Madame Pele had had her choice, she never would have moved.

DIANA LASICH HARPER

DIANA LASICH HARPER

THE LAND

Kauai, 100 miles northwest of Oahu, is the northernmost of Hawaii's six major islands and the fourth largest. It is approximately 33 miles long and 25 miles wide at its farthest points, with an area of 554 square miles and 90 miles of coastline. The island was built by one huge volcano that became extinct about six million years ago. Mount Waialeale in central Kauai is its eastern rim, and speculation holds that Niihau, 20 miles off the west coast, was at one time connected. The volcanic "hot spot" under Kauai was sealed by the weight of the island; as Kauai drifted northward the hot spot burst through again and again, building the string of islands from Oahu to Hawaii.

A simplified but chronologically accurate account of Kauai's emergence is found in a version of the Pele myth retold in the *Kumulipo*. It depicts the fire goddess as a young, beautiful woman who visits Kauai during a hula festival and becomes enraptured with Lohiau, a handsome and mighty chief. She wants him as a husband and determines to dig a fire-pit home where they can reside in contented bliss. Unfortunately, her unrelenting and unforgiving sea-goddess sister pursues her, forcing Pele to abandon Kauai and Lohiau. Thus, she wandered and sparked volcanic eruptions on Oahu, Maui, and finally atop Kilauea Crater on Hawaii, where she now resides.

Phenomenal Features of Kauai
Located almost smack-dab in the middle of the island are **Mount Kawaikini** (5,243 feet) and adjacent **Mount Waialeale** (5,148 feet), highest points on Kauai. Mount Waialeale is an unsurpassed "rain magnet," drawing an estimated 480 inches (40 feet) of precipitation per year and earning itself the dubious distinction of being "the wettest spot on earth." Don't be intimidated—this rain is amazingly localized, with only 20 inches per year falling just 20 miles away. Visitors can now enter this mist-shrouded world aboard helicopters that fly through countless rainbows and hover above a thousand waterfalls.

Draining Waialeale is **Alakai Swamp,** a dripping sponge of earth covering about 30 square miles of trackless bog (construction of an elevated boardwalk is underway). This patch of mire contains flora and fauna found nowhere else on earth. For example, ohia trees, mighty giants of upland forests, grow here as natural bonsai that could pass as potted plants.

Bordering the Alakai Swamp on the west is **Waimea Canyon,** where eons of whipping winds, pelting rain, and the incessant grinding of streams and rivulets have chiseled the red bedrock to depths of 3,600 feet and expanses 10 miles wide. On the western slopes of Waimea Canyon is the **Na Pali coast,** a scalloped, un-

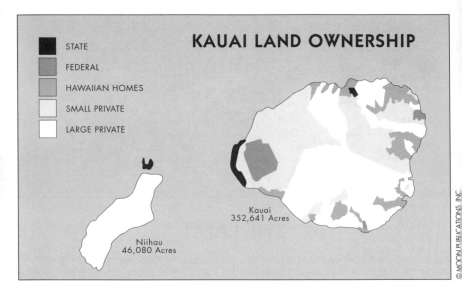

dulating vastness of valleys and *pali* forming a bulwark 4,000 feet high.

Other mountains and outcroppings around the island have formed curious natural formations. The **Hoary Head Mountains,** a diminutive range barely 2,000 feet tall south of Lihue, form a profile of Queen Victoria. A ridge just behind Wailua gives the impression of a man in repose and has been dubbed the Sleeping Giant. Another small range in the northeast, the **Anahola Mountains,** had until recently an odd series of boulders that formed "Hole in the Mountain," mythologically created when a giant hurled his spear through sheer rock. Erosion has collapsed the formation, but the tale lives on.

Land Ownership

Of Kauai's total usable land area of 398,720 acres, 62% is privately owned. Of this, almost 90% is controlled by only half a dozen or so large landholders, mainly Gay & Robinson, Amfac, Alexander & Baldwin, C. Brewer & Co., and Grove Farm. The remaining 38%, which includes a section of Hawaiian Homes land, is primarily owned by the state, and a small portion is owned by the county of Kauai and the federal government. As everywhere in Hawaii, no one owns the beaches and public access to them is guaranteed.

Channels, Lakes, and Rivers

Kauai is separated from Oahu by the **Kauai Channel.** Reaching an incredible depth of 10,900 feet and a width of 72 miles, it is by far the state's deepest and widest channel. Inland, human-made **Waita Reservoir** north of Koloa is the largest body of fresh water in Hawaii, covering 424 acres with a three-mile shoreline. The **Waimea River,** running through the floor of the canyon, is the island's longest at just under 20 miles, while the **Hanalei River** moves the greatest amount of water, emptying 150 million gallons per day into Hanalei Bay. But the **Wailua River** has the distinction of being the state's only navigable stream, although passage by boat is restricted to a scant three miles upstream. The flatlands around Kekaha were at one time Hawaii's largest body of inland water. They were brackish and drained last century when the Waimea Ditch was built to irrigate the cane fields.

Island Builders

The Hawaiians worshipped Pele, the fire goddess whose name translates equally well as "volcano," "fire pit," and "eruption of lava." Pele spit fire and spewed lava that cooled and formed islands, which in turn attracted billions of polyps whose

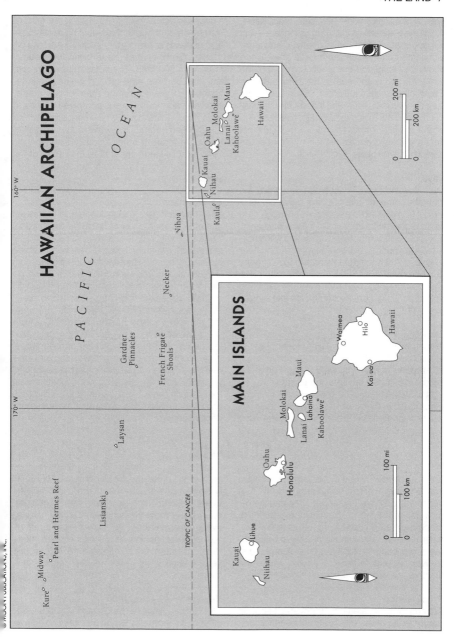

HAWAIIAN ARCHIPELAGO

PACIFIC

OCEAN

Kure○

Midway○

○Pearl and Hermes Reef

Lisianski○

Laysan○

Gardner
Pinnacles○

French Frigate
Shoals○

Necker○

Nihoa○

Kaula○

TROPIC OF CANCER

170° W

160° W

200 mi

200 km

MAIN ISLANDS

Kauai

Niihau

Lihue○

Oahu

Honolulu○

Molokai

Lanai

Lahaina○

Kahoolawe○

Maui

Hawaii

Weimea○

Hilo○

Kai ua○

100 mi

100 km

Nihau

Kauai○

Oahu○

Molokai

Lanai○

Kahoolawe

Maui

Hawaii

skeletal remains cemented into coral reefs. Kauai, like all the Hawaiian islands, is in essence a shield volcano that erupted rather gently, creating an elongated dome much like a turtle shell. Once above sea level, the tremendous weight of the newly formed island sealed the fissure below. Eventually the giant tube that carried lava to the surface sank in on itself, and the island stabilized. Wind and water took over and relentlessly sculpted the raw lava into deep crevices and cuts that became valleys, as evidenced by Koke'e, the "Grand Canyon of the Pacific."

Lava
Lava flows in two distinct types, for which the Hawaiian names have become universal geological terms: *a'a* and *pa'hoehoe*. Although easily distinguishable, chemically they're the same. *A'a* is extremely rough and spiny and will quickly tear up your shoes if you do much hiking over it. Also, if you have the misfortune to fall down, you'll immediately know why they call it *a'a*. *Pa'hoehoe,* a billowy, ropey lava resembling spilled pancake batter, often molds into fantastic shapes.

Tsunami
"Tsunami" is the Japanese word for tidal wave, a phenomenon that causes horror in most human beings. But if you were to count up all the people in Hawaii who have been swept away by tidal waves in the last 50 years, the toll wouldn't come close to those killed on bicycles in only a few Mainland cities in just five years. A Hawaiian tsunami is actually a seismic sea wave generated by an earthquake that could have originated thousands of miles away in South America or Alaska. Some waves have been clocked at more than 500 mph. The safest place during a tsunami, besides high ground well away from beach areas, is out on the open ocean where even an enormous wave is perceived only as a large swell. A tidal wave is only dangerous when it is opposed by land. The worst tsunami to strike Hawaii in modern times occurred on April 1, 1946. Maui's Hana coast bore the brunt with a tragic loss of many lives as entire villages were swept away.

Earthquakes
These rumblings are also a concern in Hawaii and offer a double threat because they cause tsunami. If you ever feel a tremor and are close to a beach, get as far away as fast as possible. Kauai very rarely experiences earthquakes, but, like the other islands, it has an elaborate warning system against natural disasters. You will notice loudspeakers high atop poles along many beaches and coastal areas; these warn of tsunami, hurricanes, and earthquakes. The loudspeakers are tested at 11 a.m. on the first working day of each month. All island telephone books contain a civil defense warning and procedures section with which you should acquaint yourself—note the maps showing which areas traditionally have been inundated by tsunami and what procedures to follow in case an emergency occurs.

CLIMATE

Kauai's climate will make you happy. Along the coastline the average temperature is 80° F in spring and summer and about 75 during the remainder of the year. The warmest areas are along the south coast from Lihue westward, where the mercury can hit the 90s in midsummer. To escape the heat any time of year, head for Koke'e, atop Waimea Canyon, where the weather is always moderate.

Precipitation
Although Mt. Waialeale is "the wettest spot on earth," in the areas most interesting to visitors, rain is not a problem. The driest section of Kauai is the southwestern desert, from Polihale to Poipu Beach, which gets from five inches per year up to a mere 20 inches around the resorts. Lihue receives about 30 inches. As you head northeast toward Hanalei, rainfall becomes more frequent but is still a tolerable 45 inches per year. Cloudbursts in winter are frequent but short-lived.

Hurricanes Iwa and Iniki
The Garden Island is much more than just another pretty face—the island and its people have

TEMPERATURE AND RAINFALL

TOWN		JAN.	MARCH	MAY	JUNE	SEPT.	NOV.
Hanapepe	high	79	80	81	84	82	80
	low	60	60	61	65	62	61
	rain	5	2	0	0	2	3
Lihue	high	79	79	79	82	82	80
	low	60	60	65	70	68	65
	rain	5	3	2	2	5	5
Kilauea	high	79	79	80	82	82	80
	low	62	64	66	68	69	65
	rain	5	5	3	3	1	5

Note: Temperature is in degrees Fahrenheit; rainfall is in inches.

integrity. Thanksgiving was not a very nice time on Kauai back in November 1982. Along with the stuffing and cranberries came an unwelcome guest who showed no *aloha,* Hurricane Iwa. What made this rude 80-mph party crasher so unforgettable was that she was only the fourth such storm to come ashore on Hawaii since records have been kept and the first since the late 1950s. All told, Iwa caused $200 million dollars' worth of damage. A few beaches were washed away, perhaps forever, and great destruction was suffered by beach homes and resorts, especially around Poipu. Thankfully, no lives were lost. The people of Kauai rolled up their sleeves and set about rebuilding. In short order, the island recovered, and most residents thought "that was that."

Unfortunately, on Friday, September 11, 1992, **Hurricane Iniki** with unimaginable ferocity ripped ashore with top wind speeds of 175 mph and slapped Kauai around like the moll in a Bogart movie. "Iniki" has two meanings in Hawaiian: "piercing winds" and "pangs of love," both devastatingly painful in their own way. The hurricane virtually flattened or tore to shreds everything in its path. No one was immune from the savage typhoon. Renowned director Steven Spielberg and his cast, including Laura Dern, Jeff Goldblum, Richard Attenborough, and Sam Neill, were on the island filming scenes for the blockbuster *Jurassic Park.* They, along with other guests, bellmen, maids, groundskeepers, and cooks, rode out the storm huddled in the ballroom of the Westin Kauai Lagoons, which

has still not recovered. Afterward, Mayor JoAnn Yukimura and her staff worked day and night from her office in Lihue, which had no roof. Hanalei taro farmers opened their humble doors to homeless neighbors and strangers alike, while a general manager of a luxury resort on the eve of his wedding pleaded with invited guests to give donations to various charitable organizations in lieu of gifts. There was hardly a structure on the entire island that wasn't damaged to one extent or another. Proud yachts were thrown like toy boats into a jangled heap; cars were buried whole in the red earth; a full third of Kauai's 20,000 homes were broken into splinters; and 4,200 hotel rooms became a tangled heap of steel and jagged glass. By the grace of God, and because of a very competent warning system, only two lives were lost and fewer than 100 people had to be admitted to the hospital due to injury. Psychologically, however, many people who lost everything were scared; special counseling services were set up to offer techniques to deal with the stress and sense of loss. Insurance companies were stressed to the breaking point, with some very slow to pay. Locals checked their policies and prayed desperately they wouldn't be "HIG-positive" (Hawaii Insurance Group), a popular island-based insurance company that literally went broke trying to pay all of the claims brought against it.

Estimates are still coming in, but *Business Trends,* a financial report published by the Bank of Hawaii, estimates that the state suffered 1.6 billion dollars' worth of damage and that Kauai ac-

*the destruction of
Hurricane Iniki*

counted for $1.58 billion of this total—a full eight times the amount of damage caused by Hurricane Iwa. Undaunted and with a pride and a will that far surpassed the fury of the storm, Kauai's inhabitants began rebuilding, while nature took care of the rest. Some philosophical souls hold that Kauai wasn't hurt at all, that only a bunch of buildings were destroyed. They contend that in her millions of years of existence, Kauai has been through many storms, and Hurricane Iniki was merely a "$1.5 billion pruning . . . for free." Trees were twisted from the ground and bushes were flattened, but Kauai is strong and fertile and the damage was only temporary. Now, Iniki is mostly a memory; Kauai has emerged a touch more self-assured and as beautiful as ever.

DIANA LASICH HARPER

FLORA AND FAUNA

Anyone who loves a mystery will be intrigued by the speculation about how plants and animals first came to Hawaii. Most people's idea of an island paradise includes swaying palms, dense mysterious jungles ablaze with wildflowers, and luscious fruits just waiting to be plucked. In fact, for millions of years the Hawaiian chain consisted of raw and barren islands where no plants grew and no birds sang. Why? Because they are geological orphans that spontaneously popped up in the middle of the Pacific Ocean. The islands, more than 2,000 miles from any continental landfall, were therefore isolated from the normal ecological spread of plants and animals. Even the most tenacious travelers of the flora and fauna kingdoms would be sorely tried in crossing the mighty Pacific. Those that made it by pure chance found a totally foreign ecosystem. They had to adapt or perish. The survivors evolved quickly, and many plants and birds became so specialized that they were limited not only to specific islands in the chain but to habitats that frequently encompassed only a single isolated valley. It was as if after traveling so far, and finding a niche, they never budged again. Luckily, the soil of Hawaii was virgin and rich, the competition from other plants or animals was nonexistent, and the climate was sufficiently varied and nearly perfect for most growing things.

The evolution of plants and animals on the isolated islands was astonishingly rapid. A tremendous change in environment, coupled with a limited gene pool, accelerated natural selection. For example, many plants lost their protective thorns and spines because there were no grazing animals or birds to destroy them. Before settlement, Hawaii had no fruits, vegetables, coconut palms, conifers, mangroves, or banyans. Tropical flowers, wild and vibrant as we know them today, were relatively few. In a land where thousands of orchids now brighten every corner, there were only four native varieties, the least in any of the 50 states. Today, the indigenous plants and animals have the highest rate of extinction anywhere on earth. By the beginning of this century, native plants growing below 1,500 feet in elevation were almost completely extinct or totally replaced by introduced species. The land and its living things have been greatly transformed by humans and their agriculture. This inexorable process began when Hawaii was the domain of its original Polynesian settlers, then greatly accelerated when the land was inundated by Western peoples.

The indigenous plants and birds of Kauai have suffered the same fate as those of the other Hawaiian islands; they're among the most endangered species on earth and disappear-

BOTANICAL GARDENS OF KAUAI

For those interested in the flora of Kauai, beyond what can be seen out of the car window, a visit to the following will be both educational and inspiring.

Koke'e Natural History Museum, tel. (808) 335-9975, just past the Koke'e State Park Headquarters, has exhibits explaining the geology and plant and animal life of the park and the surrounding upper mountain and swamp regions of the island. It is free and open daily 10 a.m.-4 p.m.

Pacific Tropical Botanical Garden, in Lawai, tel. (808) 332-7361, is the only research facility for tropical plants in the country and the premier botanical garden on Kauai (see "Lawai" in the Southwest Kauai chapter for complete details). Lasting about two and a half hours, tours are given twice daily during the week and once a day on weekends. The visitor center/museum/gift shop is open daily 7:30 a.m.-4 p.m. for walk-in visitors. You can take a short self-guided tour of the plants around this building (map provided), but to go into the gardens you need reservations in advance.

Olu Pua Gardens, formerly the manager's estate of the Kauai Pineapple Plantation, is found in nearby Kalaheo. The gardens are open to the public for a limited time daily at 9:30 a.m., 11:30 a.m., and 1:30 p.m. The 12.5-acre site includes *kau kau,* hibiscus, palm, and jungle gardens, as well as a front lawn of flowering shade trees. Reservations may be made by calling (808) 332-8182 (see "Kalaheo" in the Southwest Kauai chapter).

Kiahuna Plantation Gardens, tel. (808) 742-6411, are located at the Kiahuna Plantation Resort in Poipu. Over a 27-year period during the mid-1900s, five acres of this former plantation site were cultivated with about 2,500 plants from Africa, the Americas, the Pacific, and India, and include cactus and aloe sections. Open daily during daylight hours, free guided tours of the property are given weekdays at 10 a.m. (See "Poipu" in the Poipu and Koloa chapter for more.)

Smith's Tropical Paradise, tel. (808) 822-4654, a finely manicured and well-kept botanical and cultural garden with a bountiful, beautiful collection of ordinary and exotic plants (many labeled), is on 30 riverfront acres adjacent to the Wailua marina. Have a look here before heading upcountry. Open until 4:30 p.m. (see "Sights" in the Wailua chapter).

Limahuli Botanical Garden, tel. (808) 826-1053, on Kauai's extreme North Shore in the last valley before the beginning of the Kalalau Trail, open Tues.-Fri. and again on Sunday 9:30 a.m.-3 p.m., showcases tropical plants both ancient and modern. Part of the National Tropical Botanical Gardens, the 15 original acres were donated by Juliet Rice Wichman in 1976, and an additional 990-acre preserve was donated by her grandson, Chipper Wichman, the garden's curator, in 1994. There are both a self-guided ($10) and guided ($15) walking tours of the gardens. As you walk through this enchanted area following a three-quarter-mile loop trail, you'll pass patches of taro plants introduced to Hawaii by early Polynesians, living specimens of endangered native species, and post-contact tropicals, all while enjoying listening to the legends of the valley. For anyone planning a hiking trip into the interior, or for those who just love the living beauty of plants and flowers, a trip to Limahuli Botanical Garden is well worth the effort.

ing at an alarming rate. There are some sanctuaries on Kauai where native species still live, but they must be vigorously protected. Do your bit to save them; enjoy, but do not disturb.

PLANTS, FLOWERS, AND TREES

Hawaii's indigenous plants, flowers, and trees are fascinating and beautiful, but unfortunately, like everything else native, they are quickly disappearing. The majority of flora considered exotic by visitors was introduced either by the original Polynesians or by later white settlers. The Polynesians who colonized Hawaii brought foodstuffs including coconuts, bananas, taro, breadfruit, sweet potatoes, yams, and sugarcane. They also carried along gourds to use as containers, *awa* to make a basic intoxicant, and the ti plant to use for offerings or to string into hula skirts. Non-Hawaiian settlers over the years have brought mangos, papayas, passion fruit, pineapples, and the other tropical fruits and vegetables associated with the islands. Also, most of the flowers, including protea, plumeria, anthuriums, orchids, heliconia, ginger, and most hibiscus, have come from every continent on earth. Tropical America, Asia, Java, India, and China have contributed their most beautiful and delicate blooms. Hawaii is blessed with national and state parks, gardens, undisturbed rainforests, private reserves, and commercial nurseries that offer an exhaustive botanical survey of the island. The following is a sampling of the common native and introduced flora that add dazzling color and exotic tastes to the landscape.

Native Trees

Koa and ohia are two indigenous trees still seen on Kauai. The **koa,** a form of acacia, is Hawaii's finest native tree. It can grow to over 70 feet high and has a strong, straight trunk that can measure more than 10 feet in circumference. Koa is a quickly growing legume that fixes nitrogen in the soil. It is believed that the tree originated in Africa then migrated to Australia, where dry conditions caused the elimination of leaves. When koa came to the Pacific islands, instead of reverting to the true leaf, it just broadened its leaf stem into sickle-shaped, leaflike foliage that produces an inconspicuous, pale yellow flower. When the tree is young or damaged it will revert to the original feathery, fernlike leaf that evolved

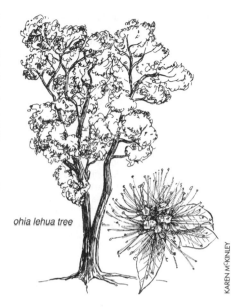

ohia lehua tree

KAREN M^cKINLEY

in Africa millions of years ago. Koa does best in well-drained soil in deep forest areas, but scruffy specimens will grow in poorer soil. The Hawaiians used koa as the main log for their dugout canoes, and elaborate ceremonies were performed when a log was cut and dragged to a canoe shed. Koa wood was also preferred for paddles, spears, and even surfboards. Today it is still, unfortunately, considered an excellent furniture wood; although fine specimens can be found in the reserve of Hawaii Volcanoes National Park on the Big Island, loggers elsewhere are harvesting the last of the big trees.

The **ohia** is a survivor and therefore the most abundant of all the native Hawaiian trees. Coming in a variety of shapes and sizes, it grows as miniature trees in wet bogs or 100-foot giants on cool, dark slopes at higher elevations. This tree is often the first life in new lava flows. The ohia produces a tuftlike flower—usually red, but occasionally orange, yellow, or white, the latter being very rare and elusive—that resembles a natural pompon. The flower was considered sacred to Pele; it was said that she would cause a rainstorm if you picked ohia blossoms without the proper prayers. The flowers

koa tree

were fashioned into lei that resembled feather boas. The strong, hard wood was used to make canoes, poi bowls, and especially temple images. Ohia logs were also used as railroad ties and shipped to the Mainland from Pahoa on the Big Island. It's believed that the "golden spike" linking rail lines between the U.S. East and West Coasts was driven into a Puna ohia log when the two railroads came together in Ogden, Utah.

Lobelia
More species of lobelia grow in Hawaii than anywhere else in the world. A common garden flower elsewhere, in Hawaii it grows to tree height. You'll see some unique species covered with hair or spikes. The lobelia flower is tiny and resembles a miniature orchid with curved and pointed ends, like the beak of the native *i'iwi*. This bird feeds on the flower's nectar; it's obvious that both evolved in Hawaii together and exhibit the phenomenon of nature mimicking nature.

Tropical Rainforests
When it comes to pure and diverse natural beauty, the U.S. is one of the finest pieces of real estate on earth. As if purple mountains' majesty and fruited plains weren't enough, it even received a tiny, living emerald of tropical rainforest. A tropical rainforest is where the earth itself takes a breath and exhales pure sweet oxygen through its vibrant, living green canopy. Though these forests—located in the territories of Puerto Rico and the Virgin Islands and in the state of Hawaii—make up only one-half of one percent of the world's total, they must be preserved. The U.S. Congress passed two bills in 1986 designed to protect the unique biological diversity of the nation's tropical areas, but their destruction has continued unabated. The lowland rainforests of Hawaii, populated mostly by native ohia, are being razed. Landowners slash, burn, and bulldoze them to create more land for cattle, agriculture, and, most distressingly, for wood chips to generate electricity! Introduced wild boar gouge the forest floor, exposing sensitive roots and leaving tiny fetid ponds where mosquito larvae thrive. Feral goats roam the forests like hoofed locusts and strip all vegetation within reach. More than half of the birds classified in the U.S. as endangered live in Hawaii, and almost all of these make their homes in the rainforests.

BIRDS

One of the great tragedies of natural history is the continuing demise of Hawaiian birdlife. Perhaps only 15 original species of birds remain of the more than 70 native families that thrived before the coming of humans. Experts believe that the ancient Hawaiians annihilated about 40 species, including seven species of geese, a rare one-legged owl, ibis, lovebirds, sea eagles, and hunting creepers. Since the arrival of Captain Cook in 1778, 23 species have become extinct, with 31 more in danger. Hawaii's endangered birds account for more than 50% of the birds listed in the U.S. Sport Fisheries and Wildlife's *Red Book,* which lists rare and endangered animals. In the last 200 years, more than four times as many birds have become extinct in Hawaii as in all of North America. These figures unfortunately suggest that a full 40% of Hawaii's endemic birds no longer exist. Almost all of Oahu's native birds are gone and few indigenous Hawaiian birds can be found on any island below the 3,000-foot level.

Native birds have been reduced in number because of multiple factors. The original Polynesians helped wipe out many species. They altered large areas for farming and burned off patches of pristine forests. Also, bird feathers were highly prized for the making of lei, for featherwork in capes and helmets, and for the large *kahili* fans that indicated rank among the *ali'i.* Introduced exotic birds and the new diseases they carried are another major reason for reduction of native bird numbers, along with predation by the mongoose and rat—especially upon ground-nesting birds. Bird malaria and bird pox were also devastating to the native species. Mosquitoes—unknown in Hawaii until a ship named the *Wellington* introduced them at Lahaina in 1826 through larvae carried in its water barrels—helped to spread infection in most native birds, causing a rapid reduction in birdlife. Feral pigs rooting deep in the rainforests knock over ferns and small trees, creating fetid pools in which mosquito larvae thrive. However, the most damaging factor by far is the assault upon native forests by agriculture and land developers. The vast majority of Hawaiian birds evolved into specialists. They lived in only one small area and ate a very limited number of plants or insects; once the food sources were removed or altered, the birds soon died.

You'll spot birds all over Kauai, from the coastal areas to the high mountain slopes. Some are found on other islands as well, but the indigenous ones listed below are found only or mainly on Kauai. Every bird listed is either threatened or endangered.

BOB RACE
pueo

Kauai's Sanctuaries

Kauai exceeds its reputation as the Garden Island. It has had a much longer time for soil building and rooting of a wide variety of plantlife, so it's lusher than the other islands. Lying on a main bird migratory route, lands such as the **Hanalei National Wildlife Sanctuary** have long been set aside for their benefit. Impenetrable inland regions surrounding Mt. Waialeale and dominated by the Alakai Swamp have provided a natural sanctuary for Kauai's own bird and plantlife. Because of this, Kauai is home to the largest number of indigenous birds extant in Hawaii, though even here they are tragically endangered. As on the other Hawaiian islands, a large number of birds, plants, and mammals have been introduced in the past 200 years. Most have either aggressively competed for, or simply destroyed, the habitat of indigenous species. As the newcomers gain dominance, Kauai's own flora and fauna slide inevitably toward oblivion.

Indigenous Forest Birds

Kauai's upland forests are still home to many Hawaiian birds; they're dwindling but holding on. You may be lucky enough to spot some of the following. The **Hawaiian owl** *(pueo)*, one of the friendliest *amakua* in ancient Hawaii, hunts both by day and night. It was an especially benign and helpful guardian. Old Hawaiian stories abound where a *pueo* came to the aid of warriors in distress. The warriors would head for a tree in which a *pueo* had alighted;

LOUISE FOOTE

once there, they were safe from their pursuers, under the protection of "the wings of an owl." There are many introduced barn owls in Hawaii, easily distinguished from *pueo* by their distinctive heart-shaped faces. The *pueo* is about 15 inches tall with a mixture of brown and white feathers. The eyes are large, round, and yellow, and the legs are heavily feathered, unlike a barn owl. *Pueo* chicks are a distinct yellow color.

The **elepaio** is an indigenous bird found around Koke'e and so named because its song sounds like its name. A small brown bird with white rump feathers, it's very friendly and can even be prompted to come to an observer offering food.

Found above 2,000 feet, feeding on a variety of insects and flowers, is the *i'iwi,* a bright red bird with a salmon-colored hooked bill. While most often sounding like a squeaking hinge, it can also produce a melodious song.

Anianiau is a four-inch, yellow-green bird found around Koke'e. Its demise is due to a lack of fear of man. The **nukupu'u,** extinct on the other islands except for a few on Maui, is found in Kauai's upper forests and bordering the Alakai Swamp. It's a five-inch bird with a drab green back and a bright yellow chest.

elepaio

Birds of the Alakai Swamp

The following scarce birds are some of the last indigenous Hawaiian birds, saved only by the inhospitability of the Alakai Swamp. All are endangered species and under no circumstances should they be disturbed. The last survivors include: the *o'u,* a chubby seven-inch bird with a green body, yellow head, and lovely whistle ranging over half an octave; the relatively common **Hawaiian creeper,** a hand-sized bird with a light green back and white belly, which travels in pairs and searches bark for insects; the *puaiohi,* a dark brown, white-bellied, seven-inch bird so rare that its nesting habits are unknown. The **O'o'a'a'**, although its name may resemble the sounds you make getting into a steaming hot tub, is an eight-inch black bird that played a special role in Hawaiian history. Its blazing yellow leg feathers were used to fashion the spectacular capes and helmets of the *ali'i*. Even before the white man came, this bird was ruthlessly pursued by specially trained hunters who captured it and plucked its feathers. The **akialoa** is a seven-inch, greenish-yellow bird with a long, slender, curved bill.

Seabirds and Shorebirds

Among the millions of birds that visit Kauai yearly, some of the most outstanding are its marine and water birds. Many beautiful individuals are seen at **Kilauea Point,** where they often nest in the trees on the cliff, or on **Moku'ae'ae Islet.** The **Laysan albatross** *(moli)* is a far-ranging Pacific flier whose 11-foot wingspan carries it in effortless flight. This bird has little fear of man, and while on the ground is easily approachable. It also nests along Barking Sands. The **wedge-tailed shearwater** *(ua'u kani)* is known as the "moaning bird" because of its doleful sounds. These birds have no fear of predators and often fall prey to feral dogs and cats. Also seen making spectacular dives for squid off Kilauea Point is the **red-footed booby,** a fluffy white bird with a blue bill and a three-foot wingspan. Kiting from the same cliffs are the **white-tailed tropic bird,** snow-white elegance with a three-foot wingspan and a long, wispy, kitelike tail. One of the most amazing is the **great frigate bird,** an awesome specimen with an eight-foot wingspan. Predominantly black, the males have a red throat pouch that they inflate like a balloon. These giants, the kings of the rookery, often steal food from lesser birds. They nest off Kilauea Point and are also seen along Kalalau Trail, and even at Poipu Beach.

Many of Kauai's water birds are most easily found in the marshes and ponds of **Hanalei National Wildlife Refuge,** though they have also been spotted on some of the island's reservoirs, especially **Menehune Fish Pond** in the **Huleia National Wildlife Refuge** and its vicinity. The **Hawaiian**

Hawaiian stilt

stilt *(ae'o)* is a 1.5-foot-tall wading bird with pink, sticklike legs. The **Hawaiian coot** *(alae ke'oke'o)* is a gray-black, ducklike bird with a white belly and face. The **Hawaiian gallinule** *(alae ula),* an endemic Hawaiian bird often found in Hanalei's taro patches, has a ducklike body with a red face tipped in yellow. It uses its huge chickenlike feet to hop across floating vegetation. The **Hawaiian duck** *(koloa maoli)* looks like a mallard and, because of interbreeding with common ducks, is becoming rarer as a distinctive species.

Introduced Common Birds

Kauai is rich in all manner of birds, from migratory marine birds to upland forest dwellers. Many live in areas you can visit; others you can see by taking a short stroll and remaining observant. Some, of course, are rare and very difficult to spot. Some of the most easily spotted island birds frequent almost all areas from the Kekaha Salt Ponds to Kalalau and the upland regions of Koke'e, including the blazing red **northern cardinal;** the comedic, brash **common mynah;** the operatic **Western meadowlark,** introduced in 1930 and found in Hawaii only on Kauai; the ubiquitous **Japanese white-eye;** sudden fluttering flocks of **house finches;** that Arctic traveler the **golden plover,** found along mudflats everywhere; the **cattle egret,** a white, 20-inch-tall heron found anywhere from the backs of cattle to the lids of garbage cans (introduced from Florida in 1960 to control cattle pests, they have so proliferated they are now considered a pest by some).

LAND ANIMALS

Hawaii had only two indigenous mammals, the monk seal found throughout the islands and the hoary bat found primarily on the Big Island. The remainder of Kauai's mammals are transplants. But like anything else that has been in the islands long enough (including people), they take on characteristics that make them "local."

Bats

The **Hawaiian hoary bats** *(ope'ape'a)* are cousins to Mainland bats, strong fliers that made it to Hawaii eons ago, where they developed their own species. Their tails have a whitish coloration, hence their name. They are found on Maui and Kauai, but mostly on the Big Island. They have a 13-inch wingspan and, unlike other bats, are solitary creatures, roosting in trees. They give birth to twins in early summer and can often be spotted darting over a number of bays just around sundown.

Hawaiian hoary bat

Introduced Fauna and Game Animals

One terribly destructive predator of native ground-nesting birds is the **mongoose.** Introduced to Hawaii last century as a cure for a rat infestation, the mongoose has only recently made it to Kauai, where a vigorous monitoring and extermination process is underway. Game mammals found in Kauai's forests include feral goats and pigs, although they too have caused destruction by uprooting seedlings and overgrazing shrubs and grasses. Game fowl that have successfully acclimatized include francolins, ring-necked pheasants, and an assortment of quail and dove. All are hunted at certain times of year (see "Hunting" under "Sports and Recreation" in the Out and About chapter).

One game animal found in Hawaii only on Kauai is the **black-tailed deer.** Kauai's thriving herd of 700 started as a few orphaned fawns from Oregon in 1961. These handsome animals, a species of western mule deer, are at home on the hilly slopes west of Waimea Canyon. Although there is little noticeable change in seasons in Hawaii, bucks and does continue to operate on genetically transmitted biological time clocks. The males shed their antlers during late winter months and the females give birth in spring. Hunting of blacktails is allowed only by public lottery in October.

MARINELIFE

Hawaiian Whales and Dolphins

Perhaps it's their tremendous size and graceful power, coupled with a dancer's delicacy of movement, that render whales so aesthetically and emotionally captivating. In fact, many people claim that they even feel a spirit-bond to these obviously intelligent mammals that at one time shared dry land with us and then re-evolved into creatures of the great seas. Experts often remark that whales exhibit behavior akin to the highest social virtues. For example, whales rely much more on learned behavior than on instinct, the sign of a highly evolved intelligence. Gentle mothers and protective "escort" males join to teach the young to survive. They display loyalty and bravery in times of distress, and innate gentleness and curiosity. Their "songs," especially those of the humpbacks, fascinate scientists and are considered a unique form of communication in the animal kingdom. Humpback whales migrate to Hawaii every year from November to May. Here, they winter, mate, give birth, and nurture their young until returning to food-rich northern waters in the spring. It's hoped that the human race can peacefully share the oceans with these magnificent giants forever. Then, perhaps, we will have taken the first step in saving ourselves.

The role of whales and dolphins in Hawaiian culture seems quite limited. Unlike fish, which were intimately known and individually named, only two generic names apply to whales: *kohola* (whale) and *palaoa* (sperm whale). Dolphins were all lumped together under one name, *nai'a;* Hawaiians were known to harvest dolphins on occasion by herding them onto a beach. Whale jewelry was worn by the *ali'i.* The most coveted ornament came from a sperm whale's tooth, called a *lei niho palaoa,* which was carved into one large curved pendant. Sperm whales have upward of 50 teeth, which range in size from four to 12 inches and weigh up to two pounds. One whale could provide numerous pendants. The most famous whale in Hawaiian waters is the humpback, but others often sighted include the sperm, killer, false killer, pilot, Cuvier's, Blainsville, and pygmy killer. There are technically no porpoises, but dolphins include the common, bottlenose, spinner, white-sided, broad-beaked, slender-beaked, and rough-toothed.

The mahimahi, a favorite eating fish found on many menus, is commonly referred to as a dolphin but is unrelated and is a true fish, not a cetacean.

Whalewatching

If you're in Hawaii from late November to early May, you have an excellent chance of spotting a humpback. You can often see a whale from a vantage point on land, but this is nowhere near as thrilling as seeing them close-up from a boat. Either way, binoculars are a must. Telephoto and zoom lenses are also useful, and you might even get a nifty photo in the bargain. But don't waste your film unless you have a fairly high-powered zoom: fixed-lens cameras give pictures with a lot of ocean and a tiny black speck. If you're lucky enough to see a whale breach (jump clear of the water), keep watching—they often repeat this a number of times. If a whale dives and lifts its fluke high in the air, expect it to be down for at least 15 minutes and not come up in the same spot. Other times they'll dive shallowly, then bob up and down quite often.

Coral

Whether you're an avid scuba diver or a novice snorkeler, you'll become aware of Kauai's underwater coral gardens and grottoes whenever you peer at the fantastic seascapes below the waves. Although there is plenty of it, the coral in Hawaii doesn't do as well as in other more equatorial areas because the water is too wild and not quite as warm. Coral looks like a plant fashioned from colorful stone, but it's the skeleton of tiny animals, zoophytes, which need algae in order to live. Coral grows best in water that is quite still, where the days are sunny, and where the algae can thrive. Many of Hawaii's reefs have been dying in the last 20 years, and no one seems to know why. Pesticides used in agriculture have been pointed to as a possible cause.

HISTORY

Kauai is the first of the Hawaiian Islands in many ways. Besides being the oldest main island geologically, it's believed that Kauai was the first island to be populated by Polynesian explorers. Theoretically, this colony was well established as early as A.D. 200, which predates the populating of the other islands by almost 500 years. Even Madame Pele chose Kauai as her first home and was content here until her sister drove her away. Her fires went out when she moved on, but she, like all visitors, never forgot Kauai.

THE ROAD FROM TAHITI

Until the 1820s, when New England missionaries began a phonetic rendering of the Hawaiian language, the past was kept vividly alive only by the sonorous voices of special *kahuna* who chanted the sacred *mele*. The chants were beautiful, flowing word pictures that captured the essence of every aspect of life. These *mele* praised the land *(mele aina)*, royalty *(mele ali'i)*, and life's tender aspects *(mele aloha)*. Chants were dedicated to friendship, hardship, and favorite children. Entire villages sometimes joined together to compose a *mele*—every word was chosen carefully, and the wise old *kapuna* would decide if the words were lucky or unlucky. Some *mele* were bawdy or funny on the surface but contained secret meanings, often bitingly sarcastic, that ridiculed an inept or cruel leader. The most important chants took listeners back into the dim past before people lived in Hawaii. From these genealogies *(ko'ihonua)*, the *ali'i* derived the right to rule, since these chants went back to the gods Wakea and Papa, from whom the *ali'i* were directly descended.

The *Kumulipo*

The great genealogies, finally compiled in the late 1800s by order of King Kalakaua, were collectively known as the *Kumulipo, A Hawaiian Creation Chant,* basically a Polynesian account of Genesis. Other chants related to the beginning of this world, but the *Kumulipo* sums it all up and is generally considered the best. The chant relates that after the beginning of time, there is a period of darkness. The darkness, however, mysteriously brims with spontaneous life; during this period plants and animals are born, as well as Kumulipo, the man, and Po'ele, the woman.

In the eighth chant, darkness gives way to light and the gods descend to earth. Wakea is "the sky father" and Papa is "the earth mother," whose union gives birth to the islands of Hawaii. First born is Hawaii, followed by Maui, then Kahoolawe. Apparently, Papa becomes bushed after three consecutive births and decides to vacation in Tahiti. While Papa is away recovering from postpartum depression and working on her tan, Wakea gets lonely and takes Kaula as his second wife; she bears him the island-child of Lanai. Not fully cheered up, but getting the hang of it, Wakea takes a third wife, Hina, who promptly bears the island of Molokai. Meanwhile, Papa gets wind of these shenanigans, returns from Polynesia, and retaliates by taking up with Lua, a young and virile god. She soon gives birth to the island of Oahu. Papa and Wakea finally decide that they really are meant for each other and reconcile to conceive Kauai, Niihau, Kaula, and Nihoa. These two progenitors are the source from which the *ali'i* ultimately traced their lineage, and from which they derived their god-ordained power to rule.

Basically, there are two major genealogical families: the **Nana'ulu**, who became the royal *ali'i* of Oahu and Kauai; and the **Ulu**, who provided the royalty of Maui and Hawaii. The best sources of information on Hawaiian myth and legend are Martha Beckwith's *Hawaiian Mythology* and the monumental three-volume opus *An Account of the Polynesian Race*, compiled by Abraham Fornander from 1878 to 1885. Fornander, after settling in Hawaii, married an *ali'i* from Molokai and had an illustrious career as a newspaperman, Maui circuit judge, and finally Supreme Court justice. For years Fornander sent scribes to every corner of the kingdom to listen to the elder *kapuna*. They returned with firsthand accounts, which he dutifully recorded.

Polynesians

Since prehistory, Polynesians have been seafaring people whose origins cannot be completely traced. They seem to have come from Southeast Asia, mostly through the gateway of Indonesia, and their racial strain pulls features from all three dominant races: Caucasian, Negro, and Asian. They learned to navigate on tame narrow waterways along Indonesia and New Guinea, then fanned out eastward into the

The Polynesians, attuned to every nuance in their environment, noticed that a migratory bird called the golden plover arrived from the north every year. They reasoned that since the plover was not a seabird, there must be land to the north.

great Pacific. They sailed northeast to the low islands of Micronesia and southwest to Fiji, the New Hebrides (now called Vanuatu), and New Caledonia. Fiji is regarded as the "cradle of Polynesian culture"; carbon dating places humans there as early as 3500 B.C. Many races blended on Fiji, until finally the Negroid became dominant and the Polynesians moved on. Wandering, they discovered and settled Samoa and Tonga, then ranged far east to populate Tahiti, Easter Island, and the Marquesas. Ultimately, they became the masters of the "Polynesian Triangle," which measures more than 5,000 miles on each leg, stretching across both the North and South Pacific studded with islands. The great Maori kingdom of New Zealand is the southern apex of the triangle, with Easter Island marking the point farthest east; Hawaii, the farthest north, was the last to be settled.

Migrations and Explorations

Ancient legends common throughout the South Pacific speak of a great Polynesian culture that existed on the island of Raiatea, about 150 miles north of Tahiti. In the Opoa district a powerful priesthood held sway in an enormous *heiau* called Toputapuatea. Kings from throughout Polynesia came here to worship. Human sacrifice was common, as it was believed that the essence of the spirit could be utilized and controlled in this life; therefore the mana of Toputapuatea was great. Defeated warriors and commoners were used as living rollers to drag canoes up onto the beach, while corpses were dismembered and hung in trees. The power of the priests of Opoa lasted for many generations, evoking trembling fear in even the bravest warrior just by the mention of their names. Finally, their power waned and Polynesians lost their centralized culture, but the constant coming and going from Raiatea for centuries sharpened the Polynesians' already excellent sailing skills and convinced them that the world was vast and that unlimited opportunities existed to better their lot.

Now explorers, many left to look for the "heavenly homeland to the north." Samoans called it "Savai'i"; Tongans "Hawai"; Rarotongans "Avaiki"; and Society Islanders "Havai'i." Others abandoned the small islands throughout Polynesia where population pressures exceeded the limits of natural resources, prompting famine. Furthermore, Polynesians were also very warlike among themselves; power struggles between members of a ruling family were common, as were marauders from other islands. So, driven by hunger or warfare, countless refugee Polynesians headed north. Joining them were a few who undoubtedly went for the purely human reason of wanderlust.

The Great Navigators

No one knows exactly when the first Polynesians arrived in Hawaii, but the great deliberate migrations from the southern islands seem to have taken place A.D. 500-800; anthropologists keep pushing the date backward as new evidence becomes available. Even before that, however, it's reasonable to assume that the first people to set foot on Hawaii were probably fishermen, or perhaps defeated warriors whose canoes were blown hopelessly northward into unfamiliar waters. They arrived by a combination of extraordinary good luck and an uncanny ability to sail and navigate without instruments, using the sun by day and the moon and rising stars by night. They could feel the water and determine direction by swells, tides, and currents. The movements of fish and cloud formations were also utilized to give direction. Since their arrival was probably an accident, they were unprepared to settle on the fertile but barren lands, having no stock animals, plant cuttings, or

women. Forced to return southward, undoubtedly many lost their lives at sea, but a few wild-eyed stragglers must have made it home to tell tales of a paradise to the north where land was plentiful and the sea bounteous. This is affirmed by ancient navigational chants from Tahiti, Moorea, and Bora Bora, which passing from father to son revealed how to follow the stars to the "heavenly homeland in the north." Possibly a few migrations followed, but it's known that for centuries there was no real reason for a mass exodus, so the chants alone remained and eventually became shadowy legend.

From Where They Came

It's generally agreed that the first planned migrations were from the violent cannibal islands Spanish explorers called the Marquesas, 11 islands In extreme eastern Polynesia. The islands themselves are harsh and inhospitable, breeding a toughness in these people that enabled them to withstand the hardships of long, unsure ocean voyages and years of resettlement. Marquesans were a fiercely independent people whose chiefs rose from the ranks because of bravery or intelligence. They must have also been a savage-looking lot. Both men and women tattooed themselves in complex blue patterns from head to foot. The warriors carried massive, intricately designed ironwood war clubs and wore carved whale teeth in slits in their earlobes that eventually stretched to the shoulders. They shaved the sides of their heads with sharks' teeth, tied their hair in two topknots that looked like horns, and rubbed their heavily muscled and tattooed bodies with scented coconut oils. They worshipped mummified ancestors while the bodies of warriors of defeated neighboring tribes were consumed. They were masters at building great double-hulled canoes launched from huge canoe sheds. Two hulls were fastened together to form a catamaran, and a hut in the center provided shelter in bad weather. The average voyaging canoe was 60-80 feet long and could comfortably hold an extended family of about 30 people. These small family bands carried all the staples they would need in the new lands.

The New Lands

For five centuries the Marquesans settled and lived peacefully on the new land, as if Hawaii's

POLYNESIAN TRIANGLE

HAWAII

Palmyra

Baker

Christmas

Phoenix

EQUATOR

Tokelau

Marquesas

Society

Tuamotu

Samoa

Niue

Tahiti

Tonga

Cook

Mangareva

Austral

Pitcairn

Rapa

Easter

Kermadec

NEW ZEALAND

Chatham

0   1000 mi

0   1000 km

aloha spirit overcame their fierceness. The tribes coexisted in relative harmony, especially since there was no competition for land. Cannibalism died out. There was much coming and going between Hawaii and Polynesia as new people came to settle for hundreds of years. It appears that then, in the 12th century, a deliberate exodus of warlike Tahitians arrived and subjugated the settled islanders. They came to conquer. This incursion had a terrific significance on the Hawaiian religious and social system. Oral tradition relates that a Tahitian priest, Paao, found the mana of the Hawaiian chiefs to be low, signifying that their gods were weak. Paao built a *heiau* at Wahaula on the Big Island, then introduced the warlike god Kukialimoku and the rigid *kapu* sys-

tem through which the new rulers became dominant. Voyages between Tahiti and Hawaii continued for about 100 years and Tahitian customs, legends, and language became the Hawaiian way of life. Then suddenly, for no recorded or apparent reason, the voyages discontinued and Hawaii returned to total isolation.

The islands remained forgotten for almost 500 years until the indomitable English seaman Capt. James Cook sighted Oahu on January 18, 1778, and stepped ashore at Waimea on Kauai two days later. At that time Hawaii's isolation was so complete that even the Polynesians had forgotten about it. On an earlier voyage, Tupaia, a high priest from Raiatea, had accompanied Captain Cook as he sailed throughout Polynesia. Tupaia demonstrated his vast knowledge of existing archipelagos throughout the South Pacific by naming over 130 islands and drawing a map that included the Tonga group, the Cook Islands, the Marquesas, and even tiny Pitcairn, a rock in far eastern Polynesia where the mutinous crew of the *Bounty* found solace. In mentioning the Marquesas, Tupaia said, *"He ma'a te ka'ata,"* which means "Food is man" or simply "Cannibals!" But remarkably absent from Tupaia's vast knowledge was the existence of Easter Island, New Zealand, and Hawaii.

The next waves of people to Hawaii would be white, and the Hawaiian world would be changed quickly and forever.

THE WORLD DISCOVERS HAWAII

The late 18th century was an extraordinary time in Hawaiian history. Monumental changes seemed to happen all at once. First, Captain James Cook, a Yorkshire farm boy fulfilling his destiny as the all-time greatest Pacific explorer, found Hawaii for the rest of the world. For better or worse, it could no longer be an isolated Polynesian homeland. For the first time in Hawaiian history, a charismatic leader named Kamehameha emerged, and after a long civil war he united all the islands into one centralized kingdom. The death of Captain Cook in Hawaii marked the beginning of a long series of tragic misunderstandings between whites and natives. When Kamehameha died, the old religious system of *kapu* came to an end, leaving the Hawaiians in a spiritual vortex. Many takers arrived to fill the void: missionaries after souls, whalers after their prey and a good time, traders and planters after profits and a home. The islands were opened and devoured like ripe fruit. Powerful nations, including Russia, Great Britain, France, and the United States, yearned to bring this strategic Pacific jewel under their own influence. The 19th century brought the demise of the Hawaiian people as a dominant political force in their own land and with it the end of Hawaii as a sovereign monarchy. An almost bloodless yet bitter military coup followed by a brief Hawaiian Republic ended in annexation by the United States. As the U.S. became completely entrenched politically and militarily, a new social and economic order was founded on the plantation system. Amazingly rapid population growth occurred with the importation of plantation workers from Asia and Europe, which yielded a unique cosmopolitan blend of races like nowhere else on earth. By the dawning of the 20th century, the face of old Hawaii had been altered forever; the "sacred homeland in the north" was hurled into the modern age. The attack on Pearl Harbor saw a tremendous loss of life and brought Hawaii closer to the U.S. by a baptism of blood. Finally, on August 21, 1959, after 59 years as a "territory," Hawaii officially became the 50th state of the United States.

Captain Cook Sights Hawaii

In 1776 Captain James Cook set sail for the Pacific from Plymouth, England on his third and final expedition into this still vastly unexplored region of the world. On a fruitless quest for the fabled Northwest Passage across the North American continent, he sailed down the coast of Africa, rounded the Cape of Good Hope, crossed the Indian Ocean, and traveled past New Zealand, Tasmania, and the Friendly Islands (where an unsuccessful plot was hatched by the *friendly* natives to murder him). On Jan-

Captain James Cook

uary 18, 1778, Captain Cook's 100-foot flagship HMS *Resolution* and its 90-foot companion HMS *Discovery* sighted Oahu. Two days later, they sighted Kauai and went ashore at the village of Waimea on January 20, 1778. Though eager to get on with his mission, Cook decided to make a quick sortie to investigate this new land and reprovision his ships. He did, however, take time to remark in his diary about the close resemblance of these newfound people to others he had encountered as far south as New Zealand, and marveled at their widespread habitation across the Pacific.

The first trade was some brass medals for a mackerel. Cook also stated that he had never before met natives so astonished by a ship, and that they had an amazing fascination with iron, which they called *toe,* Hawaiian for "adze." There is even some conjecture that a Spanish ship under one Captain Gaetano had landed in Hawaii as early as the 16th century, trading a few scraps of iron that the Hawaiians valued even more than the Europeans valued gold. It was also noted that the Hawaiian women gave themselves freely to the sailors with the apparent good wishes of the island men. This was actually a ploy by the *kahuna* to test if the white newcomers were gods or men—gods didn't need women. These sailors proved immediately mortal. Cook, who was also a physician, tried valiantly to keep the 66 men (out of 112) who had measurable cases of V.D. away from the women. The task proved impossible as women literally swarmed the ships; when Cook returned less than a year later, it was logged that signs of V.D. were already apparent on some natives' faces.

Cook was impressed with the Hawaiians' swimming ability and with their well-bred manners. They had happy dispositions and sticky fingers, stealing any object made of metal, especially nails. The first item stolen was a butcher's cleaver. An unidentified native grabbed it, plunged overboard, swam to shore, and waved his booty in triumph. The Hawaiians didn't seem to care for beads and were not at all impressed with a mirror. Cook provisioned his ships by trading chisels for hogs, while common sailors gleefully traded nails for sex. Landing parties were sent inland to fill casks with fresh water. On one such excursion a Mr. Williamson, who was eventually drummed out of the Royal Navy for cowardice, unnecessarily shot and killed a native. After a brief stop on Niihau, the ships sailed away, but both groups were indelibly impressed with the memory of each other.

Cook Returns

Almost a year later, when winter weather forced Cook to return from the coast of Alaska, his discovery began to take on far-reaching significance. Cook had named Hawaii the Sandwich Islands, in honor of one of his patrons, John Montague, the Earl of Sandwich. On this return voyage, he spotted Maui on November 26, 1778. After eight weeks of seeking a suitable harbor, the ships bypassed it, but not before the coastline was duly drawn by Lt. William Bligh, one of Cook's finest and most trusted officers. (Bligh would find his own drama almost 10 years later as commander of the infamous HMS *Bounty*.) The *Discovery* and *Resolution* finally found safe anchorage at Kealakekua Bay on the Kona coast of the Big Island. It is very lucky for history that on board was Mr. Anderson, ship's chronicler, who left a handwritten record of the strange and tragic events that followed. Even more important were the drawings of John Webber, ship's artist, who rendered invaluable impressions in superb drawings and etchings. Other noteworthy men aboard were George Vancouver, who would lead the first British return to Hawaii after Cook's death and introduce many fruits, vegetables, cattle, sheep, and goats; and James Burney, who would become a long-standing leading authority on the Pacific.

The Great God Lono Returns

By all accounts Cook was a humane and just captain, greatly admired by his men. Unlike many other supremacists of that time, he was known to have a respectful attitude toward any people he discovered, treating them as equals and recognizing the significance of their cultures. Not known as a violent man, he would use his superior weapons against natives only in an absolute case of self-defense. His hardened crew had been at sea facing untold hardship for almost three years; returning to Hawaii was truly like reentering paradise.

A strange series of coincidences sailed with Cook into Kealakekua Bay on January 16, 1779. It was *makahiki* time, a period of rejoicing and festivity dedicated to the fertility god of the earth, Lono. Normal *kapu* days were suspended and willing partners freely enjoyed each other sexually. There was also dancing, feasting, and the islands' version of Olympic games. It was long held in Hawaiian legend that the great god Lono would return to earth. Lono's image was a small wooden figure perched on a tall, mastlike crossbeam; hanging from the crossbeam were long, white sheets of *tapa*. Who else could Cook be but Lono, and what else could his ships with their masts and white sails be but his sacred floating *heiau*? This explained the Hawaiians' previous fascination with his ships, but to add to the remarkable coincidence, Kealakekua Harbor happened to be considered Lono's private sacred harbor. Natives from throughout the land prostrated themselves and paid homage to the returning god. Cook was taken ashore and brought to Lono's sacred temple, where he was afforded the highest respect. The ships badly needed fresh supplies so the Hawaiians readily gave all they had, stretching their own provisions to the limit. To the sailors' delight, this included full measures of the *aloha* spirit.

The Fatal Misunderstandings

After an uproarious welcome and generous hospitality for over a month, it became obvious that the newcomers were beginning to overstay their welcome. During the interim a seaman named William Watman died, convincing the Hawaiians that the *haole* were indeed mortals, not gods. Watman was buried at Hikiau Heiau, where a plaque commemorates the event to this day. Incidents of petty theft began to increase dramatically. The lesser chiefs indicated it was time to leave by "rubbing the Englishmen's bellies." Inadvertently many *kapu* were broken by the English, and once-friendly relations became strained. Finally, the ships sailed away on February 4, 1779.

After plying terrible seas for only a week, *Resolution's* foremast was damaged. Cook sailed back into Kealakekua Bay, dragging the mast ashore on February 13. The natives, now totally hostile, hurled rocks at the sailors. Orders were given to load muskets with ball; firearms had previously only been loaded with shot and a light charge. Confrontations increased when some Hawaiians stole a small

boat and Cook's men set after them, capturing the fleeing canoe which held an *ali'i* named Palea. The English treated him roughly; to the Hawaiians' horror, they even smacked him on the head with a paddle. The Hawaiians then furiously attacked the marines, who abandoned the small boat.

Cook Goes Down

Next the Hawaiians stole a small cutter from the *Discovery* that had been moored to a buoy and partially sunk to protect it from the sun. For the first time, Cook became furious. He ordered Captain Clerk of the *Discovery* to sail to the southeast end of the bay and stop any canoe trying to leave Kealakekua. Cook then made a fatal error in judgment. He decided to take nine armed marines ashore in an attempt to convince the venerable King Kalaniopuu to accompany him back aboard ship, where he would hold him for ransom in exchange for the cutter. The old king agreed, but his wife prevailed upon him not to trust the *haole*. Kalaniopuu sat down on the beach to think while the tension steadily grew.

Meanwhile, a group of marines fired upon a canoe trying to leave the bay. A lesser chief, Nookemai, was killed. The crowd around Cook and his men reached an estimated 20,000. Warriors outraged by the killing of the chief armed themselves with clubs and protective straw-mat armor. One bold warrior advanced on Cook and struck him with his *pahoa*. In retaliation, Cook drew a tiny pistol lightly loaded with shot and fired at the warrior. His bullets spent themselves on the straw armor and fell harmlessly to the ground. The Hawaiians went wild. Lieutenant Molesworth Phillips, in charge of the nine marines, began a withering fire; Cook himself slew two natives.

Overpowered by sheer numbers, the marines headed for boats standing offshore, while Lieutenant Phillips lay wounded. It is believed that Captain Cook, the greatest seaman ever to enter the Pacific, stood helplessly in knee-deep water instead of making for the boats because he could not swim! Hopelessly surrounded, he was knocked on the head. Countless warriors then passed a knife around and hacked and mutilated his lifeless body. A sad Lieutenant James King lamented in his diary, "Thus fell our great and excellent commander."

The Final Chapter

Captain Clerk, now in charge, settled his men and prevailed upon the Hawaiians to return Cook's body. On the morning of February 16 a grisly piece of charred meat was brought aboard: the Hawaiians, according to their custom, had afforded Cook the highest honor by baking his body in an underground oven to remove the flesh from the bones. On February 17 a group of Hawaiians in a canoe taunted the marines by brandishing Cook's hat. The English, strained to the limit and thinking that Cook was being desecrated, finally broke. Foaming with blood-lust, they leveled their cannons and muskets on shore and shot anything that moved. It is believed that Kamehameha the Great was wounded in this flurry, along with four *ali'i;* 25 *maka'ainana* were killed. Finally, on February 21, 1779, the bones of Captain James Cook's hands, skull, arms, and legs were returned and tearfully buried at sea. A common seaman, one Mr. Zimmerman, summed up the feelings of all who sailed under Cook when he wrote, ". . . he was our leading star." The English sailed next morning after dropping off their Hawaiian girlfriends who were still aboard.

Captain Clerk, in bad health, carried on with the fruitless search for the Northwest Passage. He died and was buried at the Siberian village of Petropavlovisk. England was at war with upstart colonists in America, so the return of the expedition warranted little fanfare. The *Resolution* was converted into an army transport to fight the pesky Americans; the once-proud *Discovery* was reduced to a convict ship ferrying inmates to Botany Bay, Australia. Mrs. Cook, the great captain's steadfast wife, lived to the age of 93, surviving all her children. She was given a stipend of 200 pounds per year and finished her days surrounded by Cook's mementos, observing the anniversary of his death to the very end by fasting and reading from the Bible.

THE UNIFICATION OF OLD HAWAII

Hawaii was already in a state of political turmoil and civil war when Cook arrived. In the 1780s, the islands were roughly divided into three kingdoms: venerable Kalaniopuu ruled Hawaii and the Hana district of Maui; the wily and ruthless warrior-king Kahekili ruled Maui, Kahoolawe, Lanai, and later Oahu; and Kaeo, Kahekili's brother, ruled Kauai. War ravaged the land until a remarkable chief, Kamehameha, rose and subjugated all the islands under one rule. Kamehameha initiated a dynasty that would last for about 100 years, until the independent monarchy of Hawaii was forever ended. To add a zing to this brewing political stew, Westerners and their technology were beginning to come in ever-increasing numbers. In 1786, Captain LaPerouse and his French exploration party landed in what's now LaPerouse Bay near Lahaina, foreshadowing European attention to the islands. In 1786 two American captains, Portlock and Dixon, made landfall in Hawaii. Also, it was known that a fortune could be made in the fur trade between the Pacific Northwest and Guangzhou (Canton), China; stopping in Hawaii could make it feasible. After this was reported, the fate of Hawaii was sealed.

Hawaii under Kamehameha was ready to enter its "golden age." The social order was medieval, with the *ali'i* as knights owing their military allegiance to the king, and the serflike *maka'ainana* paying tribute and working the lands. The priesthood of *kahuna* filled the posts of advisors, sorcerers, navigators, doctors, and historians. This was Polynesian Hawaii at its apex. But like the uniquely Hawaiian silversword plant, the old culture blossomed, and as soon as it did, began to wither. Ever since, everything purely Hawaiian has been supplanted by the relentless foreign influences that began bearing down upon it.

Young Kamehameha

The greatest native son of Hawaii, Kamehameha was born under mysterious circumstances in the Kohala District on the Big Island, probably in 1753. He was royal-born to Keoua Kupuapaikalaninui, the chief of Kohala, and Kekuiapoiwa, a chieftess from Kona. Accounts vary, but one claims that before his birth, a *kahuna* prophesied that this child would grow to be a "killer of chiefs." Because of this, the local chiefs conspired to murder the infant. When Kekuiapoiwa's time came, she secretly went to the royal birthing stones near Mookini Heiau and delivered Kamehameha. She entrusted her baby to a manservant and instructed him to hide the child. He headed for the rugged and remote coast

King Kamehameha

the family war god Kukailimoku—"Ku of the Bloody Red Mouth," "Ku the Destroyer." Oddly enough, Kamehameha had been born not 500 yards from Ku's great *heiau* at Kohala and had heard the chanting and observed the ceremonies dedicated to this fierce god from his first breath. Soon after Kalaniopuu died, Kamehameha found himself in a bitter war he did not seek against his two cousins, Kiwalao and Keoua, with the island of Hawaii at stake. The skirmishing lasted nine years, until Kamehameha's armies met the two brothers at Mokuohai in an indecisive battle in which Kiwalao was killed. The result was a shaky truce with Keoua, a much-embittered enemy. During this fighting, Kahekili of Maui conquered Oahu, where he built a house of the skulls and bones of his adversaries as a reminder of his omnipotence. He also extended his will to Kauai by marrying his half-brother to a high-ranking chieftess of that island. A new factor would resolve this stalemate of power—the coming of the *haole*.

The Olowalu Massacre

In 1790 the American merchant ship *Ella Nora,* commanded by Yankee Captain Simon Metcalfe, was looking for a harbor after its long voyage from the Pacific Northwest. Following a day behind was the *Fair American,* a tiny ship sailed by Metcalfe's son Thomas and a crew of five. Simon Metcalfe, perhaps by necessity, was a stern and humorless man who would brook no interference. While his ship was anchored at Olowalu, a beach area about five miles east of Lahaina, some natives slipped close in their canoes and stole a small boat, killing a seaman in the process. Metcalfe decided to trick the Hawaiians by first negotiating a truce and then unleashing full fury upon them. Signaling he was willing to trade, he invited canoes of innocent natives to visit his ship. In the meantime, he ordered that all cannons and muskets be readied with scatter shot. When the canoes were within hailing distance, he ordered his crew to fire at will. Over 100 people were slain; the Hawaiians remembered this killing as "the day of spilled brains." Metcalfe then sailed away to Kealakekua Bay and in an unrelated incident succeeded in insulting Kameiamoku, a ruling chief, who vowed to annihilate the next *haole* ship that he saw.

around Kapa'au. Here Kamehameha was raised in the mountains, mostly by men. Always alone, he earned the nickname "the lonely one."

Kamehameha was a man noticed by everyone; there was no doubt he was a force to be reckoned with. He had met Captain Cook when the *Discovery* unsuccessfully tried to land at Hana on Maui. While aboard, he made a lasting impression, distinguishing himself from the multitude of natives swarming the ships by his royal bearing. Lieutenant James King, in a diary entry, remarked that Kamehameha was a fierce-looking man, almost ugly, but that he was obviously intelligent, observant, and very good-natured. Kamehameha received his early military training from his uncle Kalaniopuu, the great king of Hawaii and the Hana District of Maui who had fought fierce battles against Alapai, the usurper who stole his hereditary lands. After regaining Hawaii, Kalaniopuu returned to his Hana district and turned his attention to conquering all of Maui. During this period young Kamehameha distinguished himself as a ferocious warrior and earned the nickname of "the hard-shelled crab," even though old Kahekili, Maui's king, almost annihilated Kalaniopuu's army at the sand hills of Wailuku.

When the old king neared death, he passed on the kingdom to his son Kiwalao. He also, however, empowered Kamehameha as the keeper of

Fate sent him the *Fair American* and young Thomas Metcalfe. The little ship was entirely overrun by superior forces. In the ensuing battle, the mate, Isaac Davis, so distinguished himself by open acts of bravery that his life alone was spared. Kameiamoku later turned over both Davis and the ship to Kamehameha. Meanwhile, while harbored at Kealakekua, the senior Metcalfe sent John Young to reconnoiter. Kamehameha, having learned of the capture of the *Fair American,* detained Young so he could not report, and Metcalfe, losing patience, marooned his own man and sailed off to China. (Metcalfe never learned of the fate of his son Thomas, and was later killed with another son while trading with the Native Americans along the Pacific coast of the Mainland.) Kamehameha quickly realized the significance of his two captives and the *Fair American,* with its brace of small cannons. He appropriated the ship and made Davis and Young trusted advisors, eventually raising them to the rank of chief. They would all play a significant role in the unification of Hawaii.

Kamehameha the Great
Later in 1790, supported by the savvy of Davis and Young and the cannons from the *Fair American* (which he mounted on carts), Kamehameha invaded Maui, using Hana as his power base. The island's defenders under Kalanikupule, son of Kahekili, who was lingering on Oahu, were totally demoralized, then driven back into the deathtrap of the Iao Valley of Maui. There, Kamehameha's forces annihilated them. No mercy was expected and none given, although mostly commoners were slain with no significant *ali'i* falling to the victors. So many were killed in this sheer-walled, inescapable valley that the battle was called *"ka pani wai,"* which means "the damming of the waters"—literally with dead bodies.

While Kamehameha was fighting on Maui, his old nemesis Keoua was busy running amok back on Hawaii, again pillaging Kamehameha's lands. The great warrior returned home flushed with victory, but in two battles could not subdue Keoua. Finally, Kamehameha had a prophetic dream in which he was told that Ku would lead him to victory over all the lands of Hawaii if he would build a *heiau* to the war god at Kawaihae.

Even before the temple was finished, old Kahekili attempted to invade Waipio, Kamehameha's stronghold. But Kamehameha summoned Davis and Young, and with the *Fair American* and an enormous fleet of war canoes defeated Kahekili at Waimanu. Kahekili had no choice but to accept the indomitable Kamehameha as the king of Maui, although he himself remained the administrative head until his death in 1794.

Now only Keoua remained in the way, and he would be defeated not by war but by the great mana of Ku. While Keoua's armies were crossing the desert on the southern slopes of Kilauea, the fire goddess Pele trumpeted her disapproval and sent a huge cloud of poisonous gas and mud-ash into the air. It descended upon and instantly killed the middle legions of Keoua's armies and their families. The footprints of this ill-fated army remain to this day outlined in the mud-ash as clearly as if they were deliberately encased in wet cement. Keoua's intuition told him that the victorious mana of the gods had swung to Kamehameha and that his own fate was sealed. Kamehameha sent word that he wanted Keoua to meet with him at Ku's newly dedicated temple in Kawaihae. Both knew that Keoua must die. Riding proudly in his canoe, the old nemesis came gloriously outfitted in the red-and-gold feathered cape and helmet signifying his exalted rank. When he stepped ashore he was felled by Kamehameha's warriors. His body was ceremoniously laid upon the altar along with 11 others who were slaughtered and dedicated to Ku, of the Maggot-dripping Mouth.

Increasing Contact
By the time Kamehameha had won the Big Island, Hawaii was becoming a regular stopover for ships seeking the lucrative sandalwood trade with China. In February 1791, Capt. George Vancouver, still seeking the Northwest Passage, returned to Kealakekua where he was greeted by a throng of 30,000. The captain at once recognized Kamehameha, who was wearing a Chinese dressing gown that he had received in tribute from another chief who in turn had received it directly from the hands of Cook himself. The diary of a crewmember, Thomas Manby, relates that Kamehameha, missing his front teeth, was more fierce-looking than ever as he approached the ship in an elegant double-hulled canoe pro-

pelled by 46 rowers. The king invited all to a great feast prepared for them on the beach. Kamehameha's appetite matched his tremendous size. It was noted that he ate two sizable fish, a king-sized bowl of poi, a small pig, and an entire baked dog. Kamehameha personally entertained the English by putting on a mock battle in which he deftly avoided spears by rolling, tumbling, and catching them in midair, all the while hurling his own spear a great distance. The English reciprocated by firing cannon bursts into the air, creating an impromptu fireworks display. Kamehameha requested from Vancouver a full table setting with which he was provided, but his request for firearms was prudently denied. Captain Vancouver became a trusted advisor of Kamehameha and told him about the white man's form of worship. He even interceded for Kamehameha with his headstrong queen, Kaahumanu, and coaxed her from her hiding place under a rock when she sought refuge at Pu'uhonua O Honaunau. The captain gave gifts of beef cattle, fowl, and breeding stock of sheep and goats. The ship's naturalist, Archibald Menzies, was the first *haole* to climb Mauna Kea; he also introduced a large assortment of fruits and vegetables. The Hawaiians were cheerful and outgoing, and showed remorse when they indicated that the remainder of Cook's bones had been buried at a temple close to Kealakekua. John Young, by this time firmly entrenched in Hawaiian society, made no request to sail away with Vancouver. During the next two decades of Kamehameha's rule, the French, Russians, English, and Americans discovered the great whaling waters off Hawaii. Their increasing visits shook and finally tumbled the ancient religion and social order of *kapu*.

Finishing Touches

After Keoua was laid to rest, it was only a matter of time until Kamehameha consolidated his power over all of Hawaii. In 1794 the old warrior Kahekili of Maui died and gave Oahu to his son, Kalanikupule, while Kauai and Niihau went to his brother Kaeo. In wars between the two, Kalanikupule was victorious, though he possessed neither the grit of his father nor the great *mana* of Kamehameha. He had previously murdered a Captain Brown, who had anchored in Honolulu, and seized his ship, the *Jackal*. With

the aid of this ship, Kalanikupule now determined to attack Kamehameha. However, while en route the sailors regained control of their ship and cruised to the Big Island to inform and join with Kamehameha. An army of 16,000 was raised and sailed for Maui, where they met only token resistance, destroyed Lahaina, pillaged the countryside, and subjugated Molokai in one bloody battle.

The war canoes sailed next for Oahu and the final showdown. The great army landed at Waikiki, and though defenders fought bravely, giving up Oahu by the inch, they were steadily driven into the surrounding mountains. The beleaguered army made its last stand at Nuuanu Pali, a great precipice in the mountains behind present-day Honolulu. Kamehameha's warriors mercilessly drove the enemy into the great abyss. Kalanikupule, who hid in the mountains, was captured after a few months and sacrificed to Ku, the Snatcher of Lands, thereby ending the struggle for power.

Kamehameha put down a revolt on Hawaii in 1796. The king of Kauai, Kaumuali'i, accepting the inevitable, recognized Kamehameha as supreme ruler without suffering the ravages of a needless war. Kamehameha, for the first time in Hawaiian history, was the undisputed ruler of all the islands of "the heavenly homeland in the north."

Kamehameha's Rule

Kamehameha was as gentle in victory as he was ferocious in battle. Under his rule, which lasted until his death on May 8, 1819, Hawaii enjoyed a peace unlike any the warring islands had ever known. The king moved his royal court to Lahaina, where in 1803 he built the "Brick Palace," the first permanent building of Hawaii. The benevolent tyrant also enacted the "Law of the Splintered Paddle." This law, which protected the weak from exploitation by the strong, had its origins in an incident of many years before. A brave defender of a small overwhelmed village had broken a paddle over Kamehameha's head and taught the chief—literally in one stroke—about the nobility of the commoner.

However, just as Old Hawaii reached its "golden age," its demise was at hand. The relentless waves of *haole* both innocently and determinedly battered the old ways into the ground. With the foreign ships came prosperity and fanciful new goods after which the *ali'i* lusted. The *maka'ainana* were worked mercilessly to provide sandalwood for trade with China. This was the first "boom" economy to hit the islands, but it set the standard of exploitation that would follow. Kamehameha built an observation tower in Lahaina to watch for ships, many of which were his own returning laden with riches from the world at large. In the last years of his life Kamehameha returned to his beloved Kona Coast, where he enjoyed the excellent fishing renowned to this day. He had taken Hawaii from the darkness of warfare into the light of peace. He died true to the religious and moral *kapu* of his youth, the only ones he had ever known, and with him died a unique way of life. Two loyal retainers buried his bones after the baked flesh had been ceremoniously stripped away. A secret burial cave was chosen so that no one could desecrate the remains of the great chief, thereby absorbing his mana. The tomb's whereabouts remain unknown, and disturbing the dead remains one of the strictest *kapu* to this day. The Lonely One's kingdom would pass to his son, Liholiho, but true power would be in the hands of his beloved but feisty wife Kaahumanu. As Kamehameha's spirit drifted from this earth, two forces sailing around Cape Horn would forever change Hawaii: the missionaries and the whalers.

MISSIONARIES AND WHALERS

The year 1819 was of the utmost significance in Hawaiian history. It marked the death of Kamehameha, the overthrow of the ancient *kapu* system, the arrival of the first whaler in Lahaina, and the departure of Calvinist missionaries from New England determined to convert the heathen islands. Great changes began to rattle the old order to its foundations. With the *kapu* system and all of the ancient gods abandoned (except for the fire goddess Pele of Kilauea), a great void permeated the souls of the Hawaiians. In the coming decades Hawaii, also coveted by Russia, France, and England, was finally consumed by America. The islands had the first American school, printing press, and newspaper west of the Mississippi. Lahaina, in its heyday, became the world's greatest whaling port, accommodating over 500 ships of all types during its peak years.

The Royal Family

Maui's Hana District provided Hawaii with one of its greatest queens, Kaahumanu, born in 1768 in a cave within walking distance of Hana Harbor. At the age of 17 she became the third of Kamehameha's 21 wives and, eventually, the love of his life. At first she proved to be totally independent and unmanageable and was known to openly defy her king by taking numerous lovers. Kamehameha placed a *kapu* on her body and even had her attended by horribly deformed hunchbacks in an effort to curb her carnal appetites, but she continued to flaunt his authority. Young Kaahumanu had no love for her great, lumbering, unattractive husband, but in time (even Captain Vancouver was pressed into service as a marriage counselor) she learned to love him dearly. She in turn became his favorite wife, although she remained childless throughout her life. Kamehameha's first wife was the supremely royal Keopuolani, who so outranked even him that the king himself had to approach her naked and crawling on his belly. Keopuolani produced the royal children Liholiho and Kauikeaouli, who became King Kamehameha II and III, respectively. Just before Kamehameha I died in 1819 he appointed Liholiho his successor, but he also had the wisdom to make Kaahumanu the *kuhina nui,* or queen regent. Initially, Liholiho was weak and became a drunkard. Later he became a good ruler, but he was always supported by his royal mother Keopuolani and by the ever-formidable Kaahumanu.

Kapu Is *Pau*

Kaahumanu was greatly loved and respected by the people. On public occasions, she donned Kamehameha's royal cloak and spear and, so attired and infused with the king's mana, she demonstrated that she was the real leader of Hawaii. For six months after Kamehameha's death, Kaahumanu counseled Liholiho on what he must do. The wise *kuhina nui* knew that the old ways were *pau* and that Hawaii could not hope to function in a rapidly changing world under the *kapu* system. In November 1819, Kaahumanu and Keopuolani prevailed upon Liholiho to break two of the oldest and most sa-

the great Queen Kaahumanu, by ship's artist Louis Choris, from the Otto Von Kotzebue expedition, circa 1816

cred *kapu* by eating with women and by allowing women to eat previously forbidden foods such as bananas and certain fish. Heavily fortified with strong drink and attended by other high-ranking chiefs and a handful of foreigners, Kaahumanu and Liholiho ate together in public. This feast became known as *Ai Noa* ("Free Eating"). As the first morsels passed Kaahumanu's lips, the ancient gods of Hawaii tumbled. Throughout the land, revered *heiau* were burned and abandoned and the idols knocked to the ground. Now the people had nothing but their weakened inner selves to rely on. Nothing and no one could answer their prayers; their spiritual lives were empty and in shambles.

Missionaries

Into this spiritual vortex sailed the brig *Thaddeus* on April 4, 1820. It had set sail from Boston on October 23, 1819, lured to the Big Island by Henry Opukahaia, a local boy born at Napoopoo in 1792. Coming ashore at Kailua-Kona, the Reverends Bingham and Thurston were granted a one-year trial missionary period by King Liholiho. They established themselves on the Big Island and Oahu and from there began the transformation of Hawaii. The missionaries were people of God, but also practical-minded Yankees. They brought education, enterprise, and, most importantly (unlike the transient seafarers), a commitment to stay and build. By 1824, the new faith had such a foothold that Chieftess Keopuolani climbed to the firepit atop Kilauea

and defied Pele. This was even more striking than the previous breaking of the food *kapu* because the strength of Pele could actually be seen. Keopuolani ate forbidden *ohelo* berries and cried out, "Jehovah is my God." Over the next decades the governing of Hawaii slipped away from the Big Island and moved to the new port cities of Lahaina and, later, Honolulu.

Rapid Conversions

The year 1824 also marked the death of Keopuolani, who was given a Christian burial. She had set the standard by accepting Christianity, and a number of the *ali'i* had followed the queen's lead. Liholiho had sailed off to England, where he and his wife contracted measles and died. Their bodies were returned by the British in 1825, on the HMS *Blonde* captained by Lord Byron, cousin of *the* Lord Byron. During these years, Kaahumanu allied herself with Reverend Richards, pastor of the first mission in the islands, and together they wrote Hawaii's first code of laws based upon the Ten Commandments. Foremost was the condemnation of murder, theft, brawling, and the desecration of the Sabbath by work or play. The early missionaries had the best of intentions, but like all zealots they were blinded by the singlemindedness that was also their greatest ally. They weren't selective in their destruction of native beliefs. *Anything* native was felt to be inferior, and they set about wiping out all traces of the old ways. In their rampage they reduced the Hawaiian culture to ashes, plucking self-will and determination from the hearts of a once-proud people. More so than the whalers, they terminated the Hawaiian way of life.

The Early Seamen

A good portion of the common seamen of the early 19th century came from the dregs of the Western world. Many a whoremongering drunkard had awoken from a stupor to find himself on the pitching deck of a ship and discover to his dismay that he had been pressed into naval service. For the most part these sailors were a filthy, uneducated, lawless rabble. Their present situation was dim, their future hopeless, and they would live to be 30 if they were lucky and didn't die from scurvy or any of a thousand other miserable fates. They snatched brief pleasure in every port and jumped ship at every opportunity, especially in an easy berth like Lahaina. They displayed the worst elements of Western culture—which the Hawaiians naively mimicked. In exchange for *aloha* they gave drunkenness, sloth, and insidious death by disease. By the 1850s the population of native Hawaiians tumbled from the estimated 300,000 reported by Captain Cook in 1778 to barely 60,000. Common conditions such as colds, flu, venereal disease, and sometimes smallpox and cholera devastated the Hawaiians, who had no natural immunities to these foreign ailments. By the time the missionaries arrived, *hapa haole* children were common in Lahaina streets.

The earliest merchant ships to the islands were owned or skippered by lawless opportunists who had come seeking sandalwood after first filling their holds with furs from the Pacific Northwest. Aided by *ali'i* hungry for manufactured goods and Western finery, they raped Hawaiian forests of this fragrant wood so coveted in China. Next, droves of sailors came in search of whales. The whalers, decent men at home, left their morals back in the Atlantic and lived by the slogan "no conscience east of the Cape." The delights of Hawaii were just too tempting for most.

Two Worlds Tragically Collide

The 1820s were a time of confusion and soul-searching for the Hawaiians. When Kamehameha II died the kingdom passed to Kauikeaouli (Kame-

Kamehameha III

hameha III), who made his lifelong residence in Lahaina. The young king was only nine years old when the title passed to him, but his power was secure because Kaahumanu was still a vibrant *kuhina nui*. The young prince, more so than any other, was raised in the cultural confusion of the times. His childhood was spent during the very cusp of the change from old ways to new, and he was often pulled in two directions by vastly differing beliefs. Since he was royal born, he was bound by age-old Hawaiian tradition to mate and produce an heir with the highest-ranking *ali'i* in the kingdom. This mate happened to be his younger sister, the Princess Nahienaena. To the old Hawaiian advisors, this arrangement was perfectly acceptable and encouraged. To the increasingly influential missionaries, incest was an unimaginable abomination in the eyes of God. The problem was compounded by the fact that Kamehameha III and Nahienaena were drawn to each other and were deeply in love. The young king could not stand the mental pressure imposed by conflicting worlds. He became a teenage alcoholic too royal to be restrained by anyone in the kingdom, and his bouts of drunkenness and womanizing were both legendary and scandalous.

Meanwhile, Nahienaena was even more pressured because she was a favorite of the missionaries, baptized into the church at age 12. She too vacillated between the old and the new. At times a pious Christian, at others she drank all night and took numerous lovers. As the prince and princess grew into their late teens, they became even more attached to each other and hardly made an attempt to keep their relationship from the missionaries. Whenever possible, they lived together in a grass house built for the princess by her father.

In 1832, the great Kaahumanu died, leaving the king on his own. In 1833, at the age of 18, Kamehameha III announced that the "regency" was over and that all the lands in Hawaii were his personally, and that he alone was the ultimate law. Almost immediately, however, he decreed that his half-sister Kinau would be "premier," signifying that he would leave the actual running of the kingdom in her hands. Kamehameha III fell into total drunken confusion, until one night he attempted suicide. After this episode he seemed to straighten up a bit and mostly kept a low profile. In 1836, Princess Nahienaena was convinced by the missionaries to take a husband. She married Leleiohoku, a chief from the Big Island, but continued to sleep with her brother. It is uncertain who fathered the child, but Nahienaena gave birth to a baby boy in September 1836. The young prince survived for only a few hours, and Nahienaena never recovered from her convalescence. She died in December 1836 and was laid to rest in the mausoleum next to her mother, Keopuolani, on the royal island in Mokuhina Pond (still in existence in modern-day Lahaina). After the death of his sister, Kamehameha III became a sober and righteous ruler. Often seen paying his respects at the royal mausoleum, he ruled longer than any other king until his death in 1854.

The Missionaries Prevail

In 1823, the first mission was established in Lahaina, Maui under the pastorage of Reverend Richards and his wife. Within a few years, many of the notable *ali'i* had been, at least in appearance, converted to Christianity. By 1828 the cornerstones for Wainee Church, the first stone church on the island, were laid just behind the palace of Kamehameha III. The struggle between missionaries and whalers centered on public drunkenness and the servicing of sailors by native women. The normally God-fearing whalers had signed on for perilous duty that lasted up to three years, and when they anchored in Lahaina they demanded their pleasure. The missionaries were instrumental in placing a curfew on sailors and prohibiting native women from their customary boarding of ships. These measures certainly did not stop the liaisons between sailor and *wahine*, but they did impose a modicum of social sanction and tolled the end of the wide-open days. The sailors were outraged; in 1825 the crew from the *Daniel* attacked the home of the meddler, Reverend Richards. A year later a similar incident occurred. In 1827, confined and lonely sailors from the whaler *John Palmer* fired their cannons at Reverend Richards' newly built home.

Slowly the tensions eased, and by 1836 many sailors were regulars at the Seamen's Chapel adjacent to the Baldwin home. Unfortunately, even the missionaries couldn't stop the pesky mosquito from entering the islands through the port of Lahaina. The mosquitoes arrived from Mexico in 1826 aboard the merchant ship *Wellington.* They were inadvertently carried as larvae in the water barrels and democratically pestered everyone in the islands from that day forward, regardless of race, religion, or creed.

Lahaina Becomes a Cultural Center

By 1831, Lahaina was firmly established as a seat of Western influence in Hawaii. That year marked the founding of Lahainaluna School, the first *real* American school west of the Rockies. Virtually a copy of a New England normal school, it attracted the best students, both native and white, from throughout the kingdom. By 1834, Lahainaluna had an operating printing press publishing the islands' first newspaper, *The Torch of Hawaii,* starting a lucrative printing industry centered in Lahaina that dominated not only the islands but also California for many years.

An early native student was David Malo. He was brilliant and well educated, but more importantly, he remembered the "old ways." One of the first Hawaiians to realize his native land was being swallowed up by the newcomers, Malo compiled the first history of precontact Hawaii, and the resulting book, *Hawaiian Antiquities,* became a reference masterpiece which has yet to be eclipsed. David Malo insisted that the printing be done in Hawaiian, not English. Malo is buried in the mountains above Lahainaluna where, by his own request, he is "high above the tide of foreign invasion." By the 1840s, Lahaina was firmly established as the "whaling capital of the world"; the peak year 1846 saw 395 whaling ships anchored here. A census in 1846 reported that Lahaina was home to 3,445 natives, 112 permanent *haole,* 600 sailors, and over 500 dogs. The populace was housed in 882 grass houses, 155 adobe houses, and 59 relatively permanent stone and wood-framed structures. Lahaina would probably have remained the islands' capital, had Kamehameha III not moved the royal capital to the burgeoning port of Honolulu on the island of Oahu.

Foreign Influence

By the 1840s Honolulu was becoming the center of commerce in the islands; when Kamehameha III moved the royal court there from Lahaina, the ascendant fate of the new capital was guaranteed. In 1843, Lord Paulet, commander of the warship *Carysfort,* forced Kamehameha III to sign a treaty ceding Hawaii to the British. London, however, repudiated this act, and Hawaii's independence was restored within a few months when Queen Victoria sent Admiral Thomas as her personal agent of good intentions. The king memorialized the turn of events by a speech in which he uttered the phrase, *"Ua mau ke ea o ka aina i ka pono"* ("The life of the land is preserved in righteousness"), now Hawaii's motto. The French used similar bullying tactics to force an unfavorable treaty on the Hawaiians in 1839; as part of these heavy-handed negotiations, they exacted a payment of $20,000 and the right of Catholics to enjoy religious freedom in the islands. In 1842, the U.S. recognized and guaranteed Hawaii's independence without a formal treaty, and by 1860 over 80% of the islands' trade was with the United States.

Kauai's Role

King Kaumuali'i of Kauai had been able, by his use of diplomacy, guile, and the large distances separating his island from the others, to remain independent even as the great King Kame-

hameha was conquering the other islands and uniting them under his rule. Finally, however, after all the other islands had been subjugated and Kaumuali'i had shrewdly joined Kamehameha through negotiations instead of warfare, Kaumuali'i retained control of Kauai—he was made governor of the island by Kamehameha. (After Kamehameha died, his successor, Kamehameha II, forced Kaumuali'i to go to Oahu, where arrangements were made for him to marry queen Kaahumanu, the greatest surviving *ali'i* of the land. Kaumuali'i never returned to his native island.)

Hawaii was in its great state of flux at the beginning of the 1800s. The missionaries were coming, along with adventurers and schemers from throughout Europe. One of the latter was George Scheffer, a Prussian in the service of Czar Nicholas of Russia. He convinced Kaumuali'i to build a Russian fort in Waimea in 1817, which Kaumuali'i saw as a means to discourage other Europeans from overrunning his lands. A loose alliance was made between Kaumuali'i and Scheffer. (The adventurer eventually lost the czar's support, and Kaumuali'i ran him off the island, but the remains of **Fort Elizabeth** still stand.) Around the same time, George Kaumuali'i, the king's son, who had been sent to Boston to be educated, was accompanying the first missionary packet to the islands. He came with Reverend Sam Whitney, whom Kaumuali'i invited to stay, and who planted the first sugar on the island and taught the natives to dig wells. **Wailoi Mission House,** just north of Hanalei, dates from 1836 and is still standing, preserved as a museum. Nearby, Hanalei Bay was a commercial harbor for trading and whaling. From here, produce such as oranges was shipped from Na Pali farms to California. In Koloa, on the opposite end of the island, a stack from the Koloa Sugar plantation, started in 1835, marks the site of the first successful sugar-refining operation in the islands. Another successful enterprise was **Lihue Plantation.** Founded by a German firm in 1850, it prospered until WW I, when anti-German sentiment forced the owners to sell out. In Lihue Town, you can still see the Haleko Shops, a cluster of four two-story buildings that show a strong German influence. The **Lihue Lutheran Church** has an ornate altar very similar to ones found in old German churches.

During the 1870s and '80s, leprosy raged throughout the kingdom and strong measures were taken. Those believed to be afflicted were wrenched from their families and sent to the hideous colony of Kalaupapa on Molokai. One famous Kauaian leper, Koolau, born in 1862 in Kekaha, refused to be brought in and took his family to live in the mountain fortress of Na Pali. He fought the authorities for years and killed all those sent to take him in. He was made popular by Jack London in his short story, "Koolau, The Leper."

When WW II came to Hawaii, Nawiliwili Harbor was shelled on December 31, 1941, but there was little damage. The island remained much the same, quiet and rural until the late 1960s when development began in earnest. The first resort destination on the island was the Coco Palms Hotel in Wailua, followed by a development in Poipu and another in Princeville. Meanwhile, Hollywood had discovered Kauai and featured its haunting beauty as a "silent star" in dozens of major films. Today, development goes on, but the island remains quiet, serene, and beautiful.

The Great Mahele

In 1840, Kamehameha III ended his autocratic rule and instituted a constitutional monarchy. This brought about the Hawaiian Bill of Rights, but the most far-reaching change was the transition to private ownership of land. Formerly, all land belonged to the ruling chief, who gave wedge-shaped parcels called *ahupua'a* to lesser chiefs to be worked for him. The commoners did all the real labor, their produce heavily taxed by the *ali'i*. The fortunes of war, the death of a chief, or the mere whim of a superior could force a commoner off the land. The Hawaiians, however, could not think in terms of "owning" land. No one could *possess* land; one could only *use* land, and its *ownership* was a strange and foreign concept. (As a result, naive Hawaiians gave up their lands for a song to unscrupulous traders, which remains an integral, unrectified problem to this day.) In 1847 Kamehameha III and his advisors separated the lands of Hawaii into three groupings: crown land (belonging to the king), government land (belonging to the chiefs), and the people's land (the largest parcels). In 1847, the sprawling Parker Ranch of the Big Island began with a two-acre grant given to John Parker. He coupled this with 360 acres given to his *ali'i* wife Kipikane by the land division known as the Great Mahele. In 1848, 245 *ali'i* entered their own land claims in the *Mahele Book,* assuring them ownership. In 1850 the commoners were given title in fee simple to the lands they cultivated and lived on as tenants, not including house lots in towns. Commoners without land could buy small *kuleana* (farms) from the government at 50 cents per acre. In 1850, foreigners were also allowed to purchase land in fee simple, and the ownership of Hawaii from that day forward slipped steadily from the hands of its indigenous people.

KING SUGAR

The sugar industry began at Hana, Maui, in 1849. A whaler named George Wilfong hauled four blubber pots ashore and set them up on a rocky hill in the middle of 60 acres he had planted in sugar. A team of oxen turned "crushing rollers" and the cane juice flowed down an open trough into the pots, under which an attending native kept a roaring fire burning. Wilfong's methods of refining were crude but the resulting high-quality sugar turned a neat profit in Lahaina. The main problem was labor. The Hawaiians, who made excellent whalers, were basically indentured workers. They became extremely disillusioned with their contracts, which could last up to 10 years. Most of their wages were eaten up by manufactured commodities sold at the company store, and it didn't take long for them to realize that they were little more than slaves. At every opportunity they either left the area or just refused to work.

Imported Labor

The **Masters and Servants Act of 1850,** which allowed importation of laborers under the contract system, ostensibly guaranteed an endless supply of cheap labor for the plantations. Chinese laborers were imported but were too enterprising to remain in the fields for a meager $3 per month. They left as soon as opportunity permitted and went into business as small merchants and retailers. In the meantime, Wilfong had sold out, releasing most of the Hawaiians previously held under contract, and his plantation fell into disuse. In 1860, two Danish brothers, August and Oscar Unna, bought land at Hana to raise sugar. They solved the labor problem by importing Japanese laborers who were extremely hardworking and easily managed. The workday lasted 10 hours, six days a week, for a salary of $20 per month with housing and medical care thrown in. Plantation life was very structured, with stringent rules governing even bedtimes and lights out. A worker was fined for being late or for smoking on the job. The workers couldn't function under these circumstances, and improvements in benefits and housing were slowly gained.

Sugar Grows

The demand for "Sandwich Island Sugar" grew as California was populated during the gold rush and increased dramatically when the American Civil War demanded a constant supply. The only sugar plantations on the Mainland were small plots confined to the Confederate states, whose products would hardly be bought by the Union and whose fields, later in the war, were destroyed. By the 1870s it was clear to Hawaii's planters—still mainly New Englanders—that the U.S. was their market; they tried often to gain closer ties and favorable tariffs. The Americans also planted rumors that the British were interested in annexing Hawaii; this put pressure on the U.S. Congress to pass the long-desired **Reciprocity Act,** which would exempt sugar from import duty. It finally passed in 1875—in exchange for U.S. long-range rights to the strategic naval port of Pearl Harbor, among other concessions. These agreements gave increased political power to a small group of American planters whose outlooks were similar to those of the post-Civil War South, where a few powerful whites were the virtual masters of a multitude of dark-skinned laborers. Sugar was now big business and the Hana District alone exported almost 3,000 tons per year. All of Hawaii would have to reckon with the "sugar barons."

Changing Society

The sugar plantation system changed life in Hawaii physically, spiritually, politically, and economically. Now boatloads of workers came not only from Japan, but also from Portugal, Germany, and even Russia. The white-skinned workers were most often the field foremen *(luna).* With the immigrants came new religions, new animals and plants, unique cuisines, and a plantation language known as pidgin, or, better, *da'kine.* Many Asians and, to a lesser extent, the other groups, including the white plantation owners, intermarried with Hawaiians. A new class of people properly termed "cosmopolitan" but more familiarly and aptly known as "locals" was emerging. These were the people of multiple-race backgrounds who couldn't exactly say *what* they were but it was clear to all just *who* they were. The plantation owners became the new "chiefs" of Hawaii who could carve up the land and dispense favors. The Hawaiian monarchy was soon eliminated.

A KINGDOM PASSES

The fate of Lahaina's Wainee Church through the years has been a symbol of the political and economic climate of the times. Its construction heralded the beginning of missionary dominance in 1828. It was destroyed by a tornado or "ghost wind" in 1858, just when whaling began to falter and the previously dominant missionaries began losing their control to the merchants and planters. In 1894, Wainee Church was burned to the ground by royalists supporting the besieged Queen Liliuokalani. Rebuilding was begun in 1897—while Hawaii was a republic ruled by the sugar planters—with a grant from H.P. Baldwin. Finally, in 1947 Wainee was completed and remodeled.

The Beginning of the End

Like the Hawaiian people themselves, the Kamehameha dynasty in the mid-1800s was dying from within. King Kamehameha IV (Alexander Liholiho) ruled 1854-63; his only child died in 1862. He was succeeded by his older brother Kamehameha V (Lot Kamehameha), who ruled until 1872. With his passing, the Kamehameha line ended. William Lunalilo, elected king in 1873 by popular vote, was of royal but not Kamehameha lineage. He died after only a year in office and, being a bachelor, left no heirs. He was succeeded by David Kalakaua, known far and wide as the "Merry

Robert Louis Stevenson with King Kalakaua, the last king of Hawaii

Monarch," who made a world tour and was well received wherever he went. He built Iolani Palace in Honolulu and was personally in favor of closer ties with the U.S., helping push through the Reciprocity Act. Kalakaua died in 1891 and was replaced by his sister Lydia Liliuokalani, last of the Hawaiian monarchs.

The Revolution

When Liliuokalani took office in 1891, the native population was at a low of 40,000 and she felt that the U.S. had too much influence over her homeland. She was known to personally favor the English over the Americans. She attempted to replace the liberal constitution of 1887 (adopted by her pro-American brother) with an autocratic mandate in which she would have had much more political and economic control of the islands. When the McKinley Tariff of 1890 brought a decline in sugar profits, she made no attempt to improve the situation. Thus, the planters saw her as a political obstacle to their economic growth; most of Hawaii's American planters and merchants were in favor of a rebellion. She would have to go! A central spokesperson and firebrand was Lorrin

Thurston, a Honolulu publisher who, with a central core of about 30 men, challenged the Hawaiian monarchy. Although Liliuokalani rallied some support and had a small military potential in her personal guard, the coup was ridiculously easy—it took only one casualty. Captain John Good shot a Hawaiian policeman in the arm and that did it. Naturally, the conspirators could not have succeeded without some solid assurances from a secret contingent in the U.S. Congress as well as outgoing President Benjamin Harrison, who favored Hawaii's annexation. Marines from the *Boston* went ashore to "protect American lives," and on January 17, 1893, the Hawaiian monarchy came to an end.

The provisional government was headed by Sanford B. Dole, who became president of the Hawaiian Republic. Liliuokalani surrendered not to the conspirators but to U.S. Ambassador John Stevens. She believed that the U.S. government, which had assured her of Hawaiian independence, would be outraged by the overthrow and would come to her aid. Incoming

Queen Liliuokalani

president Grover Cleveland *was* outraged, and Hawaii wasn't immediately annexed as expected. When queried about what she would do with the conspirators if she were reinstated, Liliuokalani said that they would be hanged as traitors. The racist press of the times, which portrayed the Hawaiians as half-civilized, bloodthirsty heathens, publicized this widely. Since the conspirators were the leading citizens of the land, the queen's words proved untimely. In January 1895 a small, ill-fated counterrevolution headed by Liliuokalani failed, and she was placed under house arrest in Iolani Palace. Officials of the republic insisted that she use her married name (Mrs. John Dominis) to sign the documents forcing her to abdicate her throne. She was also forced to swear allegiance to the new republic. Liliuokalani went on to write *Hawaii's Story* and the lyric ballad "Aloha O'e." She never forgave the conspirators and remained "queen" to the Hawaiians until her death in 1917.

Annexation

The overwhelming majority of Hawaiians opposed annexation and desired to restore the monarchy. But they were prevented from voting by the new republic because they couldn't meet the imposed property and income qualifications—a transparent ruse by the planters to control the majority. Most *haole* were racist and believed that the "common people" could not be entrusted with the vote because they were childish and incapable of ruling themselves. The fact that the Hawaiians had existed quite well for 1,000 years before white people even reached Hawaii was never considered. The Philippine theater of the Spanish-American War also prompted annexation. One of the strongest proponents was Alfred Mahon, a brilliant naval strategist who, with support from Theodore Roosevelt, argued that the U.S. military must have Hawaii in order to be a viable force in the Pacific. In addition, Japan, victorious in its recent war with China, protested the American intention to annex, and in so doing prompted even moderates to support annexation for fear that the Japanese themselves coveted the prize. On July 7, 1898, President McKinley signed the annexation agreement, and this "tropical fruit" was finally put into America's basket.

MODERN TIMES

Hawaii entered the 20th century totally transformed from what it had been. The old Hawaiian language, religion, culture, and leadership were all gone; Western dress, values, education, and recreation were the norm. Native Hawaiians were now unseen citizens who lived in dwindling numbers in remote areas. The plantations, new centers of social order, had a strong Asian flavor; more than 75% of their workforce was Asian. There was a small white middle class, an all-powerful white elite, and a single political party ruled by that elite. Education, however, was always highly prized, and by the turn of the century all racial groups were encouraged to attend school. By 1900, almost 90% of Hawaiians were literate (far above the national norm), and schooling was mandatory for all children between ages six and 15. Intermarriage was accepted, and there was a mixing of the races like nowhere else on earth. The military became increasingly important to Hawaii. It brought in money and jobs, dominating the island economy. The Japanese attack on Pearl Harbor, which began U.S. involvement in WW II, bound Hawaii to America forever. Once the islands had been baptized in blood, the average Mainlander felt that Hawaii was American soil. A movement among Hawaiians to become part of the United States began to grow. They wanted a real voice in Washington, not merely a voteless delegate as provided under their territory status. Hawaii became the 50th state in 1959, and the jumbojet revolution of the 1960s made it easily accessible to growing numbers of tourists from all over the world.

Military History

A few military strategists realized the importance of Hawaii early in the 19th century, but most didn't recognize the advantages until the Spanish-American War. It was clearly an unsinkable ship in the middle of the Pacific from which the U.S. could launch military operations. Troops were stationed at Camp McKinley, at the foot of Diamond Head, the main military compound until it became obsolete in 1907. Pearl Harbor was first surveyed in 1872 by General Schofield. (Later, a military base named in his honor, Schofield Barracks, was a main military post in central Oahu. It first housed the U.S. 5th Cavalry in 1909 and was heavily bombed in the Japanese attack at the outset of WW II.) The harbor was first dredged in 1908 and officially opened on December 11, 1911. The first warship to enter was the cruiser *California*. Ever since, the military has been a mainstay of island economy. Unfortunately, there has been long-standing bad blood between locals and military personnel. Each group has tended to look down upon the other.

Pearl Harbor Attack

On the morning of December 7, 1941, the Japanese carrier *Akagi,* flying the battle flag of the famed Admiral Togo of the Russo-Japanese War, received and broadcast over its PA system island music from Honolulu station KGMB. Deep in the bowels of the ship a radioman listened for a much different message, coming thousands of miles from the Japanese mainland. When the ironically poetic message "east wind rain" was received, the attack was launched. At the end of the day, 2,325 U.S. servicemen and 57 civilians were dead, 188 planes were destroyed, 18 major warships were sunk or heavily damaged, and the U.S. was in the war. Japanese casualties were ludicrously light. The ignited conflict would rage for four years until Japan, through Nagasaki and Hiroshima, was vaporized into total submission. By the end of hostilities, Hawaii would never again be considered separate from America.

Statehood

A number of economic and political reasons explain why the ruling elite of Hawaii desired statehood, but put simply, the vast majority of people who lived there, especially after WW II, considered themselves Americans. The first serious mention of making "The Sandwich Islands" a state was in the 1850s under President Franklin Pierce, but it wasn't taken seriously until the monarchy was overthrown in the 1890s. For the next 50 years, statehood proposals were made repeatedly to Congress, but there was stiff opposition, especially from the southern states. With Hawaii a territory, an import quota system beneficial to Mainland producers could be enacted on produce, especially sugar. Also, there was prejudice against creating a state in a place where the majority of the populace was not white. This situation was illuminated by the infamous Massie Rape Case of 1931 (see "Caucasians" under "The People" later in this chapter), which went down as one of the greatest miscarriages of justice in American history.

During WW II, Hawaii was placed under martial law, but no serious attempt to intern the Japanese population was made, as in California. There were simply too many Japanese, who went on to gain the respect of the American people by their outstanding fighting record during the war. Hawaii's own 100th Battalion became the famous 442nd Regimental Combat Team, which gained notoriety by saving the Lost Texas Battalion during the Battle of the Bulge and went on to be *the* most decorated battalion in all of WW II. When these GIs returned home, *no one* was going to tell them that they were not loyal Americans. Many of these AJAs (Americans of Japanese Ancestry) took advantage of the GI Bill and received higher educations. They were from the common people, not the elite, and they rallied grassroots support for statehood. When the vote finally occurred, approximately 132,900 voted in favor of statehood with only 7,800 votes against. Congress passed the Hawaii State Bill on March 12, 1959, and on August 21, 1959, President Eisenhower announced that Hawaii was officially the 50th state.

GOVERNMENT

Politics and government are taken seriously in the "Aloha State," which consistently turns in the best national voting record per capita. (For example, in the first state elections, 173,000 of 180,000 registered voters voted—a whopping 96% of the electorate.) In 1950, in anticipation of becoming a state, Hawaii drafted a constitution and was ready to go when statehood came. In the election to ratify statehood, hardly a ballot went uncast, with 95% of the voters in favor. The bill carried every island of Hawaii except for Niihau where, coincidentally, the majority of people (total population 230 or so) are of relatively pure Hawaiian blood. The present governor, elected in 1994, is Benjamin J. Cayetano, a Democrat who is up for reelection in 1998.

The only difference between the government of the state of Hawaii and other states is that it's "streamlined" and in theory more efficient. There are only two levels of government: the state and the county. With no town or city governments to deal with, an entire level of bureaucracy is eliminated.

Kauai County

Kauai County is composed of the inhabited islands of Kauai and Niihau and the uninhabited islands of Kaula and Lehua. Lihue is the county seat. It's represented by two state senators elected from the 24th District—a split district including north Kauai and the Wainae coast of Oahu—and the 25th District, which includes all of southern Kauai and Niihau. Kauai has three state congressmen—from the 49th District, which is again a split district with north Kauai and the Wainae coast; the 50th District around Lihue; and the 51st District, which includes all of southwestern Kauai and Niihau.

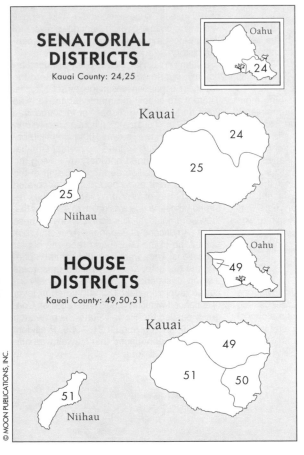

SENATORIAL DISTRICTS
Kauai County: 24,25

Oahu

Kauai

HOUSE DISTRICTS
Kauai County: 49,50,51

Oahu

Kauai

Niihau

© MOON PUBLICATIONS, INC.

ECONOMY

The Big Five Corporations

Until statehood, Hawaii was ruled economically by a consortium of corporations known as the "Big Five": **C. Brewer and Co.**—sugar, ranching, and chemicals—founded in 1826; **Theo. H. Davies & Co.**—sugar, investments, insurance, and transportation—founded in 1845; **Amfac Inc.** (originally H. Hackfield Inc.—a German firm that changed its name to American Factors and its ownership during the anti-German sentiment of WW I)—sugar, insurance, and land development—founded in 1849; **Castle and Cooke Inc.** (Dole)—pineapple, food packing, and land development—founded in 1851; and **Alexander and Baldwin Inc.**—shipping, sugar, and pineapple, founded in 1895. This economic oligarchy ruled Hawaii with a steel grip in a velvet glove.

With members on every important corporate board, they controlled all major commerce, including banking, shipping, insurance, hotel development, agriculture, utilities, and wholesale and retail merchandising. Anyone trying to buck the system was ground to dust, finding it suddenly impossible to do business in the islands. The Big Five were made up of the islands' oldest and most well-established *haole* families; all included bloodlines from Hawaii's own nobility. They looked among themselves for suitable husbands and wives, so that breaking in from the outside even through marriage was hardly possible. The only time they were successfully challenged prior to statehood was when Sears, Roebuck and Co. opened a store on Oahu. Closing ranks, the Big Five decreed that their steamships would not carry Sears' freight. When Sears threatened to buy its own steamship line, the Big Five relented.

Actually, statehood and, more to the point, tourism, broke the oligarchy. After 1960 too much money was at stake for Mainland-based corporations to ignore. Eventually the grip of the Big Five was loosened, but they are still enormously powerful and richer than ever. These days, however, they don't control everything; now their power is land. With only five other major landholders, they control 65% of the privately held land in Hawaii, and the economy of Kauai today, like that of the entire state, is based on agriculture, the military, and tourism—the fastest-growing sector.

Tourism

Kauai, in a tight race with the Big Island, is the third-most-visited island after Oahu and Maui. Regaining momentum after Hurricane Iniki, it is once again attracting about one million visitors annually, accounting for 17% of the state's total. When completely recovered, approximately 7,200

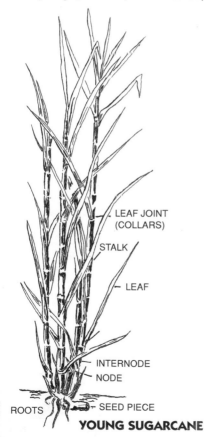

LEAF JOINT (COLLARS)

STALK

LEAF

INTERNODE

NODE

ROOTS — SEED PIECE

YOUNG SUGARCANE

LOUISE FOOTE

hotel and condo units will be available, averaging about a 70% occupancy rate. At one time, Kauai was the most difficult island on which to build a resort because of a strong grassroots antidevelopment faction. This trend has been changing due to the recession that hit everyone after Hurricane Iwa and then Iniki scared off many tourists. Island residents realized how much their livelihood was tied to tourism, and a recent ad campaign depicting tourists as visitors (rather than unwelcome invaders) has helped in their acceptance. Also, the resorts being built on Kauai are first-rate, and the developers are savvy enough to create "destination areas" instead of more high-rise boxes of rooms. Also, Kauai's "quality of room" relative to price is the state's best.

Agriculture

Agriculture still accounts for a hefty portion of Kauai's income, although **sugar,** once the backbone of the agricultural economy, has taken a downward trend and as of 1996 is no longer grown commercially on the island. Kauai produces about six percent of the state's diversified agricultural crop, with a strong yield in **papayas.** In 1982, California banned the importation of Kauai's papayas because they were sprayed with EDB, a fumigant used to control fruit flies.

The chemical is no longer used, and the papaya market has rebounded. Hanalei Valley and many other smaller areas produce five million pounds of taro, which is quickly turned into poi, and the county produces two million pounds of guavas, as well as pineapples, beef, and pork for its own use. A growing aquaculture industry produces prawns. In the mid-1980s, large acreage near Kalaheo was put into coffee, tea, and macadamia nut production. Since then, it has turned into a thriving industry. **Kauai coffee,** known to be milder than Kona coffee, is coming on strong with more and more acreage dedicated to this cash crop. Stores around the island, and more and more around the state, are retailing this hearty brew.

Military

The military influence on Kauai is small but vital. NASA's major tracking facilities in Koke'e Park were turned over to the Navy and Air Force. At **Barking Sands,** the Navy operates BARSTUR, an underwater tactical range for training in antisubmarine warfare. Also along Barking Sands (a fitting name!) is the **Barking Sands Pacific Missile Range,** operated by the Navy but available to the Air Force, Department of Defense, NASA, and the Department of Energy.

JACQUES ARAGO, CIRCA 1819, HAWAII STATE ARCHIVES

THE PEOPLE

Nowhere else on earth can you find such a kaleidoscopic mixture of people as in Hawaii. Every major race is accounted for, and over 50 ethnic groups are represented throughout the islands, making Hawaii the most racially integrated state in the country. Its population of 1.1 million includes 120,000 permanently stationed military personnel and their dependents, and it's the only state where whites are not the majority. About 60% of Hawaiian residents were born there, 25% were born in the mainland U.S., and 15% are foreign-born.

The population has grown steadily in recent times but has fluctuated wildly in the past. In 1876, it reached its lowest ebb, with only 55,000 permanent residents. This was the era of large sugar plantations; their constant demand for labor was the primary cause for importing various peoples from around the world and led to Hawaii's racial mix. World War II saw the population swell from 400,000 to 900,000. These 500,000 military personnel left at war's end, but many returned to settle after getting a taste of island living.

Population Statistics
Just over 1,200,000 people live in the state today—874,000 on Oahu, with about half of these living in the Honolulu Metropolitan Area. The rest of the population is distributed as follows: 135,500 on Hawaii, with 45,000 living in Hilo; 113,000 on Maui, with the largest concentration—52,000—in Wailuku/Kahului; 55,700 on Kauai, including 230 pure-blooded Hawaiians on Niihau; 6,700 on Molokai; and just over 2,400 on Lanai. The population density, statewide, is 173 people per square mile, slightly less than California's 191 people per square mile. The population is not at all evenly distributed; Oahu claims about 1,600 people per square mile, while Hawaii barely has 25. City dwellers outnumber those living in the country four to one.

The density of Kauai is 87 people per square mile. Kauai County's 55,700 people account for only four percent of the state's total population, making it the least populous county. Also, 325 military personnel and their dependents live on the island. The largest town is Kapa'a with 8,200 people, followed by Lihue with 5,500. Ethnically, there is no clear majority on Kauai. The people of Kauai include: 35% Caucasians, 25% Filipinos, 20% Japanese, 15% Hawaiians including those of mixed blood, and the remaining five percent is made up of Chinese, Koreans, Samoans, and a smattering of African Americans and Native Americans.

THE HAWAIIANS

The study of the native Hawaiians is ultimately a study in tragedy because it ends in their demise as a viable people. When Captain Cook first sighted Hawaii in 1778, there were an estimated 300,000 natives living in perfect harmony with their ecological surroundings; within 100 years a scant 50,000 demoralized and dejected Hawaiians existed almost as wards of the state. Today, although 140,000 people claim varying degrees of Hawaiian blood, experts say that fewer than 1,000 are pure Hawaiian, and this is stretching the point. It's easy to see why people of Hawaiian lineage could be bitter over what they have lost—strangers in their own land now, much like Native Americans. The overwhelming majority of "Hawaiians" are of mixed heritage, and the wisest take the best from all worlds. From the Hawaiian side comes simplicity, love of the land, and acceptance of people. It is the Hawaiian legacy of *aloha* that remains immortal and adds that special, elusive quality that *is* Hawaii.

Polynesian Roots

The original Polynesian stock remains an anthropological mystery, but it's believed that they were nomadic wanderers who migrated from both the Indian subcontinent and Southeast Asia through Indonesia, where they learned to sail and navigate on protected waterways. As they migrated they honed their sailing skills until they could take on the Pacific, and as they moved, they absorbed people from other cultures and races until they had coalesced into what we now know as Polynesians. Abraham Fornander, still considered a major authority on the subject, wrote in his 1885 *Account of the Polynesian Race* that he believed the Polynesians started as a white (Aryan) race, which had been heavily influenced by contact with the Cushite, Chaldeo-Arabian civilization. He estimated their arrival in Hawaii at A.D. 600—based on Hawaiian genealogical chants. Modern science seems to bear this date out, although it remains skeptical of his other surmises. The intrepid Polynesians who actually settled Hawaii are believed to have come from the Marquesas Islands, 1,000 miles south and a few hundred miles east of Hawaii. The Marquesans were cannibals and known for their tenacity and strength—attributes that would serve them well. When Captain Cook stepped ashore on Waimea, Kauai, on the morning of January 20, 1778, he discovered a population of 300,000 and an agrarian society that had flourished in the previous thousand years.

The Caste System

Hawaiian society was divided into rankings by a strict caste system determined by birth and from which there was no chance of escaping. The highest rank was the *ali'i;* the chiefs and royalty. The impeccable genealogies of the *ali'i* were traced back to the gods themselves, and the chants *(mo'o ali'i)* were memorized and sung by professionals (called *ku'auhau*) who were themselves *ali'i.* Rank passed from both father and mother, and custom dictated that the first mating of an *ali'i* be with a person of equal status.

A *kahuna* was a highly skilled person whose advice was sought before any major project was undertaken—building a house, hollowing a canoe log, even offering a prayer. The *mo'o kahuna* were the priests of Ku and Lono, and they were in charge of praying and following rituals. They were very powerful *ali'i* and kept strict secrets and laws concerning their various functions.

Besides this priesthood of *kahuna,* there were other *kahuna* who were not *ali'i* but commoners. The two most important were the healers *(kahuna lapa'au)* and the black magicians *(kahuna*

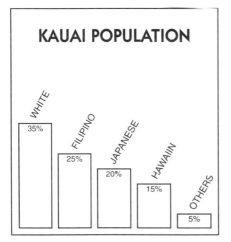

KAUAI POPULATION

- WHITE 35%
- FILIPINO 25%
- JAPANESE 20%
- HAWAIIN 15%
- OTHERS 5%

LOUISE FOOTE

The ali'i wore magnificent feathered capes which signified their rank. The noblest colors were red and yellow.

ana'ana), who could pray a person to death. The *kahuna lapa'au* had a marvelous pharmacopia of herbs and spices that could cure over 250 diseases common to the Hawaiians. The *kahuna ana'ana* could be hired to cast a love spell over a person or cause his or her untimely death. They seldom had to send out a reminder of payment!

The common people were called the *maka'ainana*, "the people of land"—farmers, artisans, and fishermen. They lived on land owned by the *ali'i* but were not bound to it. If the local *ali'i* was cruel or unfair, the *maka'ainana* had the right to leave and reside on another's lands. The *maka'ainana* mostly loved their local *ali'i*, much as a child loves a parent, and the feeling was reciprocal. *Maka'ainana* who lived close to the *ali'i* and could be counted on as warriors in times of trouble were called *kanaka no lua kaua* ("a man for the heat of battle"). They were treated with greater favor than those who lived in the backcountry, *kanaka no hii kua,* whose lesser standing opened them up to discrimination and cruelty. All *maka'ainana* formed extended families called *ohana* who usually lived on the same section of land, called *ahupua'a.* Those farmers who lived inland would barter their produce with the fishermen who lived on the shore, and thus all shared equally in the bounty of land and sea.

A special group called *kauwa* was a landless, untouchable caste confined to living on reservations. Their origins were obviously Polynesian, but they appeared to be descendants of castaways who had survived and become perhaps the aboriginals of Hawaii before the main migrations. It was *kapu* for anyone to go onto *kauwa* lands, and doing so meant instant death. If a human sacrifice was needed, the *kahuna* would simply summon a *kauwa,* who had no recourse but to mutely comply. To this day, to call someone *kauwa,* which now supposedly means only "servant," is still considered a fight-provoking insult.

Kapu and Day-to-Day Life

Occasionally there were horrible wars, but mostly the people lived quiet and ordered lives based on a strict caste society and the *kapu* system. Famine was known but only on a regional level, and the population was kept in check by birth control, crude abortions, and the distasteful practice of infanticide, especially of baby girls. The Hawaiians were absolutely loving and nurturing parents under most circumstances and would even take in a *hanai* (adopted child or oldster), a lovely practice that lingers to this day.

A strict division of labor existed among men and women. Men were the only ones permitted to have anything to do with taro: this foodstuff was so sacred that there were a greater number of *kapu* concerning taro than concerning man himself. Men pounded poi and served it to the women. Men also were the fishermen and the builders of houses, canoes, irrigation ditches, and walls. Women tended to other gardens and shoreline fishing and were responsible for mak-

Punishment of a kapu-breaker was harsh and swift.

JACQUES ARAGO, CIRCA 1819 HAWAII STATE ARCHIVES

ing *tapa* cloth. The entire family lived in the common house, called the *hale noa*.

Certain things were *kapu* between the sexes. Primarily, women could not enter the *mua* (man's house), nor could they eat with men. Certain foods such as pork, coconut, red fish, and bananas were forbidden to women, and it was *kapu* for a man to have intercourse before going fishing, engaging in battle, or attending a religious ceremony. Young boys lived with the women until they underwent a circumcision rite called *pule ipu*. After this was performed, males were required to keep the *kapu* of men. A true Hawaiian settlement required a minimum of five huts: the men's eating hut; women's menstruation hut; women's eating hut; communal sleeping hut; and prayer hut. Without these five separate structures, Hawaiian "society" could not exist, since the *ia kapu* (prohibition against men and women eating together) could not be observed.

Ali'i could also declare a *kapu,* and often did so. Certain lands or fishing areas were temporarily made *kapu* so that they could revitalize. Even today, it is *kapu* for anyone to remove all the *opihi* (a type of limpet) from a rock. The great King Kamehameha I even placed a *kapu* on the body of his notoriously unfaithful child bride, Kaahumanu. It didn't work! The greatest *kapu (kapu moe)* was afforded to the highest ranking *ali'i*: anyone coming into their presence had to prostrate himself. Lesser ranking *ali'i* were afforded the *kapu noho:* lessers had to sit or kneel in their presence. Commoners could not let their

shadows fall upon an *ali'i,* nor could they enter the house of an *ali'i* except through a special door. Breaking a *kapu* meant immediate death.

Fatal Flaws

Less than 100 years after Captain Cook's arrival, King Kalakaua found himself with only 48,000 Hawaiian subjects, down more than 80%. Wherever the king went, he would beseech his people, *"Hooulu lahui"*—"Increase the race"—but it was already too late. It was as if nature herself had turned her back on these once-proud people. Many of their marriages were barren and in 1874 when only 1,400 children were born, a full 75% died in infancy. The Hawaiians could do nothing but watch as their race faded from existence.

The Causes of Decline

The ecological system of Hawaii has always been exceptionally fragile and this included its people. When the first whites arrived they found a great people who were large, strong, and virile. But when it came to fighting off the most minor diseases, the Hawaiians proved as delicate as hothouse flowers. To exacerbate the situation, the Hawaiians were totally uninhibited toward sexual intercourse between willing partners, and they engaged in it openly and with abandon. Unfortunately, the sailors who arrived were full of syphilis and gonorrhea. The Hawaiian women brought these diseases home and, given the nature of Hawaiian society at the time, they spread like wildfire. By the time the missionaries came in 1820 and helped to halt the unbridled fornication, they estimated the native population at only 140,000—less than half of what it had been only 40 years after initial contact. In the next 50 years measles, mumps, influenza, and tuberculosis further ravaged the people. Furthermore, Hawaiian men were excellent sailors, and it's estimated that during the whaling years at least 25% of all able-bodied Hawaiian men sailed away, never to return.

But the coup de grace that really ended the Hawaiian race, as such, was that all racial newcomers to the islands were attracted to the Hawaiians and the Hawaiians were in turn attracted to them. With so many interracial marriages, the Hawaiians literally bred themselves out of existence. By 1910, there were still twice as many full-blooded Hawaiians as mixed-bloods, but by 1940 mixed-blooded Hawaiians were the fastest-growing group, and full-blooded the fastest declining.

Hawaiians Today

Many of the Hawaiians who moved to the cities became more and more disenfranchised. Their folk society stressed openness and a giving nature but downplayed the individual and the ownership of private property. These cultural traits made them easy targets for users and schemers until they finally became either apathetic or

Aloha *still shows.*

angry. Most surveys reveal that although Hawaiians number only 13% of Hawaii's population, they account for almost 50% of the financially destitute families and about half of all arrests and illegitimate births. Niihau, a privately owned island, is home to about 230 pure-blooded Hawaiians, representing the largest concentration of them, per capita, in the islands. The Robinson family, which owns the island, restricts visitors to invited guests only.

The second-largest concentration is on Molokai, where 3,300 Hawaiians, living mostly on 40-acre *kuleana* of Hawaiian Homes lands, make up 49% of that island's population. The majority of mixed-blooded Hawaiians—92,000 or so—live on Oahu, where they are particularly strong in the hotel and entertainment fields. People of Hawaiian extraction are still a delight to meet, and anyone so lucky as to be befriended by one long regards this friendship as the highlight of his or her travels. The Hawaiians have always given their *aloha* freely to all the peoples of the world, and it is we who must acknowledge this precious gift.

Mu and Menehune

Hawaiian legends give accounts of dwarflike aborigines on Kauai called the Mu and the Menehune. These two hirsute tribes were said to have lived on the island before and after the arrival of the Polynesians. The Mu were fond of jokes and games, while the Menehune were dedicated workers, stonemasons par excellence, who could build monumental structures in just one night. Many stoneworks that can still be seen around the island are attributed to these hardworking nocturnal people, and a wonderfully educational exhibit concerning them is presented at the Kauai Museum.

Anthropological theory supports the legends that say that some non-Polynesian peoples actually did exist on Kauai. According to oral history, their chief felt that too much interplay and intermarriage was occurring with the Polynesians. He wished his race to remain pure so he ordered them to leave on a "triple-decker floating island," and they haven't been seen since— though if you ask a Kauaian whether he or she believes in the Menehune, the answer is likely to be, "Of course not! But, they're there anyway." Speculation holds that they may have been an entirely different race of people, or perhaps the remaining tribes of the first Polynesians. It's possible that they were cut off from the original culture for so long they developed their own separate culture, and the food supply became so diminished their very stature became reduced in comparison to other Polynesians.

THE CHINESE

Next to Yankees from New England, the Chinese are the oldest migrant group in Hawaii, and their influence has far outshone their meager numbers. They brought to Hawaii, along with their individuality, Confucianism, Taoism, and Buddhism, although many have long since become Christians. The Chinese population, at 69,000, makes up only six percent of the state's total, and the majority (63,000) reside on Oahu. As an ethnic group they account for the least amount of crime, the highest per capita income, and a disproportionate number of professionals.

The First Chinese
No one knows his name, but an unknown Chinese immigrant is credited with being the first person in Hawaii to refine sugar. This Asian wanderer tried his hand at crude refining on Lanai in 1802. Fifty years later, the sugar plantations desperately needed workers, and the first Chinese brought to Hawaii under the newly passed Masters and Servants Act were 195 coolies from Amoy (now Xiamen), who arrived in 1852. These conscripts contracted for three to five years and were given $3 per month plus room and board. They worked 12 hours a day, six days a week, and even in 1852 their wages were the pits. The Chinese almost always left the plantations the minute their contracts expired. They went into business for themselves and promptly monopolized the restaurant and small-shop trades.

The Chinese Niche
Although many people in Hawaii considered all Chinese ethnically the same, they were actually quite different. There were two distinct ethnic groups: the Punti from Guangdong Province in southern China made up 75% of the immigrants, and the Hakka made up the remainder.

In China, they remained separate from each other, never mixing; in Hawaii, they mixed out of necessity. Hardly any Chinese women came over at first, and the ones who followed were at a premium and gladly accepted as wives, regardless of ethnic background. The Chinese were also one of the first groups who willingly intermarried with the Hawaiians, among whom they gained a reputation for being exceptionally caring spouses.

The Chinese accepted the social order and kept a low profile. For example, during the turbulent labor movements of the 1930s and '40s in Hawaii, the Chinese community produced not one labor leader, radical intellectual, or left-wing politician. When Hawaii became a state, one of the two senators elected was Hiram Fong, a racially mixed Chinese. Since statehood, the Chinese community has carried on business as usual as they continue to rise both economically and socially.

THE JAPANESE

Most scholars believe that (inevitably) a few Japanese castaways floated to Hawaii long before Captain Cook arrived and might have introduced the iron with which the islanders seemed to be familiar before the white explorers arrived. The first official arrivals from Japan were ambassadors sent by the Japanese shogun to negotiate in Washington; they stopped en route at Honolulu in March 1860. But it was as plantation workers that the Japanese were brought to the islands in large numbers. A small group arrived in 1868, and mass migration started in 1885.

In 1886, because of famine, the Japanese government allowed farmers mainly from southern Honshu, Kyushu, and Okinawa to emigrate. Among these were members of Japan's little-talked-about untouchable caste, called *eta* or *burakumin* in Japan and *chorinbo* in Hawaii. They gratefully seized this opportunity to better their lot, an impossibility in Japan. The first Japanese migrants were almost all men; between 1897 and 1908, about 70% of the immigrants were male. Afterward, migration slowed because of a "gentlemen's agreement," a euphemism for racism against the "yellow peril." By

indentured Japanese plantation workers and mounted overseer

1900 there were over 60,000 Japanese in the islands, constituting the largest ethnic group.

AJAs—Americans of Japanese Ancestry

Parents of most Japanese children born before WW II were *issei* (first generation), who considered themselves apart from other Americans and clung to the notion of "we Japanese." Their children, the *nisei,* or second generation, were a different matter altogether. In one generation they had become Americans, and they put into practice the high Japanese virtues of obligation, duty, and loyalty to the homeland; that homeland was now unquestionably America. After Pearl Harbor was bombed, the FBI kept close tabs on the Japanese community, and the menace of the "enemy within" prompted the decision to place Hawaii under martial law for the duration of the war. It has since been noted that not a single charge of espionage or sabotage was ever reported against the Japanese community in Hawaii during the war.

AJAs as GIs

Although Japanese had formed a battalion during WW I, they were insulted at being considered unacceptable American soldiers in WW II. Some Japanese-Americans volunteered to serve in labor battalions, and because of their flawless work and loyalty, it was decided to put out a call for a few hundred volunteers to form a combat unit. Over 10,000 signed up! AJAs formed two distinguished units in WW II (the 100th Infantry Battalion and the 442nd Regimental Combat Team), landed in Italy at Salerno, and even

The Japanese-American GIs returned as our boys.

fought from Guadalcanal to Okinawa. They distinguished themselves by becoming *the* most decorated unit in American military history.

The AJAs Return

Many returning AJAs took advantage of the GI Bill and received college educations. The Big Five corporations (see "Economy," earlier in this chapter) for the first time accepted AJAs—former officers—as executives, and the old order was changed. Many Japanese became involved in Hawaiian politics; the first elected to Congress was Daniel Inouye, who had lost an arm fighting in WW II. Hawaii's past governor, George Ariyoshi, elected in 1974, was the country's first Japanese-American to reach such a high office. Most Japanese, even as they climb the economic ladder, tend to remain Democrats.

Today, one out of every two political offices in Hawaii is held by a Japanese-American. In one of those weird quirks of fate, it is now the Hawaiian Japanese who are accused by other ethnic groups of engaging in unfair political practices—nepotism and reverse discrimination. Many of these accusations against AJAs are undoubtedly motivated by jealousy, but the AJAs' record in social fairness issues is not without blemish; true to their custom of family loyalty, they do stick together.

There are now 247,000 people in Hawaii of Japanese ancestry, one-fifth of the state's population. They enjoy a higher-than-average standard of living, and they—especially the men—are the least likely of any ethnic group in Hawaii to marry outside of their group.

CAUCASIANS

White people have a distinction separating them from all other ethnic groups in Hawaii: they are lumped together as one. You can be anything from a Protestant Norwegian dockworker to a Greek Orthodox shipping tycoon, but if your skin is white, in Hawaii you're a *haole*. You can have arrived at Waikiki from Missoula, Montana, in the last 24 hours, or your *kama'aina* family can go back five generations, but if you're white, you're a *haole*.

The word *haole* has a floating connotation that depends upon the spirit in which it's used. It can mean everything from a derisive "honky" or "cracker" to nothing more than "white person." The exact Hawaiian meaning is clouded, but some say it meant "a man of no background," because white men couldn't chant a genealogical *kanaenae* telling the Hawaiians who they were. The word eventually evolved to mean "foreign white man" and, today, simply "white person."

White History

Next to Hawaiians themselves, white people have the oldest stake in Hawaii. They've been there as settlers in earnest since the missionaries of the 1820s and were established long before any other migrant group. From last century until statehood, old *haole* families owned and controlled everything and, although they were generally benevolent, philanthropic, and paternalistic, they were also racist. They were established *kama'aina* families, many of whom made up the boards of the Big Five corporations or owned huge plantations and formed an inner social circle which was closed to the outside. Many managed to find mates from among close family acquaintances.

Their paternalism, which they accepted with grave responsibility, at first only extended to the Hawaiians, who saw them as replacing the *ali'i*. Asians were considered primarily instruments of production. These supremacist attitudes tended to drag on in Hawaii until quite recent times. They are today responsible for the sometimes sour relations between white and nonwhite people in the islands. Today, all individual white people are resented to a certain degree because of these past acts, even though they personally were in no way involved.

White Plantation Workers

In the 1880s, the white landowners looked around and felt surrounded and outnumbered by Asians, so they tried to import white people for plantation work. None of their schemes seemed to work out. Europeans were accustomed to a much higher wage scale and better living conditions than were provided on the plantations. Also, although they were only workers and not considered equals of the ruling elite, they still were expected to act like a special class. They were treated preferentially, which meant they received higher wages for the same jobs performed by Asians. Some of the imported workers included: 600 Scandinavians in 1881; 1,400 Germans in 1881-85; 400 Poles in 1897-98; and 2,400 Russians in 1909-12. Many proved troublesome, like the Poles and Russians, who staged strikes after only months on the job. Many quickly moved to the Mainland. A contingency of Scots, who first came as mule skinners, did become successful plantation managers and supervisors. The Germans and Scandinavians were well received and climbed the social ladder rapidly, becoming professionals and skilled workers.

The Depression years, not as bad economically in Hawaii as in the continental U.S., brought many Mainland whites seeking opportunity, mostly from the South and the West. These new people were even more racist toward brown-skinned people and Asians than the *kama'aina haole,* and they made matters worse. They also competed more intensely for jobs. The racial tension generated during this period came to a head in 1932 with the infamous Massie Rape Case.

The Massie Rape Case
Thomas Massie, a naval officer, and his young wife, Thalia, attended a party at the Officers Club. After drinking and dancing all evening, they got into a fight and Thalia rushed out in a huff. A few hours later, Thalia was at home, confused and hysterical, claiming to have been raped by some local men. On the most circumstantial evidence, Joseph Kahahawai and four friends of mixed ethnic background were accused. The highly controversial trial, rife with racial tensions, ended in a hung jury.

While a new trial was being set, Kahahawai and his friends were released on bail. Seeking revenge, Thomas Massie and Grace Fortescue—Thalia's mother—kidnapped Kahahawai with a plan of extracting a confession from him. They were aided by two enlisted men assigned to guard Thalia. While questioning Joseph, they killed him, then attempted to dump his body in the sea but were apprehended. Another controversial trial—this time for Mrs. Fortescue, Massie, and the accomplices—followed. Clarence Darrow, the famous lawyer, sailed to Hawaii to defend them. For killing Kahahawai,

these people served *one hour* of imprisonment in the judge's private chambers. The other four, acquitted with Joseph Kahahawai, maintain innocence of the rape to this day. Later, the Massies divorced, and Thalia went on to become a depressed alcoholic who eventually took her own life.

The Portuguese
The last time anyone looked, Portugal was still attached to the European continent, but for some anomalous reason the Portuguese weren't considered *haole* in Hawaii for the longest time. About 12,000 arrived between 1878 and 1887 and another 6,000 came between 1906 and 1913. Accompanied during this period by 8,000 Spanish, they were considered one and the same. Most of the Portuguese were illiterate peasants from Madeira and the Azores, and the Spanish hailed from Andalusia. They were very well received, and because they were white but not *haole,* they made a perfect "buffer" ethnic group. Committed to staying in Hawaii, they rose to become skilled workers—the *luna* class on the plantations. However, they de-emphasized education and became very racist toward Asians, regarding them as a threat to job security.

By 1920, the 27,000 Portuguese made up 11% of the population. After that, they tended to blend with the other ethnic groups and weren't counted separately. Portuguese men tended to marry within their ethnic group, but a good portion of Portuguese women married other white men and became closer to the *haole* group, while another large portion chose Hawaiian mates and grew further away. Although they didn't originate pidgin English (see "Language" below), the unique melodious quality of their native tongue did give pidgin that certain lilt it retains today. Also, the ukulele—"jumping flea"—was closely patterned after the *cavaquinho,* a stringed Portuguese folk instrument.

The White Population
Today Caucasians make up the largest racial group in the islands at 33% (about 370,000) of the population. There are heavy white concentrations throughout Oahu, especially in Waikiki, Kailua Kaneohe, and around Pearl City. The white population is the fastest growing in the islands because most people resettling in Hawaii

are white Americans—predominantly from the West Coast.

FILIPINOS AND OTHERS

The Filipinos who came to Hawaii brought high hopes of amassing personal fortunes and returning home as rich heroes. For most, it was a dream that never came true. Filipinos had been American nationals ever since the Spanish-American War of 1898 and as such weren't subject to immigration laws which curtailed the importation of other Asian workers at the turn of this century. The first to arrive were 15 families in 1906, but a large number came in 1924 as strikebreakers. The majority were illiterate peasants from the northern Philippines called *Ilocanos,* with about 10% Visayans from the central cities. The Visayans were not as hardworking or thrifty, but were much more sophisticated. From the first, Filipinos were looked down upon by all the other immigrant groups and were considered particularly uncouth by the Japanese. The value they placed on education was lower than that of any group, and even by 1930 only about half could speak even rudimentary English, the majority remaining illiterate. They were billeted in the worst housing, performed the most menial jobs, and were the last hired and first fired.

One big difference between Filipinos and other groups was that the men brought no Filipino women to marry, so they clung to the idea of returning home. In 1930 there were 30,000 men and only 360 women. This inequitable situation led to a great deal of prostitution and homosexuality; many of these terribly lonely bachelors would feast and drink on weekends and engage in their gruesome but exciting pastime of cockfighting on Sunday. When some did manage to find wives, their mates were inevitably part-Hawaiian. Today, there are still plenty of old Filipino bachelors who never managed to get home, and Sunday cockfights remain a way of life.

The Filipinos constitute 14% of Hawaii's population (169,000), with 70% living on Oahu. Many visitors to Hawaii mistake Filipinos for Hawaiians because of their dark skin; this is a minor irritant to both groups. Some streetwise Filipinos even claim to be Hawaiians, because being Hawaiian is "in" and goes over well with the tourists, especially the young women tourists. For the most part, these people are hardworking, dependable laborers who do tough work for little recognition. They remain low on the social totem pole and have not yet organized politically to stand up for their rights.

Other Groups

About 10% of Hawaii's population is a conglomerate of other ethnic groups. Of these, the largest is Korean, with 14,000 people. About 8,000 Koreans came to Hawaii between 1903 and 1905, when their government halted emigration. During the same period about 6,000 Puerto Ricans arrived, but they have become so assimilated that only 4,000 people in Hawaii today consider themselves Puerto Rican. There were also two attempts made last century to import other Polynesians to strengthen the dying Hawaiian race, but the efforts were failures. In 1869 only 126 central Polynesian natives could be lured to Hawaii, and from 1878 to 1885, 2,500 Gilbert Islanders arrived. Both groups immediately became disenchanted with Hawaii. They pined away for their own islands and departed for home as soon as possible.

Today, however, 12,000 Samoans have settled in Hawaii, and with more on the way they are the fastest-growing minority in the state. For inexplicable reasons, Samoans and native Hawaiians get along extremely poorly and have the worst racial tensions and animosity of any groups. Ostensibly, the Samoans should represent the archetypal Polynesians that the Hawaiians are seeking, but it doesn't work that way. Samoans are criticized by Hawaiians for their hot tempers, lingering feuds, and petty jealousies. They're clannish and are often the butt of "dumb" jokes. This racism seems especially ridiculous, but that's the way it is.

Just to add a bit more exotic spice to the stew, there are about 27,000 blacks, a few thousand Native Americans, and a smattering of Vietnamese refugees also living on the islands.

LANGUAGE

Hawaii is part of the U.S., of course, and people do speak English there, but that's not the whole story. If you turn on the TV to catch the evening news, you'll hear "Walter Cronkite" English—unless, of course, you happen to tune in to a Japanese-language broadcast designed for tourists from that country. You can easily pick up a Chinese-language newspaper or groove to the music on a Filipino radio station, but let's not confuse the issue. All your needs and requests at airports, car-rental agencies, restaurants, hotels, or wherever you happen to travel will be completely understood, as well as answered, in English. When you happen to overhear islanders speaking, though what they're saying will sound somewhat familiar, but you won't be able to pick up all the words, and the beat and melody of the language will be noticeably different.

Hawaii—like New England, the Deep South, and the Midwest—has its own unmistakable linguistic regionalism. All the ethnic peoples who make up Hawaii have enriched the English spoken there with words, expressions, and subtle shades of meaning that are commonly used and understood throughout the islands. The greatest influence on English has come from the Hawaiian language itself, and words such as "aloha," "hula," and "muumuu" are familiarly used and understood by most Americans.

Other migrant peoples—especially the Chinese, Japanese, and Portuguese—influenced the local dialect to such an extent that the simplified plantation lingo they spoke has become known as "pidgin." A fun and enriching part of the "island experience" is picking up a few words of Hawaiian and pidgin. English is the official language of the state, business, education, and perhaps even the mind, but pidgin is the language of the people, the emotions, and life—while Hawaiian remains the language of the heart and the soul.

Note: Many Hawaiian words are commonly used in English, appear in English dictionaries, and therefore would ordinarily be subject to the rules of English grammar. The Hawaiian language, however, does not pluralize nouns by adding an "s"; the singular and plural are differentiated by context. For purposes of this book, and to highlight rather than denigrate the Hawaiian culture, the Hawaiian style of pluralization will be followed for common Hawaiian words. The following are some examples of plural Hawaiian nouns treated this way in this book: *haole* (not haoles), hula, *kahuna,* lei, luau, and *nene*.

PIDGIN

The dictionary definition of pidgin is: "a simplified language with a rudimentary grammar used as a means of communication between people speaking different languages." Hawaiian pidgin is a little more complicated than that. It had its roots during the plantation days of last century when white owners and *luna* had to communicate with recently arrived Chinese, Japanese, and Portuguese laborers. It was designed as a simple language of the here and now and was primarily concerned with the necessary functions of working, eating, and sleeping. It has an economical noun-verb-object structure (although not necessarily in that order).

Hawaiian words make up most of pidgin's non-English vocabulary, but the language includes a good smattering of Chinese, Japanese, and Samoan as well, and the distinctive rising inflection is provided by the melodious Mediterranean lilt of Portuguese. Pidgin is not a stagnant language. It's kept alive by hip new words introduced by people who are "so radical," or especially by slang words introduced by teenagers. It's a colorful English, like the "jive" or "ghettoese" spoken by African-North Americans, and is as regionally unique as the speech of Cajuns in Louisiana's bayous. *Maka'ainana* of all socioethnic backgrounds can at least understand pidgin. Most islanders are proud of it, but some consider it a low-class jargon. The Hawaiian House of Representatives has given pidgin an official sanction, and most people feel that it adds a real local style and should be preserved.

CAPSULE PIDGIN

The following are a few commonly used words and expressions that should give you an idea of pidgin. It really can't be written properly, merely approximated, but for now, *"Brah, study da' kine an' bimbye you be hele on, brah! OK? Lesgo."*

an' den—and then? big deal; so what's next; how boring

bimbye—after a while; bye and bye. "Bimbye, you learn pidgin."

blalah—brother (but actually only refers to a large, heavy-set, good-natured Hawaiian man)

brah—brother; pal (all the bros in Hawaii are brahs). Used to get someone's attention. One of the most common words used, even among people who are not acquainted. After a fill-up at a gas station, a person might say, "Tanks, brah."

cockaroach—steal; rip off. If you really want to find out what *cockaroach* means, just leave your camera on your beach blanket when you take a little dip.

da' kine—a catchall word of many meanings that epitomizes the essence of pidgin. *Da' kine* is easily used as a euphemism for pidgin and is substituted whenever the speaker is at a loss for a word or just wants to generalize. It can mean "you know?," "watchamacallit," or "of that type."

geev um—give it to them; give them hell; go for it. Can be used as an encouragement. If a surfer is riding a great wave, the people on the beach might yell, "Geev um, brah!"

hana ho—again. Especially after a concert the audience shouts "hana ho" (one more!).

hele on—right on! hip; with it; groovy

howzit?—as in "howzit brah?" what's happening? how is it going? The most common greeting, used in place of the more formal "How do you do?"

hu hu—angry! "You put the make on the wrong da' kine wahine brah, and you in da' kine trouble, if you get one big Hawaiian blalah plenty hu hu."

kapu—a Hawaiian word meaning "forbidden." If

"kapu" is written on a gate or posted on a tree, it means "No trespassing." *Kapu*-breakers are still very unpopular in the islands.

lesgo—Let's go! Do it!

li'dis an' li'dat—like this or that; a catchall grouping, especially if you want to avoid details; like, ya' know?

lolo buggah—stupid or crazy guy (person). Words to a tropical island song go, "I want to find the lolo who stole my pakalolo."

mo' bettah—real good! great idea. An island sentiment used to be, "mo' bettah you come Hawaii." Now it has subtly changed to, "mo' bettah you visit Hawaii."

ono—number one! delicious; great; groovy. "Hawaii is ono, brah!"

pakalolo—literally, "crazy smoke"; marijuana; grass; reefer. "Hey, brah! Maui-wowie da' kine ono pakalolo."

pakiki head—stubborn; bull-headed

pau—a Hawaiian word meaning "finished"; done; over and done with. *Pau hana* means end of work or quitting time. Once used by plantation workers, now used by everyone.

stink face—basically frowning at someone; using facial expression to show displeasure. Hard looks. What you'll get if you give local people a hard time.

swell head—burned up; angry

talk story—spinning yarns; shooting the breeze; throwing the bull; a rap session. If you're lucky enough to be around to hear *kapuna* (elders) "talk story," you can hear some fantastic tales in the tradition of old Hawaii.

tita—sister (but only used to describe a fun-loving, down-to-earth country girl)

waddascoops—what's the scoop? what's up? what's happening?

Pidgin Lives

Pidgin is first learned at school where all students, regardless of background, are exposed to it. The pidgin spoken by young people today is "fo' real" different from that of their parents. It's no longer only plantation talk but has moved to the streets and picked up some sophistication. At one time there was an academic movement to exterminate it, but that idea died away with the same thinking that insisted on making left-handed people write with their right hands. It is strange, however, that pidgin has become the unofficial language of Hawaii's grassroots movement, when it actually began as a white owners' language used to supplant Hawaiian and all the languages brought to the islands.

Although hip young *haole* use pidgin all the time, it has gained the connotation of being the language of the nonwhite locals and is part of the "us against them" way of thinking. All local people, *haole* or not, do consider pidgin their own island language and don't really like it when it's used by *malihini*. If you're in the islands long enough, you don't have to bother learning pidgin; it'll learn you. There's a book sold all over the islands called *Pidgin to da Max*, written by (you guessed it) a *haole*— a Nebraskan named Doug Simonson. You might not be able to understand what's being said by locals speaking pidgin (that's usually the idea), but you should be able to *feel* what's being meant.

HAWAIIAN

The Hawaiian language sways like a palm tree in a gentle wind. Its words are as melodious as a love song. Linguists say that you can learn a lot about people through their language; when you hear Hawaiian you think of gentleness and love, and it's hard to imagine the ferocious side so evident in Hawaii's past. With its many Polynesian root words easily traced to Indonesian and Malay, Hawaiian is obviously from this same stock. The Hawaiian spoken today is very different from old Hawaiian. Its greatest metamorphosis occurred when the missionaries began to write it down in the 1820s. There is a movement to reestablish the Hawaiian language, and courses in it are offered at the University of Hawaii. Many scholars have put forth translations of Hawaiian, but there are endless, volatile disagreements in the academic sector about the real meanings of Hawaiian

THE ALPHABET.

VOWELS. Names.	SOUND. Ex. in Eng.	Ex. in Hawaii.
A a ---â	as in *father*,	la—sun.
E e ---a	— *tele*,	hemo—cast off.
I i ---e	— *marine*,	marie—quiet.
O o ---o	— *over*,	ono—sweet.
U u ---oo	—*rule*,	nui—large.

CONSONANTS.	Names.	CONSONANTS.	Names.
B b	be	N n	nu
D d	de	P p	pi
H h	he	R r	ro
K k	ke	T t	ti
L l	la	V v	vi
M m	mu	W w	we

The following are used in spelling foreign words:

| F f | fe | S s | se |
| G g | ge | Y y | yi |

Cover page of the first Hawaiian primer shows the phonetic rendering of the ancient Hawaiian language before five of the consonants were dropped.

words. Hawaiian is no longer spoken as a language except on Niihau, and the closest tourists will come to it are in place-names, street names, and words that have become part of common usage, such as *aloha* and *mahalo*. A few old Hawaiians still speak it at home, and sermons are delivered in Hawaiian at some local churches. Kawaiahao Church in downtown Honolulu is the most famous of these. (See the glossary for a list of commonly used Hawaiian words.)

Wiki Wiki Hawaiian

Thanks to the missionaries, the Hawaiian language is rendered phonetically using only 12 letters—five vowels, a-e-i-o-u, sounded as they are in Italian (see "Pronunciation Key," below), and seven consonants, h-k-l-m-n-p-w, sounded exactly as they are in English (sometimes "w" is

(continued on page 58)

CAPSULE HAWAIIAN

This brief primer is designed to give you a taste of Hawaiian and a basic vocabulary of words in common usage which you are likely to hear. Becoming familiar with them is not a strict necessity, but it will definitely enhance your experience and make it more congenial when talking with local people. You'll soon notice that many islanders spice their speech with certain words, especially when they're speaking "pidgin." You should feel free to use them, too, just as soon as you feel comfortable with the idea. You might even discover some Hawaiian words so perfectly expressive that they become a regular part of your vocabulary. Many Hawaiian words have actually made it into the English dictionary. Placenames, historical names, and descriptive terms used throughout this handbook may not appear here; for those and other applicable terms, see the glossary at the back of the book, the special topic "Capsule Pidgin," and the "Food and Drink" and "Getting Around" sections of the On the Road chapter. The definitions given are not exhaustive, but are generally considered the most common.

BASIC VOCABULARY

a'a—rough clinker lava. *A'a* has become the correct geological term to describe this type of lava wherever it is found in the world.

ae—yes

akamai—smart; clever; wise

ali'i—a Hawaiian chief or nobleman

aloha—the most common greeting in the islands. Can mean both hello and goodbye, welcome and farewell. It also can mean romantic love, affection or best wishes.

aole—no

hale—house or building; often combined with other words to name a specific place such as Haleakala (House of the Sun) or Hale Pai at Lahainaluna (Printing House).

hana—work; combined with *pau,* means end of work or quitting time

haole—a word that at one time meant foreigner but now means a white person or caucasian. Many etymological definitions have been put forth, but none satisfies everyone. Some feel that it signified a person without a background, because the first white men could not chant their genealogies as was common among Hawaiians.

hapai—pregnant. Used by all ethnic groups when a *keiki* is on the way.

hapa—half, as in a mixed-blooded person being referred to as *hapa haole*

heiau—a traditional Hawaiian temple. A platform made of skillfully fitted rocks, upon which structures were built and offerings made to the gods.

holomuu—an ankle-length dress which is much more fitted than a muumuu and which is often worn on formal occasions

hoolaulea—any happy event but especially a family outing or picnic

hoomalimali—sweet talk; flattery

hu hu—angry; irritated; mad

huli huli—barbecue, as in *huli huli* chicken

hula—a native Hawaiian dance in which the rhythm of the islands is captured in swaying hips and stories told by lyrically moving hands

hui—a group; meeting; society. Often used to refer to Chinese businessmen or family members who pool their money to get businesses started.

imu—an underground oven filled with hot rocks and used for baking. The main cooking feature at a luau, an *imu* is used to steam-bake the pork and other succulent dishes. Traditionally the tending of the *imu* was for men only.

ipo—sweetheart; lover; girl or boyfriend

kahuna—priest; sorcerer; doctor; skillful person. *Kahuna* had tremendous power in old Hawaii, which they used for both good and evil. The *kahuna ana'ana* was a feared individual because he practiced "black magic" and could pray a person to death, while a *kahuna lapa'au* was a medical practitioner who brought aid and comfort to the people.

kalua—a designation of food roasted underground in an *imu.* One island favorite is *kalua* pork.

kama'aina—a child of the land; an old-timer; a longtime island resident of any ethnic background; a resident of Hawaii or native son. Oftentimes, hotels and airlines offer discounts called *"kama'aina* rates" to anyone who can prove island residency.

kane—man, but actually used to signify a husband or boyfriend. Written on a door, it designates the men's room.

kapu—forbidden; taboo; keep out; do not touch

kapuna—a grandparent or old-timer; usually means someone who has gained wisdom. The statewide school system now invites *kapuna* to talk to the children about the old ways and methods.

kaukau—slang word meaning food or chow; grub. Some of the best eating in Hawaii is from *"kaukau* wagons," which are trucks from which plate lunches and other morsels are sold.

keiki—child or children; used by all ethnic groups. "Have you hugged your *keiki* today?"

kokua—help, as in, "Your *kokua* is needed to keep Hawaii free from litter."

kona wind—a muggy subtropical wind that blows from the south and hits the leeward side of the islands. It usually brings sticky hot weather and is one of the few times when air-conditioning will be appreciated.

lanai—veranda or porch. You'll pay more for a hotel room if it has a lanai with an ocean view.

lei—a traditional garland of flowers or vines. One of Hawaii's most beautiful customs. Given at any auspicious occasion, but especially when arriving or leaving Hawaii.

limu—varieties of edible seaweed gathered from the shoreline. It makes an excellent salad and is used to garnish many island dishes—a favorite at luau.

lomi lomi—traditional Hawaiian massage; also, a vinegared salad made up of raw salmon, chopped onions, and spices

lua—the toilet; the head; the bathroom

luau—a Hawaiian feast featuring poi, *imu*-baked pork, and other traditional foods. A good luau provides some of the best gastronomical delights in the world.

mahalo—thanks; thank you. *Mahalo nui* means "big thanks" or "thank you very much."

mahu—a homosexual; often used derisively, like "fag" or "queer"

makai—toward the sea; used by most islanders when giving directions

malihini—what you are if you have just arrived; a newcomer; a tenderfoot; a recent arrival

manauahi—free; gratis; extra

manini—stingy; tight. A Hawaiianized word taken from the name of Don Francisco Marin, who was instrumental in bringing many fruits and plants to Hawaii. He was known for never sharing any of the bounty from his substantial gardens on Vineyard Street in Honolulu—hence, the current meaning of the word.

mauka—toward the mountains; used by most islanders when giving directions

mauna—mountain. Often combined with other words to be more descriptive, as in Mauna Kea ("White Mountain").

moana—the ocean; the sea. It's a component of many business, hotel, and place-names.

muumuu—a "Mother Hubbard," a long dress with a high neckline that has become fashionable attire for almost any occasion in Hawaii. The garment introduced by the missionaries to cover the nakedness of the Hawaiians.

ohana—a family; the fundamental social division; extended family. Now used to denote a social organization with "grassroots," as in the "Save Kahoolawe Ohana."

okolehau—literally, "iron bottom"; a traditional booze made from ti root; *okole* means "rear end" and *hau* means "iron," which was descriptive of the huge blubber pots used to make the liquor. Also, if you drink too much of it, it'll surely knock you on your *okole.*

ono—delicious; delightful; the best. *Ono ono* means "extra delicious."

opu—belly; stomach

pa'hoehoe—smooth, ropey lava that looks like burnt pancake batter. *Pa'hoehoe* is now the correct geological term used to describe this type of lava wherever it may be found in the world.

pakalolo—"crazy smoke"; marijuana; grass; dope

pali—a cliff; precipice. Hawaii's geology makes them quite common. The most famous are the *pali* of Oahu, where a major battle was fought.

paniolo—a Hawaiian cowboy. Derived from the Spanish *espaniola.* The first cowboys brought in during the early 19th century were Mexicans from California.

pau—finished; done; completed. Often combined into *pau hana,* which means end of work or quitting time.

(continues on next page)

CAPSULE HAWAIIAN

(continued)

pilau—stink; smells bad; stench

pilikia—trouble of any kind, big or small; bad times

pono—righteous or excellent

poi—a glutinous paste made from the pounded corn of taro which, slightly fermented, has a light sour taste. Purplish in color, it is a staple at luau, where it is called one-, two-, or three-finger poi, depending upon its thickness.

puka—a hole of any size. *Puka* is used by all island residents and can be employed whether you're talking about a pinprick in a rubber boat or a tunnel through a mountain.

punee—bed; narrow couch. Used by all ethnic groups. To recline on a *punee* on a breezy lanai is a true island treat.

pupule—crazy; nuts; out of your mind

pu pu—appetizer; snack; hors d'oeuvres; can be anything from cheese and crackers to sushi. Oftentimes, bars or nightclubs offer them free.

tapa—a traditional paper cloth made from beaten bark. Intricate designs were stamped in using beaters, and color was added with natural dyes. The tradition was lost in Hawaii but is now making a comeback and provides some of the most beautiful folk art in the islands.

tutu—grandmother; granny; older woman. Used by all as a term of respect and endearment.

ukulele—*uku* means "flea" and *lele* means "jumping"; thus, "ukulele" means "jumping flea," which was how the Hawaiians perceived the quick finger movements on the banjo-type Portuguese folk instrument called a *cavaquinho*. The ukulele quickly became synonymous with the islands.

wahine—young woman; female; girl; wife. Used by all ethnic groups. When written on a door, it marks the women's room.

wai—fresh water; drinking water

wela—hot; *wela kahao* is "a hot time" or "making whoopee."

wiki—quickly; fast; in a hurry. Often seen as *wiki wiki* (very fast), as in Wiki Wiki Messenger Service.

USEFUL PHRASES

Aloha ahiahi—Good evening

Aloha au ia oe—I love you!

Aloha kakahiaka—Good morning

aloha nui loa—much love; fondest regards

Hauoli la hanau—Happy Birthday

Hauoli makahiki hau—Happy New Year

komo mai—please come in; enter; welcome

Mele Kalikimaka—Merry Christmas

okole maluna—bottoms up; salud; cheers; kampai

---

pronounced as "v," but this only occurs in the middle of a word and always follows a vowel). A consonant is always followed by a vowel, forming two-letter syllables, but vowels are often found in pairs or even triplets. A slight oddity about Hawaiian is the glottal stop. This is an abrupt break in sound in the middle of a word—such as "oh-oh" in English—and is denoted with an apostrophe ('). A good example is *ali'i*, or, even better, the Oahu town of Ha'iku, which actually means "abrupt break."

Pronunciation Key
For those unfamiliar with the sounds of Italian or other Romance languages, the vowels are sounded as follows:

A—in stressed syllables, pronounced as in **"ah"** (that feels good!). For example, Haleakala is pronounced "hah lay AH kah lah"). In unstressed syllables, pronounced as in "**a**gain" or "**a**bove." For example, Kamehameha is pronounced "k**a** may h**a** may h**a**."

E—short "e" as in "p**e**n" or "d**e**nt" (ha l**e**). Long "e" sounded as "ay" as in "sw**ay**" or "d**ay**." For example, the Hawaiian goose *nene* is a "nay nay."

I—pronounced "ee," as in "s**ee**" or "w**e**" (pa l**i**).

O—pronounced as in "n**o**" or "**o**h" (k**o** a or **o** n**o**).

U—pronounced "oo," as in "d**o**" or "st**ew**" (ka **pu** or P**u** na).

Diphthongs

Hawaiian also employs eight vowel pairs or diphthongs: ae, ai, ao, au, ei, eu, oi, ou. These are the sounds made by gliding from one vowel to another within a syllable. The stress is placed on the first vowel. In English, examples would be "s**oi**l" and "**eu**phoria." Common examples in Hawaiian are "lei" and *"heiau."*

Stress

The best way to learn which syllables are stressed in Hawaiian is by listening closely. It becomes obvious after a while. There are also some vowel sounds that are held longer than others; these can occur at the beginning of a word, such as the first "a" in *"aina,"* or in the middle of a word, like the first "a" in "lanai." Again, it's a matter of tuning your ear and paying attention. No one is going to give you a hard time if you mispronounce a word. It's good, however, to pay close attention to the pronunciation of street and place-names because many Hawaiian words sound alike and a misplaced vowel here or there could be the difference between getting where you want to go and getting lost.

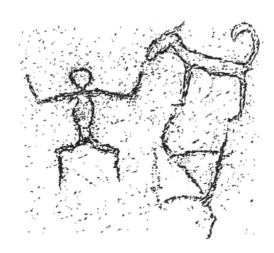

WILLIAM ELLIS, CIRCA 1791, HAWAII STATE ARCHIVES

RELIGION

The Lord saw fit to keep His island paradise secret from humans for a few million years, but once we finally arrived we were awfully thankful. Hawaii sometimes seems like a floating tabernacle; everywhere you look there's a church, temple, shrine, or *heiau*. Either the islands are a very holy place or there's a powerful lot of sinning going on that would require so many houses of prayer. Actually, it's just America's "right to worship" concept fully employed in microcosm. All the peoples who came to Hawaii brought their own forms of devotion. The Polynesian Hawaiians praised the primordial creators, Wakea and Papa, from whom their pantheon of animistically inspired gods sprang. Obviously to a modern world these old gods would never do. Unfortunately for the old gods, there were simply too many of them, and belief in them was looked upon as mere superstition—the folly of semicivilized pagans. So the famous missionaries of the 1820s brought Congregational Christianity and the "true path" to heaven.

Inconveniently, the Catholics, Mormons, Reformed Mormons, Adventists, Episcopalians, Unitarians, Christian Scientists, Lutherans, Bap-

tists, Jehovah's Witnesses, Salvation Army, and every other major and minor denomination of Christianity that followed in their wake brought their own brands of enlightenment—and never quite agreed with each other. Chinese and Japanese immigrants established the major sects of Buddhism, Confucianism, Taoism, and Shintoism. Allah is praised, the Torah is chanted in Jewish synagogues, and nirvana is sought at a variety of Hindu temples. If the spirit moves you, a Hare Krishna devotee will be glad to point you in the right direction and give you a free flower for only a dollar or two. If the world is still too much with you, you might find peace at a Church of Scientology, or meditate at a Kundalini yoga institute, or perhaps find relief at a local assembly of Baha'i. Anyway, rejoice, because in Hawaii you'll not only find paradise, you might even find salvation.

HAWAIIAN BELIEFS

The Polynesian Hawaiians worshipped nature. They saw its forces manifested in a multiplicity of forms to which they ascribed godlike powers, and based daily life on this animistic philosophy. Handpicked and specially trained storytellers chanted the exploits of the gods. These ancient tales, kept alive in a special oral tradition called *moolelo,* were recited only by day. Entranced listeners encircled the chanter and, out of respect for the gods and in fear of their wrath, were forbidden to move once the tale was begun. This was serious business where a person's life could be at stake. It was not like the telling of *kaao,* which were simple fictions, tall tales, and yarns of ancient heroes related for amusement and to pass the long nights. Any object, animate or inanimate (but especially a dead body or respected ancestor), could be a god, and all could be infused with mana.

Ohana had personal family gods called aumakua on whom they called in times of danger or strife. There were children of gods called *kupua* who were thought to live among humans and were distinguished either for their beauty and strength or for their ugliness and terror. It was told that processions of dead *ali'i,* called "Marchers of the Night," wandered through the land of the living and unless you were properly protected it could mean death if they looked upon you. There were simple ghosts known as *akua lapu* who merely frightened people. Forests, waterfalls, trees, springs, and a thousand forms of nature were the manifestations of *akua li'i,* "little spirits" who could be invoked at any time for help or protection. It made no difference who or what you were in old Hawaii; the gods were ever-present and took a direct and active role in your life.

Behind all of these beliefs was an innate sense of natural balance and order. It could be interpreted as positive-negative, yin-yang, plus-minus, life-death, light-dark, whatever, but the main idea was that everything had its opposite. The time of darkness when only the gods lived was *po.* When the great gods descended to the earth and created light, this was *ao* and humanity was born. All of these *moolelo* are part of the *Kumulipo,* the great chant that records the Hawaiian version of creation. From the time the gods descended and touched the earth at Ku Moku on Lanai, the genealogies were kept. Unlike the Bible, these included the noble families of female as well as male *ali'i.*

THE STRIFES OF MAUI

Of all the heroes and mythological figures of Polynesia, Maui is the best known. Stories of his "strifes" are like the great Greek epics and made excellent tales of daring that elders loved to relate to youngsters around the evening fire. Maui was abandoned by his mother, Hina of Fire, when he was an infant. She wrapped him in her hair and cast him upon the sea where she expected him to die. But he lived and returned home to become her favorite. She knew then that he was a born hero and had strength far beyond that of ordinary mortals. His first exploit was to lift the sky. In those days, the sky hung so low that humans had to crawl around on all fours. A seductive young woman approached Maui and asked him to use his great strength to lift the sky. In fine heroic fashion, the big boy agreed—if the beautiful woman would, euphemistically, "give him a drink from her gourd." He then obliged her by lifting the sky, and he might even have made the earth move for her once or twice.

More Land

The territory of humanity was small, and Maui decided that more land was needed, so he conspired to "fish up islands." He descended into the land of the dead and petitioned an ancestress to fashion him a hook from her jawbone. She obliged and created the mythical hook, *Manai ikalani.* Maui then secured a sacred *alae* bird, which he intended to use for bait, and bid his brothers paddle him far out to sea. When he arrived at the deepest spot, he lowered *Manai ikalani,* baited with the sacred bird, and his sister, Hina of the Sea, placed it into the mouth of "Old One Tooth," who held the land fast to the bottom of the waters. Maui then exhorted his brothers to row, but warned them not to look back. They strained at the oars with all their might and slowly a great landmass arose. One brother, overcome by curiosity, looked back and, when he did so, the land shattered into all of the islands of Polynesia.

Further Exploits

Maui still desired to serve humanity. People were without fire, the secret of which was held by the sacred *alae* birds, who learned it from Maui's far-distant mother. Hina of Fire gave Maui her burning fingernails, but Maui oafishly kept dropping them into streams until all had fizzled out and he had totally irritated his generous progenitor. Hina pursued him, trying to burn him to a cinder; Maui chanted for rain to put out her scorching fires. When she saw that they were being quenched, she hid her fire in the barks of special trees and informed the mud hens where they could be found, but first made them promise never to tell humans. Maui knew of this and captured a mud hen, threatening to wring its scrawny, traitorous neck unless it gave up the secret. The bird tried trickery and told Maui first to rub together the stems of sugarcane, then banana, and even taro. None worked, and Maui's determined rubbing is why these plants have hollow roots today.

Finally, with Maui's hands tightening around the mud hen's gizzard, the bird confessed that fire could be found in the *hau* tree and also the sandalwood, which Maui named *ili aha* (fire bark) in its honor. He then rubbed all the feathers off the mud hen's head for being so deceitful, which is why their crowns are featherless today.

The Sun Is Snared

Maui's greatest deed, however, was snaring the sun and exacting its promise to go more slowly across the heavens. The people complained that there were not enough daylight hours to fish or farm. Maui's mother could not dry her *tapa* cloth because the sun rose and set so quickly. She asked her son to help. Maui went to his blind grandmother, who lived on the slopes of Haleakala and was responsible for cooking the sun's bananas, which Maui ate every day in passing. She told him to personally weave 16 strong ropes with nooses from his sister's hair. Some say these came from her head, but other versions insist that it was no doubt Hina's pubic hair that had the power to hold the sun god. Maui positioned himself with the rope, and as each of the 16 rays of the sun came across Haleakala, he snared them until the sun was defenseless and had to bargain for his life. Maui agreed to free him if he promised to go more slowly. From that time forward the sun agreed to move slowly, and Haleakala ("The House of the Sun") became his home.

HEIAU AND IDOLS

A *heiau* is a Hawaiian temple. The basic *heiau* was a masterfully built and fitted rectangular stone wall that varied in size from about as big as a basketball court to as big as a football field. Once the restraining outer walls were built, the interior was backfilled with smaller stones and the top dressing was expertly laid and then rolled, perhaps with a log, to form a pavement-like surface. All that remains of Hawaii's many *heiau* are the stone platforms. The buildings upon them, made from perishable wood, leaves, and grass, have long since disappeared.

Some *heiau* were dreaded temples where human sacrifices were made. Tradition says that this barbaric custom began at Wahaula Heiau, on the Big Island, in the 12th century and was introduced by a ferocious Tahitian priest named Paao. Other *heiau*, such as Pu'uhonua o Honaunau, also on the Big Island, were temples of refuge where the weak, widowed, orphaned, and vanquished could find safety and sanctuary.

Idols

The Hawaiian people worshipped gods who took the form of idols fashioned from wood, feathers, or stone. The eyes were made from shells, and until these were inlaid the idol was dormant. The hair used was often human hair, and the arms and legs were usually flexed. The mouth was either gaping or in the shape of a wide figure-eight lying on its side, and more likely than not was lined with glistening dog teeth. Small figures made of woven basketry were expertly

Commoners were required to lie face down when they saw an approaching kahili, a standard that resembled a huge feather duster. This was so the mana of an ali'i would not be defiled by their touches, gazes, or even shadows.

LOUISE FOOTE

The person most instrumental in bringing the missionaries to Hawaii was a young man named Opukahaia. He was an orphan befriended by a ship's captain and taken to New England, where he studied theology. Obsessed with the desire to return home and save his people from certain damnation, Opukahaia wrote accounts of life in Hawaii that were published and widely read. These accounts were directly responsible for the formation of the Pioneer Company to the Sandwich Islands Missions in 1819. Unfortunately, Opukahaia died in New England from typhus the year before they left.

"Civilizing" Hawaii

The first missionaries had the straightforward task of bringing the Hawaiians out of paganism and into Christianity and civilization. They met with terrible hostility—not from the natives, but from the sea captains and traders who were very happy with the open debauchery and wanton whoremongering that was the status quo in the Hawaii of 1820. Many direct confrontations between these two factions even included the cannonading of missionaries' homes by American sea captains who, thanks to meddlesome "do-gooders," were denied the customary visits of island women. The most memorable of these incidents involved "Mad Jack" Percival, the captain of the USS *Dolphin*, who bombed a church in Lahaina to show his rancor. In actuality, the truth of the situation was much closer to the sentiments of James Jarves, who wrote, "The missionary was a far more useful and agreeable man than his Catholicism would indicate; and the trader was not so bad a man as the missionary would make him out to be." The missionaries' primary aim might have been conversion, but the most fortuitous by-product was education, which raised the consciousness of every Hawaiian, regardless of religious affiliation. In 40 short years, Hawaii was considered a civilized nation well on its way into the modern world, and the American Board of Missions officially ended its support in 1863.

Non-Christians

By the turn of the century, both Shintoism and Buddhism, brought by the Japanese and Chinese, were firmly established in Hawaii. The first official Buddhist temple was Hongpa Hongwanji,

BOB RACE

Kukailimoku, Kamehameha's war god, was 30 inches tall. Fashioned from feathers, it presented a horrible sight, with its gaping mouth of dog teeth, and was reputed to utter loud cries while battle was being waged.

covered with feathers. Red and yellow feathers were favorites taken from specific birds by men whose only work was to roam the forests in search of them.

MISSIONARIES ONE AND ALL

In Hawaii, when you say "missionaries," it's taken for granted that you're referring to the small and determined band of Congregationalists who arrived aboard the brig *Thaddeus* in 1820, and the follow-up groups, called "companies" or "packets," that reinforced them. They were sent from Boston by the American Board of Commissioners for Foreign Missions (ABCFM), which learned of the supposed sad and godless plight of the Hawaiian people through returning sailors and especially through the few Hawaiians who had come to America to study.

A. AGATE, CIRCA 1840, HAWAII STATE ARCHIVES

William Alexander preaching on Kauai

established on Oahu in 1889. All the denominations of Buddhism account for 17% (170,000 parishioners) of the islands' religious total, and there are about 50,000 Shintoists. The Hindu religion has perhaps 2,000 adherents, and about the same number of Jewish people live throughout Hawaii (which has only one synagogue, Temple Emanuel, on Oahu). The largest number of people in Hawaii, 300,000, remain unaffiliated, and about 10,000 people are in new religious movements and lesser-known faiths such as Baha'i and Unitarianism.

ON THE ROAD
SPORTS AND RECREATION

Kauai is an exciting island for all types of sports enthusiasts, with golf, tennis, hunting, fresh and saltwater fishing, and all manner of water sports. You can rent horses, camp and hike the hidden reaches of the Na Pali coast, or simply relax on a cruise. The following should start the fun rolling. (For Zodiacs, kayaks, etc., see "Sightseeing Tours" under "Getting Around" at the end of this chapter.)

SWIMMING AND BEACHES

With so many beaches to choose from, the problem on Kauai is picking which one to visit. If you venture farther than the immediate area of your hotel, the following will give you some help in deciding just where you'd like to romp about. This is a simple listing only. For more details, see the specific listings in the appropriate travel chapters.

Lihue Area Beaches
Kalapaki Beach, in Lihue, is one of the best on the island and convenient to Kauai's principal town center. This beach's gentle wave action is just right for learning how to bodysurf or ride the boogie board; snorkeling is fair. Two small crescent beaches lie just below the lighthouse at the far end of the beach. Water is rougher there, with much exposed rock; snorkeling should be done on calm days only. Also accessible but less frequented is **Hanamaulu Bay,** just up the coast, with a lagoon, picnic spots, and camping (with permit) at **Ahukini Recreation Pier State Park.**

Kapa'a, Wailua, and Vicinity
Like its accommodations, the beaches of Wailua are few but very good. **Lydgate Beach** has two lava pools, and the beaches below Wailua Municipal Golf Course offer seclusion in sheltered coves where there's fine snorkeling. **Waipouli Beach** and **Kapa'a Beach** flank the well-de-

veloped town of Kapa'a, while out along a cane road near Pohakuloa is the little-frequented **Donkey Beach,** known for its good surfing and snorkeling. The undertow is quite strong at Donkey Beach, so don't venture out too far if you don't swim well. (A permit issued by the Lihue Sugar Co. is technically necessary—and advised—to use the cane road.)

Anahola Beach, at the south end of Anahola Bay, has safe swimming in a protected cove, freshwater swimming in the stream that empties into the bay, picnicking, and camping (with permit). Snorkel a short distance up the shore to where the reef comes in close—an area where locals come for shore fishing. Still farther north is **Moloa'a Beach,** a little-visited half-moon swath of sand.

North Kauai Beaches

Just south of Kilauea is **Secret Beach,** all that its name implies. At the end of a tiny dirt road, the start of which eludes many people, is a huge stretch of white sand. You're sure to find it nearly empty. Camping is good, and no one is around to bother you. North of town is **Kalihiwai Beach,** great for swimming and bodysurfing during the right conditions. People camp in the ironwood trees that line the beach. There is a park at **Anini Beach**—a great place to snorkel as it has the longest exposed reef in Kauai, and a wonderful place to learn windsurfing because of the shallow water inside the reef.

Hanalei Bay is a prime spot on the north coast. Swim at the mouth of the Hanalei River (but watch out for boats) or on the far side of the bay. Experienced surfers ride the waves below the Sheraton; snorkeling is good closer to the cliffs. West of Hanalei is **Lumahai Beach,** a beautiful curve of white sand backed by cliffs and thick jungle that was the silent star of the movie *South Pacific.* The inviting water here has a fierce riptide, so enter only when the water is calm. **Haena Beach** and nearby **Tunnels** are terrific swimming and snorkeling spots.

At the end of the road is **Ke'e Beach,** a popular place with some amenities, good swimming in summer, and adequate snorkeling. Many secluded beaches at the foot of the Na Pali cliffs dot the coast to the west along the Kalalau Trail. **Hanakapi'ai Beach** is reached after one hour on the trail and fine for sunbathing; the water, es-

pecially in winter, can be torturous, so stay out. **Kalalau Beach** is a full day's hike down this spectacular coast, and some beaches here can only be reached by boat.

South Kauai Beaches

The **Poipu Beach** area is the most developed on the island—accommodating, tame, and relaxing. You can swim, snorkel, and bodysurf here to your heart's content (see "Poipu" in the Poipu and Koloa chapter).

Down the coast are **Salt Pond Beach,** one of the island's best and good for swimming and windsurfing, and **Pakala Beach,** popular with surfers but also good for swimming and snorkeling. The golden strand of **Kekaha Beach** runs for miles with excellent swimming, snorkeling, and surfing, and stretches into Barking Sands Pacific Missile Range, where you can go, with permission, for good views of Niihau when no military exercises are in progress.

Polihale Beach is the end of the road. Swimming is not the best as the surf is high and the undertow strong, but walk along the shore for a view of the south end of the great Na Pali cliffs.

SCUBA AND SNORKELING

The best beaches for snorkeling and scuba are along the northeast coast from Anahola to Ke'e. (The reefs off Poipu, roughed up by Hurricanes Iwa and Iniki, are making a remarkable comeback.) Those interested can buy or rent equipment in area dive shops and department stores. Sometimes condos and hotels offer snorkeling equipment free to their guests, but if you have to rent it, don't do it from a hotel or condo; go to a dive shop, where it's much cheaper—about $5 per day, $15 per week. Scuba divers can rent gear for about $50-60 from most shops. To get just what you need at the right price, be sure to call ahead and ask for particulars about what each company offers. For complete details on the following companies, see the appropriate travel chapters.

Scuba/Snorkel Rentals

The following full-service shops rent and sell scuba and snorkel equipment, and most offer scuba certification courses. (See the "Sports

exploring the reefs of Kauai

p.m., owned and operated by Karen Long-Olsen, is a complete diving center offering lessons, certification, and rentals. Two-tank boat dives for certified divers, including gear, are $95—$79 if you have your own equipment. Introductory dives, lesson and gear included, are $129; and a one-tank shore dive is $64. Certification courses take five days and average about $359 (group); tank refills are also available. Fathom Five also does half-day snorkeling cruises that include lessons and gear for $64. Snorkel rental is $5 per day, $15 per week.

Sea Sports Kauai, at Poipu Plaza, 2827 Poipu Rd., tel. (808) 742-9303 or (800) 685-5889, is a scuba/snorkel/surf shop. Rentals include snorkel masks, fins, and snorkels all for $5 per hour, $15 per day (includes complimentary lesson), $30 for a reef tour; surfboards for $5-10 per hour, $15-20 per day, depending on quality (surfing lessons are $30). A two-tank introductory scuba dive runs $110, a one-tank certified dive $75, and a three-day certification course $395 (dive video available at $39.95). Sea Sports Kauai is also a sports boutique with boogie boards, surfboards, underwater equipment, T-shirts, sandals, and unique bags in the form of sharks and colorful reef fish.

The **Captain's Cargo Company,** tel. (808) 338-0333, 9984 Kaumuali'i Hwy. (Rt. 50), Waimea, and office of **Liko Kauai Cruises,** is operated by Debra Hookano, wife of Captain Liko. Rental rates are $2 per hour, $5 per day for mask, fins, and snorkel.

Sea Fun, P.O. Box 3002, Lihue, HI 96766, tel. (808) 245-6400 offers guided snorkeling tours, wetsuits, optical masks, an optional video of your adventure, and juices and snacks.

Good old **Snorkel Bob,** at 4480 Ahukini Rd., in Lihue on the way to the airport, tel. (808) 245-9433, and also in old Koloa Town along Poipu Beach Rd., tel. (808) 742-2206, offers some of the best deals for snorkel rental in Hawaii (and free snorkeling maps and advice). Basic gear is $14 per week; better, silicone gear is $19-29, or $2.50 to $6.50 a day; boogie boards run $4.50-6.50 daily, $15-26 weekly. If you'll be island hopping, Snorkel Bob allows you to take the gear with you and drop it off at a Snorkel Bob location on the next island.

Other shops are **Sea Sports Divers,** tel. (808) 742-7288; **Ocean Odyssey,** tel. (808) 245-8661;

and Recreation" sections in the travel chapters for more local information.)

Kauai Water Ski and Surf Co., tel. (808) 822-3574, open daily 9 a.m.-7 p.m., in the Kinipopo Shopping Village, 4-356 Kuhio Hwy., Kapa'a, HI 96746, is a complete water-sports shop that offers snorkel gear by the day or week.

Aquatic Adventures, at 4-1380 Kuhio Hwy., Kapa'a, HI 96746, tel. (808) 822-1434, open Mon.-Fri. 7:30 a.m.-7 p.m. and Sat.-Sun. 7:30 a.m.-5 p.m., owned and operated by Janet Moore, is a dive shop offering rentals, excursions, and certification courses.

Also in Kapa'a, **Bubbles Below,** tel. (808) 822-3483, runs the most unusual dives (and perhaps the most expensive); they go to Lehua Island off Niihau—diving there, where the water is clear to depths of over 100 feet, is tops. Or you might try **Sunrise Diving Adventures,** tel. (808) 822-7333.

The second concentration of dive shops is in Koloa. **Fathom Five Divers,** about 100 yards past the left-hand turn to Poipu, tel. (808) 742-6991 or (800) 972-3078, open daily 9 a.m.-6

Pedal and Paddle, tel. (808) 826-9069, and the **Hanalei Surf Co.,** tel. (808) 826-9000, in Hanalei; and **Ray's Rentals and Activities,** 1345 Kuhio Hwy., downtown Kapa'a, tel. (808) 822-5700.

For additional information about scuba diving and diving clubs in Hawaii, contact **Hawaii Council of Dive Clubs,** P.O. Box 298, Honolulu, HI 96809.

Snuba Tours of Kauai, tel. (808) 823-8912, offers an underwater adventure free of the normal scuba tanks. You are tethered to a sea sled that carries the tanks. Depth is limited, but the fun isn't. Tours conducted off of Poipu's Lawai Beach cost $55

Snorkeling Sites

The following are examples of some of the best and safest snorkeling sites on Kauai. All of the beaches mentioned below are covered in greater detail in the travel chapters. The sites are **Anini Beach,** day-outing-friendly and terrific for windsurfing as well; near the **Beach House** along Lawai Rd. leading to the Spouting Horn; **Kee Beach,** at the end of the road at Haena (definitely stay inside the reef); **Lydgate State Park,** the safest for families and children; various spots along **Poipu Beach**—especially good toward the right side of the cove; and, **Tunnels** with its wonderful view of the mountains. *Advanced snorkelers only* should attempt the lava tubes. Beginners should stay on top of the reef.

SURFING, WINDSURFING, AND BOOGIE BOARDING

Surfing has long been the premier water sport in Hawaii. Locals and, now, "surfies" from all over the world, know where the best waves are and when they come. While Anahola Beach was a traditional surfing spot for Hawaiians of yesterday, the north shore has the beaches of choice today. The east side of Hanalei Bay provides a good roll in winter for experts, as does Tunnels. Quarry Beach, near Kilauea, and Donkey Beach, north of Kapa'a, are used mostly by locals. On the south coast, the surfers' favorite is the area in front of the Waiohai Resort, or west of there, near Pakala. Listen to local advice as to where and when to ride and why. The sea

is unforgiving—and particularly unpredictable in winter. For complete details on the companies below, see the appropriate travel chapters.

Surfing lessons are available. Companies offering them include **Mike Smith International Surfing School,** tel. (808) 245-3882; world champion **Margo Oberg**'s school on Poipu Beach, tel. (808) 742-6411 or 742-1750; and **Garden Island Windsurfing,** tel. (808) 826-9005, where Nancy Palmer offers surfing lessons at the Lawai Beach Resort.

Kauai Water Ski and Surf Co., tel. (808) 822-3574, open daily 9 a.m.-7 p.m., in the Kinipopo Shopping Village, 4-356 Kuhio Hwy., Wailua, HI 96746, is a complete water-sports shop that offers surfboard and boogie-board rentals by the day or week.

Sea Sports Kauai, located at the Poipu Plaza, 2827 Poipu Rd., tel. (808) 742-9303 or (800) 685-5889, offers rental boards and surfing lessons.

In Poipu, **Sea Star,** tel. (808) 332-8189, rents windsurfing gear (rack included) but does not offer lessons.

Hanalei Surf Co., tel. (808) 826-9000, just a few minutes from a great beginners' surfing area at Hanalei, offers surfing lessons or board rentals without lessons (boogie boards, too). Hanalei Bay goes completely flat in summer, so call ahead for surfing conditions.

The **Captain's Cargo Company,** tel. (808) 338-0333, 9984 Kaumuali'i Hwy. (Rt. 50), which is also the office of **Liko Kauai Cruises,** rents and sells surfboards and boogie boards. Rental rates are $5 per hour or $15 per day for boogie boards, $5 and $20 for surfboards.

Pedal and Paddle, tel. (808) 826-9069, in Hanalei's Ching Young Center, open daily 9 a.m.-5 p.m. in winter and 9 a.m.-6 p.m. in summer, rents body boards with fins for $8 a day, $25 a week; surfboards for $12 and $36.

Windsurfing

Windsurfing has become very popular on Kauai in the last few years. Technically called sailboarding, this sport is commonly known as windsurfing after a major manufacturer of sailboards. The best spots for beginners are Anini Beach on the north coast and Poipu Beach on the south. For the advanced only, Haena Beach on the north coast is preferred.

For windsurfing rental gear and other beach rentals and sales, contact **Hanalei Sailboards,** tel. (808) 826-9733; they're the best in the business.

Anini Beach Wind Surf Company, P.O. Box 1602, Hanalei, HI 96714, tel. (808) 826-9463, is a one-man operation. Owner Keith Kabe will load his truck with windsurfing gear and come to you. Keith is well known on the North Shore, buys and sells equipment, and will tailor your windsurfing lesson to fit your ability. Call for an appointment and to arrange a time and place for your windsurfing adventure.

Wind Surf Kauai, owned by Celeste Harvel, P.O. Box 323, Hanalei, HI 96714, tel. (808) 828-6838, specializes in beginner lessons. Three-hour group lessons (6 people maximum) are $60 with equipment (individual lessons, too).

Also contact **Sand People,** tel. (000) 020-6981, in Hanalei; **Kalapaki Beach Center,** tel. (808) 245-5595, in Nawiliwili; **Ray's Rentals and Activities,** 1345 Kuhio Hwy., downtown Kapa'a, tel. (808) 822-5700; or any of the sports shops on the island.

WATER-SKIING

When you think of recreation on Kauai, water-skiing doesn't necessarily come to mind. **Kauai Water Ski and Surf Co.,** tel. (808) 822-3574, open daily 9 a.m.-7 p.m., in the Kinipopo Shopping Village, 4-356 Kuhio Hwy., Wailua, HI 96746, has established itself as the main water-skiing company. Skimming placid Wailua River, freshwater skiers pass tour boats going to and from the Fern Grotto. Water-skiing fees include boat, driver, gas, skis, and other equipment; instruction at all levels can be arranged. They also sell beach clothes and water sports equipment. Rentals include kayaks, surfboards, boogie boards, and snorkel equipment. Inquire here about the Terheggen International Ski Club. (For complete details, see "Shopping" in the Wailua chapter.)

POWER GLIDING

Birds in Paradise, tel. (808) 822-5309, instructs you how to soar above the emerald green and azure blue of Kauai in a 70 horsepower ultra-light power glider. Instructor Gerry Charleboiss has thrilled over 2,000 brave and slightly wacky souls in the skies above Kauai. He describes his apparently skyworthy craft as a "motorcycle with wings." Safety features include a back-up rocket parachute that will bring the entire craft safely to the ground, and a surprising structural strength certified twice as strong as a Cessna and capable of withstanding 6 Gs positive load and 3 Gs negative. This state-of-the-art tandem glider needs only about 100 feet for take off and landing, and Gerry has mounted both a video and a still camera so you can write back home, "Look, Mom. No hands"—and, as she's always said, not much sense either. For those who enjoy pushing the envelope in a contraption soaring at 55 mph, prices are $75 for 30 minutes, $150 for one hour, and $250 for a tailor-made flight of over two hours.

GONE FISHING

Hawaii has some of the most exciting and productive "blue waters" in all the world. You'll find a statewide sport-fishing fleet made up of skippers and crews who are experienced professional anglers. You can also fish from jetties, piers, rocks, and shore. If rod and reel don't strike your fancy, try the old-fashioned throw net, or take along a spear when you go snorkeling or scuba diving. There's nighttime torch fishing, which requires special skills and equipment, and freshwater fishing in public areas. Streams and irrigation ditches yield introduced trout, bass, and catfish. While you're at it, you might want to try crabbing for Kona and Samoan crabs, or hunting squid (really octopus, but a tantalizing island delicacy in any case) in low-tide areas after sundown.

Deep-Sea Fishing

Most game-fishing boats work the blue waters on the calmer leeward side of the islands. Some skippers, carrying anglers who are accustomed to the sea, will also work the much rougher windward coast and island channels, where the fish bite just as well. Trolling is the preferred method of deep-sea fishing; this is done usually in waters between 1,000 and 2,000 fathoms deep (a fathom is six feet). The skipper will either "area

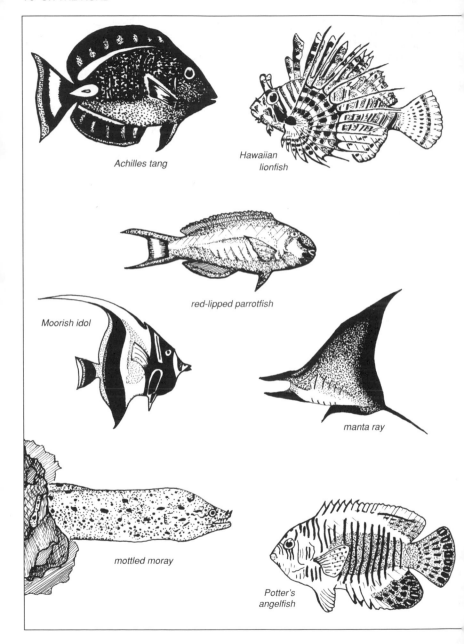

Achilles tang

Hawaiian
lionfish

red-lipped parrotfish

Moorish idol

manta ray

mottled moray

Potter's
angelfish

REEF FISH

(not drawn to scale)

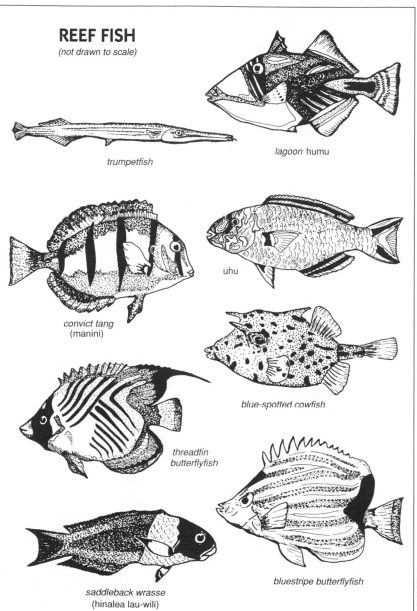

lagoon humu

trumpetfish

convict tang
(manini)

uhu

blue-spotted cowfish

threadfin
butterflyfish

saddleback wrasse
(hinalea lau-wili)

bluestripe butterflyfish

LOUISE FOOTE

fish"—which means running in a crisscrossing pattern over a known productive area—or "ledge fish," which involves trolling over submerged ledges where the game fish are known to feed. The most advanced marine technology, available on many boats, sends sonar beeps searching for fish. On deck, the crew and anglers scan the horizon in the age-old Hawaiian tradition—searching for seabirds clustered in an area, feeding on the very baitfish pursued to the surface by the huge and aggressive game fish. "Still fishing" or "bottom fishing" with hand lines can yield some tremendous fish.

The Game Fish

Kauai has excellent fishing waters year-round, with *ono, ahi,* and marlin along the ledges. The most thrilling game fish is marlin, generically known as billfish or *a'u* to the locals. The king of them is the blue marlin, with record catches well over 1,000 pounds. There are also striped marlin and sailfish, which often go over 200 pounds. The best times for marlin are spring, summer, and fall. The fishing tapers off in January but picks up again by late February. "Blues" can be caught year-round but, oddly enough, when they stop biting it seems as though the striped marlin pick up. Second to the marlin is tuna. *Ahi* (yellowfin tuna) are caught at depths of 100-1,000 fathoms. Large schools of *ahi* come to Kauai in the spring, and the fishing is fabulous, with 200-pounders possible and fish between 25 and 100 pounds common. There are also *aku* (skipjack tuna) and the delicious *ono,* which averages between 20 and 40 pounds.

Mahimahi is another strong, fighting, deepwater game fish abundant in Hawaii. This delicious fish can weigh up to 70 pounds. Shore fishing and baitcasting yield *papio,* a jack tuna. *Akule,* a scad (locally called *halalu*), is a smallish, schooling fish that comes close to shore and is great to catch on light tackle. *Ulua* are shore fish and can be found in tidepools. They're excellent eating, average two to three pounds, and are taken at night or with spears. *O'io* are bonefish that come close to shore to spawn. They're caught by bait-casting and bottom fishing with cut bait. They're bony but a favorite for fish cakes and *poki. Awa* is a schooling fish that loves brackish water. It can get up to three feet long and is a good fighter. A favorite of throw

netters, it's even raised commercially in fishponds. Besides these, there are plenty of goatfish, mullet, mackerel, snapper, various sharks, and even salmon (see "Fish and Seafood" under "Food and Drink" later in this chapter).

Freshwater Fishing

Kauai has trout and bass. Rainbow trout were introduced in 1920 and thrive in 13 miles of fishable streams, ditches, and reservoirs in the Koke'e Public Fishing Area. Large and small bass and the basslike *tucanare* are also popular game fish on Kauai. Introduced in 1908, they're hooked in reservoirs and in the Wailua River and its feeder streams.

For full- and half-day bass fishing excursions, mostly in the reservoirs around Kalaheo and Kapa'a, contact **Cast & Catch,** tel. (808) 332-9707. You'll take their 17-foot bass boat to one of Kauai's lovely freshwater reservoirs. All tackle, bait, and soft drinks are provided along with airport/hotel pick-up and delivery. Also try **J.J.'s Big Bass Tours,** tel. (808) 332-9219, with 1993 Big Bass Hawaii State Champion, John Jardin. Tackle, license, refreshments, and hotel pick-up are included.

Fishing Licenses and Regulations

No license is needed for recreational saltwater fishing. A freshwater game-fishing license is needed for certain freshwater fish during their seasons (inexpensive temporary visitors' licenses available). Licenses and a digest of fishing laws and rules are available from the State Division of Conservation and Resources Enforcement or from most sporting goods stores. For free booklets and information, write Division of Aquatic Resources, 1151 Punchbowl St., Honolulu, HI 96813. On Kauai, write to Division of Aquatic Resources, Department of Land and Natural Resources, P.O. Box 1671, Lihue, HI 96744, or stop by Room 306 of the state office building in Lihue at 3060 Giwa St., tel. (808) 241-3400.

Nearly all game fish may be taken year-round, except trout. Trout, only in the Koke'e Public Fishing Area on Kauai, may be taken for 16 days commencing on the first Saturday of August. Thereafter, for the remainder of August and September, trout can be taken only on Saturday, Sunday, and state holidays.

Fishing Charters

Some excellent fishing grounds are off Kauai, especially around Niihau, and a few charter boats are for hire. Most are berthed at Nawiliwili Harbor, with some on the north coast. Rates vary, as do the length of outings (usually four, six, or eight hours) and number of passengers allowed on the boats, so call for information before planning a trip. Some private yachts offer charters, but these come and go with the tides. Fishing excursions run in the vicinity of $75 half-day and $125 full-day shared, $350 half-day and $500 full-day exclusive.

The following charter boats have good reputations. ***Gent-Lee,*** tel. (808) 245-7504, captained by Bo Jordan, is a 36-foot full cabin cruiser complete with full galley, berths for six, and a hot shower. The *Gent-Lee* is "disabled-person friendly"—set up to take people with disabilites (who *are* encouraged to fish). *Gent-Lee* also operates the **Fisherman's Restaurant,** tel. (808) 246-4700, in Puhi, where your catch is prepared for your gustatory enjoyment; **Sea Lure Fishing Charters,** tel. (808) 822-5963, offers a modern 30-foot Radon Sportfisher departing from Nawiliwili harbor that'll take you out for the big ones; **Ahukini Charters,** tel. (808) 822-3839, operates a 32-foot Radon. Others include **Sport Fishing Kauai,** tel. (808) 742-7013, with a 38-foot Bertram; **Mana Kai Adventures,** tel. (808) 742-9849, offering a 33-foot Fiberform; and **True Blue Charters,** tel. (808) 246-6333, offers a 30-foot Force.

Sea Breeze IV, tel. (808) 828-1285, with skipper Bob Kutowski, specializes in bottom fishing. He and **Robert McReynolds,** tel. (808) 828-1379, both leave from Anini Beach. McReynolds uses medium tackle and fishes the area off Kilauea Lighthouse. Going with him is perhaps the best introduction to sportfishing in Kauai.

Only real fisherpeople need contact **Joseph "Toby" Bento,** tel. (808) 826-6319, P.O. Box 3500-151, Princeville, HI, 96722, for a day's outing; the emphasis here is on catching fish, not playing around in the ocean. Toby, who was born and raised in Hawaii, has been fishing for 35 years, having learned the trade from his dad, who has the distinction of having been twice elected Commodore of the Honolulu Yacht Club and who has designed lures that are legendary for catching marlin. Toby holds a commercial license to captain any boat up to 100 tons and, unlike many other captains, actually supports his family through fishing. Although he has caught two massive 800-pound marlins, he focuses on "what's biting," and if you are truly after fish and not a suntan, you won't find anyone more authentic than Toby Bento.

Whalewatching Cruises

For those interested in whales, boats run January through April. Many of the above charter companies, plus some of the companies listed in "Sightseeing Tours" under "Getting Around" run special whalewatching tours.

HUNTING

Most people don't think of Hawaii as a place for hunting, but actually it's quite good. Seven species of introduced game animals and 16 species of game birds are regularly hunted. Not all species of game animals are open on all islands, but every island offers hunting.

Information

Hunting rules and regulations are always subject to change. Also, environmental considerations often affect bag limits and seasons. Be sure to check with the Division of Forestry and Wildlife for the most current information. Request *Rules Regulating Game Bird Hunting, Field Trails and Commercial Shooting Preserves, Rules Regulating Game Mammal Hunting,* and *Hunting in Hawaii.* Direct inquiries to: Department of Land and Natural Resources, Division of Forestry and Wildlife Office, 1151 Punchbowl St., Honolulu, HI 96813, tel. (808) 548-2861, or, on Kauai, **Division of Forestry and Wildlife,** 3060 Eiwa St., P.O. Box 1671, Lihue, HI 96766, tel. (808) 241-3444.

General Hunting Rules

Hunting licenses are mandatory for hunting on public, private, or military land anywhere in Hawaii. They're good for one year beginning July 1 and are available to nonresidents (with special rates for senior citizens) from the Division of Forestry and Wildlife and from most sporting goods stores.

Generally, hunting hours are from a half-hour before sunrise to a half-hour after sunset. At times there are "checking stations" (Koke'e area especially) where the hunter must check in before and after hunting.

Rifles must have a muzzle velocity greater than 1,200 feet/second. Shotguns larger than .20 gauge are allowed, and muzzle loaders must have a .45-caliber bore or larger. Bows must have a minimum draw of 45 pounds for straight bows and 30 pounds for compounds. Arrows must be broadheads. Dogs are permitted only with some birds and game, and smaller caliber rifles and shotguns are permitted with their use, along with spears and knives. Hunters must wear orange safety cloth on front and back covering no smaller than a 12-inch-square area. Certain big-game species are hunted only by lottery selection; contact the Division of Forestry and Wildlife two months in advance. Guide service is not mandatory but is advised if you're unfamiliar with hunting in Hawaii. You can hunt on private land only with permission, and you must possess a valid hunting license. Guns and ammunition brought into Hawaii must be registered with the chief of police of the corresponding county within 48 hours of arrival.

Game Animals

All game animals in Hawaii have been introduced. Some are adapting admirably and becoming well entrenched, while the existence of others is still precarious. Feral pigs are escaped domestic pigs and are found on all islands except Lanai. The stock is a mixture of original Polynesian pigs and all that came later. They're hunted with dogs and usually killed with a spear or long knife; pig hunting is not recommended for the timid or tenderhearted. These beasts' four-inch tusks and fighting spirit make them tough and dangerous. Feral goats come in a variety of colors. Found on all islands except Lanai, they have been known to cause erosion and are considered pests in some areas. Openly hunted on all islands, their meat when cooked properly is considered delicious. Black-tailed deer came from Oregon. Forty were released on Kauai in 1961; the herd is now stabilized at around

feral pig

700 and they're hunted in October by public lottery. Because they thrive on island fruits, their meat is sweeter and less gamey than that of Mainland deer.

Game Birds

A number of game birds are found on Kauai. Bag limits and hunting seasons vary, so check with the Division of Forestry and Wildlife for details. Ring-necked pheasants are one of the best game birds. Francolins—gray, black, and Erkel's—from India and the Sudan, are similar to partridges. They are hunted with dogs and are great roasted. There are also chukar from Tibet, found on rugged mountain slopes; a number of quail, including the Japanese and California varieties; and spotted and zebra doves.

Hunting Excursions

Niihau Safaris, Ltd., tel. (808) 338-9869, owned by the Robinson family of Niihau and operated through their subsidiary, Niihau Helicopters, offers hunting trips to the forbidden island of Niihau. The rate is a very stiff $1,400 and includes roundtrip helicopter flight, a personal hunting guide, and a bag limit of one ram and one wild boar, which are skinned, packed, and readied for mounting. Although the game is plentiful, expect an arduous hunt with the straight-shooting skills left up to you. Also, do not expect to come into contact with any of the islands 200 Hawaiian residents. What you pay for, you get, and that's it!

HORSEBACK RIDING

You can hire mounts from **CJM Country Stables,** tel. (808) 742-6096, just past the Hyatt in Poipu. CJM offers two rides: a secret beach breakfast ride starting at 8:30 a.m. and lasting three hours for $68; and a hidden beach surprise ride at 10 a.m. and again at 2 p.m., juice provided—lasting two hours for $50.

Princeville Ranch Stables, closed Sunday, tel. (808) 826-6777, along Rt. 56 near Princeville, also offers a variety of rides—lunch, snacks, and drinks are provided on most of them. The deluxe, four-hour ride is $95 and meanders across the verdant interior land of the North Shore, ending at an inland waterfall. Shorter rides take you to overlooks of Hanalei Valley and into the foothills of the surrounding mountains.

Silver Falls Ranch, tel. (808) 828-6718, on the North Shore off Rt. 56 along Kalihiwai Ridge, offers rides daily from 9 a.m. to 4 p.m. (check in 30 minutes before). You can choose the *Hawaiian Discovery Ride,* two hours long with refreshment provided for $70, or the *Silver Falls Ride,* a three-hour ride including a picnic and swim for $95.

Note: One of the most exciting and intimate ways to discover Kauai is from atop a well-trained horse. Most of the guides are extremely knowledgable about the area's unique flora and fauna and are able to talk story about the ancient tales and legends pertaining to the ride site. For your safety and comfort, make sure to have long riding pants (jeans are the best) and closed-toed shoes (boots if possible). Also, don't forget about the tropical sun—bring a hat and sunblock as well.

Espirit De Corps Riding Academy, in the Kapaa area, tel. (808) 822-4688, appointment only, will take you on a three-hour ride for $70, a

GOLF COURSES OF KAUAI

COURSE	PAR	YARDS	FEES
Kauai Lagoons Golf Club P.O. Box 3330 Kalapaki Beach, Lihue, HI 96766 tel. (808) 241-6000 or (800) 634-6400	72 72	6942 (Lagoons) 7070 (Kiele)	$100 $145
Kiahuna Golf Course Route 1, Box 73 Koloa, HI 96756 tel. (808) 742-9595	70	6353	$53 morning $45 afternoon $35 twilight
Kukuiolono Golf Course P.O. Box 987 Lihue, HI 96766 tel. (808) 335-9940	36	2981	$7
Princeville Makai Golf Courses P.O. Box 3040 Princeville, HI 96722 tel. (808) 826-3580	36 36 36	3157 (Ocean) 3149 (Woods) 3445 (Lake)	$150 $150 $150
Princeville Prince Course P.O. Box 3040 Princeville, HI 96722 tel. (808) 826-5000	72	7309	$150
Poipu Bay Resort Golf Course 2250 Ainako St. Koloa, HI 96756 tel. (808) 742-8711 or (800) 858-6300	72	6959	$135
Wailua Municipal Golf Course P.O. Box 1017 Kapaa, HI 96746 tel. (808) 241-6666	72	6981	$25 weekdays $35 weekends

TENNIS COURTS OF KAUAI

COUNTY COURTS

Under jurisdiction of the Department of Parks and Recreation, P.O. Box 111, Lihue, HI 96766, tel. (808) 245-4751. Courts listed are in Lihue and near the Wailua and Poipu areas. There are also additional private locations around the island.

LOCATION	NAME OF COURT/LOCATION	NO. OF COURTS	LIGHTED
Hanapepe	next to stadium	2	Yes
Kekaha	next to park	2	Yes
Kalahea	Kalawai Park	2	Yes
Kapaa	New Park	2	Yes
Koloa	next to fire station	2	Yes
Lihue	next to convention hall	2	Yes
Wailua	Wailua Park	4	Yes
Waimea	next to high school	4	Yes

HOTEL AND PRIVATE COURTS THAT ARE OPEN TO THE PUBLIC

LOCATION	NAME OF COURT/LOCATION	NO. OF COURTS	LIGHTED
Hanalei	Hanalei Bay Resort	8	Yes
Kapaa	Aston Kauai Beachboy	1	No
Poipu	Poipu Kai Resort (fee for nonguests)	9	No
Poipu	Hyatt Regency	4	Yes
Poipu Beach	Kiahuna Tennis Club (fee)	10	Yes
Princeville	Princeville Resort Tennis Club	6	No

four- hour ride with snacks for $90, and a deluxe eight-hour ride with lunch for $150.

GOLF

Kauai offers varied and exciting golfing all around the island. Kukui O Lono Golf Course, a mountaintop course in Kalaheo, is never crowded and is worth visiting just to see the gardens. Wailua Municipal Golf Course is a public course with a reasonable greens fee, considered excellent by visitors and residents. Princeville boasts 46 magnificent holes sculpted around Hanalei Bay. A favorite for years, Kauai Lagoons Golf Club has recently added Kiele Course, designed by Jack Nicklaus. In Poipu, Kiahuna Golf Course and the new Poipu Bay Resort Golf Course, designed by Robert Trent Jones, Jr., are fabulous courses.

Oftentimes, if you are a guest of one the hotels affilated with a golf course, you are offered guest golfing rates at substantial savings. Also worth checking out is the **Kauai Golf Challenge,** a booklet of coupons that allows you to golf at Princeville's Prince Course, the Lagoons Kiele Course, and the Poipu Bay Resort Golf Course for reduced rates. Call any of the courses listed for details.

TENNIS

The accompanying chart lists private and public tennis courts. Many hotel tennis courts are open to nonguests, usually for a fee. The Mirage Princeville Tennis Club has a few clay courts for those who prefer that surface.

FITNESS CENTERS

If you are interested in staying fit or getting fit while vacationing, Kauai has the facilities.

Large and well equipped, the **Kauai Athletic Club,** tel. (808) 245-5381, is across from the Kukui Grove Center outside Lihue.

The **Princeville Health Club and Spa,** in the Princeville Golf Course clubhouse, tel. (808) 826-5030, keeps you healthy with aerobic classes, free weights, Nautilus machines, a swimming pool, jacuzzi, steam room, sauna, and massage by appointment. Nutrition programs can be set up with the staff, who also have information about running courses.

The **Anara Spa and Fitness Center,** at the Hyatt in Poipu, tel. (808) 742-1234, offers a total immersion into health and fitness along with therapeutic massage, water treatments, herbal wraps, and general pampering of aching muscles, overworked egos, and jangled nerves.

CAMPING AND HIKING

Kauai is very hospitable to campers and hikers. More than a dozen state and county parks offer camping, and a network of trails leads into the interior. There are different types of camping to suit everyone: you can drive right up to your spot at a convenient beach park or hike for a day through incredible country to build your campfire in total seclusion. A profusion of "secret beaches" have unofficial camping, and the State Division of Forestry even maintains free campsites along its many trails. Koke'e State Park provides affordable self-contained cabins, and RV camping is permitted at Koke'e and Polihale State Parks, and at Haena, Hanamaulu, and Niumalu County Parks.

Hikers can take the Kalalau Trail—perhaps the premier hiking experience in Hawaii—or go topside to Koke'e and follow numerous paths to breathtaking views over the bared-teeth cliffs of Na Pali. Hunting trails follow many of the streams into the interior; or, if you don't mind mud and rain, you can pick your way across the Alakai Swamp (boardwalk under construction). Wherever you go, enjoy but don't destroy, and leave the land as beautiful as you find it.

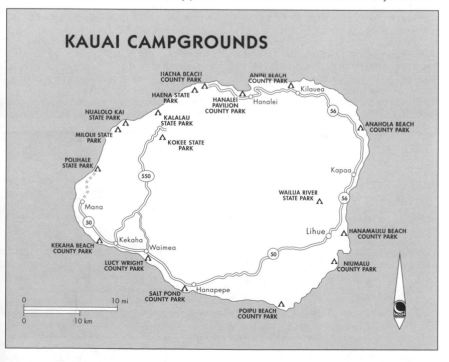

KAUAI CAMPGROUNDS

General Camping Information

All the campgrounds, except for the state parks along Na Pali, provide grills, pavilions (some with electricity), picnic tables, cold-water showers, and drinking water. No one can camp "under the stars" at official campgrounds; you must have a tent. Campsites are unattended, so be careful with your gear—especially radios, stereos, and cameras (your tent and sleeping bag are generally okay). Always be prepared for wind and rain, especially along the north shore.

Note: Recently, the police have been aggressively issuing tickets and fines of $50-300 for illegal camping, especially along North Shore beaches. Multiple offenders can even be sentenced to 30 days in jail. *Sometimes* they will merely issue a warning, but definitely do not count on it!

County Parks

A permit is required for camping at all county-maintained parks. The cost is $3 per person per day, children under 18 free if accompanied by parent or guardian. Permits are good for four nights, with one renewal possible, for a total of seven nights per campground. Camping is limited to 60 days total in any one-year period. The permit-issuing office is the Division of Parks and Recreation, 4193 Hardy St., Lihue, HI 96766, tel. (808) 241-6670, open Mon.-Fri. 7:45 a.m.-4:15 p.m. (at all other times, including weekends and holidays, you can pick up your permit at the Kauai Police Dept., Lihue Branch, 3060 Umi St., tel. 808-245-9711). Write in advance for information and reservations, but do not send money. They'll send you an application. Return it with the appropriate information, and your request will be logged in their reservations book. You'll also receive brochures and maps of the campgrounds. When you arrive, you must pick up and pay for your permit at the Parks and Recreation office or the police station.

State Parks

A camping permit (free) is required at all state parks. Camping is restricted to five nights within a 30-day period per campground, with two- and three-night maximums at some of the stopovers along the Kalalau Trail. You can pick up the permits at the Dept. of Land and Natural Resources (DLNR), Division of State Parks, 3060 Eiwa St., Rm. 306, Lihue, HI 96766, tel. (808) 241-3444. Permits can be picked up Mon.-Fri. 8 a.m.-4 p.m. only. *No* permits will be issued without proper identification. You can write well in advance for permits which will be mailed to you, but you must include photocopies of identification for each camper over 18. Children under 18 will not be issued a permit, and they must be accompanied by an adult. Allow at least one month for the entire process, and no reservations are guaranteed without at least a seven-day notice. Include name, dates, number of campers (with ID photocopies!), and number of tents.

Camping is allowed at Koke'e State Park, and the **Koke'e Lodge** also provides self-contained

Polihale State Park

housekeeping cabins. They are furnished with stoves, refrigerators, hot showers, cooking and eating utensils, bedding, and linen; wood is available for the fireplaces. The cabins vary from one large room which accommodates three to two-bedroom units which sleep seven. The cabins are tough to get on holidays, during trout-fishing season (August and September), and during the wild plum harvest in June and July. For reservations, write Koke'e Lodge, P.O. Box 819, Waimea, Kauai, HI 96796, tel. (808) 335-6061. (For complete information, see "Waimea Canyon and Koke'e State Parks," under "Hanapepe to Polihale" in the "Southwest Kauai" chapter.)

Hiking

Over 90% of Kauai is inaccessible by road, making it a backpackers' paradise. Treks range from overnighters requiring superb fitness and preparedness to 10-minute nature loops just outside your car door. Most trails are well marked and maintained, and all reward you with a swimming hole, waterfall, panoramic overlook, or botanical or historical information.

Through its various divisions, the Department of Land and Natural Resources, 3060 Eiwa St., Lihue, Kauai, HI 96766, provides free detailed maps and descriptions of most trails. For state park trails (Kalalau and Koke'e), direct letters to the Department's Division of State Parks; for forest reserve trails, the Division of Forestry; for hunting trails, the Division of Fish and Game.

Tips and Warnings

Many trails are used by hunters of wild boar, deer, or game birds. Oftentimes, the forest reserve trails, maintained by the State Division of Forestry, have check-in stations at the trailheads. Trekkers and hunters must sign a logbook, especially if they intend to use the camping areas along the trails. The comments by previous hikers are worth reading for up-to-the-minute information on trail conditions. Many roads leading to the trailheads are marked for 4WD vehicles only. Heed the warnings, especially during rainy weather, when roads are very slick and swollen streams can swallow your rental car. Also remember: going in may be fine, but a sudden storm can leave you stranded.

See "Health and Safety" for important hiking and camping precautions.

Maps of the trails are usually only available in Lihue from the various agencies, not at trailheads. Water found along the trails is unsafe to drink unless treated, so carry your own or drink only from catchment barrels. Expect wind and rain at any time along the coast or in the interior. Make sure to log in at the check-in stations and leave your itinerary. A few minutes of filling in forms could save your life.

Koke'e State Park Trails

Maps of Koke'e's trails are available at the ranger's booth at the park headquarters, and the Koke'e Natural History Museum also has additional maps and information.

Never attempt to climb up or down the park's *pali*. You *cannot* go from Koke'e down to the valleys of Na Pali. Every now and again someone attempts it and is killed. The cliffs are impossibly steep and brittle, and your handholds and footholds will break from under you. Don't be foolish.

If you're going into the Alakai Swamp, remember that all the birds and flora you encounter are unique and most of them are fighting extinction. Also, your clothes will become permanently stained with swamp mud—a wonderful memento of your trip. Before attempting any of the trails, please sign in at park headquarters.

A number of trails start along Koke'e Road or the dirt roads that lead off from it; most are marked and well maintained. The first you encounter heading up from the coast is **Cliff Trail,** only a few hundred yards long and leading to a spectacular overview of the canyon. Look for feral goats on the canyon ledges. **Canyon Trail** continues off Cliff Trail for 1.5 miles. It's a strenuous trail that dips down to Waipoo Waterfall before climbing out of the canyon to Kumuwela Lookout. **Halemanu-Koke'e Trail** begins off a secondary road from the old ranger station just before the military installation. It travels just over a mile and is a self-guiding nature trail. With plenty of native plants and trees, it's a favorite area for indigenous birds.

One of the best trails off Koke'e Road is the **Kukui Trail.** The well-marked trailhead is between mile markers 8 and 9. The trail starts with the **Iliau Nature Loop,** an easy, 10-minute, self-guided trail that's great for sunset lovers. Notice the pygmy palms among the many varieties

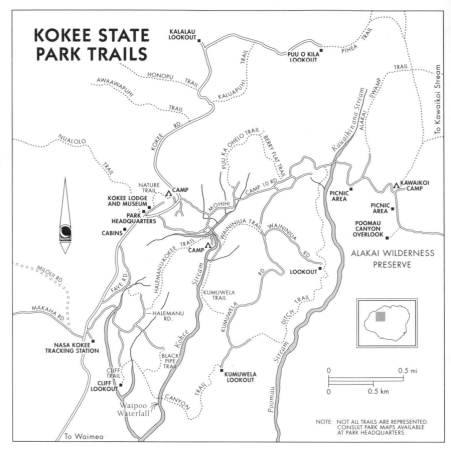

KOKEE STATE PARK TRAILS

KALALAU LOOKOUT

PUU O KILA LOOKOUT

PIHEA TRAIL

TRAIL

HONOPU TRAIL

AWAAWAPUHI

KALUAPUHI TRAIL

To Kawaikoi Stream

TRAIL

KOKEE RD.

NUALOLO

PUU KA OHELO TRAIL

BERRY FLAT TRAIL

Kauaikinana Stream

ALAKAI SWAMP

TRAIL

NATURE TRAIL

CAMP

KAWAIKOI CAMP

KOKEE LODGE AND MUSEUM

PARK HEADQUARTERS

CABINS

MOHIHI

CAMP 10 RD.

WAININIUA TRAIL

WAININIUA

PICNIC AREA

PICNIC AREA

POOMAU CANYON OVERLOOK

CAMP

ALAKAI WILDERNESS PRESERVE

MILOLII RD.

MAKAHA RD.

FAVE RD.

HALEMANUKOKEE TRAIL

Kokee Stream

KUMUWELA TRAIL

RD.

LOOKOUT

DITCH TRAIL

NASA KOKEE TRACKING STATION

HALEMANU RD.

KUMUWELA TRAIL

KUMUWELA LOOKOUT

Poomau Stream

0   0.5 mi

0   0.5 km

CLIFF TRAIL

CLIFF LOOKOUT

BLACK PIPE TRAIL

TRAIL

CANYON TRAIL

Waipoo Waterfall

NOTE: NOT ALL TRAILS ARE REPRESENTED. CONSULT PARK MAPS AVAILABLE AT PARK HEADQUARTERS.

To Waimea

of plants and flowers. The sign-in hut for the Kukui Trail is at the end of the Nature Loop. Read some of the comments before heading down. The trail descends 2,000 feet through a series of switchbacks in 2.5 miles. It ends on the floor of the canyon at Wiliwili Campsite. From here the hale and hardy can head up the Waimea River for one-half mile to the beginning of the **Koaie Canyon Trail.** The canyon trail is three miles and takes you along the south side of Koaie Canyon, where there are plenty of pools and campsites. This trail *should not* be attempted during rainy weather because of the risk of flash flooding. You can also branch south

from the Kukui Trail and link up with the **Waimea Canyon Trail,** which takes you eight miles to the town of Waimea. Because it crosses private land, you must have a special permit (available at the trailhead). There is no camping south of Waialeale Stream.

At pole 320 near park headquarters, you find the beginning of **Mohihi Camp 10 Road.** This road is recommended for 4WDs; it can be crossed with a regular car *only* in dry weather. It leads to a number of trails, some heading into valleys, others out along ridges, and still others into the Alakai Swamp. **Berry Flat,** a one-mile trail, and **Puu Ka Ohelo,** under a half mile, are easy loops that give you an up-close look at a vibrant upland forest. Under the green canopy are specimens such as sugi pine, California redwood, eucalyptus from Australia, and native koa. Locals come here in June to harvest the methley plums, for which the area is famous. Off the Camp Road is the entrance to the Forest Reserve at **Sugi Grove,** where camping is limited to three days. **Kawaikoi Stream Trail** begins three-quarters of a mile past Sugi Grove. This 3.5-mile trail is moderately strenuous and known for its scenic beauty. It follows the south side of the stream (trout), crosses over, and loops back on the north side. Avoid it if the stream is high.

The **Alakai Swamp Trail** is otherworldly, crossing one of the most unusual pieces of real estate in the world. It begins off Camp Road at a parking area one-quarter mile north of the Na Pali Forest Reserve entrance sign. The trail descends into the swamp for 3.5 miles and is very strenuous. Because you cross a number of bogs, be prepared to get wet and muddy. Good hiking shoes that won't be sucked off your feet are a must! The trail follows abandoned telephone poles from WW II and then a series of brown and white (keep an eye out) trail markers. If you smell anise along the way, that's the *mokihana* berry, used with *maile* in fashioning wedding lei. The trail ends at Kilohana, where there's an expansive vista of Wainiha and Hanalei Valley.

One of the most rewarding trails for the time and effort is **Awaawapuhi Trail.** The trailhead is after park headquarters, just past pole no. 152 at the crest of the hill. It's three miles long and takes you out onto a thin finger of *pali,* with the sea and an emerald valley 2,500 feet below. The sun dapples the upland forest that still bears the scars of Hurricane Iniki. Everywhere flowers and fiddlehead ferns delight the eyes, while wild thimbleberries and passion fruit delight the taste buds. The trail is well marked and slightly strenuous. Connecting with the Awaawapuhi at the three-mile marker, the **Nualolo Trail,** which starts near park headquarters, is the easiest trail to the *pali,* with an overview of Nualolo Valley.

Pihea Trail begins at the end of the paved road near the Puu O Kila Overlook. It's a good general-interest trail because it gives you a great view of the Kalalau Valley, then descends into

the Alakai Swamp where it connects with the Alakai Swamp Trail. It also connects with the Kawaikoi Stream Trail, and from each you can return via Mohihi Camp 10 Road for an amazing loop of the area.

East Kauai Trails

All these trails are in the mountains behind Wailua. Most start off Rt. 580, which parallels the Wailua River. Here are an arboretum and some fantastic vistas from Nounou Mountain, known as the Sleeping Giant.

Nounou Mountain Trail, East Side, begins off Haleilio Road just north of the junction of Rts. 56 and 580, at the Kinipopo Shopping Village. Follow Haleilio Road for 1.2 miles to telephone pole 38. Park near a water pump. The trailhead is across the drainage ditch and leads to a series of switchbacks which scale the mountain for 1.75 miles. The trail climbs steadily through native and introduced forest and ends at a picnic table and shelter. From here you can proceed south through a stand of monkeypod trees to a trail that leads to the Giant's face. The going gets tough, and unless you're very sure-footed, stop before the narrow ridge (500-foot drop). The views are extraordinary and you'll have them to yourself.

Nounou Mountain Trail, West Side, is found after turning onto Rt. 580 at the Coco Palms Hotel. Follow it a few miles to Rt. 581, bear right for just over a mile, and park at pole 11. Follow the right-of-way until it joins the trail. This will lead you through a forest of introduced trees planted in the 1930s. The West Trail joins the East Trail at the 1.5-mile marker and proceeds to the picnic table and shelter. This trail is slightly shorter and not as arduous. For either, bring water; there is none on the way.

Follow Rt. 580 until you come to the University of Hawaii Experimental Station. Keep going until the pavement ends and then follow the dirt road for almost a mile. A developed picnic and freshwater swimming area is at Keahua Stream. On the left is a trailhead for **Keahua Arboretum.** The moderate trail is one-half mile through a forest reserve maintained by the Division of Forestry; marked posts identify the many varieties of plants and trees. The **Kuilau Trail** begins about 200 yards before the entrance to the arboretum, on the right. This trail climbs the ridge for 2.5 miles, en route passing a picnic area and shelter. Here are some magnificent views of the mountains; continue through a gorgeous area replete with waterfalls. After you cross a footbridge and climb the ridge, you come to another picnic area. A few minutes down the trail from here you join the **Moalepe Trail,** which starts off Olohena Rd. 1.5 miles down Rt. 581 after it branches off Rt. 580. Follow Olohena Road to the end and then take the dirt road 1.5 miles to the turnaround. The last part can be extremely rutted and slick in rainy weather. The Moalepe is a popular horseback-riding trail. It gains the heights and offers some excellent panoramas before joining the Kuilau Trail.

The Kalalau Trail

This is *the* trail on Kauai. The Kalalau is a destination in and of itself, and those who have walked these phenomenal 11 miles never forget

it. The trail leads down the Na Pali coast—as close as you can get to the Hawaiian paradise of old. Getting there is simple: follow Rt. 56 until it ends and then hike (see "Sightseeing Tours" under "Getting Around" at the end of this chapter for alternative rides in or out of Kalalau). But before you start, be aware that the entire area falls under the jurisdiction of the Division of State Parks, and a ranger at Kalalau Valley oversees matters. The trailhead has a box where you sign in. Day-use permits are required beyond Hanakapi'ai (two miles in); camping permits are required to stay overnight at Hanakapi'ai, Hanakoa, or Kalalau. You can camp for five nights, but no two consecutive nights are allowed at either Hanakapi'ai or Hanakoa.

You need a good waterproof tent, sleeping bag, repellent (fierce mosquitoes), first-aid kit, biodegradable soap, food, and toiletries. There are many streams along the trail, but the water

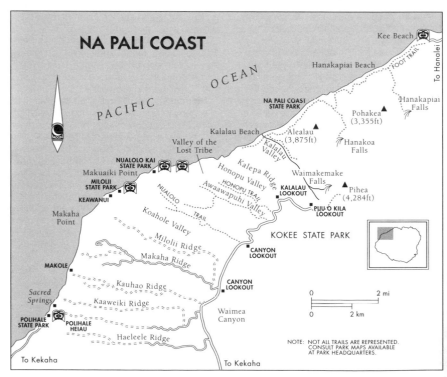

can be biologically contaminated and cause horrible stomach distress. Boil it or use purification tablets. Little firewood is available, and you can't cut trees, so take a stove. Don't litter; carry out what you carried in.

The trail is well marked by countless centuries of use, so you won't get lost, but it's rutted, root strewn, and muddy. Remnants of mileage posts are all along the way. Streams become torrents during rains but recede quickly—just wait! Mountain climbing is dangerous because of the crumbly soil, and the swimming along the coast is unpredictable, with many riptides. Summers, when the wave action returns sand to the beach, are usually fine, but stay out of the water from September to April. At Hanakapi'ai, a grim reminder reads, "This life-saving equipment was donated by the family and friends of Dr. Rulf Fahleson, a strong swimmer, who drowned at Hanakapi'ai in March 1979." Pay heed! Also, in keeping with the tradition of "Garden of Eden," many people go au naturel at Kalalau Beach. Private parts unaccustomed to sunshine can make you wish you hadn't.

Many people hike in as far as **Hanakapi'ai.** This is a fairly strenuous two-mile hike, the first mile uphill, the last down, ending at the beach. Camp at spots on the far side of the stream up from the beach. You can also camp in the caves at the beach, but only during the summer and at low tide. The unmaintained **Hanakapi'ai Trail** leads two miles up the valley to the splendid **Hanakapi'ai Falls,** taking you past some magnificent mango trees and crumbling stone-walled enclosures of ancient taro patches. One mile up you cross the stream. If the stream looks high and is running swiftly, turn back; the trail up ahead is narrow and dangerous during periods of high water. If it's low, keep going—the 300-foot falls and surrounding amphitheater are magnificent. You can swim in the pools away from the falls, but not directly under—rocks and trees can come over at any time.

Hanakapi'ai to **Hanakoa** is two miles of serious hiking (two to three hours) as the trail climbs steadily, not returning to sea level until reaching Kalalau Beach nine miles away. Switchbacks take you 600 feet out of Hanakapi'ai Valley. Although heavily traversed, the trail can be very bad in spots. Before arriving at Hanakoa, you must go through **Hoolulu** and **Waiahuakua**

Hanakapi'ai Stream

hanging valleys. Both are lush with native flora and are parts of a nature preserve. Shortly, Hanakoa comes into view. Its many wide terraces are still intact from when it was a major food-growing area. Coffee plants gone wild can still be seen. You can use the old walls as windbreaks, or you can spend the night in the roofed shelter. Nearby is a Forestry Service trail-crew shack that's open to hikers if the crew isn't using it. Hanakoa is rainy, but the rain is intermittent and the sun always follows. The swimming is fine in the many stream pools. A one-third-mile hike up the east fork of the stream, just after the six-mile marker, takes you past more terraces good for camping before coming to **Hanakoa Falls.** The terraces are wonderful, but the trail is subject to erosion and is treacherous with many steep sections.

Hanakoa to **Kalalau Beach** is under five miles but takes about three tough hours. Start early in the morning; it's hot, and although you're only traveling five miles, it gets noticeably drier and more open as you approach Kalalau. The views along the way are ample reward. The power and spirit of the incomparable *aina* become predominant. Around the seven-mile marker you enter lands that until quite recently were part of the Makaweli cattle ranch. The vegetation turns from lush foliage to lantana and sisal, a sign of the aridness of the land. After crossing Pohakuao Valley, you climb the *pali;* on the other side is Kalalau. The lovely valley, two miles wide and three deep, beckons with its glimmering freshwater pools. It's a beauty among beauties and was cultivated until the 1920s. Many terraces and house sites remain. Plenty of guava, mango, and Java plum trees can be found. You can camp in the trees fronting the beach or in the caves west of the waterfall. You are not allowed to camp along the stream, at its mouth, or in the valley. The waterfall has a freshwater pool, where feral goats come in the morning and evening to water.

A *heiau* is atop the little hillock on the west side of the stream. Follow the trail here up-valley for two miles to **Big Pool.** Big Pool is really two pools connected by a natural water slide. Riding it is great for the spirit but tough on your butt. Enjoy! Along the way you pass Smoke Rock, where *pakalolo* growers at one time came to smoke and talk story.

Note: The Kalalau Trail, because of heavy use and environmental concerns, has been closed from time to time over the last year for trail repairs. There has also been a problem finding the funds needed to perform the trail repairs. So make sure to check with the DLNR at tel. (808) 241-3446 for an update on use and accessibility.

Hiking and Camping Equipment

Like everything else you take to Kauai, your camping and hiking equipment should be lightweight and durable. The size and weight of your camping equipment should not cause a problem with baggage requirements on airlines: if it does, it's a tip-off that you're hauling too much. One odd piece of luggage you might consider is a small plastic foam cooler packed with equipment. Exchange these for food items when you get to Hawaii; if you intend to car camp successfully and keep food expenses down, you'll definitely need a cooler. (You can also buy one

on arrival for only a few dollars.) You'll need a lightweight tent, preferably with a rainfly and a sewn-in waterproof floor. This will save you from getting wet and miserable and will keep out mosquitoes, cockroaches, ants, and the few stinging insects on Kauai.

Sleeping bags are a good idea, although you can get along at sea level with only a blanket. Down-filled bags are necessary for high-altitude camping. Campstoves are needed because there's very little available wood; it's often wet in the deep forest, and open fires are often prohibited. If you'll be car camping, take along a multiburner stove and, for trekking, a backpacker's stove will be necessary. The grills found only at some campgrounds are popular with many families that go often to the beach parks for an open-air dinner. You can buy a very inexpensive charcoal grill at many variety stores throughout Hawaii. It's a great idea to take along a lantern. This will also increase safety for car campers. Definitely take a flashlight, replacement batteries, and a few small candles. A complete first-aid kit can be the difference between life and death and is worth the extra bulk. Hikers, especially those leaving the coastal areas, should take rain gear, a plastic ground cloth, utility knife, compass, safety whistle, mess kit, water-purification tablets, a canteen, nylon twine, and waterproof matches.

Rental Equipment and Sales

Na Pali Outfitters, a division of Kayak Kauai (see "Kayaks," under "Getting Around"), P.O. Box 508, Hanalei, HI 96714, tel. (808) 826-9844, and in Kapa'a at tel. (808) 822-9179, open daily 8 a.m.-5 p.m., sells and rents camping equipment. At both locations you can find all sorts of camping gear including metal cups and dishes, insect repellent, backpacks, day packs, ground cloths, camping gas, candles, and tube tents.

Pedal and Paddle, tel. (808) 826-9069, in Hanalei's Ching Young Center, open daily 9 a.m.-5 p.m. in winter, 9 a.m.-6 p.m. in summer, rents and sells backpacking equipment. Rental rates are two-person dome tent $10 a day, $30 a week; backpack $5 and $20; light blanket $3 and $10; and day packs $4 and $12. A rental day begins at the time you rent and ends at 5 p.m. the following day. Bikes, snorkel gear, surfboards, and boogie boards are also available.

The **Wainiha Store,** just a few miles before the beginning of the Kalalau Trail, open daily 9:30 a.m.-6:30 p.m., tel. (808) 826-6251, sells a few supplies and sundries. Campers and cyclists heading down the Kalalau Trail can store bags here for $2 per bag per day and bikes for $5 a day. A three-day camping equipment package including tent, lantern, stove, utensils, and backpack is $30 (no sleeping bags). Remember that camping permits must be picked up at the DLNR at the State Building way back in Lihue.

Other camping supply outlets are **Dan's Sports Shop,** in the Kukui Grove Center, tel. (808) 246-0151, and **Jungle Bob's,** in Hanalei, tel. (808) 826-6664. Also try the very local **Mandala Store,** at 3122 Kuhio Hwy. in Lihue, which carries mosquito nets and hammocks.

Helpful Departments, Organizations, and Guidebooks

For trail maps, accessibility information, hunting and fishing regulations, and general forest rules, write to the Dept. of Land and Natural Resources, Division of Forestry and Wildlife, 1151 Punchbowl St., Honolulu, HI 96813, tel. (808) 548-2861. Their *Kauai Recreation Map* is excellent and free. The following organizations can provide general information on wildlife, conservation, and organized hiking trips, although they are not based on Kauai: Hawaiian Trail and Mountain Club, P.O. Box 2238, Honolulu, HI 96804; Hawaiian Audubon Society, P.O. Box 22832, Honolulu, HI 96822; Sierra Club, 1212 University Ave., Honolulu, HI 96826, tel. (808) 946-8494.

For a well-written and detailed hiking guide, complete with maps, check out *Kauai Trails,* by Kathy Morey, or try *Hawaiian Hiking Trails* by Craig Chisholm. For hikers and boaters, *On the Na Pali Coast,* by Kathy Valier, is indispensable. Along with a description of the Kalalau Trail, it will enlighten you about the coast's natural history, plant and animal life, legends, tales, and archaeological sites.

Topographical and Nautical Charts

For in-depth topographical maps, write U.S. Geological Survey, Federal Center, Denver, CO 80225. In Hawaii, a wide range of topographical maps can be purchased at Trans-Pacific Instrument Co., 1406 Colburn St., Honolulu, HI 96817, tel. (808) 841-7538. For nautical charts, write National Ocean Survey, Riverdale, MD 20240.

ARTS AND ENTERTAINMENT

Referring to Hawaii as "paradise" is about as hackneyed as you can get, but when you combine it into "artists' paradise" it's the absolute truth. Something about the place evokes art (or at least personal expression) from most people. The islands are like a magnet: they draw artists to them, and they also draw art from the artists.

Sometimes the artwork is overpowering in itself and in its sheer volume. Though geared mostly to the tourist market of cheap souvenirs, there is hardly a shop in Hawaii that doesn't sell some item that falls into the general category of "art." You can find everything from carved monkey-face coconut shells to true masterpieces.

The Polynesian Hawaiians were master craftsmen, and their legacy still lives in a wide variety of woodcarvings, basketry, and weavings. The hula is art in swaying motion, and the true form is studied rigorously and taken very seriously. There is hardly a resort area that doesn't offer the "bump and grind" tourist hula, but even these revues are accompanied by proficient local musicians. Nightclubs offer "slack-key" balladeers, and island music performed on ukuleles and Hawaii's own steel guitars spills from many lounges. Vibrant fabrics catch the spirit of the islands and are rendered into muumuu and aloha shirts (both almost mandatory purchases!) at countless local factories. Pottery, heavily influenced by the Japanese, is well developed at numerous kilns. Local artisans fashion delicate jewelry from coral and olivine, while some ply the whalers' legacy of etching called scrimshaw. There is a fine tradition of quilt making, flower art in lei, and street artists working in everything from airbrush to glass.

ARTS OF OLD HAWAII

Since everything in old Hawaii had to be fashioned by hand, almost every object was either a work of art or at least the product of a highly refined craft. With the "civilizing" of the natives, most of the old ways disappeared, including the old arts and crafts. Most authentic Hawaiian art exists only in museums, but with the resurgence of Hawaiian roots, many old arts are being revitalized, and a few artists are becoming proficient in them.

Magnificent Canoes

The most respected artisans in old Hawaii were the canoe makers. With little more than a stone adze and a pump drill, they built canoes that could carry 200 people and last for generations—sleek, well proportioned, and infinitely seaworthy. The main hull was usually a gigantic koa log, and the gunwale planks were minutely drilled and sewn to the sides with sennit rope. Apprenticeships lasted for years, and a young man knew that he had graduated when one day he was nonchalantly asked to sit down and eat with the master builders. Small family-sized canoes with outriggers were used for fishing and perhaps carried spear racks; large oceangoing double-hulled canoes were used for migration and warfare. On these, the giant logs had been adzed to about two inches thick. A mainsail woven from pandanus was mounted on a central platform, and the boat was steered by two long paddles. The hull was dyed with plant juices and charcoal, and the entire village helped launch the canoe in a ceremony called "drinking the sea."

Carving and Weaving

Wood was a primary material used by Hawaiian craftsmen. They almost exclusively used koa because of its density, strength, and natural luster. It was turned into canoes, woodware, calabashes, and furniture used by the ali'i. Temple idols were a major product of woodcarving. Carved stone artifacts included poi pounders, mirrors, fish sinkers, and small idols. Hawaiians became the best basket makers and mat weavers in all of Polynesia. Ulana (mats) were made from lau hala leaves. The leaves were

split, had the spines removed, and were stored in large rolls. When needed, they were soaked, pounded, and then fashioned into various floor coverings and sleeping mats. Intricate geometrical patterns were woven in, and the edges were rolled and well fashioned.

Coconut palms were not used to make mats in old Hawaii, but a wide variety of basketry was made from the aerial root ie'ie. The shapes varied according to use. Some were tall and narrow, some were cones, others were flat like trays, and many were woven around gourds and calabashes. A strong weaving tradition has survived in Hawaii, and the time-tested materials of lau hala are still the best, although much is now made from coconut fronds. You can purchase anything from beach mats to a woven hat and all share the qualities of strength, lightness, and ventilation.

Feather Work

This highly refined art was found only on the islands of Tahiti, New Zealand, and Hawaii, while the fashioning of feather helmets and idols was unique to Hawaii alone. Favorite colors were red and yellow, which came only in a very limited number on a few birds such as the o'o, i'iwi, mamo, and apapane. Professional bird hunters in old Hawaii paid their taxes to ali'i in prized feathers. The feathers were fastened to a woven net of olona cord and made into helmets, idols, and beautiful flowing capes and cloaks. These resplendent garments were made and worn only by men—especially during battle, when a fine cloak became a great trophy of war. Feather work was also employed in the making of kahili as well as lei, which were highly prized by the noble ali'i women.

Tapa Cloth

Tapa, cloth made from tree bark, was common throughout Polynesia and was considered a woman's art. A few trees such as the wauke and mamaki produced the best cloth, but a variety of other barks could be utilized. First the raw bark was pounded into a feltlike pulp and beaten together to form strips (the beaters had distinctive patterns that helped to make the cloth supple). They were then decorated by stamping, using a form of block printing, and dyed with natural colors made from plants and sea animals, in shades of gray, purple, pink, and red. They were even painted, using natural brushes made from pandanus fruit, with an overall gray color made from charcoal. The *tapa* cloth was sewn together to make bed coverings, and fragrant flowers and herbs were either sewn or pounded in to produce a permanent fragrance. *Tapa* cloth is still available today, but the Hawaiian methods have been lost, and most comes from other areas of Polynesia.

HULA AND LEI

The Lei of the Land

Every major island is symbolized by its own lei, made from a distinctive flower, shell, or fern. Each island has its own official color as well, though it doesn't necessarily correspond to the color of the island's lei. Kauai, oldest of the main islands, is represented by the *mokihina lei* and the regal color purple. The *mokihina* tree produces a small cubelike fruit that smells like anise. Green when strung into Kauai's lei, they then turn a dark brown and keep their scent for months.

Hula

The hula is more than an ethnic dance; it is the soul of Hawaii expressed in motion. It began as a form of worship during religious ceremonies and was only danced by highly trained men. It gradually evolved into a form of entertainment, but in no regard was it sexual. The hula was the opera, theater, and lecture hall of the islands all rolled into one. It was history portrayed in the performing arts. In the beginning, an androgynous deity named Laka descended to earth and taught men how to dance the hula. In time, the male aspect of Laka departed for the heavens, but the female aspect remained. The female Laka set up her own special hula *heiau* at Haena Point on the Na Pali coast of Kauai, where it still exists. As time went on, women were allowed to learn the hula. Scholars surmise that men became too busy wresting a living from the land to maintain the art form.

Hawaiian hula was never performed in grass skirts; *tapa* or ti-leaf skirts were worn. Grass skirts came to Hawaii from the Gilbert Islands, and if you see grass and cellophane skirts in a "hula revue," it's not traditional. Almost every major resort offering entertainment or a luau also offers a hula revue, which most times is young island beauties accompanied by local musicians putting on a floor show for the tourists; it'll be fun, but it won't be traditional. A hula dancer has to learn how to control every part of her or his body, including the facial expressions, which help to set the mood. The hands are extremely important and provide instant background scenery. For example, if the hands are thrust outward in an aggressive manner, this can mean a battle; if they sway gently overhead, they refer to the gods or to creation; they can easily become rain, clouds, the sun, sea, or moon. Watch the hands to get the gist of the story, though the advice of one wiseguy is, "You watch the parts you like, and I'll watch the parts I like!"

Swaying hips, depending upon their motion, can signify a long walk, a canoe ride, or sexual intercourse. The foot motion can portray a battle,

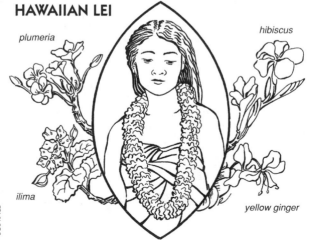

HAWAIIAN LEI

plumeria

hibiscus

ilima

yellow ginger

BOB RACE

ART INFORMATION RESOURCES

This section includes the names and addresses of guilds, centers, and organizations that dispense information on Hawaiian arts and crafts.

Arts Council of Hawaii, P.O. Box 50225, Honolulu, HI 96850, tel. (808) 524-7120; Karl Ichida, executive director. A citizens' advocacy group for the arts providing technical assistance and information to individuals and groups. Publishes *Cultural Climate,* a newsletter covering what's happening in the arts of Hawaii including a calendar of events, feature articles, and editorials. Membership fee, $15, includes newsletter (50 cents per issue to nonmembers).

Bishop Museum, 1525 Bernice St., Honolulu, HI 96819, tel. (808) 847-3511. The world's best museum covering Polynesia and Hawaii. Exhibits, galleries, archives, demonstrations of Hawaiian crafts, and a planetarium. On the premises, Shop Pacifica has a complete selection of books and publications on all aspects of Hawaiian art and culture. Shouldn't be missed.

Contemporary Arts Center, 605 Kapiolani Blvd., Honolulu, HI 96813, tel. (808) 525-8047. Promotes public awareness of contemporary art by providing gallery space, publicity, and exposure for local artists. Also houses a permanent collection and monthly exhibitions.

East Hawaii Cultural Council, P.O. Box 1312, Hilo, HI 96721. Publishes *The Center Newspaper,* a monthly newsletter of what's happening artistically and culturally in Hawaii (primarily on the Big Island). Includes a good monthly calendar of events with listings from exhibit openings to movies.

East-West Center Culture Learning Institute, Burns Hall 4076, 1777 East-West Rd., Honolulu, HI 96848, tel. (808) 944-7691. At University of Hawaii campus. Dedicated to the sharing, exhibition, and appreciation of arts, culture, and crafts from throughout Asia and the Western world. Their bimonthly *Centerviews* includes an events calendar and topical editorials on the Pacific. Free.

East-West Journal, 1633 Kapiolani Blvd., Honolulu, HI 96814. Yearly guide to exhibition galleries featuring the work of locally renowned artists.

Hawaii Craftsmen, P.O. Box 22145, Honolulu, HI 96823, tel. (808) 523-1974. Increases awareness of Hawaiian crafts through programs, exhibitions, workshops, lectures, and demonstrations.

Honolulu Academy of Arts, 900 S. Beretania St., Honolulu, HI 96814, tel. (808) 532-8700. Collects, preserves, and exhibits works of art. Offers public art education programs related to their collections. Also offers tours, classes, lectures, films, and a variety of publications.

Honolulu Symphony Society, 1000 Bishop St., Honolulu, HI 96813, tel. (808) 537-6171. Provides professional-caliber music, primarily symphonic concerts.

Pacific Handcrafters Guild, P.O. Box 15491, Honolulu, HI 96818, tel. (808) 538-7227. Focuses on developing and preserving handicrafts in Hawaii and the Pacific. They sponsor three major crafts fairs annually.

State Foundation on Culture and the Arts, 335 Merchant St., Room 202, Honolulu, HI 96813, tel. (808) 586-0300. Established by state legislature in 1965 to preserve Hawaii's diverse cultural and artistic heritage. Publishes *Hawaii Cultural Resource Directory,* which lists most of the art organizations, galleries, councils, co-ops, and guilds throughout Hawaii. Very complete.

University of Hawaii at Manoa Art Gallery, 2535 The Mall, Honolulu, HI 96822, tel. (808) 948-6888. Showcases contemporary artwork. Theme changes periodically.

a walk, or any kind of conveyance. The overall effect is multidirectional synchronized movement. The correct chanting of the *mele* is an integral part of the performance. These story chants, combined with accompanying musical instruments, make the hula very much like opera—especially similar in the way the tale unfolds.

ARTS TO BUY

Alohawear
A wild Hawaiian shirt or a bright muumuu, especially when worn on the Mainland, has the magical effect of making the wearer "feel" as if he is in Hawaii, while at the same time eliciting spontaneous smiles from passersby. Maybe it's the colors, or the vibe that says "hang loose," but nothing says Hawaii like alohawear does. More than a dozen fabric houses in Hawaii turn out distinctive patterns, and dozens of factories create their own designs. Oftentimes these factories have retail outlets, but in any case hundreds of shops in the islands sell alohawear.

Aloha shirts were the great idea of a Honolulu Chinese merchant who hand-tailored and sold them to tourists who arrived by ship in the glory days before World War II. They were an instant success. Muumuu, or "Mother Hubbards," were the idea of missionaries who were scandalized by Hawaiian women running about au naturel and insisted on covering the new Christian converts from head to foot. Ironically, the roles are now reversed, and it's Mainlanders who come to Hawaii and immediately strip down to as few clothes as possible.

Alohawear was at one time exclusively made of cotton or rayon. These materials are still the best for tropical wear, but slowly polyester has crept into the market. No material could possibly be worse than polyester for the island climate, so check the label! Muumuu now come in various styles and can be worn for the entire spectrum of social occasions in Hawaii. Aloha shirts are still basically cut the same, but the patterns have changed; apart from the original flowers and ferns, modern shirts might depict an island scene, giving the impression of a silk-screen painting. A basic, good-quality muumuu or aloha shirt starts at about $25 and is guaranteed to be worth its price in good times and happy smiles. The connoisseur might want to purchase *The Hawaiian Shirt, Its Art and History* by R. Thomas Steele. It's illustrated with pictures of more than 150 shirts now considered works of art by collectors the world over.

Scrimshaw
The art of etching and carving on bone and ivory has become an island tradition handed down from the times of the great whaling ships. Examples of this Danish sailor's art date all the way back to the 15th century but, like jazz, it was really popularized and raised to an art form by Americans—whalers on decade-long voyages from "back east" plying vast oceans in search of great whales. Frederick Merek, who sailed aboard the whaling ship *Susan,* was the best of the breed; however, most sailors only carved on the teeth of great whales to pass the time and have something to trade for whiskey, women, and song in remote ports of call. When sailors, most of whom were illiterate, sent

scrimshaw

scrimshaw back to family and friends, it was considered more like a postcard than an artwork. After the late 1800s, scrimshaw faded from popular view and became a lost art form until it was revived, mostly in Lahaina, during the 1960s.

Today, scrimshaw can be found throughout Hawaii, but the center remains the old whaling capital of Lahaina, Maui. Here, along Front Street, numerous shops specialize in scrimshaw. Today, many pieces are carved on fossilized walrus and woolly mammoth ivory, gathered by Inuits in Alaska and shipped to Hawaii. It comes in a variety of shades from pure white to mocha, depending upon the mineral content of the earth in which it was buried. Elephant ivory or whale bone is no longer used because of ecological considerations, but there is a "gray market" in Pacific walrus tusks. Inuits can legally hunt the walrus. They then make a few minimal scratches on the harvested tusks, which technically makes them "Native American art," a form free of most governmental restrictions. The tusks are then sent to Hawaii, where immediately the superficial scratches are removed and the ivory is reworked by scrimshanders. Other fossilized ivory from walrus, mammoth, and mastodon comes mainly from Siberia. Fossilized ivory being a finite resource, people in the trade predict there is only a 20-year supply left. But this is hard to estimate since new finds may add to the present treasure trove.

Scrimshaw is used in everything from belt buckles to delicate earrings and even coffeetable centerpieces. Prices go from a few dollars up to thousands. The shop on Kauai that handles the largest volume of scrimshaw art pieces and acts as the outlet for local scrimshanders is **Ye Old Ship Store** in the Coconut Plantation Market Place in Kapa'a. Ye Old Ship Store sponsors the **Hawaii International Scrimshaw Competition,** held every February at the Coconut Marketplace. This competition brings the best scrimshanders from around the country, presenting phenomenal works of art for judgment. Make sure to attend if possible.

Woodcarving
One Hawaiian art that has not died out is woodcarving. The preferred koa wood is becoming increasingly scarce, but many items are still available (although they are pricey). Milo and monkeypod, also excellent woods for carving, have largely replaced koa. You can buy tikis, bowls, and furniture at numerous shops. Variety stores sell countless inexpensive carved items, such as little hula girls or salad servers, but most of these are imported from Asia or the Philippines.

Weaving
The minute you arrive in Hawaii you should spend $2 for a woven beach mat. This is a necessity, not a frivolous purchase, but the mat won't have been made in Hawaii. What is made in Hawaii is *lau hala,* traditional Hawaiian weaving from the leaves *(lau)* of the pandanus *(hala)* tree. These leaves vary greatly in length, with the largest being over six feet; their thorny spine must be removed before they can be worked. The leaves are cut into strips from one-eighth to one inch wide, then woven; colors range from light tan to dark brown.

Lau hala makes great purses, mats, baskets, and absolutely superb hats—not to be confused with a palm-frond hat. A *lau hala* hat is amazingly supple—when squashed it'll pop back into shape. A good one, though expensive ($25), with proper care will last for years. All *lau hala* should be given a light application of mineral oil on a monthly basis, especially if it is exposed to the sun. Iron flat items over a damp cloth, and keep purses and baskets stuffed with paper when not in use. Palm fronds are widely used in weaving. They too are a great raw material, but not as good as *lau hala.* Almost any item woven from palm makes a good, authentic yet inexpensive gift or souvenir.

Gift Items
Jewelry is always an appreciated gift, especially if it's distinctive, and Hawaii has some of the most exotic. The sea provides the basic materials of pink, gold, and black coral, and it's so beautiful that it holds the same fascination as gems. Harvesting the coral, however, is very dangerous work. The Lahaina beds have one of the best black coral lodes in the islands, but unlike reef coral these trees grow at depths which are at the outer limits of a scuba diver's capabilities. Only the best and bravest risk diving the 180 feet after the black coral, and at least one diver loses his life each year. Conservationists

have brought great pressure to restrict the harvesting of these deep corals, and the state strictly regulates the firms and divers involved.

Puka (shells with little naturally occurring holes) and *opihi* shells are also made into jewelry. Generally, these items are very inexpensive, but they're authentic handicrafts and great purchases. Hanging macrame planters festooned with shells are usually affordable and sold at roadside stands along with shells.

Hawaii also produces some unique food items appreciated by most people: jars of macadamia nuts and butters, as well as tins of rich, gourmet Kona coffee (one of only two coffees produced in the United States). Island fruits like guava, pineapple, passion fruit, and mango are often gift-boxed into assortments of jams, jellies, and spicy chutneys. And for that special person in your life, you can bring home island fragrances, perfumes, and colognes with the exotic smells of gardenia, plumeria, and even island ginger. All of the above items are reasonably priced, lightweight, and travel well.

THAT GOOD OLD ISLAND MUSIC

The missionaries usually take a beating when it's recounted how much Hawaiian culture they destroyed while civilizing the natives. However, they seem to have done one thing right. They taught the Hawaiians the diatonic musical scale and immediately opened a door for latent and superbly harmonious talent. Before the missionaries, the Hawaiians knew little about melody. Though sonorous, their *mele* were repetitive chants where the emphasis was placed on historical accuracy and not on "making music." The Hawaiians, in short, didn't *sing*. But within a few years of the missionaries' arrival, they were belting out good old Christian hymns, and one of their favorite pastimes became group and individual singing.

Early in the 1800s, Spanish *vaqueros* were imported from California to run the wild cattle that had grown steadily in numbers ever since killing them was made *kapu* by Kamehameha I. The cattle, a gift of the white man, had become a menace, growing in numbers to the point where they were even attacking grass houses for fodder. The Spanish cowboys roped, branded,

and corralled them and, further living up to the cowboy image, would pass lonesome nights on the range singing and playing the guitars they had brought with them. The Hawaiians made excellent cowboys *(paniolos)* and also, with ears recently tuned by the missionaries, picked up the melodies accompanied by the strange new instrument—and quickly "Hawaiianized" them.

Immigrants who came along a little later in the 19th century, especially from Portugal, helped create a Hawaiian-style music. The biggest influence was a small four-stringed instrument called a *braga* or *cavaquinho*. One owned by Augusto Dias was the prototype of a homegrown Hawaiian instrument that became known as the ukulele. "Jumping flea," the translation of "ukulele," is an appropriate name devised by Hawaiians impressed by how nimbly players' fingers "jumped" over the strings.

The "Merry Monarch" (King Kalakaua) and Queen Liliuokalani were both patrons of the arts who furthered the Hawaiian musical identity at the turn of the century. Kalakaua revived the hula and was also a gifted lyricist and balladeer. He wrote the words to "Hawaii Pono," which became the anthem of the nation of Hawaii and, later, the state anthem. Liliuokalani wrote the hauntingly beautiful "Aloha O'e," which is often pointed to as the "spirit of Hawaii" in music. Detractors say that its melody is extremely close to that of the old Christian hymn, "Rock Beside the Sea," but the lyrics are so beautiful and perfectly fitted that this doesn't matter.

Just prior to Kalakaua's reign, a Prussian bandmaster, Captain Henri Berger, was invited to head the fledgling Royal Hawaiian Band, which he turned into a very respectable orchestra lauded by many visitors to the islands. Berger was open-minded and learned to love Hawaiian music. He collaborated with Kalakaua and other island musicians to incorporate their music into a Western format. He headed the band for 43 years, until 1915, and was instrumental in making music a serious pursuit of talented Hawaiians.

Popular Hawaiian Music

Hawaiian music has a unique twang, a special feeling that says the same thing to everyone who hears it: "Relax, sit back in the moonlight, watch the swaying palms as the surf sings a lullaby." This special sound is epitomized by the bouncy ukulele, the falsetto voice of Hawaiian crooners, and the smooth ring of the "steel" or "Hawaiian" guitar. The steel guitar is a variation that was originated by Joseph Kekuku in the 1890s. Stories abound of how Kekuku devised this instrument; the most popular versions say that Joe dropped his comb or pocket knife on his guitar strings and liked what he heard. Driven by the faint rhythm of an inner sound, he went to the machine shop at the Kamehameha School and turned out a steel bar for sliding over the strings. To complete the sound he changed the cat-gut strings to steel and raised them so they wouldn't hit the frets. Voila!—Hawaiian music as the world knows it today.

The first melodious strains of **slack-key guitar** *(ki ho'alu)* can be traced back to the time of Kamehameha III and his California *vaqueros*. The Spanish had their way of tuning the guitar, and played difficult and aggressive music that did not sit well with Hawaiians, who were much more gentle and casual in their manners.

Hawaiians soon became adept at making their own music. At first, one person played the melody, but it lacked fullness. There was no body to the sound. So, as one *paniolo* fooled with the melody, another soon learned to play bass, which added depth. But players were often alone; by experimenting, they learned that they could get the right hand going with the melody and at the same time could play the bass notes with the thumb to improve the sound. Singers also learned that they could "open tune" the guitar to match their rich voices.

Hawaiians believed that knowledge was sacred and that what is sacred should be treated with utmost respect—which meant keeping it secret, except from sincere apprentices. Guitar playing became a personal art form whose secrets were closely guarded, handed down only to family members who showed ability and determination. When old-time slack-key guitar players were done strumming, they loosened all the strings so that no one could figure out how they had had it tuned. If they were playing and some folks came by who were interested and weren't part of the family, the Hawaiians stopped what they were doing, put the guitars down, and put their feet across the strings to wait for the passerby to go away. As time went

on, more and more Hawaiians began to play slack key, and a common repertoire emerged.

Accomplished musicians could easily figure out the simple songs, once they had figured out how the family had tuned the guitar. One of the most popular tunings was the "open G." Old Hawaiian folks called it the "taro patch tune." Different songs came out, and if you were in their family and interested in the guitar, they took the time to sit down and teach you. The way they taught it was straightforward—and a test of your sincerity at the same time. The old master would start to play. They just wanted you to listen and get a feel for the music—nothing more than that. You brought your guitar and listened. When you felt it, you played it, and the knowledge was transferred. Today, only a handful of slack-key guitar players know how to play the classic tunes classically. The best-known and perhaps greatest slack-key player was Gabby Pahinui, with the group Sons of Hawaii. He passed away not many years ago, but left many recordings behind. A slack-key master still singing and playing is Raymond Kane. Raymond now teaches a handful of students his wonderful and haunting music. Not one of his students is from his own family, and most are *haole* musicians trying to preserve the classical method of playing.

Hawaiian music received its biggest boost from a remarkable radio program known as *Hawaii Calls*. This program sent out its music from the Banyan Court of Waikiki's Moana Hotel from 1935 until 1975. At its peak in the mid-1950s, it was syndicated on over 700 radio stations throughout the world. Ironically, Japanese pilots heading for Pearl Harbor tuned in island music as a signal beam. Some internationally famous classic tunes came out of the '40s and '50s. Jack Pitman composed "Beyond the Reef" in 1948; over 300 artists have recorded it and it has sold well over 12 million records. Other million-sellers include "Sweet Leilani," "Lovely Hula Hands," "The Crosseyed Mayor of Kaunakakai," and "The Hawaiian Wedding Song."

By the 1960s, Hawaiian music began to die. Just too corny and light for those turbulent years, it belonged to the older generation and the good times that followed WW II. One man was instrumental in keeping Hawaiian music alive during this period. Don Ho, with his Tiny Bubbles, became the token Hawaiian musician of the '60s and early '70s. He's persevered long enough to become a legend in his own time, and his Polynesian Extravaganza at the Hilton Hawaiian Village packed visitors in until the early 1990s. He's now at the Waikiki Beachcomber. Al Harrington ("The South Pacific Man") until his retirement in the early '90s had another Honolulu "big revue" which drew large crowds. Of this type of entertainment, perhaps the most Hawaiian is Danny Kaleikini, still performing at the Kahala Hilton on Oahu, who entertains his audience with dances, Hawaiian anecdotes, and tunes on the traditional Hawaiian nose flute.

The Beat Goes On

Beginning in the mid-'70s, islanders began to assert their cultural identity. One of the unifying factors was the coming of age of "Hawaiian" music. It graduated from the "little grass shack" novelty tune and began to include sophisticated jazz, rock, and contemporary rhythms. Accomplished musicians whose roots were in traditional island music began to highlight their tunes with this distinctive sound. The best embellish their arrangements with ukuleles, steel guitars, and traditional percussion and melodic instruments. Some excellent modern recording artists have become island institutions. The local people say that you know if the Hawaiian harmonies are good if they give you "chicken skin."

Each year special music awards, Na Hoku Hanohano ("Hoku" for short), are given to distinguished island musicians. The following are Hoku winners considered by their contemporaries to be among the best in Hawaii. Though most do not perform on Kauai, if they're playing on one of the other islands while you're in Hawaii, don't miss them. **Barney Isaacs and George Kuo** won Instrumental Album of the Year for *Hawaiian Touch.* **Na Leo Pilimihana** *(Flying With Angels)* won Song of the Year, Album of the Year, Contemporary Album of the Year, and Group of the Year. **Robi Kahakalau's** *Sistah Robi* earned Female Vocalist and Island Contemporary Album of the Year. "Friend In

Me" won Single of the Year for **Brothers and Sisters.** Keali'i Reichel's *Lei Hali'a* was voted Popular Hawaiian Album of the Year (and the artist also won Male Vocalist of the Year and Favorite Entertainer of the Year). *Broken Hearts* earned **Darren Benitez** a Most Promising Artist of the Year award; **Sonny Kamahele** received a Lifetime Achievement Award; and **Ledward Ka'apana** is a Slack Key Award winner.

Past Hoku winners who have become renowned performers include **Brothers Cazimero,** who are blessed with beautiful harmonic voices; **Krush,** who are highly regarded for their contemporary sounds; **The Peter Moon Band,** fantastic performers with a strong traditional sound; **Karen Keawehawai'i,** who has a sparkling voice and can be very funny when the mood strikes her; and **Henry Kapono,** formerly of Cecilio and Kapono, who keeps a low profile but is an incredible performer and excellent songwriter (his shows are noncommercial and very special). **Cecilio** is now teamed up with **Maggie Herron;** they are hot together and have a strong following in Honolulu. **The Beamer Brothers** are excellent performers and can be seen at various nightspots. **Loyal Garner,** who was awarded Female Vocalist of the Year for *I Shall Sing,* is a truly wonderful artist. **Del Beazley** is a talented energized performer. **Makaha Sons Of Niihau,** led by Israel Kamakawiwoole, are the best traditional Hawaiian band and shouldn't be missed. **Hawaiian Style Band** is known for *Vanishing Treasures,* a terrific album filled with contemporary music. **Bryan Kessler & Me No Hoa Aloha** performs songs like "Heiau," a haunting melody. **Susan Gillespie** and **Susi Hussong** are first-rate instrumentalists, and **Kealohi,** who recorded *Kealohi,* is very promising.

Other top-notch performers with strong followings are Ledward Kaapana; Mango; Oliver Kelly; Ka'eo; Na Leo Pilimehana, whose "Local Boys" won a Hoku for Best Single; Freitas Brothers; Brickwood Galuteria, who won a double Hoku for Best Male Vocalist and Most Promising Artist; and Third Road Delite.

SUE STRANGIO EVERETT

FESTIVALS, HOLIDAYS, AND EVENTS

In addition to all the American national holidays, Hawaii celebrates its own festivals, pageants, ethnic fairs, and a multitude of specialized exhibits. They occur throughout the year—some particular to only one island or locality, others, such as Aloha Week and Lei Day, celebrated on all the islands. Some of the smaller local happenings are semi-spontaneous, so there are no exact dates on which they're held. These are some of the most rewarding because they provide the best opportunities to have fun with the local people. At festival time, everyone is welcome. Check local newspapers and the free island magazines for exact dates.

January
The **Kauai Loves You Triathlon** is held at lovely Hanalei Bay. Amateurs and professionals are welcome. Covered by CBS, it can alternatively occur in December.

February
The **Hawaii International Scrimshaw Competition,** held throughout the entire month of February and sponsored by Ye Old Ship Store at the Coconut Marketplace, brings the best scrimshanders from around the world to display their phenomenal artwork. An excellent opportunity to experience this revived sailors' art.

The **Carole Kai Bed Race** is a fund-raising race of crazies pushing decorated beds down Front Street in Lahaina, Maui, and at the Kukui Grove Center in Lihue. (Another is held in Honolulu in early March.)

The three-day **Captain Cook Festival,** a.k.a. Waimea Town Celebration, is held at Waimea, the spot where this intrepid Pacific explorer first made contact. Food, entertainment, canoe races, and a partial marathon add to the fun. Sometimes occurs in March.

March
Midmonth features feminine beauty, grace, and athletic ability at the **Miss Kauai Pageant,** at the Kauai War Memorial Convention Hall, Lihue.

The **Prince Kuhio Festival,** at Prince Kuhio Park in Koloa and in Lihue, features festivities from the era of Prince Kuhio along with canoe races, a 10k run, and a royal ball in period dress.

The **Prince Kuhio Rodeo** is held at Po'oku Stables, in Princeville. Call (808) 826-6777 for details.

The **LPGA Women's Kemper Open Golf Tournament** is held at the Princeville Prince Golf Course in late February or early March.

April

Wesak, or **Buddha Day,** is on the closest Sunday to April 8 and celebrates the birthday of the Buddha. Ornate offerings of tropical flowers are placed at temple altars throughout Hawaii. Enjoy the flower festivals, pageants, and dance programs at many island temples.

May

May 1 is May Day to the communist world, but in Hawaii red is only one of the colors when everyone dons a lei for **Lei Day.** Festivities abound throughout Hawaii; check out the activities at the Kauai Museum in Lihue.

Armed Forces Week brings military open houses, concerts, and displays in and around the islands. Hawaii is the most militarized state in the country, and that fact becomes obvious this week. Call Military Relations at (808) 438-9761 for details.

Filipino Fiesta is a month-long celebration of the islands' Filipino population. Food, various festivities, and a beauty contest are parts of the fiesta.

Memorial Day in Hawaii is special, with military services held at Honolulu's National Memorial Cemetery of the Pacific on the last Monday in May. Call (808) 546-3190 for details.

June

King Kamehameha Day, June 11, is a state holiday honoring Kamehameha the Great with festivities on all islands. Check local papers for times and particulars. On Kauai, enjoy parades, *hoolaulea,* and arts and crafts, concentrated around the Kauai County Building and the Kukui Grove Center.

Koke'e Wilderness Festival is an event that combines a 5k and a 10k footrace and a mountain-bike race. Events start in Poipu in mid-June.

July

The week of the **Fourth of July** offers the all-American sport of rodeo along with parades, carnivals, and contests on every island.

The **Trans Pacific Race** from Los Angeles to Honolulu sails during odd-numbered years. Yachties arrive throughout the month and converge on Ala Wai Yacht Basin, where "party" is the password. They head off for Hanalei Bay to begin the year's yachting season.

The **Na Hula O Kaohikukapulani** features Hawaiian hula and Polynesian dances performed by the children of this well-known hula *halau.* Held in Lihue.

August

The **Annual Hanalei Stampede** is held at the Po'oku Stables, Princeville.

MUSEUMS AND LIBRARIES

Grove Farm Homestead, P.O. Box 1631, Lihue, HI 96766, tel. (808) 245-3202. Open by appointment only. Records and business and personal papers of early sugar planter George N. Wilcox. Plantation owner's house, workers' cottages, outbuildings, and garden. Definitely worth a visit. Personalized tours.

Hanalei Museum, P.O. Box 91, Hanalei, HI 96714, tel. (808) 826-6783. Local history on display. Small collection of native items, but many turn-of-the-century photos. Open 10 a.m.-5 p.m.; no admission charge.

Kauai Museum, 4428 Rice, Lihue, HI 96766, tel. (808) 245-6931. Open Mon.-Fri. 9:30 a.m.-4:30 p.m. Two buildings. The story of Kauai told through art and ethnic exhibits. Hawaiiana books, maps, and prints available at museum shop.

Koke'e Natural History Museum, P.O. Box NN, Koke'e State Park, Lihue, HI 96752, tel. (808) 335-9975. Open daily 10 to 4; free. Exhibits interpreting the geology and unique plants and animals of Kauai's mountain wilderness. Great to visit while at Waimea Canyon.

Waioli Mission House, Waioli Corporation, P.O. Box 1631, Lihue, HI 96766, tel. (808) 245-3202 for information. Open Tuesday, Thursday, and Saturday 9 a.m.-3; free.

The Central Library, 4344 Hardy St., Lihue, HI 96766, tel. (808) 245-3617. Branch libraries are in Hanapepe, Kapa'a, Koloa, and Waimea.

August 17 is **Admissions Day,** a state holiday recognizing the day that Hawaii became a state.

At the **Kauai County Fair,** gardeners, stockmen, and craftspeople of the Garden Island display their wares at the War Memorial Center in Lihue. There are pageantry, great local foods, and terrific bargains to be had.

The **West Kauai Summer Festival** in Waimea features a beach party, luau, hula, arts and crafts booths, games, races, concerts, a beauty pageant, and more.

September

In early September, the **Garden Island Marathon and Half-Marathon** starts in Kapa'a.

Aloha Week, in late September, brings festivities on all of the islands as everyone celebrates Hawaii's own intangible quality, *aloha.* There are parades, luau, historical pageants, balls, and various other entertainments. The spirit of *aloha* is infectious and all are welcome to join in. Check local papers and tourist literature for happenings near you.

The **Mokihana Festival,** held in late September mainly in Lihue and Waimea with festivities at some of the big hotels, is a grassroots festival featuring lei making, hula, and ukulele competitions, along with folk-arts workshops and local entertainment.

October

The **Kauai Taro Festival,** held in Hanalei, honors taro, the staple of ancient Hawaii still actively cultivated along the North Shore. Festivities also include entertainments, arts and crafts, and a farmer's market.

November

November 11, **Veterans Day,** is a national holiday celebrated with a large parade from Fort DeRussy to Queen Kapiolani Park in Waikiki, Oahu. All islands have parades, though; for information about the one on Kauai, contact the Kauai Chamber of Commerce, tel. (808) 245-7363.

December

The **Kauai Junior Miss Presentation,** at the Kauai War Memorial Convention Hall, Lihue, is where young hopefuls get their first taste of the "big time."

The **Festival of Trees** is when the business community pitches in and markets gaily decorated Christmas trees, giving the proceeds to charity. It's held in Wailua, at the Coco Palms Hotel's Queen's Audience Hall.

The **Kauai Museum Holiday Festival** is an annual Christmas event known for attracting the island's best in handcrafted items and home-baked goodies. At the Kauai Museum, Lihue, tel. (808) 245-6931.

Bodhi Day is ushered in with ceremonies at Buddhist temples to commemorate Buddha's day of enlightenment. All islands.

The **Christmas Concert** by the Kauai High School Band and Chorus includes a medley of classic, contemporary, and Hawaiian Christmas carols and other tunes. At the Kauai War Memorial Convention Hall, Lihue, tel. (808) 245-6422.

SHOPPING

Kauai has plenty of shops of all varieties: food stores in every town, boutiques, and specialty stores here and there. There are health-food stores and farmers' markets, two extensive shopping malls, and even a flea market. The following is merely an overview; specific stores, with their hours and descriptions, are covered in the appropriate travel sections. For food markets, health-food stores, farmers' markets, and fresh fish, see these specific topics in "Food and Drink" later in this chapter.

SHOPPING CENTERS

In and around Lihue

The **Kukui Grove Shopping Center,** tel. (808) 245-7784, is one of the two largest malls on Kauai. It's a few minutes west of Lihue along the Kaumualii Hwy. (Rt. 50). Clustered around an open courtyard, its more than 50 shops have everything from food to fashions, sports gear to artwork. Across Rt. 58 and toward the city from this complex is a cluster of offices and shops that includes fast-food restaurants, banks, boutiques, shoe stores, and a nearby Kmart.

Lihue has four small shopping centers off Rice Street. **Lihue Shopping Center,** tel. (808) 245-3731, is a small clutch of shops, a restaurant or two, a bank, supermarket, and discount store. The **Rice Shopping Center,** tel. (808) 245-2033, features variety stores, a natural food and nutrition center, a laundromat, and a karaoke bar. In Nawiliwili is the **Pacific Ocean Plaza** and, just across the road, at 3416 Rice St., is the **Anchor Cove Shopping Center,** bright and new with clothing stores, several good restaurants, a convenience store, and various boutiques.

Kauai has been "martinized": Wal-Mart is here, along with Kmart, causing a bit of "folding, spindling, and malling" of the local small retail shops, although to some these shopping meccas have had a positive effect on the island—sort of. For years, the people of Kauai felt deprived lacking the opportunity to spend their hard-earned money accompanied by the crackle of a public address system announcing, "Attention shoppers, the manager is offering a blue-light special with 10% off in toilet accessories." These retail behemoths have definitely lowered prices and made more goods available, but with an eye toward corporate gain have put the squeeze on local "mom and pop" shops—the traditional retailers of Kauai. But, as is often heard, "progress is our most important product" and, in truth, the demise of the neighborhood store has been repeated uncountable times in towns and cities around the nation. However, in the encapsulated island economy of Hawaii, it has had a particularly devastating effect, especially given the limited number of "tourist shoppers" whose dollars are the lifeblood of the small shops. In a free economy, all have the right to trade, and you might even feel that the coming of the "big boys" was inevitable. However, some of their business practices seem to be aimed specifically at crushing the competition. For example, both large stores have added an "Hawaiiana section" offering traditional Hawaiian arts and crafts. In the past, part of the enjoyment in purchasing a traditional Hawaiian craft was obtaining it either directly from the person who made it or from the bare wood shelves of a local

store that was very close to the source. Since the "marts" have entered the retail scene, plenty of locally owned stores and boutiques have gone under. Keep this in mind when making that "special purchase," which can just as easily be had from a local merchant tending his or her counter as from a blue-smocked, name-tagged assistant manager in training striding the antiseptic aisles. The Wal-Mart is located along Rt. 56 as you're entering Lihue from the airport; the Kmart is adjacent to the Kukui Grove Shopping Center.

In and around Kapa'a

The Coconut Market Place, tel. (808) 822-3641, an extensive shopping mall, is along the Kuhio Hwy. (Rt. 56) in Waipouli between Wailua and Kapa'a. The Market Place is even larger than Kukui Grove and offers over 70 shops in a very attractive open-air setting. Aside from the clothing and gift shops, there is a bookstore, a cinema, a good activity and information center, and over a dozen eateries. In its courtyard is a huge banyan tree, a lookout tower, and colorful sculptures made of pipes, fittings, and machinery from old sugar mills.

The **Kauai Village,** built on the theme of an 18th-century Main Street and boasting its own museum, is modern, large, and diverse. One of Kauai's newest shopping centers, the Kauai Village, at 4-831 Kuhio Hwy. between Wailua and Kapa'a, offers a **Safeway** supermarket, open 24 hours; **Long's,** a complete variety store with photo equipment and a **pharmacy;** an **ABC Store,** for everything from suntan lotion to beach mats; a well-stocked **Waldenbooks; Blockbuster Video,** for home/condo entertainment; a cluster of fast-food restaurants and small inexpensive eateries; **Papaya's Market Cafe,** the island's best natural health-food store; and the **Pacific Cafe,** a fantastic restaurant featuring Pacific Island cuisine prepared by master chef Jean-Marie Josselin (see "Food" in the Kapa'a chapter). Other stores are **Mango's for Men,** featuring gentlemen's alohawear; **Sunglass Hut,** where you can buy all kinds of sunglasses; **Kahn Gallery,** resplendent with some of the finest artworks in Hawaii; and the always good **Crazy Shirts.**

Along the Kuhio Hwy. in Wailua, Waipouli, and Kapa'a, are six smaller shopping centers. Starting from the Rt. 580 turnoff, they are the

Kinipopo Shopping Center just across from Sizzler; **Waipouli Town Center, Waipouli Plaza,** and **Waipouli Complex,** all on the *mauka* side of the highway in rapid succession. Finally, just before the main part of Kapa'a, is **Kapa'a Shopping Center,** tel. (808) 245-2033, the largest of these complexes, with the greatest variety of stores.

In and around Poipu

Across the road from the Kiahuna Plantation Condominiums in Poipu is the **Poipu Shopping Center,** tel. (808) 851-1200, an attractive cluster of shops and restaurants geared toward the tourist. The proletarian **Ele'ele Shopping Center,** tel. (808) 245-2033, at the Rt. 541 turnoff to the Port Allen harbor, is the only one farther west along the south shore.

Along the North Shore

The north coast has but two shopping centers. **Princeville Center,** tel. (808) 826-3320, the newest, largest, and open to everyone, provides the main shopping for the residents of this planned community. In Hanalei, you'll find limited shopping at the **Ching Young Shopping Center,** tel. (808) 826-7222.

SPECIALTY SHOPS AND BOUTIQUES

Fine Art Galleries

The longest-lasting part of a journey is the memory of that journey, which can instantly transport you through space and time to recapture the sublime beauty of the moment. One of the best catalysts for recapturing this memory is an inspirational work of art. **Kahn Galleries** specializes in original artworks and limited-edition prints created by some of the finest artists Hawaii has to offer. The Kahn Galleries, open daily 9 a.m.-10 p.m., are located in Hanalei Town right in the old schoolhouse, tel. (808) 826-6677; in Koloa in the main building that faces you as you enter town, tel. (808) 742-2277; at the Kilohana Plantation, just west of Lihue, tel. (808) 246-4454; and in the Kauai Village Shopping Center, tel. (808) 822-4277. Some of the master artists and works displayed by Kahn Galleries include **Tabora,** who creates dramatic seascapes of wind-whipped palms and crashing surf made

magically mysterious by the light of a translucent moon or illuminated by a glorious sunset; H. **Leung** and his sons, Thomas and Richard, are landscape impressionists who blend the techniques of east and west into paintings of provocative, dazzling beauty; world-famous **George Sumner,** a much-copied but never equaled environmental impressionist who insists on historical correctness and who brings us, among other images, the beauty of whales like cosmic ballerinas twisting to the surface to drink deep of life-giving oxygen; the finely detailed sculptures of **Randy Puckett;** and the extremely talented **Makk** family—Meriko, Eva, and A.D.—who work in oil on canvas rendering soulful portraits of American presidents and first ladies as well as immense murals in cathedrals around the world. Kahn Galleries also offer unbelievable prints produced by a computer-based method called *giclee.* A picture of the original is made into a transparency that is scanned to match subtle strokes and color variations perfectly, and then airbrushed at four million droplets per second (each one-fourth the diameter of a human hair) on to paper or canvas, creating a cyberspace copy of near-perfect similarity to the original.

If the price of original artwork puts too much of a strain on your budget, then **Island Images,** offering fine-art prints and posters, might have just what you need at an affordable price. Island Images, tel. (808) 822-3636, open daily 9 a.m.-5 p.m., is at Kapa'a's Coconut Market Place. Posters average $30, with framing and shipping available. Island Images also has *some* original artwork sold at discount prices.

Old Hanapepe Town has a string of fine-art shops and studios along the main drag. The first is the **James Hoyle Gallery,** housed in a two-story building just as you enter town, tel. (808) 335-3582, open daily 9 a.m.-6 p.m. and by appointment. James Hoyle has been able to capture the spirit of Hawaii through color and movement. His medium is a mixture of oil, pastel, and polymer, which he applies to canvas in a distinctive style of macro-pointillism. Each daub, like a melted jelly bean, is a fantastic color of deep purple, orange, magenta, yellow, and various shades of green. The result is a blazing sunset swirling with color backlighting a tortured lava mountain that broods over a tiny pool of water speckled with olive-green taro. Another painting may be palm trees laid low by the wind while storm clouds whistle overhead, and below, in humble elegance, is the bare wood home of a Filipino plantation family clinging to life in a lovely tropical setting. The sense that permeates all of Hoyle's work is that in Hawaii humanity cannot conquer nature but must learn to live in harmony with the *aina,* which is very much alive. These fine works range in price from $800 to $40,000.

A minute down the road is the **Lele Aka Studio and Gallery,** wild with fantastic demons rising from the sea and goddesses with silvery moonbeams emanating from their foreheads. In stark contrast, there are also portraits depicting the lovely bright faces of Kauai's children.

Another minute's stroll brings you to **Kauai Fine Arts,** 3848 Hanapepe Rd., P.O. Box 1079, Hanapepe, HI 96716, tel. (808) 335-3778, open Mon.-Fri. 10 a.m.-5 p.m. and Saturday and Sunday by appointment. The interior gives the impression that you are inside a handcrafted jewelry box. When you view it yourself, you'll see what I mean. From floor to wall to ceiling, it's all natural wood. The floor is hardwood and the walls and ceiling are pine. Owned and operated by Caribbean islander Mona Nicolaus, Kauai Fine Arts specializes in original engravings, original antique prints mainly of the Pacific Islands, antique maps, and vintage natural science photos from as far afield as Australia and Egypt. The shelves also hold a collection of antique bottles.

A co-op of four goldsmiths displays its craftsmanship at **The Goldsmith's Gallery,** tel. (808) 822-4653, in the Kinipopo Shopping Village, Waipouli.

Nearly three dozen first-rate island artists display their artwork at the **Artisans' Guild of Kauai,** tel. (808) 826-6441, in Hanalei.

Specialty Shops and Boutiques

You can't go wrong in the following shops. The **Kauai Museum Shop,** on Rice Street in Lihue, tel. (808) 245-6931, has perhaps the island's best selection of Kauaian arts and crafts at reasonable prices, as well as books on Hawaii. **Kapaia Stitchery,** tel. (808) 245-2281, has beautiful handmade quilts, embroideries, and 100% cotton alohawear. Many shops can be found at **Kilohana,** tel. (808) 245-5608, west of Lihue on the way to Puhi. Most rooms in this 1930 plantation estate of Gaylord Wilcox have been turned into high-end boutiques featuring gifts, artwork, clothing, jewelry, antiques, or plants. **Remember Kauai,** tel. (808) 822-0161, at 4-734 Kuhio Hwy. between Wailua and Kapa'a, sells a very wide selection of coral and shell necklaces, featuring famous Niihau shellwork, bracelets, earrings, buckles, and chains.

The old standby in Kilauea is **Kong Lung Store,** which prides itself on being an ever-changing consignment store. One section offers such things as jewelry and upscale gift items, while another has been taken over by the Indo Pacific Trading Co. (see "Shopping" in the Lihue chapter for a complete description).

Kilauea is also home to the **Island Soap Co.,** owned and operated by Stephen and Marlena Connella at P.O. Box 846, Kilauea, HI 96754, tel. (808) 828-1120 or (800) 300-6067. Here, the husband and wife team hand-pours soap and perfumes the raw bars with heady fragrances like coconut, plumeria, and ginger. They also produce self-pampering products like scented coconut oils, lotions, and bath gels capturing the scents of the islands. Island Soap Co. products are available at boutiques throughout Hawaii and can also be purchased by mail order.

Flea Markets

Excellent bargains are found at **Spouting Horn Flea Market** near Poipu Beach, where vendors set up stalls selling cut-rate merchandise.

The **Roxy Swap Meet,** held every Saturday, tel. (808) 822-7027, is in the middle of Kapa'a with tables set up under numerous tents. People from all over come to barter and sell everything and anything.

Bookstores

The most extensive bookstores on Kauai are the **Waldenbooks** shops at the Kukui Grove Shopping Center in Lihue, tel. (808) 245-7162, the Coconut Market Place in Waipouli, tel. (808) 822-9362, and the Kauai Village between Wailua and Kapa'a, tel. (808) 822-7749, all generally open Mon.-Sat. 9 a.m.-8 p.m. and Sunday 9 a.m.-5 p.m. and featuring racks of books on everything from Hawaiiana to travel, along with maps, postcards, stationery, and some souvenirs.

Borders Books and Music, tel. (808) 246-0862, in the Kukui Grove Shopping Phase II, near the Kmart, is an excellent full-service bookstore, music center, and coffee bar. Shelves, attended by a very knowledgeable staff, hold bestsellers, Hawaiiana, children's books, travel guides, and a wide variety of special-interest publications. There is a computer center and a fine coffee lounge where you can revitalize with a latte and a sweet while perusing your new purchase.

Perhaps the place with the widest selection of Hawaiiana, Kauaiana, and guidebooks is the **Kauai Museum Shop;** other stores to check for books on these subjects are the **Koke'e Natural History Museum,** in Koke'e State Park, the **Hawaiian Art Museum and Bookstore** and **Kong Lung Store,** in Kilauea; and **Happy Talk** and **Hanalei Camping and Backpacking,** in Hanalei. Books on metaphysics, spiritualism, self-help, health, cooking, and natural foods can be found at **Papaya's Natural Food Cafe,** in Kapa'a, and at **Hanalei Health and Natural Foods,** in Hanalei.

DIANA LASICH HARPER

hibiscus

ALPHONSE PELLION, CIRCA 1817, HAWAII STATE ARCHIVES

ACCOMMODATIONS

When it comes to places to stay, Kauai is blessed by a combination of happenstance and planning. The island was not a major Hawaiian destination until the early '70s. By that time, all concerned had wised up to the fact that what you *didn't do* was build endless miles of high-rise hotels and condos that blotted out the sun and ruined the view of the coast. Besides that, a very strong grassroots movement insisted on tastefully done low-rise structures that blend into and complement the surrounding natural setting. This concept mandates "destination resorts," the kinds of hotels and condos that lure visitors because of their superb architecture, artistic appointments, and luxurious grounds. There is room for growth on Kauai, but the message is clear: Kauai is the most beautiful island of them all, and the preservation of this delicate beauty benefits everyone. The good luck doesn't stop there. Kauai leads the other islands in offering the best-quality rooms for the price.

Hotels

Even with the wide variety of other accommodations available, most visitors, at least first-timers, tend to stay in hotels. At one time, hotels were the only places to stay and characters like Mark Twain were berthed at Kilauea's rude Volcano House, while millionaires and nobility sailed for Waikiki, Oahu, where they stayed in luxury at the Moana Hotel or Royal Hawaiian; both still stand as vintage reminders of days past. Today, there are 60,000 hotel rooms statewide, and every year more hotels are built and older ones renovated. The hotels come in all shapes and sizes, from 10-room, family-run affairs to high-rise giants. Whatever accommodations you want, you'll generally find them on Kauai.

Types of Hotel Rooms

Most readily available and least expensive is a bedroom with bath—the latter sometimes shared, in the less-expensive hotels. Some hotels can also offer you a studio (a large sitting room that converts to a bedroom), a suite (a bedroom with sitting room), or an apartment with full kitchen plus at least one bedroom. Kitchenettes are often available and contain refrigerators, sinks, and stoves usually in a small corner nook or fitted together as one space-saving unit. Kitchenettes cost a bit more but save you a bundle by allowing you to prepare some of your own meals. To get that vacation feeling while keeping costs down, eat breakfast in, pack a lunch for the day, and go out to dinner. If you rent a kitchenette, make sure all the appliances work as soon as you arrive. If they don't, notify the front desk immediately; if the hotel will not rectify the situation, ask to be moved or for a reduced rate. Hawaii has cockroaches, so put all food away.

Hotel Rates: Add 10% Room Tax

Every year, Hawaiian hotels welcome the New Year by hiking their rates about 10%. A room that was $90 this year will be $99 next year, and so on. Hawaii, because of its gigantic tourist flow and tough competition, offers hotel rooms at universally lower rates than most developed resort areas around the world; so, even with the 10% room tax, there are still many reasonable rates to be had. Package deals, especially to Waikiki, almost throw in a week's lodging for the price of an air ticket. The basic **daily rate** is geared toward double occupancy; singles are hit in the pocketbook. Single rates are cheaper than doubles, but never as low as half the double rate; the most you get off is 40%. **Weekly and monthly** rates will save you approximately 10% off the daily rate. Make sure to ask because this information won't be volunteered. Many hotels will charge for a double and then add an additional charge ($3 to $25) for extra persons. Some hotels—and not always the budget ones—let you cram in as many as can sleep on the floor with no additional charge, so, again, ask. Others have a policy of **minimum stay,** usually three days, but their rates can be cheaper; **business/corporate rates** are usually offered to anyone who can at least produce a business card.

Hawaii's **peak season** runs from just before Christmas until after Easter and then again in early summer. Rooms are at a premium then, and peak-season rates are an extra 10% above

the normal daily rate. Often, hotels also suspend weekly and monthly rates during peak season. The **off-peak** season is in late summer and fall, when rooms are easy to come by and most hotels offer rates about 10% below the normal rate.

In Hawaiian hotels, you always pay more for a good view. Terms vary slightly, but usually, "oceanfront" means your room faces the ocean and your view is mostly unimpeded. "Ocean view" is slightly more vague. It could be a decent view or it could require standing on the dresser and craning your neck to catch a tiny slice of the sea sandwiched between two skyscrapers. Rooms are also designated and priced upward as **standard, superior,** and **deluxe.** As you go up, this could mean larger rooms with more amenities or it can merely signify a better view.

Plenty of hotels offer the **family plan,** which allows children under a certain age to stay in their parents' room free if they use the existing beds. If another bed or crib is required, there is an additional charge. Only a limited number of hotels offer the **American plan,** where breakfast and dinner are included with the night's lodging. In many hotels, you're provided a refrigerator and a heating unit to make coffee and tea at no extra charge.

Note: Senior citizens, aged 55 and older, are often offered special discounts at some of Kauai's resorts. A hotel won't volunteer this information, though, so it's up to you to inquire. Sometimes it is required that you be a member of the American Association of Retired Persons (AARP), but not always. Discounts can range from 10% to a hefty 20%.

Paying, Deposits, and Reservations

The vast majority of Hawaiian hotels accept foreign and domestic traveler's checks, personal checks preapproved by the management, foreign cash, and most major credit cards. Reservations are always the best policy, and they're easily made through travel agents or by contacting the hotel directly. In all cases, bring documentation of your confirmed reservations with you in case of a mix-up.

Deposits are not always required to make reservations but do secure them. Some hotels require the first night's payment in advance. Reservations without a deposit can be legally released if the room is not claimed by 6 p.m. Remember, too, that letters "requesting reservations" are not the same as confirmed reservations. In letters, include your dates of stay, type of room you want, and price. Once the hotel answers your letter, *confirm* your reservations with a phone call or follow-up letter and make sure that the hotel sends you a copy of the confirmation. All hotels and resorts have **cancellation requirements** for refunding deposits. The time limit on these can be as little as 24 hours before arrival or as much as a full 30 days. Some hotels require full **advance payment** for your length of stay, especially during peak season or during times of crowded special events. Be aware of the time required for a cancellation notice *before* making your reservation deposit—especially when dealing with advance payment. If you have confirmed reservations, especially with a deposit, and there is no room for you, or a room that doesn't meet prearranged requirements, you should be given the option of accepting alternate accommodations. You are owed the difference in room rates, if there is any. If there is no room whatsoever, the hotel is required to find you one at a comparable hotel and to refund your deposit in full.

Your Choices

Kauai has approximately 75 properties with a total of 7,200 rooms available, of which 35% are condominium units. Almost all the available rooms on Kauai are split between four major destinations: Poipu Beach, Lihue, Wailua/Kapa'a, and Princeville/Hanalei. Except for Koke'e Lodge overlooking Waimea Canyon and Waimea Plantation Cottages in Waimea, little is available west of Poipu. Specialized and inexpensive accommodations are offered inland from Poipu at Kahili Mountain Park, but these very basic cottages are just a step up from what you'd find at a Boy Scout camp. Long stretches along the coast between the major centers have no lodgings whatsoever. The north shore past Hanalei has one resort, a few condos, and some scattered guest homes, but you won't find any large concentration of rooms. Aside from hotel/condo or cottage rooms, rental homes are peppered throughout the island.

Poipu, the best general-purpose beach and most popular destination on Kauai, has three

major hotels (two are rebuilding following Hurricane Iniki) and a host of condos. Prices are reasonable to expensive, and most of the condos offer long-term discounts.

For years, Lihue had only one luxury hotel, the Kauai Surf, which became the fabulous Westin Kauai. Heavily hit by Iniki, its fate is still undetermined. In and around Lihue are also most of Kauai's inexpensive hotels, guest cottages, and one mandatory fleabag. Small hotels, and especially the guest cottages, are family run. They're moderately priced, very clean, and more than adequate. However, they are in town and you have to drive to the beach. Just a few minutes away is the Outrigger Beach Hotel and its neighbor, the Aston Kauai Beach Villas, two fine and affordable properties.

Wailua/Kapa'a, on the east coast, has good beaches and a concentration of accommodations, mostly hotels. Here you'll find the Kauai Resort, which traditionally has brought most of the big-name entertainment to Kauai. The Coco Palms in Wailua is a classic. Used many times as a Hollywood movie set, it has a very loyal clientele—the sure sign of a quality hotel. Unfortunately, the Coco Palms was heavily hit by Iniki, and it, too, has not yet recovered. The Coconut Plantation is just east of Coco Palms and includes an extensive shopping center, three large hotels, and a concentration of condos. Almost all sit right on the beach and offer superior rooms at a standard price.

Princeville is a planned "destination resort." It boasts a commuter airport, shopping center, 1,000 condo units, and the Sheraton Princeville Hotel—a showcase resort overlooking Hanalei Bay. From here to Haena are few accommodations until you get to the Hanalei Colony Resort—literally the last resort.

Hotel Amenities

All hotels have some, and some hotels have all of them. Air-conditioning is available in most, but under normal circumstances you won't need it. Balmy trade winds provide plenty of breezes, which flow through louvered windows and doors in many hotels. Casablanca room fans are better. TVs are often included in the rate, but not always. In-room phones are provided, but a service charge is usually tacked on, even for local calls. Swimming pools are very common, even though the hotel may sit right on the beach. There is always a restaurant of some sort, a coffee shop or two, a bar, a cocktail lounge, and sometimes a sundries shop. Some hotels also offer tennis courts or golf courses either as part of the premises or affiliated with the hotel; usually an "activities desk" can book you into a variety of daily outings. Plenty of hotels offer laundromats on the premises, and hotel towels can be used at the beach. Bellhops get about $1 per bag, and maid service is free, though maids are customarily tipped $1-2 per day—a bit more if kitchenettes are involved, or if you've been a piggy. Parking is free. Hotels can often arrange special services like babysitters, all kinds of lessons, and special entertainment activities. A few even have bicycles and snorkeling equipment to lend. They'll receive and send mail for you, cash your traveler's checks, and take messages.

Condominiums

The method of paying for and reserving a condo is just about the same as for a hotel. However, requirements for deposits, final payments, and cancellation charges are much stiffer than in hotels. Make absolutely sure you fully understand all of these requirements when you make your reservations. The main qualitative difference between a condo and a hotel is in amenities. At a condo, you're more on your own. You're temporarily renting an apartment, so there won't be any bellhops and there'll rarely be a bar, restaurant, or lounge on the premises, though many times you will find a sundries store. The main lobby, instead of having that grand-entrance feel of many hotels, is more like an apartment-house entrance, although there might be a front desk. Condos can be efficiencies (one big room), but mostly they are one- or multiple-bedroom affairs with complete kitchens. Reasonable housekeeping items should be provided: linens, furniture, and all needed kitchen equipment. Most have TVs and phones, but remember that the furnishings provided are up to the individual owner. You may find brand-new furnishings that are top of the line or garage-sale bargains. Inquire about the furnishings when you make your reservations. Maid service might be included on a limited basis (for example, once weekly), or you might have to pay extra for it.

Condos usually require a minimum stay, although some will rent on a daily basis, like hotels. Minimum stays, when applicable, are often three days, but seven is also commonplace, and during peak season two weeks isn't unheard of. Swimming pools are common, and depending on the "theme" of the condo, you can find saunas, weight rooms, jacuzzis, and tennis courts. Rates are about 10-15% higher than at comparable hotels, with hardly any difference between doubles and singles. A nominal extra fee is charged for more than two people; condos can normally accommodate four to six guests. You can find clean, decent condos for as little as $200 per week, all the way up to exclusive apartments for well over $1,500. Their real advantage is for families, friends who want to share, and especially long-term stays, for which you will always get a special rate. The kitchen facilities save a great deal on dining costs, and it's common to find units with their own mini-washers and dryers. Parking space is ample for guests and, as at hotels, plenty of stay/drive deals are offered.

Hotel/Condominium Information

The best source of hotel/condo information is the **Hawaii Visitors Bureau (HVB).** While planning your trip, either visit one nearby or write to them in Hawaii. (Addresses are given in the "Information and Services" section later in this chapter.) Request a copy of their (free) current *Member Accommodation Guide.* This handy booklet lists all the hotel/condo members of the organization, with addresses, phone numbers, facilities, and rates. General tips are also given.

Hotel/Condo Booking and Reservations

Another way to find vacation or long-term rentals is through a rental/real estate agent. This can be handled either on Kauai or through the mail. If handled through the mail, the process may take considerably longer, and you risk not getting the type of place that you want. Throughout the island, everything from simple beach homes to look-alike condominiums and luxurious hideaways are put into the hands of rental agents. The agents have descriptions of the properties and terms of the rental contracts, and many will furnish photographs. When contacting an agency, be as specific as possible about your needs, length of stay, desired location, and how much you're willing to spend. Write several months in advance. Be aware that during high season, rentals are at a premium; if you're slow to inquire there may be slim pickings.

The following is a partial list of booking agents handling a number of properties on Kauai.

Aloha Rental Management, tel. (808) 826-7288 or (800) 487-9833

Aston Hotels and Resorts, 2250 Kuhio Ave., Honolulu, HI 96815, tel. (808) 931-1400 or (800) 922-7866 Mainland, (800) 445-6633 Canada, or (800) 321-2558 in Hawaii

Grantham Resorts, P.O. Box 983, Poipu, HI 96756, tel. (808) 742-1412 or (800) 325-5701

Kauai 800, P.O. Box 295, Lawai, HI 96765, tel. (800) 443-9180

Kauai Paradise Vacations, tel. (808) 826-7444 or (800) 826-7782

Kauai Vacation Rental and Real Estate, 4480 Ahukini Rd., Lihue, HI 96766, tel. (808) 245-8841 or (800) 367-5025

Marc Resorts Hawaii, 2155 Kalakaua Ave., Honolulu, HI 96815, tel. (808) 926-5900 or (800) 535-0085

North Shore Properties and Vacation Rentals, Princeville Center, Princeville, HI 96714, tel. (808) 826-9622 or (800) 488-3336

R.R. Realty and Rentals, 2827 Poipu Rd., Koloa, HI 96756, tel. (808) 742-7555 or (800) 367-8022

Bed and Breakfasts

Bed-and-breakfast inns are hardly a new idea. The Bible talks of the hospitable hosts who opened the gates of their homes and invited the wayfarer in to spend the night. B&Bs have a long tradition in Europe and were commonplace in 18th-century America. Now, lodging in a private home called a bed and breakfast is becoming increasingly fashionable throughout America, and Hawaii is no exception. Not only can you visit Kauai, you can also "live" there for a time with a host family and share an intimate experience of daily life.

Points to Consider: The primary feature of B&Bs is that every one is privately owned, and therefore uniquely different from every other. The range of B&Bs is as wide as the living standards in America. You'll find everything from a semi-mansion in the most fashionable residential area to a little grass shack offered by a down-home fisherman and his family. This means that it's particularly important for the guest to choose a host family with whom his or her lifestyle is compatible.

Unlike at a hotel or a condo, you'll be living *with* a host (usually a family), although your room will be private, with private baths and separate entrances quite common. You don't just "check in" to a B&B. In Hawaii, you go through agencies (listed below) which act as go-betweens in matching host and guest. Write to them and they'll send you a booklet with a complete description of the

cabin at Kahili Mountain Park

B&B, its general location, the fees charged, and a good idea of the lifestyle of your host family. With the reservations application they'll include a questionnaire that will basically determine your profile (Are you single? Do you have children? Are you a smoker? etc.) as well as arrival and departure dates and all pertinent particulars.

Since B&Bs are run by individual families, the times that they will accept guests can vary according to what's happening in their lives. This makes it imperative to write well in advance: three months is good, but farther ahead too many things can change. Four weeks is about the minimum time required to make all necessary arrangements. Expect to encounter a minimum stay (three days is common) and a maximum stay. B&Bs are not long-term housing, although it's hoped that guest and host will develop a friendship and that future stays can be as long as both desire.

B&B Agencies: A top-notch B&B agency is **Bed and Breakfast Hawaii,** operated by Evelyn Warner and Al Davis. They've been running this service since 1978, and their reputation is excellent. They charge a membership fee of $10 yearly. For this, they mail you their *Directory of Homes,* a periodic "hot sheet" of new listings, and all pertinent guest applications; add $1 for handling. Write Bed and Breakfast Hawaii, P.O. Box 449, Kapa'a, HI 96746, or call (808) 822-7771 or (800) 733-1632.

One of the most experienced agencies, **Bed And Breakfast Honolulu Statewide,** at 3242 Kaohinanai Dr., Honolulu, HI 96817, tel. (808) 595-7533 or (800) 288-4666, owned and operated by Marylee and Gene Bridges, began in 1982. Since then, they've become masters at finding visitors the perfect accommodations to match their desires, needs, and pocketbooks. Their repertoire of guest homes includes more than 400 rooms, with half on Oahu and the other half scattered around the state. Accommodations from Marylee and Gene are more personally tailored than hotel rooms. When you phone, they'll match your needs to their computerized in-house guidelines.

Other well-known agencies include the following. **Go Native Hawaii** will send you a directory and all needed information if you write to them at 65 Halaulani Pl., P.O. Box 11418, Hilo, HI 96721, or call (808) 935-4178 or (800) 662-8483.

Volcano Reservations, owned and operated by Graham and Judy Millar, P.O. Box 160, Volcano, HI 96785, tel. (808) 967-7244 or (800) 736-7140, is an agency specializing in the Volcano area of the Big Island, but with rentals available throughout the state. **Pacific Hawaii Bed And Breakfast** at 19 Kai Nanai Pl., Kailua, HI 96734, tel. (808) 486-8838 or (800) 999-6026, lists homes throughout the state but especially around Kailua/Kaneohe on Oahu's upscale windward coast. **Hawaiian Islands Vacation Rentals,** 1277 Mokulua Dr., Kailua, HI 96734, tel. (808) 261-7895 or (800) 258-7895, is owned and operated by Rick Maxey, who can arrange stays on all islands and help with interisland flights and car rental. **Babson's Vacation Rentals and Reservation Service,** 3371 Keha Dr., Kihei, Maui, HI 96753, tel. (808) 874-1166 or (800) 824-6409, is owned and operated by Ann and Bob Babson, a delightful couple who will try hard to match your stay with your budget. **Affordable Paradise,** 226 Pouli Rd., Kailua, HI 96734, tel. (808) 261-1693 or (800) 925-9065, specializes in Oahu B&Bs but can arrange stays on all islands.

Agencies specializing in beachfront villas, luxury condominiums, and exclusive estates are **Villas of Hawaii,** 4218 Waialae Ave., Suite 203, Honolulu, HI 96816, tel. (808) 735-9000, and **Vacation Locations Hawaii,** P.O. Box 1689, Kihei, HI 96753, tel. (808) 874-0077. Information on B&Bs can also be obtained from the **American Board of Bed and Breakfast Associations,** P.O. Box 23294, Washington, D.C. 20026.

Hostels
Kauai offers one hostel, the **Hawaii International Hostel,** at 4532 Leihua St., Kapa'a HI 96746, tel. (808) 823-6142, just across from the Kapa'a Library.

Home Exchanges
One other method of staying in Hawaii, open to homeowners, is to offer the use of your home for use of a home in Hawaii. This is done by listing your home with an agency that facilitates the exchange and publishes a descriptive directory. To list your home and to find out what is available, write **Vacation Exchange Club,** 12006 111 Ave., Youngtown, AZ 85363, or **Interservice Home Exchange,** P.O. Box 87, Glen Echo, MD 20812.

FOOD AND DRINK

Hawaii is a gastronome's Shangri-La, a sumptuous smorgasbord in every sense of the word. The varied ethnic groups that have come to Hawaii in the last 200 years have each brought their own special culture and enthusiasms—and, lucky for all, they didn't forget their cook pots, hearty appetites, and exotic taste buds. The Polynesians who arrived first found a fertile but uncultivated land. Immediately, they set about growing taro, coconuts, and bananas and raising chickens, pigs, fish, and even dogs, though consumption of the latter was reserved for the nobility. The harvests were bountiful and the islanders thanked the gods with the traditional feast called the luau. The underground oven, the *imu,* baked most of the food. Participants were encouraged to feast while relaxing on straw mats and enjoying the hula and various entertainments. The luau is as popular as ever and a treat that's guaranteed to delight anyone with a sense of eating adventure.

The missionaries and sailors came next; their ships' holds carrying barrels of ingredients for puddings, pies, dumplings, gravies, and roasts—the sustaining "American foods" of New England farms. The mid-1800s saw the arrival of boat-loads of Chinese and Japanese peasants, who wasted no time making rice instead of bread the staple of the islands. The Chinese added their exotic spices, cooking complex Sichuan dishes as well as workers' basics like chop suey. The Japanese introduced *shoyu* (soy sauce), sashimi, boxed *(bento)* lunches, delicate tempura, and rich, filling noodle soups. The Portuguese brought their luscious Mediterranean dishes of tomatoes, peppers, and plump, spicy sausages; nutritious bean soups; and mouth-watering sweet treats like *malasadas* (holeless donuts) and *pao dolce* (sweet bread). Koreans carried crocks of zesty kimchi and quickly fired-up barbecue pits for *pulgogi,* a traditional marinated beef cooked over an open fire. Filipinos served up their delicious *adobo* stews—fish, meat, or chicken in a rich sauce of vinegar and garlic.

Recently, Thai and Vietnamese restaurants have been offering their irresistible dishes next door to restaurants serving fiery burritos from Mexico and elegant cream sauces from France. The ocean breezes of Hawaii not only cool the skin but also waft some of the most delectable aromas on earth to make the taste buds tingle and the spirit soar.

THE CUISINES OF HAWAII

Hawaiian cuisine, the oldest in the islands, consists of wholesome, well-prepared, and delicious foods. All you have to do on arrival is notice the size of some of the local boys (and women) to know immediately that food to them is indeed a happy and serious business. An oft-heard island joke is that "local men don't eat until they're full; they eat until they're tired." Many Hawaiian dishes have become standard fare at a variety of restaurants and are eaten at one time or another by anyone who spends time in the islands. Hawaiian food in general is called *kaukau,* cooked food is *kapahaki,* and something broiled is described as *kaola.* Any of these prefixes on a menu will let you know that Hawaiian food is served. Usually inexpensive, it will definitely fill you and keep you going.

Traditional Favorites

In old Hawaii, although the sea meant life, many more people were involved in cultivating beautifully tended garden plots of taro, sugarcane, breadfruit, and various sweet potatoes *(uala)* than with fishing. They husbanded pigs and barkless dogs *(ilio),* and prized *moa* (chicken) for their feathers and meat (but found eating the eggs repulsive). Their only farming implement was the *o'o,* a sharpened hardwood digging stick. The Hawaiians were the best farmers of Polynesia, and the first thing they planted was taro—a tuberous root created by the gods at the same time they created humans. This main staple of the old Hawaiians was made into poi. Every luau will have poi, a glutinous purple paste made from pounded taro root. It comes in liquid consistencies referred to as one-, two-, or three-finger poi. The fewer fingers you need to eat it, the thicker it is. Poi is one of the most nutritious carbohydrates known, but people unaccustomed to it find it bland and tasteless. Some of the best, fermented for a day or so, has an acidic bite. Poi is made to be eaten *with* something, but locals who love it pop it in their mouths and smack their lips. Those unaccustomed to it will suffer constipation if they eat too much.

A favorite popular dessert is *haupia,* a custard made from coconut. *Limu* is a generic term for edible seaweed, which many people still gather from the shoreline and eat as a salad or mix with ground *kukui* nuts and salt to make a relish. A favorite Hawaiian snack is *opihi,* small shellfish (limpets) that cling to rocks. People gather them, always leaving some on the rocks for the future. Cut from the shell and eaten raw by all peoples of Hawaii, they sell for $150 per gallon in Honolulu—a testament to their popularity. A general term that has come to mean hors d'oeuvres in Hawaii is *pu pu.* Originally the name of a small shellfish, it is now used for any finger food. A traditional liquor made from ti root is *okolehao.* It literally means "iron bottom," reminiscent of the iron blubber pots used to ferment it.

Pacific Rim Specialties
(a.k.a. "Hawaiian Regional") Cuisine

At one time the "tourist food" in Hawaii was woeful. Of course, there have always been a handful of fine restaurants, but for the most part the food lacked soul, with even the fine hotels opting to offer secondhand renditions of food more appropriate to large mainland cities. Surrounded by some of the most fertile and pristine waters in the Pacific, you could hardly find a restaurant offering fresh fish, and it was a onetime misdirected boast that even the fruits and vegetables lying limp on your table were "imported." Beginning with a handful of extremely creative and visionary chefs in the early 1980s who took the chance of offending the perceived simple palates of visitors, a delightfully delicious new cuisine was born. Based upon the finest traditions of continental cuisine—including, to a high degree, its sauces, pastas, and presentations—the culinary magic of Pacific Rim cuisine boldly adds the pungent spices of Asia, the fantastic fresh vegetables, fruits, and fish of Hawaii, and, at times, the earthy cooking methods of the American Southwest. The result is a cuisine of fantastic tastes, subtle yet robust, satiating but health-conscious—the perfect marriage of fresh foods and fresh preparations. Now, restaurants on every island proudly display menus labelled Hawaiian Regional. As always, some are better than others, but the general result is that the "tourist food" has been vastly improved and everyone benefits. Many of these exemplary chefs left lucrative and prestigious positions at Hawaii's five-diamond hotels and opened signature restaurants of their own, making this fine cuisine more available and affordable. The list is growing all the time, but some of the best are Roy Yamaguchi of Roy's Restaurant on Oahu, Maui, and Kauai; Jean-Marie Josselin of the Pacific Cafe on Kauai, Maui, and Oahu; Beverly Gannon of the Hailimaile General Store, Maui; David Paul's on Maui; Mark Ellman of Avalon on Maui; Phillipe Padovani currently on Lanai at the Manele Bay Hotel's formal Ihilani Dining Room; Sam Choy of Sam Choy's, Big Island and Oahu; and Alan Wong presiding at Alan Wong's Restaurant on Oahu.

TROPICAL FRUITS, NUTS, AND VEGETABLES

Some of the most memorable taste treats from the islands require no cooking at all: the luscious tropical and exotic fruits and vegetables sold in markets and roadside stands or just found hanging on trees, waiting to be picked. Make sure to experience as many as possible. The general rule in Hawaii is that you are allowed to pick fruit on public lands, but you should limit your picking to personal consumption. The following is a sampling of some of Hawaii's best produce.

Bananas
No tropical island is complete without them. There are over 70 species in Hawaii, with hundreds of variations. Some are for peeling and

common banana

eating, others are cooked. A "hand" of bananas is great for munching, backpacking, or picnicking. Available everywhere—and cheap.

Avocados
Brought from South America, avocados were originally cultivated by the Aztecs. They have a buttery consistency and nutty flavor. Hundreds of varieties in all shapes and colors are available fresh year-round. They have the highest fat content of any fruit next to the olive.

Coconuts
What would a tropical paradise be without coconuts? Indeed, these were some of the first plants brought by the Polynesians. When a child was born, a coconut tree was planted to provide fruit for the child throughout his or her lifetime. Truly tropical fruits, coconuts know no season. Drinking nuts are large and green, and when you shake them you can hear the milk inside. You get about a quart of fluid from each. It takes skill to open one, but a machete can handle anything. Cut the stem end flat so that it will stand, then bore a hole in the pointed end and put in a straw or hollow bamboo. Coconut water is slightly acidic and helps balance alkaline foods. Spoon meat is a custardlike gel on the inside of drinking nuts. Sprouted coconut meat is also an excellent food. Split open a sprouted nut, and inside is the yellow fruit, like a moist sponge cake. "Millionaire's salad" is made from the heart of a coconut palm. At one time an entire tree was cut down to get to the heart, which is just inside the trunk below the fronds and is like an artichoke heart except that it's about the size of a watermelon. In a downed tree, the heart stays good for about two weeks.

Breadfruit
This island staple provides a great deal of carbohydrates, but many people find the baked, boiled, or fried fruit bland. It grows all over the islands and is really thousands of little fruits growing together to form balls.

Mangos
These are some of the most delicious fruits known to humans. They grow wild all over Hawaii; the ones on the leeward sides of the islands ripen April–June, while the ones on the

windward sides can last until October. They're found in the wild on trees up to 60 feet tall. The problem is to stop eating them once you start!

Papayas
This truly tropical fruit has no real season but is mostly available in the summer. Papayas grow on branchless trees and are ready to pick as soon as any yellow appears. Of the many varieties, the "solo papaya"—meant to be eaten by one person—is the best. Split them in half, scrape out the seeds, and have at them with a spoon.

breadfruit

Passion Fruit
Known by their island name of *lilikoi,* passion fruit make excellent juice and pies. The small yellow fruit (similar to lemons but smooth-skinned) is mostly available in summer and fall. Many grow wild on vines, waiting to be picked. Slice off the stem end, scoop the seedy pulp out with your tongue, and you'll know why they're called "passion fruit."

Guavas
These small, round, yellow fruits are abundant in the wild, where they ripen from early summer to late fall. The plant is considered a pest, so pick all you want. A good source of vitamin C, they're great for juice, jellies, and desserts.

Macadamia Nuts
The king of nuts was brought from Australia in 1892. Now it's the state's fourth-largest agricultural product. Available roasted, candied, or buttered.

Litchis
Called nuts but really small fruit with thin red shells, litchis have sweet, juicy white flesh when fresh and appear nutlike when dried.

Potpourri
Along with the above, you'll find pineapples, oranges, limes, kumquats, thimbleberries, and blackberries in Hawaii, as well as carambolas, wild cherry tomatoes, and tamarinds.

FISH AND SEAFOOD

Anyone who loves fresh fish and seafood has come to the right place. Island restaurants specialize in seafood, and it's available everywhere. Pound for pound, seafood is one of the best dining bargains on Kauai. You'll find it served in every kind of restaurant, and often the fresh catch-of-the-day is proudly displayed on ice in a glass case. The following is a sampling of the best.

Mahimahi
This excellent eating fish is one of the most common and least expensive in Hawaii; the flesh is light and moist. It's referred to as "dolphin" but is definitely a fish, not a mammal. Mahimahi can weigh 10-65 pounds. This fish is broadest at the head. When caught it's a dark olive color, but after a while the skin turns iridescent shades of blue, green, and yellow. It can be served as a main course or as a patty in a fish sandwich.

A'u
This true island delicacy is a broadbill swordfish or marlin. It's expensive even in Hawaii because the damn thing's so hard to catch. The meat is moist and white and truly superb. If it's offered on the menu, order it. It'll cost a bit more, but you won't be disappointed.

Ono
Ono means "delicious" in Hawaiian, so that should tip you off to the taste of this wahoo, or king mackerel. *Ono* is regarded as one of the finest eating fishes in the ocean, and its flaky white meat lives up to its name.

Manini
These five-inch-long fish are some of the most abundant in Hawaii and live in about 10 feet of water. They school and won't bite a hook but are easily taken with spear or net. Not often on menus, they're still favorites with local people who know best.

HAWAIIAN GAME FISH

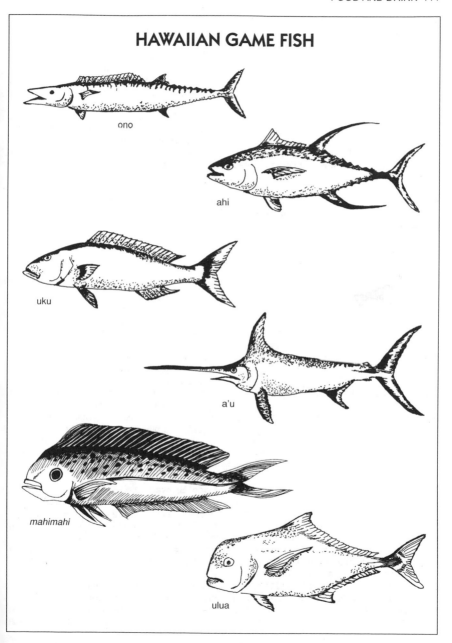

ono

ahi

uku

a'u

mahimahi

ulua

Ulua

This member of the crevalle jack family ranges 15-100 pounds. Its flesh is white and has a steaklike texture. Delicious and often found on the menu.

Uku

This gray snapper is a favorite with local people. The meat is light and firm and grills well.

Ahi

A yellowfin tuna with distinctive pinkish meat, *ahi* is a great favorite either cooked or served raw in sushi bars.

Moi

This is the Hawaiian word for "king." The fish has large eyes and a sharklike head. Considered one of the finest eating fishes in Hawaii, it's best during the autumn months.

Seafood Potpourri

Some other island seafood found on the menu includes *limu,* edible seaweed; *opihi,* a small shellfish considered one of the best island delicacies, eaten raw; *aloalo,* like tiny lobsters; crawfish, plentiful in taro fields and irrigation ditches; *ahipalaka,* albacore tuna; various octopuses (squid or calamari); and sharks of various types.

UNIQUE ISLAND DRINKS

To complement the fine dining in the islands, the bartenders have been busy creating their own tasty concoctions. The full range of beers, wines, and standard drinks is served in Hawaii, but for a real treat you should try mixed drinks inspired by the islands.

Coffee

Kona coffee at one time held the distinction of being "the only coffee grown in the U.S.A." It comes from the Kona District of the Big Island and is a rich, aromatic, truly fine coffee. Recently however, **Kauai coffee** has entered the market. More and more acreage, formerly used to grow sugarcane, is being turned to coffee production. Kauai coffee is milder than its Kona cousin and can be found at gift shops throughout Kauai. One of the main outlets is the **Island**

Coffee Co., P.O. Box 8, Eleele, Kauai, HI 96705, tel. (808) 335-5497 or (800) 545-8605.

Drinking Laws

There are no state-run liquor stores in Hawaii; all kinds of spirits, wines, and beers are available in markets and shops, which are generally open during normal business hours seven days a week. The drinking age is 21, and no towns are "dry." Legal hours for serving drinks depend on the type of establishment. Hours generally are: hotels, 6 a.m.-4 a.m.; discos and nightclubs where there is dancing, 10 a.m.-4 a.m.; bars and lounges where there is no dancing, 6 a.m.-2 a.m. Most restaurants serve alcohol, and in many that don't, you can bring your own.

Exotic Drinks

To make your island experience complete, you must order one of these colorful drinks. Most look very innocent because they come in pineapples, coconut shells, or tall frosted glasses. They're often garnished with little umbrellas or sparklers, and most have enough fruit in them to give you your vitamins for the day. Rum is used as the basis of many of them. It's been an island favorite since it was introduced by the whalers of the last century. Here are some of the most famous: mai tai (a mixture of light and dark rum, orange curaçao, orange and almond flavoring, and lemon juice); chi-chi (a simple concoction of vodka, pineapple juice, and coconut syrup—a real sleeper because it tastes like a milk shake); Blue Hawaii (vodka and blue curaçao); and planter's punch (light rum, grenadine, bitters, and lemon juice—a great thirst quencher). A Singapore Sling is a sparkling mixture of gin, cherry brandy, and lemon juice.

Local Brews

A locally brewed beer, **Primo,** manufactured under the auspices of the Joseph Schlitz Brewing Co. of Milwaukee, is a serviceable American brew in the German style but lacks the full, hearty flavor of the European imports. In the early '70s, it enjoyed an estimated 65% of the local market, but after a bad batch was inadvertently released, sales plummeted and the local share fell to five percent, where it has remained. In the early 1990s, two local breweries folded: the Pacific Brewing Company, which produced **Maui Lager,** and the Honolulu Brewing Company, which produced **Koolau Lager,** among others. Both breweries were critically acclaimed but geared their beers to the full-bodied European taste. Local beer drinkers enjoy a much lighter brew, so sales of the new beers never really took off.

Undaunted, Paula Thompson, a young and energetic ad executive turned *bier meister,* has been brewing small batches of beer in her Kula home for years. A visiting uncle involved in an Oregon brewery suggested after tasting and enjoying one of her beers that Maui was perfect for a microbrewery of its own. Paula agreed, but to keep start-up costs down, she is brewing her **Whale Ale,** and **Aloha Lager** at the Blitz Weinhard Brewery in Portland, Oregon. Once the beer has been established, she hopes to move operations to Maui.

Khalsa and Cameron Healy, a father and son team known to their friends and family as "Spoon" and "Pops," are the owners and hands-on brewmasters at **Kona Brewing Company,** 75-5629 Kuakini Hwy., Kailua-Kona, Big Island, Hawaii 96740, tel. (808) 334-1133, tours offered Mon.-Fri. 3-5 p.m. Originally from Portland, Oregon, they moved to Hawaii on a whim about four years ago. Spoon, who called himself a beach bum, was in reality, like other self-professed beach bums, a highly intelligent and energetic young man who was searching for a worthwhile life mission. In the midst of meditating on his future, he noticed there were no locally brewed beers to quaff. With this fact in mind he approached Pops with an idea to "make a really better beer." Pops considered the proposition and concluded that Spoon was a chip off the old block (Pops had had a similar idea a few years earlier, when he felt much improvement could be made to the "too common" potato chip. Like his son, Pops decided to make "really great ones," and started producing now famous Kettle Chips.) About two years ago, Spoon and Pops started producing a home brew that barely covered their own needs. With plenty of hard work, mixed with experimentation and a dollop of luck, their efforts have yielded a small, spotless state-of-the-art brewery producing about 500 barrels per month of absolutely excellent beer. At this stage, they produce three basic beers available on all the islands: *Lilikoi Wheat Beer,* a fruity

yet hearty beer made with lilikoi and passion fruit; *Pacific Golden Ale,* a classic malty ale, light and ideal for sipping at the beach; and *Firerock Pale Ale,* a darker, hoppy beer, great with a meal. Spoon and Pops are still hard at work perfecting new brews for your ultimate enjoyment. You can find beer from the Kona Brewing Co. at many bars and fine restaurants throughout Hawaii. Do yourself a flavor and order a frosty mug of this truly wonderful beer.

MUNCHIES AND ISLAND TREATS

Certain finger foods, fast foods, and island treats are unique to Hawaii. Some are meals in themselves, others are snacks. Here are some of the best and most popular.

Pu Pu
Pronounced as in "Winnie the Pooh Pooh," these are little finger foods and hors d'oeuvres. They can be anything from crackers to cracked crab. Often, they're given free at lounges and bars and can even include chicken drumettes, fish kebabs, and tempura. At a good display of them you can have a free meal.

Crackseed
A sweet of Chinese origin, crackseed is preserved and seasoned fruits and seeds. Favorites include coconut, watermelon, pumpkin seeds, mango, plum, and papaya. Distinctive in taste, they take some getting used to but make great trail snacks. Available in all island markets. Also look for dried fish (cuttlefish) on racks, usually near the crackseed. These are nutritious and delicious and make great snacks.

Shave Ice
This real island institution makes the Mainland "snow cone" melt into insignificance. Special machines literally shave ice to a fluffy consistency. It's mounded into a paper cone, and your choice from dozens of exotic island syrups is generously poured over it. Given a straw and spoon, you just slurp away.

Malasadas and *Pao Dolce*
Two sweets from the Portuguese, *malasadas* are holeless donuts and *pao dolce* is sweet

bread. Sold in island bakeries, they're great for breakfast or as treats.

Lomi Lomi Salmon
Sometimes referred to as *lomi,* this salad of salmon, tomatoes, and onions with garnish and seasonings often accompanies "plate lunches" and is featured at buffets and luau.

MONEY-SAVERS

Only one thing is better than a great meal: a great meal at a reasonable price. The following are island institutions and favorites that will help you eat well and keep costs down.

Kaukau Wagons
These are lunch wagons, but instead of slick, stainless-steel jobs, most are old delivery trucks converted into portable kitchens. Some say they're remnants of WW II, when workers had to be fed on the job; others say that the meals they serve were inspired by the Japanese *bento* boxed lunch. You'll see the wagons parked along beaches, in city parking lots or on busy streets. Usually a line of local people will be

The coconut was very important to the Hawaiians and every part was utilized. A tree was planted when a child was born as a prayer for a good food supply throughout life. The trunks were used for building homes and heiau *and carved into drums to accompany hula. The husks became bowls, utensils, and even jewelry.* 'Aha, *sennit rope braided from husk fiber, was renowned as the most saltwater-resistant natural rope ever made.*

DIANA LASICH HARPER

placing their orders, especially at lunchtime—a tip-off that the wagons serve delicious, nutritious island dishes at reasonable prices. They might have a few tables, but basically they serve food to go. Most of their filling meals are about $3.50, and they specialize in the "plate lunch."

Plate Lunch
One of the best island standards, these lunches give you a sampling of authentic island food that can include teriyaki chicken, mahimahi, *lau lau,* and *lomi* salmon, among others. They're on paper or styrofoam plates, are packed to go, and usually cost less than $3.50. Standard with a plate lunch is "two-scoop rice" and a generous dollop of macaroni or other salad. Full meals, they're great for keeping food costs down and for instant picnics. Available everywhere, from *kaukau* wagons to restaurants.

Saimin
Special "saimin shops" as well as restaurants serve this hearty, Japanese-inspired noodle soup. Saimin is a word unique to Hawaii. In Japan, these soups would be called *ramin* or *soba,* and it's as if the two were combined in "saimin." A large bowl of noodles in broth, stirred with meat, chicken, fish, or vegetables, costs only a few dollars and is big enough for an evening meal. The best place to eat saimin is in a local hole-in-the-wall shop run by a family.

Tips
Even some of the island's best restaurants in the fanciest hotels offer early-bird specials—the regular-menu dinners offered to diners who come in before the usual dinner hour, which is approximately 6 p.m. You pay as little as half the normal price and can dine in luxury on some of the best foods. The specials are often advertised in the free tourist books, which might also include coupons for two-for-one meals or limited dinners at much lower prices. Just clip them out.

Luau and Buffets
The luau is an island institution. For a fixed price of about $45, you get to gorge yourself on a tremendous variety of island foods. On your luau day, skip breakfast and lunch and do belly-stretching exercises! Buffets are also quite common in Hawaii, and like the luau they're all-you-

can-eat affairs. Offered at a variety of restaurants and hotels, they usually cost $12 and up. The food, however, ranges from quite good to only passable. At lunchtime, they're even cheaper, and they're always advertised in the free tourist literature, which often include discount coupons.

FOOD STORES

Supermarkets

Groceries and picnic supplies can be purchased in almost every town on the island. Many of the markets in the smaller towns also sell a limited selection of dry goods and gifts. The general rule is the smaller the store, the bigger the price. The largest and cheapest stores with the biggest selections are in Lihue and Kapa'a. **Big Save Value Centers** sell groceries, produce, and liquors in Ele'ele, Hanalei, Kapa'a, Koloa, Lihue, and Waimea. Most stores are open weekdays 8:30 a.m.-9 p.m., weekends until 6 p.m.

Large **Foodland** supermarkets, open 5 a.m.-midnight, operate at the Waipouli Town Center and the Princeville Center. The Princeville store is the largest and best-stocked market on the north shore.

Star Super Market is a well-stocked store in the Kukui Grove Shopping Center, while the smaller but well-stocked **Menehune Food Marts** are found in Kekaha, Kalaheo, and Kilauea.

Safeway, open 24 hours, in the Kauai Village Shopping Center, along the Kuhio Hwy., in Waipouli between Wailua and Kapa'a, is a large well-stocked supermarket.

Smaller individual markets around the island include **Kojima's** and **Pono Market** in Kapa'a, where you can stock up not only on food items and dry goods, but also on local color. North from Kapa'a are **Whalers General Store** in Anahola, the **farmers' market** in Kilauea, and the limited-selection "last chance" **Wainiha Store** in Wainiha.

Note: The following stores in and around the Poipu area are all making a comeback since Hurricane Iniki. Some are up and running, while others are still under repair. Along the south coast look for the **Sueoka Store** in Koloa, the **Kukuiula Store** at the turnoff to Spouting Horn, **Whalers General Store** in the Kiahuna Shopping Village, **Matsuura Store** in Lawai, **Mariko's Mini Mart** in Hanapepe, and the **Ishihara Market** in Waimea.

Health-Food Stores

Papaya's Natural Food Cafe, at the Kauai Village Shopping Center, 4-831 Kuhio Hwy., open daily except Sunday 9 a.m.-8 p.m., tel. (808) 823-0190, is not only the largest but also the best natural-food store on Kauai. Coolers and shelves are stocked with organic fruits and vegetables, beers and wines, whole-grain breads, organic teas and flavored coffees, grains, dried beans, spices, homeopathic medicines, cruelty-free cosmetics, vitamins, minerals, and an assortment of biodegradable cleaning products. The cafe section has a display case filled with cheesecakes and other goodies, salads and entrees by the pound, and freshly made sandwiches, all packed and ready to go. If you are into healthy organic food, there is no place better than Papaya's!

The best fruit drinks come from small roadside stands like Banana Joe's.

If not the best, at least the most down-to-earth health-food store on Kauai is **Ambrose's Kapuna Natural Foods,** tel. (808) 822-7112 or 822-3926, along the Kuhio Hwy. across from the Foodland Supermarket in Kapa'a. Ambrose is a character worth visiting just for the fun of it. He's well stocked with juices, nuts, grains, island fruits, vitamins and minerals, and plenty of bananas. Ambrose has one of the largest collections of the big old boards on the island (he has new surfboards too). If he's not in the store just give a holler around the back. He's there!

General Nutrition Center, tel. (808) 245-6657, in the Kukui Grove Center, is a full-service health-food store.

Hale O' Health, tel. (808) 245-9053, in the Rice Shopping Center in Lihue, open Mon.-Fri., 8 a.m.-5 p.m. and Sat.-Sun. until 3 p.m., specializes in vitamins and minerals. The shelves are stocked with everything from whole-wheat flour to spices, organic pastas, oils, and a good selection of teas. The back deli case holds a small selection of fresh organic vegetables and prepared deli sandwiches.

On the north shore, try **Hanalei Health and Natural Foods,** in the Ching Young Shopping Village, open daily 8:30 a.m.-8:30 p.m., tel. (808) 826-6990. Although cramped, this little store has a good vibe and a reasonable selection of bulk foods, fresh produce, hand-squeezed juices, vitamins, and books. They also have a good selection of cosmetics, incense, candles, and massage oils.

Farmers' Markets and Fresh Fish

Farmers' markets are also found on Kauai; each must have at least 20 vendors. The **Sunshine Farmers' Market,** featuring backyard produce from people's garden surplus, is held six days a week: Monday at noon at the baseball field in Koloa; Tuesday at 3 p.m. at the Kalaheo Neighborhood Center; Wednesday at 3 p.m. at the beach park in Kapa'a; Thursday at the Kilauea Neighborhood Center and in Old Hanapepe from 4:30 p.m. (get there early; the best pickings are gone in the first hour); Friday at 3 p.m. in Lihue at Vidinha Stadium; and Saturday at 9 a.m. at the Kekaha Neighborhood Center. Local gardeners bring their produce to town; a large selection of island produce can be had at very good prices. The stories and local color are even more delicious than the fruit. Contact the County Information and Complaint Office, tel. (808) 245-3213, for exact times and places.

Every Tuesday from 3 to 5 p.m. pick up some farm-fresh fruit and vegetables from the **Hawaiian Farmers of Hanalei** farmers' market located one-half mile west of Hanalei, in Waipa, on the road to Haena. Look for the sign along the road on the left.

An excellent fish store is the **Pono Fish Market,** in Kapa'a, open Mon.-Sat. 9 a.m.-8:30 p.m. and Sunday till 6 p.m. They have fresh fish daily and often offer specials.

G's Fishco, 4361 Rice St., Lihue, tel. (808) 246-4440, open weekdays 10 a.m.-8 p.m., Saturday until 7 p.m., and Sunday until 5 p.m., offers cold cases filled with whole fish, *poki,* sashimi, and assorted seafood.

Ara's Sakamaya, open Mon.-Sat. 9 a.m.-7 p.m. and Sunday 9 a.m. 5 p.m., tel. (808) 245-1707, in the Hanamaulu Plaza in Hanamaulu (clearly marked along Rt. 56), is a takeout deli-restaurant that offers plate lunches, Japanese *bento,* and **fresh fish** daily.

Other stores include **The Fish Express** at 3343 Kuhio Hwy. in Lihue, and **Nishimura's Market** in Hanapepe.

HEALTH AND SAFETY

In a recent survey published by *Science Digest,* Hawaii was cited as the healthiest state in the U.S. in which to live. Indeed, Hawaiian citizens live longer than anywhere else in America: men to 74 years and women to 78. Lifestyle, heredity, and diet help with these figures, but Hawaii is still an oasis in the middle of the ocean, and germs just have a tougher time getting there. There are no cases of malaria, cholera, or yellow fever. Because of a strict quarantine law, rabies is also nonexistent. On the other hand, tooth decay—perhaps because of a wide use of sugar and the enzymes present in certain tropical fruits—is 30% above the national average. With the perfect weather, a multitude of fresh-air activities, soothing negative ionization from the sea, and a generally relaxed and carefree lifestyle, everyone feels better there. Hawaii is just what the doctor ordered: a beautiful, natural health spa. That's one of its main drawing cards. The food and water are perfectly safe, and the air quality is the best in the country.

Handling the Sun

Don't become a victim of your own exuberance. People can't wait to strip down and lie on the sand like beached whales, but the tropical sun will burn you to a cinder if you're silly (the worst part of the day is 11 a.m.-3 p.m.). The burning rays come through easier in Hawaii because of the sun's angle, and you don't feel them as much because there's always a cool breeze. You'll just have to force yourself to go slowly. Don't worry; you'll be able to flaunt your best souvenir—your golden Hawaiian tan—to your green-with-envy friends when you get home. It's better than showing them a boiled lobster body with peeling skin! If your skin is snowflake white, 15 minutes per side on the first day is plenty. Increase by 15-minute intervals every day, which will allow you a full hour per side by the fourth day. Have faith; this is enough to give you a deep golden, uniform tan.

Haole Rot

A peculiar condition caused by the sun is referred to locally as *haole* rot. It's called this because it supposedly affects only white people, but you'll notice some dark-skinned people with the same condition. Basically, the skin becomes mottled with white spots that refuse to tan. You get a blotchy effect, mostly on the shoulders and back. Dermatologists have a fancy name for it, and they'll give you a fancy prescription with a not-so-fancy price tag to cure it. It's common knowledge throughout the islands that Selsun Blue shampoo has some ingredient that stops the white mottling effect. Just wash your hair with it and then make sure to rub the lather over the affected areas, and it should clear up.

Bugs

Everyone, in varying degrees, has an aversion to vermin and creepy crawlers. Hawaii isn't infested with a wide variety, but it does have its share. Mosquitoes were unknown in the islands until their larvae stowed away in the water barrels of the *Wellington* in 1826 and were introduced at Lahaina. They bred in the tropical climate and rapidly spread to all the islands. They are a particular nuisance in the rainforests. Be prepared; bring a natural repellent like citronella oil (available in most health stores on the islands) or a commercial product available in any grocery or drugstore. Campers will be happy to have mosquito coils to burn at night as well. Cockroaches are very democratic insects. They hassle all strata of society equally. They breed well in Hawaii, and most hotels are at war with them, trying desperately to keep them from being spotted by guests. One comforting thought is that in Hawaii they aren't a sign of filth or dirty housekeeping. They love the climate like everyone else, and it's a real problem keeping them under control.

Hiking and Camping Precautions

To stay safe in Hawaii, there are two things you must keep your eye on: humans and nature. The general rule is that the farther you get away from towns, the safer you'll be from human-induced hassles. If possible, don't hike or camp alone, especially if you're a woman. Don't leave your valuables in your tent, and always carry your money, papers, and camera with you. Don't tempt the locals by being overly friendly or unfriendly, and make yourself scarce if they're drinking.

Many trails are well maintained, but trailhead markers are often missing. The trails themselves can be muddy, which can make them treacherously slippery and often knee-deep. Always bring food because you cannot, in most cases,

forage from the land. Water in most streams is biologically polluted and will give you bad stomach problems if you drink it without purifying it first; either boil it or treat it with tablets. For your part, please don't use the streams as a toilet.

Always tell a ranger or other official of your hiking intentions. Supply an itinerary and your expected route, then stick to it. Twilight is short in the islands, and night sets in rapidly. In June, sunrise is around 6 a.m. and sunset 7 p.m.; in December, these occur at 7 a.m. and 6 p.m. If you become lost at night, stay put, light a fire if possible, and stay as dry as you can. Hawaii is made of brittle, crumbly volcanic rock, so never attempt to climb steep *pali*. Every year people are stranded, and fatalities have occurred. If lost, walk on ridges and avoid the gulches, which have more obstacles and make it harder for rescuers to spot you.

Heat can cause your body to lose water and salt. If you become woozy or weak, rest, take salt, and drink water as you need it. Remember, it takes much more water to restore a dehydrated person than to stay hydrated as you go; take small, frequent sips. Be mindful of flash floods: small creeks can turn into raging torrents with upland rains. Never camp in a dry creek bed. Fog is only encountered at the 1,500- to 5,000-foot level, but be careful of disorientation. Generally, stay within your limits, be careful, and enjoy yourself.

WATER SAFETY

Hawaii has one very sad claim to fame: more people drown here than anywhere else in the world. Moreover, dozens of swimmers yearly end up with broken necks and backs or injuries from scuba and snorkeling accidents. These statistics shouldn't keep you out of the sea—it is indeed beautiful, benevolent in most cases, and a major reason to go to Hawaii. But if you're foolish, the sea will bounce you like a basketball and suck you away for good. The best remedy is to avoid situations you can't handle. Don't let anyone dare you into a situation that makes you uncomfortable. "Macho men" who know nothing about the power of the sea will be tumbled into Cabbage Patch Kids dolls in short order. Ask lifeguards or beach attendants about conditions, and follow their advice. If local people refuse to go in, there's a good reason. Even experts get in trouble in Hawaiian waters. Some beaches, such as Waikiki, are as gentle as lambs and look as if you would have to tie an anchor around your neck to drown there. Others, especially on the north coasts during the winter months, are frothing giants.

While beachcombing, or especially when walking out on rocks, never turn your back to the sea. Be aware of undertows (the waves drawing back into the sea). They can knock you off your feet. Before entering the water, study it for rocks, breakers, reefs, and riptides. Riptides are powerful currents, like rivers in the sea, that can drag you out. Mostly they peter out not too far from shore, and you can often see their choppy waters on the surface. If caught in a "rip," don't fight to swim directly against it; you'll lose and only exhaust yourself. Swim diagonally across it, while going along with it, and try to stay parallel to the shore. Don't waste all your lung power yelling, and rest by floating.

When bodysurfing, never ride straight in; come to shore at a 45° angle. Remember, waves come in sets. Little ones can be followed by giants, so watch the action awhile instead of plunging right in. Standard procedure is to duck under a breaking wave. You can survive even thunderous oceans using this technique. Don't try to swim through a heavy froth and never turn your back and let it smash you. Don't swim alone if possible, and obey all warning signs. Hawaiians want to entertain you and they don't put up signs just to waste money. The last rule is, "If in doubt, stay out."

Yikes!

Sharks live in all the oceans of the world. Most mind their own business and stay away from shore. Hawaiian sharks are well fed—on fish—and don't usually bother with unsavory humans. If you encounter a shark, don't panic! Never thrash around because this will trigger their attack instinct. If they come close, scream loudly.

Portuguese man-of-wars put out long, floating tentacles that sting if they touch you. Don't wash the sting off with fresh water, as this will only aggravate it. Hot salt water will take away the sting, as will alcohol—either the drinking or rubbing kind—after-shave lotion, and meat tenderizer (MSG), which can be found in any supermarket and many Chinese restaurants.

Coral can give you a nasty cut, and it's known for causing infections because it's a living organism. Wash the cut immediately and apply an antiseptic. Keep it clean and covered, and watch for infection.

Poisonous sea urchins, such as the lacquer-black *wana,* can be beautiful creatures. They are found in shallow tidepools and will hurt you if you step on them. Their spines will break off, enter your foot, and burn like blazes. There are cures. Vinegar and wine poured on the wound will stop the burning. If those are not available, the Hawaiian solution is urine. It might seem ignominious to have someone pee on your foot, but it'll put the fire out. The spines will disintegrate

This "denizen of the deep" is much more afraid of you than you are of him.

in a few days, and there are generally no long-term effects.

Hawaiian reefs also have their share of moray eels. These creatures are ferocious in appearance but will never initiate an attack. You'd have to poke around in their holes while snorkeling or scuba diving to get them to attack. Sometimes, this is inadvertent on the diver's part, so be careful where you stick your hand while underwater.

Present in streams, ponds, and muddy soil, **Leptospirosis** is a *freshwater*-borne bacteria, deposited by the urine of infected animals. From two to 20 days after the bacteria enter the body, there is a *sudden* onset of fever accompanied by chills, sweats, headache, and sometimes vomiting and diarrhea. Preventive measures include: staying out of fresh water sources where cattle and other animals wade and drink; not swimming in freshwater if you have an open cut; and not drinking stream water. There have been only 32 reported cases on Kauai since 1979, so infection is rare. Don't become number 33!

HAWAIIAN FOLK MEDICINE AND CURES

Hawaiian folk medicine is well developed, and its cures for common ailments have been used effectively for centuries. Hawaiian *kahuna* were highly regarded for their medicinal skills, and Hawaiians were by far some of the healthiest people in the world until the coming of the Europeans. Many folk remedies and cures are used to this day and, what's more, they work. Many of the common plants and fruits that you'll encounter provide some of the best remedies. When roots and seeds and special exotic plants are used, the preparation of the medicine is as painstaking as in a modern pharmacy. These prescriptions are exact and take an expert to prepare. They should never be prepared or administered by an amateur.

Common Curative Plants

Arrowroot, for diarrhea, is a powerful narcotic used in rituals and medicines. The pepper plant *(Piper methisticum)* is chewed and the juice is spit into a container for fermenting. Used as a medicine for urinary tract infections, rheumatism, and asthma, it also induces sleep and

KAREN McKINLEY

KUKUI (CANDLENUT)

Reaching heights of 80 feet, the *kukui* (candlenut) tree was a veritable department store to the Hawaiians, who made use of almost every part of this utilitarian giant. Its nuts, bark, or flowers were ground into potions and salves and taken as a general tonic, applied to ulcers and cuts as an effective antibiotic, or administered internally as a cure for constipation or asthma attacks. The bark was mixed with water and the resulting juice was used as a preservative for fishnets and as a dye in tattooing, tapa-cloth making, and canoe painting. The oily nuts were burned in stone holders as a source of light and ground and eaten as a condiment called *inamona*. Polished, the nuts took on a beautiful sheen and were strung as lei. Lastly, the wood itself was hollowed into canoes and used as fishnet floats.

cures headaches. A poultice for wounds is made from the skins of ripe bananas. Peelings have a powerful antibiotic quality and contain vitamins A, B, and C, phosphorous, calcium, and iron. The nectar from the plant was fed to babies as a vitamin juice. Breadfruit sap is used for healing cuts and as a moisturizing lotion. Coconut is used to make moisturizing oil, and the juice was chewed, spat into the hand, and used as a shampoo. Guava is a source of vitamins A, B, and C. Hibiscus has been used as a laxative. *Kukui* nut oil makes a gargle for sore throats and a laxative, and the flowers are used to cure diarrhea. *Noni,* an unappetizing, hand-grenade-shaped fruit that you wouldn't want to eat unless you had to, reduces tumors, diabetes, and high blood pressure, and the juice is good for diarrhea. Sugarcane sweetens many concoctions, and the juice of toasted cane was a tonic for sick babies. Sweet potato is used as a tonic during pregnancy and juiced as a gargle for phlegm. Tamarind is a natural laxative and contains the most acid and sugar of any fruit on earth. Taro has been used for lung infections and thrush and as suppositories. Yams are good for coughs, vomiting, constipation, and appendicitis.

SERVICES FOR VISITORS WITH DISABILITIES

A person with a disability can have a wonderful time in Hawaii; all that's needed is a little pre-planning. The following is general advice that should help you plan.

Commission on Persons with Disabilities

This commission was designed with the express purpose of aiding handicapped people. It is a source of invaluable information and distributes self-help booklets free of charge. Any handicapped person heading to Hawaii should write first or visit their offices on arrival. For the *Aloha Guide To Accessibility* ($3) write or visit the head office at: Commission on the Handicapped, 500 Ala Moana Blvd., Honolulu, HI 96813, tel. (808) 586-8121; on Maui, 54 High St., Wailuku, HI 96793, tel. (808) 243-5441; on Kauai, 3060 Eiwa St. #207, Lihue, HI 96766, tel. (808) 241-3308; on Hawaii, P.O. Box 1641, Hilo, HI 96820, tel. (808) 933-7747.

When contacting the Kauai office, ask for their *Kauai Traveler's Guide for Physically Handicapped Persons* and *A Key to Resources Serving the Handicapped on Kauai.*

General Information

The key for a smooth trip is to make as many arrangements ahead of time as possible. Tell the transportation companies and hotels you'll be dealing with the nature of your disability in advance so that they can make arrangements to accommodate you. Bring your medical records and notify medical establishments of your arrival if you'll be needing their services. Travel with a friend or make arrangements for an aide on arrival (see "Kauai Services," following). Bring your own wheelchair if possible, and let airlines know if it is battery-powered. Boarding interisland carriers requires steps; no problem—they'll board you early on special lifts—but they must know that you're coming. Many hotels and restaurants accommodate persons with disabilities, but always call ahead just to make sure.

Kauai Services

At Lihue Airport, handicapped parking is available in an adjacent lot and across the street in the metered area.

For **emergency services,** call (808) 245-3773; visitor info is available at (808) 246-1440. For medical services, **Kauai Medical Group** at Wilcox Hospital will refer, tel. (808) 245-1500. For emergency room, long-term, and acute care contact Wilcox Memorial Hospital, 3420 Kuhio Hwy., Lihue, tel. (808) 245-1100.

To get around, arrangements can be made if the following are contacted well in advance: the county **Office of Elderly Affairs,** tel. (808) 245-7230, and **Akita Enterprises,** tel. (808) 245-5314; **Avis** will install hand controls on cars, but they need a month's notice. There are very few sidewalks and fewer cut curbs on Kauai—and none in Lihue. Special **parking permits** (legal anywhere, anytime) are available from the police station in Lihue. Medical equipment rentals are available from: **American Cancer Society,** tel. (808) 245-2942; **Pay 'n Save,** tel. (808) 245-6776; and **Easter Seals,** tel. (808) 245-6983. For medical support and help contact **Kauai Center for Independent Living,** tel. (808) 245-4034.

MEDICAL SERVICES

Hospitals

Medical help is available at **Wilcox Memorial,** 3420 Kuhio Hwy., Lihue, tel. (808) 245-1100; **Kauai Veterans,** in Waimea at (808) 338-9431; and **Samuel Mahelona Hospital,** in Kapa'a at (808) 822-4961.

Medical Clinics and Physicians

Medical services are also available from **Kauai Medical Group,** 3420 B Kuhio Hwy., tel. (808) 245-1500; after hours call 245-1831. The urgent-care clinic runs Mon.-Sat. 9 a.m.-6 p.m. and Sunday 10 a.m.-4 p.m.; the regular clinic runs weekdays 8 a.m.-5 p.m. and weekends 8 a.m. to noon. There are additional offices located in Kapa'a, Koloa, Kukui Grove Shopping Center, Kilauea, and Princeville.

Garden Island Medical Group is in Waimea, tel. (808) 338-1645; after hours call 338-9431. Office hours are weekdays 8 a.m.-5 p.m., and weekends 8 a.m. to noon. Offices are also in Ele'ele and Koloa.

Hawaiian Planned Parenthood can be reached at (808) 245-5678.

For the **Natural Health and Pain Relief Clinic,** call (808) 245-2277.

A fine **pediatrician** (with four young children of his own) is Dr. Terry Carolan, at 4491 Rice St., Lihue, tel. (808) 245-8566.

Pharmacies

Southshore Pharmacy in Koloa, tel. (808) 742-7511, gives senior discounts. Other drugstores include **Westside Pharmacy,** in Hanapepe, tel. (808) 335-5342; **Shoreview Pharmacy,** in Kapa'a, tel. (808) 822-1447; **Longs Drugs,** in the Kukui Grove Shopping Center, tel. (808) 245-7771; and **Pay 'n Save,** in Lihue, tel. (808) 245-8896. All the hospitals and medical groups also have their own pharmacies.

Alternative Health Care

Aunty Daisy, Tongan-born but raised on Fiji, affirms that she is alive today because of the *aloha* hands of her grandmother, Tama Tuiileila. At the age of 10, Aunty Daisy contracted German measles, which left her young body painfully crippled. Although her English-born father took her to the best doctors available, nothing could be done. For five years her young body degenerated until she was a total invalid in chronic pain. Finally, an interisland steamer brought Grandmother Tama on a long-awaited visit. Grandmother Tama laid eyes for the first time upon her granddaughter and knew what must be done. With total focus, she began her ancient incantations while laying hands upon the child. For two torturous days and nights she continu-

ously massaged, all the while infusing the twisted little body with the *aloha* that flowed through her hands. From that day forward, Daisy began to blossom. Within a few years, the lovely young woman was married with children of her own. For the next 20 years, Daisy lived her life as a wife and mother in Australia, where she had moved with her husband. But when Grandmother Tama passed away, Aunty Daisy was suddenly filled with the desire to help people through massage and knew innately that she was somehow imbued with the *aloha* touch. Aunty Daisy is never far from Tama, whom she carries in her heart and memory. Wherever she goes, even in her tiny massage studio, Grandmother Tama is there, too. You can feel this touch at **Aunty Daisy's Polynesian Massage,** in the small Waipouli Complex at 971 D Kuhio Hwy., tel. (808) 822-0305, open Tuesday and Wednesday 8:30 a.m.-5:30 p.m.; Thursday and Friday 11 a.m.-10 p.m., and Saturday 9:30 a.m.-2:30 p.m. If your heart, spirit, or body aches, give them to "the lady with *aloha* hands."

The **Healing Arts Resources of Kauai,** a.k.a. HARK, at P.O. Box 160, Kapa'a HI, 96746, tel. (808) 822-5488 or (800) 599-5488, is directed by Joan Levy, who, as an independent practitioner, offers transformational, psychospiritual, intensive healing workshops. Joan's clients are the life-tossed and road-weary who have come to the point in their lives where they are willing to take action to make a positive change. Joan's method is an *intensive* program lasting one to two weeks. The belief is that you must remove yourself from your daily situation so as to focus on the deep-seated issues and create a positive change. After a telephone interview, Joan attempts to isolate the problem. She'll invite you to her own practice or direct you to one of Kauai's other excellent practitioners that she feels can help. Joan is well respected by the healing community and has a longstanding network of practitioners proficient in everything from massage to metaphysics. She is extremely adept at referring you to the practitioner who she feels can offer you the maximum benefit. Joan's creation of HARK, and her ability to bring the healing community of Kauai into this cooperative referral system is a testament to her own abilities and continued purpose of creating harmony.

Lomi Mai Ka Na'au ("Massage From Center"), P.O. Box 302, Kilauea, HI 96754, tel. (808) 828-6813 or 822-0919, offers sessions in the Hawaiian healing arts with *lomi lomi* massage as the basis. This powerful body and soul work is performed by the capable hands of practitioners Penny Kahelani Prior and Joy Finch, assisted by *kuma hula* Ku'uipo Latonio. Two-week intensive workshops, typically given in June and February, are also offered to those who wish to be trained in this healing work. Extremely vigorous, the workshops have been called "Massage Boot Camp" by some who have attended. For the workshop, Lomi Mai Ka Na'au makes use of a taro patch as a classroom and leads arduous brush-busting walks along mountainous pig trails just to soften you up so that the lomi and lifestyle philosophy penetrate deeper. The food is vegetarian and the accommodations spartan, so as to completely focus you on the task at hand. The course is designed for the serious student only, and after two weeks of being kneaded into shape physically, spiritually, and emotionally, you at least come away with a basic understanding of what *lomi* and the Hawaiian healing arts are really about. For those visiting Kauai who would like to experience this powerful bodywork medium, call the above telephone numbers to set up a session.

Kauai Speaks Quarterly, P.O. Box 230 Kilauea, Kauai, HI, tel. (808) 828-1213, is available free in many shops and restaurants. Its storehouse of information for those seeking the inner path, alternative healers, spiritualism, inner growth, and the healing of Parent Earth, with an especially strong focus on women-related issues. Inside, the "Island Directory" points you to everything from astrology to workshops and retreats, and the "Calendar of Events" lets you know what's happening when and where on the island.

ILLEGAL DRUGS

The use and availability of illegal, controlled, and recreational drugs are about the same in Hawaii as throughout the rest of the United States. Cocaine constitutes the fastest-growing recreational drug, and it's available on the streets of the main cities, especially Honolulu. Al-

though most dealers are small-time, the drug is brought in by organized crime. The underworld here consists mostly of men of Asian descent, and the Japanese *yakuza* is said to be displaying a heightened involvement in Hawaiian organized crime. Cocaine trafficking fans out from Honolulu.

One drug menace is known as "ice." Ice is smokable methamphetamine which will wire a user for up to 24 hours. The high lasts longer and is cheaper than the one obtained with cocaine or its derivative, crack. Users become quickly dependent, despondent, and violent because ice robs them of their sleep along with their dignity. Its use is particularly prevalent among late-night workers. Many of the violent deaths in Honolulu have been linked to the growing use of ice.

However, the main drug available and most commonly used in Hawaii is marijuana, which is locally called *pakalolo.* There are also three varieties of psychoactive mushrooms that contain the hallucinogen psilocybin. They grow wild but are considered illegal controlled substances.

Pakalolo Growing

About 25 years ago, mostly *haole* hippies from the Mainland began growing pot in the more remote sections of the islands, such as Puna on Hawaii and around Hana on Maui. They discovered what legitimate planters had known for 200 years: plant a broomstick in Hawaii, treat it right, and it'll grow. *Pakalolo,* after all, is only a weed, and it grows in Hawaii like wildfire. The locals quickly got into the act when they realized that they, too, could grow a "money tree." As a matter of fact, they began resenting the *haole* usurpers, and a quiet and sometimes dangerous feud has been going on ever since. Much is made of the viciousness of the backcountry growers of Hawaii. There are tales of booby traps and armed patrols guarding plants in the hills, but mostly it's a cat-and-mouse game between the authorities and the growers. If you as a tourist are tramping about in the forest and happen upon someone's "patch," don't touch anything. Just back off and you'll be okay. Pot has the largest monetary turnover of any crop in the islands, and as such is now considered a major source of agricultural revenue. There are all kinds of local names and varieties of pot in

Hawaii, the most potent being Kona Gold, Puna Butter, and Maui Wowie. Actually, these names are all becoming passé. Dealers will sometimes approach you. Their normal technique is to stroll by and in a barely audible whisper offer, "Buds?"

Hawaiian *pakalolo* is sold slightly differently here from the way it is on the Mainland; dealers package it in heat-sealed Seal-a-Meal plastic bags. The glory days are over, and many deals are rip-offs.

THEFT AND HASSLES

From the minute you sit behind the wheel of your rental car, you'll be warned about not leaving valuables unattended and locking your vehicle up tighter than a drum. Signs warning about theft at most major tourist attractions help to fuel your paranoia. Many hotel and condo rooms offer safes, so you can lock your valuables away and be able to relax while getting sunburned. Stories abound about purse snatchings and surly locals who are just itching to give you a hard time. Well, the stories are all true to a degree, but Hawaii's reputation is much worse than the reality. In Hawaii, you'll have to observe two golden rules: (1) if you look for trouble, you'll find it, and (2) a fool and his camera are soon parted.

Theft

The majority of theft in Hawaii is of the "sneak thief" variety. If you leave your hotel-room door unlocked, a camera sitting on the seat of your rental car, or valuables on your beach towel, you'll be inviting a very obliging thief to pad away with your stuff. You'll have to learn to take precautions, but they don't have to be anything like those employed in rougher areas like South America or Southeast Asia—just normal North American precautions.

If you must walk alone at night, stay on the main streets in well-lit areas. Always lock your hotel-room door and windows and place all valuable jewelry in the hotel safe. When you leave your hotel for the beach, there is absolutely no reason to carry all your traveler's checks, credit cards, or a big wad of money. Just take what you'll need for drinks and lunch. If you're uptight about leaving any money in your beach bag, just stick it in your bathing suit or bikini.

American money is just as negotiable if it's damp. Don't leave your camera or portable stereo on the beach unattended. Ask a person nearby to watch them for you while you go for a dip. Most people won't mind at all, and you can repay the favor.

While sightseeing in your shiny new rental car (which immediately brands you as a tourist), again, don't take more than what you'll need for the day. Many people lock valuables away in the trunk, but remember that most good car thieves can jimmy it as quickly as you can open it with your key. If, for some reason, you must leave your camera or valuables in your car, consider putting them under the hood. Thieves usually don't look there, and on most modern cars you can only pop the hood with a lever on the inside of the car. It's not failsafe, but it's worth a try.

Campers face special problems because their entire scene is open to thievery. Most campgrounds don't have any real security, but who, after all, wants to fence an old tent or a used sleeping bag? Many tents have zippers that can be secured with a small padlock. If you want to go trekking and are afraid to leave your gear in the campgrounds, take a large green garbage bag with you. Transport your gear down the trail and then walk off through some thick brush. Put your gear in the garbage bag and bury it under leaves and other light camouflage. That's about as safe as you can be. You can also use a variation on this technique instead of leaving your valuables in your rental car.

Hassles

Another self-perpetuating myth about Hawaii is that "the natives are restless." An undeniable animosity exists between locals—especially those with some Hawaiian blood—and *haole.* Fortunately, this prejudice is directed mostly at the group and not at the individual. The locals are resentful against those *haole* who came, took their land, and relegated them to second-class citizenship. People realize that this does not include the average tourist and they can tell who you are at a glance. Tourists usually are treated with understanding and given a type of immunity. Besides, Hawaiians are still among the most friendly, giving, and understanding people on earth.

Haole who live in Hawaii might tell you stories of their children having trouble at school, even mention an unhappy situation at some schools called "beat-up-a-*haole*" day—and you might hear that if you're a *haole* it's not a matter of *if* you'll be beaten up, but *when*. Truthfully, most of this depends upon your attitude and your sensitivity. The locals feel infringed upon, so don't fuel these feelings. If you're at a beach park and there is a group of local people in one area, don't crowd them. If you go into a local bar and you're the only one of your ethnic group in sight, you shouldn't have to be told to leave. Much of the hassle involves drinking. Booze brings out the worst prejudice on all sides. If you're invited to a beach party and the local guys start getting drunk, make that your exit call. Don't wait until it's too late.

Most trouble seems to be directed toward white men. White women are mostly immune from being beaten up, but they have to beware of the violence of sexual abuse and rape. Although plenty of local women marry white men, it's not a good idea to try to pick up a local girl. If you're known in the area and have been properly introduced, that's another story. Also, girls out for the night in bars or discos can be approached if they're not in the company of local guys. If you are with your bikini-clad girlfriend and a bunch of local guys are, say, drinking beer at a beach park, don't go over and try to be friendly and ask, "What's up?" You (and especially your girlfriend) might not want to know the answer. Maintain your own dignity and self-respect by treating others with dignity and respect. Most times you'll reap what you sow.

SUE STRANGIO EVERETT

WHAT TO TAKE

It's a snap to pack for a visit to Kauai. Everything is on your side. The weather is moderate and uniform on the whole, and the style of dress is delightfully casual. The rule of thumb is to pack lightly: few items, and clothing light in both color and weight. What you'll need will depend largely on your itinerary and your desires. Are you drawn to the nightlife, the outdoors, or both? If you forget something at home, it won't be a disaster. You can buy everything you'll need in Hawaii. As a matter of fact, Hawaiian clothing, such as muumuu and aloha shirts, is one of the best purchases you can make, both in comfort and style. It's quite feasible to bring only one or two changes of clothing with the express purpose of outfitting yourself while there. Prices on bathing suits, bikinis, and summer wear in general are quite reasonable.

Matters of Taste
A grand conspiracy in Kauai adhered to by everyone—tourist, traveler, and resident—is to "hang loose" and dress casually. Best of all, alohawear is just about all you'll need for comfort and virtually every occasion. The classic muumuu is large and billowy, and aloha shirts are made to be worn outside the pants. The best of both are made of cool cotton. Rayon is a natural fiber that isn't too bad, but polyester is hot, sticky, and not authentic. Not all muumuu are of the "tent persuasion." Some are very fashionable and form-fitted with peek-a-boo slits up the side, down the front, or around the back. *Holomuu* are muumuu fitted at the waist with a flowing skirt to the ankles. They are not only elegant but perfect for "stepping out."

In the Cold and Rain
Two occasions for which you'll have to consider dressing warmly are visits to mountaintops and boat rides where wind and ocean spray are factors. You can conquer both with a jogging or sweat suit and a featherweight, water-resistant windbreaker. If you intend to go interisland and visit Mauna Kea or Mauna Loa on the Big Island, or Maui's Haleakala, it'll be downright chilly. Your jogging suit with a hooded windbreaker/raincoat will do the trick for all occasions. If you're going to camp or trek, you should add another layer—a woolen sweater being one of the best. Wool is the only natural fiber that retains most of its warmth-giving properties even

if it gets wet. Several varieties of "fleece" synthetics currently on the market also have this ability. If your hands get cold, put a pair of socks over them. Tropical rain showers can happen at any time so you might consider a fold-up umbrella, but the sun quickly breaks through and the warming winds blow.

Shoes

Dressing your feet is hardly a problem. You'll most often wear zoris (rubber thongs) for going to and from the beach, leather sandals for strolling and dining, and jogging shoes for trekking and sightseeing. A few discos require dress shoes, but it's hardly worth bringing them just for that. If you plan on heavy-duty trekking, you'll definitely want your hiking boots. Lava, especially a'a, is murder on shoes. Most backcountry trails are rugged and muddy, and you'll need those good old lug soles for traction. If you plan moderate hikes, you might want to consider bringing rubberized ankle supports to complement your jogging shoes. Most drugstores sell them, and the best are a rubberized sock with toe and heel cut out.

Specialty Items

The following is a list of specialty items that you might consider bringing along. They're not necessities but most will definitely come in handy. A pair of binoculars really enhances sightseeing—great for viewing birds and sweeping panoramas, and almost a necessity if you're going whalewatching. A folding, Teflon-bottomed travel iron makes up for cotton's one major shortcoming—wrinkles—and you can't always count on hotels to have irons. Nylon twine and miniature clothespins are handy for drying garments, especially bathing suits. Commercial and hotel laundromats abound, but many times you'll get by with hand-washing a few items in the sink. A transistor radio/tape recorder provides news, weather, and entertainment and can be used to record impressions, island music, and a running commentary for your slide show. An inflatable raft for riding waves, along with flippers, mask, and snorkel, can easily be bought in Hawaii but don't weigh much or take up much space in your luggage. If you'll be camping, trekking, or

boating with only seawater available for bathing, take along Sea Saver Soap, available from good sporting goods stores. This special soap will lather in seawater and rinse away the sticky salt residue with it.

For the Camper

If you don't want to bring it with you, all necessary camping gear can be purchased or rented while in Hawaii. Besides the above, you should consider taking the following: a frame backpack or a convertible pack that turns into a suitcase, daypack, matches in a waterproof container, all-purpose knife, mess kit, eating utensils, flashlight (remove batteries), candle, nylon cord, and sewing kit (dental floss works as thread). Take a first-aid kit containing Band-Aids, all-purpose antiseptic cream, alcohol swabs, tourniquet string, cotton balls, elastic bandage, razor blade, Telfa pads, and a small mirror for viewing private nooks and crannies. A light sleeping bag is good, although your fleecy jogging suit with a ground pad and light blanket or even your rain poncho should be sufficient. Definitely bring a down bag for mountainous areas. In a film container pack a few nails, safety pins, fishhooks, line, and bendable wire. Nothing else does what these do and they're all handy for a million and one uses.

Basic Necessities

As previously mentioned, you really have to consider only two "modes" of dressing in Hawaii: beachwear and casual clothing. The following is designed for the midrange traveler carrying one suitcase or a backpack. Remember that there are laundromats and that you'll be spending a considerable amount of time in your bathing suit. Consider the following: one or two pairs of light cotton slacks for going out and about, and one pair of jeans for trekking—or, better yet, corduroys which can serve both purposes; two or three casual sundresses—muumuu are great; three or four pairs of shorts for beachwear and sightseeing; four to five short-sleeved shirts or blouses and one long-sleeved; three or four colored and printed T-shirts that can be worn for anything from trekking to strolling; a beach coverup—the short terrycloth type is the best; a brimmed hat for rain and sun—the crushable floppy type is great for purse or daypack; two or three pairs of socks are sufficient—nylons you won't need; two bathing suits (nylon ones dry quickest); plastic bags to hold wet bathing suits and laundry; five to six pairs of underwear; towels (optional, because hotels provide them, even for the beach); a first-aid kit (pocket-size is sufficient); suntan lotion and insect repellent; a daypack or large beach purse. And don't forget your windbreaker, perhaps a shawl for the evening, and an all-purpose jogging suit.

Babies and Toddlers

No need to leave home without the baby—no matter how appealing a few weeks away from that little bundle of joy might seem. **Baby's**

Away, tel. (808) 245-6259 or (800) 996-9030, specializes in the needs of little ones. They rent everything from cribs to rocking chairs.

Pets and Quarantine

Hawaii has a very rigid pet-quarantine policy designed to keep rabies and other Mainland disease from reaching the state. All domestic pets are subject to 90 days' quarantine, regardless of the fact that they may have current veterinary shot certificates. Unless you are contemplating a move to Hawaii, it is not feasible to take pets. For complete information, contact the Department of Agriculture, Animal Quarantine Division, 99-770 Moanalua Rd., Honolulu, HI 96701, tel. (808) 488-8461.

INFORMATION AND SERVICES

HAWAII VISITORS BUREAU OFFICES

In 1903, the Hawaiian Promotion Committee thought tourism could be the economic wave of the future. They began the Hawaii Tourist Bureau, which became the Hawaii Visitors Bureau. The HVB is now a top-notch organization providing help and information to all of Hawaii's visitors. Anyone contemplating a trip to Hawaii should visit or write the HVB and inquire about any specific information that might be required. Their advice and excellent brochures on virtually every facet of living in, visiting, or simply enjoying Hawaii are free. The material offered is too voluminous to list, but for basics, request individual island brochures (including maps) and ask for copies of their *Member Accommodation Guide,* and *Member Restaurant Guide.* Allow two to three weeks for requests to be answered.

Statewide HVB offices include the **HVB Administrative Office,** Waikiki Business Plaza, 2270 Kalakaua Ave., Suite 801, Honolulu, HI 96815, tel. (808) 923-1811; **Big Island HVB Hilo,** 250 Keawe St., Hilo, HI 96720, tel. (808) 961-5797; **Big Island HVB Kona Branch,** 75-5719 W. Alii Dr., Kailua-Kona, HI 96740, tel. (808) 329-7787; **Kauai HVB,** 3016 Umi St.,

Suite 207, Lihue, HI 96766, tel. (808) 245-3971; **Maui HVB,** 1727 Wili Pa Loop, Wailuku, HI 96793, tel. (808) 244-3550.

Two other helpful organizations are the **Molokai Visitors Association,** P.O. Box 960, Kaunakakai, Molokai, HI 96748, tel. (808) 553-3876, (800) 800-6367 Mainland, or (800) 553-0404 interisland, and **Destination Lanai,** P.O. Box 700 Lanai City, HI 96763, tel. (808) 565-7600.

Before you leave for the islands, information can be accessed from the *Official Recreation Guide* through travel agents who have a Sabre hookup. Among other items, information can be garnered on transportation, travel activities, and cultural events; reservations can be made at the same time.

North American Offices

HVB Canada, c/o Comprehensive Travel, 1260 Hornby St. #104, Vancouver, B.C. V6Z1W2, tel. (604) 669-6691

HVB New York, Empire State Bldg., 350 5th Ave. Suite 1827, New York, NY 10018, tel. (212) 947-0717

HVB Washington D.C., 3975 University Dr., #335, Fairfax, VA 22030, tel. (703) 691-1800

HVB San Diego, 11835 Carmel Mountain Rd., # 1304-353, San Diego, CA 92128, tel. (619) 485-7278

European Offices

HVB United Kingdom, P.O. Box 208, Sunbury on Thames, Middlesex, England TW165RJ, tel. 44-181-941-4009

HVB Germany, c/o Herzog HCGmbH, Borsigalee 17, 60388 Frankfurt/Main Germany, tel. 49-69-42-089-089

Asia/Pacific Offices

HVB Japan, Kokusai Bldg. 2F, 1-1, Marunouchi, 3-chome, Chiyoda-ku, Tokyo 100, tel. 011-81-3-3201-0430

HVB Korea, c/o Travel Press, Samwon Bldg. 10th Fl., 112-5, Sokong Dong, Chung-ku, Seoul, Korea, tel. 82-2-773-6719

HVB New Zealand, c/o Walshes World, 87 Queen St., 2nd Fl., Dingwall Bldg., Auckland, New Zealand, tel. 64-9-379-3708

HVB Taiwan, c/o Federal Transportation Co., 8th Fl., Nanking E. Rd., Section 3, Taipei, tel. 886-2-506-7043

HVB Thailand, c/o ADAT Sales, 8th Fl., Maneeya Center Bldg., 518/5 Ploenchit Rd., Bangkok 10330, tel. 66-2-652-0507

LOCAL RESOURCES

Emergencies

For the police, fire, and ambulance anywhere on Kauai, dial **911.**

Coast Guard Search and Rescue on Kauai: tel. (808) 245-4521 or (800) 552-6458.

Civil defense. In case of natural disaster such as hurricanes or tsunami on Kauai call (808) 241-6336.

Crisis Intervention Helpline: tel. (808) 245-3411.

Rape Crisis Hotline: tel. (808) 245-4144.

Ask-2000 Information and Referral Service, tel. (808) 275-2000, dispenses a wide variety of information on subjects from health to legal topics.

Aloha Pages, tel. (808) 246-8934, is a free 24-hour "talking telephone" information service on a variety of topics including entertainment, sports, health, weather, and community services. For specific information, dial the above number or check your local Hawaiian phone book for a complete listing of available topics.

The "HVB Warrior" is posted alongside the roadway, marking sites of cultural and historical interest.

Weather, Surf, and Time

For a recorded message 24 hours a day call Aloha Pages—tel. (808) 246-8934—then dial ext. 1520 for local weather, 1521 for surf reports, 1522 for marine weather. For the time, call (808) 245-0212.

Consumer Protection

If you encounter problems finding accommodations, bad service, or downright rip-offs, try the following: the Chamber of Commerce, tel. (808) 245-7363; the Hawaii Hotel Association, tel. (808) 923-0407; the Office of Consumer Protection, tel. (808) 241-3365; and the Better Business Bureau of Hawaii on Oahu, tel. (808) 942-2355.

Parks

For **state parks** on Kauai, contact the Department of Land and Natural Services, Division of State Parks, State Bldg., 3060 Eiwa St., P.O. Box 1671, Lihue, HI 96766, tel. (808) 241-3444. For **lodging** at Koke'e State Park, write Koke'e Lodge, P.O. Box 819, Waimea, HI 96796, tel. (808) 335-6061. For **county parks** contact the Division of Parks and Recreation, 4193 Hardy St., Lihue, HI 96766, tel. (808) 241-6670, open for permits Mon.-Fri. 7:45 a.m.-4:15 p.m.; when it's closed, permits are available at the Lihue Police Station, 3060 Umi St., Lihue, HI 96766, tel. (808) 245-6721.

Post Offices
Normal business hours are Mon.-Fri. 8 a.m.-4:30 p.m., Saturday 8 a.m.-noon. The central post office on Kauai is at 4441 Rice St., Lihue, tel. (808) 245-4994. Main branches are located at Kapa'a, tel. (808) 822-5421, and Waimea, tel. (808) 338-9973, with 13 others scattered throughout the island. Most larger hotels also offer limited postal services.

Reading Material
The central **library** is at 4344 Hardy St., Lihue, tel. (808) 245-3617. Branch libraries are located in Hanapepe, Kapa'a, Koloa, and Waimea. Check with the main library for times and services.

Free **tourist literature,** such as *This Week Kauai, Spotlight Kauai,* and *Kauai Beach Press,* is available at all hotels and most restaurants and shopping centers around the island. They come out every Monday and contain money-saving coupons and up-to-the-minute information on local events. *Kauai Drive Guide* is available from the car rental agencies and contains tips, coupons, and good maps. The Hawaii AAA *Tourbook* is also very useful.

There are two island newspapers, *The Garden Island,* published four times weekly, and the *Kauai Times,* appearing once a week. Hawaii's two main English-language dailies are the *Honolulu Star Bulletin* and the *Honolulu Advertiser*. The Japanese-English *Hawaii Hochi* and the Chinese *United Chinese Press* are also available. The last four are published on Oahu, but available on Kauai.

Menu is an informative magazine that lists restaurants and details of their menus. Other publications of interest that have ads, stories, and information, about all the islands are *Art to Onions,* a fine art and leisure magazine, and the inflight magazines of Aloha and Hawaiian Airlines.

Kauai Speaks Quarterly, P.O. Box 230 Kilauea, Kauai, HI, tel. (808) 828-1213, available free at various locations, is an excellent resorce for those seeking the inner path, alternative healers, spiritualism, inner growth, and the healing of Parent Earth. Its "Island Directory" points you to everything from astrology to workshops

and retreats, and its calendar of events lets you know what's happening when and where on the island. Especially helpful to women.

Telephone
As they do everywhere else in the U.S., long-distance rates go down at 5 p.m. and again at 11 p.m. until 8 a.m. the next morning. Rates are cheapest from Friday at 5 p.m. until Monday at 8 a.m. Local calls from public telephones (anywhere on the same island is a local call) cost 25 cents. Calling between islands is a toll call, and the price depends on when and from where you call and how long you speak. Emergency calls are always free. The area code for the entire state of Hawaii is 808. For directory assistance: local, 1-411; interisland, 1-555-1212; Mainland, (area code) 555-1212; toll free, (800) 555-1212.

> **The area code for all Hawaii is 808.**

Time Zones
There is no daylight saving time in Hawaii. When daylight saving time is not observed on the Mainland, Hawaii is two hours behind the West Coast, four hours behind the Midwest, and five hours behind the East Coast. Hawaii, being just east of the international date line, is almost a full day behind most Asian and Oceanian cities. Hours behind these countries and cities are: Japan, 19 hours; Singapore, 18 hours; Sydney, 20 hours; New Zealand, 22 hours; Fiji, 22 hours.

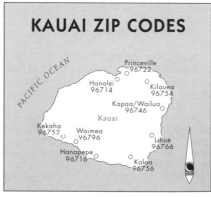

KAUAI ZIP CODES

Princeville 96722
Hanalei 96714
Kilauea 96754
Kapaa/Wailua 96746
Kauai
Kekaha 96752
Waimea 96796
Lihue 96766
Hanapepe 96716
Koloa 96756

PACIFIC OCEAN

© MOON PUBLICATIONS, INC.

RADIO STATIONS

STATION	DIAL NUMBER	REMARKS
OAHU		
KCCN	AM 1420	Hawaiian music 24 hours. Indiscriminate selections will either delight or exasperate.
KDEO	AM 940, FM 102	Country
KPOI	FM 98	Rock
MAUI		
KAIM	AM 870, FM 95.5	Contemporary
KAOI	FM 95	Stereo
KPOA	FM 93.5	Hawaiian music 19 hours a day. Tropical jazz five hours a day.
HAWAII		
KBIG	FM 98	
KHLO	AM 850	Country
KIPA	AM 620	Contemporary and requests
KKON	AM 700	Contemporary
KPUA	AM 670	Contemporary
KOAS	FM 92.1	Contemporary
KAUAI		
KFMN	FM 97	Contemporary, oldies
KONG	AM570,FM93.5	Contemporary and requests; Hawaiian music Friday evenings and Sunday mornings
KUAI	AM720	Contemporary and Hawaiian oldies; surf report

Note: Not all stations may be received on all islands.

Electricity

The same electrical current is in use in Hawaii as on the U.S. Mainland and is uniform throughout the islands. The system functions on 110 volts, 60 cycles of alternating current (AC). Appliances from Japan will work, although there is some danger of burnout; those requiring the normal European voltage of 220 will not work.

Distance, Weights, and Measures

Hawaii, like all of the U.S., employs the "English method" of measuring weights and distances. Basically, dry weights are in ounces and pounds; liquid measures are in ounces, quarts, and gallons; and distances are measured in inches, feet, yards, and miles. The metric system is known but is not in general use. The conversion chart at the back of this book should be helpful.

Laundromats

Self-service laundromats are Lihue Washerette, in the lower level of the Lihue Shopping Center, and Kapa'a Laundry Center, in the Kapa'a Shopping Center.

Island Facts

Kauai's nickname is "The Garden Isle," and it is the oldest of the main Hawaiian islands. Its lei is made from the *mokihana,* a small native citrus fruit purple in color.

MONEY AND FINANCES

Currency

U.S. currency is among the drabbest in the world—it's all the same size and color. Those unfamiliar with it should spend some time getting acquainted so that they don't make costly mistakes. U.S. coinage in use is: one cent, five cents, 10 cents, 25 cents, 50 cents, and $1 (uncommon); paper currency is $1, $2 (uncommon), $5, $10, $20, $50, $100. Bills larger than $100 are not in common usage.

Banks

Full-service banks tend to open slightly earlier than Mainland banks, at 8:30 a.m. Mon.-Friday. Closing is at 3 p.m., except on Friday, when most banks remain open until 6 p.m. Of most value to travelers, banks sell and cash traveler's checks, give cash advances on credit cards, and exchange and sell foreign currency.

Traveler's Checks

Traveler's checks are accepted throughout Hawaii at hotels, restaurants, and car-rental agencies and in most stores and shops. However, to be readily acceptable they should be in American currency. Banks accept foreign-currency traveler's checks, but it'll mean an extra trip and inconvenience. Some larger hotels that deal often with Japanese and Canadians will accept the currency of those two nations.

Credit Cards

More and more business is transacted in Hawaii using credit cards. Almost every form of accommodation, shop, restaurant, and amusement accepts them. For renting a car they're almost a must. With "credit card insurance" readily available, they're as safe as traveler's checks and sometimes even more convenient. Don't rely on them completely, because there are some establishments that won't accept them—or perhaps won't accept the kind you carry.

BOB RACE

orchid tree

HAWAII STATE ARCHIVES

GETTING THERE

With the number of visitors each year approaching six million—and double that number just passing through—the state of Hawaii is one of the easiest places in the world to get to . . . by plane. About 10 large U.S. airlines (and other small ones) fly to and from the islands. About the same number of foreign carriers, mostly from Asia and Oceania, also touch down here on a daily basis. In 1978, airlines were deregulated. In 1984, the reign of the Civil Aeronautics Board (CAB), which controlled exactly which airlines flew where and how much they could charge, ended. Routes, prices, and schedules were thrown open to free competition. Airlines that had previously monopolized preferred destinations found competitors prying loose their strangleholds. Thus, Hawaii is now one of the most hotly contested air markets in the world. The competition among carriers is fierce, and this makes for sweet deals and a wide choice of fares for the money-wise traveler. It also makes for pricing chaos. It's impossible to give airline prices that will hold true for more than a month—if that long. But it's comforting to know that flights to Hawaii are cheaper today than they have been in years and mile for mile are one of the

best travel bargains in the industry. Familiarize yourself with the alternatives at your disposal so that you can make an informed travel selection. Now more than ever, you should work with a sharp travel agent who's on your side.

Airlines servicing Hawaii, both domestic and foreign, land at Honolulu International Airport and then carry on to Kauai or offer connecting flights on "interisland carriers." In most cases they're part of the original ticket price with no extra charge. Different airlines have "interline" agreements with different Hawaiian carriers so check with your travel agent. All major and most smaller interisland carriers service Kauai from throughout Hawaii.

Note: Airlines usually adjust their flight schedules about every three months to account for seasonal differences in travel and route changes. Before planning a trip to and around the islands, be sure to contact the airlines directly or go through your travel agent for the most current information on routes and flying times.

When to Go
The prime tourist season starts two weeks before Christmas and lasts until Easter. It picks up

again with summer vacation in early June and ends once more in late August. Everything is usually booked solid and prices are inflated. Hotel, airline, and car reservations, which are a must, are often hard to coordinate at this time of year. You can save 10-50% and a lot of hassling if you go in the artificially created off-season—September to early December, and mid-April (after Easter) until early June. Recently, the drop in numbers of tourists during the off-season has not been nearly as substantial as in years past, indicating the increasing popularity of the island at all times of the year, but you'll still find the prices better and the beaches, trails, campgrounds, and even restaurants less crowded. The people will be happier to see you, too.

Travel Restrictions on Airlines

There are two categories of airlines that you can take to Hawaii: **domestic** (meaning American-owned) and **foreign**-owned. An American law, penned at the turn of the century to protect American shipping, says that "only" an American carrier can transport you to and from two American cities. In the airline industry, this law is still very much in effect. It means, for example, that if you want a roundtrip between San Francisco and Honolulu, you *must* fly on a domestic carrier, such as United or American. If, for example, you are flying from San Francisco to Tokyo, you are at liberty to fly a "foreign" airline, and you may even have a stopover in Hawaii, but you must continue to Tokyo or some other foreign city and cannot fly back to San Francisco on the foreign airline. Canadians have no problem flying Canadian Pacific roundtrip from Toronto to Honolulu because this route does not connect two American cities; so it is with all foreign travel to and from Hawaii. Travel agents know this, but if you're planning your own trip be aware of this fact; if you're traveling roundtrip it must be on a domestic carrier.

Kinds of Flights

The three kinds of flights available to Hawaii are "milk run," direct, and nonstop. Milk runs are the least convenient. On these, you board a carrier—say in your home town—fly it to a gateway city, change planes and carriers, fly on to the West Coast, change again, and then fly to

Hawaii. They're a hassle—your bags have a much better chance of getting lost, you waste time in airports, and to top it off, they're not any cheaper. Avoid them if you can.

On direct flights you fly from point A to point B without changing planes; it doesn't mean that you don't land in between. Direct flights do land, usually once, to board and deboard passengers, but you sit cozily on the plane along with your luggage until you reach your destination. Nonstop is just that but can cost a bit more; you board and take your seat and when the doors open again you're in Hawaii. All flights from the West Coast gateway cities are nonstop "God willing"—because there is only the Pacific in between!

Travel Agents

At one time people went to a travel agent the same way they went to a barber or beautician—loyally sticking with one. Most agents are reputable professionals who know what they're doing. They should be members of the American Society of Travel Agents (ASTA) and licensed by the Air Traffic Conference (ATC). Most have the inside track on the best deals, and they'll save you countless hours calling 800 numbers and listening to elevator music while on hold. Unless you require them to make very special arrangements, their services are free—they are paid a commission by the airlines and hotels that they book for you.

If you've done business with a travel agent in the past and were satisfied with the services and prices, by all means stick with him or her. If no such positive rapport exists, then shop around. Ask friends or relatives for recommendations; if you can't get any endorsements go to the Yellow Pages. Call two or three travel agents to compare prices. Make sure to give all of them the same information and be as precise as possible. Tell them where and when you want to go, how long you want to stay, which class you want to travel, and any special requirements. Write down their information. It's amazing how confusing travel plans can be when you have to keep track of flight numbers, times, prices, and all the preparation info. When you compare, don't look only for the cheapest price. Check for convenience of flights, amenities in hotels, and any other fringe benefits that might be included. Then make your choice of agent and, if he or she is willing to give you individualized service, stick with that agent from then on.

Agents become accustomed to offering the same deals to many clients because they're familiar with the arrangements and because the deals have worked well in the past. Sometimes these are indeed the best, but if they don't suit you, don't be railroaded into accepting them. Any good agent will work with you. After all, it's your trip and your money.

Package Tours

For the independent traveler, practical package deals that include only flight, car, and lodging are okay. Agents put these together all the time and they might be the best, but if they don't work for you, make arrangements separately. A package *tour* is totally different. On these, you get your hand held by escorts, eat where they want you to eat, go where they want you to go, and watch Hawaii slide by your bus window. For some people, especially groups, this might be the way to do it, but everyone else should avoid the package tour. You'll see Hawaii best on your own, and if you want a tour you can arrange one there, often more cheaply. Once arrangements have been made with your travel agent, make sure to take all receipts and letters of confirmation (hotel, car) with you to Hawaii. They probably won't be needed, but if they are, nothing will work better in getting results.

Mainland and International Fares

There are many categories of airline fares, but only three apply to the average traveler: first class, coach, and excursion (APEX). Traveling **first class** seats you in the front of the plane, gives you free drinks and movie headsets, a wider choice of meals, more legroom, and access to VIP lounges, if they exist. There are no restrictions, no penalties for advance-booking cancellations or rebooking of return flights, and no minimum-stay requirements.

Coach, the way most people fly, is totally adequate. You sit in the plane's main compartment, behind first class. Your seats are comfortable, although you don't have as much legroom or as wide a choice of meals. Movie headsets and drinks cost you a few dollars. Coach offers many of the same benefits as first

class and costs about 30% less. You can buy tickets up until takeoff, you have no restrictions on minimum or maximum stays, you receive liberal stopover privileges, and you can cash in your return ticket or change your return date with no penalties.

Excursion, or advance-payment excursion (APEX), fares are the cheapest. You are accommodated on the plane exactly the same as if you were flying coach. There are, however, some restrictions. You must book and pay for your ticket in advance (7-14 days). You must book your return flight at the same time, and under most circumstances you can't change either without paying a penalty. Also, your stopovers are severely limited and you will have a minimum/maximum stay period. Only a limited number of seats on any one plane are set aside for APEX fares, so book as early as you can. Also, if you must change travel plans, you can go to the airport and get on as a standby passenger using a discounted ticket, even if the airline doesn't have an official standby policy. There's always the risk that you won't get on, but you do have a chance, as well as priority over an actual standby customer.

Standby is exactly what its name implies: you go to the airport and wait around to see if any flights going to Hawaii have an empty seat. You can save some money this way but cannot have a firm itinerary or limited time. Since Hawaii is such a popular destination, standbys can wait days before catching a plane.

Active and retired **military personnel** and their dependents are offered special fares on airlines and in military hostels. An excellent resource book listing all of these special fares and more is *Space-A* ($11.75 for book and first-class postage), available from Military Travel News, P.O. Box 9, Oakton, VA 22124. Plenty of money-saving tips.

Charters

Charter flights were at one time only for groups or organizations that had memberships in travel clubs. Now they're open to the general public. A charter flight is an entire plane or a block of seats purchased at a quantity discount by a charter company and then sold to customers. Because they are bought at wholesale prices, charter fares can be the cheapest available. As in package deals, only take a charter flight if it is a "fly only," or perhaps includes a car. You don't need one that includes a guide and a bus. Most importantly, make sure that the charter company is reputable. They should belong to the same organizations as most travel agents (ASTA and ATC). If not, check them out at the local chamber of commerce.

More restrictions apply to charters than to any other flights. You must pay in advance. If you cancel after a designated time, you can be penalized severely or lose your money entirely. You cannot change departure or return dates and times. However, up to 10 days before departure the charter company is legally able to cancel, raise the price by 10%, or change time and dates. They must return your money if cancellation occurs, or if changed arrangements are unacceptable to you. Mostly they are on the up-and-up and flights go smoothly, but there are horror stories. Be careful. Be wise. Investigate!

Tips
Flights from the West Coast take about five hours; you gain two hours over Pacific Standard Time when you land in Hawaii. From the East Coast it takes about 11 hours and you gain five hours over Eastern Standard Time. Try to fly Mon.-Thurs., when flights are cheaper and easier to book. Pay for your ticket as soon as your plans are firm. If prices go up, there will be no charge added, but merely booking doesn't guarantee the lowest price. Make sure that airlines, hotels, and car agencies get your phone number, too—not only your travel agent's—in case any problems with availability arise (travel agents are often closed on weekends). It's not necessary, but it's a good idea to call and reconfirm flights 24-72 hours in advance.

First-row (bulkhead) seats are good for people who need more legroom but bad for watching the movie. Airlines will give you special meals (vegetarian, kosher, low cal, low salt) often at no extra charge, but you must notify them in advance. If you're "bumped" from an overbooked flight, you're entitled to a comparable flight to your destination within one hour. If more than an hour elapses, you get denied-boarding compensation, which goes up proportionately with the amount of time you're detained. Sometimes this is cash or a voucher for another flight to be used in the future. You don't have to accept what an airline offers on the spot if you feel they aren't being fair.

Traveling with Children
Fares for children ages 2-12 are 50% of the adult fares; children under two not occupying a seat travel free. If you're traveling with an infant or active toddler, book your flight well in advance and request the bulkhead seat or first row in any section and a bassinet if available. Many carriers have fold-down cribs with restraints for baby's safety and comfort. Toddlers appreciate the extra space provided by the front-row seats. Be sure to reconfirm and arrive early to ensure this special seating. On long flights you'll be glad that you took these extra pains.

Although most airlines have coloring books, puppets, etc., to keep your child busy, it's always a good idea to bring your own. These can make the difference between a pleasant flight and a harried ordeal. Also, remember to bring baby bottles, formula, diapers, and other necessities, as many airlines may not be equipped with exactly what you need. Make all inquiries ahead of time so you're not caught unprepared.

Baggage
You are allowed two free pieces of luggage—one large, the other smaller—and a carry-on bag. The two main pieces can weigh up to 70 pounds each; an extra charge is levied for extra weight. The larger bag can have an overall added dimension (height plus width plus length) of 62 inches; the smaller, 55 inches. Your carry-on must fit under your seat or in the overhead storage compartment. Purses and camera bags are not counted as carry-ons and may be taken aboard. Surfboards and bicycles are about $15 extra. Although they make great mementos, remove all previous baggage tags from your luggage; they can confuse handlers. Attach a sturdy holder with your name and address on the handle, or use a stick-on label on the bag itself. Put your name and address inside the bag, and the address where you'll be staying in Hawaii if possible. Carry your cosmetics, identification, money, prescriptions, tickets, reservations, change of underwear, camera equipment, and perhaps a clean shirt or blouse in your carry-on.

Visas

Entering Hawaii is like entering anywhere else in the United States. Foreign nationals must have a current passport and proper visa, an ongoing or return air ticket, and sufficient funds for the proposed stay in Hawaii. Canadians do not need a visa or passport but must have proper identification (such as a passport, driver's license, or birth certificate).

Leaving Hawaii

Remember that before you leave Hawaii for the Mainland, all of your bags are subject to an **agricultural inspection,** usually a painless procedure taking only a minute or two. To facilitate your departure, leave all bags unlocked until after inspection. There are no restrictions on beach sand, coconuts, dried flower arrangements, froph flower lei, pineapples, certified pest-free plants, seashells, seed lei, and wood roses. However, avocado, litchi, and papaya must be treated before departure. Some other restricted items are berries, fresh gardenias, roses, jade plants, live insects, snails, cotton, plants in soil, soil itself, and sugarcane.

Kauai's Airports

Lihue Airport, less than two miles from downtown Lihue, receives the vast majority of Kauai's flights. No public transportation to or from the airport is available, so you must either rent a car or hire a taxi. The terminal, long and low, has a restaurant and cocktail lounge, snack shop, flower shop, gift shop, restrooms, and a handful of suitcase-size coin lockers ($1) in the lobby. The gift shop sells pre-inspected island fruit that's boxed and ready to transport; tel. (808) 245-6273. All major car rental agencies and a good number of local firms maintain booths just outside the main entranceway; other agencies send vans to the airport to pick up customers. Baggage pick-up is at either end of the building, Aloha and United to the left as you enter the terminal from the plane, Hawaiian Airlines to the right—follow the signs. Check-in counters are along the outside corridor—Hawaiian Airlines on the left and Aloha and United on the right as you look at the terminal building. All non-carry-on baggage must go through an agricultural inspection at the terminal entrance; carry-on luggage is run through X-ray machines.

Kauai's Lihue Airport is connected to all the Hawaiian islands by direct flight, but no non-stop flights from the Mainland are currently operating. All Mainland and international passengers arrive via Honolulu, from which three major interisland carriers offer numerous daily flights.

Average flying times to Kauai are 27 minutes from Honolulu, one to two hours from the Big Island depending upon stops, and just over one hour from Maui, including the stop in Honolulu. Outgoing and incoming flights are dispersed equally throughout the day.

Princeville Airport is basically an airstrip servicing Princeville. Located along Rt. 56 just east of town, it is used only by Aloha Island Air and Papillon Helicopters. The terminal is a cute little building made inconspicuous by the immense beauty surrounding it. There's a toilet, telephone, Amelia's Cafe and lounge, and Hertz and Avis car rental offices. Located on the second floor, with windows looking out onto the runway and open to the lobby below, Amelia's serves drinks, sandwiches, hot dogs, nachos, and chili—most for under $7. The rental car booths stay open until the last incoming flight has arrived.

Stopover Flights

All the major carriers have arrangements for getting you to Kauai. United States carriers such as Hawaiian Airlines, Western, Continental, and American, along with foreign carriers like Canadian Pacific, Qantas, and Japan Airlines, land at Honolulu. There they have an interline agreement with island carriers, including Hawaiian and Aloha Airlines, which then take you to Kauai. This sometimes involves a plane change, but your baggage can be booked straight through. Hawaiian Airlines has expanded to Mainland flights from San Francisco and Los Angeles, with connecting flights in Honolulu to Lihue. They offer the added convenience of dealing with just one airline.

INTERISLAND CARRIERS

Getting to and from Kauai via the other islands is easy and convenient. The only effective way for most visitors to travel between the Hawaiian islands is by air. Luckily, Hawaii has an excellent air transportation system which boasts one of the industry's safest flight records. The following airlines have competitive prices, with interisland flights for about $75 one-way. You can also save money (about $15) if you take the first or last daily scheduled flight. This offer usually applies only to flights to and from Honolulu, but do check because the policy often changes. Another alternative is to purchase a booklet of six flight vouchers. You save about $7 per ticket, and they are *transferable.* Just book a flight as normal and present the filled-in voucher to board the plane. Perfect for families or groups of friends, vouchers can be purchased at any ticket office or at Honolulu International Airport.

Note: Although every effort has been made for up-to-the-minute accuracy, remember that schedules are constantly changing. The following should be used only as a point of reference. Please call the airlines listed below for their latest schedules.

Hawaiian Airlines
Hawaiian Airlines, tel. (808) 245-1813 on Kauai, (800) 367-5320 nationwide, or (800) 882-8811 in

Hawaii, offers the largest number of daily flights. From Honolulu, Oahu, 26 nonstop flights go 5:45 a.m.-8 p.m.; from Kahului, Maui, 15 flights run 6:55 a.m.-7:10 p.m., two nonstop; from Kona, Hawaii, six flights are available 6:45 a.m.-3:20 p.m. with a stopover in Maui or Honolulu; from Hilo, Hawaii, eight flights leave 6:45 a.m.-6:40 p.m. but all stop in Maui or Honolulu; from Lanai, two afternoon flights run via Honolulu;

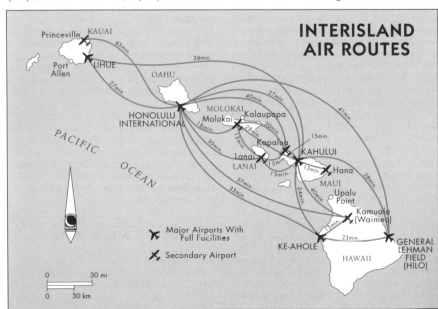

Air travel is one of the best ways to see the islands.

and from Molokai, there are two flights—at 7:05 a.m. and 11 a.m.—via Honolulu.

Aloha Airlines

Aloha Airlines, tel. (808) 245-3691 or (800) 367-5250 nationwide, has a jet fleet of 737s connecting Kauai to Honolulu, Maui, and both Kona and Hilo on Hawaii. Aloha's routes to Lihue are: from Honolulu, 22 flights 5:30 a.m.-8 p.m.; from Maui, 24 flights via Honolulu, 6:12 a.m.-7 p.m.; from Kona, 16 flights via Honolulu and/or Maui, 6:50 a.m.-6:15 p.m.; and from Hilo, 10 flights, 6:30 a.m.-6:35 p.m.

Charter Airlines

If you've got the bucks or just need to go when there's no regularly scheduled flight, try **Paragon Air,** tel. (808) 244-3356 or (800) 428-1231; **Trans Air,** tel. (808) 833-5557, only carries cargo.

DOMESTIC CARRIERS

The following are the major domestic carriers to and from Hawaii. The planes used are primarily DC-10s and 747s, with smaller 727s flown now and again. A list of the gateway cities from which they fly direct and nonstop flights is given, but connecting cities are not. All flights, by all carriers, land at Honolulu International Airport except the limited direct flights to Maui and Hawaii. Only the established companies are listed. Entrepreneurial small airlines such as the now-defunct Hawaii Express pop up now and again and specialize in dirt-cheap fares. There is a frenzy to buy their tickets and business is great for a while, but then the established companies lower their fares and the gamblers fold.

Hawaiian Airlines

One of Hawaii's own domestic airlines has entered the Mainland market. They operate a daily flight from Los Angeles and San Francisco to Honolulu, with periodic flights from Anchorage, Las Vegas, Portland, and Seattle. The "common fare" ticket price includes an ongoing flight to any of the neighbor islands, and if you're leaving Hawaii, a free flight from a neighbor island to the link-up in Honolulu. Senior citizen discounts for people age 60 or older are offered on transpacific and interisland flights. Hawaiian Air's transpacific schedule features flights between Honolulu and points in the South Pacific nearly every day: flights depart for Pago Pago and American Samoa, half of them continuing on to Apia, Western Samoa, and the rest flying to Tonga, with additional flights to New Zealand, Guam, Tahiti, and Rarotonga. Hawaiian Airlines offers special discount deals with Dollar rental cars and select major-island hotels. Contact Hawaiian Airlines at (800) 367-5320 Mainland or (800) 882-8811 in Hawaii.

United Airlines

Since their first island flight in 1947, United has become top dog in flights to Hawaii. Their Mainland routes connect over 100 cities to Honolulu. The main gateways are direct flights from San Francisco, Los Angeles, San Diego, Seattle, Portland, Chicago, New York, Denver, and Toronto. They also offer direct flights to Maui from San Francisco, Los Angeles, and Chicago, and from Los Angeles to the Big Island. United offers a number of packages, including flight and hotel on Oahu, and flight, hotel, and car on the Neighbor Islands. They interline with Aloha Airlines and deal with Hertz rental cars. They're the big guys and they intend to stay that way—their packages are hard to beat. Call (800) 241-6522.

American Airlines
American offers direct flights to Honolulu from Los Angeles, San Francisco, Dallas, and Chicago. They also fly from Los Angeles and San Francisco to Maui, with a connection in Honolulu. Call (800) 433-7300.

Continental
Flights from all Mainland cities to Honolulu connect via Los Angeles and San Francisco. Call (800) 525-0280 or (800) 231-0856 for international information.

Northwest
Northwest flies from Los Angeles, San Francisco, and Portland via Seattle. There are onward flights to Tokyo, Osaka, Okinawa, Manila, Hong Kong, Taipei, and Seoul. Call (800) 225-2525.

Delta Air Lines
In 1985, Delta entered the Hawaiian market; when it bought out Western Airlines its share became even bigger. They have nonstop flights to Honolulu from Dallas/Ft. Worth, Los Angeles, San Francisco, and San Diego; now they have flights to Kahului, Maui, via Los Angeles or Honolulu. Call (800) 221-1212.

FOREIGN CARRIERS

The following carriers operate throughout Oceania but have no U.S. flying rights. This means that in order for you to vacation in Hawaii using one of these carriers, your flight must originate or terminate in a foreign city. You can have a stopover in Honolulu with a connecting flight to a Neighbor Island. For example, if you've purchased a flight on Japan Air Lines from San Francisco to Tokyo, you can stop in Hawaii, but you must then carry on to Tokyo. Failure to do so will result in a stiff fine, and the balance of your ticket will not be refunded.

Canadian Airlines International
Nonstop flights from Canada to Honolulu originate in Vancouver and Toronto; nonstop Pacific flights go to Fiji, Auckland, and Sydney, with connecting flights to other Pacific cities. Call (800) 426-7007.

Air New Zealand
Flights link New Zealand, Australia, and Fiji with Los Angeles via Honolulu. Also offered are a remarkable APEX fare from Los Angeles to New Zealand, with stops in Honolulu and Fiji; and a Super Pass fare that lets you stop in eight cities between Los Angeles and Australia. Occasionally, other special fares are offered. Call (800) 262-1234 for current information.

Japan Air Lines
The Japanese are the second-largest group, next to Americans, to visit Hawaii. JAL flights to Honolulu originate in Tokyo, Nagoya, and Osaka. There are no JAL flights between the Mainland and Hawaii. Call (800) 525-3663.

Philippine Airlines
Philippine Airlines flies between Los Angeles or San Francisco and Manila via Honolulu. Connections in Manila are available to most Asian cities. Call (800) 435-9725.

Qantas
Daily flights depart from San Francisco and Los Angeles for Sydney via Honolulu. Stopovers are possible in Fiji and Tahiti. Call (800) 622-0850.

China Airlines
Routes from Los Angeles to Taipei with stopovers in Honolulu and Tokyo are possible but not available year-round. Connections are available from Taipei to most Asian capitals. Call (800) 227-5118.

Korean Air
Korean Air offers some of the least expensive

flights to Asia. Flights leave only from Los Angeles, stop in Honolulu, then continue either directly to Seoul or stop over in Tokyo. Connections to many Asian cities. Call (800) 421-8200.

Asiana Air
Direct flights are offered from Honolulu to Seoul, then continue throughout the Pacific and Asia, with limited flights to Europe and Russia. Call (800) 227-4262.

TRAVEL BY SHIP

American Hawaii Cruises
This American cruise ship company operates one 800-passenger ship, the SS *Independence*. This ship offers a seven-day itinerary that circumnavigates and calls at the four main islands. Fares range from an inside "thrifty cabin" at $1,145 to a luxury "owner's suite" for $3,195. Children under 16 are often given special rates and cruise free June-Sept. when they share a cabin with their parents. You board the ship in Honolulu after a plane flight to the islands arranged by American Hawaii Cruises. This ship is a luxury seagoing hotel and gourmet restaurant; swimming pools, health clubs, movies, and nightclubs are all parts of the amenities. For details, contact: American Hawaii Cruises, 2 N. Riverside Plaza, Chicago, IL 60606, tel. (800) 765-7000.

Alternatives
Other companies offering varied cruises include **P&O Lines,** which operates the *Sea Princess* through the South Pacific, making port at Honolulu on its way from the West Coast once a year.

Royal Cruise Line, out of Los Angeles or Auckland, sails the *Royal Odyssey,* which docks in Honolulu on its South Pacific and Orient cruise, $2200-4000.

The **Holland America Line** sails a year-long World Cruise, calling at Honolulu. Call (800) 426-0327.

Society Expeditions offers a 42-day cruise throughout the South Pacific departing from Honolulu. Fares range $3,000-9,000. Call (800) 426-7794.

Information
Most travel agents can provide information on the above cruise lines. If you're especially interested in traveling by freighter, contact: **Freighter Travel Club of America,** P.O. Box 12693, Salem, OR 97309; or **Ford's Freighter Travel Guide,** P.O. Box 505, 22151 Clarendon St., Woodland Hills, CA 91367.

TOUR COMPANIES

Many tour companies advertise packages to Hawaii in large city newspapers every week. They offer very reasonable airfares, car rentals, and accommodations. Without trying, you can get roundtrip airfare from the West Coast and a week in Hawaii for $400-500 using one of these companies. The following companies offer great deals and have excellent reputations. This list is by no means exhaustive.

SunTrips
This California-based tour and charter company sells vacations all over the world. They're primarily a wholesale company but will work with the general public. SunTrips often works with Rich International Air, tel. (305) 871-5113. When you receive your SunTrip tickets, you are given discount vouchers for places to stay that are convenient to the airport of departure. Many of these hotels have complimentary airport pickup service and will allow you to park your car, free of charge, for up to 14 days, which saves a considerable amount on airport parking fees. SunTrips does not offer assigned seating until you get to the airport. They recommend that you get there two hours in advance, and they ain't kidding! This is the price you pay for getting such inexpensive air travel. SunTrips usually has a deal with a car-rental company. Remember that everyone on your incoming flight is offered the same deal, and all make a beeline for the rental car's shuttle van after landing and securing their baggage. If you have a traveling companion, work together to beat the rush by leaving your companion to fetch the baggage and heading directly for the van as soon as you arrive. Pick your car up, then return for your partner and the bags. Even if you're alone, you could zip over to the car-rental center and then

return for your bags without having them sit very long on the carousel. Contact SunTrips, 2350 Paragon Dr., P.O. Box 18505, San Jose, CA 95158, tel. (800) 786-8747 in California, (808) 941-2697 in Honolulu.

Council Travel Services
These full-service budget-travel specialists are a subsidiary of the nonprofit Council on International Educational Exchange and the official U.S. representative to the International Student Travel Conference. They'll custom-design trips and programs for everyone from senior citizens to college students. Bona fide students have extra advantages, however, including eligibility for the International Student Identification Card (CISC), which often gets you discount fares and waived entrance fees. Groups and business travelers are also welcome. For full information, call (800) 226-8624, or write to Council Travel Services at one of these offices: 530 Bush St., San Francisco, CA 94108, tel. (415) 421-3473, or 205 E. 42nd St., New York, NY 10017, tel. (212) 661-1450. Other offices are in Austin, Berkeley, Boston, Davis, Long Beach, Los Angeles, Miami, Portland, San Diego, and Seattle.

STA Travel
STA Travel is a full-service travel agency specializing in student travel, regardless of age. Those under 26 do not have to be full-time students to get special student fares. Older independent travelers can avail themselves of services and, although you are ineligible for student fares, STA works hard to get you discounted or budget rates. STA's central office is at 7202 Melrose Ave., Los Angeles, CA 90046, tel. (213) 934-8722, or (800) 777-0112. STA maintains 39 offices throughout the USA, Australasia, and Europe, along with **Travel Cuts,** a sister organization operating in Canada. Many tickets issued by STA are flexible, allowing changes with no penalty, and are open-ended for travel up to one year. STA also maintains **Travel Help,** a service available at all offices designed to solve all types of problems that may arise while traveling. STA is a well-established travel agency with an excellent and well-deserved reputation.

Nature Expeditions International
These quality tours have nature as the theme. Trips are nine- or 15-day, four-island, natural-history expeditions with an emphasis on plants, birds, and geology. Their guides are experts in their fields and give personable and attentive service. Contact Nature Expeditions International at 6400 E. El Dorado, Suite 200, Tuscon, AZ 85714, tel. (520) 721-6712 or (800) 869-0639.

Ocean Voyages
This unique company offers seven- and 10-day itineraries aboard a variety of yachts in the Hawaiian Islands. The yachts, equipped to carry two to 10 passengers, ensure individualized sail training. The vessels sail throughout the islands, exploring hidden bays and coves, and berth at different ports as they go. This opportunity is for anyone who wishes to see the islands in a timeless fashion, thrilling to sights experienced by the first Polynesian settlers and Western explorers. For rates and information contact Ocean Voyages, 1709 Bridgeway, Sausalito, CA 94965, tel. (415) 332-4681.

Pleasant Hawaiian Holidays
A California-based company specializing in Hawaii, Pleasant Hawaiian Holidays makes arrangements for flights, accommodations, and transportation only. At 2404 Townsgate Rd., Westlake Village, CA 91361, tel. (800) 242-9244.

Others
A Plus Travel, a local Kauai firm, tel. (808) 742-9541 in Koloa, (808) 826-4022 in Hanalei, and (808) 822-3858 in Kapa'a, is a budget travel agency owned by husband and wife team Ervin and Angeletta Green. A Plus specializes in discounted tickets to the entire South Pacific including Indonesia, the Philippines, and Kong Hong, discounted tickets to and from the Mainland, and discounted interisland tickets as well. They offer ticket delivery service on Kauai and can also make arrangements for a discounted rate at many hotels and condos.

Travelers with Disabilities
Wheelers of Hawaii, 186 Mehani Circle, Kihei, HI 96753, tel. (808) 879-5521 or (800) 303-3750, is a private company owned and operated by Dave McKown, who has traveled the world with his brother, who is a paraplegic. Dave knows

firsthand the obstacles faced by people with disabilities. Wheelers of Hawaii is a full-service travel agency, with bookings into hotels, condos, and private homes set up for the physically disabled. The focus is mainly on Honolulu, Kona, and Maui, but Dave is a good source of information to any traveler with a disability.

Ecotours to Hawaii

Sierra Club Trips offers Hawaii trips for nature lovers who are interested in an outdoor experience. Various trips include hikes over Maui's Haleakala and, on Kauai, a kayak trip along the Na Pali coast and a family camping spree in the Koke'e region. All trips are led by experienced guides and are open to Sierra Club members only ($35 per year to join). For information, contact the Sierra Club Outing Department, 85 2nd St., Second Floor, San Francisco, CA 94105, tel. (415) 977-5500.

Earthwatch allows you to become part of an expeditionary team dedicated to conservation and the study of the natural environment. An expedition might include studying dolphins in the Kewalo Basin Marine Mammal Laboratory or diving Maui's threatened reefs. You become an assistant field researcher—your lodgings may be a dorm room at the University of Hawaii, and your meals may come from a remote camp kitchen. Fees vary and are tax deductible. If you are interested in this learning experience, contact Earthwatch, 680 Mt. Auburn St., P.O. Box 403-P, Watertown, MA 02272, tel. (617) 926-8200.

Backroads, 1516 Fifth St., Suite PR, Berkeley, CA 94710, tel. (510) 527-1555 or (800) 462-2848, arranges easy-on-the-environment bicycle and hiking trips on the Big Island. Basic tours include a six-day hiking/camping tour ($698), a six-day hiking/inn tour ($1,295), an eight-day bicycle/inn tour ($1,495), and a five-day bicycle/camping tour ($649). Prices include hotel/inn accommodations or tent when applicable, most meals, and professional guide service. Airfare is not included, and bicycles and sleeping bags can be rented (BYO okay) for reasonable rates.

Crane Tours, 15101 Magnolia Blvd., Sherman Oaks, CA 91403, tel. (800) 653-2545, owned and operated by Bill Crane, has been taking people kayaking and backpacking to the Big Island, Maui, Kauai, and Molokai since 1976. Basic prices for these eco-adventures start at $650 and rise to around $1,145 (airfare not included).

DIANA LASICH HARPER

GETTING AROUND

The most common way to get around Kauai is by rental car. The abundance of agencies keeps prices competitive. As always, reserve during peak season, but in the off-season you may take your chances by shopping around to score a good deal. Kauai also has limited shuttle-bus service; expensive taxis; reasonable bicycle, moped and scooter rentals; and the good old (legal) thumb.

RENTAL CARS

The best cars to rent on Kauai happen to be the cheapest: subcompacts with standard shift (if you can drive a standard). Kauai's main roads are broad and well paved, but the back roads, where all the fun is, are narrow, twisty affairs. You'll appreciate the downshifting ability of standard transmissions on curves and steep inclines. If you get a big fatso luxury car, it'll be great for puttin' on the ritz at the resort areas, but you'll feel like a hippopotamus in the backcountry. (If you've got that much money to burn, rent two cars!) Try to get a car with cloth seats; vinyl is too sticky, although sitting on your towel will help. Air-conditioning is necessary.

The mile markers on back roads are great for pinpointing sites and beaches. The lower number on these signs is the highway number, so you can always make sure that you're on the right road.

Requirements

A variety of requirements are imposed on the renter by car agencies, but the most important clauses are common. Some of the worst practices (being challenged) are no rentals to people under 25 or over 70 and no rentals to military personnel or Hawaii residents! Before renting, check that you fulfill the requirements. Generally, you must be 21—although some agencies rent to 18-year-olds and others require you to be 25. You must possess a valid driver's license (licenses from most countries are accepted, but if you are not American, get an International Driver's License to be safe). You should also have a major

credit card in your name. This is the easiest way to rent a car. Some companies will take a deposit, but it will be very stiff—easily $50 per day on top of your rental fees, and sometimes much more. In addition, the agency may require a credit check on the spot, complete with phone calls to your employer and bank. If you damage the car, charges will be deducted from your deposit, and the car company itself determines the extent of the damages. Some companies will not rent you a car without a major credit card in your name, no matter how much of a deposit you are willing to leave.

When to Rent

On this one, you'll have to make up your own mind; it's a bet that you can either win or lose big. But it's always good to know the odds before you plop down your money. You can reserve your car in advance, when you book your air ticket, or play the field when you get there. If you book in advance, you'll obviously have a car waiting for you, but the deal you made is the deal you'll get—it may or may not be the best around. On the other hand, if you wait, you can often take advantage of excellent on-the-spot deals. However, you're betting that cars are available. You might make a honey of a deal, or you might be totally disappointed and not be able to rent a car at all.

If you're arriving during the peak seasons of Christmas, Easter, or late summer vacation, absolutely *book your car in advance*. They are all accounted for during this period, and even if you can find a junker from a fly-by-night, they'll price-gouge you mercilessly. If you're going off-peak, you stand a good chance of getting the car you want at a price you like. It's generally best to book ahead, and it is easy to do so as the majority of car companies have toll-free numbers (listed below). At least call them for an opinion of your chances of getting a car upon your intended arrival.

Rates

If you pick up a car-rental brochure at a travel agency, notice that the prices for Hawaii rentals are about the lowest in the United States. The two rate options for renting are mileage and flat rate. A third type, mileage/minimum, is generally a bad idea unless you plan to do some heavy-duty driving. Mileage rate costs less per day, but you are charged for every mile driven. Mileage rates are best if you drive less than 30 miles per day—but even on an island that isn't much! The flat rate is best, providing a fixed daily rate and unlimited mileage. With either rate, you buy the gas; don't buy the cheapest; the poor performance from low octane eats up your savings.

Discounts of 10-15% for weekend, weekly, and monthly rentals are available. It's sometimes cheaper to rent a car for the week even if you're only going to use it for five days. Both weekly and monthly rates can be split between Neighbor Islands.

The average price of a subcompact standard shift, without a/c, is $30 per day, $120 per week (add about $8 per day—$50 per week—for an automatic), but rates vary widely. Luxury cars are about $10 per day more. Most of the car companies, local and national, offer special rates and deals. These deals fluctuate too rapidly to give any hard-and-fast information. They are common, however, so make sure to inquire. Also, peak periods have "blackouts," during which normally good deals no longer apply.

Warning: If you keep your car beyond your contract, you'll be charged the highest daily rate unless you notify the rental agency beforehand. *Don't keep your car longer than the contract specifies without notifying the company.* Companies are quick to send out their repossession specialists. You might find yourself in a situation with the car gone, a warrant issued for your arrest, and an extra charge on your bill. A simple courtesy call notifying them of your intentions saves a lot of headaches and hassle.

What Wheels to Rent

The super-cheap rates on the eye-catcher brochures refer to subcompact standard shifts. The price goes up with the size of the car and with an automatic transmission. As with options on a new car, the more luxury you get, the more you pay. If you can drive a standard shift, get one. They're cheaper to rent and operate, and a standard shift gives you greater control. AM/FM radios are good to have for entertainment and for weather and surf conditions.

Insurance

Before signing your car-rental agreement, you'll be offered "insurance" for around $10 per day. Since insurance is already built into the contract (don't expect the rental agency to point this out), what you're really buying is a waiver on the deductible ($500-1,000) in case you crack up the car. If you have insurance at home, you will almost always have coverage on a rental car—including your normal deductible—although not all policies are the same, so check with your agent. Also, if you haven't bought their waiver and you do have a mishap, the rental agencies will put a claim against your credit card on the spot for the amount of the deductible, even if you can prove that your insurance will cover the charge. They'll tell *you* to collect from your insurance company because they don't want to be left holding the bag on an across-the-waters claim. If you have a good policy with a small deductible, it's hardly worth paying the extra money for the waiver, but if your own policy is inadequate, buy the insurance. Also, most major credit cards offer complimentary car-rental insurance as an incentive for using their cards to rent the car. Simply call the toll-free number of your credit card company to see if this service is included.

Driving Tips

Protect your children as you would at home, with car seats. Their rental prices vary considerably: Alamo offers them free; National charges $3 per day; Hertz needs 48 hours notice; Dollar gives them free but they're not always available at all locations. Almost all the agencies can make arrangements if you give them enough notice. Check before you go and if all else fails, bring one from home.

There are few differences between driving in Hawaii and on the Mainland. Just remember that many people on the roads are tourists and can be confused about where they're going.

Since many drivers are from somewhere else, there's hardly a regular style of driving in the islands. A farmer from Iowa accustomed to poking along on back roads can be sandwiched between a frenetic New Yorker who's trying to drive over his roof and a super-polite but horribly confused Japanese tourist who normally drives on the left.

In Hawaii, drivers don't honk their horns except to say hello or signal an emergency. It's considered rude, and honking to hurry someone might earn you a knuckle sandwich. Hawaiian drivers reflect the Hawaiian climate: they're relaxed and polite. Oftentimes, they'll brake to let you turn left when they're coming at you. They may assume you'll do the same, so be ready for another driver, after a perfunctory turn signal, to turn across your lane. The more rural the area, the more apt this is to happen.

It may seem like common sense, but remember to slow down when you enter the little towns strung along the circle-island route. It's easy to bomb along on the highway and flash through these towns, but you'll be missing some of Hawaii's best scenery. Also, rural children expect *you* to be watchful and will assume that you are going to stop for them when they dart out into the crosswalks.

BYOC

If you want to bring your own car, write for information to: Director of Finance, Division of Licenses, 1455 S. Beretania St., Honolulu, HI 96814. However, unless you'll be in Hawaii for a bare minimum of six months and will spend all your time on one island, don't even think about it. It's an expensive proposition and takes time and lots of arrangements. From California, the cost is at least $600 to Honolulu International Airport and an additional $100 to any other island. To save on rental costs, it would be better to buy and sell a car there, or to lease for an extended period.

Auto Rental Companies

The following are major firms that maintain either a booth or courtesy pick-up vans at Lihue Airport. **Dollar,** tel. (808) 245-3651, (800) 342-7398 statewide, or (800) 800-4000 worldwide, has an excellent reputation and very competitive prices. Dollar rents all kinds of cars as well as jeeps and convertibles. Great weekly rates, and all major credit cards accepted.

Alamo has good weekly rates, tel. (808) 245-8953 or (800) 327-9633.

National Car Rental, tel. (808) 245-3502 or (800) 227-7368 nationwide, features GM and Nissan cars and accepts all major credit cards. They sometimes rent without a credit card if you leave a $100/day deposit—less if you take full insurance coverage.

Avis, tel. (808) 245-3512, 826-9773 in Princeville, or (800) 831-8000 nationwide, features late-model GM cars as well as most imports and convertibles.

Budget, tel. (808) 245-1901 or (800) 527-0700, offers competitive rates on a variety of late-model cars.

Hertz, tel. (808) 245-3356 or (800) 654-3131, is competitively priced with many fly/drive deals. They also maintain desks at the Princeville Airport.

A local company with a reliable reputation is **Westside-U-Drive,** tel. (808) 332-8644.

Scooters and Mopeds

These tiny two-wheelers are available from **South Shore Activities,** tel. (808) 742-6873, at Poipu Beach, and from **Budget** at Kiahuna Plantation in Poipu.

BUSES AND TAXIS

One of the benefits to come out of the destruction caused by Hurricane Iniki was the establishment of limited public transportation. The **Iniki Express,** free at one time, has become the **Kauai Bus,** 4396 Rice St., #104, Lihue, HI 96766, tel. (808) 241-6410 for current routes. Operating times are Mon.-Sat. 6 a.m.-6:30 p.m. (no operation Sunday and holidays); fare is $1; 50 cents for seniors, students, and people with disabilities (with I.D.); $25 for a monthly pass. Wait at any of the designated bus stops. The bus will not allow large bags or items—including backpacks and boogie boards—nor will it stop or pick up at undesignated spots, so be aware. The bus runs main routes only from the airport to Lihue, as far north as Hanalei, as far west as Kekaha, and as far south as Poipu. Running approximately every 40 minutes during the morning and slowing to once an hour in the afternoon, it is not uncommon for there to be a lapse of two hours between buses. The "Iniki Express" should be running at least until 1998. In September 1996, the U.S. Dept. of Transportation passed an appropriations bill allocating $3.2 million for Kauai's public transportation.

Taxis are all metered and charge a hefty price for their services; all have the same rates. Airport taxis have a monopoly on pick-ups at the airport, although others can drop off there. Sample fares are $5.50 from Lihue and $35 from Poipu to the airport, $30 from Lihue to Poipu, $60 from Lihue to Princeville, and $25 from Princeville to Ke'e Beach and the Kalalau trailhead. Reputable taxi companies include **Akiko's,** tel. (808) 822-3613, in Wailua; **A-1,** tel. (808) 742-1390, in Poipu; **North Shore Taxi,** tel. (808) 826-6189, in Hanalei; and **Kauai Cab,** tel. (808) 246-9554, in Lihue.

ALTERNATIVES

Bicycles

Riding a bike around Kauai is fairly easy, thanks to the lack of big hills—except for the road up to Koke'e State Park. Traffic is moderate, especially in the cool of early morning, when it's best for making some distance. Roads are generally good, but shoulders aren't wide and are sometimes nonexistent. Peak season brings a dramatic increase in traffic and road congestion. Take care! Perhaps the best riding is by mountain bike on the cane haul roads that head into the interior.

Shipping your own bicycle interisland costs about $20, and another $25 from the Mainland if it goes on a different airline. You must provide your own box and pack the bike yourself.

Outfitters Kauai, an ecology-minded sports shop specializing in kayaking and mountain biking, is owned and operated by Rick and Julie Havilend in the Poipu Plaza, at 2827-A Poipu Rd., P.O. Box 1149, Poipu Beach, HI 96756, tel. (808) 742-9667, open Mon.-Sat. 9 a.m.-5 p.m. and Sunday by arrangement. Their Poipu "interpretive bike course," self-guided with map and narrative information, is $20-33, depending upon the grade of bicycle chosen ($35 tandem). Mountain-bike rentals include helmet and water bottles for $20 a day and up (multiday

discounts). Biking and kayaking incidentals are also available for purchase along with Patagonia clothing.

An excellent choice is **Bicycle John's,** a full-service bicycle shop offering sales, repairs, and rentals. Located along Rt. 56 as you enter Lihue, tel. (808) 245-7579, the shop is open Mon.-Fri. 9 a.m.-5 p.m., Saturday 10 a.m.-4 p.m., and Sunday noon-4 p.m. Rental bicycles range from an 18-speed basic cruiser to a custom road bike, and prices range from $25 per day to $65 for four days with a price break for multiday rentals.

You're not required to salute John Sargent, the **Bike Doctor,** in Hanalei, tel. (808) 826-7799, open Mon.- Sat. 9 a.m.-5 p.m., who has a shop stocked with everything for both casual and serious cyclists. John sells road bikes, sells and rents Marin mountain bikes, and offers special wiki wiki repair service to visiting cyclists whose equipment has broken down. Rental prices are $25 a day, $100 per seven-day week, including helmet, tool box, and water bottle. The Bike Doctor is intimately familiar with roads and trails all over the island and is happy to give advice on touring. Happy pedaling!

Bicycle Kauai, at 1379 Kuhio Hwy., Kapa'a, tel. (808) 822-3315, open Mon.-Fri. 9 a.m.-6 p.m., Saturday 9 a.m.-4 p.m., and Sunday 10 a.m.-3 p.m., is a complete bicycle shop with sales, repairs, helmets, riding clothes, and rentals. Trek mountain bikes are $20 per day or $100 per week, including helmet, lock, and a car rack. The staff is friendly and knowledgeable, offering plenty of advice on bike routes and where and when to ride.

Pedal and Paddle, tel. (808) 826-9069, in the Ching Young Center in Hanalei, open daily 9 a.m.-5 p.m. in winter, 9 a.m.-6 p.m. in summer, rents bicycles as well as camping gear, snorkel gear, and surfboards. Prices are $10 per day, $40 per week for a cruiser bike and $50 and $80 for a mountain bike; prices include lock, helmet, and car rack if desired.

Or try **Dan's Sport Shop,** tel. (808) 246-0151, a full-service sporting goods store located at the Kukui Grove Shopping Center.

Hitchhiking

Using your thumb to get around is legal on Kauai, but you must stay off the paved portion of the road. For short hops in and around the towns—like from Koloa to Poipu or from the airport to Lihue—thumbing isn't difficult. But getting out to the Kalalau Trail or to Polihale on the west end, when you're toting a backpack and appear to be going a longer distance is tough. As on all the islands, your best chance of being picked up is by a visiting or local *haole*. Sometimes locals in pickup trucks will stop to give you a ride for short distances. Women *should not* hitch alone!

SIGHTSEEING TOURS

Magnificent Kauai is fascinating to explore by land, sea, or air. Looking around on your own is no problem, but some of the most outstanding areas are more expediently seen with a professional guide. Some of the options are discussed below.

Van and Bus Tours

On Kauai, most tour companies run vans, but some larger companies also use buses. Though cheaper, tours on full-sized coaches are generally less personalized. Wherever a bus can go, so can your rental car—but on a tour you can relax and enjoy the scenery without worrying about driving. Also, tour drivers are very experienced with the area and know many stories and legends with which they annotate and enrich your trip. Coach tours vary, but typical trips go to Hanalei and the north coast, to Waimea Canyon and south coast sights, or combine one of these tours with a trip to the Wailua River. Each agency has its own routes and schedules, but all hit the major tourist sites.

Rates sometimes include entrance fees and lunch. Half-day fares run $55-65, while full-day fares run $75-85; children's fares are about 25% less. Fares also vary according to area of pick-up and route. Often a tour to the Fern Grotto is considered the highlight—that should say it all! Companies offering these tours include **Trans Hawaiian,** tel. (808) 245-5108, **Robert's Hawaii,** tel. (808) 245-9558, **Kauai Paradise Tours,** tel. (808) 246-3999 (German-speaking guide available), and **Polynesian Adventure Tours,** tel. (808) 246-0122.

One unique tour company is **Kauai Mountain Tours, Inc.,** tel. (808) 245-7224 or (800) 452-1113, P.O. Box 3069, Lihue, HI 96766. It alone is licensed to operate tours in the Na Pali Kona Forest Reserve. Knowledgeable guides take you into the back country over dirt roads by air-conditioned 12-passenger 4WD vans, with an informed narrative on the way. They let you see a part of Kauai not reached by anyone who doesn't walk in. Traveling is rough, but the sights are unsurpassed; truly, this is one of the few ways in Kauai to get off the beaten path. The company's guides, all local people, are excellent and have a tremendous amount of knowledge about the island's flora, fauna, and history. Their seven-hour adventure costs $84 plus tax ($56 for children under 12) and includes a deli/picnic lunch (vegetarian too!) Tours start about 8 a.m. with free pick-up in the Wailua and Poipu areas.

Bicycle Tours

Outfitters Kauai (see "Bicycles," under "Alternatives," above), tel. (808) 742-9667, offers mountain bike and hike ecotours to Koke'e on Wednesday from 7:30 a.m. to 1:30 p.m., or by special arrangement. The 16-mile relaxed-pace ride contains a few vigorous climbs and focuses on the natural history of the area. Cold drinks and a full lunch are included for $78 per person. Rick and Julie are excellent athletes who know the mountains and seas of Kauai intimately. Their tours are educational as well as highly adventuresome; you couldn't find a better outfit to travel with.

Air Tours

Flying in a chopper is a thrilling experience, like flying in a light plane —with a twist. It can take you into all kinds of otherwise inaccessible little nooks and crannies. Routes cover the entire island, but the highlights are flying through Waimea Canyon, into the Mount Waialeale crater—where it almost never stops raining—and over the Alakai Swamp, where you see thousands of waterfalls and even 360-degree rainbows floating in midair. Then, to top it off, you fly to the Na Pali coast, swooping along its ruffled edge and dipping down for an up-close look at its caves and giant seacliffs. Earphones cut the noise of the aircraft and play soul-stirring music as a background to the pilot's narration. The basic one-hour around-the-island flight runs about $150 per person; other flights are 45-75 minutes in length and cost from $100-130. Some companies tailor flights to your interests; a flight might include a swim at a remote pool along with a champagne lunch. But these are, of course, more costly. Niihau Helicopters also flies periodically to points on Niihau. Its flights are more expensive, but it's the only way to get to see this island up close. Discounts of up to 15% from some of the companies are always featured in the ubiquitous free tourist brochures and are also occasionally offered through tourist-activity and information centers.

Outdoor purists disparage this mode of transport, saying, "If you can't hike in you shouldn't be there"—but that's tunnel vision and not always appropriate. To go deep into the mist-shrouded interior, especially through the Alakai Swamp, the average traveler "can't get there from here"—it's just too rugged and dangerous. The only reasonable way to see it is by helicopter and, except for the noise, choppers actually have less of an impact on the ecosystem than hikers do! A compromise—limiting numbers and times of flights—seems to be the best answer.

Everyone has an opinion on which company offers the best ride, the best narration, or the best service. All the helicopter companies on Kauai are safe and reputable, and most fly A-Stars, with a few Bell Jet Rangers still in use. Some helicopters accommodate only four passengers, while others take five; some have two-way microphones so you can ask questions of the pilot. Remember, however, that the seating arrangement in a helicopter is critical to safety. The pre-flight crew is expertly trained to arrange the chopper so that it is balanced, and with different people in various sizes flying every day, their job is very much like a chess game. This means that the seating goes strictly according to weight. If you are not assigned the seat of your choice, for safety's sake, please do not complain. Think instead that you are part of a team whose goal is not only enjoyment but also to come back safe and sound. It's very difficult not to have a fascinating flight—no matter where you sit.

Of the nearly two dozen helicopter companies on Kauai, the majority operate from Lihue Airport, with a handful flying from Burns Field in Hanapepe. The following have top-notch reputations. **Ohana Helicopter Tours,** at the An-

chor Cove Shopping Center, 3416 Rice Street, tel. (808) 245-3996 or (800) 222-6989, is an owner-operated company that gives personalized service. Ohana offers complimentary shuttle service (Kapa'a and Poipu areas) to their office, where flight procedures are explained. They want you to have the time of your life—not hard to achieve with this experience. The owner, Bogart Kealoha, has years of commercial and military experience and *knows* this island of his birth. Kealoha's hands-on approach, coupled with a flawless flight record since the day he opened for business over 10 years ago, has allowed Ohana Helicopters to grow into one of the largest and best-regarded helicopter companies on the island. Ohana now employs five pilots running three modern A-Stars into Kauai's wondrous interior. All pilots are handpicked and trained by Bogart, whose chief task has become the maintenance and safety of the crafts. The pilots use his wealth of knowledge as they point out historical, geological, and mythological areas during your flight. From smooth liftoff to gentle landing, you are in good hands with Ohana.

The granddaddy of them all is **Jack Harter Helicopters,** P.O. Box 306, Lihue, HI 96766, tel. (808) 245-3774 or (888) 245-2001, www.helicopters-kauai.com. Jack, along with his wife, Beverly, literally started the helicopter business on Kauai and has been flying the island for over 20 years. Jack doesn't advertise but he is always booked up. He knows countless stories about Kauai and just about everywhere to go on the island. He gives you a full hour and a half in the air, and his slogan—"Imitated by all, equalled by none"—says it all.

Safari Helicopter, tel. (808) 246-0136 or (800) 326-3356, is owned and operated by pilot Preston Myers, who learned to fly in the '60s and has been flying over Kauai for more than 10 years. Safari prides itself on offering a luxury tour in its state-of-the-art A-Star helicopters, complete with two-way sound system, unobstructed view , air-conditioned compartments, and an all-seeing video camera system that records your trip for future enjoyment. Prices range from a 40 minute mini-tour for $89 to a one hour flight including video of your tour for $148.

Other companies with good reputations and competitive prices flying out of Lihue Airport are: **Island Helicopters,** P.O. Box 3101, Lihue,

HI 96766, tel. (808) 245-8588, owned and piloted by Curt Lofstedt, who also employs Rudy Dela Cruz, a local instructor with the Air National Guard; **South Sea Helicopters,** P.O. Box 1445, Lihue, HI 96766, tel. (808) 245-7781 or (800) 367-2914, is owned and operated by Dennis Esaki, a local pilot with plenty of knowledge and experience; **Will Squyre Helicopters,** tel. (808) 245-8881, a one-man operation with personalized service from an owner who loves his work.

Several reputable companies fly from Burns Field in Hanapepe. **Bali Hai,** tel. (808) 332-7331, is one; **Niihau Helicopters,** P.O. Box 370, Makaweli, HI 96769, tel. (808) 335-3500, is another. The primary purpose of Niihau Helicopters is to provide medical and emergency treatment for the residents of Niihau. However, to defray costs, occasional nonscheduled tourist charters are offered on its twin-engine Agusta 109A. Two of their flights last 90 and 110 minutes, each with 30-minute stops on secluded beaches on Niihau; fares are $185 and $235, respectively. Two other options are an overflight of Niihau for $135 and a tour of the Na Pali coast with a Niihau overflight for $235. While it cannot compete with helicopter companies that regularly fly only over Kauai, it does offer you the only way to see Niihau up close. Let pilot Tom Mishler show you a bit of this Forbidden Island.

Fly Kauai and **Kumulani Air,** tel. (808) 246-9123, will take you above Kauai's sand and surf in their fixed-wing Cessna aircraft. A variety of tours are offered including flyovers of Niihau.

Special Note
On October 26, 1995, the FAA instituted regulation S472, stipulating that all commercial air-tour operators fly at an elevation of no less than 1,500 feet and maintain a lateral standoff of 1,500 feet from canyon walls. The majority of the helicopter tour operators now have been granted an elevation deviation of 1,000 feet, but the lateral standoff remains. If you have flown on Kauai before and remember descending deep into the canyons and hovering within an arm's length of waterfalls, don't expect a repeat performance. Don't be discouraged, though; despite the new restrictions, the tours are still outstanding and offer the thrill of a lifetime.

Wailua River Cruises
You too can be one of the many cruising up the Wailua River on a large, canopied, motorized barge. The Fern Grotto, where the boat docks, is a natural amphitheater festooned with hanging ferns—one of the most touristed spots in Hawaii. The oldest company is **Smith's Motor Boat Service,** tel. (808) 822-4111, in operation since 1947. The extended Smith family still operates the business, and members serve in every capacity. During the 20-minute ride upriver you're entertained with music and a recounting of legends, and at the Fern Grotto a small but well-

tourist boat on the Wailua River cruising to the Fern Grotto

A Zodiac ride is an
adventurous way to
see the Na Pali coast.

done medley of island songs is performed. Daily cruises depart every half hour from Wailua Marina 9 a.m.-2:30 p.m., to 3:30 p.m. Monday, Wednesday, and Friday. Adults cost $10, children $5, discounts for seniors and kama'aina available. Evening cruises are only offered to large groups by special request.

Waialeale Boat Tours, tel. (808) 822-4908, is Smith's only competition. Also at the marina, they're a smaller operation with competitive rates. Daily tours leave approximately every half hour between 9 a.m. and 3:30 p.m. and cost $15 adults, $7.50 children; senior and kama'aina rates available.

Zodiacs

The exact opposite experience from the tame Wailua River trip is an adventurous ride down the Na Pali coast in a very tough, motorized rubber raft that looks like a big horseshoe-shaped inner tube that bends and undulates with the waves like a floating waterbed. These seaworthy craft, powered by twin engines, have five separate air chambers for unsinkable safety. Seating 12 or so, they'll take you for a thrilling ride down the coast, pausing along the way to whisk you into caves and caverns. Once at Kalalau Valley, you can swim and snorkel before making the return ride; the roundtrip, including the stop, takes about five hours. If you wish, you can stay overnight and be picked up the next day, or hike in or out and ride only one-way; this service is $60 one-way, $105 roundtrip.

You roll with the wind and sea going down the coast and head into it coming back. The wind generally picks up in the afternoon, so for a more comfortable ride, book the morning cruise.

Other Zodiac trips include a hike to an archaeological site at Nualolo Kai Beach, a whale-watching tour, and a trip to Kipu Kai or up little-visited rivers on the south coast. All are popular so make reservations. Rates vary with the season and particular expedition, but the ultimate once-in-a-lifetime ride is around $120. Shorter trips run $60-65. Bring a bathing suit, snorkel gear (rental available), lunch, drinks (cooler provided), camera (in a plastic bag for protection), sneakers for exploring, and a windbreaker for the return ride. Summer weather permits excursions almost every day, but winter's swells are turbulent and these experienced seamen won't go if it's too rough. Take their word for it! Pregnant women and individuals with bad backs are not advised to ride.

Oldest and best known of the Zodiac companies is **Na Pali Zodiac,** P.O. Box 456, Hanalei, HI 96714, tel. (808) 826-9371 or (800) 422-7824, owned and operated by "Captain Zodiac," Clancy Greff. They now operate on Maui and Hawaii, too.

Another reputable company offering Zodiac tours is **Hanalei Sea Tours,** tel. (808) 826-7254 or (800) 733-7997, P.O. Box 1447, Hanalei, HI 96714. Their trips include: a Nualolo Day Trip; a five- to six-hour trip down the Na Pali coast for $100, lunch and snorkeling gear included; a four-hour trip down the Na Pali coast for $75; a two-and-a-half-hour mini-tour, which includes whalewatching in season, for $55 (beverages provided). For the Zodiac tours, children ages five to 12 are about $20 cheaper. Hanalei Sea Tours also offers Kalalau Valley camper drop-off service May-Sept. for $60 one-way, $130 roundtrip, and drop-off service to Milolii State Park for $130 roundtrip, including a state camping permit. The minimum age for children on the Zodiac tour is five.

Kayaks
Outfitters Kauai (see "Bicycles," under "Alternatives," above), tel. (808) 742-9667, offers a South Shore Sea Kayaking Tour on Thursday or by arrangement; check in at 1:15 p.m., return by 5 p.m. Single or double kayaks are available, and the adventure includes snacks and cold drinks for $48 per person. Also offered are the Na Pali Kayak Adventure and the River Kayak Adventure, which take you up Kauai's navigable rivers; $45 for a double kayak, $30 for a single.

Kayak Kauai, P.O. Box 508, Hanalei, HI 96714, tel. (808) 826-9844, and in Kapa'a at tel. (808) 822-9179, open daily 8 a.m.-5 p.m., has extensive experience—its owners are world-class kayak experts and the staff are sensitive people who provide good service while having a good time. Two-person kayaks rent for $48-60 per day, and one- and three-person kayaks for $35-75. From May to October, the company leads ocean tours up the Na Pali coast for $130. It also rents and sells surf-skis, boogie boards, masks, fins, *tabi* (robber-soled water shoes great for walking reefs), tents, and other beach and camping gear. Staff will rig your car to carry the kayak and will provide drop-off and pick-up service at Ke'e Beach for $8, or at Polihale State Park for $40—when it's safe to be on the ocean. During the summer, guided tours are taken along the Na Pali coast, and when conditions are too harsh there, trips are run to Kipu Kai along the south coast. All of the above provide good family-style fun.

Kauai Water Ski and Surf, tel. (808) 822-3574, open daily 9 a.m.-7 p.m., in the Kinipopo Shopping Village, 4-356 Kuhio Hwy., Wailua, HI 96746, is a complete water-sports shop that offers kayak rentals.

Ray's Rentals and Activities, 1345 Kuhio Hwy., downtown Kapa'a, tel. (808) 822-5700, rents kayaks at reasonable prices, and **Kayak Kauai** (see above) has a rental outlet across the road from Ray's, open daily 9 a.m.-4 p.m., tel. (808) 822-9179.

Cabin Cruisers and Sailing Ships
For those who want an adventure but a smooth ride, try a cabin cruiser, Boston whaler, or catamaran. Boston whalers are stable, V-hulled ships—the fastest on the coast—while catamarans ride on two widely spaced hulls. Both provide smooth sailing down the coast and get you back in great comfort. Like the Zodiacs, each ventures into the sea caves (sea conditions permitting), stop for you to snorkel, and provide complimentary snacks after your swim. Tours vary, but typically a half day runs $65; five hours, with a hike to an ancient fishing village site at Nualolo Kai, costs $90; whalewatching trips on the north or south coast are $45-65; and, during the summer, sunset tours run $80. When calling, be sure to ask about the particulars of each trip and what extras each company provides.

Liko Kauai Cruises, P.O. Box 18, Waimea, HI 96796, tel. (808) 338-0333, is a new cruise company owned and operated by native Hawaiian Captain Liko Hookano. Unlike all the other cruises, Liko Kauai takes you down the Na Pali coast from the *west end* departing from Kikiaola Harbor just two miles from Waimea, offering vistas and sights unseen by any of the other companies. Born and raised on Kauai, Captain Liko worked for 10 years as a supervising lifeguard on the west end, and no one knows these waters better than he. After boarding the 38-foot cabin cruiser and setting sail down the coast, Captain Liko begins telling Hawaiian tales, especially about Niihau, the island of his ancestors. En route you pass Barking Sands Pacific Missile Range, Polihale, the secluded Milolii Beach, and the little-visited Marconi or Treasure Beach, where the snorkeling is superb. The tour offers a lunch of sandwiches, chips, sides, and soft drinks (BYO beer okay). On the way back, since the boat is completely outfitted for fishing charters, some lucky person gets to reel in whatever bites. The boat, built not only for speed, but also for comfort, has a large, comfortable bathroom and freshwater showers for rinsing off. The four-to-five-hour tour meets at

8:30 a.m. at the offices of **Captain's Cargo Company,** 9984 Kaumuali'i Hwy. (Rt. 50). It is clearly marked just as you enter Waimea from the east end. Rates are $85 adults, $65 children 4-14, free under age four. Captain Liko's wife, Debra, *capo de captain,* runs this boutique and the office for the tours.

Paradise Adventure Cruises, Inc., P.O. Box 1379, Hanalei, HI 96714, tel. (808) 826-9999, owned by Byron Fears, runs the most personalized charter boat trips on the island, taking a maximum of six passengers on his Boston whalers. All his captains know the coast well, and one may even take out his guitar and serenade you while you're scarfing down the provided crackers, cheese, and soft drinks. Byron is the only operator to provide free use of simple underwater cameras—bring ASA 400 film.

Hanalei Sea Tours, tel. (808) 826-7254 or (800) 733-7997, P.O. Box 1447 Hanalei, HI 96714, offers Zodiac (see earlier mention) and catamaran trips along the spectacular Na Pali coast. This reputable company features comfortable boats with limited passengers, knowledgable skippers, and friendly crews. Definitely one of the best.

Na Pali Adventures, tel. (808) 826-6804 or (800) 659-6804, P.O. Box 1017, Hanalei, HI 96714, provides environmentally responsible interpretive tours in their specially outfitted catamarans on which you can sail, snorkel, or whale watch in season. Based primarily in Hanalei, they will also sail from Nawilwili or Port Allen, depending upon ocean conditions. Rates are $55-80 ($60 for children 3-12), depending on which tour you choose, and include a snorkel stop with instructions and equipment, snacks, beverages, and deli sandwiches. Also try **Catamaran Kahanu,** tel. (808) 826-4596, at the Kauhale center in Hanalei. They'll give you an intimate experience of Na Pali on their power catamaran.

Blue Odyssey Kauai, tel. (808) 826-9033, runs a 50-foot cabin cruiser on both the north and south coasts, half-day trips for $75—$85 when combined with a one-way Zodiac ride on the north coast. Their dinner cruise is $49.95. From Port Allen, the **Na Pali Cruise Line** operates the island's finest cruise ship. This 130-foot liner takes you from Port Allen around the west end of the island and up the Na Pali coast in comfort and elegance for $85, $110 if you combine it with a Zodiac ride partway along the coast. A sunset dinner cruise is also available—very romantic.

Running under sail is also possible around Kauai. Captain Andy of **Captain Andy's Sailing Adventures,** tel. (808) 822-7833, lets the wind power his 46-foot catamaran along the south coast in winter and the north coast in summer. A real jolly fellow, he will take you for a half day of sailing, snorkeling, and beachcombing for $75 or for a two-hour sunset cruise for $45.

Bluewater Sailing, tel. (808) 828-1142, runs a 42-foot ketch-rigged yacht also on the south coast in winter and the north coast in summer. This is Kauai's only monohull charter sailing

A Boston whaler stops along the Na Pali coast to get a better look at playing dolphins.

vessel. Half-day rates are $75, all day $115, a sunset sail is $45. Hourly, daily, and weekly charters can be arranged.

Blue Dolphin Charters, tel. (808) 246-4482, welcomes you aboard a 49-passenger, 56-foot trimaran named *Tropic Bird,* on which you can sail, snorkel, and watch the sun go down.

Ecotourism in Hawaii

The following is a partial list of organizations, both public and private, that offer environmentally sound tours and outings throughout the Hawaiian Islands.

American Friends Service Committee, 2426 O'ahu Ave., Honolulu, HI 96822, tel. (808) 988-6266 (Hawaii "Land Seminars").

Eye of the Whale/Earthwalk Tours, P.O. Box 652, Davisville, RI 02854, tel. (401) 539-2401 (sailing and hiking).

Hawaii Audubon Society, 212 Merchant St., Suite 320, Honolulu, HI 96813, tel. (808) 528-1432.

The Nature Conservancy, 1116 Smith St., Suite 201, Honolulu, HI 96817, tel. (808) 537-4508 (hikes).

To contact the local Kauai Chapter of the **Sierra Club,** call hike leader Bob Nishek, tel. (808) 822-9238, for monthly hikes to some of the best and least-known areas on Kauai

Terran Tours, owned and operated by nature guide David Kuhn, tel. (808) 335-3313, offers birdwatching expeditions into the Alakai Swamp. You'll see some of the earth's rarest and most endangered birdlife. David guides everyone from single trekkers to larger groups on one- to three-day excursions. Rates vary depending on the number of people and the duration of the tour.

Gambel's quail

KEITH PERKINS

LIHUE

The twin stacks of the **Lihue Sugar Company** let you know where you are: in a plantation town on one of the world's most gorgeous islands. Lihue ("Open to Chill") began growing cane in the 1840s, and until the last cane harvest in 1996, its fields were among Hawaii's most productive. The town has correspondingly flourished and boasts all the modern conveniences including chrome-and-glass shopping centers, libraries, museums, and a hospital. But the feel is still that of a company town. Lihue, the county seat, has 4,000 residents and two traffic lights. It isn't the geographical center of the island (Mount Waialeale has that distinction), but it is halfway along the coastal road that encircles the island, making it a perfect jumping-off point for exploring the rest of Kauai. It has the island's largest concentration of restaurants and the most varied shopping, a major resort, and right-priced accommodations. If you're going to find any nightlife at all on Kauai, beyond the lounges at the big resorts, it'll be here (don't expect much) Good beaches are within a five-minute drive, and you can be out of town and exploring long before your shave ice begins to melt.

SIGHTS

KAUAI MUSEUM

If you really want to enrich your Kauai experience, this is the first place to visit. Spending an hour or two here infuses you with a wealth of information regarding Kauai's social and cultural history. The two-building complex is at 4428 Rice St. in downtown Lihue, tel. (808) 245-6931, open Mon.-Fri. 9:30 a.m.-4:30 p.m. and Saturday until 1 p.m.; admission is $5, $4 seniors 65 and older, $1 children 6-17, and free under six. The main building was dedicated in 1924 to Albert Spencer Wilcox, son of pioneer missionaries at Hanalei. It has a Greco-Roman facade and was the public library until 1970. Its two floors house the main gallery, devoted to ethnic heritage and island art exhibits that are changed on a regular basis. The **Museum Shop** sells books, Hawaiiana prints, and a fine selection

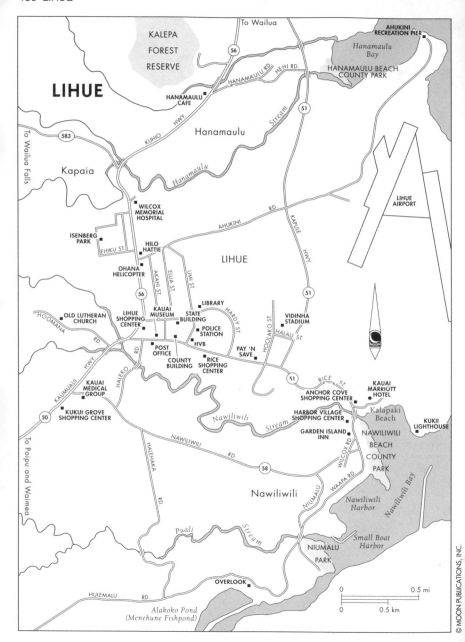

LIHUE

KALEPA FOREST RESERVE

To Wailua

To Wailua Falls

Kapaia

Hanamaulu

Hanamaulu Stream

HANAMAULU CAFE

KUHIO HWY

HANAMAULU RD.

HEHI RD.

AHUKINI RECREATION PIER

Hanamaulu Bay

HANAMAULU BEACH COUNTY PARK

LIHUE AIRPORT

WILCOX MEMORIAL HOSPITAL

ISENBERG PARK

EHIKU ST.

HILO HATTIE

OHANA HELICOPTER

AKAHI ST.

EIUA ST.

UMI ST.

AHUKINI RD.

KAPULE HWY

LIHUE

OLD LUTHERAN CHURCH

HOOMANA RD.

HALEKO RD.

LIHUE SHOPPING CENTER

KAUAI MUSEUM

LIBRARY

STATE BUILDING

POLICE STATION

HVB

PAY 'N SAVE

HARDY ST.

HOOLAKO ST.

HALAU ST.

VIDINHA STADIUM

MooN

POST OFFICE

COUNTY BUILDING

RICE SHOPPING CENTER

KAUMUALII HWY

KAUAI MEDICAL GROUP

KUKUI GROVE SHOPPING CENTER

To Poipu and Waimea

HAELEKA RD.

NAWILIWILI RD.

Nawiliwili Stream

ANCHOR COVE SHOPPING CENTER

HARBOR VILLAGE SHOPPING CENTER

GARDEN ISLAND INN

RICE ST.

KAUAI MARRIOTT HOTEL

Kalapaki Beach

NAWILIWILI BEACH COUNTY PARK

KUKII LIGHTHOUSE

WILCOX RD.

WAAPA RD.

NIUMALU RD.

Nawiliwili

Puali Stream

Nawiliwili Harbor

Nawiliwili Bay

Small Boat Harbor

NIUMALU PARK

HULEMALU RD.

OVERLOOK

Alakoko Pond (Menehune Fishpond)

0   0.5 mi

0   0.5 km

© MOON PUBLICATIONS, INC.

of detailed U.S. Geological Survey maps of the entire island. Some inexpensive but tasteful purchases include baskets, wooden bowls, and selections of *tapa*. (The *tapa* is made in Fiji, but native craftspeople are studying Fijian techniques and hope to re-create this lost art.) The main room contains an extensive and fascinating exhibit of calabashes, koa furniture, quilts, and feather lei. One large calabash belonged to Princess Ruth, who gave it to a local child. Its finish, hand rubbed with the original *kukui* nut oil, still shows a fine luster. The rear of the main floor is dedicated to the **Senda Gallery,** with its collection of vintage photos shot by W.J. Senda, a Japanese immigrant from Matsue who arrived in 1906. These black and whites are classics, opening a window onto old Kauai.

Kauai's fascinating natural and cultural history begins to unfold when you walk through the courtyard into the second half of the museum, the **William Hyde Rice Building.** Notice the large black iron pot used to cook sugarcane. The exhibits are self-explanatory, chronicling Kauai's development over the centuries. The windows of the Natural History Tunnel show the zones of cultivation on Kauai, along with its beaches and native forests. Farther on is an extensive collection of Kauai shells, old photos, and displays of classic muumuu. The central first-floor area has a model of a Hawaiian village, an extensive collection of weapons, some fine examples of adzes used to hollow canoes, and a model of HMS *Resolution* at anchor off Waimea. An excerpt from the ship's log records Captain Cook's thoughts on the day that he discovered Hawaii for the rest of the world.

As you ascend the stairs to the second floor, history continues to unfold. Missionaries stare from old photos, their countenances the epitome of piety and zeal. Just looking at them makes you want to repent! Most old photos record the plantation era. Be sure to see the **Spalding Shell Collection,** gathered by Colonel Spalding, an Ohio veteran of the Civil War who came to Kauai and married the daughter of Capt. James Makee, owner of the Makee Sugar Company. Besides shells from around the world are examples of magnificent koa furniture, table settings, children's toys, dolls, and photos of Niihau—about all that the outside world ever sees.

Follow the stairs to the ground floor and notice the resplendent examples of feather capes on the wall. On the main floor, in an alcove by the front door, push the button to begin a 15-minute aerial-view video of Kauai. This pictorial is a treat for the eyes; soothing Hawaiian chanting in the background sets the mood. If you're seeking further enrichment, (bring the children) the museum staff conducts a tour (free with admission) Wednesday at 10:30 a.m. and upon request. Time permitting, they will also take you on private tours if you call in advance. On Friday, there is an orchid sale in the museum yard, where you can delight in the magic of these lovely flowers. Outside in the courtyard is **A Matter of Taste,** an espresso bar where you can refresh yourself with a coffee, cool drink, or light lunch.

GROVE FARM HOMESTEAD

Grove Farm is a plantation started in 1864 by George Wilcox, the son of missionaries who worked for the original owner of the surrounding acreage. The first owner saw no future in the parched land and sold 500 acres to Wilcox for $1,000. Through a system of aqueducts, Wilcox brought water down from the mountains and began one of the most profitable sugar plantations in Hawaii. The homestead was a working plantation until the mid-1930s, when George died and operations were moved elsewhere. The remaining family continued to occupy the dwellings and care for the extensive grounds. In 1971, Mabel Wilcox, a niece of the founder, dedicated the family estate to posterity. Well advanced in years but spirited in mind, she created a nonprofit organization to preserve Grove Farm Homestead as a museum. Reap the benefits of her efforts by visiting this self-sufficient farm Monday, Wednesday, or Thursday. Well-informed guides take you on a two-hour tour of the grounds and various buildings; admission $3 adults, $1 children under 12. Tours are *by reservation only!* Drop-in visitors will be turned away. Telephone (808) 245-3202 at least 24 hours in advance to make arrangements. Mail reservations are accepted up to three months in advance; write to Grove Farm Homestead, P.O. Box 1631, Lihue, HI 96766. The homestead is located off Nawiliwili Road; precise directions are given when you call. Group size is limited to give full attention to detail and minimize wear and tear on the buildings. Tours begin at 10 a.m. and 1 p.m. Please be prompt!

Living History

The first thing you notice when entering Grove Farm is the rumble of your tires crossing a narrow-gauge railroad track. The tracks meant sugar, and sugar meant prosperity and change for old Hawaii. The minute you set foot upon Grove Farm Homestead you can feel this spirit permeating the place. This is no "glass-case" museum. It's a real place with living history, where people experienced the drama of changing Hawaii.

George Wilcox never married. In love once, he was jilted, and that ended that. In 1870, his brother Sam came to live on the homestead. In 1874, Sam married Emma, daughter of missionaries from the Big Island. She had been educated in Dearborn, Michigan, and had recently returned to Hawaii. The couple had six children—three boys and three girls. Two of the boys survived to manhood and managed the farm, but both met later with tragic deaths. Of the girls, only Henrietta, the oldest, married. The two other sisters, Miss Elsie and Miss Mabel, were single all their lives. Elsie became very involved in politics, while Mabel went to Johns Hopkins University and earned a degree as a registered nurse. Her parents wouldn't let her leave home until she was 25 years old, when they felt she could cope with the big, bad world. She returned in 1911 and opened a public health office on the grounds.

The Tour

You meet your guide at the plantation office. The buildings, furnishings, orchards, and surrounding lands are part of what was the oldest intact sugar plantation in Hawaii. The office contains a safe dating from 1880, when it was customary to pay for everything in cash. On top sits a cannonball that's been there as long as anyone can remember. Perhaps it was placed there by Mr. Pervis, the original bookkeeper. As time went on the safe's combination—which is in letters, not numbers—was lost. A safecracker was eventually hired to open it, and inside was the combination written in a big, bold hand: "B-A-L-L."

You cross the grounds to a simple dwelling and enter the home of the Moriwakis. Mrs. Moriwaki came to Grove Farm as a "picture bride," though she was born in Hawaii and taken back to Japan as a child. She was the cook at the big house for almost 50 years. After the grounds opened to the public and until her death in 1986, she returned on tour days to explain her role in running the homestead. Her home is meticulously clean and humble, a symbol of Japanese plantation workers' lives on Hawaii. Notice the food safe; most workers in Hawaii had no iceboxes and kept vermin away by placing sar-

The sunny Wilcox living room is filled with embroidery, fine koa furniture, and books.

dine cans filled with water or kerosene inside, into which the pests fell and were drowned. A small print of Mt. Fuji and a geisha doll in a glass case are simple yet meaningful touches. Together they signify the memory of the past along with the hope of a brighter future which all plantation workers sought for their children.

As you walk around, notice how lush and fruitful the grounds are, with all sorts of trees and plants. At one time the workers were encouraged to have their own gardens. A highlight is a small latticework building half submerged in the ground. This is the **fernery,** at one time a status symbol of the good life in Hawaii. There was great competition among the ladies of Victorian Hawaii, who were proud of their ferns, and you became an instant friend if you presented a new and unique variety while on a social visit. Behind the Wilcox Home is a small schoolhouse built in 1900. It later became Mabel Wilcox's public health office; now a depository for all sorts of artifacts and memorabilia, it's called the **Trunk Room.** A photo of Mabel shows her in a Red Cross uniform. By all accounts, Mabel was a serious but not humorless woman. Her dry and subtle wit was given away only by her sparkling eyes, which are evident in the photo.

Wilcox Home

Shoes are removed before entering this grand mansion. The Wilcoxes were pleasant people given to quiet philanthropy, but their roots as New England missionaries made them frugal. The women always wore homemade cotton dresses and in the words of a tour guide, "nothing was ever thrown away by this family." The home is comfortable and smacks of culture, class, and money—in the old-fashioned way. As you enter, you'll be struck with the feeling of space. The archways were fashioned so they get smaller as you look through the house. This shrinking perspective gives an illusion of great length. The walls and staircase are of rich, brown koa. Much of the furniture was bought secondhand from families returning to the Mainland. This was done not out of a sense of frugality, but simply because it was often the only good furniture available.

The piano here belonged to Emma Wilcox; the profusion of artwork includes many original pieces, often done by visitors to the homestead.

One longtime visitor, a sickly girl from the East Coast, did some amazing embroidery. Her finest piece on display took 10 years to complete. Portraits of the family include a good one of George Wilcox. Notice a Japanese chest that Miss Mabel won in a drawing while she was in Japan with her sister Elsie and Uncle George in 1907. Notice, too, the extensive collection of Hawaiiana that the family accumulated over the decades. In the separate kitchen wing is a stove that is still functional after 100 years of hard use. A porch, obviously homey during rainstorms, looks out onto a tea house. Everything in the home is of fine quality and in good taste. It's a dwelling of peace and tranquillity.

The Cottage

Finally you arrive at the private home of a private man, George Wilcox himself. It is the picture of simplicity. Only an old bachelor would have chosen these spartan surroundings. An inveterate cigar smoker along with his brother Sam, both

George's desk

were forbidden by the ladies to smoke in the main house. Here, he did as he pleased. Maybe the women were right; George died of throat cancer . . . in 1933 at the age of 94!

The first room you enter is his office. George was a small man and a gentleman. Whenever he left the house, he donned a hat. You'll notice a collection of his favorites hanging on pegs in the hallway. One of his few comforts was a redwood tub he'd soak in for hours. This self-made millionaire kept his soap in an old sardine tin, but he did use fine embroidered towels. His bedroom is simple, bright, and airy. The mattress is of extremely comfortable horse hair. Outside his window is a profusion of fruit trees, many of which George planted himself. As the tour ends you get the feeling that these trees are what Grove Farm is all about—a homestead where people lived, and worked, and dreamed.

OTHER SIGHTS

Kilohana Plantation

The manor house at Kilohana Plantation was built in 1935 by the wealthy *kama'aina* planter, Gaylord Wilcox, to please his wife, Ethel. She was enamored with Hollywood and its glamorous Tudor-type mansions, which were the rage of the day. Sparing no expense, Gaylord spent $200,000 building an elaborate 16,000-square-foot home; estimates are that it would cost about $3 million by today's standards. A horse and carriage waits to take visitors on a tour (nominal fee) of the 35 lush acres that surround the home, which was the center of a working farm—a feeling that lingers. Inside, **Gaylord's Restaurant** occupies the actual dining room (see "Fine Dining" under "Food," later in this chapter). Original furniture includes a huge table that seats 22 and a stout sideboard fit for a truly regal manor house. As you pass from room to room—some of which are occupied by fine boutiques, jewelry shops, and art galleries—notice the coved ceiling, lustrous wood molding, and grand staircase. A mirror from the '30s (mirrors in Hawaii have a tough time holding up because of the moisture) still hangs just inside the tiled, atriumlike main entranceway. Walk straight through a set of double doors onto the flagstone veranda (also occupied by Gaylord's

for alfresco dining) to view a living tapestry of mountain and cloud, even more ethereal when mist shrouds magical Mt. Waialeale in the distance. To arrive, take Rt. 50 (Kaumuali'i Hwy.) west from Lihue for about two miles toward the tiny village of Puhi, and look on the mountain side for the clearly marked entrance.

Lihue's Churches

When Rt. 56 becomes Rt. 50, just as you pass the Lihue Sugar Mill, look for the HVB Warrior pointing you to the **Old Lutheran Church.** Just before the bridge, follow Hoomana Road to the right through a well-kept residential area. Built in 1883, it has everything a church should have, including a bell tower and spire, but it's all miniature-sized. The church reflects a strong German influence that dominated Lihue and its plantation until WW I. The turn-of-the-century pastor was Hans Isenberg, brother of the plantation founder and husband to Dora Rice from the old *kama'aina* family. Pastor Isenberg was responsible for procuring the Lihue Horse Trough, an ornate marble work imported from Italy in 1909 and now on display at the Haleko Shops' botanical gardens in downtown Lihue (see below). The outside of the church is basic New England, but inside, the ornate altar is reminiscent of baroque Germany. Headstones in the yard to the side indicate just how old this congregation is.

On a nearby hill is **Lihue Union Church,** which was mostly attended by workers and their families. Its cemetery is filled with simple tombstones, and plumeria trees eternally produce blossoms for the departed ones. If you follow the main road past the Lutheran church, it deadends at an enormous cane field. This sea of green runs to the mountains and lets you know just how much sugar still dominates the way of life in Lihue and on Kauai in general.

Around Town

Across the street from Lihue Shopping Center, a stone's throw from the twin stacks of the sugar mill, are four solid-looking buildings known as the **Haleko Shops.** Once the homes of German plantation managers—before they gave up their holdings during WW I—they're now occupied by restaurants and shops; part of the shopping center across the road. Around them is a botanical garden. Each plant carries a description of its

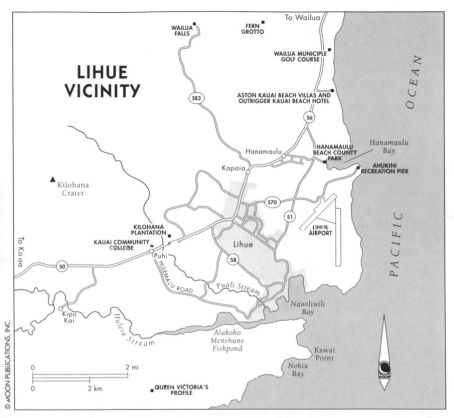

LIHUE VICINITY

To Wailua

WAILUA FALLS

FERN GROTTO

WAILUA MUNICIPLE GOLF COURSE

583

ASTON KAUAI BEACH VILLAS AND OUTRIGGER KAUAI BEACH HOTEL

56

OCEAN

Hanamaulu

HANAMAULU BEACH COUNTY PARK

Hanamaulu Bay

Kapaia

AHUKINI RECREATION PIER

▲ Kilohana Crater

570

51

To Ko'oa

50

KILOHANA PLANTATION

KAUAI COMMUNITY COLLEGE

Puhi

HULEMALU ROAD

58

Lihue

LIHUE AIRPORT

PACIFIC

Puali Stream

Nawiliwili Bay

Kipu Kai

Huleia Stream

Alakoko Menehune Fishpond

Kawai Point

Nohiu Bay

0   2 mi

0   2 km

QUEEN VICTORIA'S PROFILE

© MOON PUBLICATIONS, INC.

traditional use and which ethnic group brought it to the island. (Look for the Lihue Horse Trough imported by Pastor Isenberg.)

Follow Umi Street off Rice to Hardy Street. At the corner is the **Kauai Library.** In the entrance is a batik wall hanging by Jerome Wallace—the largest painting of its type in the world.

Follow Rice Street toward Nawiliwili Harbor and it turns into Rt. 51, known as Waapa Road. You'll come to the junction with Rt. 58 (Nawiliwili Road). Take Nawiliwili to Niumalu Road and turn left, following it to Hulemalu Road. You pass the predominantly Hawaiian settlement of Niumalu. Along Hulemalu Road is a lookout, below which is **Alakoko ("Rippling Blood") Pond,** commonly known as Menehune Fishpond. You have a sweeping view of

Huleia Stream, the harbor, and the Hoary Head Mountains in the background. The 900-foot mullet-raising fishpond is said to be the handiwork of the Menehune. Legend says that they built this pond for a royal prince and princess and made only one demand: that no one watch them in their labor. In one night, the indefatigable Menehune passed the stones needed for the project from hand to hand in a double line that stretched for 25 miles. But the royal prince and princess could not contain their curiosity and climbed to a nearby ridge to watch the little people. They were spotted by the Menehune, who stopped building, leaving holes in the wall, and turned the royal pair into the twin pillars of stone still seen on the mountainside overlooking the pond.

Wailua Falls

Wailua Falls

Heading north, in Kapaia, Rt. 583 branches from Rt. 56 and heads into the interior. As the road lifts up and away from the ocean, you realize that the rolling terrain surrounded by lofty mountain peaks is completely given over to sugarcane. To the left and right are small homes with the usual patches of tropical fruit trees. Route 583 ends at mile marker 3. Far below, Wailua Falls tumbles 80 feet over a severe *pali* into a large round pool. It's said that the *ali'i* would come here to dive from the cliff into the pool as a show of physical prowess; commoners were not considered to be infused with enough *mana* to perform this feat.

Many of the trees here are involuntary trellises for rampant morning glory. Pest or not, its blossoms are still beautiful as it climbs the limbs. A trail down to the falls is particularly tough and steep. If you make it down, you'll have the falls to yourself, but you'll be like a goldfish in a bowl with the tourists—perhaps jealously—peering down at you.

BEACHES AND PARKS

Lihue has very convenient beaches. You can sun yourself within 10 minutes of anywhere in town, with a choice of beaches on either Nawiliwili or Hanamaulu Bay. Few tourists head to Hanamaulu Bay, while Nawiliwili Bay is a classic example of "beauty and the beast." There is hardly a more beautiful harbor than Nawiliwili's, with a stream flowing into it and verdant mountains all around. However, it is a working harbor complete with rusting barges, groaning cranes, and petrochemical tanks. Private yachts and catamarans bob at anchor with their bright colors reflecting off dappled waters, and as your eye sweeps the lovely panorama it runs into the dull gray wall of a warehouse where raw sugar is stored before being shipped to the Mainland to be processed. It's one of those places that separates perspectives: some see the "beauty," while others focus on the "beast."

Kalapaki Beach

This most beautiful beach at Nawiliwili fronts the lavish Kauai Marriott (formerly the Westin Kauai). Just follow Rice Street until it becomes Rt. 51; you'll soon see the bay on your right and the entrance to the hotel on your left. The hotel serves as a type of giant folding screen, blocking out most of the industrial area and leaving the lovely views of the bay. Park in the visitors' area at the hotel entrance, or to the rear of the hotel at the north end of Nawiliwili Beach Park, where a footbridge leads across the Nawiliwili Stream to the hotel property and the beach. Access to the beach is open to anyone, but if you want to use the hotel pool and showers, you'll have a lot less hassle if you order a light breakfast or lunch at one of the restaurants. The homemade ice cream at the hotel ice cream shop is delicious!

The wave action at Kalapaki is gentle at most times, with long swells combing the sandy-bottomed beach. Kalapaki is one of the best swimming beaches on the island, fair for snorkeling, and a great place to try bodysurfing or begin with a board. Two secluded beaches in this area are generally frequented by local people. Head through the hotel grounds on the road to the right past the few private homes that overlook this bay. From here you'll see a lighthouse on

Ninini Point. Keep the lighthouse to your left as you walk across the golf course to the bay. Below are two small crescent beaches, both good for swimming and sunbathing. The right one has numerous springs that flow up into the sand. You can also head for **Nawiliwili Beach County Park** by following Rt. 51 downhill past the Kauai Marriott until you come to the water; on the left is the beach park. Here are showers, picnic tables, and a pavilion along with some shady palm trees for a picnic. A seawall has been erected here, so for swimming and sunning it's much better to walk up to your left and spend the day at Kalapaki Beach.

Niumalu Beach County Park

This county-maintained beach park lies along the Huleia Stream on the west end of Nawiliwili Harbor. Many small fishing and charter boats are berthed nearby and local men use the wharf area to fish and "talk story." There is no swimming and you are surrounded by the industrial area. However, you are very close to Lihue and there are pavilions, showers, toilets, and camping both for tents and RVs (permit required). To get there, take Rt. 51 to Nawiliwili Harbor. Continue on Waapa Road along the harbor until you arrive at the beach park.

Ahukini Recreation Pier

As the name implies, this state park is simply a pier from which local people fish. And it's some of the best fishing around. Follow Rt. 57 to Lihue Airport. With the airport to your right, keep going until the road ends at a large circular parking lot and fishing pier. The scenery is only fair, so if you're not into fishing give it a miss.

Hanamaulu Beach County Park

This is a wonderful beach, and although it is very accessible and good for swimming, very few tourists come here. There is not only a beach, but to the right is also a lagoon area with pools formed by Hanamaulu Stream. Local families frequent this park, and it's particularly loved by children as they can play Tom Sawyer on the banks of the heavily forested stream. There are picnic tables, showers, toilets, a pavilion, and camping (county permit). In Hanamaulu, turn *makai* off Rt. 56 onto Hanamaulu Road, take the right fork onto Hehi Road, and follow it to the beach park.

ACCOMMODATIONS

If you like simple choices, you'll appreciate Lihue; only two fancy resorts are here, the rest are either family-run hotel/motels or apartment hotels. Prices here are also better than on the other islands because Lihue isn't considered a prime resort town. But it makes an ideal base, because from Lihue you can get *anywhere* on the island in less than an hour. Although it's the county seat, the town is quiet, especially in the evenings, so you won't have to deal with noise or hustle and bustle.

Inexpensive

Motel Lani, owned and operated by Janet Naumu, offers clean, inexpensive rooms at 4240 Rice St.; for reservations write Motel Lani, P.O. Box 1836, Lihue, HI 96766; tel. (808) 245-2965. The lobby is actually an extension of Janet's home, where she and her children often watch TV. There are 10 sunburn-pink units and, although close to the road, they're surprisingly quiet. Each room has a small desk, dresser, bath, fan, and refrigerator and is cross-ventilated. Some have air-conditioning. No TVs. Janet usually doesn't allow children under three years old, especially if they misbehave, but she's reasonable and will make exceptions. A small courtyard with a barbecue is available to guests. Rates for two nights are $32-40 double, $40 and up triple, $14 for an additional person, slightly more for one night.

The loved but worse-for-wear Ocean View Motel, built and operated by the irascible but lovable Spike Kanja, several years ago reopened as the refurbished and very attractive **Garden Island Inn,** at 3445 Wilcox Rd., Nawiliwili, HI 96766, tel. (808) 245-7227 or (800) 648-0154. The new owners, Steve and Susan Layne, did a wonderful job of turning the once character-laden hotel into a bright and cheery inn. Head down Rice Street toward Nawiliwili; the inn is at the corner of Wilcox Road, across from

Nawiliwili Beach Park, just a stroll from Kalapaki Beach. Each room has a color TV, microwave, refrigerator, and coffeemaker with Lappert's Kona coffee complimentary. The Inn also provides boogie boards, snorkeling gear, beach mats, bicycles (if you're nice), and ice chests for a day's outing. The ground floor rooms, $55 d, are appointed with textured bamboo-motif wallpaper and are cooled by louvered windows and ceiling fans. Second floor rooms, $65 d, are about the same, but each has its own lanai. The best rooms ($75-85) are on the third floor, from where you look down on a fully matured banana grove. Is this the tropics or what! More like mini-suites, third-floor rooms give you two full rooms that can easily accommodate four people comfortably. The front sitting room, doubling as a kitchen, is bright with a wraparound lanai from where you can watch the goings on in Nawiliwili Harbor and have an unobstructed view of the cement works! Fortunately, Kauai always seems to give more than it takes. Walk out to the cement works in the evening and look over the seawall. You're likely to spot green sea turtles as they breaststroke through the darkening sunset waters looking for food and a quiet nook in which to relax. Across the street from the inn is a family-oriented playground great for the kiddies and a new volleyball court kept green by a year-round sprinkler system. For the money, the Garden Island Inn is one of the best deals on Kauai.

The **Kauai Inn,** formerly the Hale Niumalu Motel, is off the main drag near the boat harbor in Niumalu. The buildings were at one time overflow accommodations for a big hotel but are now independently owned. The rooms are large and well kept but plain. The best feature is a screened lanai with a profusion of hanging plants in the old building. No longer the deal it used to be, charges are $69-89, with weekly rates available. Located across from Niumalu Park at the corner of Niumalu and Hulemalu Roads. The Kauai Inn was battered by Iniki but hopes to reopen; for information, call (800) 326-5242 or (808) 245-3316.

The **Hale Lihue,** 2931 Kalena St., Lihue, HI 96766, tel. (808) 245-2751, *was* a quiet, clean, and basic motel owned and operated for many years by a lovely Japanese couple, Mr. and Mrs. Morishige, whose hospitality made it an institution. They retired in 1984 and sold the hotel to a "man from Los Angeles," whose name Mrs. Morishige couldn't remember. She was assured, however, that he would keep "everything the same," but the Hale Lihue went on the skids for a few years. It has now made an excellent comeback! Don't expect anything fancy from this pink, two-story, cinder-block hotel, but the manager, Benki M. Somera (cellular tel. 808-639-8896 for emergencies), runs a well-managed, clean hotel with a screened-in lobby. Perfect for no-frills, budget accommodations. Rates are $22 s, $25 d, $30 t; with kitchenettes, $30 s, $40 d, and good weekly rates.

The **Tip Top Motel,** 3173 Akahi St. (for reservations, write P.O. Box 1231, Lihue, HI 96766), tel. (808) 245-2333, is a combination lounge, restaurant, and bakery popular with local folks. It's a functional, two-story, cinder-block building painted light gray. The lobby/cafe/bakery is open daily except Monday 6:45 a.m.-9 p.m. The rooms are antiseptic in every way—a plus, as your feet stay cool on the bare linoleum floor— and all are air-conditioned. Just to add that mixed-society touch, instead of a Gideon's Bible in the dresser drawer, you get *The Teachings of Buddha,* placed by the Sudaka Society of Honolulu. Rates are $50 for four, with a few cheaper rooms available.

Moderate/Deluxe Accommodations

The **Aston Kauai Beach Villas,** at 4330 Kauai Beach Dr., Lihue, HI 96766, tel. (808) 245-7711, (800) 922-7866 Mainland, (800) 445-6633 Canada, or (800) 321-2559 Hawaii, are perfectly located midway between the airport and Kapa'a. It is a fine condominium resort that has consistently earned the AAA "Three-Diamond Award." The spacious units, a signature of Aston Resorts, differ slightly, but expect a terra-cotta foyer leading to a living room with comfortable bamboo furniture with puff pillows, a fold-out couch, and remote-control color TV. The dining area has a marble-topped table with high-back chairs adjacent to the full kitchen with refrigerator, dishwasher, garbage disposal, coffeemaker, four-burner electric stove, hood fan, microwave oven, toaster, and all the necessary utensils. A washer-dryer combination is tucked into its own utility closet. Master bedrooms have queen-size beds, private baths, plenty of closet space, and complimentary safes. Ceiling fans, air-conditioning, and phones are part of the amenities. Each unit has a lanai with outdoor tables, chairs, and lounges. Rates are $99 for a studio with kitchen, $140 for one-bedroom units, $195 for a two-bedroom with a garden view, and $255 for a two-bedroom, two-bath suite with ocean view. The Aston Kauai Beach Villas are adjacent to the Outrigger Kauai Beach Hotel (a former Hilton), with which it shares all amenities including the free-form pool.

The **Outrigger Kauai Beach Hotel** is one of Kauai's newest hotel/condos. On 25 landscaped acres overlooking Hanamaulu Beach, it offers 350 hotel rooms—all with mini-refrigerators—and 136 villas with full kitchens and laundry facilities. The hotel pool is in three sections connected by tiny waterfalls and cascades. Dining amenities include late-night room service, lobby lounge, pool bar and restaurant, **Gilligan's** for drinks and dancing, and the casual **Jacaranda Terrace,** the hotel's main dining hall. There are four tennis courts, two whirlpools, and watersports equipment. Prior to the nightly luau, a torchlighting ceremony is performed, and a wide range of events is run by the activities desk. Rates are $125-175 hotel, $140-200 one-bedroom villa, $190-250 two-bedroom villa (up to four people). Special honeymoon, tennis, and golf packages are available. For information, write 4331 Kauai Beach Dr., Lihue, HI 96766; tel. (800) 445-8667 or (808) 245-1955.

The **Kauai Marriott on Kalapaki Beach,** at Kalapaki Beach, Lihue, Kauai, HI. 96766, tel. (808) 245-5050 or (800) 228-9290, is a testament to man's perseverance coupled with the forgiving personality of Mother Nature. In 1987, the hotel was completely refurbished and rebuilt, emerging as the Westin—at the time, the most luxurious property on Kauai. Hurricane Iniki then furiously blew ashore, raking the island and mangling the hotel. Afterward, the Marriott chain purchased the property and set about restoring it to its former grandeur. The result is, once again, a fabulous hotel that cooperates as a time-share condominium. Upon arrival, you are greeted with valet parking and enter through a grand foyer. Descending the escalator you emerge on a flagstone path, which winds along the perimeter of *Kamalao Kalapaki,* a formal garden that says "Hawaii" unmistakably. Enter

the garden and immediately you're embraced by the foliage and the feeling that you're walking the grounds of a grand estate where you can enjoy a quiet moment or a slow meditative stroll enhanced by twittering birds and the soft swish of palms tussled by sea breezes. Suddenly you'll see a delightful burst of flowers amidst the subtle shades of tranquil green that carpets the gardens. You'll be serenaded by a small, lava-rock waterfall that showers the surrounding ferns and foliage with mist. If you continue straight along the colonnaded main walkway, you'll soon descend a flight of marble stairs into the reception area. Displayed here is a lustrous original *koa* canoe that belonged to royal Prince Kuhio. In the care of a local Hawaiian family over the generations, the canoe was leased to Marriott with the understanding that funds be used in a scholarship that directly benefits a child of Hawaiian ancestry. The central area of the hotel is an extensive free-form pool surrounded by five neoclassical thrust proscenium porticos bubbling with soothing jacuzzis.

Rooms are classified into garden view ($229), pool/ocean view with car and complimentary health club ($269/$285), and deluxe ocean ($375); all prices include breakfast for two. Although the Marriott considers itself "family deluxe," the rooms are pure luxury. A comfy bed with six puffy pillows faces an entertainment center complete with remote-control color TV. The walls are painted a muted sand color reminiscent of the beach and brightened by Hawaiian-themed paintings and prints, while the carpeting is the soft green of new-mown grass. Some rooms have reclining chairs with footrests, others have love seats that convert to double beds. The furniture is generally a blend of bent bamboo and rattan. Each room boasts air-conditioning, a mini-fridge, tiled full bath with separate dressing area, a steam iron and ironing board, coffee maker with complimentary Kona coffee, and mailbox. Full-service amenities include in-room dining and cocktails, an activities desk, concierge service, and complimentary airport shuttle. The hotel's mini-mall (most shops open daily 9 a.m.-9 p.m.) includes **Lamonts Gifts and Sundries,** for everything from grocery items to glass anthuriums; **Aveda Concept Salon,** where owner April Lane offers hair styling, facials, manicures, and pedicures; **Tropical Tantrum,** for ladies' original resort and alohawear; **The Sandal Tree,** where you can dress your feet in anything from elegant pumps to flip-flops; the **Marriott Logo Shop,** for an assortment of articles including those fashioned from comfortable, wrinkle-resistant "micro-wear"; **Collections,** with alohawear, hats, and ladies' and men's bathing suits and bikinis, presented by Liberty House.

The hotel also offers a cocktail lounge, a poolside snack bar, and the **Kukui Buffet,** an indoor/outdoor restaurant for breakfast, lunch, and dinner overlooking the central pool area. Although you're surrounded by luxury at the Marriott, you experience the feeling of a quieter, more casual place. The hotel is very much like the stunning sister who decided to stay close to home instead of heading for the bright lights where her beauty would easily have dazzled everyone.

FOOD

Dining in Lihue is a treat—good to your palate and your budget. The roster of restaurants in and around town is the most extensive on the island. You can have savory snacks at saimin shops or at bargain-priced eateries frequented by local people. You'll find pizza parlors and fast-food chains. Stepping up in class, there are continental, Italian, and Japanese restaurants, while moderately priced establishments serve up hearty dishes of Mexican, Chinese, and good old American fare. Fancier dining is found in some of the big hotels.

Inexpensive in and around Lihue

If you ask anyone in Lihue where you can chow down for cheap, they'll send you to **Ma's Family Inc.,** an institution owned and operated by matriarch Akiyo Honjo, a third-generation Kauaian, who is assisted at times by her great-grandchildren. To arrive make a right off of Rice Street onto Kress Street and follow Kress to the corner, where you'll find Ma's at 4277 Halenani St., open weekdays 5 a.m.-1:30 p.m. and Saturday, Sunday, and holidays 5-10 a.m. (or until customers stop coming), tel. (808) 245-3142. The building is old and a bit run-down, but clean. A few tourists find it, but mostly it's local working people who come here for a hearty and filling meal. Lunches are good, but the super deals are breakfast and the Hawaiian specialties. The coffee, free with breakfast and served with condensed milk, arrives in a large pot about as soon as your seat hits the chair. The menu is posted above the kitchen. You can start the day with The Works, which includes either potatoes or fried noodles, bacon or sausage, and toast for $5. From the Hawaiian menu, try *kalua* pork with two eggs and rice, poi, and *lomi* salmon, or

Kauai sausage—all for under $6. For the famished (or a traveling wrestling team), the menu also offers a pound of *kalua* pork. (If this last item is ordered by one guy who appears grumpy before his gallon of morning coffee, don't bother him!) Ma also serves hamburgers from $1.75 and an assortment of sandwiches including teriyaki beef—the most expensive at $2.50.

Hamura Saimin Stand, at 2956 Kress St., tel. (808) 245-3271, open daily 10-2 a.m. (depending upon business), is just around the corner from Ma's. People flock to the orange countertops of this restaurant all day long, where they perch on short stools to eat giant steaming bowls of saimin. But the real show is around 2 a.m., when all the bars and discos let loose their revelers. There is no decor here (beyond the sign admonishing, "Please do not stick gum under counter"), just good food. Your first time, try the Saimin Special, which gives you noodles, slivers of meat and fish, vegetables, won ton, and eggs, all floating in a golden broth. Other items on the small menu are variations on the same theme, with nothing over $5. On the counter will be hot sauce, mustard, and shoyu—condiments that you mix yourself in the small bowls that accompany your soup. Enjoy not only the saimin, but also the truly authentic Kauai experience.

Halo Halo Shave Ice occupies a second counter in the same building—use the side entrance. Here you can get some of the best throat coolers on the island.

A replica of a 1920's delivery truck sets the theme at **Ye Old Espresso Court,** open Mon.-Sat. 8 a.m.-5 p.m., directly behind the Exotic Bird Emporium at Paena Court. Here at the bottom of Rice Street, Billie Ann Walker serves up steaming mugs of espresso, cappuccino and café latte, along with Italian sodas, sun tea, real Ghirardelli cocoa, and spiced *chai*. After you and your taste buds are caffeine-dancing, take care of those early-morning hunger pangs with a fresh pastry baked by the local gourmet Garden Island Bakery. If time permits, Billie will join you at one of the outside tables to "talk story." A great stop for a revitalizing pick-me-up.

A Matter of Taste, located at the Kauai Museum, 4428 Rice St., open during museum hours, (Mon.-Fri. 9:30 a.m.-4 p.m., Sat. until 1 p.m.) is nestled in the quiet museum courtyard. Owner Barbara Watts is a travel enthusiast and will be happy to pour you a house coffee, latte, mocha, cappuccino, or refreshing piña colada or mocha slush. Nibbles include luscious cappuccino and lilikoi cheesecake and chocolate-macadamia nut croissants, while light lunches include quiche, minestrone soup, and feisty turkey chili.

Yokozuna's Ramen, a cafeteria-style ramen shop with long communal tables and a few potted plants for decor, is located along Rt. 56 as you enter Lihue, just across from McDonald's, tel. (808) 246-1008, and open Mon.-Sat. 10:30 a.m.- 2 p.m. and and 4:30 p.m.-10 p.m. Try *wakame* (seaweed) ramen for $5.60, Yokozuna ramen, the house specialty for $6.75, or cold ramen for $5.35. Plate lunches and dinners include breaded shrimp for $5.75, beef curry and rice for $5.95, grilled mahi-mahi $5.85, or chicken tofu for $6.55. Yokozuna's Ramen is very local, very clean, and known for its good food.

Da Box Lunch, along Rt. 56 as you are entering Lihue from the airport, open for breakfast and lunch Mon.-Sat. 5:30 a.m.-2 p.m., is a small local place appointed in blue with picnic-table seating that has made a pretty good attempt at being "downhome chic." The limited menu presents Belgian waffles or two eggs with a choice of bacon, Portuguese sausage, or buttermilk pancakes, all priced around $5. Box lunches, priced $4-6, might include teriyaki meat, fresh noodles, rice, and the mandatory scoop of mac-salad.

Tip Top Restaurant/Bakery, at 3173 Akahi St. between Rice and Rt. 57, open daily except Monday 6:45 a.m.-9 p.m., tel. (808) 245-2333, doubles as the downstairs lobby of the Tip Top Motel. A local favorite with unpretentious but clean surroundings, the food is wholesome but uninspired—just like the service. Breakfast is the best deal, at around $5, and the macadamia

nut pancakes are delish! Plate lunches are under $6 and dinners under $8. You can choose anything from pork chops to teriyaki chicken, and you get soup, salad, rice, and coffee. The *bento* (box lunches), either American-style or Asian, are a good deal. Visit the bakery section and let your eyes tell your stomach what to do. The *malasadas* are fresh daily.

Dani's, 4201 Rice St., toward Nawiliwili near the fire department, open Mon.-Fri. 5 a.m.-1:30 p.m., Saturday 5 a.m.-1 p.m., closed Sunday, tel. (808) 245-4991, is a favorite with local people. It's been around a while and has a good reputation for giving you a hearty meal for a reasonable price. The food is American-Hawaiian-Japanese. Most full meals range from $4.50 to $8, and you have selections like *lomi* salmon, tripe stew, teri beef and chicken, and fried fish. Unpretentious, the cafeteria-style interior displays formica-topped tables and linoleum floors. Service is friendly, and the food is good.

You won't have to wonder what the future will bring as far as your evening meal if you choose the **Fortune Cookie Restaurant,** 4261 Rice St., tel. (808) 246-0855, open Mon.-Thur. 9:30 a.m.-8 p.m., Friday 9 a.m.-9 p.m., and Saturday 10 a.m.- 9 p.m., free delivery in the Lihue area with a $10 minimum purchase. The menu offers a "super *bento*" of deep-fried prawns, kaugee, spare ribs, crispy chicken, mixed vegetables, chow mein, and steamed rice for $6.45, deep-fried vegetarian egg rolls $5.25, deep fried wanton soups $7.25, house fried rice $6.50, shrimp Canton $6.50, and a variety of chow meins from $5.95 to $6.45. Fortune Cookie caters to vegetarians with items like braised tofu and Sichuan broccoli (each $5.95). The decor in this one room restaurant is lean and practical.

The **Garden Island Barbecue,** across from the newly renovated Yoneji Bldg. at 4252 Rice St., tel. (808) 245-8868, open Mon.-Sat. 10:30 a.m.-9 p.m., is a simple, clean, and economical eat-in or takeout restaurant. The menu offers varied dishes from the mix of ethnic groups on Kauai including crispy *kaugee* mein at $6.25, pot-roast chicken for $5.95, shrimp and vegetables for $6.25, and oxtail soup for $5.95. Cheaper but equally filling items include loco moco at $5.50, an array of sandwiches and hamburgers priced from only $1.25 to $2.25, and "mini" and regular plate lunches heaped with barbecued short ribs, shrimp curry, or mahi from $3.75 to $5.75, depending on your choices. The food is good, the surroundings adequate, and the service friendly.

Kunja's Korean Restaurant, open Mon.-Sat. 9:30 a.m.-8 p.m. at 4100 Rice St., in the small shopping center next door to Ben Franklin's, tel. (808) 245-8792, is a sit-down or takeout restaurant that serves authentic Korean food. Dishes include short ribs, marinated beef strips, mixed rice and vegetables, and various noodle soups, priced from $3.50 to $6.75. Many are made with the Hawaiian palate in mind, but for a really spicy dish try O-jing-o Po Kum for $5.50 or kimchi soup for $5.50. Clean and tidy, with only a few tables.

Look for an anchor chain marking the two-tone blue **Beach Hut,** open daily except Sunday 7 a.m.-4 p.m. at the bottom of Rice St., just before Nawiliwili Harbor. This upscale window-restaurant offers limited seating in the upstairs "crow's nest," from where you get a great view of the harbor. With a good reputation among local clientele, it serves breakfast and lunches of fish and chips, mahimahi, and charbroiled chicken for under $7.50. The specialty is large, juicy buffalo burgers with all the fixings, but turkey burgers and traditional beef burgers are also offered. Unpretentious, the Beach Hut is an excellent choice for lunch in the Nawiliwili area.

The Nawiliwili Tavern, housed in the old Hotel Kuboyama, at the bottom of Rice St. along Paena Loop Rd., tel. (808) 245-7267, open 11 a.m.- 2 a.m., is a friendly neighborhood bar and restaurant where you can mix with local people and tourists alike who are having fun playing pool, shuffleboard, or darts. Enjoy a cold beer in the casual and attractive surroundings, or satisfy your appetite by ordering a teriyaki burger for $6.50, pastrami and Swiss for $6.95, various plate lunches for $8.95, *pu pu* like sashimi at $7.95, or chicken strips for $3.95 (daily lunch special is $5.50).

Don't let the name **Lihue Bakery and Coffee Shop** fool you into thinking of just the familiar styrofoam cup of coffee and powdered donut. Located in the Rice Shopping Center and open Mon.-Sat. 5:30 a.m.-6 p.m. and Sunday 5 a.m.-1 p.m., this storefront restaurant specializes in Filipino foods and pastries. Choose your selection from a hot table laden with ethnic dishes like

pinkabet and chicken or pork *adobo*. You can have from one to three selections for $4, $4.50, and $5, and top it off with a Filipino pastry.

The **Kukui Grove Shopping Center** has a number of sit-down and sidewalk restaurants. They include the **Deli and Bread Connection,** a kitchenware store with a deli counter offering sandwiches for around $3 and an assortment of soups and salads; **Kauai Cinnamons,** a bake shop specializing in cinnamon rolls; **Si Cisco's,** a Mexican restaurant nicely appointed with a tile floor and a full bar; **Joni Hana,** a walk-up counter with *bento* and plate lunches priced $2-5; and **J.V. Snack Bar,** featuring shave ice and light sandwiches.

One of the mall's best restaurants for Cantonese food at very reasonable prices is **Ho's Garden,** where most dishes are under $7.

Fast Foods

Yes, the smell of the colonel's frying chicken overpowers the flower-scented air, and the golden arches glimmer in the bright Kauai sun. **Pizza Hut, Jack in the Box, McDonald's, Kentucky Fried Chicken, Zack's Frozen Yogurt, Domino's, Baskin-Robbins,** and **Subway Sub Shop** are all located along Route 56 as you are entering Lihue. **Burger King** and **Taco Bell** are at the Kukui Grove Shopping Mall, and a **Dairy Queen** brazier can be found on Rice St. across from the Rice Street Shopping Center.

Moderate in and around Lihue

The restaurants in and around Lihue charge as little as $5 for an entree, with the average around $10. Most of these restaurants advertise specials and discounts in the free tourist literature.

Restaurant Kiibo serves authentic Japanese meals without a big price tag. Many Japanese around town come here to eat. The low stools at the counter are reminiscent of a Japanese *akachochin* or *sushiya*. In fact, the sushi bar is a recent addition. The menu listing savory offerings of udon, tempura, teriyaki, and a variety of *teishoku* (specials) includes pictures showing you just what you'll get. The service is quick and friendly; most offerings are under $10. Restaurant Kiibo is *ichiban!* Located just off Rice St., at 2991 Umi St.; it's open for lunch 11 a.m.-1 p.m. (attracts many office workers) and for dinner 5:30-9 p.m., closed Sunday and holidays; tel. (808) 245-2650. Just around the corner is the **Lihue Cafe** for Japanese and Chinese food. Unpretentious setting, basic food. Open Mon.-Sat. 4:30-9 p.m. (to 10 p.m. on Friday); tel. (808) 245-6471.

The **Barbecue Inn** has been in business for three decades, and if you want a testimonial, just observe the steady stream of local people, from car mechanics to doctors, heading for this restaurant. Word has it that it's better for lunch than dinner. The atmosphere is "leatherette and formica," but the service is homey, friendly, and prompt. Japanese and American servings are huge. Over 30 entrees include a chicken platter, seafood, even prime rib. The Friday teriyaki platter is a good choice. The scampi is perhaps the best for the price on the island. Most meals come complete with soup or salad, banana bread, vegetables, beverage, and dessert for around $6 and up. Breakfast goes for a reasonable $2, with lunch at bargain prices. The homemade pies are luscious. Cocktails. No credit cards accepted; 2982 Kress St., open daily 7:30 a.m.-8:45 p.m.; tel. (808) 245-2921.

Tokyo Lobby, in Nawiliwili, at the Pacific Ocean Plaza, 3501 Rice St., Suite 103, tel. (808) 245-8989, open Mon.-Sat. for lunch 11 a.m.-2 p.m., dinner daily 5-9:30 p.m., prides itself on the freshness of the food, especially the seafood. Appointed with shoji screens, a pagoda-style roof over the sushi bar, paper fans, and paper lanterns, the Tokyo Lobby creates an authentic Japanese atmosphere. Most meals are presented in small wooden boats, the signature of the restaurant. For lunch, start with combination *nigiri* sushi or sashimi priced around $9.50, various *don buri* (a bowl of rice with savory bits of meat, egg, and vegetables on top) for $6.50-11.95, or *nabeyaki,* assorted seafood with vegetables, and noodles in a broth for $8.95. The dinner menu starts with appetizers like chicken teriyaki or deep-fried soft-shell crab for $3.75-8.95. Soups and salads include miso for $1.50, or *sunomono,* seafood and cucumber in a light vinegar sauce, for $6.50. Sashimi and sushi platters are served with soup and *tsukemono* (cabbage salad), and range from $8.95 to $19.95 for the deluxe combination. Dinner entrees include calamari steak, curried chicken, and beef teriyaki, all priced under $13.95, or combination dinners like sesame chicken with

sashimi for $19.95. The house specialty is the Tokyo Lobby Love Boat (minimum two people), including soup, steamed rice, New York steak, teri chicken, California roll, sashimi, and tempura for $21.50 per person.

Kauai Chop Suey, tel. (808) 245-8790, open daily except Monday for lunch 11 a.m.-2 p.m. and for dinner 4:30-9 p.m., is a reasonably priced Chinese restaurant also located in Nawiliwili's Pacific Ocean Plaza. The restaurant's two dining rooms, separated by a keyhole archway, are alive with plants and brightened by Chinese lanterns hanging from the open-beamed ceiling. The simple but pleasing decor also features tables set with white linen, all dominated by large lazy Susans, perfect for easy sampling of the savory dishes chosen from the menu. Begin with scallop soup or rainbow tofu soup, priced under $7.50. Entrees include sizzling shrimp with lobster sauce for $8.15 (Mama Lau, the owner, says this is the best!), boneless chicken with mushrooms for $7.75, or beef or pork with tomato for under $8.00. House specials are Kauai Chop Suey for only $7.25, and a variety of noodle dishes, all under $7.50 Kauai Chop Suey also offers plate lunches and dinners to go, and has a steady local clientele, a sure sign of good food at reasonable prices.

Rob's Goodtime Grill is one of Lihue's only "neighborhood bars," where you can watch sports on a big screen TV, hobnob with the locals, sing your heart out when the karaoke fires up, and have a reasonable meal. Located in the Rice Shopping Center, open daily 10-2 a.m., with takeout orders available 10 a.m.-midnight; tel. (808) 246-0311. The menu includes zucchini sticks, shrimp cocktail, chef's salad, or Pacific catch salad (seafood, crabmeat, and jumbo shrimp), all priced $5-6.75. Sandwiches run from pastrami and Swiss for $5.50 down to a veggie for $5.25, while burgers are under $6. Entrees include a mahi platter or stir-fry for $6.75, with a special offered daily. The interior is a mixture of booths, tables, and bar seating, and the service and atmosphere are friendly. (See also "Entertainment," below).

The Beach Club, at the Anchor Cove Shopping Center in Nawiliwili, owned and operated by Charlie Vespoli, is open daily 8-11 a.m. for breakfast, 11 a.m.- 5 p.m. for lunch, and 5 a.m.-10 p.m. for dinner with the bar open until closing.

However, time permitting, Charlie, the chief cook, will serve you whatever you want at any hour. Breakfast starts with a veggie omelette for $6.95, shrimp omelette for $8.95, or the normal bacon, Portuguese sausage, or green onion and cheddar cheese for $7.95. An espresso bar opens your eyes with cappuccino, espresso Roma, latte, or mocha, all priced from $1.95 to $2.95. There is wine by the glass or the bottle, along with beer and mixed drinks from the full-service bar. Lunch brings cowboy ribs at $6.95, ham-wrapped shrimp for $7.95, special won ton for $5.95, or New England clam chowder for $9.95. Lunch specialties include Caesar salad for $5.95 or sandwiches such as barbecued beef, grilled ahi, or a sirloin burger—each $8.95. More hearty dinner dishes inspired by Southern Italian cuisine include Vespoli esposito marinara for $11.95, eggplant parmigiana for $14.95, or scampi at $19.95. Island-style entrees include fresh local fish for $19.95 done with macnut breading, Cajun cream sauce, or garlic champagne. Although the food is good, the Beach Club is still trying to find its niche. The interior, designed originally as a supper club, features a parquet floor, track lighting, and giant windows that open to the beauty of Nawiliwili. But overall, the place has a transitional feeling. The waitpeople are enthusiastic and friendly but still need some training in the finer points of service.

The **Fisherman's Galley,** along Rt. 50 in Puhi (look for the blue marlin and yellowfin tuna on the roof), tel. (808) 246-4700, open daily for lunch and dinner, is the seafood restaurant affiliate of Gent-Lee fishing charters. Here, you can dine on the freshest of fish, creamy chowders, steak and lobster, and, for the landlubber, even burgers (takeout available). The full bar serves bottled and draught beers, wine, and cocktails. Choices include smoked or fresh fish salad for $8.95, fish and chips in various sizes priced $5.95-8.95, and a fresh tuna melt for $6.95. Larger meals include a Hawaiian fish platter for $15.95, a New York Steak at $13.95, or the whopping Captain Bo's Platter, with prawns, steak, and fresh fish, for $25.95.

Hanamaulu Dining
Heading north, in Hanamaulu and clearly marked along Rt. 56, is the **Hanamaulu Restaurant and Tea House and Sushi Bar,** where they must be doing something right—they've lasted in the same location for over 70 years! Open 9 a.m.-1 p.m. for lunch and 4:30-9 p.m. for dinner; tel. (808) 245-2511. The menu, which includes sushi, *yakiniku,* and a variety of other Japanese and Chinese dishes, is priced right. Ho Tai, the pudgy happy buddha, greets you as you enter the room, which has shiny parquet flooring and is partitioned by shoji screens and hanging plants. Next door and part of the same restaurant is a sushi bar with tatami-floored rooms that look over a fishpond and a lovely Japanese garden. In the sushi-bar section is an elevated tatami made private by sliding screens. The gardens behind and next door to the restaurant are wonderful and well worth a stroll.

The Planter's also sits along Rt. 56 in Hanamaulu, tel. (808) 245-1606. The menu is long and varied, but the specialty is *kiawe*-broiled prime rib and steak. Most meals run in the $12-18 range. Open windows let in the breeze as well as the traffic noise along the highway. The bar is open 3:30-10:30 p.m., happy hour runs until 5:30 p.m., and dinner is served daily except Sunday 5-9:30 p.m. In the large green building next door (built 1908) are the post office, a few shops, and the **Big Wheel Donut Shop** for a quick sugar fix.

The Hanamaulu Plaza in Hanamaulu is also clearly marked along Rt. 56. It is a small but practical shopping center featuring a laundromat and **Ara's Sakamaya,** open Mon.-Sat. 9 a.m.-7 p.m. and Sunday 9 a.m.-5 p.m.; tel. (808) 245-1707. It is a takeout deli-restaurant that offers plate lunches, Japanese *bento,* and fresh fish daily.

Across the street is a **7-Eleven** and a **Shell** gas station.

Fine Dining
The rear flagstone veranda and original dining room at Kilohana, the restored 1935 plantation estate of Gaylord Wilcox, have been turned into the breezy **Gaylord's,** at 3-2087 Kaumuali'i Hwy., Lihue, tel. (808) 245-9593, open daily for lunch 11 a.m.-3 p.m., for dinner from 5 p.m., and Sunday for brunch 9:30 a.m.-2:30 p.m.; reservations recommended. Visiting the vintage estate is a must, and if you can't stay for dinner, lunch starts with salads and munchies like a Kilohana fruit platter, fresh shrimp cocktail,

baked brie in phyllo, or honey-baked brie with macadamia nuts served with fresh fruit and baguette slices for $8.95. The sandwich board offers turkey, beef, and brie, or hot teriyaki or Cajun chicken croissant, at $8.95, along with standards like a grilled cheese or peanut butter sandwich for the children for $3.95. More substantial yet still health-conscious choices include Cajun and regular chicken Caesar salads for $8.95, peppered *ahi* Caesar at $9.95, Gaylord's Papaya Runneth—a papaya stuffed with turkey salad or bay shrimp salad at $7.95—and the very popular Oriental chicken salad at $9.95. The dinner menu begins with appetizers like blackened prawns and pan-seared sashimi priced around $8.95. Dinner entrees include herb-crusted whole rack of lamb ($24.95), blackened prime rib ($19.95 or $21.95), and chicken *moutard* and free-range Cornish game hen (either $16.95). Fish and game lovers will greatly enjoy the seafood rhapsody, where your taste buds will thrill to Mozart for $26.95; one of three choices of fresh fish (market price) that can be char-broiled, sautéed, or sesame crusted; or Gaylord's famous farm-raised venison marsalla—medallions of tender, lean venison (saddle cuts) sautéed and served with artichoke hearts, sun-dried tomato, and basil. Twirl your fork into savory pasta dishes like angel-hair pasta with marinara sauce, Greek-style pasta with grilled chicken, or seafood linguine, all priced $16.95-18.95. For dessert, choose a fabulous Kilohana mud pie, a rich cheesecake, or fantastic banana cream pie, all guaranteed to please. Finish your meal with a cappuccino or coffee mocha prepared on a century-old espresso machine, resplendent in its battered yet burnished glory. Gaylord's also prides itself on having one of the largest wine cellars on Kauai, featuring over 100 vintages from around the world representing more than two dozen varietals.

Sunday brunch, basically a la carte, features the hearty Plantation Breakfast, cheese blintzes, French toast, Gaylord's eggs Benedict, and Gaylord's waffle topped with real maple syrup or the specially prepared topping of the day. Breakfast meats, served with all types of eggs and omelettes, include ham, bacon, Portuguese sausage, and even spring ham. Prices for a complete brunch are $9.95-14.95 and include a fresh-baked sweet roll, potatoes, and a fresh fruit cup. If you want to move away from the breakfast menu, there is a special Sunday pasta, teriyaki chicken, or even a hamburger. Gaylord's is a wonderful restaurant to visit just to spend a quiet afternoon. The dining facility is indoor/outdoor, utilizing the plantation home's generous veranda, with a more formal dining room inside. Formal tables, surrounded by upholstered chairs, are graced with floral displays set upon fine starched linens. The feeling is one of gentility, as if you were a guest at a very civilized garden party. (For a complete description of the home, see "Kilohana Plantation" under "Sights," earlier in this chapter. Also, see "Shopping" for the fine stores, art galleries, and boutiques on premises.)

J.J.'s Broiler, in the Anchor Cove Shopping Center at 3410 Rice St., tel. (808) 246-4422, open daily 11 a.m.-5 p.m. for lunch, until 10 p.m. for dinner, and until midnight for cocktails and light meals, was known in Kapa'a for over 30 years as Kauai's original steak house and famous for its juicy Slavonic steak; it has now moved to Nawiliwili. Richard Jasper, son of the original owner, lolled in his crib to the sizzle of barbecue and the aroma of heady spices, and now owns and operates the restaurant, assisted by executive chef Mark Caeson. The menu offers grain-fed aged beef from the Midwest and four daily choices of fish caught by local captains and delivered fresh to this long-established restaurant. Upon entering, the living landscape of Nawiliwili Bay glistening through the huge windows creates the backdrop for the bi-level interior, done in light wood counterpointed by blue carpeting. The first level is more casual, with a full bar, wooden tables, and bentwood chairs. You can also dine alfresco on the veranda under large yellow umbrellas, but wherever you choose, you are not far from the sea. The tiered upstairs offers horseshoe booths and intimate tables, along with another full bar and wrap-around windows that open to cooling sea breezes. Hanging from the ceiling are replicas of 12-meter racing yachts, exactly like those entered in the America's Cup (not models, these authentic, seaworthy craft are more like one-person go-carts for the ocean). Lunch at J.J.'s starts with potato skins for $7.25, a clam bucket for $6.75, or mozzarella sticks for $6.95. There are also calamari ringers for $6.95, and soups including specialties French onion and Hawaiian Ocean Chowder, each for $5.25. You can also have a very reasonable soup and dinghy sandwich (one tuna or one turkey on croissant) for $6.95. Salads include Oriental chicken ($8.50), Italian tortellini ($8.75), and Fisherman's Net—crab, shrimp, and smoked fish on a bed of greens—for $9.95. Sandwiches range from the Kalapaki Yacht Club (turkey, bacon, and avocado for $8.25) to J.J.'s steak sandwich for $9.75. Burgers range from $6.25 to $7.50. Dinner can begin with J.J.'s house escargot or crab cakes (each $8.95). From the broiler, choose New York steak for $19.95, prime rib of beef for $20.25, roasted macadamia or lamb rack for $23.95, or broiled scallops with crisp taro for $18.95. Specialties include a Chinese Fajita platter at $19.95, medallions of beef tenderloin for $29.95, and seafood linguine for $22.95. For those wondering about Slavonic steak, it's broiled tenderloin dipped in a special sauce of butter, wine, and garlic and ordered alone or in combination with teriyaki chicken or lobster tail. Daily specials for both lunch and dinner are offered to help save money at this fine steak and seafood restaurant.

The heady aroma of sautéed garlic mixed with the sweet scents of oregano and rosemary floats from the kitchens of **Cafe Portofino**. This authentic Italian restaurant, owned and operated by Giuseppi Avocadi, is located on the second level of the Pacific Ocean Plaza, tel. (808) 245-2121, and is open for lunch Mon.-Fri. 11 a.m.-2 p.m. and daily for dinner 5-10 p.m. Sliding wooden doors open to the distinctive wooden bar—a bold statement of high chic topped with pink-and-black marble and surrounded by marble-topped tables and floral upholstered captain's chairs. The open-beamed wooden ceiling is dotted with fancy fans, track lighting, and a baby spot illuminating a rosewood piano. The main dining room, encased in beveled glass windows, is studded with gray-on-pink tables formally set, and counterpointed by a black-and-white tiled floor. Flowers and ferns add island color, and an outdoor veranda is perfect for a romantic evening. The dinner menu begins with antipasto Portofino for $8, and offers choices like steamed clams, calamari friti, or escargot from $6.50 to

$8.75. Salads include the house salad for $4.25 and the ensalate de patate—a warm potato salad with bacon strips—for $5.25, while soups of the day, like minestrone Portofino, are priced at $4.25. Tempting Italian entrees include spaghetti marinara at $13.75, fettuccine Cafe Portofino (noodles sautéed in tomato, mushroom, garlic, butter, oregano, and cheese sauce) for $19, and specialties of the house like scampi with fettuccine for $19, or eggplant parmigiana at $15. Fresh fish, broiled, baked, or sautéed, is served with fresh homemade condiments (daily quote), while an assortment of chicken dishes, from cacciatore to al forno, are all priced around $14.50. There is a full wine list, and desserts are complemented by a cup of coffee or cappuccino from the full espresso bar. The lunch menu is smaller, both in portion size and price, with most offerings available for under $12. Every night, you are serenaded with live contemporary music, including light jazz, or soloists on saxophone, piano, or harp. Cafe Portofino's newest addition is a formal but comfortable banquet room that can seat up to 100 people. Cafe Portofino is an excellent choice for an evening of romance and fine dining. Buon appetito!

Duke's Canoe Club, tel. (808) 246-9599, on Kalapaki Bay at the Kauai Marriott Resort, open daily 5-10 p.m. for dinner and 4 p.m.-12:30 a.m. for drinks, *pu pu,* and light meals at the Barefoot Bar, with live Hawaiian music nightly, is as much an Hawaiian class act as its namesake, the legendary Duke Kahanamoku. Duke's is one of those places, with an exemplary setting just off the beach, a lustrous wood and thatched interior illuminated by torches and moonlight, that pleasantly overwhelm you with the feeling that you're *really in Hawaii.* At the Barefoot Bar, you feel compelled to quaff a frothy brew and, well . . . kick off your shoes as you listen to the natural melody of wind and waves just a palm tree away. You can order sandwiches, plate lunches, pizza, burgers, and salads, all for well under $10, and you can enjoy a variety of island drinks prepared at the full-service bar. Upstairs, still casual but elegant enough for a romantic evening, the menu offers fresh catch ($17.95-19.95) expertly baked in a glaze of lemon and basil, or ginger, orange, and macadamia, or offered teriyakied, sautéed, or simply broiled. You can also order prime rib for $19.95, shrimp scampi for $17.95, or twist your fork into pasta primavera for a reasonable $9.95. Duke's is Hawaii at its best: relaxed, charming, idyllic, and offering fine cuisine.

Farmers' Market

If you're making your own meals while visiting Kauai, remember that locally grown fresh fruit and vegetables are available from vendors at the farmers' market every Friday at 3 p.m. at Vidinha Stadium in Lihue.

ENTERTAINMENT

Lihue is not the entertainment capital of the world, but if you have the itch to step out at night, there are a few places where you can scratch it.

The **Outrigger Kauai Beach Hotel** has dancing and entertainment at **Gilligan's.** Weekends are popular here with locals from Lihue and Kapa'a who are looking for a night out on the town. The music seems to get louder as the night wears on, and the dance floor is seldom empty. Open Sun.-Thurs. 8 p.m.-2 a.m., Fri.-Sat. 8 p.m.-4 a.m. Dress code.

If you desire slower dancing and quieter music, find your way to the **Lihue Neighborhood Center,** tel. (808) 822-4836, any Friday evening from 7:30 to 9:30 for downhome square dancing. A $1 donation is requested at the door. Records provide the music, and a caller helps even the novice become proficient by the end of the evening.

Sometimes the **Kukui Grove Shopping Center** presents free entertainment, usually of a Hawaiian nature. The schedule varies, but these shows mainly occur on weekends. Check the free tourist literature to see if anything's going on—these events are worth the effort!

Enjoy a night of shared karaoke fun at **Rob's Goodtime Grill** (formerly Kay's Pub), open Mon.-Sat. 10 a.m.-1 a.m. in the Rice Street Shopping Center. A would-be crooner is given the microphone and sings along with the music—the video and words to which are projected on a screen in the corner. A funky, dark little place with booths and formica tables, it's become a local hangout. Even if your mom used to ask you to stop singing in the shower, here you can join in the fun. Everyone gets applause, and beer and drinks are reasonably priced.

If you're lucky, you can "strike out" at the **Lihue Lanes Bowling Alley,** in the Rice Shopping Center, 4303 Rice St., tel. (808) 245-5263, open daily 9 a.m.-11 p.m.

Hap's Hideaway Tavern is a friendly neighborhood bar where you can have a quiet beer. The address is 2975 Ewalu St., tel. (808) 245-3473, and although you'll see the sign on Rice Street, you have to go around back to enter.

For 20 years, the **Kauai Community Players** have presented the island with virtually its only theatrical performances. Four times a year—November, February, April, and July—this nonprofessional community theater group puts on well-known and experimental plays, usually in the Lihue Parish Hall across Nawiliwili Road from the Kukui Grove Shopping Center. Curtain time is 8 p.m., and ticket prices are $7 adults, $5 students and senior citizens (a dollar less with advance purchase). For information on what's currently showing, call (808) 822-7797.

Another possibility for evening entertainment is the nightly luau and torchlighting ceremony at the Outrigger Kauai Beach Hotel.

SHOPPING

Lihue makes you reach for your wallet—with good cause. A stroll through one of the city's four shopping centers is guaranteed to send you home with more in your luggage than you came with. Kauai's best selections and bargains are found here in the city. It helps that Lihue is a *resort* town—second to being a *living* town. Kauaians shop in Lihue, and the reasonable prices that local purchasing generates are passed on to you.

Shopping Centers

The **Rice Shopping Center,** at 4303 Rice St., tel (808) 245-2033, features a **laundromat,** a bowling alley, inexpensive eateries, a health-food store, a pet center, and a karaoke bar.

The **Lihue Shopping Center,** in downtown Lihue along Rt. 56, features **Gem,** a large discount store filled with everything from sporting goods to alohawear, and the **Big Save Supermarket,** open daily 7 a.m.-11 p.m.

The **Kukui Grove Shopping Center,** tel. (808) 245-7784, along Rt. 50 just a few minutes west of Lihue, is Kauai's largest shopping mall. The center's main stores include **Liberty House,** for general merchandise and apparel (may be closing); **Longs Drugs** and **Woolworths** for sundries, sporting goods, medicines, and photo needs; **Sears; Foot Locker** and **Kinney Shoes,** where you can dress your tootsies appropriately; and **Waldenbooks,** a first-class complete bookstore. Some distinctive boutiques and shops found at the mall include **Alexandra Christian,** which has racks of ladies' high fashion including cocktail dresses and evening gowns; **Deja Vu,** a surf shop with T-shirts, sun hats, glasses, wrap-around dresses, bikinis, boogie boards, surfboards, sandals, and a smattering of dress shirts and shoes; **Easy Discount Store,** with sundries and souvenirs from sunglasses to beach balls for the kids; **Shades of California** will protect your eyes with a large assortment of sunglasses, while **Zales** and **Prestige Jewelers** offer fine jewelry. To pick up classic, contemporary, or island tunes, head for **Tempo Music Shop;** for anything electronic that beeps or buzzes, head for **Radio Shack.**

Other shops include **Pictures Plus** for island prints and custom framing; **Rave,** another store for the younger set with dresses, bikinis, and alohawear; **Kauai Beach Co.,** a great shop for T-shirts and distinctive men's and women's fashions; **Dan's Sports Shop,** tel. (808) 246-0151, for golf clubs, tennis rackets, baseball caps, mitts, dartboards, and water gear; **General Nutrition Center** for the health conscious; **Kaybee Toys,** for children, with a large selection of stuffed animals and games; the **IndoPacific Trading Co.,** the most intriguing store in the mall (see "Arts, Crafts, and Souvenirs," following); and, finally, the **Kauai Product Store,** which offers muumuu, dolls, koa boards, carvings, art work, post cards, and a smattering of jewelry, all made on Kauai.

The **Anchor Cove Shopping Center,** at 3416 Rice Street, just a minute from Kalapaki Beach and Nawiliwili Harbor, is Lihue's newest shopping and dining mall. Among the semidetached kiosks, you will find an **ABC Store,** open daily 7 a.m.-10:30 p.m., selling sundries, beachwear, groceries, film, drugs, cosmetics, and also liquor; **Aloha Wear,** open daily 9 a.m.-5 p.m. and until 6 on Monday and 9 Sunday, selling discounted alohawear for the entire family; **Feet First,** open daily 9 a.m.-9 p.m., where you can not only dress your tootsies in anything from froufrou golden slippers to tough but tasteful Tevas, but also find aloha shirts, matching cabana sets, discounted bathing suits, beach cover-ups, and shorts; another store is **Crazy Shirts,** open daily 9 a.m.-9 p.m., with well made and distinctive designed T-shirts; **Sunglass Hut International,** open daily 9 a.m.-9 p.m., which can protect your eyes and enhance your image with sunglasses from famous makers like Revo, Ray Ban, Oakley, and Maui Jim—with 1,700 stores in their chain, they offer excellent prices, and satisfaction is guaranteed even at a store in your home area; **Royal Hawaiian Heritage,** open 10 a.m.- 9 p.m. Monday through Saturday and 10 a.m.- 6 p.m. on Sunday, sparkles with Hawaiian-inspired jewelry including personalized pendants and bracelets all in solid 14-karat gold; **Sophisticated You,** owned and operated by former beauty queen Therese Jasper and open daily 10 a.m.- 5 p.m. and Sunday 11 a.m.- 3 p.m., features ladies' fine apparel for sale or rent, and rents wedding gowns and tuxedos, just in case the tropical sun goes to your head and you decide to tie the knot. Other establishments in the center include **Ohana Helicopter Tours** (see "Air Tours" under "Sightseeing Tours" in the "Getting Around" section of the On the Road chapter); **J.J.'s Broiler** (see "Fine Dining," under "Food," above), and **The Beach Club,** a newcomer to the dining scene trying to get established.

Pay 'n Save is on Rice Street with a row of shops including Daylight Donuts. In Nawiliwili is the **Pacific Ocean Plaza,** just across from Anchor Cove, with clothing stores, several restaurants, and an art gallery.

Along Rt. 56 just as you enter Lihue, you'll see a classic building dating from 1923. Once the home of Garden Island Motors Limited, it's now a mini-mall housing **Subway Sandwich Shop,** a national chain; **Photo Spectrum,** offering one-hour film processing; and **Baskin-Robbins 31 Flavors.**

Clothing and Specialty Shops

Don't pass up **Hilo Hattie,** an institution of alohawear, to at least educate yourself on products and prices. Though their designs may not be one-of-a-kind, their clothing is very serviceable and well made. Specials are always offered in the free tourist literature and on clearance racks at the store itself. They also have a selection of gifts and souvenirs. Among the abundance of incentives to get you in is the free hotel pick-up from Poipu to Kapa'a, a tour of the factory, free refreshments while you look around, and free on-the-spot alterations. Look for the store at 3252 Kuhio Hwy., at the intersection with Rt. 57. Open every day 8:30 a.m.-5 p.m., tel. (808) 245-3404.

Kapaia Stitchery is where you find handmade and distinctive fashions. This shop is along Rt. 56 in Kapaia, a tiny village between Hanamaulu and Lihue. The owner is Julie Yukimura, who, along with her grandmother and a number of very experienced island seamstresses, creates fashions, quilts, and embroideries that are beautiful, painstakingly made, and priced right. You can choose a garment off

the rack or have one tailor-made from the Stitchery's wide selection of cotton fabrics. You can't help being pleased with this fine shop!

Clothing at discount prices is found at **Garment Factory to You** in the Lihue Shopping Center. This store is as practical as its name.

Bamboo Lace, tel. (808) 245-6007, in the **Pacific Ocean Plaza** at 3501 Rice St., almost in Nawiliwili, open Mon.-Sat. 11 a.m.-7 p.m., offers dresses, blouses, hats, jewelry, and a smattering of alohawear. It's owned and operated by Nadine, who handpicks fashionable clothing from the continent. Shelves also hold bath and skin-care products, gift items, lingerie, fancy shoes, and straw hats. Basically, Bamboo Lace is a women's fine apparel store, which Nadine says resembles her closet, only a lot bigger.

You can find everything you need to try your luck in Kauai's waters at **Lihue Fishing Supply,** 2985 Kalena St., open Mon.-Fri. 8:30 a.m.-5 p.m. and Saturday 8:30 a.m.-4:30 p.m., tel. (808) 245-4930.

Arts, Crafts, and Souvenirs

The longest-lasting part of a journey is the memory of that journey, capable of instantly transporting you through space and time to recapture the sublime beauty of the moment. One of the best catalysts for recapturing this memory is an inspirational work of art.

Kahn Galleries specializes in original artworks and limited-edition prints created by some of the finest artists Hawaii has to offer. The Kahn Galleries, open daily 9 a.m.-10 p.m., are located in Hanalei Town right in the old schoolhouse, tel. (808) 826-6677; in Koloa in the main building that faces you as you enter town, tel. (808) 742-2277; at the **Kilohana Plantation,** just west of Lihue, tel. (808) 246-4454; in the Kauai Village Shopping Center, tel. (808) 822-4277; and at Kapaa Coconut Marketplace, in a slightly different venue called Island Images, where some of the great art is sold at discount prices. Some of the master artworks shown by Kahn Galleries include Tabora's dramatic seascapes of wind-whipped palms and crashing surf, made magically mysterious by the light of translucent moon or illuminated by a glorious sunset; the landscapes of father and sons H., Thomas, and Richard Leung, impressionists who blend the techniques of East and West into paintings of provocative, dazzling beauty; the environmental impressionism of world-famous George Sumner; and the finely detailed sculptures of Randy Puckett. Kahn Galleries also offer unbelievable prints produced by a computer-based operation called **giclee,** where a picture of the original is made into a transparency that is scanned to match subtle strokes and color variations perfectly, and then airbrushed at 4 million droplets per second (each 4 times smaller than a human hair) to paper or canvas, creating a cyberspace copy of amazing exactness.

The Country Store, at the Kilohana Plantation, open daily 9 a.m. to late evening, specializes in Hawaiian-inspired souvenirs, wind chimes, wicker picnic baskets, cutlery, Hawaiian quilted pillows, vintage fabric handbags, hand-blown and hand-etched glass, and lovely silver jewelry. Master crafts from local artists include koa boxes by Robert Brackbill and Roy Tsumoto; koa, camphor, and kamani bowls by Robert Bouman; throws (small blankets) by local artist Anne Oliver, who hand-dyes and -sews her work; and cobalt blue glass, hand-blown and -etched by Jennifer Pontz.

Upstairs and down (the koa banister is a delight to run your hand over) in the vintage Kilohana Plantation Home you will also find **Sea Reflections,** glimmering with glass, jewelry, and carvings; **Grande's,** for that impulse purchase of a gold bracelet or pearl necklace; **Kilohana Gallery,** offering eye-catching *tapa* prints, wooden bowls, and inexpensive souvenir items; and the somehow politically-incorrect-sounding **Dolls and Furry Little Critters** (whose name, said in the wrong context, could get your face slapped), selling fuzzy-wuzzies and doll babies.

If you're after just filling a shopping basket with trinkets and gimcracks for family and friends back home, go to **Gem** in Lihue or **Longs Drugs** in the Kukui Grove Shopping Center. Their bargain counters are loaded with terrific junk for a buck or two.

The IndoPacific Trading Co. at the Kukui Grove Shopping Center (also at the Coconut Market Place in Kapa'a and at Kong Lung Complex in Kilauea), tel. (808) 246-2177, is a distinctive boutique selling artifacts, incense, local island perfumes, and cotton and rayon clothing mostly from Indonesia and Thailand, including replicas of classic Hawaiian shirts. Artworks include sculpted ducks, fish, primitive artwork

from New Guinea, Borneo, and Australia and a beautiful collection of Balinese masks. Richly embroidered Burmese tapestries, baskets, hammocks, and wind chimes imported from Java, Sumatra, and other parts of Oceania hang on the walls. Amazing pieces of furniture including hand-carved teak chests, a beveled glass mirror intricately etched, a Balinese temple door, prancing horses, and bentwood chairs are also on display.

For better-quality souvenirs, along with custom jewelry, try **Linda's Creation,** at 4254 Rice Street. This shop, owned and operated by Joe and Linda Vito, is well stocked with items ranging from silk wallets for $2 to lovely vases for over $100.

Kauai Museum Shop, at the Kauai Museum has authentic souvenirs and items Hawaiian with competitive prices.

The Gift Gallery, at the Pacific Ocean Plaza at 3501 Rice St., just near Nawiliwili Harbor, open Tues.-Sat. 10 a.m.-9 p.m., is filled with stuffed animals, koa woodwork, tile whales, and decorative exotic birds, mugs, wind chimes, serving platters, glasswork, and a good collection of postcards.

Longi's Crackseed Center, in the Rice Shopping Center, open Mon.-Fri. 8:30 a.m.-9 p.m., Saturday 8:30 a.m.-4:30 p.m., and Sunday 10 a.m.-4 p.m., is packed with large glass jars filled with crackseed, preserved and spiced fruits, seeds, and nuts.

Listen for the chatter of a cheeky cockatoo leading you into **Exotic Bird Emporium,** at 3470 Paena Loop Road at the bottom of Rice St. just before the harbor, tel. (808) 246-6707, open Mon.-Sat. 9 a.m-8 p.m. and Sunday 10 a.m.-6 p.m., where owners Bob & Geri Jasper are proud to offer "the world's finest hand-fed baby birds" (read "spoiled rotten"). These magnificently plumed "living feather dusters" include everything from Moluccan cockatoos to hyacinth macaws and range in price from $1,000 to $20,000. All are U.S. bred from incubated eggs, so the Emporium's birds are no threat to the deterioration of the rain forest or the natural populations of their wild relatives. The health of all birds is 100% guaranteed, and they are imprinted from birth to accept human contact. Bob and Geri will ship them anywhere in the continental U.S.

In the humble and poorly marked Kalapaki Shopping Center, just a minute from the Anchor Cove Shopping Center towards Nawiliwili Harbor, is the **Bead Store,** open daily from 9 a.m. to 5 p.m., tel. (808) 245-8713, sparkling from floor to ceiling with baubles, bangles, and beads. Look for a couple of hanging shell baskets and a makeshift sign reading "Beads." Inside, the shimmering faux jewels—some pre-strung, others waiting for nimble fingers—come from all over the world, including the Philippines, Czechoslovakia, and Native American beads from throughout the southwest. Other items include Hawaiian fishhooks, a case full of sterling silver, gaping shark jaws, crystals, and plenty of carvings of horses, fish, and turtles. A grab bag called "findings" offers bits and pieces of the various baubles at a large markdown.

The **Kalapaki Bay Gallery,** at Pacific Ocean Plaza, open daily noon to 10 p.m., tel. (808) 245-5125, features a collection of works which attempt to capture the lighted soul of Hawaii. Here are the famed seascapes, waterfalls, and landscapes of Edgardo Garcia and the oils of famed Maui artist James O'Neill. The owner is artist D.J. Khamis, who, in a collaboration with O'Neill, brings to life a cavorting humpback whale rising from the deep along Kauai's dramatic Na Pali Coast, and in a solo piece raises Madame Pele triumphantly from her ancient volcano home on Kauai. Khamis has another gallery just across the courtyard called **Kauai Collections,** filled with the works of aspiring artists capturing scenes from around the entire state. One artist, Mark D'Amato, works in fossilized ivory, creating amazing miniatures of fishhooks, roses, and even feathers. Another is Roman Hubbel, a sculptor/potter who is just as adept at working in free-form as he is in classic form. Some of the paintings are by a recent arrival, Rafal Chlodzinski, an internationally known watercolorist and graduate architect who renders Hawaii in a bright and whimsical style.

The soothing rich aroma of a premium cigar wafts from the **Kapaia Trading Company** into the big dip along Rt.56, just at the turnoff to Wailua Falls, at 3-601 A Kuhio Highway, Lihue, HI 96766, open daily 9 a.m. to sunset, tel. (808) 246-6792. Owned and operated by Bill Carl, this one-time gas station is a great place for both men and women to peruse. The swirl of burly koa and other native woods lend natural luster to the handmade humidors and fine furniture that Bill has crafted. If you enjoy a fine cigar, write or call Bill in advance to get a list of the cigars he carries (which includes Mackanudos, Fuente, Partigas, Fonseca, and Griffins, among many others). You can pack your purchases in one of many styles of humidors boasting brass hinges, a built-in sponge and bentonite clay holder to keep the humidity constant, a humidity gauge, drawers perfectly designed to hold different shapes of cigars, and a lifetime guarantee (from the builder). From cigar-box-size to a desktop model, these beauties go for from $250 to $1,650. The hand-built furniture on display includes everything from a dining set to an ice bucket of solid koa and a wine rack with glass holder and built-in fruit and cheese tray. Kapaia Trading Company also hosts a monthly cigar tasting for $45 that includes three excellent cigars, fine port, wine, whiskey or cognac, and gourmet hors d'oeuvres. The Kapaia Trading Company, more than just a shopping stop, is a "real" working man's gallery, where years of carpentry experience has been called upon to create exquisite pieces of fine art.

Photo Needs

For a full-line photo store go to **Don's Camera Center,** 4286 Rice St., tel. (808) 245-6581. You'll find all you'll need from a wide selection of famous brands to camera repair and one-day processing. **Longs Drugs, Woolworths,** and **Kauai 1-hour Photo** at the Kukui Grove Shopping Center have inexpensive film and processing. **Senda Studio,** at 4450 Hardy St., is a studio and supply shop.

Supermarkets and Health Food Stores

The **Big Save Supermarket,** 4444 Rice St., tel. (808) 245-6571, is open daily 7 a.m.-11 p.m. The well-stocked **Star Super Market** is in the Kukui Grove Shopping Center.

Also in the Kukui Grove Shopping Center is **General Nutrition Center,** a full-service health food store.

Hale O' Health, tel. (808) 245-9053, in the Rice Shopping Center, open Mon.-Fri. 8 a.m.-5 p.m. and Sat.-Sun. until 3 p.m., specializes in vitamins and minerals. The shelves are stocked with everything from whole-wheat flour to spices, organic pastas, and a good selection of teas. The back deli case holds a small selection of fresh organic vegetables and prepared deli sandwiches.

KEITH PERKINS

WAILUA

Wailua ("Two Waters") is heralded by the swaying fronds of extra-tall royal palms; whenever you see these, like the *kahili* of old, you know you're entering a special place. The Hawaiian *ali'i* knew a choice piece of real estate when they saw one, and they cultivated this prime area at the mouth of the Wailua River as their own. Through the centuries they built many *heiau* in the area, some where unfortunates were slaughtered to appease the gods, others where the weak and vanquished could find succor and sanctuary. The road leading inland along the Wailua River was called the King's Highway. Commoners were allowed to travel only along this road and to approach the royal settlement by invitation only. The most exalted of the island's *ali'i* traced their proud lineage to Puna, a Tahitian priest who, according to the oral tradition, arrived in the earliest migrations and settled here.

Even before the Polynesians came, the area was purportedly settled by the semimythical Mu. This lost tribe may have been composed of early Polynesians who were isolated for such a long time that they developed different physical characteristics from their original ancestral stock. Or perhaps they were a unique people altogether, whom history never recorded. But like another island group, the Menehune, they were said to be dwarfish creatures who shunned outsiders. Unlike the industrious Menehune, who helped the Polynesians, the Mu were fierce and brutal savages whose misanthropic characteristics confined them to solitary caves in the deep interior along the Wailua River, where they led unsuspecting victims to their deaths.

Wailua today has a population of over 2,000, but you'd never know that driving past it, as most houses are scattered in the hills behind the coast. Though an older resort area, it's not at all overdeveloped. The natural charm is as vibrant as ever. Depending on conditions, the beaches can be excellent, and there're shops, restaurants, and nightlife close at hand. With development increasing both to the east and west, perhaps now, as in days of old, the outstanding beauty of Wailua will beckon once again.

SIGHTS

Wailua is famous primarily for two attractions, one natural, the other manmade. People flock to these, but there also exist, in the hills behind the settlement along King's Highway, deserted *heiau,* sacred birthing stones, old cemeteries, and vantages for meditative views of the river below.

Fern Grotto

Nature's attraction is the Wailua River itself, Hawaii's only navigable stream, which meanders inland toward its headwaters atop forbidding Mt. Waialeale. Along this route is the Fern Grotto, a tourist institution of glitz, hype, and beauty rolled into one. Two local companies run sightseeing trips to the grotto on large motorized barges. As you head the two miles up-

river, the crew tells legends of the area and serenades visitors with Hawaiian songs. A hula demonstration is given, where you are encouraged to get up and swing along. The grotto itself is a huge rock amphitheater, whose ever-misty walls create the perfect conditions for ferns to grow. And grow they do, wildly and with abandon, filling the cavern with their deep musty smell and penetrating green beauty. Partially denuded of its lush green coat by Hurricane Iniki, the grotto is slowly filling in and becoming again the beauty it once was. Although the grotto is smaller than one might imagine, the resonating acoustics are wonderful from inside. Here in the natural cathedral, musicians break into the Hawaiian Wedding Song; over the years a steady stream of brides and grooms have

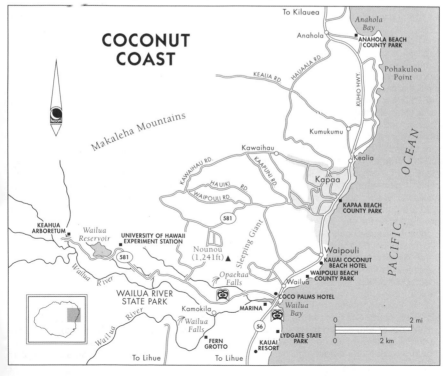

come to exchange vows. The Fern Grotto trip is an amusement ride, but it's also the only way to get there. It's enjoyable and memorable, but you have to stay in the right frame of mind; otherwise, it's too easy to put down. (For tour information, see "Sightseeing Tours" under "Getting Around" in the On the Road chapter.)

Smith's Tropical Paradise

Set along the Wailua River is this 30-acre botanical and cultural garden. A large entranceway welcomes you and proclaims it a "tropical paradise." Inside, most plants are labeled; many are ordinary island foliage, but others are rare and exotic even for the Garden Island. The entire area is sheltered and well watered, and it's easy to imagine how idyllic life was for the original Hawaiians. The array of buildings includes a luau house and a lagoon theater used in the evenings for an international musical show and luau. Peacocks and chickens pecking beneath the trees are natural groundskeepers, preventing insects and weeds from overpowering the gardens. The "villages"—Japanese-, Philippine-, and Polynesian-inspired settlements—are merely plywood facsimiles. However, the grounds themselves are beautifully kept and very impressive. For those who won't be trekking into the Kauai backcountry (especially for those who will), this garden provides an excellent opportunity to familiarize yourself with Kauai's plants, flowers, and trees. You are welcome to walk where you will, but signs guide you along a recommended route. Scheduled mini-trams carry tourists around the grounds for an additional fee. Entrance fees are $5 adults, $2.50 children two to 11; the tram tour is an additional $3 for adults, $2 for children. The entrance fee is good 8:30 a.m.-4:30 p.m., after which the gardens are readied for the evening entertainment. The luau/musical show costs $43.75 for adults and $26 for children ($10.50 and $5.25 for the show only). Reservations are necessary for both. Rated the favorite luau show on the island, this spectacle includes Hawaiian music, a fiery volcanic eruption, and dances from all over the Pacific. For information, call (808) 822-4654, 822-9599, or 822-3467, or pick up tickets at the Smith's booth across from the entrance to the Coco Palms Hotel on the north side of the river mouth. To get to the gardens, follow the road past the Wailua Marina on the south side of the river and park in the large lot.

Kamokila Hawaiian Village

Situated at a bend in the Wailua River on the way to the Fern Grotto is Kauai's only re-created folk village. Kamokila ("Stronghold") has been cut from the jungle on the site of an *ali'i* village, the first of seven ancient villages in this valley; the villages farther up were for common laborers. The prominent ridge across the river indicates the boundary past which the ordinary man could not tread for fear of his losing his life.

The old village sat on terraces on the hillside above the river, and fields were cultivated where the village now lies. Kamokila has been resurrected to give visitors a glimpse of what island life was like for the ancient Hawaiians. Created in 1981, it was destroyed almost immediately by Hurricane Iwa in 1982, and badly knocked around again by Hurricane Iniki in 1992. Though currently closed, it is continually going through renovation to make it more authentic; there are examples of buildings, agricultural plots, fruit trees and medicinal plants, and demonstrations of ancient crafts and activities of everyday life. Taro is grown and poi made, mats and skirts are woven, and traditional medicines prepared. A *hale noa* (chief's sleeping quarters), *hale koa* (warrior's house), *pahoku hanau* (birthing house), *hale ali'i akoakoa* (assembly hall), *laola pa'au* (herbal medicine office), and *lana nu'u mamao* (oracle tower) have been erected. The *imu* pits for cooking are functional, and there is an athletic ground used for games at festive times of the year. There are also *tiki* (spirit containers) and *amakua* (ancestral spirit icons) set up at propitious spots around the village.

A guide escorts you and explains the importance of each site, the methods of creating handicrafts and tools, the use of both the ordinary and medicinal plants, and how the village operated on a daily basis. You may drive down to the village by following a steep one-lane track that skirts the ridge—the turnoff is just above the Opaeka'a Falls overlook on Rt. 580. A free shuttle bus service is available from hotels in the Wailua and Kapa'a area. Future plans include a ferry ride from the Wailua Marina to the village. The entrance fee is $5 for adults, $2.50 for children under 12; open Mon.-Sat. 9 a.m.-5 p.m.

A trip to this inspiring village is well worth the time and effort and will certainly add to your knowledge of the roots of Hawaiian life. For more information, call (808) 822-4866 or 822-3350 in the hope that it has reopened.

Historical Sites and *Heiau*

The King's Highway (Rt. 580), running inland from Wailua, and Rt. 56, the main drag, have a number of roadside attractions and historical sites dating from the precontact period. Most are just a short stroll from your car and well worth the easy effort. The mountains behind Wailua form a natural sculpture of a giant in repose, aptly called the **Sleeping Giant.** You have to stretch your imagination just a little to see him (his outline is clearer from farther up, toward Kapa'a), and although not entirely a bore, like most giants, he's better left asleep. This giant and his green cover are part of the Nounou Forest Reserve.

Along Rt. 56 just before the Coco Palms Hotel, a tall stand of palms on the east side of the Wailua River is part of Lydgate State Park and marks the spot of **Hauola O' Honaunau,** a temple of refuge that welcomed offending *kapu*-breakers of all social classes. Here miscreants could atone for their transgressions and have their spiritual slates wiped clean by the temple priests, enabling them to return to society without paying with their lives. Both the refuge and **Hikina Heiau** are marked by a low encircling wall. The area is extremely picturesque here,

where the Wailua River meets the sea. Perhaps it's knowledge about the temple of refuge that creates the atmosphere, but here, as at all of these merciful temple sites, the atmosphere is calm and uplifting, as if some spiritual residue has permeated the centuries. It's a good spot to relax in the cool of the grove, and there are picnic tables available.

As Rt. 580 meanders inland, you pass **Wailua River State Park.** Then immediately look for **Poaiahu Arboretum** and its convenient turnout. The arboretum is merely a stand of trees along the roadside. Across the road is **Holo Holo Ku Heiau,** where the unfortunate ones who didn't make it to the temple of refuge were sacrificed to the never-satisfied gods. This temple is one of Kauai's most ancient; the altar itself is the large slab of rock near the southwest corner. Behind the *heiau,* a silver guardrail leads up the hill to a small, neatly tended Japanese cemetery. The traditional tombstones chronicling the lives and deaths of those buried here have turned green with lichens against the pale blue sky. As if to represent the universality of the life-death cycle, **Pohaku Hoo Hanau,** the "royal birthing stones," are within an infant's cry away. Royal mothers came here to deliver the future kings and queens of the island. The stones somehow look comfortable to lean against, and perhaps their solidity reinforced the courage of the mother.

Back on Rt. 580, you start to wend your way uphill. You can see how eroded and lush Kauai is from this upland perch. On your left is the

From the bell stones you can look over the Wailua River and Coco Palms Resort to the sea.

verdant Wailua Valley, watered by the river, and on your right, separated by a spit of land perhaps only 200 yards wide, is a relatively dry gulch. Notice, too, the dark green freshwater as it becomes engulfed by the royal blue of the ocean in the distance. As you climb, look for an HVB Warrior pointing to **Opaeka'a Falls.** The far side of the road has an overlook; below is the Wailua River and the Kamokila Hawaiian Village. Take a look around to see how undeveloped Kauai is. Across the road and down a bit from the Opaeka'a turnoff is **Poliahu Heiau,** supposedly built by the Menehune. Nothing is left but a square wall enclosure that is overgrown on the inside. Do not walk on the walls as it's believed that the spirits of the ancestors are contained in the rocks. Down the ridge, at the end of a gravel track, are the **bell stones;** pounded when a royal *wahine* gave birth, their peals could be heard for miles. From here, there is a great view over the river and down to the coast.

Beaches, Parks, and Recreation

Wailua has few beaches, but they are excellent. **Wailua Municipal Golf Course** skirts the coast, fronting a secluded beach, and because of its idyllic setting is perhaps the most beautiful public links in Hawaii. Even if you're not an avid golfer, you can take a lovely stroll over the fairways as they stretch out along the coastline. The greens fee is a reasonable $18 weekdays, $20 weekends, with carts and clubs for rent. The driving range is open until 10 p.m. For the convenience of golfers, the clubhouse has a dining room and snack bar open daily. For information or links reservations call (808) 241-6666. Below the links is a secluded beach. You can drive to it by following the paved road at the western end of the course until it becomes dirt and branches toward the sea. The swimming is good in the sheltered coves and the snorkeling is better than average along the reef. Few people ever come here, and plenty of nooks and crannies are good for one night's bivouac.

Lydgate Beach is a gem. It's clearly marked along Rt. 56 on the south side of the Wailua River, behind the Kauai Resort complex. Two large lava pools make for great swimming even in high surf. The smaller pool is completely protected and perfect for tots, while the larger is great for swimming and snorkeling. Stay off the slippery volcanic rock barrier. This beach is never overcrowded, and you can find even more seclusion by walking along the coast away from the built-up area. If you head to the river, the brackish water is refreshing, but stay away from the point where it meets the ocean; the collision creates tricky, wicked currents. **Lydgate State Park** also provides sheltered picnic tables under a cool canopy provided by a thick stand of ironwoods, plus grills, restrooms, and showers, but no camping. The beach across the river fronting the Coco Palms is treacherous and should only be entered on calm days when lifeguards are in attendance.

ACCOMMODATIONS

The hotels in Wailua are like the beaches—sparse but good. Your choices are the famous Coco Palms (not scheduled to reopen until 1998) and the Kauai Resort, with its admirable location fronting Lydgate State Park. Wailua also has one B&B.

The **Kauai Resort,** at 3-5920 Kuhio Hwy., Wailua, HI 96746, reservations (through Hawaiian Pacific resorts), tel. (808) 245-3931 or (800) 367-5004, has a lovely setting above Lydgate Park, with the Hauola Temple of Refuge adjacent to the grounds. Incorporated into the architecture are a series of cascading pools and a koi pond that boils with frenzied color at feeding time. The main lobby is a huge affair with swooping beams in longhouse style. Rooms are well decorated, and most have ocean views. Rates are $99 standard, $145 deluxe oceanfront, and $75 for cabanas with kitchenettes, which are separate from the main facility and have unobstructed views of the beach.

A unique lodging alternative is the **Fern Grotto Inn,** a bed and breakfast surrounded by Wailua River State Park. This plantation home on the Wailua River offers three tastefully furnished bedrooms with private baths, gourmet breakfast especially tailored for the health-conscious traveler, and a private garden perfect for an evening stroll. Rates range $80-100 per night, or the entire home can be rented for $1,250 per week. For information, contact the Fern Grotto Inn at 4561 Kuamoo Rd., Wailua, HI 96746, tel. (808) 822-2560, or on Oahu at (808) 521-5521.

The **Coco Palms Resort,** tel. (808) 823-0760, is a classic Hawaiian hotel, one of the first tourist destinations built on the island, but it took a terrible beating during Hurricane Iniki. Promising to reopen soon (but don't hold your breath), the Polynesian-inspired buildings are interspersed through a monumental coconut grove planted by a German immigrant in the early 1800s. His aspiration was to start a copra plantation, and although it failed, his plantings matured into one of the largest stands of coconut trees in the islands. Nightly, the hostelry's famous torchlighting ceremony takes place under the palm canopy, which encircles a royal lagoon once used to fatten succulent fish for the exclusive use of the ali'i. Everyone, hotel guest or not, is welcome to the ceremony, and you should definitely go if you're in the area around sundown. The Lagoon Terrace Lounge, which also offers soft evening entertainment, and the Lagoon Dining Room have superb front-row seats. Some may put the performance down as fake traditional, but it's the *best* fake traditional on the island—both dramatic and fun. It was started by the recently retired Grace Guslander, the congenial hostess famous for her cocktail parties.

The hotel grounds are inspiring, and often when Hollywood needed "paradise" they came here. Parts of several old movie sets still remain. Notice the authentic-looking cement palm trees used to blend in the construction of some of the buildings. There's a small zoo, a museum, and a chapel built by Columbia Pictures for Rita Hayworth in the movie *Sadie Thompson.* More than 2,000 marriages have been performed in this chapel since—and not all involved Zsa Zsa Gabor or Liz Taylor! After Tattoo used to inform Mr. Rorque of the arrival of "De plane, boss," in the popular TV series *Fantasy Island,* it was into the Coco Palms grove that he drove the jeep. Elvis came here to film *Blue Hawaii,* and segments of *South Pacific* were shot on the grounds. Frank Sinatra found out who the chairman of the board *really* was when he was swept out to sea from a nearby beach one day. Old Blue Eyes used his velvet voice to scream for help and was rescued by local men from the fire department using a surfboard. After the rescue, Sinatra discovered that they had no boat; showing the class for which he's famous, he bought them a spanking new CrisCraft. The hotel bought the beachhouse in which Sinatra had been staying and rented it out as the "Sinatra House." The singer was later upstaged when John Kennedy visited a number of times, and the house was renamed "President's House." The hotel divested itself of this property recently. As soon as you walk onto the Coco Palms grounds you feel romantic. You can't help it—and no one's immune. The Coco Palms is a peaceful garden. Let it surround you.

FOOD

Inexpensive
In the Wailua Shopping Center behind Sizzler is the pick-and-choose, hot-table-style **Manila Fastfood Restaurant,** tel. (808) 823-0521, serving breakfast 7-9:30 a.m., lunch 10 a.m.-3 p.m., and dinner 4-7 p.m. A mixture of Filipino and American dishes are served for around $5.

Wah Kung Chop Suey, in the Kinipopo Shopping Village just across from the Sizzler Steakhouse, open daily 11 a.m.-8:30 p.m., tel. (808) 822-0560, is a clean, no-decor restaurant offering Chinese and local food. Lunch specials 11 a.m.-2 p.m. (all around $5) include items like kung pao with vegetables, rice or noodles; beef broccoli; fried chicken; lemon chicken; and egg foo yong. Soups made from scallops, abalone, and pork are $4.50-5.50. Standards like chop suey and chow mein are under $6, and at $7.50 shrimp, scallops, and mahimahi are the most expensive dishes on the menu. Wah Kung has a good reputation with local people, so they must be doing something right!

Moderate
The **Wailua Marina Restaurant,** tel. (808) 822-4311, overlooking the Wailua River, offers inexpensive to moderately priced "local-style" food and free hotel pick-up in the Wailua area for

dinner. If you're going on a Fern Grotto boat trip, consider eating here. Breakfast, 8:30-11 a.m., is under $5; lunches, until 2 p.m., include dishes like a small tenderloin, fries, and a tossed green salad for $7.25; dinner, 5-9 p.m., features entrees like Korean barbecued ribs or breaded veal cutlets in mushroom sauce for under $11. It's convenient, and there's never a wait after the last boat upriver.

Mema's Thai Chinese Restaurant, in Wailua Shopping Plaza behind Sizzler, is open Mon.-Fri. 11 a.m.-2 p.m. for lunch and nightly 5-9:30 p.m. for dinner, tel. (808) 823-0899, and is a casual family-operated restaurant with a touch of class. The ornate chairs and tables, made of imported wood from Thailand sets the theme. Waiters, dressed in green silk shirts, carry their trays past a profusion of potted plants and flowers. The booklike menu starts with crispy noodles at $6.95, fish cakes for $7.95, satay for $7.95-9.95 depending upon choice of fish or meat, fried calamari at $7.95, and exotic Thai soups ($7.95-10.95) like spicy lemongrass or Thai ginger coconut. Most entrees can be prepared vegetarian but might include cashew chicken at $8.25; garlic with mixed vegetable, chicken, pork, shrimp, or beef for $7.95-9.50; spicy sweet and sour chicken, beef, vegetables, seafood, or pork for $7.95-14.95; or savory curries—red, green, or yellow—$8.95-15.95. The assortment also includes rice and noodle dishes to please all palates and pocketbooks. If you are overwhelmed by choices, try the fixed dinners for two to six people ranging in price from $32.95 to $89.95. Mema's offers complete wine, beer, and dessert menus. If you are looking for a restaurant with excellent exotic food where you can enjoy a romantic evening for a reasonable price, Mema's should be at the top of your list.

Some will be happy, others sad, to hear that the aroma of fast food wafts on the breezes of Wailua. Just past the venerable Coco Palms is the **Sizzler Steakhouse,** at 4361 Kuhio Hwy., tel. (808) 822-7404, open Fri.-Sat. 6 a.m.-11 p.m. and Sun.-Thurs. 6 a.m.-10 p.m., serving breakfast and the familiar steaks, burgers, and salad bar, in this better-than-average fast-food environment.

Expensive
The Japanese legend of Kintaro, a pint-sized boy born to an old couple from inside a peach pit, is slightly less miraculous than the excellent and authentic Japanese restaurant named for him, owned and operated by a Korean gentleman, Don Kim. From the outside, **Restaurant Kintaro** is nothing special, but inside it transforms into the simple and subtle beauty of Japan. The true spirit of Japanese cooking is presented, with the food as pleasing to the eye as to the palate. The sushi bar alone, taking up an entire wall, is worth stopping in for. The dinners are expertly and authentically prepared, equaling those served in fine restaurants in Japan. If you have never sampled Japanese food before, Restaurant Kintaro is Kauai's best place to start. Those who *are* accustomed to the cuisine can choose from favorites like tempura, sukiyaki, a variety of soba, and the old standby teriyaki. Open daily 5:30-9:30 p.m. for dinner only, along Rt. 56 just past the Coco Palms. Reservations often necessary; call (808) 822-3341.

SHOPPING

The **Kinipopo Shopping Village,** a diminutive seaside mall, at 4-356 Kuhio Hwy., just across from Sizzler, offers most of Wailua's one-stop shopping. Here you can find the **Goldsmith's Gallery,** tel. (808) 822-4653, open Mon.-Sat. 9:30 a.m.-5:30 p.m. and Friday until 7 p.m., a store shimmering with brilliant jewelry. Five jewelers make the individual pieces, and for their artistry were named the 1992 "Jewel Designers of the Year" for the State of Hawaii. Diamonds, gold, and Australian opals add brilliance (and hefty price tags) to the artwork. Much of the jewelry is commissioned, but there is plenty on display to choose from. One of their distinctive lines, all with island motifs, features pieces shaped like flowers, clam shells, sailfish, petroglyphs, birds, and tropical fish, all fashioned into bracelets, earrings, brooches, and charms.

Kauai Water Ski and Surf Co., tel. (808) 822-3574, open daily 9 a.m.-7 p.m., also in the Kinipopo Shopping Village, is a complete watersports shop. Bathing suits, bikinis, sun visors, men's shorts, surfboards, boogie boards, wet-suits, fins, masks, snorkels, underwater watches, and even a few backpacks and daypacks line the shelves of this small but jam-packed shop. A water-skiing rental package comes complete with boat, professional driver, all equipment, and instruction for beginners to advanced for $85 an hour; kayaks rent for $25 a day single, $50 a day double; snorkel gear is $5 a day, $20 per week; boogie boards are $5 and $20; and surfboards are $10 and $30.

Bachman's, also in the Kinipopo Village, handles clothes, shells, and gift items, while **A Unique Emporium,** open daily except Monday 10 a.m.-5 p.m., tel. (808) 823-0455, is a cutesy-pie shop. Dolls, umbrellas, quilts, pillows, some wicker furniture, and a few display cases filled with jewelry make it as sweet as a double-fudge brownie.

Tony's Minit Mart and the **Shell Station Mini-Mart,** just next door, sell sundries, snacks, beer, and packaged foods.

May and Joy of Hawaii, tel. (808) 823-6276, just across the street, is a surprisingly neat souvenir stand. Inside you will find cut flowers and lei, and a good selection of touristy "junque" including some fine lei fashioned from amethyst and semiprecious stones.

The **Kinipopo General Store** sells groceries, sundries, and liquors.

D.S. Collections, next to Restaurant Kintaro, just past the Kinipopo Shopping Center, is a women's fine apparel store with a smattering of jewelry and some lovely ceramic bowls.

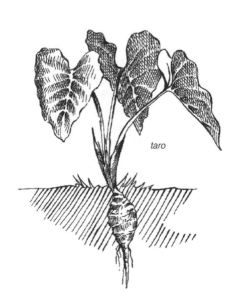

taro

BOB RACE

KAPA'A

Kapa'a means "fixed," as in "fixed course." In the old days, when the canoes set sail to Oahu, they'd always stop first at Kapa'a to get their bearings, then make a beeline directly across the channel to Oahu. Yachts still do the same today. Kapa'a is a town of unusual contrasts. At the south end along the main drag is **Waipouli** ("Dark Water"), actually a separate municipality (though you'd never know it). Clustered here are newish hotels, condos, a full-service shopping mall, restaurants, nightlife—all in all sort of a live-in resort atmosphere. The heart of Kapa'a itself is a workers' settlement, with modest homes, utilitarian shops, some downhome eateries, and a funky hotel.

Actually, a few more people live here than do in Lihue, and the vibe is a touch more local. There are no sights per se. You spend your time checking out the shops, scanning the color-mottled mountains of the interior, and combing the beaches, especially those to the north, toward Hanalei. Two minutes upcoast you're in wide-open spaces. Cane roads cut from Rt. 56 and rumble along the coast. Small oceanside communities pop up, their residents split between beachhouse vacationers and settled *kama'aina*.

What distinguishes Kapa'a is its unpretentiousness. This is "everyday paradise," where the visitor is made to feel welcome and stands in line with everyone else at the supermarket. Generally, the weather is cooperative throughout the area, prices on all commodities and services are good, beaches are fair to spectacular, and the pace is unhurried. Kapa'a isn't the choicest vacation spot on the island, but you can have a great time here and save money.

BEACHES AND PARKS

Central Kapa'a's beaches begin at **Waipouli Beach County Park,** fronting the cluster of hotels just north of the Coconut Market Place Shopping Center, and end near the royal coconut grove by the Kauai Coconut Beach Hotel. The town interrupts the beach for a while south of the Waikaea Canal, and then the beach picks up again at **Kapa'a Beach County Park,** running north for almost a mile until it ends near a community swimming pool and the Kapa'a Library. A number of small roads lead off the beach from Rt. 56. Kapa'a Beach County Park has just over 15 acres, with a pavilion, picnic tables, showers, toilets, and grills. The beach is pretty to look at, but this section of town is run-down. The feeling here is that it belongs to the locals, although no undue hassles have been reported.

As soon as you cross the Kapa'a Stream on the north end of town you're in the one-store village of Kealia. Past mile marker 1, look for Ray's Auto Saloon, and turn off onto the cane road. At the junction is **Kealia Beach.** This wide, white strand curves along the coast for a half-mile. It's not a beach park, so there are no facilities, but during calm weather the swimming is good—particularly at the north end—and few people are ever here except for some local fishermen and surfers.

Continue along Rt. 56 heading north, and just past mile marker 12 you'll find cars parked along the side of the road. Walk to the nearby cane road and continue for 10 minutes until you come to a surfing beach that the locals call **Donkey Beach.** Look for a tall stand of ironwoods, a rutted, makeshift pulloff, and a wide sandy beach below. A footpath leads down to it. This area is very secluded and good for unofficial camping. Unfortunately, the undertow is severe, especially during rough weather, and only experienced surfers challenge the waves here. You can sunbathe and take dips, but remain in the shallows close to shore. (**Note:** There is access to the cane roads from Kealia Beach, but these are often chained and locked. Technically, you need (and should get) a permit issued at the Lihue Sugar Co. office in Lihue to travel them. As you skirt the coastline on this road, heading for **Pohakuloa Point** and Donkey Beach, the ride is much more picturesque than Rt. 56. Continue north on the cane road until it intersects Rt. 56 again.)

ACCOMMODATIONS

Inexpensive
Hawaii International Hostel, at 4532 Leihua St., Kapa'a, HI 96746, tel. (808) 823-6142, just across from the Kapa'a Library, welcomes international guests with a friendly staff that speaks German, French, and good old English. Rates are $16 for a dorm bunk (no reservations, 40 bunks, private female dorm available), and $40 for a private room (reservations accepted, 6 rooms). Although open 24 hours, "lights out" (read "no more noise") is at 11 p.m.; checkout is by 10 a.m., with a loss of $10 key deposit if you're late. Occasionally, staff members or guests organize an impromptu barbecue/luau, and the hostel runs van tours ($20)—mostly hikes to waterfalls, canyons, and pristine beaches, along with airport pickup on arrival before 10 a.m. and after 6 p.m. Facilities include a communal kitchen with good appliances, a lounge with comfortable couches and cable TV, and a laundry room. Dorm rooms, each with its own sink and private bath, contain either four or six bunks. The private rooms are small but cheery (shared bath). The hostel is clean and well managed and has a maximum seven-night stay.

Hotel Coral Reef, at 1516 Kuhio Hwy., Kapa'a, HI 96746, tel. (808) 822-4481 or (800) 843-4659, is relatively inexpensive and definitely has character. Toward the north end of Kapa'a between the main road and the beach, this family-style hotel, one of the first built in the area, has a deluxe view of the bay, is clean, and attracts a decent clientele. Enter the office past a mini-garden, and notice a seascape mural of the bay as you recline on the covered lanai. The rates (based on double occupancy) for the recently refurbished rooms are: oceanfront $89, ocean view $59, two-room suite $79, mountain or garden view $49 ($10 charge for additional guests). The hotel offers "room and car packages" and senior citizen discounts. Rooms, outfitted in tropical decor, feature refrigerators, sliding glass doors, daily maid service, free parking, a pay telephone in the lobby, color television, complimentary coffee, activity bookings and equipment rental, and private beachfront lanai. The Hotel Coral Reef is family run, neat as a pin, and very affordable for a family vacation.

For those island visitors "who value their personal health, and who seek inner growth and the opening of creative potential," the **Keapana Center,** at 5620 Keapana Rd., Kapa'a, HI 96746, tel. (808) 822-9978 or (800) 822-7968, may be the place for you. Gabriela, the multitalented owner, has had varied careers from college professor to dance instructor but now calls herself simply an artist. Living on Kauai for over 20 years and being an avid hiker and outdoor person, Gabriela is accommodating and helpful in giving tips on hikes and nature trails and is also well-versed on the Hawaiian culture, especially the healing arts. In touch with local practitioners, she can make arrangements for instruction or sessions of massage and body work, naturopathic medicine, yoga, tai chi, 12-step programs, and other healing and wellness programs in this restful but stimulating (and non-smoking) environment. Guest rooms are very island, very Hawaiian. Floors are covered with sisal matting, and most furniture is rattan or wicker. Shoji-screen paper lanterns add soft lighting, and beautiful floral displays brighten every room. Beds are covered with batik bedspreads, while Balinese masks, Chinese peasant hats, and hula skirts hang from the walls. The common area, open to the elements, is serene with its own indoor/outdoor garden. The lanai offers sweeping vistas over the lush hillside, which descends to the beach only five minutes away. A solar jacuzzi waits to knead the muscles of any intrepid hikers. Rooms with shared/private baths are $40/$65 s, $55/$70 d, with weekly rates available. Each morning the continental breakfast includes homemade bread, health-conscious muffins, and unique island fruits like sour sop or star fruits which grow on the property and are delightfully unfamiliar to most guests. Bowls of papayas and hands of bananas, all organic and all also from the property, are left in the downstairs area for the guests. There is a kitchenette, with refrigerator and microwave available. Gabriela also offers a freestanding 24-foot yurt with its own kitchen and hot outdoor shower. The rate is $60 (maximum four people), with a five-day minimum, (discount thereafter). The yurt can accommodate children, whereas the house is an adult-only atmosphere to ensure the serenity of the environment.

The **Royal Drive Cottages,** at 147 Royal Dr., Kapa'a, HI 96746, tel. (808) 822-2321, owned and operated by Bob Levine, are nestled in the mountains high above Kapa'a. Very private, the self-contained cottages are complete with kitchenettes; $75 d, with weekly discounts available.

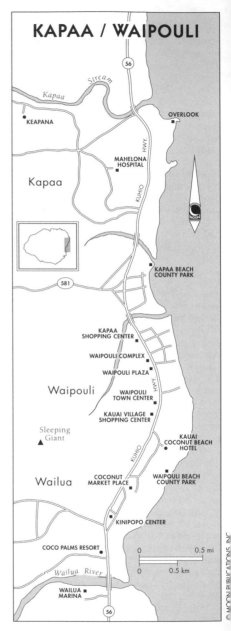

Moderate

Part of the Hawaiian-owned Sand and Seaside Hotels, **Kauai Sands** is a better-than-average budget hotel with a convenient location, spacious grounds, accommodating staff, large, relaxing lobby, budget restaurant, two pools, and beach access. All rooms have two double beds, a refrigerator, air conditioning, ceiling fans, TVs, telephones, and lanais. What the hotel lacks in luster it makes up in price. Daily rates range from $75 for a standard room to $135 for a junior suite. Excellent room and car packages are offered. For reservations, write Sand and Seaside Hotels, 2222 Kalakaua Ave., Suite 714, Honolulu, HI 96815, or call tel. (800) 367-7000. Located just behind the Coconut Market Place, at 420 Papaloa Rd., Wailua, HI 96746, tel. (808) 822-4951.

For a better-than-average hotel at moderate prices, you can't go wrong with the **Aston Kauai Beachboy Hotel,** located along the coastline at the Coconut Plantation, 4-484 Kuhio Hwy. #100, Kapa'a, HI 96746, tel. (808) 931-1400, (800) 922-7866 Mainland, or (800) 321-2558 Hawaii. Cool and quiet, the hotel surrounds a central courtyard and pool that is quite secluded from the main road, offering an oasis of peace and quiet. The oversize rooms, decorated in a pleasant Hawaiian style, offer separate dressing room and vanity areas, mini-fridges, double closets, coffeemakers, and safes. In the sleeping area you'll find a king-size bed, daybed, business desk, remote-control color TV, and louvered doors that open to a private lanai overlooking the ocean or into the central pool area. Rates are $98-138 d for a standard room, and $145-185 for a one bedroom with kitchen. The hotel also offers a poolside bar, open daily 11 a.m.-7 p.m., full-service bar, shuffleboard, volleyball, tennis facilities, laundry room, sundries store, and free daily scuba lessons for guests. The hotel's **Beach Boy Restaurant** offers breakfast, lunch, and dinner buffets at reasonable prices.

Between the Beachboy and the Kauai Sands is the **Islander on the Beach Hotel,** a bright white structure with a front veranda on all levels, giving it a Southern plantation look. The studio apartments have been changed into hotel rooms with wet bars, refrigerators, coffeemakers, color TVs, and lanais. Set right on the beach, the

hotel has a pool, a beach activities center, and a gift shop. Room rates are $95 for a standard to $185 for an oceanfront suite; add $10 during high season. Write Islander on the Beach, 484 Kuhio Hwy., Kapa'a, HI 96746, or call (808) 822-7417 or (800) 847-7417.

Kapa'a also has several condos in the moderate price range. The **Kapa'a Shore Condo** is along the main road just north of the Coconut Plantation, at 40-900 Kuhio Hwy., Kapa'a, HI 96746, tel. (808) 822-3055. These one- and two-condo units offer a swimming pool, heated jacuzzi, tennis courts, and maid service on request. All units are bright and cheerful, with full kitchens and dishwashers. One-bedroom garden-view units accommodate up to four for $110, one-bedroom oceanview units run $120, and two-bedroom oceanview units house up to six for $150. For reservations, call Kauai Vacation Rentals, tel. (808) 245-8841 or (800) 367-5025.

Other reasonably priced condominiums in the area include the **Kapa'a Sands,** with pool and maid service. The oldest condo on the island—since 1968—Kapa'a Sands is kept clean and up-to-date and has been completely refurbished since Hurricane Iniki. It is situated on old Japanese grounds that once were the site of a Shinto shrine. The Japanese motif is still reflected in the roofline of the units and the *torii* design above each door number. Each unit has a full kitchen, ceiling fans in all rooms, and a lanai. Two-bedroom units occupy two levels, and even the garden units have limited views of the ocean. Room rates are $75 for garden studios, $85 for oceanfront studios, $99 for two-bedroom garden units, and $109 for two-bedroom oceanfront units. Monthly rates are available; minimum stay is three days except during winter, when it is seven days. For reservations, write Kapa'a Sands, 380 Papaloa Rd., Kapa'a, HI 96746, or call (808) 822-4901 or (800) 222-4901.

The **Pono Kai,** at 1250 Kuhio Hwy., Kapa'a, HI 96746, is a step up in class, offering one-bedroom units at $109-135, and two bedrooms at $135-160. All units have full kitchens, color cable TVs, and lanais. For reservations, call Kauai Vacation Rentals, tel. (808) 245-8841 or (800) 367-5025.

The **Plantation Hale,** at 484 Kuhio Hwy., Kapa'a, HI 96746, tel. (808) 822-4911 or (800)

462-6262 on Kauai, is a condominium that also offers daily rates. It's across the street from Waipouli Beach County Park just beyond the Coconut Market Place. There are only one-bedroom units; however, each is like a small apartment with full kitchen, bath, dining room, and living area. Rates for up to four people are $105-120.

Expensive

Amidst a huge grove of swaying palms, encircling a central courtyard, sits the sand-colored, low-rise **Kauai Coconut Beach Hotel,** at P.O. Box 830, Coconut Plantation, Kapa'a, HI 96746, tel. (808) 822-3455 or (800) 222-5642. The palm grove once belonged to the family of the famous swimmer and actor Buster Crabbe, of *Buck Rogers* fame. He and his twin brother, Bud, were born and raised right here, and Buster learned to swim along this very coast. After entering the main lobby, turn around and look at the grove—a natural buffer offering peace and tranquillity—and notice the diminutive indoor coconut trees placed here and there, creating the illusion that the grove continues inside. The lobby is alive with trees, flowers, and vines trellised from the balconies. Wicker chairs, stained glass depicting a sailing canoe departing at sunset, and a 40-foot waterfall, reminiscent of the real thing at Hanakapi'ai add comfort and grandeur. A bas relief encircles the reception area, and as your eyes sweep from panel to panel it tells the story of how the Hawaiians became a "people," migrating originally from Indonesia until they found their fabled "homeland in the north." All rooms have a remote control color TVs, air conditioning, mini-fridges, safes, coffeemakers with complimentary Kona coffee, private lanais, and room service available from 7 a.m to 9:30 p.m. The pastel green walls are decorated with an original painting in a Hawaiian theme, and the headboards in the upgraded rooms are carved with palm tree motifs repeated in the armoires. Carpets are bluish-green, and bed quilts are bright with printed flowers and ferns. Large pedestal lamps light conversation nooks made comfortable with high-backed armchairs surrounding marble-topped tables. The junior suites (all fronting the ocean) are massive, and feature separate dressing nooks just off the baths, ceiling fans, and Victorian wicker *punees,* perfect to while away the afternoon reclining and sipping a refreshing mint julep. Rates are $95 for a standard room to $250 for a VIP suite, which includes a full buffet breakfast.

For your convenience, the hotel offers two full-service activity desks where you can arrange everything from helicopter rides to horseback riding, with concierge service taking care of all travel details. Wednesday evenings during whale watching season (late November through early May), a marine slide show comes to the Chart Room, a comfortable, quiet area hung with authentic maps and charts from the days of the tall ships. A lobby table is always reserved for local craftspeople, who offer their authentic handmade creations—anything from carvings to quilts. The hotel's three tennis courts, free to guests, are supervised by Coco, the onsite tennis pro. The hotel's Voyage Room/Flying Lobster is an indoor/outdoor restaurant featuring original artwork. Have a drink and listen to nightly entertainment at the Royal Coconut Grove Lounge, or try the hotel luau, one of the best on the island.

Colony Resorts manages two deluxe condos in and around the Coconut Plantation. A touch more classy than their Plantation Hale is the **Lae Nani,** offering one- and two-bedroom units on the beach. The rich decor varies by unit, but all have full kitchens, lanais, ceiling fans, and one and a half baths; most have ocean views. There is a laundry room, daily maid service, a swimming pool, tennis courts, and barbecue grills on the lawn. A small *heiau* is on the property beachside. One-bedroom units for up to four people are $150-179, and the two-bedroom units are $185-205, maximum six persons; rates are $20 cheaper during low season. The hotel is at 410 Papaloa Rd., Kapa'a, HI 96746. For reservations, call (808) 822-4938 or (800) 367-6046. The **Lanikai** is next door at 390 Papaloa Rd., tel. (808) 822-7456. Here there are only two-bedroom, two-bath units that rent for $200 a day, $20 cheaper during low season. For reservations, contact Colony Resorts, 32 Merchant St., Honolulu, HI 96813, tel. (800) 367-6046.

FOOD

From the Coconut Market Place to the north edge of Kapa'a, there are dozens of places to eat. The vast majority are either inexpensive diners or mid-priced restaurants, but there are one fine restaurant, several luau and buffets, the ubiquitous fast-food chains, and several bakeries, fruit stands, markets, and grocery stores.

Inexpensive Food in Shopping Malls
Surrounded by hotels and condos, the **Coconut Market Place** is the island's largest shopping center. In this huge complex are more than a dozen eateries.

For a quick, cool snack try **Lappert's** for ice cream, or **Rainbow Frozen Yogurt** for a more healthful snack, and for quick counter food try **The Fish Hut** or **Island Chicken**.

For more substantial food, check out **South of the Border**, a restaurant and cantina serving steak and Mexican food and even live music now and again, especially on weekends; **Tradewinds Bar**, tel. (808) 822-1621, open 10 p.m.-2 a.m., serving drinks and food and offering karaoke nightly; **Taco Dude**, receiving high praise from local people, is open for lunch and dinner and serves beef, chicken, or bean tacos for $1.75, tostadas for $2.25, burritos at $3.75-4.75, and taco salad for $4.75. A counter restaurant, it serves fresh food made to order at reasonable prices. Others include the **Banyan Tree Cafe** and **Aloha Kauai Pizza**. At **Don's Deli and Picnic Basket** you can get a large sandwich for $2.50-4.50, subs, or a picnic basket for your day on the beach or your trip to the north coast. **Auntie Sophie's Grill** serves burgers, hot dogs, and sandwiches, while **Harley's Ribs and Chicken** says it all with its name. For a cup of fine coffee and a selection of baked goods, try the **Cafe Espresso**. For your sweet tooth, step in to see what mouthwatering delicacies the **Rocky Mountain Chocolate Factory** and **Nut Cracker Sweet** shops have to offer, or go healthy with **Zack's Frozen Yogurt**.

A short way up the highway, *mauka* from the road, is the **Waipouli Town Center**, marked by **McDonald's** and **Pizza Hut**. Near the yogurt shop is **Waipouli Restaurant**, a favorite local eatery open daily 7 a.m.-7 p.m. except Monday, when it closes at 3 p.m. The daily breakfast special, served 7 a.m.- 11a.m., brings a pancake, two pieces of bacon, and eggs for $2.99. Or choose a menu item like papaya for $1.39, or omelettes with a choice of bacon, ham, Portuguese sausage, or Spam for $5.49. Sandwiches range from hamburgers to teriyaki beef and are all priced under $3. For a local treat, try the Kauai Super Saimin at $5.79, or miso saimin at $4.79. The lunch menu, mostly under $7, features shrimp tempura, beef broccoli, or a mixed plate of barbecued steak, fried chicken, and fried noodles. The best deals are the daily specials, priced at only $6.39, offering choices like fresh ono, chicken cutlet, and beef stew. The dinner menu ranges from $8.49 to $12.99 for a sirloin steak or shrimp tempura—the most expensive items listed. You can also order a rice bowl topped with anything from the menu for only $2.79. The Waipouli Restaurant is basic, friendly, and clean—and the prices can't be beat!

The Waipouli Town Center has one of the best moderately priced restaurants on the island, **The King and I**, tel. (808) 822-1642, open Sun.-Thurs. 4:30-9:30 p.m. and Friday and Saturday 4:30-10 p.m. This Thai restaurant serves wonderful food that will make your taste buds stand up and be counted. Most dinners are $5-8. Also in the center is the Chinese restaurant the **Dragon Inn**, which has a well-deserved reputation for filling meals at reasonable prices. There is a menu as long as your arm, and most dinners go for $5-7. Stop in for lunch Tues.-Sat. 11 a.m.-2 p.m., for an all-you-can-eat buffet at $6.95, and nightly for dinner 4:30-9:30 p.m.

Recently opened in the center is the **Lizard Lounge and Deli**, tel. (808) 821-2205, open 7 a.m.-1 a.m., and offering everything from a limited breakfast buffet, to deli sandwiches and pizza by the slice.

In the Waipouli Complex, another tiny mall along Kuhio, is the **Aloha Diner**, tel. (808) 822-3851. Open daily except Sunday 11:30 a.m.-3 p.m. and 5:30-9 p.m., this diner serves Hawaiian food. It offers a la carte selections like *kalua* pig, chicken luau, *lomi* salmon, rice and poi, *haupia,* and *kulolo.* Dinner specials run $5-6, with full dinners $7.50-9.50. Takeout is available. There is no atmosphere, the service is slow but friendly, and most people eating here are residents. Next door is the Japanese **Restaurant Shiroma,** which also serves Chinese standards. The daily lunch and dinner specials include items like shrimp tempura, pork tofu, teriyaki steak, or seafood combo. A money-saving lunch is a huge bowl of *wonton min* and a side of rice. And you must have a slice of the homemade pineapple or passion fruit chiffon pie for $1. Shiroma is open Fri.-Sun. 7 a.m.-9 p.m., and Monday, Wednesday, and Thursday 7 a.m.-2 p.m.; closed Tuesday.

For inexpensive plate lunches, try the **Barbeque House,** in the Kapa'a Shopping Center, open Mon.-Sat. 10:30 a.m.-8 p.m., where most selections are under $5.

Papaya's, a natural-food cafe and market, at the Kauai Village, 4-831 Kuhio Hwy., open daily except Sunday 9 a.m.-8 p.m., tel. (808) 823-0190, is not only the largest, but also the best natural-food store and cafe on Kauai. From the cafe section (outdoor tables available) come daily specials like vegan baked tofu over brown rice with green salad for $4.95, a tri-plate with your choice of three salads (one pound total) for $8.50, soup du jour $1.95-4.95 depending upon the size, and two-fisted sandwiches like veggie with cheese ($5.50), nutty burger ($6), or a good old-fashioned tempe burger for $5.50. Gourmet coffees, herbed teas, and fresh juices are also a specialty. Papaya's is famous for its hot entrees, including stuffed peppers, vegetarian lasagna, chicken enchiladas, spanakopita—a Greek dish with feta cheese and filo dough—and stuffed baked potatoes, all sold by the pound for about $4 and up; all can be packed to go. If you are into healthy organic food, there is no place better than Papaya's!

Inexpensive Eateries in and around Kapa'a

In Kapa'a, you'll find **Local's Fast Food,** open daily 6 a.m.-midnight, where you can get items like a "loco-moco"—hamburger, two fried eggs, brown gravy, and rice—for $3.49, hamburger steak plate lunch for $2.99, and a variety of topped hot dogs. The food isn't great, but the prices are right and it's not the typical fast-food styrofoam junk.

Almost next door is **Margarita's.** Billed as a "Mexican restaurant and watering hole," it's open daily from 4:00 p.m. for cocktails and from 5 p.m. for dinner.

Marilyn Monroe, skirt tossed by the Kauai breeze, and the big bow tie and bigger smile of owner and chief soda jerk Chris Erickson welcome you to **Beezers,** a vintage '50s soda fountain, open daily 11 a.m.-10 p.m., tel. (808) 822-4411, along Rt. 56 in downtown Kapa'a. Chris, a bartender for two decades, researched the soda-fountain idea for years before opening Beezers—and actually got his best idea after visiting Disneyland. He scoured Hawaii and then finally the Mainland before finding a real soda fountain. The floor of red, black, and white tiles leads to low stools facing a counter made from glass brick and featuring a light show inside that matches the tunes coming from a real jukebox in the corner. The ice cream served is Hawaii's own Lappert's—some of the best in the world. Besides standard cones, Beezers serves an old-fashioned banana split for $7.95, a Mustang Sally—a rich chocolate brownie with two scoops of creamy vanilla—for $6.25, and an American Bandstand deluxe—a decadent combination of white chocolate, macadamia nuts, Kona coffee, and chocolate ice cream all covered with hot fudge, hot butterscotch, and marshmallow toppings, whipped cream, chopped nuts, and a cherry—for $7.95. Chris also handmakes malts, shakes, and flavored Cokes, and serves brownie wedges, oatmeal molasses cookies, coffee, tea, lemonade, and juices. Beezers is the kind of place where if you're not smiling going in, you're definitely smiling coming out.

Look for yellow and white umbrellas shading a few picnic tables that mark **Bubba's,** at 1384 Kuhio Hwy., tel. (808) 823-0069, open Mon.-Sat. 10:30 a.m.-6 p.m. and sometimes on Sunday, where you can have a Bubba burger for $2.75 or a Big Bubba for $5 Other menu items include a "Slopper," an open-faced burger smothered in Bubba's famous Budweiser beer chili, for $4.50; a Hubba Bubba, a scoop of rice, hamburger, and grilled hot dog smothered in beer chili with diced onion for $5.50; or a simple order of fish and chips, chicken burger, or corn dog, all for under $4.50. Sides include French fries, onion rings, and "frings," a combo of both. On entering, you can try your hand at a coin toss, and if you manage to place your coin in the right slot, you win a soda, lunch, or a free T-shirt. Also, check out the community bulletin board to see what's happening and what's for sale in the Kapa'a area. Bubba's is a throwback to the days when a diner owner was also the short-order cook and all the burgers were handmade. Rock 'n' roll, grease, and Elvis lives, man! Enjoy!

Kapaa Bagelry and Espresso Bar, just near Bubba's at 1384 Kuhio Hwy., tel. (808) 823-6008, open Mon.-Fri. 7 a.m.-3 p.m. and Sat.-Sun. 7:30 a.m.-2:30 p.m., occupies an old bank building and, to keep up with the catch-your-eye local paint jobs, is bright orange. Here too, everything is handmade, but instead of old-fashioned burgers, the offerings are mostly organic and healthful. All sandwiches are served on hand-rolled bagels boiled in the traditional way. Choose one of the many flavors and then have a sandwich like the Napili, with green onion spread, cukes, tomato, and sprouts for $2.75; the Kilohana, a combo of hummus, olives, red onions, and sprouts for $2.95; or the Kalalau, with roast turkey, avocado, red onions, and sprouts for $3.75. Lighter appetites will enjoy a bagel (90 cents plain) covered with roasted red peppers for $1, smoked marlin for $1.25, or lomi lomi salmon for $1 25. You can also enjoy homemade soup like spring garlic and potato, and black bean chili over rice with sour cream, both including bread, for $3.75. Drinks from espresso to hot chocolate, priced $1.50-2.95, fresh organic juices priced $1.50-3.95, and even iced *chai* and tropical smoothies ($2.50) are offered. The Kapaa Bagelry is unpretentious, homey, healthful, and "culinarily correct," a welcome haven for yuppies and born-again-hippies. Peace, brotherhood, Birkenstocks, and Volvos forever!

Hana-Ya Sushi, in downtown Kapa'a, at 1394 Kuhio Hwy., tel. (808) 822-3878, open Mon.-Fri. 11:30 a.m.-2 p.m. for lunch and Mon.-Sat. 5:30-9:30 p.m. for dinner, is an authentic sushi bar owned by sushi chef Matomu Hanaya and serves up tasty tidbits and classic Japanese dishes. For lunch, try *oyaku donburi* or chicken katsu (each $5.95), or a 16-piece tray of as-sorted sushi for $8.55. Dinner prices are about $1 more for the fixed dishes, and $16.55 for a tray of 19 pieces of assorted sushi. Hanaya *san* has no liquor license, but it's okay to bring your own sake or beer. *Itadakemas!*

The Olympic Cafe, a fixture in Kapa'a for over half a century but torn up by Hurricane Iniki (then painted purple, perhaps to ward off the wrath of future "big wind goddesses" with the right vibes), is back in business at 1387 Kuhio Hwy., tel. (808) 822-5731, open daily 6 a.m.-2 p.m. for breakfast and lunch and 5-9 p.m. for dinner. This linoleum and formica restaurant fixes American, Japanese, and Hawaiian standards. Breakfasts of eggs, meats, rice, and potatoes are under $6, and lunches of chopped steak or breaded pork cutlets are under $7. Island favorites like saimin and pork soup are about $4.50, and the mahi plate is under $6.50. The dinner menu, priced $6.95-11.95, includes shrimp tempura, chicken or pork katsu, pork or chicken hecca, and the fresh catch of the day. A children's menu offers nothing priced over $5. Beer, wine, and cocktails are served. There's no atmosphere, but the service is friendly, the restaurant clean, and the food plentiful and good.

Sideout Bar and Grill, tel. (808) 822-0082, a neighborhood bar and restaurant in downtown Kapa'a, open daily 11 p.m.-1:30 a.m., offers inexpensive sandwiches, burgers, and light meals along with cold drafts, wine, liquor, and imported beer. Sideout patrons are a fun-filled potpourri of sunburned tourists, tattooed locals, and multi-earringed men and women of various sexual persuasions. The restaurant has a dining deck out back where you can enjoy local fare like meat loaf, pork adobo, fish cakes, and fresh catch when available. Prices for all are only around $7.

A diner with formica tables and a lunch counter, **T. Higashi Store** also caters mostly to local residents, tel. (808) 822-5982. Serving everyday Japanese food, it's open 6 a.m.-8 p.m.

Moderate

The **Ono Family Restaurant,** downtown Kapa'a, at 4-1292 Kuhio Hwy., open daily 7 a.m.-3 p.m., tel. (808) 822-1710, is cozy and functional, with nice touches like carpeted floors, ceiling fans, and even a chandelier. Creative breakfasts include eggs Canterbury, with turkey, tomatoes, and hollandaise sauce over poached eggs on an English muffin; pancakes; and a variety of omelettes like a Local Boy, which combines Portuguese sausage and kimchi. Lunch salads run about $4.50, and the Island's Best Burger is $5.50. You can't go wrong with a mushroom melt burger for $6.95, and from the broiler or grill try sirloin steak, barbecued ribs, or teri chicken. For those with a taste for the exotic, you can even get a real buffalo burger here, from American bison raised in Hanalei and Kansas. The daily fish special is always terrific and, depending upon the catch, goes for about $13.

If the moon hits your eye like a big pizza pie, go to **Rocco's Italian Restaurant** at the Pacific House Complex in downtown old Kapa'a across from the ABC store, tel. (808) 822-4422, open Mon.-Sat. 11 a.m.-4 p.m. for lunch and daily 5-10 p.m. for dinner. Enter to a valiant attempt at creating a homey Italian atmosphere— red and green curtains, Chianti bottles hanging from an open beamed ceiling, and a recessed bar separated from the downstairs dining area by a glass brick wall. Upstairs, you'll find a more intimate seating area where you can look over a balcony railing festooned with artificial grapes and garlic bunches to the flagstone floor below. Lunch specials are Caesar salads with shrimp, fresh fish, or chicken, priced from $7.95 to 9.95, as well as soups like minestrone or onion for around $3.50 and sandwiches, including Sofia's Garden Sub at $6.50, or Cynthia's Chicken Parmesan Sub, at $7.95. Pizza by the slice goes for $2.50 and up, depending on toppings. Or choose lasagna at $7.95 or ravioli at $6.95. The dinner menu starts with sautéed mushrooms for $5, white pizza for $6, or their ravedabout sautéed garlic shrimp at $9.95. Pastas offered include linguine, manicotti, and cannelloni, ranging from $8.95 to $12.95, while entrees of eggplant, chicken, or pork parmigiana go from $11.95 to $12.95, and a specialty of chicken "franchisee" (like marsala) is $12.95. For snacks to go with a beer or a glass of wine from the full-service bar, order garlic bread with ricotta cheese for $7.50, or meatballs with marinara sauce for $3.50. Satisfy your sweet tooth with New York cheesecake or tiramisu, priced $2.25-4.00. Rocco's food is better than average, and the atmosphere is friendly, with the strong appeal of a cozy neighborhood ristorante.

Look for the blue and white awning on the left as you're leaving Kapa'a heading north. It marks **Charlie's Place,** tel. (808) 822-3955, open for breakfast Tues.-Sun. 7:30-11:30 a.m., for lunch Tues.-Fri. 11:30 a.m.-3 p.m., and for dinner Tues.-Sat. 6-10 p.m. (they plan to have dinner on Sunday nights as well, so check). The bar is open Tues.-Sat until midnight or so, with happy hour 3-6 p.m., during which well drinks are $2 and draft Steinlager is $1.50. Charlie's hops with live music from local bands, and features changing themes like "songwriters round" on Tuesday, female country rock Wednesday, folk rock Thursday, rock and roll on Friday, and Saturday-night potpourri. Charlie's is an indoor/outdoor restaurant/bar right across the street from Kapa'a Beach Park. They have a lanai, where you can catch the breeze, and inside are hanging plants, blue tables, and an old piano in the corner. The breakfast menu at Charlie's Place includes eggs with bacon or ham and sausage for $5.25, eggs Benedict for $7.50, omelettes $4.50-5.95, and waffles $2.95-3.95. Lunch brings a tropical seafood burrito for $8.95, fish and chips for $7.95, barbecued ribs for $7.95, a full range of burgers from $5, a garden vegetarian sandwich at $6.95, and a small children's menu. For dinner choose Cajun-style fresh catch—the house specialty—at $13.95, tropical seafood plate or ginger chicken for $11.95, teriyaki chicken for $10.95, or a vegetarian platter for $10.95. Charlie's is a good-time local bar with a mixed clientele where you can have a toe-tapping evening or a quiet beer and a chat.

When you don't want to fool around deciding where to get a good meal, head for the north end of Kapa'a and the local favorite, **Kountry Kitchen.** Open daily 6 a.m.-9 p.m., the tables are usually packed with regulars during peak dining hours. Breakfasts are full meals of hefty omelettes for $3-4 or the Hungryman Special, for over $6. Lunches range $4-6, and full dinners of country ribs, sesame shrimp, or baked ham served with soup, bread, potatoes or rice, and veggies are $7-9. The food is tasty, the service prompt and friendly, and the portions large. The Kountry Kitchen is at 1485 Kuhio Hwy., tel. (808) 822-3511.

Nearby is the **Makai Restaurant,** tel. (808) 822-3955, which serves Hawaiian, Mediterranean, and continental food. Try their fish and chips, gyros, or moussaka (you can get it to go). The open windows let in the breeze and morning sunlight but, as the place is close to the road, they also let in the sounds of passing cars.

Norberto's El Cafe, at the intersection of Kukui St. and Rt. 56 in downtown Kapa'a, tel. (808) 822-3362; open daily 5:50-9:00 p.m., is a family-run Mexican restaurant. Then what's it doing on a side street on a Pacific Island, you ask? Hey, gringo, don't look a gift burro in the face! They serve nutritious, delicious, wholesome food, and they cater to vegetarians—all dishes are prepared without lard or animal fats. The smell of food wafting out of the front door around dinnertime is its best advertisement. They serve the best Mexican food on the island. Full-course meals of burritos, enchiladas, and tostadas are $11.50-12.95, children's plates are $6.95, and a la carte dishes are $2.95-6.95. The best deals are the chef's specials of *burrito el cafe,* Mexican salad, and chiles rellenos, all for under $7, or fajitas for $13.95. Other entrees are rellenos tampico, chimichangas, tacos, and quesadillas. Dinners are served with soup, beans, and rice; chips and salsa are complimentary. There's beer on tap, or if you really want to head south of the border (by way of sliding under the table), try a pitcher of margaritas. If you have room after stuffing yourself like a chimichanga, try a delicious chocolate-cream pie or homemade rum cake. The cafe is extremely popular with local folks and tables fill as soon as they're empty.

At the Coconut Market Place is **Buzz's Steak and Lobster** restaurant, tel. (808) 922-7491, open for lunch 11 a.m.-3 p.m., *pu pu* and happy hour 3-5 p.m., and dinner 5-10:30 p.m. They offer an early-bird special 5-6:30 p.m. with your choice of teriyaki chicken, ground sirloin, or fried island fish, for $7.95. Buzz's started serving steaks and seafood in Waikiki in 1957 and, with its signature restaurant still open on Oahu, continues to do the same. You enter through large *koa* doors into a subdued interior rich with more *koa* and highlighted by lava rock. An open kitchen presides over a comfortable dining area with high-backed wicker chairs, while palm fronds and a hanging canoe add a Polynesian flair. Take time to notice the collection of artifacts, paintings, basketry, lei, and antiques gathered from Tahiti and the islands of the South Pacific. Word on the street says the salad bar here is the best. For lunch, Buzz's offers soup of the day at $2.95, tuna and avocado salad at $6.95, a tuna salad sandwich for $4.95, and a mahi mahi burger for $6.50. Desserts include New York-style cheesecake and homemade ice-cream pie, both priced at $3.95. Appetizers, served at both lunch and dinner, include calamari at $5.95, deep-fried zucchini and teriyaki beef sticks both priced at $4.50. Dinner entrees are ground sirloin for $8.95, various steaks priced $12.95-17.95, prime rib (Fri.-Sat. only) at $17.95, golden fried chicken for $10.95, and baby-back pork ribs for $14.95. Seafood offered is lobster tail (daily quote), oven-broiled mahi for $11.95, fish and fries for $8.95, and various fresh catch at market price. As an added benefit, you can sit at the bar after dinner and listen to nightly entertainment 9 p.m.-midnight.

The **Jolly Roger Restaurant,** open 6 p.m.-2 a.m., claims to have the longest happy hour on the island—6:30 a.m.-7 p.m. They're not known for exceptional food, but you always get hearty, substantial portions no matter what time of day you come to dine. A breakfast special brings pancakes, eggs, and bacon for $3.99, while a steak and shrimp dinner special is $7.99. Evening entertainment features a lively karaoke bar. You can find Jolly Roger behind the Coconut Market Place Shopping Center, near the Islander on the Beach Hotel, tel. (808) 822-3451.

Al and Don's Restaurant, in the Kauai Sands Hotel, is open daily 7 a.m.-8 p.m., tel. (808) 822-4221. The service and food are good but not memorable. However, the view from the spacious booths overlooking the seacoast is magnificent. Prices are reasonable for their numerous dinner and breakfast selections. Perhaps this is the problem: though you don't get the bum's rush, the place feels like one of those feeding troughs in Waikiki that caters to everyone and pleases no one. However, you can't complain about the large portions; breakfast is $3.85 for all-you-can-eat hotcakes, one egg, grilled ham, and coffee. And you won't be disappointed with their build-your-own omelette. Most breakfasts are under $4, and there are plenty of evening specials, with most dinners under $10. Dinner includes soup and salad bar with adequate entree choices like *ahi,* swordfish, top sirloin, and chicken exotica. The bar serves good drinks for reasonable prices. When you leave Al and Don's, you won't feel like complaining, but you won't rush back either.

The **Bull Shed** is known for prime rib; its chicken and seafood dishes are also praised ($9.95-18.95). The wine list is better than average and includes Domaine Chandon champagne ($22.95). Insiders go for the extensive salad bar for only $6.95—but be forewarned: the pickings get all jumbled together as the night goes on, and the salad bar peaks out by 7:30. The Bull Shed is open for cocktails and dinner daily 5:30-10 p.m. at 796 Kuhio Hwy., down the little lane that is across from McDonald's, tel. (808) 822-3791.

Diners at **Noe's,** in the Kauai Village Shopping Center, tel. (808) 821-0110, open daily for lunch 11 a.m.- 5 p.m., for dinner 5 p.m.-10:30 p.m., and for happy hour 4-6 p.m., get plenty of hands-on attention from owner Linda Chong. Appetizers begin at $4.95 and include mozzarella sticks, quesadilla rolls, breaded dill pickles, and standards like wing dings or onion rings at $6.95. The lunch menu continues with Cobb salad at $8.95, fish and chips for $7.95, steak sandwich for $9.95, burgers made your way from $5.95, or a bacon cheeseburger for $6.50. Well priced dinner specials include stir-fry local-style beef, chicken, or shrimp for $12.95, scampi at $14.95, and mahi magic for $12.95. A house specialty is *shri island pie,* made with Oreos and Kona coffee ice cream, all covered with fudge for $3.50. Noe's interior is island casual with a touch of Dublin and sports a long bar with green stools, and booths or tables with bamboo captains' chairs. A huge hammerhead shark leers beady-eyed from the wall, somewhat like a "hammered" tourist leering at the bikini babes.

Walk the gangplank to enter the **Kapa'a Fish and Chowder House,** in a two-tone blue building on Kapa'a's north end, tel. (808) 822-7488, offering a happy hour daily 4-6 p.m. and dinner from 5:30 p.m. Tastefully appointed, the interior of this comfortably casual restaurant is nautical, featuring a ship's wheel, hanging nets, and ocean-blue carpet. Start with steamed clams (market price), Pacific shrimp cocktail at $7.95, a pot of clam or fish chowder at $4, or a Caesar salad for $6.95. Seafood selections are coconut shrimp, Alaska snow crab clusters, charbroiled lobster tails, or tiger prawns priced $14.95-18.95.

Landlubbers can order New York strip steak at $19.95, ginger chicken for $10.95, or New York pepper steak for $20.95, along with multiple combination plates for around $21.95. A selection of pasta dishes like calamari sauté or shrimp scampi is $14.95-15.95. The full bar serves wine, beer, and exotic drinks and offers a special every night. The Kapa'a Fish and Chowder House is a decent restaurant, with good value for the money.

Fine Dining

Master chef Jean-Marie Josselin knows a good thing when he sees it and, moreover, knows how to prepare it exquisitely. You can enjoy his excellent food at the **Pacific Cafe,** at the Kauai Village, 4-831 Kuhio Hwy., tel. (808) 822-0013, open 5:30-10 p.m. Although it's in a shopping center, the Pacific Cafe creates a casually elegant atmosphere appointed with a cove and molded ceiling, ferns and flowers placed here and there, bamboo chairs, and an open kitchen so that you can witness the food preparation. Appetizers range from $7.25 to $9.75 and include such delicacies as deep-fried tiger-eye sushi with wasabi ($9.75) or *beurre blanc* pan-fried shrimp or salmon with sweet Thai pepper sauce for $8.25. Soups and salads are mouth-watering; a special Thai coconut curry basil soup with fresh island fish and shrimp is $5.75, seared spicy ahi salad with Kauai, romaine, and Caesar dressing is $7.45. Order from the woodburning grill—you can't go wrong! Try grilled ahi marinated in coriander, fennel seeds, white truffle mashed potatoes, and peppercorn sauce for $22.95, or the grilled rack of lamb—Hunan style—with dried cherry port sauce for $24. Specialties of the Pacific Cafe include wok-charred mahimahi with garlic sesame crust and lime ginger sauce for $24, or herb crust of opakapaka with black rice and basil, and coconut chardonnay vinaigrette for $22.50. The Pacific Cafe is an excellent restaurant with the perfect mixture of fine food, fine service, and superb presentation; by far the best that the area has to offer.

Luau and Buffet

The **Voyage Room,** at the Kauai Coconut Beach Hotel, offers a sumptuous breakfast buffet including vegetarian and health-conscious fare like fresh fruit, yogurt, and cereal along with the traditional breakfast fixings of sausage, home-fried potatoes, eggs, and a good assortment of croissants and pastries. An excellent way to save money is to choose from the hotel's dining plans: one includes breakfast, another includes both breakfast and dinner.

In the evenings, the Voyage Room transforms into **The Flying Lobster.** The surf-and-turf oriented menu begins with *pu pu* such as jumbo shrimp cocktail for $7.50, sashimi at market price, or deep-fried wonton for $3.75. Seafood lovers will enjoy featured entrees like the spiny lobster dinner—one tail for $19.75, or a 10-ounce dinner for $23.95—or choose a filling combination like lobster and mahi for $22.50, and top sirloin teriyaki steak and lobster for $25.50. From the broiler, you can dine on New York steak at $19.75, or try a Hawaiian Luau sampler—a trio of *imu* baked pork, teriyaki beef, and *mahi* served with *lomi* salmon and *poi* for $16.25. Other selections include the fresh catch of the day, which can be broiled, sautéed with lemon butter, or stuffed with crab and priced $17.50-20, or try Chinese-style shrimp and scallops—a true delight for $22.50. For lighter appetites and the budget conscious, choose from a selection of pastas that include Italian sausage and fettucini at $11.25 and shrimp and sausage over fettucine for $14.15. Salads and sandwiches include a lobster bisque and salad bar for $9.75 and a seafood salad sandwich for $9.50. Top off your meal with a scrumptious dessert like Coconut Beach sand pie, a trio of coffee, chocolate, and vanilla ice creams for $3.75, or a real island special such as "tutu's" banana treat—bananas flambéed in brown sugar and butter, and topped with a blend of fine liqueurs over vanilla ice cream for $3.75. Follow the example of the locals who come to the Flying Lobster on Friday and Saturday evenings from 5:30-9:30 p.m. for the seafood and prime-rib buffet—lobster, crab, shrimp, oysters, prime rib, and fresh fish cooked to order before your very eyes. Prices are extremely reasonable at $19.95 adults, $10.95 children ages 6-10, and free for little ones under five. Sunday evenings bring the prime rib *paniolo* barbecue buffet, a Hawaiian cowboy cookout, also priced at $19.95. Make reservations at tel. (808) 822-3455; they're recommended because both are very popular with local people, who know quality and a fantastic price when they see them.

The real treat is the **Kauai Coconut Beach Hotel Luau,** which everyone agrees is one of the best on the island. It's held every night in the special luau *halau* under a canopy of stars and palm trees. The luau master starts the *imu* every morning; stop by and watch. He lays the hot stones and banana stalks so well that the underground oven maintains a perfect 400°. In one glance, the luau master can gauge the weight and fat content of a succulent porker and decide just how long it should be cooked. The water in the leaves covering the pig steams and roasts the meat so that it falls off the fork. Local wisdom has it that "All you can't eat in the *imu* are the hot stones." The dining begins at 7 p.m., with cocktails ongoing until 8 p.m., when the show begins. Tables are laden with pork, chicken, Oriental beef, salmon, fish, exotic fruits, salads, coconut cake, and *haupia*. Afterwards, you lean back and watch authentic Hawaiian hula and entertainment choreographed by Kawaikapookalawai (a.k.a. Frank Hewett). The enthusiastic entertainment is a combination of *kahiko* (ancient hula) and *awana* (modern hula), performed by an accomplished troupe of both men and women. Most numbers are *kahiko*—dignified, refined and low-keyed portrayals of the tales and myths of ancient Hawaii. Intermixed are a few *awana* numbers, startling, colorful, and reminiscent of the days when Elvis was still the gyrating king of *Blue Hawaii.* Prices are $49 adults, half-price for children under 12, discounts available for seniors, and Tuesday and Saturday family nights, on which one child is admitted free; reservations suggested, tel. (808) 822-3455.

On a day that you can eat a lot, want to try a little bit of everything, and don't want to bust your wallet, stop in at the **Beach Boy Restaurant,** at the Aston Kauai Beachboy Hotel, in Kapa'a, tel. (808) 822-7163, which offers an extremely economical and well presented buffet, open daily for breakfast ($6.95) 6:30-10 a.m., lunch ($7.95) 11 a.m.-1:30 p.m., and dinner ($11.95) 5-9 p.m., with discounts offered for seniors and children. Breakfast is a full array of eggs, meats, coffee, croissants, toast, and fresh fruit, while lunch consists of platters of roasted chicken with Cajun spice, baked mahi, beef stew, and a complete salad bar including cakes, fresh fruits, and various desserts. Dinner changes its theme every day with dishes from Japan, the Philippines, China, Hawaii, and typical American standards including main courses like roast turkey, baked mahi with wasabi glaze, kailua pork and cabbage, an assortment of pasta and sauces, and, again, the full salad bar. The room itself is large but not impersonal, with floor-to-ceiling windows open to the courtyard of the hotel. The food is good quality, well presented, and you certainly get your money's worth.

OTHER PRACTICALITIES

ENTERTAINMENT

The night scene in Kapa'a isn't very extensive, but there is enough to satisfy everyone.

The **Jolly Roger Restaurant** at the Coconut Market Place offers karaoke nightly. You can listen, sing, and even dance nightly 9 p.m.-1:30 a.m. The atmosphere is casual, the talk friendly. A good watering hole, where you can find cool drinks and good conversation, is the **Tradewinds Bar,** also at the Coconut Market Place. **South of the Border,** a Mexican cantina in the same center, sometimes has live music (especially on weekends). Nearby, **Buzz's** also has nightly entertainment—usually a small band playing contemporary, original, and country-and-western music. You can sit at the bar and enjoy the casual Polynesian setting.

The Coconut Market Place also hosts a free **Polynesian Hula Show** Monday, Wednesday, Friday, and Saturday at 5 p.m. The young local dancers and musicians put as much effort into their routines as if this were the big time. (Be forewarned that local sneak thieves rifle cars in the parking lot, knowing that their owners are occupied watching the show.) The shopping center also has something to offer moviegoers: the **Plantation Cinema 1 and 2.**

The **Kauai Coconut Beach Hotel** offers a little of everything. You can enjoy free *pu pu* and entertainment at Royal Coconut Grove Lounge, just off the gardens and pool deck—happy hour is 4-6 p.m. Every evening form 8 to 11 p.m., listen to pop, contemporary, and standard hits by local musicians. The dinner show in the Paddle Room presents a full performance of Hawaiian dance and music. Swing, rock, and Hawaiian music, as well as hula of the Polynesian Show, also accompany the luau.

Margarita's, along the Kuhio Hwy., just near the Waipouli Shopping Center, jams with live entertainment on the weekends.

SHOPPING

Kapa'a teems with shopping opportunities. Lining Kuhio Highway are a major shopping mall—the Coconut Market Place—and several other smaller shopping plazas. All your needs are met by a variety of food stores, health stores, drugstores, a farmers' market, fish vendors, and some extraordinary shops and boutiques tucked away here and there. You can easily find photo supplies, sporting equipment, "treasures," and inexpensive lei to brighten your day. Like dealing with the sun in Hawaii, enjoy yourself but don't overdo it.

The Coconut Market Place

Prices at this cluster of over 70 shops, restaurants, galleries, and movie theaters are kept down because of the natural competition of so many shops, each of which tries to specialize, which usually means good choices for what strikes your fancy. As you walk around, notice the blown-up photos that give you a glimpse into old Hawaii. **Ye Old Ship Store** displays the best collection of scrimshaw on Kauai and some sea paintings by local artists. Any of the jewelry shops has enough stock on hand to drop even Mr. T to his knees. With so many apparel and footwear shops, the job of finding just the right aloha shirt, muumuu, or sports clothing shouldn't be a problem. **Pottery Tree** overflows with everything from junk to fine pieces. Select from stained-glass chandeliers, I Love Hawaii mugs, and cheap yet nice shell mobiles. **Kauai Gold Limited** sells scrimshaw and Niihau shells, while **Kauai Vision Kites** allows you to fly with the breezes over the island, and the **Ship Store Gallery** sets sail for adventure with nautical artwork of tall-masted ships and contemporary Japanese art in a gallery that'a filled with cannons, pistols, and swords.

If the price of original artwork puts too much of a strain on your budget, then **Island Images,** offering fine art prints and posters, might have what you need at an affordable price. Island Images, open daily 9 a.m.-5 p.m., tel. (808) 822-3636, offers posters for around $30, with framing and shipping available, and a smattering of original artwork at discounted prices.

Some other specialty shops include **Pure Hawaiian,** with *tapa* cloth, drums, koa bowls, straw hats, muumuu, and casual dresses; **Golden Nugget,** for fine jewelry; **Kii Hale,** selling dolls from around the world but specializing in Hawaiian dolls; **Coconut Coast,** for women's and children's casual wear; **Island Surf Shop,** where you can purchase a boogie board, travel bag, a pareo, beach hat, and T-shirts; if yours becomes one of the sunburned bodies, you might be interested in the **Aloe Connection; Russian Treasures** is filled with Russian dolls; and **Collectors Corner** sells shells; mailboxes shaped like mermaids, cats, and cockatoos; aloha shirts, and Hawaiian dolls.

If your heart desires Hawaiian delicacies like Kona coffee, Maui onion mustard, macadamia nuts, island candy, Kauai Kookies, Kukui jams and jellies, or whatever else, head for **The Nut Cracker Sweet** and just see if you can pull yourself away. For the ordinary purchase, head for **Whaler's General Store. Fox One-Hour Photo** will develop film, and the **Kauai Visitors Center** can give you information about things to see, places to go, and adventures to explore.

Kauai Village

Built around a theme of an 18th-century Main Street, this very modern, very large, and very diverse shopping center, one of the newest and best that Kauai has to offer, complete with its own museum, is at 4-831 Kuhio Hwy. It contains a **Safeway** supermarket, open 24 hours; **Longs Drugs,** open Mon.-Sat. 8 a.m.-9 p.m. and Sunday until 6 p.m., a complete variety store with photo equipment and a pharmacy; an **ABC** store, for everything from suntan lotion to beach mats; a **Waldenbooks,** tel. (808) 822-7749, open Mon.-Sat. 9 a.m.-8 p.m. and Sunday 9 a.m.-5 p.m., well stocked with everything from Hawaiiana to travel; a cluster of fastfood restaurants and small, inexpensive eateries; also located here are **Papaya's,** the island's best natural health-food store, and the **Pacific Cafe,** a fantastic restaurant featuring Pacific Island cuisine prepared by master chef Jean-Marie Josselin. Other stores are **Mango's for Men,** featuring gentlemen's alohawear; **Sunglass Hut,** where you can buy all kinds of sunglasses; a **Kahn Gallery,** resplendent with some of the finest artworks in Hawaii; and the always good **Crazy Shirts.**

Kapa'a Shopping Center

Marked by a **Shell** station and a **Burger King** at 4-1105 Kuhio Hwy., is this bite-size, functional shopping center. Here, you'll find a **Big Save Market,** a well-stocked food store, open daily 7 a.m.-10 p.m.; **Clic Photo,** for inexpensive film and fast developing; **Kapa'a Bakery,** filled with goodies; **Kapa'a Laundry,** for do-it-yourselfers; **Kapa'a Sports Center** with all kinds of sporting goods; and **Kauai Video.** Also in this shopping

courtyard of the Coconut Market Place

center are the Kapa'a clinic of the **Kauai Medical Group,** a full-service **post office,** an inexpensive restaurant or two, and **Mail Boxes Kauai** for mailboxes, faxes, and mailings of all sorts.

Small Shopping Malls

Across the highway from another Shell station, in the **Waipouli Complex,** is Popo's Cookies. Closed Mon.-Wed., it is open Thurs.-Fri. 8 a.m.-5 p.m., Saturday until 3 p.m., and Sunday until 2 p.m. Nearby, in the **Waipouli Plaza,** are several clothing shops and a seashell merchant who sells retail and wholesale. Farther down the road, in the **Waipouli Town Center,** you'll find **Foodland,** open 5a.m.-midnight; **Fun Factory** arcade for games; **Blockbuster Video,** for home/condo entertainment; and **JM's** jewelry store.

Boutiques and Souvenirs

Right next door to Ambrose's Kapuna Natural Foods and across from Foodland is **Marta's Boat,** open Mon.-Sat. 10:30 a.m.-6 p.m., tel. (808) 822-3926. Primarily a children's boutique, the overflowing shelves also hold handmade quilts by local ladies, T-shirts, shorts, casual wear, elegant evening wear, and beautiful lingerie. A rack of games and educational items will help to keep the little ones happy on a return plane voyage or during an evening in the condo.

Follow the reggae beat and your dancing feet to **Jamaican Style,** in the Waipouli Town Center, open daily noon- 9 p.m., tel. (808) 823-6100, owned and operated by Jimmy Dread. Racks hold Jamaican Style's own brand of 100% cotton, preshrunk T-shirts and the island's largest selection of junior bikinis. The wall is filled with CDs and tapes of reggae music from Alpha Blonde to Ziggy Marley.

Ye Old Ship Store, located in the Coconut Market Place, and distinguished as the center's oldest retail store, is the premier shop on Kauai for scrimshaw. The shelves are filled with collectors' pieces and museum-quality artwork scrimmed from fossilized walrus, mammoth, and mastodon ivories which have been worked by extremely talented contemporary artists. Every February, Ye Old Ship Store sponsors the **Hawaii International Scrimshaw Competition,** drawing competitors from throughout the U.S. and Canada. Pieces created by these master *scrimshanders* are like any other original works

of art, carrying price tags up to $10,000 and beyond. Some of the top scrimshanders on display are Jerry DuPont who won the top color nautical category; Ray Peters from Hawaii, winner of the black and white category; Kelly Mulford, a fine artist who took top honors in color whale, and Best of Hawaii category; Anna Good, winner of the Niihau Award for most unique in the open category with her rendering of a geisha at a tea ceremony; and the phenomenal Jesus Arick, who captured the drama and pathos of the Greek hero Prometheus. Cases hold other items, not just scrimshaw, in a wide variety of price ranges—Hawaiian fishhooks made from wild pig bone by local hunters ($66); copies of fishhooks from the Philippines ($20); turtles, whale tails, and money clips priced $9.95-75. Another local artist on display is Curt Danette, who specializes in *tiki* fashioned in the traditional way, from native woods like milo, koa, and even the very scarce sandalwood. Ye Old Ship Store has other interesting items that will delight the entire family. If scrimmed knives, letter openers, and fine jewelry isn't enough, look for the distinctive "Spirit of Aloha Kauai Bottle," made from Kauai's land, sea, and air, and each blessed with a Hawaiian prayer, or for an extremely accurate Hawaiian Islands map T-shirt depicting Hawaii during the times of first contact, made more fancy with a border of ancient Hawaiian tattooing. Ye Old Ship Store is a perfect stop to make a purchase that says "Hawaii," or just to have a close-up look at a very intriguing artform.

Remember Kauai, 4-734 Kuhio Hwy., open daily 9:30a.m.-5:30 p.m., tel. (808) 822-0161, just past the Kauai Coconut Beach Hotel, specializes in unique Hawaiian jewelry, like necklaces made from shells, beads, wood, and gold. The counters shine with belt buckles, pins, and a large collection of gemstones from around the world. Niihau shellwork is available, and fine specimens run up to $12,000. The scrimshaw, worked by Kauai artists on fossilized walrus ivory, adds rich texture to everything from knives to paperweights. Any place like this, with a rainbow painted on its roof, is worth a look.

Cathy and Karlos travel to Indonesia where they purchase the magnificent fabrics they design of 100% cotton or rayon for exclusive clothing to bring back to their shop **Bokumarue,** at 1388 Kuhio Hwy., Kapa'a, HI 96746, tel. (808)

822-1766, open 10 a.m.-6 p.m. They have taken on a new partner, Zayda, who helps with the designs and in the retail shop. Cathy, who has been in the garment design business for over 20 years, offers affordable yet classy garments that include casual dresses, lace dresses, and is-land-style shirts. Karlos specializes in pareo and sarongs all of which are either handstamped or handpainted, and boasts the largest and best-priced selection on Kauai. Kathy also offers a personal line of lotions, potions, and bath gels called **Body Paradise Kauai.** She blends and bottles over 25 different essential oils on the premises from which to choose and create your own distinctive scent. Other items include *ikat* blankets (a real deal at $20), temple carvings, and gaily painted masks, angels, and winged creatures priced $30-50. There is even some amazing primitive basketry from Borneo, and handpainted 100% cotton quilts from Indone-sia for $175. Bokumarue, although not typically Hawaiian, is a real find!

Earth Beads, owned by Angelika Riskin, just a step from Bokumarue, tel. (808) 822-0766, open daily except Sun. 10 a.m.-6 p.m., special-izes in beads and imported items from India, Africa, and South America. Shimmering in the tiny shop are earrings, belts, incidental bags, and sterling silver jewelry from Thailand, as well as locally made designs. A smattering of primi-tive basketry, incense, perfumed oils, T-shirts, "jungle" umbrellas and very unusual greeting cards complete the stock of this great little shop.

Walk into the **Island Hemp and Cotton Com-pany,** tel. (808) 821-0225, open Mon.-Sat.10 a.m.- 6 p.m., and suddenly you're in Asia. Stride across the reed mat floor while the soulful eyes of a Buddha sitting serenely atop a glass counter follow you in. Across from the ABC store in downtown Kapa'a, the shop is owned and op-erated by Nancee McTernan, a long distance traveler and "old Asia hand" who has personal-ly chosen every item in the store. Some spe-cial items include: tall drums made by Sage Adamson, a local artisan who sold one of his creations to Mickey Hart of Grateful Dead fame; Buddhas from Borneo; baskets from Bali; purs-es from Southeast Asia; carved bone necklaces from New Zealand; local puka shell jewelry; Ni-ihau shellwork; and antique wood carvings from all parts of Indonesia. The clothing, all made from organic cotton, hemp, and linen, is ma-chine washable and requires no ironing. Items include everything from casual shirts to elegant dresses ranging in price from $34 to $150. If you are after a truly distinctive gift, one-of-a-kind clothing, or an original artifact, you can't do better than visiting Nancee at Island Hemp and Cotton Company.

Far Fetched Designs, in downtown Kapaa across from the Olympic Cafe, open daily 10 a.m.- 6 p.m., tel. (808) 823-8235, sells art, curios, curiosities, and bric-a-brac from around the world. The jam-packed shop offers clocks bear-ing angels, rabbits, and mythical paintings; carved furniture from Indonesia; babushka dolls from Russia; glassware, kaleidoscopes, and island jewelry. There's a smattering of postcards and a good selection of local art by Kimberlin Blackburn, who works on handmade paper with pastels to create stylized seascapes and land-scapes; Terri Scarborough, who employs pig-ments from local plants, roots, and fibers to dye her paper, which is then laid down in a silkscreen fashion to create Hawaii's flora, fauna, and water-falls; and Sally French, who works in reverse acrylic on glass.

Kamaaina Clothing and Vintage Prints, lo-cated next to Beezers in downtown Kapa'a, open daily 9 a.m.- 6 p.m., tel. (808) 822-0916, sells T-shirts with distinctive turn-of-the-century travel poster prints, "red dirt" T-shirts, and actu-al prints (framed in koa, if you like).

Look for **M. Miura Store,** at the north end of Kapa'a, mountain side, open Mon.-Sat. 9 a.m.- 5 p.m. Local people shop at this dry goods store for alohawear, T-shirts, caps, men's and wom-en's shorts, and a good selection of bikinis.

As shiny and glittering as the sunbeams pour-ing through the windows, **Kela'a Glass Gallery,** in the Hefat Market Place, at 4-1354 Kuhio Hwy, Kapa'a, HI 96746, tel. (808) 822-4527, owned and operated by Larry Barton, is a showcase for over 60 contemporary artists working in glass. A few of the more famous are Daniel Lotton, Cohn-Stone, Bruce Freund, Bob Eickholt, and Steve Schlanser. The gallery features every-thing from classic vases to free-form sculptures ranging in price from $10-2000. Kela's also sells and ships (disassembled but with pieces num-bered for easy re-assembly) wooden flowers that are hand-carved and hand-painted in Indonesia. There are 30 different flowers represented including hibiscus, irises, calla lilies, various ginger, and heliconia. Prices range between $8 and $45, with the bulk priced $12 to $25.

If you are an aficionado of old Hawaii, make sure to drop into the **Tin Can Mailman,** at 4-1353 Kuhio Ave., downtown Kapa'a, tel. (808) 822-3009, open daily except Sun. 10 a.m-5:30 p.m. The Tin Can Mailman has definitely found a heart for out-of-print books on Hawaii and Polynesia, battered travel guides filled with memories, antique maps, vintage menus, early botanical prints, rare Missionary items, and even new books. The shop is small, jam-packed, and bursting with ancient voices still quietly singing their songs.

The **Roxy Swap Meet,** held every Saturday and during the week (days to be announced), tel. (808) 822-7027, is in the middle of Kapa'a with tables set up under numerous tents. People from all over come to barter and sell everything and anything.

Photo Needs

Across from Remember Kauai is **Cameralab,** tel. (808) 822-7338, for all your photofinishing needs. In downtown Kapa'a, **Pono Studio** also develops film, carries photographic equipment, and has a studio for portraits. At the Coconut Market Place, **Fox One-Hour Photo** and **Plantation Camera and Gifts** also do photo developing.

Small Food Shops

Papaya's, a natural-food cafe and market, at the Kauai Village, 4-831 Kuhio Hwy., is open daily except Sunday 9 a.m.-8 p.m., tel. (808) 823-0190. Coolers and shelves hold items like wild tropical guava juice, organic sprouted hot-dog buns, and mainstays like organic fruits and vegetables, yogurt, whole-grain bread and bulk foods. The new owners, Eric and Leslie Wing, have added an extensive collection of premium microbrewery beers, along with racks of fine wines, and boast the best selection and prices on Kauai. There is also a good selection of organic teas and flavored coffees. Spices, oils, vinegars, organic salad dressings, homeopathic medicines, cruelty-free cosmetics, vitamins, minerals, and an assortment of biodegradable cleaning products are also well represented. A large display case holds all kinds of goodies like cheesecakes, pumpkin and carrot cake, mango moussecake, and chocolate flan. If you are into healthy organic food, there is no place better than Papaya's.

There are several other markets and groceries in the Waipouli/Kapa'a area where you can pick up food if you're cooking for yourself. **Ambrose's Kapuna Natural Foods** (in a funky yellow building), tel. (808) 822-7112 or 822-3926, across from Foodland in the Waipouli Town Center, serves the community's produce and bulk- and health-food needs. Ambrose and his friends are real storehouses of information

Ambrose's Kapuna Natural Foods is perfect for all your whole-grain needs.

about the island; they have the "scoop" on what's happening and where. While visiting Ambrose, take a peek just next door at the **Kapa'a Missionary Church,** made from beautifully laid lava rock. If you have kids, check **Marta's Boat.**

There's a **farmers' market** every Wednesday at 3 p.m. at the Kapa'a Beach Park, while the local **Pono Market,** open Mon.-Sat. 7 a.m.-9 p.m. and Sun. 8 a.m.-4 p.m., is stuffed to the gills with grocery items, along with takeout sushi, bento, and deli sandwiches. As you're coming into Kapa'a heading north look for the **Sunnyside Farmers Market,** open daily 8 a.m.-8 p.m., where you can get fresh fruits and vegetables from around the island. **Kojima's** grocery, for produce, meat, liquor, beer, and picnic supplies, is beyond the Aloha Lumber yard at the north end of town. Currently painted blue, this well-stocked store is on the mountain side of the road.

Sports and Recreation
One of the best bike shops on the island for sales and repair is **Bicycle Kauai,** tel. (808) 822-3315, at 1379 Kuhio Hwy. in Kapa'a, open Mon.-Fri. 9 a.m.-6 p.m., Saturday 9 a.m.-4 p.m., and Sunday 10 a.m.- 1 p.m. Stop in and talk to the guys; they can give you great advice on where to ride for your type of bike. Cannondale mountain bikes rent for $20 a day or $85 per seven-day week, including helmet, lock, and a car rack. You can also arrange a mountain-bike tour of 3-6 hours (full-day tours by appointment only) for $50-100, depending on the length and location of the tour (price includes a lunch prepared by Anahola's famous Duane's Ono Charburger).

Aquatic Adventures, at 4-1380 Kuhio Hwy., Kapa'a, HI 96746, tel. (808) 822-1434, open daily 7:30 a.m.-5 p.m., owned and operated by Janet Moore, is a full-service dive shop offering rentals, excursions, and certification courses. PADI courses, lasting three to five days for open-water certification, are $450 for the total package ($300 for a refresher course). Beginners can start with an introductory shore dive for $100 or a boat dive for $140. Other possibilities include a two-tank boat dive ($80, $95 with equipment), a one-tank shore dive or a one-tank night dive ($70 and $80); and a three-tank dive to Niihau, Thursday 7 a.m.- 5 p.m. ($200 and $215). All dives are on a 30-foot Raddon especially designed for scuba diving and comfort

with an onboard hot shower. Janet also sells a full complement of underwater gear including knives, wet suits, masks, fins, spearfishing gear, and carry bags.

Chris The Fun Lady, at 4-746 Kuhio Hwy. across from the Waipouli Shopping Center, tel. (808) 822-7759, open daily 8 a.m.-6 p.m., offers boogie-board rentals at $5-8 a day; kayaks for $25 single, $50 double with coolers, dry bags, life vests, car racks, and waterproof maps included; top-of-the-line snorkel gear (prescription masks, too), golf clubs, fishing equipment, and surfboards at $10 per day. Chris is an expert at arranging all ocean, air, and luau activities, claiming that her years of experience on Kauai don't always get you the cheapest but do always gets you the best.

There's no problem planning a fun-filled day with the help of **Ray's Rentals and Activities,** 1345 Kuhio Hwy., in downtown Kapa'a, tel. (808) 822-5700. Ray's rents boogie boards, snorkel gear, bicycles, surfboards, and kayaks. It also rents Harleys for the macho, Hondas for the minnow, and mopeds for the micro. The big Harleys are $175 per day, small Harleys are $150, Hondas $125, and mopeds $35 (longer-use discounts are available). Ray's functions as a booking agency for activities like helicopter rides, scuba diving, snorkeling, and luau. They claim to beat all prices, so it's worth calling to see what they can do.

Kayak Kauai, across the road from Ray's, open daily 8 a.m.-5 p.m., tel. (808) 822-9179, rents two-person kayaks for $48-60 per day and single kayaks for $25-35. Its owners are world-class kayak experts, and the staff are sensitive people who provide good service while having a good time. From May to October they lead ocean tours up the Na Pali coast for $130. They also rent and sell surf-skis, boogie boards, masks, fins, *tabi,* tents, and other beach and camping gear. They will rig your car to carry the kayak and provide drop-off and pick-up service at Kee Beach for $8 or at Polihale State Park for $40—when it's safe to be on the ocean. During the summer, guided tours are taken along the Na Pali coast, and when conditions are too harsh up there, trips are run to Kipu Kai along the south coast. All of the above are good family-style fun. Kayak Kauai has another shop in Hanalei, tel. (808) 826-9844, which provides the same services.

Ambrose of **Ambrose's Kapuna Natural Foods,** in the funky yellow building across from Foodland in the Waipouli Town Center is a surfer's advocate, philosopher, and generally good guy. He has one of the largest collections of big boards and old surfboards on the island, and some new ones, too. If you are a surfer coming on vacation and you let Ambrose know in advance what you want and are qualified to use, he'll have it waiting when you get here. He doesn't rent boards, but he'll buy back the ones he sells at a very equitable rate. On his neighborhood beaches, Ambrose also offers surfing lessons tailor-made to the individual beginner or advanced board rider. Rates are $25 per hour.

INFORMATION AND SERVICES

Aside from the hotel activity desks, there are four places in Waipouli/Kapa'a where you can get tourist information. Very helpful is the **Kauai Visitors Center** in the Coconut Market Place, tel. (808) 245-3882. They have a complete range of free information on all the island's activities, are able to make reservations, and have an eye for the deals.

K.B.T.C. also has the full range of information and sometimes gets discount deals. Stop in at their main booth at the Pono Kai Condo or at their cubbyhole office below Jimmy's Grill in downtown Kapa'a, or call (808) 822-7447.

Your Kauai Office, open Mon.-Sat. 8 a.m.-6 p.m., tel. (808) 822-5504, can answer all of your shipping and office needs, including fax, photocopies, and UPS.

For a rejuvenating and revitalizing massage contact **Aunty Daisy's Polynesian Massage.** Aunty Daisy is "the lady with the *aloha* hands" and works in the small Waipouli Complex at 971 D Kuhio Hwy., tel. (808) 822-0305, open Tuesday and Wednesday 8:30 a.m.-5:30 p.m., Thursday and Friday 11 a.m.-10 p.m., and Saturday, 9:30 a.m.-2:30 p.m.

THE NORTH SHORE

The north shore is a soulful song of wonder, a contented chant of dream-reality, where all the notes of the Garden Island harmonize gloriously. The refrain is a tinkling melody, rising, falling, and finally reaching a booming crescendo deep in the emerald green of Na Pali. In so many ways this region is a haven: tiny towns and villages that refused to crumble when sugar pulled out; a patchwork quilt of diminutive *kuleana* of native Hawaiians running deep into luxuriant valleys, where ageless stone walls encircle fields of taro; a winter sanctuary for migrating birds, and gritty native species desperately holding on to life; a refuge for myriad visitors—the adventuring, vacationing, life-tossed, or work-weary who come to its shores seeking a setting conducive to finding peace of body and soul.

The north shore is only 30 miles long, but, oh, what miles! Along its undulating mountains, one-lane roads, and luminescent bays are landlocked caves still umbilically tied to the sea; historical sites, the remnants of peace or domination once so important and now reduced by time; and living movie sets, some occupied by villas of stars or dignitaries, enough to bore even the worst name-dropper. Enduring, too, is the history of old Hawaii in this fabled homeland of

the Menehune, overrun by the Polynesians who set up their elaborate kingdoms built on strict social order. The usurpers' *heiau* remain, and from one came the hula, swaying, stirring, and spreading throughout the island kingdoms.

Starting in **Kilauea,** an old plantation town, you can search out the spiritual by visiting two intriguing churches, browse an "everything" general store, or marvel at the coastline from bold promontories pummeled by the sea. Then there are the north shore beaches—fans of white sand, some easily visited as official parks, others hidden, the domains of simplicity and free spirits. **Princeville** follows, a convenient but incongruous planned community, vibrant with its own shopping mall, airport, and flexing condo muscles. Over the rise is **Hanalei,** even more poetic than its lovely name, a tiny town, a yachties' anchorage with good food, spirited, slow, a bay of beauty and enchantment. Movie cameras once rolled at neighboring **Lumahai Beach** and an entire generation shared the dream of paradise when they saw this spot in *South Pacific.* Next in rapid succession are **Wainiha,** and **Haena** with its few amenities, the last available indoor lodging, a restaurant, a bar, and a little of the world's most relaxed lifestyle. The road ends at **Ke'e Beach,** where adventure begins with the start of the Na Pali Coast Trail. The north shore remains for most visitors the perfect setting for seeking and maybe actually finding peace, solitude, the dream, yourself.

HEADING NORTH: ANAHOLA AND VICINITY

Route 56 north from Kapa'a is a visual treat. Out your window, the coastline glides along in an ever-changing panorama. Development is virtually nonexistent until you get to Kilauea in the Hanalei District. To your left are the **Anahola Mountains,** jagged, pointed, and intriguing. Until recently, you could crane your neck and see **Hole-in-the-Mountain,** a natural arrangement of boulders that formed a round *puka* (legend says it was formed by an angry giant who hurled his spear with such force that he made

Anahola Village church, backdropped by the distinctive Anahola Mountains

the hole), but time and storms have taken their toll and the hole has collapsed.

Villages, Beaches, and Practicalities
The first village that you come to is **Anahola.** Just before mile marker 14 is the **Whaler's General Store,** open daily 6:30 a.m.-9:30 p.m., selling groceries, souvenirs, vegetables, and liquor. If you'd like to brighten your day or evening with an inexpensive orchid or plumeria lei, call ahead and order one from **Albert Christian** in Anahola at (808) 822-5691.

Next door to the general store is a **post office** and **Duane's Ono Charburger,** open Mon.-Sat. 10 a.m.-8 p.m. and Sunday 11 a.m.-6 p.m., a clean, friendly roadside stand where you can get burgers or fish 'n' chips. Some of the double-fisted burgers include the Ono at $3.90; an Old Fashioned, with cheddar, onions, and sprouts on a Kaiser roll, at $4.95; the Local Boy, made with teriyaki, cheddar cheese, and pineapple for $5.65; and a Local Girl, made with teriyaki and Swiss cheese. The burgers are oversize, and heavy with cheese and trimmings. For an extra treat, try a delicious marionberry shake. Tables are available, but hold your appetite for a few minutes and make it a picnic at the nearby beach.

Across the road from Duane's, look for the Anahola Baptist Church and a small lane leading to **Hawaiian Barbecue Chicken,** owned and operated by Lee and his family, open Tues.-Sun. when the family is there, tel. (808) 822-7144. The Hawaiian Barbecue is a hut in a grove of trees with two green picnic tables out front. Cooking is done on an enormous barbecue Lee fashioned from an old flatbed truck, its grills flipped by a motorized chain. Lee and his family offer plate lunches such as a half chicken with a scoop each of rice and mac salad for only $6.50. Treats include shave ice, smoothies, cold coconut, and, for a touch of beauty, fresh lei. Hawaiian Barbecue is downhome, clean, friendly, inexpensive, delicious, and filled with the aloha spirit. You can't go wrong.

Just a minute up the road, look to your right for Aliomanu ("Oil of the Shark") Road and follow it for a few minutes to the mouth of the Anahola River as it spills into the bay. Or take Anahola Road off Rt. 56 just before the Whaler's General Store to a long strand of white sand that forms one of the best beaches on the north shore. The south end of the bay is **Anahola Beach County Park,** with a developed picnic area, shower, grills, restrooms, and camping (county permit). Tall ironwood trees provide a natural canopy. The swimming is safe in the protected cove near the beach park and in the freshwater river, good for a refreshing dip. As you walk north the waves and rips get tougher—Anahola means "easily broken." It's not advisable to enter the water, although some experienced board riders do challenge the waves here, as the Hawaiians did long ago. However, the reef comes close to shore at this end, and wherever you can find a sheltered pocket is good for snorkeling. Local anglers love this spot for nearshore fishing. The entire area is popular with local people, and at times begins to look like a tent city of semipermanent campers and squatters. This is a place to camp for a few days, or just to stop in for a refreshing plunge on the way to or from the north shore.

The turnoff to **Moloa'a ("Matted Roots") Bay** is between mile markers 16 and 17. Turn down the rough Koolau Road, follow it to Moloa'a Road, and take this narrow but paved road to the end. Look for the brilliant poinsettias blooming in early winter along Koolau Road— they are the island's clue that Christmas and New Year are near. Moloa'a Bay is a magnificent but rarely visited beach. The road leading down is a luscious little thoroughfare, cutting over domed hillocks in a series of switchbacks. The jungle canopy is thick and then opens into a series of glens and pastures. Off to the sides are vacation homes perched on stilts made from telephone poles. A short drive takes you to road's end and a small cluster of dwellings where there is limited space to put your vehicle. Park here and follow the right-of-way to the beach signs. Here, a stream comes into the bay providing a great place to wash off the ocean water after a dip. The beach is lovely, bright, and wide, forming a crescent moon. To the north the beach ends in a grassy hillock; south, it's confined by a steep *pali* (this is where the swimming is best). As at all north shore beaches, swimming is advised only during calm weather. Snorkeling is good, but you'll have to swim the channel out to the base of the *pali,* which is unadvisable if the waves are rough. Although a few homes are around, Moloa'a is a place of peaceful solitude. Sunsets are light shows of changing color, and you'll probably be a solitary spectator.

KILAUEA

There's no saying *exactly* where it begins, but Kilauea is generally considered the gateway to the north shore. The village proper was built on sugar, but that foundation melted away almost 20 years ago. Now the town holds on as a way station to some of the most intriguing scenery along this fabulous coast. Notice the bright, cheery, well-kept homes as you pass through this community. The homeowners may be short on cash but are nonetheless long on pride and surround their dwellings with lovingly tended flower gardens. The bungalows—pictures of homey contentment—are ablaze with color.

To get into town, look for mile marker 23 and a **Shell** gas station on your right, along with the **Menehune Food Market,** a small store selling sundries and general groceries. This is where you turn onto Kolo Road, following the signs to Kilauea Lighthouse and National Wildlife Refuge. The promontory that it occupies, Kilauea Point, is the northernmost point of the main Hawaiian Islands.

A second way into Kilauea is by turning off the highway just before mile marker 23 at Ho'okui Rd., which is marked by **Mango Mama's Fruit Stand** (a farmers' market is held every Saturday at noon in the Crater Hills schoolyard next door). Go one block and turn left. Pass St. Sylvester's Church and proceed over a bridge, past the Kilauea School, and on into town.

Alternatively, just before you arrive at the turnoff to Kilauea, look left to see a sign pointing to **Kai Guava Plantation,** open daily 9 a.m.-5 p.m., where you can take a (free) self-guided map tour through lush gardens. Proceed along the access road lined with ferns, banana trees, ironwoods, and flowering bushes, and stop in at the gift shop to pick up a map of the grounds. They also sell guava products, T-shirts, and sundries. Follow a well-trodden path through a

KAUAI'S NORTH SHORE

© MOON PUBLICATIONS, INC.

covered archway where tropical plants grow, and cross a tiny stream to find many of Hawaii's flowers and plants labeled by name. The path winds along for just 10 minutes and leads to a pond surrounded by taro, bird of paradise, hibiscus, torch ginger, ferns, and various palms. Near the pond, you'll find a round, thatched gazebo, and a picnic table for your enjoyment. Finally, cross the stream on two rustic, wooden half-moon bridges while listening to the babbling water and whispering wind, just as the ancient Hawaiians did while tending their water-terraced fields.

SIGHTS

As you head down Kolo Road from the gas station, you pass the post office. Where Kolo intersects Kilauea Road sits **Christ Memorial Episcopal Church** on the right. Hawaii seems to sprout with as many churches as bamboo shoots, but this one is special. The shrubbery and flowers immediately catch your eye, their vibrant colors matched by the stained-glass windows (imported from England). The present church was built in 1941 from cut lava stone. Inside is a hand-hewn altar, and surrounding the

church is a cemetery with several tombstones of long-departed parishioners. Go in, have a look, and perhaps meditate for a moment.

Before turning on Kilauea Road have a look at **St. Sylvester's Catholic Church.** This house of worship is octagonal, with a roof resembling a Chinese hat. Inside are murals painted by Jean Charlot, a famous island artist. The church, built by Friar John Macdonald, was an attempt to reintroduce art as one of the bulwarks of Catholicism.

Head down Kilauea Road past the Kong Lung Store and keep going until Kilauea Road makes a hard swing to the left. Proceeding straight ahead up Mihi Road brings you to a little Japanese cemetery on your right. This road has been blocked—it's now privately owned and closed to the public—but it leads to Mokolea Point's **Crater Hill,** where, 568 feet straight down, is the Pacific, virtually unobstructed until it hits Asia. The seacliff is like a giant stack of pancakes, layered and jagged, with the edges eaten by age, and covered with a green syrup of lichen and mosses. The cliff is undercut and gives the sensation of floating in midair. There is a profusion of purple and yellow flowers all along the edge. The cliffs serve as a giant rookery for seabirds and, along with Mokolea Point to the east, are now part of the

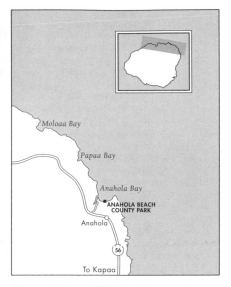

ing a beam 90 miles out to sea. The clamshell lens has not been used since the mid-'70s, however, and a small, high-intensity light now shines as an important reference point for mariners.

The area is alive with permanent and migrating birds. Keep your eyes peeled for the great frigate bird kiting on its eight-foot wingspan, and the red-footed booby, a white bird with black wingtips darting here and there, always wearing red dancing shoes. At certain times of the year, Hawaiian monk seals and green turtles can be seen along the shore and around Moku'ae'ae Island just off Kilauea Point. Dolphins and whales are also spotted offshore. Information at the visitors center gives you a fast lesson in birdlife and a pictorial history of the lighthouse—worth reading. Also available are a good selection of books on Hawaiian flora, fauna, history, and hiking, as well as maps of the islands, are available. The center also signs out binoculars for free to view the birds, and there are usually informative docents in the yard with monoculars trained on particular birds or nesting sites on the nearby cliffs.

The Kilauea Wildlife Refuge is attempting to relocate albatross from the Midway Islands, where they nest on runways. The refuge has successfully relocated more than 40, and you can watch them floundering around on nearby Albatross Hill.

A leisurely walk takes you out onto this amazingly narrow peninsula, where you can learn more about the plant- and birdlife in the area. Don't keep your eyes only in the air, however. Look for the coastal *naupaka* plants, which sur-

Kilauea National Wildlife Refuge, which also encompasses Kilauea Point.

For a more civilized experience of the same view with perhaps a touch less drama, head down Kilauea Road to the end and park at **Kilauea Lighthouse,** a designated national historical landmark. This facility, built in 1913, was at one time manned by the Coast Guard but is now under the jurisdiction of the Department of the Interior's Fish and Wildlife Service. Boasting the largest "clamshell lens" in the world, it is capable of send-

Kilauea Lighthouse

ROBERT NILSEN

round the parking lot and line the walk to the lighthouse. Common along the seashore and able to grow even in arid regions, these plants have bunches of bright green, moisture-retaining, leathery leaves; at their center are white half-flowers the size of a fingernail and small white seeds.

The refuge plans to establish a four-mile-long walking trail from Kilauea Point around Crater Hill to Mokolea Point that will be used strictly for tours led by refuge personnel.

This facility is open Mon.-Fri. 10 a.m.-4 p.m., closed weekends and federal holidays. The entrance fee is $2 adults, free for children under 16, $10 for an annual refuge permit; the Golden Eagle Pass, Golden Access Pass, Golden Age Pass, and a Federal Duck Stamp are also honored for free entrance.

BEACHES

The Kilauea area has some fantastic beaches. One is a beach park with full amenities and camping, one is hidden and rarely visited, others are for fishing or just looking.

Kauapea Beach, more commonly called **Secret Beach,** deserves its name. After passing through Kilauea, look for Banana Joe's tropical fruit stand on the left; just past it is Kalihiwai Road. Make a right onto Kalihiwai and then take the very first dirt road on the right. Follow this tiny road for about one mile, until it turns right at an iron gate. Continue down the hill to a parking area and a little homemade sign announcing the beach trail. Follow the signs (if there are signs it can't be too secret, right?). Even some local residents ruefully admit that the secret is out. However, if you venture to this beach, be conscious that there are private homes nearby and that it's a place locals come to enjoy away from the crowds of tourists.

Walk beside the barbed-wire fence and start down the slippery slope to the beach. You pass through some excellent jungle area before emerging at Secret Beach in less than 15 minutes. If you expect Secret Beach to be small, you're in for a shock. This white-sand strand is huge. Off to the right you

can see Kilauea Lighthouse, dazzling white in the sun. Along the beach is a fine stand of trees providing shade and perfect for pitching a tent. (Recently the police have been patrolling and issuing tickets for camping without a permit! Sometimes, they issue a warning only, but don't count on it.) A stream coming into the beach when you come down the hill is okay for washing in, but not drinking. For drinking water, head south along the beach and keep your eyes peeled for a freshwater spring coming out of the mountain. What more can you ask for? The camping is terrific and generally free of hassles.

Kilauea Bay offers great fishing, unofficial camping, and beautiful scenery. Proceed through Kilauea along Kilauea Road and pass Kong Lung Store. Take the second dirt road to the right; it angles through cane fields about 100 yards past the Martin Farm produce stand. Follow this rutted road 1.5 miles down to what the local people call **Quarry Beach,** also known as Kahili Beach. At the end of the road is the now-abandoned Kahili Quarry. Although easy to get to, this wide sandy beach is rarely visited. Characteristic of Kauai, Kilauea Stream runs into the bay. From the parking lot, you must wade across the stream to the beach. The swimming is good in the stream and along the beach, but only during calm periods. Some local residents come here to surf or use boogie boards; do this only if you have been on the bay before and are experienced with Hawaiian water. Plenty of places along the streambank or on the beach are good for picnicking and camping. Many local fishermen come here to catch a transparent fish called *o'io,* which they often use for bait. It's too bony to fry, but they have fig-

great frigate bird

ured out an ingenious way to get the meat. They cut off the tail and roll a soda pop bottle over it, squeezing the meat out through the cut. They then mix it with some water, hot pepper, and bread crumbs to make delicious fish balls.

Kalihiwai Beach is just past Kilauea, off Rt. 56 and down Kalihiwai Road. If you go over the Kalihiwai River, you've gone too far—even though another section of the Kalihiwai Road also leads from there down to the coast. This road was once part of the coastal road, but the devastating tsunami of 1946 took out the lower bridge and the road is now divided by the river. As on many such rivers in Kauai, a ferry was used here to ease early transportation difficulties. In less than half a mile down the first Kalihiwai Road you come to an off-the-track, white sand beach lined with ironwoods. The swimming and bodysurfing are outstanding, given the right conditions. The river behind the iron woods forms a freshwater pool for rinsing off, but there are no amenities whatsoever. People can camp among the ironwoods without a problem. The second Kalihiwai Road leads you to the beach on the west side of the river where some people come to fish.

Go over the bridge and turn right on the second Kalihiwai Road. Follow this to a Y, take the left fork—Anini Road—and follow it to its end at the remarkable **Anini Beach County Park.** The reef here is the longest exposed reef off Kauai; consequently, the snorkeling is first-rate. Anini was traditionally called *Wanini.* It was known as one of the best fishing grounds and was reserved for the exclusive use of the *ali'i.* But time and sea air weathered a latter-day sign until the "W" rusted off completely. Newcomers to the area mistakenly called it Anini, and the name stuck. It's amazing to snorkel out to the reef in no more than four feet of water and then to peer over the edge into waters that seem bottomless. Windsurfers also love this area, and their bright sails can be seen year-round. Those in the know say this is the best spot on Kauai for beginning windsurfers as the winds are generally steady, the water is shallow, and the beach protected. Several shops in Hanalei give lessons here.

Follow the road to the end, where a shallow, brackish lagoon and a large sandbar make the area good for wading. This beach has full amenities—toilets, picnic tables, grills, and a pavilion.

There are private homes at both ends of this beach, so be considerate when coming and going.

A polo ground is across the road from the open camping area, and several Sundays each month matches are held here beginning at 3 p.m. and lasting until 5 p.m. Admission is $3 per person or $6 per car, and the exciting matches are both fun and stylish. The local horsemen are excellent players who combine with their trusty mounts to perform amazing athletic manuevers.

PRACTICALITIES

Accommodations

The **Mahi Ko Inn,** General Delivery, Kilauea, HI 96754, tel. (808) 828-1103 or (800) 458-3444, is a restored plantation home where you're hosted by Cathy and Doug Weber. Rates are $75-135, with continental breakfast included.

The **Kai Mana,** P.O. Box 612, Kilauea, tel. (808) 828-1280, is filled with the healing vibrations of its internationally acclaimed owner, Shakti Gawain, author of *Creative Visualization,* and of the powerful natural forces so evident on Kauai. Here, the emphasis of your vacation is not only on relaxation, but also on revitalization. Part of your stay can involve private counseling with Shakti when she is in residence, a session with a massage practitioner or meditation instructor, or a simple nature-attunement excursion. Rates are $75 s, $95 d standard room; $95 s, $115 d deluxe corner room; self-contained cottage for $125 per night, $750 per week. All rooms have their own private entrances and private baths; light breakfast food is provided, and a kitchenette is open to guests.

Food, Shopping, and Services

In Kilauea across from the **Shell** station look for **Shared Blessing Thrift Shop,** open Tuesday and Thursday 2-5 p.m. and Wednesday and Saturday 9 a.m.-noon in a vintage plantation building, a good place to pick up secondhand treasures or curios from Kauai here among everything from binoculars to boogie boards.

The **Hawaiian Art Museum,** housed in a plantation building on the left about 50 yards past the sign pointing to Kilauea Lighthouse in downtown Kilauea, tel. (808) 828-1253, open Mon.-Fri.

1-5 p.m. and Sunday 10-11 a.m., offers "talk story" on Sunday morning by Serge King, an internationally known author and lecturer proficient in his knowledge of *huna* and ancient Hawaiian arts and crafts. The shelves and counters are filled with artifacts like *poi* pounders and bowls, a remarkable carved statue of a god doing a handstand, a model village alive with dancers and warriors, descriptions of different canoes, *makini* masks with their distinctive owl-like eyes, ferocious-looking *palau* war clubs, and Hawaiian musical instruments. The museum is also the home of **Aloha International,** founded by Serge King and dedicated to the practice and philosophy of *huna.* You can contact the center for a free brochure listing the weeklong summer courses offered and a list of their various products. The curator, Bev Brody, a certified instructor in *huna,* is also intimately familiar with the fauna and flora in the area, and may lead you on a nature hike if you call in advance to make arrangements and if time permits.

Look for the blue and white kiosk in a banana grove marking **Mango Mama's Fruit Stand** at the south entrance to Kilauea along Rt. 56. Mango Mama's is ripe with papayas, bananas, mac nuts, fresh juices, sugarcane, honey, and health-conscious sandwiches.

An institution in this area is **Kong Lung Store,** located along Kilauea Lighthouse Road at the intersection of Keneke Street, tel. (808) 828-1822, open Mon.- Fri. 10 a.m.-6 p.m., Saturday 9 a.m.-6 p.m., and Sunday 10 a.m.- 5 p.m., which has been serving the needs of the north shore plantation towns for almost a century. But don't expect bulk rice and pipe fittings. The upstairs section of the store is called **Reinventions** and sells consignment clothing for both men and women; downstairs, the items change constantly, but there are always hats, furniture, bath products, and artworks. The **Indo Pacific Trading Co.,** a store featuring arts and artifacts from throughout Asia and Polynesia, also has a section of the old Kong Lung Store (see "Arts, Crafts, and Souvenirs" under "Shopping" in the Lihue chapter for a full description).

The **Roadrunner Bakery and Cafe,** at 2430 Oka St. (turn at Garden Isle Missionary Baptist Church just before Kong Lung), open Mon.-Fri. 7 a.m.-8 p.m., to 8:30 p.m. Saturday, tel. (808) 828-8226, would make even Wile E. Coyote give up Acme Exploding Enchiladas with its excellent and very affordable Mexican food. Shuffle across a sand floor and spin like a piñata to view the interior painted floor and a ceiling with a Mexican motif. Chew your chimichanga while Aztec Indians tend their crops, horses gallop past, buses laden with chickens and baggage cruise along through cactus fields, and *charro* roast a side of beef over a campfire. Owned and operated by Denis Johnston, who arrives at 3 a.m. to fire up the ovens. You order through a window that looks back into the bakery, then sit at green tables amidst full-size trees and strings of hanging chilies. Breakfast gets you rolling with *huevos*—rancheros, Mexicana, or Americano—all priced under $6. Lunch brings appetizers like chips and salsa at $4.75, guacamole and chips at $5.25, and entrees like chicken flautas at $4.75. A range of salads priced $5.75-6.75 includes grilled vegetable and mahi selections. Regular Mexican fare includes tostadas smothered with roasted chicken, pork, steak, or fresh catch, all under $7.75; or *tortas* bulging with pinto beans, rice, lettuce, salsa fresca, and your choice of steak, roast pork, or roast chicken, all at $5.25. Roadrunner also offers tacos, tamales, and enchiladas, all handmade fresh on the premises. Beverages are coffee, iced tea, and fresh-squeezed orange juice. From the bakery you can order Hanalei taro rolls, bagels, sourdough, cracked pepper, honey wheat, and Rhine molasses bread, along with all sorts of goodies. Roadrunner is a hands-on business run with pride, friendliness, and a commitment to fresh and excellent food at reasonable prices.

Windows all around open to a miniature garden and lanai where you can dine alfresco at **Casa di Amici Ristorante.** Located next door to Kong Lung Store, open for dinner 5:30-9 p.m., tel. (808) 828-1555, it is the best Italian restaurant on the north shore. Chef Randall Yates and his professional staff make you feel right at home in this "house of friends." Inside, the ristorante is classic, with green-topped tables trimmed in wood and comfortable chairs with padded armrests. In the center, a diminutive fountain performs a tinkling melody while an ensemble of magnificent Hawaiian flowers dances gently in the breeze. Start with antipasti, a plate laden with greens, pepperoncini, olives, eggs, provolone, salami, prosciutto, and anchovies for $10, or try the gorgonzola mushroom polenta served with Roma tomatoes, or the risotto quatro fromagio with fresh basil and tomatoes, each at $8. Soups and salads include minestrone for $5, the savory *zuppa di casa*—New Zealand mussels with fresh tomatoes, capers, tri-colored bell peppers, and leeks in a rich *femet depoission* for $6, or Caesar salad $6, and mixed salad for $5. Pasta dishes are a choice of linguine, fettuccine, capellini, tortellini, or penne covered in zesty sauces like pesto, marinara, arabiato, or alfredo; entrees include lasagna, chicken cacciatore, veal marsala, and chicken picatta, all priced $16-22. The ristorante also has a full-service bar serving top-shelf liquors and imported draft beers, along with a fine wine selection prominently displayed for your perusal. There's espresso or cappuccino to complete your meal, and, to add to your dining pleasure, soothing piano music is performed Thurs.-Saturday.

Just behind Casa di Amici is the **Kilauea Bakery and Pau Hana Pizza,** open daily except Sunday 6:30 a.m.-9 p.m., tel. (808) 828-2020. Using all natural ingredients, Kilauea Bakery supplies some of the best restaurants along the north shore. The extensive selection of baked goods is tempting, and occasionally they put out something a bit offbeat like pumpkin coconut muffins (the breadsticks are great). As with the other shops in this little complex, Kilauea Bakery succeeds in offering something special. Their pizzas are made with organically grown California olive oil and whole-milk mozzarella on a wholewheat or sourdough crust. All are gourmet, topped with sautéed mushrooms, feta cheese, grated Parmesan, homemade pesto, sun-dried tomatoes, or locally grown peppers, priced $7.25 for a small to $16.25 for a 16-inch large, or $2.75 by the slice. Enjoy your treat inside, or sit on the tiny veranda under a shade umbrella. Coffee, made by the cup, is also served.

Next door to Casa di Amici is the Kilauea neighborhood center and theater, and beyond that is **The Farmers' Market,** a deli/grocery store, open 9 a.m.-9 p.m. The deli carries food items and beverages and makes filling homemade soups and sandwiches for those who want something substantial but don't want a full sit-down meal. Much of their produce is organic, when possible, and they have a gourmet section with imported cheeses and fine food items. Behind the center is a small community park.

Kilauea is also home to the **Island Soap Co.,** owned and operated by Stephen and Marlena Connella, at P.O. Box 846, Kilauea, HI 96754, tel. (808) 828-1120 or (800) 300-6067. The husband and wife team hand-pours its soap, perfuming the raw bars with heady fragrances like coconut, plumeria, and ginger. They also produce self-pampering products like scented coconut oils, lotions, and bath gels capturing the scents of the islands. Island Soap Co. products are available at boutiques throughout Hawaii and can also be purchased by mail.

To experience the living beauty of your trip to Kauai, try a bouquet of lovely orchids from **Makai Farms,** tel. (808) 828-1874, open Sat.-Tues. 9 a.m.-4 p.m., or by appointment. Look for the sign to the entrance past mile marker 21, *makai* along a white fence.

Martin Farm Produce Stand is just beyond town. Open Mon.-Sat. 9 a.m.-5 p.m., it operates on the self-service honor system. Select what you want, add up the cost marked on each item, and drop your payment in the box. Nearby, at the corner of Oka Street, is the Kilauea clinic of the **Kauai Medical Group.**

After visiting all these places, you need a rest. The perfect stop is just west of town at **Banana Joe's** fruit stand, *mauka* of the highway, tel. (808) 828-1092. Run by Joe Halasey, his wife, and friends, this little yellow stand offers fresh fruit, smoothies and other drinks, packaged fruit baskets, baked goods with fruit, and other fruit products. They have more kinds of fruit than you've ever heard of—try something new. If you're interested and they have the time, you may be able to visit the farm behind the stand and talk to Banana Joe himself, but you'll have to ask first. Not to be outdone in the related-to-a-tropical-fruit department, just before Banana Joe's is **Mango Mama's Fruit Stand.** What's next? Sister Soursop and Brother Breadfruit?

PRINCEVILLE

Princeville is 11,000 acres of planned luxury overlooking Hanalei Bay. Last century, the surrounding countryside was a huge ranch—Kauai's oldest, established in 1853 by the Scotsman R.C. Wyllie. After an official royal vacation to the ranch by Kamehameha IV and Queen Emma in 1860, the name was changed to Princeville in honor of the royal son, Prince Albert. The young heir unfortunately died within two years, and his heartbroken father soon followed.

Since 1969, Consolidated Gas and Oil of Honolulu has taken these same 11,000 acres and developed them into a prime vacation community designed to keep the humdrum world far away. Previously owned by the Princeville Development Corporation, a subsidiary of Quitex Australia, and now owned by the Japanese firm Santuri and the Mitsui Corporation, the community provides everything: accommodations, shopping, dining, recreational facilities (especially golf and tennis), even a fire and police force and an airport. First-rate condos are scattered around the property, and a new multitiered Sheraton Mirage Hotel perches over the bay. The guests expect to stay put, except for an occasional daytrip. Management and clientele are in league to provide and receive satisfaction. And without even trying, it's just about guaranteed.

Note: Mile markers on Hwy. 56 going west are renumbered from one at Princeville. It is 10 miles from here to the end of the road at Ke'e Beach.

RECREATION

Golf, Tennis, and Other Athletic Clubs
Those addicted to striking hard, dimpled white balls or fuzzy soft ones have come to the right spot. In Princeville, golf and tennis are the royal couple. The **Princeville Makai Golf Course** offers 27 holes of magnificent golf designed by Robert Trent Jones, Jr. This course, chosen as one of America's top 100, hosted the 26th annual World Cup in 1978 and is where the LPGA Women's Kemper Open is played. Radiating from the central clubhouse are three nine-hole, par-36 courses you can use in any combination. They include the **Woods, Lake,** and **Ocean** courses—the names highlighting the special focus of each.

Opened in 1987, the 18-hole **Prince Course,** tel. (808) 826-3580, also welcomes the public. It's located off Hwy. 56 just east of the Woods course and has its own clubhouse. For this course, accuracy and control are much more important than power and distance. Many expert golfers judge the Prince extremely difficult— perhaps the most challenging in Hawaii; there's one par-six hole, another hole with the tee 300 feet above the fairway, and ravines and streams among the obstacles. Nine-hole twilight golf is available on any course weekdays after 3 p.m. for a reduced fee. The clubhouse has an extensive pro shop, a snack shop, and club storage. The driving range

The airport marks the beginning of the planned community of Princeville.

is open during daylight hours. Plenty of package deals to the resort include flights, accommodations, rental car, and unlimited golf.

You can play on six professional tennis courts at the **Princeville Resort Tennis Club,** tel. (808) 826-3620. There's a pro shop, lessons and clinics, racket rental, ball machines, and even video playback so you can burn yourself up a second time reviewing your mistakes. (Several condos in Princeville, such as The Cliffs and the Hanalei Bay Resort, also have tennis courts, but these are for their guests only.)

In the Princeville clubhouse is the **Princeville Spa and Health Club,** open weekdays 6:30 a.m.-8 p.m., Saturday 8 a.m.-8 p.m., and Sunday 8 a.m.-6 p.m., tel. (808) 826-5030. Available are aerobics classes, Cybex and Polaris machines, freeweights, an outdoor pool, jacuzzi, sauna and steam, and spa services. It also has designated running courses throughout the Princeville resort area. Daily, weekly, and monthly rates are available. For those with small children, a babysitting service is available 8:30-10:30 a.m. weekdays.

Other Activities

Two miles east of Princeville is the Princeville Airport. **Papillon Helicopters,** tel. (808) 826-6591, operates its magical mystery tours deep into Kauai's interior from here. Once-in-a-lifetime, unforgettable experiences, flights range from the "Discover"—at 30 minutes—to the "Odyssey," which includes a complete view of the island and a two-hour picnic stop.

If flying isn't your pleasure, how about loping along on horseback? **Pooku Stables,** tel. (808) 826-6777, is located a half-mile east of Princeville Center, open Mon.-Sat. 7:30 a.m.-4 p.m.. You can rent a mount here for one of three group rides that take you throughout the area's fascinating countryside. Prices are $30, $50, and $75 for the Hanalei Valley, shoreline, and waterfall picnic rides. The Hanalei Stampede, Kauai's largest rodeo, is held at the stables in early August. Call for details.

ACCOMMODATIONS

The condos and hotel rooms in Princeville all fall into the high-moderate to expensive range. The best deals naturally occur off-season (fall), especially if you plan on staying a week or more. Oddly enough, a project like Princeville should make booking one of its many condos an easy matter, but it's sadly lacking on this point. Lack of a centralized organization handling reservations causes the confusion. Each condo building can have half a dozen booking agents, all with different phone numbers and widely differing rates. The units are privately owned and the owners simply choose one agency or another. If you're going through a travel agent at home, be aware of these discrepancies and insist on the least-expensive rates. A situation that reduces the number of units available is that many of the condos are moving to exclusively time-share programs while others still offer rental units along with their time-share units, so check out the possibilities.

The **Princeville Hotel,** 5520 Kahaku Rd., Princeville, HI 96722, tel. (808) 826-9644, (800) 826-4400, or (800) 782-9488, is a dramatic architectural opus, built in cascading tiers on an extreme point of rugged peninsula. From its perch, all but 16 of the 250 rooms offer breathtaking views of the frothing azure of Hanalei Bay as it stretches toward the emerald green of Bali Hai Peak down the coast. The other rooms offer panoramic views of Puu'poa Marsh, a wildlife conservation wetlands area that offers sanctuary to exotic birdlife. The main lobby offers elegance on a grand scale. The living natural treasures of Kauai spill intimately into the immense room, which is completely encircled by glass. Gold-capped Corinthian columns seem to support banks of clouds as they wander past colossal skylights. Teardrop chandeliers softly illuminate magical fans of tropical flora surrounding a central reflecting pool, its waters lapping the edges in natural syncopation to the wind that whispers through the entire majestic chamber. Here and there are gold-tinged mirrors, Louis XIV chairs, plush couches, and stout coffee tables, and a floor of swirled black and white marble. One special spot is **the Living Room,** a dignified area serving as library, cocktail lounge, and music room. Choose a plush chair just before sunset, and sip a cocktail as the sun streaks the sky with lasers of light dancing across the endless blue of the wide Pacific. There is entertainment every night: a pianist comes to play Hawaiian and contemporary music, you can enjoy twice-weekly sonorous Hawaiian chanting, and sometimes you can watch the exotic sway of accomplished hula dancers. Cocktails and beverages are served 4 p.m.-midnight, *pu pu* and hors d'oeuvres 5-9 p.m., and dessert 5-10:30 p.m. The hotel has a small mini-mall with a cluster of shops that include the **Princeville Resort Shop,** the hotel's logo boutique, where you can purchase everything from hats to incidental bags, all emblazoned with the hotel's logo; **Lamont's Gifts and Sundries,** stocked with sundresses, bathing suits, film, suntan lotion, and books and magazines; a beauty salon; and **Collectors Fine Arts,** representing internationally acclaimed artists.

All rooms feature bathrooms with double vanities, gold fixtures, lotions, potions, terry robes, slippers, and deep immersion tubs, some of which are mini-spas. Bathroom doors are of liquid crystal that can be controlled to change from opaque for privacy to clear so that you can enjoy the view while you soak. Rooms also feature mini-bars, refrigerators, remote-controlled color TVs, and 24-hour room service. In addition, there are three restaurants (see following), two lounges, romantic beachside dinners, prepared picnic lunches, and an activities desk. The Princeville also offers full pool service—with poolside food service—and a white sand beach fronting the hotel that is perfect for swimming. The reef below, alive with tropical fish, is excellent for snorkeling. At dusk, descend to the pool area and immerse yourself in one of the jacuzzis to watch the sun melt into the Pacific as you

melt into the foaming bubbles. Free shuttle service is provided to and from the golf course, tennis courts, shopping center, and Princeville Airport. A standard room ranges $290-465, suites are $925 for an executive to $3,500 for a royal, with a $35 third-person charge.

Set high on the bluff overlooking the Pacific Ocean and having one of the nicest views in the area is **The Cliffs at Princeville,** tel. (808) 826-6219 or (800) 367-7052. These one-bedroom condo units have full-size baths and small wet bars. At the far end of the L-shaped living and dining room is the fully equipped kitchen; you can prepare everything from a fresh pot of morning coffee to a five-course meal at your leisure and in the comfort of your own living space. Two large lanai, one at each end of the unit, offer both ocean and mountain views. Carpets run throughout the unit and the furniture is of contemporary style. Fresh flowers, potted plants, Hawaiian prints, and artwork counter the pastel colors and the subdued floral patterns of the bedroom linen. The bedrooms have king-size beds and the cushy living-room couch pulls out to sleep two more. Units have color TVs, video and stereo systems, compact washers and dryers, irons and ironing boards, small safes for valuables, and daily maid service. Some third-floor units have two bedrooms. These are basically the same as the one-bedroom units except that the second bedroom is in a loft and the living-room ceiling slants up to the second floor. One-bedroom units are $120-150; one-bedroom units with lofts run

entrance to The Cliffs at Princeville

$155-200. The property also has a pool and tennis courts free to guests and a breezy common room off the pool with a large-screen TV, reading material, and a laundry room.

The best deal in Princeville is offered by **Sandpiper Village** condominiums. By chance, they stumbled onto a good thing. When they first opened, they priced their units low to attract clientele. The response was so good, with so many repeat visitors, that they have decided to keep it that way . . . for the time being. For $80-200, you get a roomy one-bedroom unit (one to two people); a two-bedroom, two-bath unit (one to four people); or a three-bedroom unit. (Minimum stay is often required, so ask. *Kama'aina* and long-term stay discounts, are available.) A few unadvertised one-room studios with baths but no kitchens run $45 per night; available on a limited basis; you must specifically ask about these. Most units have garden views, with a few offering ocean views. Each has a full kitchen with dishwasher, laundry facilities, color TV, and private lanai. Maid service (fee) is available on request, and a cleaning charge ($65-85) is added to your bill at checkout. On the grounds are a pool, jacuzzi, barbecue grills, and recreational building, all surrounding well-tended gardens. For reservations and information, contact booking agents Oceanfront Realty at (800) 222-5541.

The **Hanalei Bay Resort,** P.O. Box 220, Hanalei, HI 96714, physically at 5380 Honoiki Rd., tel. (808) 826-6522 or (800) 827-4427, is a condo resort with some private units. You enter through a spacious open area paved with flagstone and face the **Bali Hai Bar,** done in longhouse style with a palm-frond roof, magnificent koa long bar, and matching koa canoe. From the bar, you have a spectacular panorama of Bali Hai Peak dappled by passing clouds and Hanalei Bay, a sheet of foam-fringed azure. Evening brings live music, with everything from jazz to a local slack-key combo. Stepping down the hillside from the bar is the resort's free-form pool complete with a 15-foot waterfall—all surrounded by landscaping inspired by the area's natural beauty. The resort buildings are like two outstretched arms ready to embrace the bay, and all units are guaranteed to have stupendous views. Amenities include laundry facilities, full kitchens in the condo units, TV, phone, tennis courts, and air conditioning. The resort condo offers single rooms, studios, and one-, two-, and three-bedroom suites in categories from mountain view to ocean deluxe. Rates start at $140 for a mountain-view room to $650 for a three-bedroom suite.

Other condos in the development are expensive, charging a minimum of $100 per night. They're out to please and don't skimp on the luxuries. For example, the **Ka'eo Kai,** tel. (800) 367-8047, gives you a massive, 2,300-square-foot unit with lanai, custom kitchen, fireplace, stereo, and big-screen TV. The units accommodate seven comfortably. The **Pali Ke Kua** condos sit right on the cliffs and, along with the nearby **Pu'u Po'a** and **Hale Moi** condominiums are managed by Marc Resorts Hawaii, tel. (800) 535-0085. The Pali Ke Kua boasts one of the best restaurants on the north coast, the units at the Pu'u Po'a are more luxurious and slightly more expensive, and the Hale Moi overlooks the golf course for about half the price.

The **Hanalei Bay Villa,** located just next to the prestigious Princeville Resort, is the area's newest vacation rental and offers large luxury suites at affordable prices. Rates are $140, $175, and $230 for a one-, two-, or three-bedroom unit (weekly and longer-stay discounts available). For reservations and information, contact Oceanfront Realty at tel. (808) 826-6585 or (800) 222-5541.

Other good locations include the **Alii Kai II,** where all units are around $100; the **Paniolo;** and weathered gray Cape Cod-ish **Sealodge.** Reservations can be made by calling Hanalei Aloha Rental Management, P.O. Box 1109, Hanalei, HI 96714, tel. (808) 826-9833 or (800) 367-8047.

Princeville Vacation Rental, tel. (808) 826-6244, offers deluxe, nonsmoking rooms on the Princeville Golf Course for $80 a night, $500 a week, three-day minimum.

FOOD

The **Bali Hai,** open daily, tel. (808) 826-6522, at the Hanalei Bay Resort, open for breakfast 7-11 a.m., lunch 11:30 a.m.-2 p.m., and dinner 5:30-10 p.m., enjoys an excellent reputation not only for its food but also for its superb atmosphere and prizewinning view of the sunset through the wraparound windows of this bilevel and informal yet elegant restaurant. The Bali Hai chefs grow their own herbs on the premises and insist on fresh local vegetables, meat, and fish prepared in a mixture of continental and Pacific Rim cuisine. Settle comfortably into high-backed wicker chairs in the inviting room, which is reminiscent of a Polynesian longhouse, with a vaulted thatched roof from which hangs a koa outrigger canoe. Drink in the spectacular view of Hanalei Bay while a tinkling waterfall keeps a soothing rhythm in the background. Start your day with a chilled fresh coconut for $4.75, a half island papaya for $3.50, or a continental breakfast that includes fresh fruit juices, bakery items, and Kona coffee for $7.25. Go local with a taro patch breakfast of two fried eggs, Portuguese sausage, poi pancakes, and taro hash browns for $8.25, or try specialties like the Bay Breakfast—eggs, ham, bacon or sausage, hash browns, and white rice for $7.25—or the Bay Benedict for $12.50. Lunchtime brings Kauai onion soup for $4, soup and salad for $7.50, and filling salads like spicy beef salad with smoked tofu for under $10. The sandwich board has a Monte Cristo with ham, turkey, and Swiss cheese—for $9.75 and an assortment of burgers, including the Bali Hai, charbroiled and served with cheese and onions, for $8.25. You can start with appetizers like blackened ahi sashimi (market price), sesame-crusted chicken for $8, or a *pu pu* platter for $11. Soup selections include soup de jour at $4, gazpacho at $5, and seafood chowder for $6, or try a garden salad with Kilauea organic greens and a choice of dressing for $5.50, or salad entrees like a crab Caesar for $14 ($16 with snow crab legs). Entree specialties are fresh island fish prepared in a variety of tempting sauces including Thai sesame, papaya salsa, and Drambuie herbed butter. Standard but wonderful offerings are teriyaki chicken at $21, spicy scampi for $23, and petite Australian lamb with fresh mint sauce for $25. Nightly, a luau and Hawaiian revue featuring hula and reenactments of Hawaiian legends is offered. You're greeted with cocktails and music provided by a local duet 6-7 p.m., and the luau buffet opens at 6:45 p.m. Tables are laden with Hawaiian favorites like *lomi* salmon, chicken long rice, fresh island catch,

kalua pork, hapia, coconut cake, and hot bread pudding. A cocktail show begins seating at 7:45 p.m., and the revue begins at 8:45 p.m. Prices for luau and revue are $49.95 adults and $12.95 children ages 5-12, $19.50 and $14 for the cocktail show and revue only.

The **Happy Talk Lounge,** also at the Hanalei Bay Resort, mixes its fantastic views of Hanalei Bay with exotic drinks, wine by the glass, and frothy beers for a night of relaxation and entertainment. A limited menu served 3-10 p.m. offers tortilla chips at $4.50, jalapeño poppers at $7.25, a *pu pu* platter for two at $11, and sesame-crusted chicken for $8. Sandwiches and salads served daily 11:30 a.m.-10 p.m. include a bay burger made with the fresh catch of the day for $10.75, chicken breast marinated in teriyaki sauce for $9, honey dipped chicken at $8.75, and a fruit and cheese plate, enough for two at $9.25.

The **Beamreach Restaurant,** in a freestanding building on the grounds of the Pali Ke Kua condo complex, open nightly for dinner 5:30-9:30 p.m., tel. (808) 826-6143 (reservations suggested), is a casual fine dining restaurant where chef Catalano Domingo offers a mix of island-style and classic American dishes. The bilevel dining room, subdued in shades of tan and brown, is lightly appointed with hanging baskets, throw nets, frescoes depicting Hawaiian mythology, and a display case holding ancient artifacts. A very good sign is that all soups and salad dressings are made on the premises, and fresh organic greens and vegetables are used as much as possible. Stimulate your palate with poke, offered raw or seared, at $6.95; teriyaki meat sticks at $5.95; or a pot of fresh steamed clams for $6.95. Move on to entrees, priced $12.95-21.95, like ground sirloin, filet mignon, macadamia nut chicken with tropical sauce, or fresh fish sautéed, broiled, or blackened. Your sweet tooth will be happy with desserts such as Tahitian Lime Pie at $4.50, tropical fruit sherbet for $2.75, or a rum, caramel, or chocolate sundae for $4.50. The Beamreach also has a full-service bar stocked with fine wine, a good selection of beer, and house specialty tropical drinks.

The **Princeville Hotel** is home to three restaurants. The **Cafe Hanalei,** open for breakfast 6:30-11 a.m., lunch 11 a.m.-2:30 p.m., dinner 6-9:30 p.m., and Sunday brunch, tel. (808) 826-9644, offers indoor or outdoor seating in a casual setting. Breakfast at the Hanalei is either continental for $14.95 or full for $20.95. The continental breakfast is much more than you might expect—a buffet table set with lox and bagels, cream cheese, fresh island fruits, fresh-squeezed juices, an assortment of cereals, yogurt, pastries, and coffee. The full breakfast buffet is complete with an omelette station, and an array of savory breakfast meats. Lunch may be chilled shrimp with rice noodles for $11.50, Thai chicken and beef satay for $10.95, a Caesar salad with croutons and Parmesan for $7.95, sushi nigiri and California rolls for $14, or any of a number of gourmet sandwiches and burgers. Dinner entrees are roasted rack of lamb for $27.95, grilled moon fish *(opa)* for $24.95, seared spicy pepper ahi at $27.95, breast of chicken or steamed Kona lobster at $35.95. Finish with desserts like apple cinnamon cheesecake, mango creme brûlé, or flourless chocolate cake, all delicious and prepared daily.

La Cascata, open daily for dinner 6-9:30 p.m., tel. (808) 826-9644, offers tremendous views of the island's inland waterfalls as you dine in this elegant ristorante. Designed after a famous restaurant in Positano, Italy, it features elegant decor including hand-painted terra-cotta floors, inspiring murals, and formally set tables. The Meditarranean-inspired menu features capellini pasta with rosemary chicken and penne primavera with roasted seasonal vegetables, both priced around $24. Grilled island ahi with roasted garlic polenta and mushroom medley, garlic-bread-crumb-baked island snapper, or crisp, slow-roasted duck with stewed lentils are all around $28. Meals are perfectly finished with desserts like classic tiramisu or a chocolate bourbon pecan tart, or with a cup of espresso or cappuccino, or a glass of fine port. For light meals, try the hotel's casual, pavilion-type **Beach Bar and Restaurant,** where you can order snacks, sandwiches, or complete meals. They offer such entrees as grilled Black Angus sirloin steak, grilled salmon or opacapaca, and barbecued pork ribs, all priced $30-35. A children's menu, priced $2 for every year of age between 3 and 12, helps keep prices down. For a sunset drink, try the hotel's **Living Room** or swim up to the pool's water bar for a mid-lap mai tai.

At the Princeville Center you'll find **Chuck's Steak House,** open for lunch Mon.-Fri. 11:30 a.m.-2:30 p.m., nightly for dinner 6-10 p.m., tel. (808) 826-9700. Chuck has a very loyal cleintele that come not only for the juicy steaks but for the fresh fish as well. Chuck's is "casual country," with an open-beamed ceiling, a choice of booth or table inside or on the lanai, and a few saddles and barrels placed here and there for effect. The lunch menu has *pu pu* and salad like "loaded fries," which are covered with bacon, cheese, and sour cream for $4.25; Caesar salad for $5.25; tuna salad $8.95; shrimp Louis for $10.50; and crab Louis for $12.50. Burgers and sandwiches go from a simple burger for $4 to a barbecue prime rib sandwich for $6.75. Dinner is delicious, with the fresh catch charbroiled or sautéed for $18.50, shrimp Hanalei for $21.50, juicy prime rib from $16.95-24.50 depending on the cut, teriyaki chicken breast at $15.75, an assortment of combination dinners priced $19.50-26, and the mouth-watering house specialty—barbecued pork ribs. A senior and children's menu relieves the bottom-line total. Chuck's has a full-service bar separate from the dining area and features a local Hawaiian woman who comes to sing and play her ukulele on weekends. Chuck's is a good choice for a family-style restaurant offering hearty portions.

Follow the rich aroma of brewing coffee to **Hale O Java,** an upscale, friendly, indoor/outdoor, casual restaurant behind Chuck's Steak House, open daily 6:30-10:30 a.m. for breakfast, 10:30 a.m.-5:30 p.m. for lunch, and until 9:30 p.m. for dinner, tel. (808) 826-7255; it will even deliver from 5 p.m. until closing. The breakfast menu offers an early-bird special (6:30-8 a.m.—two eggs, bacon, toast, and Americano coffee for $3.95), Belgian waffles $3.95-5.50, and tropical granola for $4.50; steaming coffee, latte, cappuccino, or mocha in large Italian-style cups cost around $2; or try a fruit slush or smoothie just to cool off. A glass case is filled with pastries—from sticky buns to bagels—made fresh on the premises and all priced under $2. Lunch menu is basically *panini,* Italian sandwiches made with an assortment of lunch meats and smothered with mozzarella, sliced tomatoes, and fresh pesto, served on focaccia bread for about $6. Pizza, a specialty of Hale O Java, is priced $8.50-18.50, depending on size and toppings. Dinner brings spaghetti or fettucini with marinara, white wine sauce, or pesto, priced $8.50-10.50, with a daily lasagna priced at $8.75. This place is a step or two off the normal tourist track, but it's quiet and offers well-prepared food and decent prices with a friendly staff to make you feel welcome.

Auntie Sophies, just near Hale O Java, open daily 11 a.m.-9 p.m., is a Mexican restaurant with seating indoors or outdoors on the lanai. Lunch-menu items like chicken, beef, or cheese enchiladas ($6.95), burrito ($7.95), or taco salad ($7.95), are all served with Spanish rice and beans. You can also have a chili rice bowl for $4.50, or a gringo hamburger or hot dog with different fixings for $5.95-7.50. Dinner brings a chile relleno for $11.95, baby back ribs for $14.95, or fried chicken at $11.95. Daily specials like fajitas round out the menu.

Also at the Princeville Center, **Lappert's Ice Cream** will fill a cone for you. You can order guess-what at the **Pizza Burger.**

Don't forget **Amelia's,** open daily 11:30 a.m.-6:30 p.m. at the Princeville Airport, convenient on your way into or out of town. This friendly pub serves sandwiches, hot dogs, chili, and nachos and has four TVs for live satellite sports.

ENTERTAINMENT

There is little in the way of evening entertainment in Princeville, so you may have to be creative and make your own. However, the following are definitely worth checking out. The **Bali Hai Restaurant** at the Hanalei Bay Resort swings with nightly entertainment Tues.-Sat. 6:30-9:30 p.m.—everything from contemporary music to Hawaiian ballads performed by slack-key artists. A very special performance that shouldn't be missed is the free jazz combo every Sunday 3-6 p.m. Local musical talent is fantastic, but to make things even better, top-name musicians who happen to be on the island are frequently invited to join in. If you love jazz, you can't find a more stunning venue than the Bali Hai.

Weekends bring live music to the **Princeville Golf Course Clubhouse,** where a good mix of local people and tourists come to dance the night away.

The Living Room, in the main lobby of the Princeville Hotel, is a dignified venue for a variety of island-themed entertainment including Hawaiian music, chanting, and hula.

SHOPPING AND SERVICES

Aside from the few shops in some of the larger resorts, the shopping in Princeville is clustered in the **Princeville Center,** with most shops (although not all) open daily 8 a.m.-8 p.m. Since Princeville is a self-contained community, many of these are practical shops: bank, hardware store, sporting-goods outlet, real-estate offices, Kauai Medical Group clinic, post office, restaurants. **Foodland,** open daily 6 a.m.-11 p.m., is important because it offers the cheapest food prices on the North Shore. Before it was built, the local people would drive to Kapa'a to shop; now they come here.

Some of the shops here include **Lappert's Ice Cream,** for a quick pick-me-up; **J Ms Jewels** for a quick pick-*her*-up; the **Kauai Kite Company,** a bursting crayon box filled with stuffed animals, toys, and, of course, kites for a quick lift-it-up; **Hanalei Photo Company,** a full-service photography store offering developing, cameras, and photo supplies and gadgets for a quick pin-it-up; and **Sand Dunes,** a clothing boutique for men and women with sandals, sun hats, waterproof watches, perfume, ladies' dresses, jewelry, T-shirts, and beach bags. **Pretty Woman,** open Mon.-Sat. 9:30 a.m.-6 p.m., is in the rear of the center, so you'll have to search them out. They sell name-brand ladies' fashions, jewelry, evening dresses, hats, and accessories. Not-so-pretty men are also welcome—especially if they have rolls of wrinkled-up bills bearing pictures of dead presidents—who were not so pretty either. **Restrooms,** handicapped friendly, are on the first floor of the shopping center just near the Mail Service Center.

The **Princeville Medical Clinic,** specializing in preventive medicine, is open Mon.-Fri. 9 a.m.-5 p.m. and alternating Saturdays 9 a.m.-1 p.m., tel. (808) 826-7228. Mornings are best for walk-in patients.

The last gas station on the north shore is **Princeville Chevron.** If your gauge is low make sure to tank up if you're driving back down the coast. They're open Mon.-Thurs. 7 a.m.-7 p.m., Friday and Saturday until 8 p.m., and Sunday until 6 p.m.

The **Princeville Health Club and Spa,** located at the Princeville Golf Club, open Mon.-Fri. 7 a.m.-8 p.m., Saturday 8 a.m.-8 p.m., and Sunday 8 a.m.-6 p.m., tel. (808) 826-5030, is open to the general public with a charge of $12 a day, and $40 a week. Besides a complete set of exercise equipment, the spa offers massage, body treatments, facials, and aromatherapy wraps.

HANALEI

If Puff the Magic Dragon had resided in the sunshine of Hanalei instead of the mists of Hanalee, Little Jackie Paper would still be hangin' around. You know you're entering a magic land the minute you drop down from the heights and cross the Hanalei River. The narrow, one-lane bridge is like a gateway to the enchanted coast, forcing you to slow down and take stock of where you are. To add to your amazement, as you look up valley over a sea of green taro, what else would you expect to find but a herd of buffalo? (They've been imported by a local ontrepreneur trying to cross-breed them with beef cattle.)

Hanalei ("Lei-making Town") compacts a lot into a little space. You're in and out of the town in two blinks, but you'll find a small shopping center, some terrific restaurants, beach and ocean activities, historical sites, and a cultural and art center. You also get two superlatives for the price of one: the epitome of a laid-back north shore village, and a truly magnificent bay. In fact, if one were forced to choose the most beautiful bay in all of Hawaii, Hanalei (and Lumahai, the silent star of the movie *South Pacific,* just north of town), would definitely be among the finalists.

SIGHTS

The sights around Hanalei are exactly that—beautiful sweeping vistas of Hanalei Valley and the sea, especially at sunset. People come just for the light show and are never disappointed. When you proceed past the Princeville turnoff, keep your eyes peeled for the Hanalei Valley scenic overlook. Don't miss it! Drifting into the distance is the pastel living impressionism of Hanalei Valley—most dramatic in late afternoon, when soft shadows from deeply slanting sunrays create depth in this quilt of fields. Down the center, the liquid silver Hanalei River flows until it meets the sea where the valley broadens into a wide flat fan. Along its banks, impossible shades of green vibrate as the valley steps back for almost nine miles, all cradled in the protective arms of 3,500-foot *pali.* Controlled by rains, waterfalls either tumble over the *pali* like lace curtains billowing in a gentle wind or with the blasting power of a fire hose. Local wisdom says, "When you can count 17 waterfalls, it's time to get out of Hanalei." The valley has always been

taro fields in Hanalei Valley, from which the majority of Hawaii's poi is made

one of the most accommodating places to live in all of Hawaii, and its abundance was ever-blessed by the old gods. Madame Pele even sent a thunderbolt to split a boulder so that the Hawaiians could run an irrigation ditch through its center to their fields.

In the old days, Hanalei produced taro, and deep in the valley the outlines of the ancient fields can still be discerned. Then the white man came and planted coffee that failed and sugar that petered out, and raised cattle that overgrazed the land. During these times, Hanalei had to *import* poi from Kalalau. Later, when Chinese plantation laborers moved in, the valley was terraced again, but this time the wet fields were given to rice. This crop proved profitable for many years and was still grown as late as the 1930s. Then, amazingly, the valley began to slowly revert back to taro patches.

In 1972, 917 acres of this valley were designated **Hanalei National Wildlife Sanctuary;** native water birds such as the Hawaiian coot, stilt, duck, and gallinule loved it and reclaimed their ancient nesting grounds. Today, the large, green, heart-shaped leaves of taro carpet the valley, and the abundant crop supplies about half of Hawaii's poi. You can go into Hanalei Valley; however, you're not permitted in the designated wildlife areas except to fish or hike along the river. Never disturb any nesting birds. Look below to where a one-lane bridge crosses the river. Just there, Ohiki Road branches inland. Drive along it slowly to view the simple and quiet homesteads, old rice mill, nesting birds, wildflowers, and terraced fields of this enchanted land.

Overlooking the bay, on a tall bluff, are the remains of an old Russian fort (1816) from the days when Hawaii was lusted after by many European powers. It's too difficult to find, but knowing it's there adds a little spice.

For a real cultural event, the North Shore co-operative, operating the **Waipa Taro Farm,** tel. (808) 826-6192, graciously invites lucky volunteers (maximum 15) to help with the final preparation of their famous taro every Thursday from 7 a.m. to noon. You must remember that you are there to help, not to observe. You are there to do a job and should hold your questions until work is done when you are free to take a walk through the taro patch.

Down the block, on the right next to Napali Zodiac, an old building (the old Ching Young Store) houses the **Native Hawaiian Trading and Cultural Center.** Don't get *too* excited, though, because this good idea doesn't have its act together yet. Aside from a very small museum (open daily 10 a.m.-5 p.m.), it has some authentic Hawaiian crafts and some awful touristy junk, too. You can buy handmade jewelry, shells, clothes, and sweets, but some of the really worthwhile items are lovely fresh plumeria lei and flowers. Upstairs is the Artisans Guild of Kauai, a fine co-op where local artists display and sell their arts and crafts.

Waioli Mission House Museum

As you leave town, look to your left to see **Waioli Hui'ia Church.** If you're in Hanalei on Sunday, do yourself a favor and go to the 10 a.m. service; you will be uplifted by a choir of rich voices singing enchanting hymns in Hawaiian. They do justice to the meaning of *waioli,* which is "healing or singing waters." The Waioli Mission House is a must-stop whenever you pass through. You know you're in for a treat as soon as you pull into the parking lot, which is completely surrounded by trees, creeping vines, ferns, and even papaya. You walk over steppingstones through a formal garden with the jagged mountains framing a classical American homestead; the acreage was also a self-sufficient farm where the owners raised chickens and cattle. Most mission homes are New England-style, and this one is, too, inside. But outside, it's Southern, because the missionary architect, Rev. William P. Alexander, was a Kentuckian who arrived with his wife, Mary Ann, in 1834 by double-hulled canoe from Waimea. Although a number of missionary families lived in the home in the first few years after it was built in 1837, in 1846 Abner and Lucy Wilcox arrived, and the home became synonymous with this family. Indeed, it was owned and occupied by the *kama'aina* Wilcox family until very recently. It was George, the son of Abner and Lucy, who founded Grove Homestead over by Lihue. Miss Mabel Wilcox, his niece—who died in 1978—and her sister, Miss Elsie, who was the first woman representative of Hawaii in the '30s, set up the nonprofit educational foundation that operates the home.

Your first treat will be meeting Joan, the lovely tour guide. A fusspot in the best sense of the word, she's like a proper old auntie who gives you the "hairy eyeball" if you muss up the doily on the coffee table. Joan knows an unbelievable amount of history and anecdotes, not only about the mission house, but also about the entire area and Hawaii in general. The home is great, and she makes it better. The first thing she says to Mainlanders, almost apologetically, is "Take off your shoes. It's an old Hawaiian custom and feels good to your feet."

You enter the parlor, where Lucy Wilcox taught native girls who'd never seen a needle and thread to sew. (Within a few years, their nimble fingers were fashioning muumuu to cover their pre-Christian nakedness.) In the background, an old clock ticks. In 1866, a missionary coming to visit from Boston was given $8 to buy a clock; here it is keeping time more than 120 years later. The picture on it is of the St. Louis Courthouse. Paintings of the Wilcoxes line the walls. Lucy looks like a happy, sympathetic woman. Abner's books line the shelves. Notice old copies of *Uncle Tom's Cabin* and *God Against Slavery*. Mr. Wilcox, in addition to being a missionary, was a doctor, teacher, public official, and veterinarian. His preserved letters show that he was a very serious man, not given to humor. He and Lucy didn't want to come to Waioli at first, but they learned to love the place. He worried about his sons and about being poor. He even wrote letters to the king urging that Hawaiian be retained as the first language, with English as a second. He and Lucy returned to New England for a visit in 1869, where both took sick and died.

During the time that this was a mission household, nine children—eight of them boys—were born in the main bedroom. Behind it is a nursery, the only room that has had a major change; Lucy and Mabel had a closet built and an indoor bathroom installed there in 1921. Upstairs is a guest bedroom that the Wilcoxes dubbed the "room of the traveling prophet," because it was invariably occupied by visiting missionaries. It was also used by Abner Wilcox as a study, and the books in the room are the original primers printed on Oahu. The homestead served as a school for selected boys who were trained as teachers.

The house has been added to several times and is surprisingly spacious. Around the home are artifacts, dishes, and knickknacks from the last century; notice candle molds, a food locker, a charcoal iron, and the old butter churn. Lucy Wilcox churned butter, which she shipped to Honolulu in buckets and which brought in some good money. Most of the furniture is donated period pieces; only a few were actually used by the Wilcoxes. From an upstairs window, you can still see the view that has remained unchanged from the last century: Hanalei Bay, beautifully serene and timeless. The Waioli Mission House is open Tuesday, Thursday, and Saturday 9 a.m.-3 p.m., and is free! There is a bucket for donations; please be generous.

The spacious guest bedroom at the Waioli Mission House Museum is filled with period furniture.

BEACHES

Since the days of the migrating Polynesians, Hanalei Bay has been known as one of the Pacific's most perfect anchorages. Used as one of Kauai's three main ports until very recently, it's still a favorite port of call for world-class yachts. They start arriving in mid-May, making the most of the easy entrance and sandy bottom, and stay throughout the summer. They leave by October, when even this inviting bay becomes rough, with occasional 30-foot waves. When you drive to the bay, the section under the trees near the river is called **Black Pot.** It received this name from an earlier time, when the people of Hanalei would greet the yachties with island *aloha,* which, of course, included food. A fire was always going with a large black pot hanging over it, into which everyone contributed and then shared in the meal. Across the road and upriver a few hundred yards is **Hanalei Canoe Club.** This small local club has produced a number of winning canoe teams in statewide competitions, oftentimes appearing against much larger clubs.

The sweeping crescent bay is gorgeous. The Hanalei River and three smaller streams empty into it, and all around it's protected by embracing mountains. A long pier is in the center, and two reefs front the bay: **Queen** to the left and **King** to the right. The bay provides excellent sailing, surfing, and swimming—mostly in the summer. The swimming is good near the river (but watch out for boats and Zodiac rafts, which are launched from here) and at the west end, but rip currents can appear anywhere, even around the pier area, so be careful. The best surf rolls in at the outside reef below Pu'u Po'a Point on the east side of the bay, but it's definitely recommended only for expert surfers. Beginners should try the middle of the bay during summer, when the surf is smaller and gentler. The state maintains three parks on the bay: Black Pot, at the Hanalei River mouth, Pine Trees, in the middle of the bay, and Waipa, on the west side. Black Pot and Pine Trees have picnic areas, restrooms, and showers. Camping is permitted only at Pine Trees. A small *kaukau* wagon sells plate lunches near the river; local fishermen launch their boats in the bay and are often amenable to selling their catch.

Lumahai Beach is a femme fatale, lovely to look at but treacherous. This hauntingly beautiful beach (whose name translates as "Twist of Fingers") is what dreams are made of: white sand curving perfectly at the bottom of a dark lava cliff with tropical jungle in the background. The riptides here are fierce even with the reef, and the water should never be entered except in very calm conditions during the summer. Look for a vista point between mile markers 4 and 5. Cars invariably park here. It's a sharp curve, so make sure to pull completely off the road or the police may ticket you. An extensive grove of hala trees appears just as you set off down a steep and often muddy footpath leading down to the east end of the beach. The best and easiest place to park is amongst the ironwood trees at the west end of the beach near the bridge that crosses the Lumahai River; an emergency phone is across the road from this parking area. From here you can walk to the south end if you want seclusion.

ACCOMMODATIONS

The inexpensive **Mahikoa's Hanalei Bay Inn** is on the west side of town across from the school. It's tucked in amongst flowering bushes and trees; with only six units, it's a quiet, relaxing place. Five units have living/bedroom areas with queen-size or pairs of twin beds, efficiency kitchens sufficient to make light meals, and full baths; one of the units has an additional separate bedroom. The efficiencies run $55 ($45 after two days) and the one-bedroom is $65 ($55 after two days). In addition, a bed-and-breakfast room maintained in the innkeeper's cottage goes for $50 plus tax. Maid service is available after four days. For more information, call (808) 826-9333 or write to Edmund Gardien, Innkeeper, Mahikoa's Hanalei Bay Inn, P.O. Box 122, Hanalei, HI 96714.

Bed, Breakfast, and Beach, P.O. Box 748, Hanalei, HI 96714, tel. (808) 826-6111, owned by Caroly Barnes, is a neo-classic trilevel plantation-style home, located in a quiet residential area only a minute's walk from the beach. It gives you a strong feeling that you are part of the community. Upstairs offers a wide, covered lanai, perfect for catching the breeze or listening to the soft patter of a morning shower while eating breakfast—served 8:30-9:30 a.m. and consisting of your choice of piping hot coffee, herbal teas, and fresh island fruits, juices or smoothies, accompanied by muffins, and fresh-baked bread. On the upper levels you'll find plenty of windows from which to enjoy a postcard view of the surrounding mountains scratching the soft bellies of passing clouds causing showers that turn into lace waterfalls cascading from the green luminescent heights. The common area, a casual lounging parlor, is cool and inviting with smooth parquet floors, an open beamed ceiling, and knotty-pine paneling. The decor throughout is a mixture of classic Hawaiian and tasteful New England antique appointed with items like a bent glass china closet, wooden refrigerator, and reclining bamboo chairs and couches covered in floral patterned puff pillows. Nooks and crannies are filled with objets d'art and plenty of reading material. From the common area, a staircase ascends to the Bali Hai Suite. At 700 square feet, it occupies the entire top floor and is divided into a master bedroom, day room/conversation nook, and bath. Off the central area is the Pualani Suite—smaller, but alive, like a living floral arrangement with pastel blooms from ceiling to bedspread. At ground level, two units, called the Garden Lanai and Maki, offer kitchenettes and outdoor showers (Garden Lanai has an indoor shower as well). The decor in both is island themed, with bamboo or rattan furniture and louvered windows and ceiling fans for catching the breezes. Bed, Breakfast, and Beach is an excellent choice of accommodations for relaxation, a feeling of homeyness, and extremely good value. Rates are $70-90 d; children are welcome except in the Bali Hai Suite.

You can still smell the sweet incense that permeates **Historic Bed and Breakfast, Hanalei,** 5-5067 Kuhio Hwy., P.O. Box 1662, Hanalei, HI 96714, tel. (808) 826-4622. Housed in Kauai's oldest Buddhist Temple, the simple but elegant structure built in 1901 served the Japanese community until 1985, when it began to fall into disrepair. Neglected and deteriorating, the temple was saved by a consortium of local business people and now has the distinction of being listed in both the National and State Historic Registers. This painstaking and extensive effort refurbished more than 95% of the original structure including the lustrous hardwood floor, polished over the decades by the stockinged tread of devout parishioners. This remarkable B&B is now owned and operated by Jeff and Belle Shepherd, who welcome you to three bright and airy rooms cooled by ceiling fans. Decorated with original art, the two downstairs and one upstairs rooms, priced $55 s, $65 d, are separated by shoji screens and feature beds covered with antique quilts. You are free to relax in the comfortable common area—part of which serves as a dining room for breakfast—or to stroll outdoors to a small garden, perfect for an evening cup of tea. The shared bathrooms have deep Japanese-style *ofuro* tubs where you can soak away to your heart's content. Historic Bed and Breakfast, offering a perfect opportunity to become part of Kauai 's living history, is centrally located, with only a five minute walk to the downtown area or the beach.

Private rental homes, generally listed through property and rental agencies, are also available in town (and farther along the coast). For information, contact **Na Pali Properties, Inc.,** P.O. Box 475, Hanalei, HI 96714, tel. (808) 826-7272; **North Shore Properties and Vacation Rentals,** P.O. Box 607, Hanalei, HI 96714, tel. (808) 826-9622; or **Ironwood Rentals,** tel. (808) 826-7533.

FOOD AND FOOD SHOPPING

Hanalei has a number of eating institutions, ranging from excellent restaurants to *kaukau* wagons. The food is great at any time of day, but those in the know time their meals to coincide with sunset. They watch the free show and then go for a great dinner.

The **Hanalei Gourmet,** in the old schoolhouse at the Hanalei Center, open Mon.-Thurs. 10 a.m.-10:30 p.m. for lunch and dinner and Fri.-Sun. 8 a.m.- 11:30 p.m., tel. (808) 826-2524, is a born-again-hippie, semi-yuppie, one-stop nouveau cuisine deli, gourmet food shop, and good-time bar. To top it off, it's friendly, the food is exceptionally good, the prices are right, and there's even live entertainment. It is broken into two sections; to the right is the deli, with cases filled with lunch meats, cheeses, salads, and smoked fish, while to the left is the bar/dining area. Here, ceiling fans keep you cool, while blackboards, once used to announce hideous homework assignments, now herald the daily specials. Behind the bar, windows through which reprimanded childhood daydreams once flew now open to frame green-silhouetted mountains. Original hardwood floors, white walls bearing local artworks and hanging plants, two big-screen TVs for sports enthusiasts, and a wide veranda with a few tables for dining alfresco complete the restaurant. Breakfast, served from 8 a.m., offers a half-papaya with other fresh fruit for $4.75; bagels, lox, and cream cheese for $6.95, muesli topped with fresh fruit for $4.25, and huevos Santa Cruz for $6.25. You can also enjoy a cup of Lappert's coffee and a pastry for around $3. Lunch sandwiches, all around $7, are huge wedges filled with pastrami, smoked ham, gourmet cheeses, and more. Lunch and dinner are served 5:30-9:30 p.m. and features specials like Oregon Bay shrimp served open-face on brown bread with melted cheese and remoulade sauce for $7.50, or smoked Alaskan king salmon on a French baguette for $10.50, and fresh catch made in a variety of ways at market price. You can also order a picnic lunch to go, side salads, plenty of baked goods, and even a fine bottle of wine. The Hanalei Gourmet definitely lives up to its name and is the perfect spot for a meal or a social beer.

Bubba Burger, first opened in Kapa'a and now with a branch in Hanalei at the Hanalei Center, open daily 10 a.m.-6 p.m., is still doing what it's always done: serve up double-fisted burgers, individually made, at great prices. Mostly a window restaurant, there is seating on the lanai, with a few tables inside. Bubba's burgers range in price $2.50-4.25, with other offerings on the menu like Italian sausage or a fish burger at $4.50, a Hubba Bubba—rice, a burger patty, and hot dog, all smothered with chili for $5. Try side orders like chili fries or Caesar salad, all light on the wallet but not so light on the waistline.

Papagayo Azul, open 11 a.m.-9 p.m., tel. (808) 826-4494, a north shore institution, features good food at reasonable prices. Before the devastation of Hurricane Iniki, Papagayo Azul was located along the main street, but this spotless *nuevo Mexicano* restaurant has since moved to the back court of the Hanalei Center, where you should definitely seek it out. Inside, the new restaurant boasts an open kitchen, thatched roof, wooden floor, ceiling fans, and the mandatory sombreros, serape, and strung chili peppers of a Mexican restaurant. Lunch brings a regular burrito for $5.95, carnitas burrito at $7.95, fish taco for $4.50, tostadas $6.95, and good old nachos at $4.95. The dinner menu (you can order from the lunch menu at dinner) starts with ceviche at $6.95, quesadilla with a chicken or beef at $4.95, *ensaladas de nopalitos*— a cactus marinated in herbs and spices— at $5.95, and *ensaladas de jicama,* marinated in orange juice for $5.95. Entrees include *pollo borracho,* a boneless breast of chicken grilled in tequila sauce at $9.95, *pescado asado,* charbroiled ahi in a light chile wine sauce at $11.95, or beef steak ranchero at $12.95. All items are served a la carte; beans and rice are $1.95 extra. Papagayo Azul has always had a loyal local following and still deserves the distinction of a people's choice restaurant.

If you want a romantic evening, head for the silvery beams of **Cafe Luna,** open daily in the Hanalei Center 5-9:30 p.m. tel. (808) 826-1177, an avant-garde, cosmopolitan restaurant where you can dine alfresco under a wooden pavilion or inside at classically set tables. Begin your meal with seafood bisque for $6, classic Caesar for $7, or polenta with shrimp for $8. Move on to pasta like *aglio e olio* for $11; primavera made with fresh vegetables, sherry, and choice of marinara, white, oglio, or *blu,* a gorgonzola-based sauce with sage, tomato, and cream. The main entrees range in price $14-21 and include choices like filet mignon, grilled fish, and vegetarian lasagna. There is a full selection of pizzas priced $9-12 with a wonderful array of toppings including marinated shrimp, caramelized onions, and sun-dried tomato. To top off your meal, choose a dessert like light and refreshing fresh berries, banana rum crepes, or the Italian standard, tiramisu. Cafe Luna is a fine dining restaurant, offering a perfect mixture of nouvelle and classic dishes that won't cost you the moon.

In a freestanding building in the Hanalei Center follow the aroma of fresh brewed coffee to the **Old Hanalei Coffee Company,** open daily 8 a.m.-5 p.m., tel. (808) 826-6717 where you can revitalize with a cup of espresso, cappuccino, latte, au lait, or an old-fashioned hot chocolate made with Hershey's syrup and milk. If you're in the mood for something else, try a frosted mocha or a flavored Italian soda. The Hanalei Coffee Co. serves breakfast and lunch until 2 p.m.; you can eat inside or out on the lanai. The good but limited menu consists of Kauai waffles, three-egg scramble, assorted bagels, homemade soup, and sandwiches like hot cordon bleu or hot turkey, everything priced $2.50-6.50. Smaller items—all made on the premises—include muffins and cheesecake, or you might like to bring home a pound of bulk coffee. Just outside is **Shave Ice Paradise,** which is owned by the same man who owns the Coffee Company (you'll see him scurrying back and forth). Here you can choose from 17 flavors of traditional shave ice including coconut and papaya, with fruit cocktail and adzuki beans thrown in for good measure. There's ice cream and a signature drink called a Summer Breeze, somewhat like an Orange Julius with a special twist. They scoop the ice cream and make the shave ice as if they were doing it for family and friends. Your only problem is to lick faster than these hefty babies can melt.

You've got to stop at the **Tahiti Nui,** tel. (808) 826-6277, if just to look around and have a cool drink. The owner, Louise Marston, a real Tahitian although her name doesn't sound like it, is dedicated to creating a friendly family atmosphere and she succeeds admirably. Inside, it's pure Pacific Island. The decorations are modern Polynesian longhouse, with blowfish lanterns and stools carved from palm tree trunks. The bar, open from noon to midnight, is the center of action and features live music Wed.-Sat. nights. Old-timers drop in to "talk story," and someone is always willing to sing and play a Hawaiian tune. The mai tais are fabulous. Just sit out on the porch, kick back, and sip away. The lunch and dinner menu ($10-21) is limited but includes fresh fish, beef, and chicken—all prepared with an island twist. You sit at long tables and eat family-style. The Tahiti Nui is famous for its luau-style parties Wednesday and Friday at 6:30 p.m. There's singing, dancing, and good cheer all around—a perfect time to mingle with the local people. The food is real Hawaiian, and the show is no glitzy extravaganza or slick production. This luau is very

down to earth, casual, Kauaian; everybody has a good time; price is $40 adults, $17 children, free under age five.

Located next to Tahiti Nui, in the Kauhale Center, the **Hanalei Wake-Up Cafe,** open daily 6 a.m.-2:30 p.m., tel. (808) 826-5551, owned and operated by Lani, is the perfect breakfast place in Hanalei. Cubbyhole small, it also has a few tables out on the veranda. The cheery help, the smell of freshly brewed coffee, and the good home cookin' should help start your day off on the right foot. Try a giant muffin for $2, Over the Falls French toast for $4.75, and Hanalei in the Tube, which is a quesadilla with scrambled eggs, onions, and bell peppers in a flour tortilla with rice or hash browns for $6.50. You can also have a veggie tofu sautè of fresh vegetables, served with rice or hash browns for $5.75. Baked goods include bagel with cream cheese for $2, or have a nutritious sunrise smoothie flavored with fresh pineapple, banana, or papaya for $2.75.

Just down the walkway in this group of shops is the **Black Pot Luau Hut** restaurant and bar, tel. (808) 826-9871, serving mostly Hawaiian food. Open on a variable schedule for lunch and dinner, usually 11:30 a.m.-2:30 p.m. and then again 5:30-9 p.m., Black Pot offers saimin for $2.55-4.25, teri chicken or beef sticks at $1, hamburgers for $2.55-3.40, and a selection of sandwiches like fishmelt, crabmelt, teri beef, or teri chicken for under $5. The Hawaiian and local food choices, served with two scoops of rice and potato or macaroni salad, include *kalua* pig for $7.95, stir-fry chicken for $6.50, or a teri chicken plate at $4.95. Downhome basic Black Pot is very friendly, very local, and very good.

At the Hanalei Trader, the first building on the left as you enter town, look for a hanging golden dolphin marking the **Hanalei Dolphin Restaurant,** open daily 5:30-10 p.m., tel. (808) 826-6113, almost hidden in the dense tropical foliage on the banks of the Hanalei River. The interior is casual, with an open beamed ceiling, wood trim, and *tapa*-like formica tables with blue captain's chairs. Appetizers include ceviche at $5, stuffed mushrooms for $6.50, and seafood cocktails at market price. Seafood, mainly from the owners' fish market around back, includes fresh catch at market price (try the seared teriyaki ahi), teriyaki shrimp for $19.50, calamari for $16, fresh fish and chips for $15. Other entrees include Hawaiian chicken for $15, *haole* chicken, a boneless breast of chicken with seasonings and Parmesan for $15, and New York steak at $19.50. Light dinners like broccoli casserole and seafood chowder run $10.50. All entrees are served with family-style salads, steak fries or rice, and hot homemade bread.

The **Hanalei Dolphin Fish Market,** at the Hanalei Trader, open daily 11 a.m.-6 p.m., sells fresh, locally caught fish, perfect for a private dinner or beach luau.

Tropical Taco is a *kaukau* wagon open daily except Monday 11 a.m.-4 p.m. It dispenses great food at cheap prices and is usually parked next to the Hanalei Trader as you enter town. Roger, the owner and an avid surfer, came to the north shore 20 years ago. He's never too busy to "talk story" and is a font of wit and wisdom about Hanalei and the surrounding area. A family man who has proudly sent his daughters off to university through his one-man operation, Roger will take the time—especially with families—to direct you to safe swimming, snorkeling, and hiking areas. Roger has just painted his truck bright green to fit in with the foliage, and from the window dispenses tasty and filling baby burritos for $2, regular tacos for $4, large overstuffed fish tacos for $7, ice cream, and 100% cotton Tropical Taco T-shirts.

A great place to write home is the covered veranda of the 100-year-old plantation home that was once the Hanalei Museum. The owners of **Postcards,** tel. (808) 826-1191, a cafe and mostly-Mexican restaurant, have refurbished the mansion to a condition as close to the original as possible, and today it is listed on the National Register. Breakfast here with a steaming cup of cappuccino and a homemade muffin, or sweet roll, and watch north shore life go by. Postcards is an upbeat, health-conscious vegetarian restaurant that prides itself on using organic ingredients and making every dish from scratch. It roasts all its own peppers, make its own salsa, and drenches its enchiladas in four different types of sauces simmered from three different types of chili peppers. Dishes are simple but hearty, and the price, especially for the quality, is good. Postcards is wheelchair friendly, while smokers are completely prohibited even from lighting up outside. The food is so pure and the vibes so harmonious that the present owner and staff plan to serve people for at least the next 200 or 300 years.

Zelo's, established in Princeville for seven years, moved to Hanalei in late 1995 after the hurricane; it's open daily 11 a.m.-9:30 p.m. with happy hour 3:30-5:30 p.m. and sometimes music on weekends, tel. (808) 826-9700. The interior of this indoor/outdoor restaurant is distinctive, with a bamboo bar covered with a corrugated roof supported by old beams and tree trunks, and lauhala matting on the walls. The lunch menu offers salads ranging from a petite for $3.95 to a Chinese chicken salad for $9.50. Sandwiches include grilled cheese for $4.75, a Philadelphia steak sandwich for $8.95, and turkey and cheese at $6.25. There is a full range of burgers with all the fixings—including teriyaki, pesto, and a Cajun fish burger—priced $5-8. Other items are nachos at $5.95, gourmet onion rings for $4.95, all-you-can-eat spaghetti at $8.95, fettucine alfredo for $8.95, and linguine with clams and pine nuts at $11.95. The atmosphere is pleasant, the staff friendly, and the prices reasonable.

In the Ching Young Shopping Center, **Pizza Hanalei,** open daily 11 a.m.-9 p.m., tel. (808) 826-9494, serves Hanalei's only pizza, and it's delicious. Made with thin, white, or whole-wheat crust, these pizzas run $8-30 (for the Lizzy Special). There is pizza by the slice 11 a.m.-4 p.m. Green and pasta salads, garlic bread, lasagna, and pizzarittos (pizza filling rolled up in a pizza shell like a burrito) are also on the menu. They also do cholesterol-free tofu pizza using Tofurella.

Next to Pizza Hanalei is **Hanalei Health and Natural Foods,** open daily 8:30 a.m.-8:30 p.m. in summer, 9 a.m.-7 p.m. in winter, tel. (808) 826-6990. Inside are bulk foods, fresh fruits and vegetables, a variety of baked breads, freshly squeezed juices, deli foods, and sandwiches, as well as books and vitamins. They also have a good selection of cosmetics, incense, candles, rolling papers, and massage oils. If you're into natural foods and healthful living, stop in, look around, and chat.

If the little hunger monster gets hold of you and a slab of tofu just won't do, walk across the courtyard to **the Village Snack and Bake Shop.** Open daily 6 a.m.-6 p.m., it serves just what its name implies, along with light breakfasts.

Papa Al's Buffalo Burger and Euro-Asian Mixed Plates, in a freestanding building in the Ching Young Village, serves up burgers, veggie burgers, barbecued steaks, Korean barbecue, and pretzels. They also have unusual items like funnel cakes from New Jersey and fried bologna sandwiches—if burgers of buffalo (raised in Hanalei), $5.65, aren't unusual enough. Papa Al's is basically a window restaurant with outdoor seating where prices are very reasonable, ranging from $2.95 for the fried bologna to $6.75 for stir-fried chicken. Next door is **Zababaz,** where you can refresh yourself with a shave ice or a Lappert's ice cream cone.

Every Tuesday 3-5 p.m., pick up some farm-fresh fruit and vegetables from the **Hawaiian Farmers of Hanalei** farmers' market, located a half-mile west of town, in Waipa, on the road to Haena. Look for the sign along the road on the left.

SHOPPING

The **Hanalei Trader** is the first building as you enter town. Here you'll find **Ola's,** tel. (808) 826-6937, open daily 10 a.m.- 9:30 p.m., an "American" craft store with items from all 50 states, like glass work from Oregon, ceramics from California, wood products from Hawaii, and jewelry from New York. Some of the unique items are tiny tots' leather moccasins, wildflower honey foaming bath, greeting cards, hairbrushes, wooden hearts, leather purses, cutting boards, and silver and gold jewelry.

Ke Kane Kai, a.k.a. The Water Man, also in the Hanalei Trader, tel. (808) 826-5594, open daily 9 a.m -9:30 p.m., not only catches your eye but also helps keep the sun out of it with a display of hats for both men and women. It also sells a large selection of alohawear and casual beachwear. Glass cases hold watches and sunglasses, while a canoe fashioned from breadfruit hangs overhead and surfboards line the walls. Although Ke Kane Kai doubles as a clothing shop, its primary function is as a surf shop. Upstairs is filled with surfboards fashioned by legendary shapers like Terry Chung and Billy Hamilton, along with a wide selection of wet suits, leashes, and shorts. Ke Kane Kai does not rent surfboards but does rent top-notch silicone snorkel gear at $5 per day or $20 per week

The **Ching Young Village** in the center of town is a small shopping center. Among its attractions are a **Big Save Supermarket,** open daily 7 a.m.-9 p.m.; a number of variety and gift stores; **public restrooms;** a few clothing shops; **Flying Fish Film Processing;** a **Bank of Hawaii; Hanalei Video and Music;** and a **See Kauai** activity and information booth; the **post office** is next door.

Two shops located just near the Tahiti Nui Restaurant are the **Hanalei Photo Company,** with one-hour developing, cameras, and a fax service; and **Kiki Bikini,** where ladies might want to find that just-right swimsuit.

The **Hanalei Center,** the newest in town, has an excellent assortment of shops and boutiques. Some impressive ones are **Rainbow Ducks,** specializing in children's wear; **Sand People,** which offers island casual clothing for men and women; **Bamboo Silks,** a ladies' shop with elegant and casual dresses; **Yellowfish Trading Company,** which is stuffed from floor to ceiling with Hawaiiana, antiques, collectibles, hula-doll lamps, classic Hawaiian aloha shirts, kuchi-kuchi dolls, costume and silver jewelry, floral colored day bags, candles, swords, antique hats, Matson Steamship Line posters, and koa carvings and incidentals. Yellowfish is a terrific place to browse and get a taste of classic Hawaii. Here, too, is **Whalers General Store,** open daily 8 a.m.-8 p.m., selling groceries, liquor, sundries, and souvenirs.

The most distinctive shop, **Kahn Galleries,** open daily 9 a.m.-10 p.m., in the Hanalei Town Center, tel. (808) 826-6677, specializes in original artworks and limited edition prints created by some of the finest artists Hawaii has to offer.

Tropical Tantrum, in the Hanalei Center, open 9 a.m.-9 p.m. and until 7 p.m. in winter, tel. (808) 826-6944, is part of a small chain (others are in Kapa'a and on Maui) that designs its own fabrics which are then turned into original clothing in Indonesia. At Tropical Tantrum, women can rage in the most vibrant colors of purple, blue, red, green, and yellow, transforming themselves into walking rainforests. Prices for original designs, perfect for either casual or elegant evenings, range $40-120. Complete the ensemble with earrings, necklaces, or bracelets from their selection. Gentlemen may browse through a rack of aloha shirts, priced around $60, stuck off in the corner.

Victor Bailey, a.k.a. **Treasure Chest,** P.O. Box 178, Kealia, HI 96751, tel. (808) 826-1492, offers strings of beads and seashells, mixing in a sprinkling of semiprecious gemstones for color and style. His distinctive creations are affordable—bracelets and anklets at $10, necklaces $20-40. You're going to have to find Victor mostly by chance, since like the wind that bathes Kauai, he's at any beach where the sun shines (although mostly he prefers the north shore).

SPORTS AND RECREATION

Hanalei is alive with outdoor activities. The following is merely a quick list of what's available.

Na Pali Zodiac, the oldest and best-known Zodiac company, offers stupendous rides up the Na Pali coast in a seagoing rubber raft, with hiking drop-off service also available. It's owned and operated by "Captain Zodiac," Clancy Greff, P.O. Box 456, Hanalei, HI 96714, tel. (808) 826-9371 or (800) 422-7824.

Hanalei Sea Tours, tel. (808) 826-7254 or (800) 733-7997, P.O. Box 1447, Hanalei, HI 96714, offers a Nualolo Day Trip; a five- to six-hour trip down the Na Pali coast for $100, lunch and snorkeling gear included; a four-hour trip down the Na Pali coast for $75; a mini-tour, two and a half hours, which includes whalewatching in season, for $55, beverages provided; and a catamaran adventure for the same price as the zodiac. Hanalei Sea Tours offers Kalalau Valley camper drop-off service May-Sept. for $60 one-way, $130 roundtrip, and drop-off service to Milolii State Park for $130 roundtrip including a state permit to camp.

For boat rides up the coast, contact **Na Pali Adventures,** tel. (808) 826-6804, or (800) 659-6804, P.O. Box 1017, Hanalei, HI 96714. They provide environmentally responsible interpretive tours in their specially outfitted catamarans. You can sail, snorkel, or whalewatch in season. Based primarily in Hanalei, they also sail from Nawilwili or Port Allen, depending on ocean conditions. Rates are $55-80, depending upon which tour you choose, and include a snorkel stop with instructions and equipment, snacks, beverages, and deli sandwiches.

The company to see for a kayaking adventure up the Hanalei River or during summer, along the coast, is **Kayak Kauai,** tel. (808) 826-9844.

A variety of sailing and fishing adventures are available from **Hawaiian Z-boat Co.,** tel. (808) 822-5113; **Robert McReynolds,** tel. (808) 822-5113; and Captain Andy's **Bluewater Sailing** tel. (808) 822-0525. The sailboats run only during the summer.

The **Hanalei Surf Co.,** in the Hanalei Center, tel. (808) 826-9000, is a water-sports shop that rents and sells snorkeling equipment, boogie boards, and surfboards. Rental rates are surfboards for $15 per day, boogie boards for $7, snorkel equipment for $5; money-saving weekly rates are available on all rentals. The store is also stocked with a good selection of shirts, shorts, thongs, bathing suits, pareo, incidental bags, sunglasses, sunblock, and dresses.

Pedal and Paddle, tel. (808) 826-9069, in the Ching Young Center, open daily 9 a.m.-5 p.m. in winter, 9 a.m.-6 p.m. in summer, rents and sells snorkel gear, bikes, boogie boards, and surfboards. Prices are: snorkel gear $7 a day, $20 per week; body board with fins $8 and $25; surf boards $12 and $36; cruiser bikes $10 and $40; mountain bikes $50 and $80 (all bike rentals include lock, helmet, and car rack if desired); two-person dome tents $10 and $30; backpacks $5 and $20; light blankets $3 and $10; day packs $4 and $12 . A rental day begins the hour you rent and ends at 5 p.m. the following day. Pedal and Paddle does not sell bikes or kayaks, but snorkel and camping gear is for sale. Kayaks available for rent, too.

John Sargent's **Bike Doctor,** in Hanalei, tel. (808) 826-7799, open Mon.- Sat. 9 a.m.-5 p.m., is stocked with everything for the casual and serious cyclist. John is also intimately familiar with roads and trails all over the island and is happy to give advice on touring.

Ke Kane Kai is a full-service surf shop.

SERVICES AND INFORMATION

The **North Shore Taxi,** tel. (808) 826-6189, not only runs a pick-up and delivery service, but also does tours. The ordinary fare from Hanalei to Princeville is under $10, to the end of the road at Ke'e Beach is about $20. Owner Dave Sammann will pick you up and take you to or from the North Shore or to the airport in a taxi, mini van, or station wagon for $63. North Shore Taxi also offers luxury service with one of their Cadillac or Lincoln stretch limos for $135. You must pre-arrange the luxury service and Dave will be waiting, resplendent in his chauffeur's cap and surfing shorts.

ROAD'S END

Past Hanalei you have six miles of pure magic until the road ends at Ke'e Beach. To thrill you further and make your ride even more enjoyable, you'll find historical sites, natural wonders, a resort, restaurant, grocery store, and the *heiau* where the hula was born, overlooking a lovely beach.

Sights, Accommodations, and Services

As you drive along, you cross one-lane bridges and pass little beaches and bays, one after another, invariably with a small stream flowing in. Try not to get jaded peering at "just another gorgeous north shore beach."

Over a small white bridge is the village of **Wainiha** ("Angry Water"), with its tiny **Wainiha Store,** open daily 9:30 a.m.-6:30 p.m., tel. (808) 826-6251, where you can pick up a few supplies and sundries. You can also rent beach equipment like boogie boards ($5 a day), snorkel gear ($6), and surfboards ($12)—a cash deposit is required for any rental. Campers and cyclists heading down the Kalalau Trail can store bags for $2 per bag per day and bikes for $5 a day. A three-day **camping equipment** package, including tent, lantern, stove, utensils, and a backpack (no sleeping bags), runs $30. Remember that camping permits must be picked up at the DLNR at the State Building way back in Lihue! Talk to Janet if you're looking for a place to stay; people from around the area come to the store to post fliers if they have rooms to rent. You can still get a shack on the beach or in amongst the banana trees.

Attached to the store are **Wainiha Sandwiches** and a T-shirt and gift shop. Sandwiches, all around $5, include turkey and Swiss, roast beef, ham, or tuna, all with sprouts, tomatoes, mustard, mayonnaise, and veggie salt. It's not hard to find a bunch of local guys hanging around, perhaps listening to Jahawaiian reggae music, who could brighten your day by selling you some of the local produce!

Next up, look for signs to the **Hanalei Colony Resort**—literally the last resort. You can rent very comfortable, spacious, two-bedroom condos here, each with a full kitchen, shower/tub, and lanai. The brown board-and-batten buildings blend into the surroundings. The resort has a jacuzzi and swimming pool, barbecue grills, coin-operated washers and dryers, Hawaiiana classes, complimentary slide shows, and twice-weekly maid service. The beach in front of the resort is great for a stroll at sunset, but be very careful swimming during winter months or periods of high surf. Based on single or double occupancy, units rent for $110-130 for a garden view, $185-205 for a premium oceanfront, with the seventh night free for a weeklong stay. Car-rental packages are available if arranged before arriving on Kauai. For information, contact Hanalei Colony Resort, P.O. Box 206, Hanalei, HI 96714, tel. (808) 826-6235 or (800) 628-3004.

On the premises is **Charo's Restaurant**—yes, *that* Charo! Heavily damaged by Hurricane Iniki, it has recently reopened and serves lunch and dinner 11:30 a.m.-9 p.m. Next door is **Charro's Gift Shop** where you can buy a T-shirt or poster emblazoned with the famous "hoochi-koochi" girl, as well as cassettes and CDs of Charro's music. Another case displays bangles, bracelets, and beads.

Just past Hanalei Resort, between mile markers 7 and 8 on the highway, look for the entrance to **YMCA Camp Naue.** The turnoff is at the road entrance by the phone booth. Here, several buildings are filled with bunks and a separate toilet area and cooking facilities. The camp caters to large groups but is open to single travelers for the staggering sum of $10 per night. Kauai residents are $9; children are half price; a tent and the first person costs $8; each additional person in the tent is $5. The bunkhouses lie under beachside trees, campers stay in the yard. As with most YMCAs, there are many rules to be followed. You can get full information from YMCA headquarters in Lihue or by writing YMCA of Kauai, P.O. Box 1786, Lihue, HI 96766, tel. (808) 246-9090, 742-1200, or 826-6419 in Haena.

About six-tenths of a mile past YMCA, a driveway turns off the highway to **Tunnels Beach** (look for a two-story house with a green roof). It's superb for snorkeling and scuba, with a host of underwater caves off to the left as you face the sea. Both surfing and windsurfing are great, and so is the swimming if the sea is calm. Watch out for boats that come inside the reef to anchor. Off to the right and down a bit is a nude beach. Be careful not to sunburn delicate parts!

Haena Beach County Park, just before the road's end, is a large, flat, fieldlike area, where you carve out your own camping site. For your convenience, the county provides tables, a pavilion, grills, showers, and camping (permit required). The sand on this long crescent beach is rather coarse, and the swimming is good only when the sea is gentle, but in summertime a reef offshore is great for snorkeling. Some Zodiac boats are launched a few hundred yards down the beach to the east. The cold stream running through the park is always good for a dip. Kuulei's *kaukau* wagon is usually parked in this lot every day from about 10 a.m.

Tassa Hanalei B&B, P.O. Box 856 Hanalei, HI 96714, tel. (808) 826-7298, owned by Ileah Von Hubbard, is dedicated to the rejuvenation of your body, mind, and spirit. Located along the river in Wainiha Valley, the tranquil surroundings of flowers, foliage, birdlife, and waterfalls create a natural healing balm. Rates, paid in cash or traveler's check only, are $65 s, $85 d for the smaller suite or $105 d, $125 family, and $150 group for the larger. During the last week of every month, Ileah offers a healing retreat. You can also make an appointment between 10 a.m. and 7 p.m. for a variety of therapies including massage, yoga, and colonics. Tassa Hanalei may not be for everyone, but if you have come to Kauai not only to relax but to rejuvinate, it may be perfect for you

Across the road is **Maniniholo dry cave.** Notice the gorgeous grotto of trees, and the jungle wild with vines. You walk in and it feels airy and very conducive as living quarters, but it has never been suggested that the cave was used as a site of permanent habitation. Luckily, even with all the visitors going in and out, it hasn't been trashed. For the past few years, on a night of a full moon, people have gathered in the cave just at sunset for group *sufi* dancing. Unfortu-

nately, there have been communication problems with the local people of the area. The gathering was open to all who wished to join the circle of peaceful humanity, but no one *formally* invited the local people to attend because no one person was the *formal* head of this very independent group. News of the dance spread by word of mouth, and those inclined to come were welcomed. Many of the the *sufi* dancers were alternative types and some very misinformed local people believed that some kind of unholy ritual was going on. Most of these feelings have been smoothed over by now, but since the gathering can attract a relatively large crowd, the local constabulary took notice and made their authoritative presence very much felt. It is lamentable that this peaceful and harmonious gathering has caused negative feelings. Perhaps if we all keep dancing in the circle of inner light, the darkness will disappear.

Up the road, just after entering **Haena State Park,** an HVB Warrior points the way to the **wet caves;** right along the road is **Waikanaloa,** and 150 yards up the side of a hill is **Waikapala'e.** Their wide openings are almost like gaping frogs' mouths, and the water is liquid crystal. Amazingly, the dry cave is down by the sea, while Waikapala'e, subject to the tides, is inland and uphill. Look around for ti leaves and a few scraggly guavas. Straight up, different lavas that have flowed over the eons create a stacked pancake effect. The best time to come is in the hour before and the hour after noon, when the sun shoots rays into the water. If azure could bleed, it would be this color.

Limahuli Botanical Garden, in the last valley before the beginning of the Kalalau Trail, a half-mile past mile marker 9, not far from the caves, open Tues.-Fri. and again on Sunday 9:30 a.m.-3 p.m., tel. (808) 826-1053, showcases tropical plants both ancient and modern. Part of the **National Tropical Botanical Gardens,** the 15 original acres were donated by Juliet Rice Wichman in 1976, and an additional 990-acre preserve was donated by her grandson, Chipper Wichman, the garden's curator, in 1994. There are both self-guided ($10) and guided ($15) walking tours of the gardens (wear good shoes; umbrellas are provided). As you walk through this enchanted area you'll pass taro patches, plants introduced to Hawaii by the early Polynesians, living specimens of endangered native Hawaiian species, and post-contact tropicals; your guide treats you to legends of the valley (or you can read them in your brochure) as you follow the three-quarter-mile loop trail. For anyone planning a hiking trip into the interior, or for those who just love the living beauty of plants and flowers, a trip to Limahuli Botanical Garden is well worth the effort.

The road ends at **Ke'e Beach,** a popular spot with restrooms and showers. Here is the beginning of the Kalalau Trail. As always, the swimming is mostly good only in the summertime. A reef offshore is also great for snorkeling. If conditions are right and the tide is out, you can walk left around the point to get a dazzling view of the Na Pali cliffs. Don't attempt this when the sea is rough! This path takes you past some hidden beach homes. One was used as the setting for the famous love rendezvous in the miniseries *The Thorn Birds.* Past the homes, another path takes you up the hill to the site of the ancient Ka Ulu A Paoa Heiau, birthplace of the hula. The views from up here are remarkable and worth the climb, especially during winter, when the sun drops close to the cliffs and backlight Lehua Island, then sinks into its molten reflection. In the past, after novitiates had graduated from the hula *heiau,* they had to jump into the sea below, swimming around to Ke'e Beach as a sign of dedication. Tourists aren't required to perform this act.

bird of paradise

DIANA LASICH HARPER

BOB RACE

POIPU AND KOLOA

Poipu/Koloa is the most well-established and developed tourist area on Kauai, but it's now fielding competition from developments in Kapa'a and Princeville. On the site of what was the island's oldest sugar mill—a stone chimney remains to mark the spot—Koloa has been transformed from a tumbledown sugar town to a thriving tourist community where shops, restaurants, and boutiques line its wooden sidewalks. Nearby is the site of Hawaii's first Catholic mission. On the oceanfront in Poipu, luxury accommodations and fine restaurants front the wide beach, the water beckons, and the surf is gentle. Flanking this resort community on the east is Pu'uhi Mount, where the last volcanic eruption occurred on the island; to the west, beyond Prince Kuhio's birthplace, is the Spouting Horn, a plume of water that jets up through an opening in the volcanic rock shore with every incoming wave. Whether you're exploring the sights, cultivating a tan on the beach, combing the shops for your gift list, or sampling island treats, Poipu and Koloa will not fail to provide.

KOLOA

Five miles west of Lihue, Maluhia Road (Rt. 520) dips south off Rt. 50 and heads for Koloa. As you head down Maluhia Road, you pass through **Tunnel of Trees,** a stand of rough-bark *Eucalyptus robustus,* sometimes referred to as "swamp mahogany." Brought from Australia, they're now very well established, adding beauty, a heady fragrance, and shade to over a mile of this narrow country lane.

Koloa Town attracts a large number of tourists and packs them into a small area. There are plenty of shops, restaurants, and water-sport equipment rentals in town. Nearly all the old shops are remodeled plantation buildings. Dressed in red paint and trimmed with white, they are festooned with strings of lights as if decorated for a perpetual Christmas festivity.

The traffic is hectic around 5:30 p.m. and parking is always a problem, but you can easily solve it. Just as you are entering town, look to your right to see a weathered stone chimney standing alone in a little field. Park here and simply walk across the street, avoiding the hassles. This unmarked edifice is what's left of the **Koloa Sugar Plantation,** established in 1835, site of the first successful attempt at refining sugar in the islands. Although of major historical significance, the chimney is in a terrible state of disrepair—many broken beer bottles litter the inside. Notice, too, that shrubs are growing off the top and a nearby banyan has thrown off an aerial root and is engulfing the structure. Unless action is taken soon, this historical site will be lost forever.

On this overgrown corner lot is a circle of over a dozen varieties of sugarcane, each with a short explanation of its characteristics and where it was grown. A plaque and sculpture have recently been added to this site. Reading the plaque will give you an explanation of and appreciation for the sugar industry on Hawaii, the significance of the Koloa Sugar Plantation, and the people who worked the fields. The bronze sculpture portrays individuals of the seven ethnic groups that provided the greatest manpower for the sugar plantations of Hawaii: Hawaiians, Chinese, Japanese, Portuguese, Puerto Ricans, Koreans, and Filipinos. (From the 1830s to the first decade of this century, smaller numbers of Englishmen, Scots, Germans, Scandinavians, Poles, Spaniards, American blacks, and Rus-

sians also arrived to work. All in all, about 35,000 immigrants came to Hawaii to make the sugar industry the success it has been.) Koloa is the birthplace of the Hawaiian sugar industry, the strongest economic force in the state for over a century. More than anything else, it helped to shape the multiethnic mixture of Hawaii's population. While the original mill is gone, the fields surrounding Koloa still produce cane for the McBryde Sugar Co., Ltd., which has a mill to the east of town.

The tall steeple on the way to Poipu belongs to **Koloa Church,** locally known as the White Church. Dating from 1837, it was remodeled in 1929. For many years the steeple was an official landmark used in many land surveys. If you turn left on Koloa Road, right on Weliweli Road, and then follow Hapa Road to its end, you come to **St. Raphael's Catholic Church,** marking the spot where a Roman Catholic mission was first permitted in the islands, in 1841. The stone church itself dates from 1856, when it was built by Friar Robert Walsh. The roof of the church can be seen sticking above the trees from Kiahuna Golf Course in Poipu.

PRACTICALITIES

Most of the accommodations, restaurants, and shopping in the Koloa area are centered around

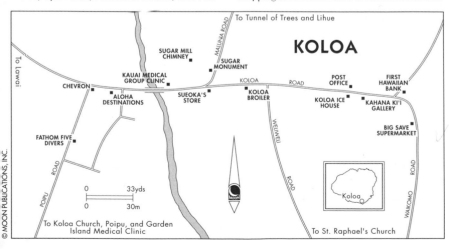

Poipu. Please refer to the "Poipu" section, following, for information.

Accommodations

Kahili Mountain Park is a gem, *if* you enjoy what it has to offer: it's like a camp for big people, at P.O. Box 298, Koloa, HI 96756, tel. (808) 742-9921. To get there, follow Rt. 50 west about one-half mile past the turnoff to Koloa, and look for the sign pointing mountainside up a cane road. Follow it for about one mile to the entranceway. The surroundings are absolutely beautiful, and the only noises, except for singing birds, are from an occasional helicopter flying into Waimea Canyon and the children attending the school on the premises. The high meadow is surrounded by mountains, with the coast visible and Poipu Beach about 15 minutes away. In the middle of the meadow is a cluster of rocks, a mini replica of the mountains in the background. A spring-fed pond is chilly for swimming, but great for catching bass that make a tasty dinner. There are three types of accommodations: cabinettes, cabins, and deluxe cabins. A cabinette is a one-room unit, usually with a double or two twin beds and full kitchen; they rent for $36.95 d, $11 per extra person. A few of the original rustic cabinettes still remain, with no running water, bare wood walls, open ceilings, and cement floors, but the majority didn't survive Hurricane Iniki. The cabinettes are in a cluster facing a meadow, and each is surrounded by flower beds and trees. All dishes and utensils are provided, but you must do all your own housekeeping. Bathrooms and showers are in a central building, with separate laundry facilities available. A relaxing Japanese *ofuro* (hot tub) is also open to guests. The cabins are raised, wooden-floored houses with full kitchens, bedrooms with chairs, tables, and dressers, private toilets, and outdoor showers, priced reasonably at $49.95 d, plus $11 for an extra person. Deluxe cabins, renting at $59.95 (luxury cabins are available, for $88), are about the same but a bit larger and upgraded with queen-size and two twin beds, indoor showers, and complete kitchens with large refrigerators. The park has been open for about 25 years and has recently been purchased by the Seventh-Day Adventist Church, which runs the school while retaining the rental units. The grounds and the facility are beautifully kept by the original caretakers, Ralph and Veronica.

Food

A classic building, complete with covered veranda and koi pond, houses **Tom Kats Restaurant and Bar,** open daily for dining 11 a.m.- 10 p.m., bar open later depending upon business. Attracting a mixture of local and tourist clientele, the indoor/outdoor restaurant serves appetizers like jumbo onion rings, plump zucchini, mozzarella sticks, chicken fingers, and buffalo wings, all for $4.75-5.50. Salads ranging $6.50-8.50, include chef's, Caesar, and seafood. The broiler serves burgers priced $5.75-6.75 topped with blue cheese, bacon, mushrooms, and Swiss cheese, while the sandwich board offers a classic Reuben, ham and cheese, French dip, and grilled chicken priced $6.50-8.25. Happy hour is daily 4-6 p.m., when you can order domestic beers at $1.75, and mixed drinks, margaritas, and mai tais for $2.50. The full bar, along with wine and liquor, has an excellent selection of imported and microbrews like Sierra Nevada, Kona Pacific, Golden Hill, and Harper Lager.

Lappert's Aloha Ice Cream, downtown Koloa, dishes up creamy scoops of delicious Kauai made ice cream. Connoisseurs of the dripping delight consider it among the best in the world. The ice-cream parlor doubles as an espresso bar with pastries thrown in for good measure.

Adjacent to Sueoka's Store in downtown Koloa is a **plate-lunch window** that dishes out hearty, wholesome food until early afternoon. It's difficult to spend more than $5.

Rosie's Kaukau Wagon, parked at the entrance to Koloa's baseball diamond (near the firehouse), especially on Monday when the **farmers' market** is operating, dishes up traditional island favorites weighty enough to sink a Boston whaler for only $5.

If you want pampering, keep walking past the **Koloa Broiler,** but if you want a good meal at an unbeatable price, drop in. The decor is the weatherbeaten, wainscoted building itself with a few neglected potted ferns here and there because someone probably told them they ought to. This cook-it-yourself restaurant is centrally located on Koloa Road and is open daily 11 a.m.-10 p.m. for lunch, dinner, and cocktails,

3:30-6 p.m. for happy hour , tel. (808) 742-9122. At the Koloa Broiler, *you* are the chef. Order top sirloin, beef kebab, mahimahi, and barbecued chicken for $10.95-12.95, fresh fish and ribs at $14.95, or a beef burger for $6 until 4 p.m., and $7 after. Your uncooked selection is brought to your table, and you take it to a central grill where a large clock and a poster of cooking times tell you how long your self-made dinner will take. The feeling is like being at a potluck barbecue, and you can't help making friends with the other "chefs." There is a simple salad bar with sticky rice and a huge pot of baked beans to which you can help yourself. Waiters bring fresh-baked bread and a pitcher of ice water. Put your selection on the grill, fix and eat a salad, and it's just about time to turn your meat on the barbecue. Just before it's done, toast some bread on the grill. The Koloa Broiler Bar attracts a good mixture of tourists and local people with its friendly neighborhood atmosphere. After dinner, order a cup of coffee or one of the special house drinks like Mighty Mai Tai, Passionate Margarita, Forbidden Fruit, or the famous Konanut Cooler. The bartenders and patrons are friendly, and you couldn't find a better place for a beer while shooting the breeze.

Follow the raised wooden sidewalk to the **Koloa Cultural Center,** where you will find **Taisho Restaurant,** open Mon.-Sat. for dinner only, from 5 p.m., where you can enjoy a full Japanese meal or pick and choose tidbits from the sushi bar. Classic entrees include tempura at $12.95, chicken *katsu* for $7.95, and mushroom chicken for $8.95. A specialty is Taisho *bento,* a full meal with tempura, sesame chicken, sashimi, gyoza, salad, and rice soup for $13.95. A full menu of *donburi* (a bowl of rice topped with vegetables, egg, tofu, or meat) starts at only $5.50, with the most expensive—10 *donburi*—for $8.95. This intimate restaurant with only a dozen or so tables is very simple with a few strokes of Japanese decor like shoji and wooden partitions.

Shopping

In Koloa, shops and boutiques are strung along the road like flowers on a lei. You can buy everything from original art to beach towels. Jewelry stores, surf shops, gourmet stores, even a specialty shop for sunglasses are just a few examples; Old Koloa Town packs a lot of shopping into a little area. Besides, it's fun just walking the raised sidewalks of what looks very much like an old Western town.

Koloa Town has some fine shops along the main street and for a few hundred yards down Poipu Road. Look for **Island Images,** tel. (808) 742-7447, offering fine art prints and posters, open daily 9 a.m.-5 p.m., next to Lappert's Aloha Ice Cream—posters average $30, with framing and shipping available; **Crazy Shirts,** a Hawaiian firm selling some of the best T-shirts and islandwear available; **Koloa Gold** and **Koloa Jewelry,** offering rings, necklaces, and scrimshaw; **Progressive Expressions,** for surfboards, surf gear, and islandwear; and **Kahana Ki'i Art Gallery** if you're looking for quality island art.

Along Koloa's elevated walkway, make sure to stop into **Kauai Fine Arts,** open daily 10 a.m.-6 p.m., tel. (808) 742-7608. Owned by Caribbean islander Mona Nicolaus, who operates the original Kauai Fine Arts, in Hanapepe, the boutique specializes in original engravings, antique prints mainly of the Pacific Islands, antique maps, and vintage natural science photos from as far afield as Australia and Egypt, and is also home to a collection of antique bottles. Recently added hand-embroidered pillows and quilts are designed in Hawaii but made on Bali; a smattering of handbags is also on offer, as is *tapa* imported from Tonga or Fiji. Kauai Fine arts offers framing and worldwide shipping. If not purchasing, at least stop to browse in the museum-like atmosphere, where fine vintage items reach back in time to touch the face of old Hawaii and the Pacific as a whole.

Also along the strip you'll find **Atlantis Gallery and Frames,** featuring prints, posters, and framing. Casual resortwear is available from **Paradise Clothing,** open daily 10 a.m.-7 p.m., where shirts by Tommy Bahama are featured along with a good assortment of bathing suits, beach dresses, men's and women's hats and shorts, and a sampling of clothing for children.

Just before the elevated walkway begins, you'll find **Hula Moon Gifts,** owned by Diana Soong, the proprietress of the Kauai Products store at the Kukui Grove Shopping Center. The shelves at Hula Moon bear mostly arts and crafts made in Hawaii, with some of the gift items fashioned in Indonesia. Featured items include vests imprinted with a *tapa* design and antique print; life-like Hawaiian dolls made from resin by Patty Kanaar; tiles, platters, and red-dirt pottery; handmade (and numbered) ukulele made by Jim Adwell; koa bowls by Wayne Jacintho; and less-expensive items like shark-teeth necklaces, barrettes, bracelets, mirror and comb sets, and koa bookmarks.

Kauai One Hour Photo, tel. (808) 742-1719, along Poipu Road in Koloa, offers camera needs, film, and processing.

The Blue Orchid at the end of the raised wooden sidewalk in the Koloa Cultural Center, open Mon.-Sat. 9:30 a.m.-5:30 p.m., is a lady's boutique selling dresses, alohawear, earrings, jewelry, and fresh-cut flowers. Arlene, the owner, handpaints the dresses and T-shirts, all of which are made from cotton, rayon, or silk. Prices start at $30 for the dresses and $12 for the T-shirts.

When you see Weliweli Road at the end of the raised wooden sidewalk, look for a sign pointing to St. Raphael's Church and follow it for a minute to **Chang's Tao Wai,** a.k.a. Koloa Variety Store, a discount variety store. Inside is a tangle of touristy junk and nifty items including beach mats, T-shirts, hats, fishing supplies, and inexpensive cotton aloha shirts.

Stuck in a corner near Chang's is **Nileen's Enterprises,** tel. (808) 742-9727, a nutrition center about as large as your average closet. Open Monday, Wednesday, and Friday 12:30-5 p.m. and Saturday 9:30 a.m.-2:30 p.m., Nileen's sells nutritional supplements, vitamins, minerals, homeopathic remedies, and skin-care products.

Food Shopping
In Koloa, a **Big Save Supermarket** is on Koloa Road, at the junction of Waikomo Road. **Sueoka's Store,** in downtown Koloa, is a local grocery and produce market. Both carry virtually everything that you'll need for condo cooking.

Pick up fresh fruits and vegetables at the **farmers' market** held every Monday at noon at the baseball field in Koloa (turn near the fire station). Depending on what's happening on the farms, you can get everything from coconuts to fresh-cut flowers while enjoying a truly local island experience.

Services
Koloa's **public restrooms** are in the courtyard housing the Koloa History Center, just near Crazy Shirts.

The Koloa **post office** is along Koloa Road, tel. (808) 742-6565. At the end of Koloa Road is **First Hawaiian Bank,** the area's only bank.

Note: Also see "Services and Information" in the Poipu section, below. For recreation in and around Koloa, see "Sports and Recreation," also under "Poipu."

POIPU

Poipu Road continues south from Koloa for two miles until it reaches the coast. En route it passes a cane road (with a traffic signal), which reaches Hanapepe via Numila, and a bit farther passes Lawai Road, which turns right along the coast and terminates at the Spouting Horn. Poipu Road itself bends left past a string of condos and hotels, into what might be considered the town, except that nothing in particular makes it so. Both Hoonani and Hoowili Roads lead to different sections of the beach. As you pass the mouth of Waikomo Stream (along Hoonani Road), you're at **Koloa Landing,** once the island's most important port. When whaling was king, dozens of ships anchored here to trade with the natives for provisions. Today nothing remains. Behind Poipu is **Pu'uhi Mount,** believed to be the site of the last eruption to have occurred on Kauai.

Along Poipu Road, look for the driveway into the Kiahuna Plantation Resort on the right across from the Poipu Shopping Village. This is the site of the **Kiahuna Plantation Gardens,** formerly known as the Moir Gardens (the central area still maintains this name). The 35 lovely acres are adorned with over 3,000 varieties of tropical flowers, trees, and plants, and a lovely lagoon. The gardens were heavily battered by Hurricane Iwa and again by Iniki, but the two dozen full-time gardeners have restored them to their former beauty. These grounds, originally part of the old sugar plantation, were a "cactus patch" started by the manager, Hector Moir, and his wife back in 1938. Over the years, the gardens grew more and more lavish until they became a standard Poipu sight. The Kiahuna Plantation has greatly expanded the original gardens, opening them to the public during daylight hours, free of charge. Many plants are identified.

The **Koloa-Poipu bypass road** has recently been completed and takes you from Koloa Town to Poipu, emerging just near the Hyatt. In Koloa, turn left along the main street, then make a right on Weliweli Rd. past St. Raphael's Church where you will see signs for the bypass.

The Great Poipu Beaches

Although given a lacing by Hurricane Iniki, **Poipu Beach County Park** is on the mend and is Poipu's best-developed beach park. Located at the eastern end of Poipu, it provides a pavilion, tables, showers, toilets, a playground, and lifeguards. The swimming, snorkeling, and bodysurfing are great. A sheltered pool rimmed by lava boulders is gentle enough for anyone, and going just beyond it provides the more exciting wave action often used by local surfers. Follow the rocks out to Nukumoi Point, where there are a number of tidepools.

Following the shoreline around to the east you'll end up at **Brennecke's Beach,** a great spot for boogie boarding and surfing. The county has purchased all of the land fronting the beach and is establishing a revetment that will be filled with sand. The entire area is slated to become a public beach park with full amenities and should be up and running by late 1997.

At the eastern end of the Hyatt is an access road leading to **Shipwreck Beach,** now improved with a pavilion containing restrooms and showers. The Hyatt Hotel has also developed a nearby walkway affording fantastic seascapes as you amble along. Shipwreck Beach is a long strand of white sand. One of the only beneficiaries of Hurricanes Iwa and Iniki, the beach was broadened and widened with huge deposits of sand making it bigger and better than ever. The swimming and snorkeling are good, but, as always, use caution.

Continue along Poipu Road past the golf course and take a right on the dirt road towards CJM Stables. Park before the hill gets too steep (unless you're in a 4WD vehicle), then walk 10 minutes down to **Mahaulepu Beach,** a wonderful strand with breaks in the reef that make it good for swim-

ming. Remember, however, that beach access is across private land, and the landowner sometimes posts a security guard who asks to see your driver's license and may have you sign a liability release. There is no official camping here, but local people sometimes bivouac in the ironwoods at the east end; beyond is a rocky bluff from which you have a fine view of the coastline east of here. The only people who frequent the beach are fishermen, au naturel sunbathers, and, when the waves are right, surfers.

West End

Turn onto Lawai Road to pass **Kuhio Park,** the birthplace of Prince Kuhio. Loved and respected, Prince Cupid—a nickname by which he was known—was Hawaii's delegate to Congress from the turn of the century until his death in 1922. He often returned to the shores of his birth whenever his duties permitted. Containing a statue and monument, terraced lava walls, palm trees, and a pool, this well-manicured acre faces the sea. Just beyond the park near the beach house is a family-safe snorkeling area. Farther along is **Kukui'ula Bay.** Before Hurricane Iwa and later Iniki pummeled this shoreline, the bay was an attractive beach park where many small boats anchored. Today, it's coming back, and you can still launch a boat here, but the surrounding area is still recovering from the storm. The pavilion hasn't yet been rebuilt, but there are showers and portable restrooms. The comfort station is slated to be back by the summer of 1997. Sailing cruises leave from this harbor in winter, shore fishermen come to try their luck, and scuba divers explore the coral reef offshore.

In a moment, you arrive at the **Spouting Horn.** A large parking area has many stalls marked for tour buses. (At the **flea market** here, you can pick up trinkets and souvenirs.) Don't make the mistake of looking just at the Spouting Horn. Have "big eyes" and look around at the full sweep of this remarkable coastline. The Spouting Horn is a lava tube that extends into the sea, with its open mouth on the rocky shore. The wave action causes the spouting phenomenon, which can blow spumes quite high, depending on surf conditions. They say it shot higher in the old days, but when the salt spray damaged the nearby cane fields plantation own-

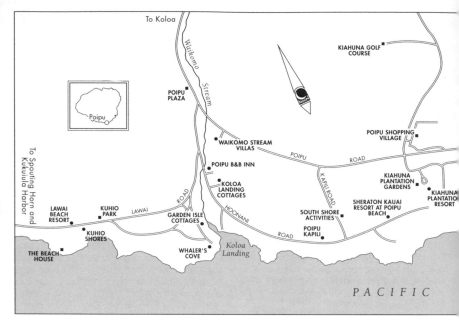

ers supposedly had the opening made larger so the spray wouldn't carry as far. Photographers wishing to catch the Spouting Horn in action have an ally. Just before it shoots, a hole behind the spout makes a large belch—a second later, the spume flies. Be ready to click.

ACCOMMODATIONS

Most of Poipu's available rooms are found in medium- to high-priced condos; however, there are first-class hotels, a handful of cottages, and bed and breakfasts.

Note: Also see "Accommodations" under "Koloa," preceding.

Cottages, Cabins, and B&Bs

Koloa Landing Cottages, at 2749 Hoonani Rd., are modern units in a quiet residential area, and some of Poipu's least-expensive accommodations. Two-bedroom, two-bath units for up to five people are available, each with a full kitchen, dishwasher, and color television. Rates are $65 for one or two people, $75 for three or

four, and $5 for an additional person beyond that. Studios, also equipped with kitchen and color TVs, run $45 for one or two people. Laundry facilities are on the premises. Reservations are suggested; four nights' deposit is required, 25% for stays longer than 14 days. Contact Sylvia at (808) 742-1470, Hans at (808) 742-6436, or write to Koloa Landing Cottages, RR1, Box 70, Koloa, HI 96756.

Garden Isle Cottages are tucked away at the west end along Hoona Road between Poipu Beach and the Spouting Horn. They sit on the beach surrounded by lush foliage, offering privacy. The cottages are operated by artists Robert and Sharon Flynn, whose original works highlight each of the units. All the units are self-contained and fully equipped. Prices range from $52-75 for a single or double in a studio with bath and lanai but no kitchen (refrigerator, coffee pot, and toaster only) to $130-135 for a two-bedroom, two-bath unit for up to four people ($6 per additional person in any unit). Weekly maid service is provided for the studios. Four nights' deposit is required, 25% if staying over 14 days. Call (808) 742-6717 daily 9 a.m.-noon,

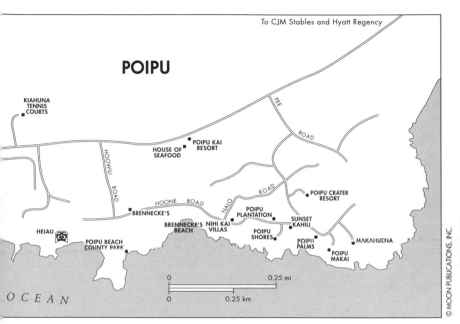

To CJM Stables and Hyatt Regency

POIPU

KIAHUNA
TENNIS
COURTS

PEE ROAD

HOOWILI ROAD

HOUSE OF
SEAFOOD

POIPU KAI
RESORT

HOONE ROAD

BRENNECKE'S

NALO

ROAD

POIPU CRATER
RESORT

POIPU
PLANTATION

SUNSET
KAHILI

HEIAU

POIPU BEACH
COUNTY PARK

BRENNECKE'S
BEACH

NIHI KAI
VILLAS

POIPU
SHORES

POIPU
PALMS

MAKAHUENA

POIPU
MAKAI

0   0.25 mi
0   0.25 km

OCEAN

© MOON PUBLICATIONS, INC.

or write Garden Isle Cottages, 2666 Puuholo Rd., Koloa, HI 96756.

You will find no bedroom closer to the gentle surf than at **Gloria's Spouting Horn Bed and Breakfast.** Leveled by Hurricane Iniki, the one-time humble plantation house has come back as a perfectly designed and highly attractive B&B, with your comfort and privacy assured. Created by Bob and Gloria with the help of a California architect, the stout, hurricane-resistant, natural-wood post-and-beam structure supports a Polynesian longhouse-style roof. None of the three guest rooms share a common wall, and the entire home is designed for maximum exposure to the outdoors. Wide bay windows with louvers underneath bring you as close as possible to the outdoors when opened simultaneously. A nubbed burgundy carpet (all shoes outside, please) massages your feet as you pad the hall to your cross-ventilated suite, which is further cooled by ceiling fans in the main bedroom and in your private bath. Skylights let in the sun or stars as you lie in bed or recline in an easy chair to watch a movie from the extensive video collection on your remote-control color TV. Floral wallpaper and antique tables topped with doilies and cut flowers suggest a Victorian theme. Every suite opens to a private lanai where the rolling surf and dependable whoosh of the Spouting Horn serenade you throughout the evening. All baths are private, spacious, and offer a shower, commode, and Japanese *ofuro* in which you can soak away all cares and worries. Descend a central stairway to a small bar that holds port, brandy, and different liqueurs for your evening enjoyment. Breakfast is a combination of fresh fruits, fresh juices, piping hot coffee and teas, and perhaps a pizza pancake crunchy with macadamia nuts and smothered with home-made banana topping. Contact Gloria's Spouting Horn Bed and Breakfast at 4464 Lawai Beach Rd., Poipu, HI 96756, tel. (808) 742-6995. Rates are $150 per night double occupancy, with long-term discounts offered. Only a few steps from the Spouting Horn, near the end of this cul-de-sac, traffic disappears at night and the quiet settles in at this absolutely excellent accommodation.

Poipu Bed and Breakfast Inn and Vacation Rentals is a large and spacious renovated plantation house. Stained in tropical colors, this wooden house has all the comforts of home, plus antiques, art, and crafts from the island. If you have that childlike affection for carousel rides, you'll love this place because there are several carousel horses in the house. The bedrooms are on either side of the large, central sitting room. Each has a color TV, refrigerator, and private bath. The sitting room also has a TV, videotapes, books, and games. There is no smoking allowed inside the house; sit out on the large, comfortable lanai or walk in the garden. Children are welcome. Daily room rates, including a continental breakfast, are $65-100. Rooms combined into two-bedroom, two-bath suites are $140 and $155; the entire house can be rented for $250. An extra $10 is charged for a child or additional person, $5 is subtracted for single occupancy. For information and reservations, call (808) 742-1146 or (800) 552-0095, or write to Poipu Bed and Breafast Inn, 2720 Hoonani Rd., Koloa, HI 96756.

Pua Hale (Flower House), at 2381 Kipuka St., Koloa, HI 96756, tel. (808) 742-1700 or (800) 745-7414, is a lovely, deluxe 750-square-foot house where your privacy and serenity are assured. With a touch of Japan, Pua Hale features shoji screens, cool wooden floors, a relaxing *ofuro,* custom furniture and decorating, and a complete kitchen and laundry. This self-contained unit, only minutes from Poipu, is surrounded by a privacy fence and a manicured garden, so you can choose whether you want to

socialize or simply enjoy the glorious quietude on your own. Rates are a reasonable $100 per night, or $650 per week. You can't find better.

Perched on a cliff and next door to the National Botanical Gardens is **Marjorie's Kauai Inn,** P.O. Box 866, Lawai, Kauai, HI 96765, tel. (808) 332-8838 or (800) 717-8838, with a choice of three private accommodations each with private mini-kitchen, cable TV, radio, and phone. Also included are access to a hot tub, a barbecue, and laundry facilities.

Moderate

Although the prices in Poipu can be a bit higher than elsewhere on Kauai, you get a lot for your money. Over a dozen well-appointed modern condos are lined up along the beach and just off it, with thousands of units available. Most are a variation on the same theme: comfortably furnished, fully equipped, with a tennis court here and there, always a swimming pool, and maid service available. Most require a minimum stay of at least two nights, with discounts for longer visits. The following condos have been chosen to give you a general idea of what to expect and because of their locations. Prices average about $140 s or d for a one-bedroom apartment, up to $200 for a two- or three-bedroom, with extra persons ($10) charged only in groups of more than four or six people in the multiple-bedroom units. Rates during high season (mid-December through mid-April) are approximately 10% higher. You can get excellent brochures listing

For peace and quiet, few places in Poipu can beat the Halemanu Bed and Breakfast Inn.

most Poipu-area accommodations by writing to **Poipu Beach Resort Association,** P.O. Box 730, Koloa, HI 96756, tel. (808) 742-7444.

The **Kiahuna Plantation Resort,** RR 1, Box 73, Koloa, HI 96756; tel. (808) 742-6411 or (800) 688-7444, now operated by Hawaii's own Outrigger Resorts, first opened its doors and grounds to the public in 1972. Previously, it was the estate of Mr. and Mrs. Edward Moir, the founders of the Kaloa Sugar Company. Their private home, now serving as the reception center, is a breezy but stout lava-rock structure in the classic plantation style. Their living room, appointed in lustrous *koa,* now serves as the main dining room of the **Plantations Garden Restaurant.** Mrs. Moir was a horticulturist enamored of cacti. Whenever she went to the mainland she collected these amazing plants, mainly from Texas and the Southwest, and transported them back to Hawaii to be planted in her cactus garden. However, before planting them she would invite a *kahuna* to bless the land and to pray for their acceptance. The cactus garden flourished, and by magic or mystery was the only thing in the entire area left untouched when Hurricane Iniki swept away everything else in sight like a huge broom. The property, comprising 35 lush acres fronting Poipu Beach, houses just over 300 units, divided into separate buildings. Furniture differs from one unit to another since each is individually owned, but certain standards must be met and in most cases the decor is well above acceptable. You enter the one-bedroom, 800-square-foot apartments through louvered doors. Sliding doors at the other end of the apartment allow breezes to filter through, assisted by ceiling fans in every room. In master bedrooms, most with king- or queen-size beds, you can expect to find rattan furniture, Hawaiian-style quilts, bedside phones, and remote color TVs. Bathrooms feature showers and tubs, dressing areas, and handy hallway closets with complimentary safes. The main living rooms, separated from the kitchens by large dining areas, have their own TVs (video library available), phones, and comfortable furniture perfect for relaxation. The modern full kitchens are complete with garbage disposals, dishwashers, electric ranges, ice-making refrigerators, and all the dinnerware and flatware required for family meals. Each unit has a covered lanai with table, chairs, and lounges overlooking the grounds. With the sea in the distance you'll feel like a transplanted flower in this magnificent garden. The two-bedroom bi-level units—at 1,700 square feet, the size of most homes—are wonderful, easily accommodating up to six guests. In the upstairs area, you will find a sitting room, formal dining area, modern kitchen, bath, and lanai. Like all units on the property, they feature ceiling fans in every room, and cross-ventilation through louvered doors and windows. Downstairs are two bedrooms—one master bedroom, and a smaller but still quite large guest bedroom, each with its own bath, phone, and TV. A ground-level lanai lets you step out into the sunshine. All units are only a minute's walk from the beach, home to the Hawaiian monk seal March-July. Full beach service is provided including towels, lounge chairs, boogie boards, and snorkel masks. The Kiahuna Plantation also boasts a concierge service which will make arrangements for any activity on the island and tennis courts with their own **Courtside Cafe,** open 7 a.m.-2 p.m. for breakfast and lunch. The units are broken into a number of categories, from a one-bedroom garden view (accommodates up to four) to a two-bedroom oceanfront (up to six). Prices range $155-450, mostly depending on the view. The Kiahuna Plantation Resort is a first-rate condominium, expertly managed, and a terrific value.

With 110 acres, **Poipu Kai Resort** has the largest grounds in the area—one corner of which runs down to the ocean. Set amongst broad gardens, most units look out onto a swimming pool or the tennis courts. Light color schemes, bright and airy rooms, wicker furniture, ceiling fans, woven pandanus items decorating walls and tables, and Hawaiian art prints typify the room decorations. Most units have queen-size beds and walk-in closets with chests of drawers; bathrooms have large shower/tubs and double sinks. For your convenience, color TVs, economy washer-and-dryer units, irons and ironing boards, and floor safes are in all units. Daily maid service is provided. Kitchens are fully equipped with electric utilities and sufficient cookware to prepare a full-course meal. Dining rooms adjoin spacious living rooms, which open onto broad lanai. There are one- and two-bedroom units, in 15 different floor plans. Some are Hawaiian in theme; others are

Spanish, with stucco and arched entryways; modern units show more glass and chrome; and a few may resemble your own Mainland abode. A handful of three-bedroom homes are also available in the adjacent housing estate. Room rates are $130-150/$115-135 (high/low season) for one-bedroom units, $175-240/$160-210 for two bedrooms and two baths, and $205/$180 for the homes. Facilities on the grounds include nine tennis courts (free for guests), a pro shop (open 8 a.m.-noon and 2-6 p.m.) with a resident tennis pro, five swimming pools, one outdoor jacuzzi, and numerous barbecue grills. The activity center (open, to nonguests as well, 8 a.m.-1 p.m. and 2:30-4 p.m.) can arrange everything from a towel for the beach to a helicopter tour of the island. Across the walkway from the resort office is the House of Seafood, the area's premier seafood restaurant, open only for dinner. For reservations, write to Poipu Kai Resort, RR 1, Koloa, HI 96756, or call (808) 742-6464 or (800) 777-1700.

The **Poipu Shores** condo is at the east end of the beach, surrounded by other small condos. They're slightly less expensive than the rest, allowing up to six people at no extra charge in certain two- and three-bedroom units. Their one-bedroom units run $110; a standard two-bedroom is $150, a deluxe two-bedroom is $160, and a three-bedroom unit runs $165. Rates are $10-20 cheaper off-season. There is a three-night minimum stay. Maid service is provided free every other day. All units are clean, spacious, and airy, and the area's best beaches are a short stroll away. Write Poipu Shores, 1775 Pee Rd., Koloa, HI 96756; tel. (808) 742-7700 or (800) 367-8047.

Poipu Kapili is a three-story condo that looks more like a "back-East" bungalow. Directly across the road from the beach, all units have ocean views. The pool is located in the center of the property. Also on the premises are free, lighted tennis courts, and rackets and balls are provided. The bedrooms are huge, with ceiling fans and wicker headboards; kitchens are spacious with full stoves, dishwashers, and a private lanai for each unit. Rates range $125-225 for a one-bedroom unit to $185-300 for a two-bedroom; monthly and weekly discounts are available. The condo also offers a convenient activities desk, which will book you into any activity that strikes your fancy. Write Poipu Kapili, 2221 Kapili Rd., Koloa, HI 96756, tel. (808) 742-6449 or (800) 443-7714.

Other condos also stretch along this wonderful shore. The smaller ones generally cluster at the east end of the beach; others are near Koloa Landing and Kuhio Park: **Makahuena** sits on Makahuena Cliff, with the crashing waves below, tel. (808) 742-7555 or (800) 367-8022. **Poipu Crater Resort** snuggles inside a small seaside caldera, tel. (800) 367- 8020. **Poipu Makai**, tel. (800) 367-5025; **Poipu Palms**, tel. (800) 367-8022; **Sunset Kahili**, tel. (800) 827-6478; **Poipu Plantation**, tel. (808) 742-6757 or (800) 733-1632; and **Nihi Kai Villas**, tel. (800) 367-5025, all run in quick succession across the cliff at the east end of Poipu Beach. On the west end, **Grantham Resorts** and **Waikomo Stream Villas** (also managed by Grantham Resorts) are next door to each other along the stream, tel. (800) 325-5701. On the far side of Koloa Landing is **Whaler's Cove,** managed by Village Resorts, at 264 Peuhalo Rd., Koloa, HI 96756, tel. (808) 742-7571 for (800) 225-2683, a deluxe accommodation with only 38 units offering you an excellent sense of privacy and manageability; and at Lawai Beach are **Lawai Beach Resort,** tel. (800) 777-1700, and **Kuhio Shores,** tel. (808) 742-1319.

Deluxe

A parade of royal palms lines the grand boulevard that ends at the elegant porte cochere where towering panes of glass open to a roiling sea frothing against the periwinkle sky that fronts the **Hyatt Regency Kauai Resort and Spa,** 1571 Poipu Rd., Koloa, HI 96756, tel. (808) 742-1234 or (800) 233-1234. This magnificent, 600-room hotel, deceptive in size, is architecturally designed so that its five floors rise no taller than the surrounding palms. A bellman pulls the golden frond handles on double doors opening to the main hall, where a floor of green and white marble is covered with an enormous Persian rug bearing a tropical island motif. To left and right, larger-than-life replicas of poi bowls specially fashioned for the royal *ali'i* mark a formal sitting area illuminated by a magnificent chandelier of cut crystal. Ahead is a central courtyard, tiled to create a sundial effect. As you progress through the heart of the hotel, greenery and flowers, both wild and tamed, compose a liv-

*Hyatt Regency
Resort and Spa*

ing lei of floral beauty. Lustrous koa tables bear gigantic anthuriums and torch gingers ablaze with color, Artworks, *tapa* wall hangings, and birdcages filled with flitting plumage and trilling songs line the hallways, while the interplay of marble floors and rich carpets is counterpointed by weathered bronze. Enter the **Stevenson Library,** one of the Hyatt's bars, to find overstuffed chairs, beveled glass windows, pool and billiard tables, a grand piano, and ornate chess sets waiting for the first move. Outdoors, walking paths scented by tropical blooms lead through acres of pools, both fresh- and saltwater, featuring slides, a rivulet flowing through a "gorge," and the watery massaging fingers of cascading waterfalls and bubbling whirlpools.

Heavy mahogany doors open into guest rooms, all done in soothing pastels with white on tan textured wallpaper. Each room features a full entertainment center with remote-control color TV, private lanai with outdoor furniture, a mini-bar, and double closets. Mahogany furniture, overstuffed chairs and footstools, and Chinese-style lamps insure tasteful relaxation. Spacious bathrooms contain separate commodes with their own telephones, double marble-top sinks, hair dryers, large soaking tubs, and cotton *yukata* (robes). Rates are from $230 for a garden view to $345 for a deluxe oceanfront; $410 Regency Club; and $425 to $1,800 suites.

Restaurants at the Hyatt range from casual to elegant (see "Food," following, for a complete description). **Dondero's,** the hotel's signature restaurant, offers superb Italian food, while the **Tidepool Restaurant,** in South Pacific style, offers fresh fish and seafood. The **Ilima Terrace,** at the bottom of a sweeping staircase, is open for breakfast, lunch, and dinner and presents everything from a Philadelphia cheese steak to a children's menu. The **Seaview Terrace,** with its vaulted ceiling, magnificent chandeliers, and carved marble-topped tables is perfect for a sunset drink, while **Kuhio's,** with its sunken parquet dance floor, is perfect for an intimate rendezvous.

In its own facility fronted by a courtyard is the distinctive green tile roof of the horseshoe-shaped Anara Spa. The treatment rooms offer ancient Hawaiian remedies for energy and rejuvenation. You begin with *kapu kai* (sacred sea), a steam bath followed by a body scrub with *alae* clay and Hawaiian sea salt. Next you may be immersed in a tub of *limu* and then kneaded by a massage therapist who specializes in *lomi lomi,* the Hawaiian massage favored by the *ali'i.* All therapy rooms are indoor/outdoor, with mini-gardens and the serenade of falling waters to help unjangle nerves. Hibiscus tea and cool water are always available, and once finished you are conducted into the locker rooms, where you can shower and pamper yourself with lotions and potions. The Amara Spa also offers health-conscious cuisine, a lap pool, aerobics room, and complete training equipment including Lifecycles, treadmills, and StairMasters.

Embassy Vacation Resort at Poipu Point, 1613 Pee Rd., Kalaheo, HI 96750, tel. (808) 742-1888, (800) 922-7866 Mainland and Canada, and (800) 321-2558 Hawaii, is a marriage of concepts between Embassy Suites, known for their luxury hotels, and Aston Resorts, a Hawaiian company that knows how to deliver the aloha spirit. The property, sitting on 23 manicured, oceanfront acres, further combines the concept of a luxury resort with time-share condominiums. Upon arrival, you enter through a white porte cochere trimmed in light wood framing beveled glass windows offering a view of the landscaping spreading past windswept palms to a reflecting pool fed by a tiny rivulet. In the main lobby you find guest reception, a concierge desk, and a sitting area brightened by immense floral displays framed by arched French doors opening to the gardens below. The grounds are a dramatic combination of water and lava stone forming a mosaic sculpture reminiscent of both the taro fields of ancient Hawaii and the natural beauty of wild Kauai. The 10 neoclassic plantation-style buildings housing the two-bedroom, 1,200-square-foot units are no taller than a palm tree. They surround a central courtyard where you will discover, fronting a sandy beach, a large pool with one side tiled side and the other sand-bottomed. Poolside, you will find complete amenities including lounge chairs, umbrellas, a jacuzzi, and, nearby, a complete fitness center. Mornings bring a complimentary health-conscious breakfast served 8-9:30 a.m. in an outdoor dining area near the pool, complete with coffee, various juices, Hawaiian fruits, bagels, toast, and sweet breads. Late risers can enjoy a more limited buffet in the reception area until 10 a.m., and juice is available throughout the day. Here and there throughout the property you'll find little picnic nooks complete with tables and barbecue grills for your enjoyment. Notice a thick grove of ironwoods completely surrounded by a hedge; these protect the site of an ancient *heiau* that the resort is dedicated to preserving. Guests can look but are not permitted inside—a right reserved for native Hawaiian groups who, on occasion, still come to pray. Just below the pool area lies a stretch of dramatic coastline pounded by heavy wave action, frothing misty azure against the coal-black lava. The area, long known as a productive fishing site, lures local anglers who have embedded pole holders in the rock. From March to July, this coastal area is a favorite lounging spot for Hawaiian monk seals, who arrive just as humpback whales leave the offshore waters for their trek back to the Arctic. These waters are too treacherous for recreational swimming, but a two-minute walk takes you to Shipwreck Beach, one of the premier beaches of Poipu. The two-bedroom units, air conditioned with ceiling fans throughout, are brightened by white tile and textured carpeting and feature full kitchens with marble-topped counters, electric stoves, fridges with ice makers and cold water dispensers, coffee makers, toasters, microwaves, double stainless steel sinks, pine cabinetry, trash compactors, and dishwashers. For added convenience, every room includes a shopping list of basic staples available for *wiki wiki* delivery from a local market. The dining/living room features comfortable bamboo furniture with puff pillows, fold-out couch, distinctive drum-top tables, and floor-to-ceiling glass doors that open to a wraparound lanai. There is a wet bar complete with wine glasses and bar utensils and an entertainment center containing remote-control color TV, CD player, tape deck, and VCR. The master bedroom, large and spacious, offers a queen-size bed with carved headboard, private bedside phone, entertainment center complete with remote-control color TV, and a huge bath with separate commode, hair dryer, extra deep tub, and two-person shower stall. The guest bedroom holds two single beds, a large closet, ceiling fan, and private bath with vanity and shower. Each unit has its own washer and dryer, along with steam iron and board. Room charges, based on double occupancy (no extra charge for up to six) range $275 s for a standard garden view to $590 for an ocean view. The Embassy Resort also offers a discounted "Mini-Vac" for those wishing to consider purchasing a time share on property (call for complete details; professional, no-pressure salespeople guaranteed).

Coming Back

The following properties in and around Poipu were extensively damaged by Hurricane Iniki. Although physically battered, their spirits are intact, and all will be reopening as soon as renovations are completed. Call directly, or check with

Kauai Today, tel. (800) 262-1400. All are excellent choices.

The **Sheraton Kauai Resort at Poipu Beach,** tel. (808) 742-2442 or (800) 325-3535, is the new name for the storm-ravaged Sheraton Kauai Gardens and the Sheraton Kauai Beach, which are being combined into one luxury hotel. Plans are to reopen in the Fall of 1997 with 492 rooms, all of which will have ocean views. Mindful of the ecological impact on the area, Sheraton plans to install underground parking.

Stouffer Waiohai Beach Resort and the **Stouffer Poipu Beach Resort** are not open at this time. Stouffer Resorts has indicated no plans for their reopening thus far.

FOOD

Inexpensive

On your right as you approach Poipu is a small complex called the Poipu Plaza. There, at **Taqueria Norteños,** you can fill up on Mexican fast food for under $4. They make their tacos and burritos a bit differently from most Mexican food stands: a taco is simply rice and beans in a taco shell. If you want the standard cheese, tomato, and lettuce, you have to ask for it—and pay an extra charge. The flavorful food is homemade but precooked, waiting in heating trays. Vegetarian meals are also served. Order at the walk-up window and take your tray to one of the picnic tables in the next room; they do takeout as well. Filling and good but nothing special, Taqueria Norteños is open daily except Wednesday 11 a.m.-10:30 p.m.

Shipwreck Subs in the Poipu Shopping Village can fix you up with a sub sandwich like a tuna delight, cheese combo, or vegetarian—$6 for a large and $4.50 for a small.

Brennecke's Snack Bar is located just off Poipu Beach, below Brennecke's restaurant and open 10:30 a.m.-4 p.m. The best deals are takeout hot dogs, burgers, and filling plate lunches. For a bit more sophistication, try one of the hotel's poolside grills and cafes for a light lunch.

Joe Brennecke is a football fanatic from Cleveland, Ohio, who spent many a fall afternoon in that city's "Dog Pound." After the game, Joe and his buddies wanted to wrap their meaty fists around man-sized sandwiches and wash

them down with cold ones. No froufrou food for these bruisers. So Joe moved to Kauai and opened **Joe's Courtside Cafe,** adjacent to the Kiahuna Tennis Club (look for a sign *mauka* just past the Poipu Shopping Plaza), tel. (808) 742-6363, open for breakfast 7-11 a.m., lunch 11 a.m.-2 p.m., and cocktails daily. Joe serves up his fare on an elevated portico with a brick and tile floor. For breakfast, start with eggs Benedict for $8.75, tofu scramble for $7.50, a croissant breakfast sandwich (O.K. nobody's perfect) for $4.95, or French toast at $5.50. You can also create your own omelettes for $6.95 or gnosh on a blueberry muffin or cinnamon roll with a steaming mug of coffee. For health conscious "weenies," there's even granola for $1.75. Lunch brings a personalized house salad that you build yourself for $12.50, grilled chicken breast at $7.50, Caesar salad with anchovies at $5.95, or a bowl of Portuguese bean soup for $3.50 (now you're talkin'). Sandwiches, priced $5.50-9, include a tuna melt, turkey breast, a South Shore steak, a Reuben, or fresh island fish. The grill serves a Joe Mama burger for $5.75, a grilled chicken breast for $6.25, or a Dog Named Joe for $4.75, served with a wedge of Kosher pickle and authentic stadium mustard imported from Cleveland. Joe takes personal pride in his restaurant and from behind the bar serves drinks like Joe Jones' Juice—a mai tai that includes dark Malibu and 151 rum—a good selection of beers including microbrews like Hawaii's own Kona Pacific, and Chico, California's, Sierra Nevada, along with wine, champagne, and fruit smoothies. Joe's Courtside Cafe is a sleeper, known mostly to local people who come time and again to get a fine breakfast or lunch at a reasonable price.

La Grillia, at the Poipu Shopping Village, open 11 a.m.-10 p.m., tel. (808) 742-2147, offers American standards and Italian dishes directly from Calabria created by owner Cathy Gargalonne. There is a full espresso bar open all day, and breakfast brings omelettes and eggs for around $6. Delicious with a latte or mocha, the homemade cinnamon buns and various muffins sell out quickly. Also available are Hawaiian smoothies made from papaya, lime, banana, and tropical juice, priced around $2.50. For lunch, served 3-5 p.m., you can enjoy a *bambino* burger with pasta for $3.25, rotinni with marinara for $3.25, chop chop salad for $7.95, a blackened burger with Cajun sauce, various *panini* with Italian lunch meats, and a meatball sandwich with marinara and mozzarella for $6.95. An "express lunch," which changes daily, is $6.50. Dinner, served 5-10 p.m., starts with focaccia at $3.95 or stuffed mushrooms or shrimp crustini at $5.95. Dinner entrees include meat or spinach lasagna, manicotti, or chicken or eggplant Parmesan for $12.95; pastas including angel hair, linguine, or spaghetti, smothered in a variety of sauces are $10.95. Beside the espresso bar, beverages include wines by the bottle or glass and beer.

Moderate

Located on the terrace of the Kiahuna Plantation Resort (once the plantation manager's home), under towering trees and surrounded by lush greenery, the **Plantation Garden Cafe** emanates a strong Hawaiian atmosphere. *Pu pu* run $3.95-6.95 and just whet your appetite for the meal to come. For a main course, try Hawaiian chicken, shrimp tempura, or the pasta special, each $12.95. Or sample the seafood or vegetable salads or sandwiches. After dinner, have a mouthwatering dessert or walk across the lobby for a tropical drink in the lounge.

Brennecke's Beach Broiler, an open-air, second-story deck directly across from Poipu Beach County Park, offers a view that can't be beat. Seafood is the dinner specialty but pasta and *kiawe*-broiled meat and chicken are also served. Prices range $9.95-22.50. All entrees are served with soup, salad, pasta primavera (instead of regular old potatoes), and garlic bread. Salads and sandwiches are served for lunch, and *pu pu* until dinner starts. There is a children's menu for both lunch and dinner. Lunch is 11:30 a.m.-3 p.m., happy hour 2-4 p.m., and dinner 5-10:30 p.m.; tel. (808) 742-7588.

Keoki's Paradise, at the Poipu Shopping Village, tel. (808) 742-7534, is an excellent choice for dinner or a night's entertainment. Enter past a small fountain into the longhouse-style interior with stone floor and thatched roof. Choose a seat at the long bar for a casual evening or at one of the tables overlooking the garden surrounding the restaurant. The varied menu lists savory items including Thai shrimp sticks for $8.95, fresh catch prepared a variety of ways including baked, herb-sautéed, teriyaki-grilled, or in an orange ginger sauce at market price; shrimp and steak $19.95; or beef dishes like top sirloin at $16.95 and prime rib for $23.95. A daily Sunset Special, served 5:30-6:15 p.m., offers items like Balinese chicken and teriyaki sirloin for prices ranging from $9.95 to $14.95. The Cafe Menu (available until closing), includes *pu pu,* burgers, salads, and sandwiches like a Reuben at $6.95, grilled chicken salad $9.95, chicken quesadilla for $8.95, and buffalo wings for $7.95. "Aloha Fridays" brings food and drink specials from 4:30 to 7 p.m. Margaritas are $2.50, draft beer is $1.50, and all the food on the Cafe Menu over $5 is $2 off. Desserts are the original Hula Pie, Keoki's Triple Chocolate Cake, or Haagen Daz Non-Fat Sorbet. A great selection of beer and mixed drinks adds to an enjoyable evening. The seafood and taco bar (a good place for conversation for single travelers) is open 4:30-midnight. Have an island drink before going in to dinner, served 5:30-10 p.m. Live entertainment is offered Thurs.-Sat. by local bands specializing in contemporary Hawaiian music.

An indoor/outdoor cafe, **Pattaya Asian Cafe,** at the Poipu Shopping Village, tel. (808) 742-8818, open 11:30 a.m.-2:30 p.m. for lunch and 5:30-9:30 p.m. for dinner, is a very tasteful, moderately priced restaurant appointed with a flagstone floor, and Thai mahogany tables and chairs. The ornate mahogany bar, covered by a pagoda roof, flashes with mirrors embedded in two gold and blue swans. The exotic menu starts with *mee grop,* a dish of crispy noodles, chicken, bean sprouts, and green onions; Bangkok wings, a concoction of long rice, onion, black mushrooms, carrots, and ground pork served with the house peanut sauce; and delicious fish cakes or sautéed calamari, ranging in price from $7.95 to $9.25. Soups and salads are spicy lemongrass soup for $10.95, a Thai ginger coconut soup with chicken or seafood at $7.25-10.95, and fresh island papaya salad for $5.95. More substantial meals include *pad Thai,* a traditional noodle dish for $9.25; spicy fried rice ranging from $6.95- $9.25 depending upon ingredients; red, green, and yellow curry made with chicken, pork, beef, or shrimp $7.95-14.95; and plenty of vegetarian selections. Although it is in a shopping center, Pattaya Asian Cafe is a terrific and authentic restaurant with friendly service and good prices.

If you want south-of-the-border food, try the homey **Cantina Flamingo,** tel. (808) 742-9505, on Nalo Rd. in amongst the condos—follow the pink flamingos! Sizzling fajitas are the specialty of the house and a real treat; other items on the menu are enchiladas tasca, flamingo burritos, taquitos rancheros, flautas Kauai, appetizers, soups, and salads. Chips and salsa are free. Nothing on the menu is over $9.95. You can't go wrong here. How about deep-fried ice cream for dessert? If not, head to the next room, beyond the wall aquarium, for a cool-down drink at the cantina. There you can choose one of at least nine kinds of fruit margaritas. (Imagine what it's like to peer through the distortion of the aquarium divider after a few of these potent concoctions!) Food is served 3:30-9:30 p.m. daily; *pu pu* is free 3:30-5:30 p.m.; takeout is available for some menu items. Hanging greenery, pink flamingos (of course!), and piñatas lend this eatery its distinctive air.

You can find other mid-priced restaurants at the hotels and clubhouses in Poipu. Try the **Poipu Bay Grill,** in the clubhouse of the Poipu Bay Resort Golf Course, open for breakfast and lunch. This moderately priced restaurant serving American standards has fantastic views of the surrounding mountains and sea.

Fine Dining

Exquisite dining can be enjoyed at various restaurants, some overlooking Poipu's beaches—perfect for catching the setting sun—and others in elegant gardens bathed by tropical breezes. Prices are high, but you definitely get a full measure of what you pay for.

In a freestanding building at the Poipu Shopping Village, culinary magic is created at **Roy's Poipu Bar and Grill,** at 2360 Kiahuna Plantation Dr., open nightly for dinner 5:30-9:30 p.m., reserva-

tions recommended, tel. (808) 742-5000. Here, in an open kitchen—one of Roy's trademarks—chef de cuisine Mako Segawa-Gonzales and a superbly trained staff create an array of marvelous dishes from the island's freshest meats, fish, poultry, fruits, and vegetables. Founder Roy Yamaguchi, along with a number of extremely talented chefs throughout Hawaii, is a master of Pacific Rim/Hawaiian regional cuisine. He combines and presents the best recipes of Asia, the Southwest, and the Continent with a flair and creativity that are astounding. The restaurant, easily transformed from indoor to outdoor by huge surrounding glass doors, features marble-topped wooden tables with cushioned chairs. Tropical flowers on each table, muted pink walls, and baby spotlights enhance the atmosphere. The chef's "special sheet" changes nightly, but a sampling of the delectable dishes that you may enjoy includes dim sum appetizers like crispy smoked duck *gyoza,* crispy Asian spring roll, sweet basil-crusted beef sauté, and ravioli with shiitake and spinach, all priced $5.95-7.95. Garden-fresh island greens are the base for spicy Thai beef salad ($6.95), sweet Maui onion salad ($5.95), and crispy calamari Caesar salad ($6.95). *Imu*-baked pizzas range from $4.95 for a child's pie to $6.95 for the deluxe mesquite-grilled-chicken feast. A few entrees usually on the menu are lemongrass-crusted chicken at $14.95, Roy's grilled shrimp at $17.95, and pot roast for $15.95 trimmed with mashed potatoes and old-fashioned apple ginger pineapple sauce. The special sheet always has fresh fish and seafood, like basil-seared *ono* with Thai red curry and lobster sauce, macadamia-nut-crusted *hevi* with a mango and coconut sauce, and sesame-seared *uku* with a shiitake cream sauce, all at market price. Roy's offers a memorable dining experience.

Another superb restaurant recently opened in Poipu is the **Beach House Restaurant,** tel. (808) 742-1424, open daily for dinner 5:30-10 p.m, run under the tutelage of master chef Jean-Marie Josselin, the owner of the Pacific Cafe in Kapa'a. The on-site chef, preparing exquisite Pacific Rim/Hawaiian regional dishes, is Linda Yamada, former executive chef at the Westin Kauai. The menu varies nightly, but expect a blending of East and West with a Mediterranean flair. This is another restaurant where your dining enjoyment is assured.

The **House of Seafood** has windows framing living still-lifes of palm fronds, flower gardens against a background of the distant ocean. It consistently has the largest selection of fresh fish in the area (generally from eight to 12 varieties), and its dishes are very creative—baked in puff pastry, sautéed with macadamia nut sauce, or steamed in a ginger sauce, to name a few. Ask the waiter for the best choice of the day. Start your meal off with an appetizer, soup, or salad, and finish with a creamy island-fruit dessert or drink. Entrees run $17-35, a children's menu $9-11. Located at Poipu Kai Resort; call (808) 742-5255 for reservations.

The main dining room at the Hyatt, tel. (808) 742-1234, is the **Ilima Terrace,** open daily for breakfast, lunch, and dinner. Descend a formal staircase and step onto a slate floor covered with an emerald green carpet. The tables, bright with floral-patterned tablecloths, have highback wicker chairs. Floor-to-ceiling beveled glass doors look out onto the lovely grounds, while lighting is provided by massive chandeliers fashioned like flowers. Start your day with a choice of fresh chilled juices and move on to hearty omelettes and servings of eggs accompanied by Paniolo corned beef or chicken hash for $8.50. Other selections are Belgian waffles or buckwheat or buttermilk pancakes for around $7.50, or simple sides like English muffins, hash browns, and steamed rice for around $3. The Ilima Breakfast Buffet at $14.75 daily, $17 on Sunday, is wonderful and offers specialties like eggs Benedict, stuffed blintzes, freshly made omelettes, fresh fish, and a wide assortment of breakfast meats. The health-conscious can choose homemade muesli, granola, or an assortment of fresh island fruit. Lunch brings starters like quesadillas, tossed salad, and *ahi* sashimi for $4.25-8. Salads include lemon-barbecued chicken, and niçoise salad with albacore tuna for around $8. Move on to grilled salmon with Bibb lettuce, tomato, and sprouts for $9.25, or you can have a personal pizza topped with mushrooms, pepperoni, and cheese for $12. A daily pasta could be linguine with roasted chicken for $9.75; sandwiches range from a Philly cheese steak to a Reuben for around $9. Dinner offers fresh Hawaiian fish prepared with *hulakoi* pineapple sauce for $19, grilled chicken for $17, and vegetable and shrimp tempura for $18. Desserts include papaya cheesecake,

triple chocolate torte, or coconut cream pie. There is a full-service bar, with wines, beers, and cappuccino, and the children's menu is loaded with goodies like alphabet soup, grilled-cheese sandwiches and chips, and hamburgers, all for under $4.

Dondero's, featuring classic Italian cuisine, is the Hyatt's signature restaurant, open for dinner only. To enter, you descend a marble staircase highlighted with green tiles into which have been embedded sea scallop shells. The continental room is formal with high-backed upholstered armchairs and tables covered in white linen and set with crystal and silver. Each has a view through floor-to-ceiling windows facing the manicured gardens. Dinner begins with antipasti, or crêpes with porcino mushrooms for $7.50, or sautéed shrimp with lemon and spinach pasta for $9.50. There is open ravioli with seafood, a Caesar salad for $4.50, or fresh buffalo mozzarella with tomato and basil for $5. Soups include minestrone or delicate pasta squares in chicken broth for $4. Entrees are pasta primavera for $18, whole-wheat pizza topped with feta cheese for only $12, and special dishes like spaghettini, gnocchi, farfal, penne, or risotto del giorno for under $22. An excellent dish is cioppino, a heady mixture of sautéed scallops, shrimp, lobster, and clams in a tomato broth, for $26. Slightly more casual is the hotel's **Tidepool Restaurant,** a mushroom cluster of thatched "huts" supported by huge beams forming an indoor/outdoor restaurant overlooking the tidepools. The Tidepool boasts the island's freshest fish, broiled, seared, grilled, or steamed, with a medley of sauces and toppings to choose from.

ENTERTAINMENT

If, after a sunset dinner and a lovely stroll along the beach, you find yourself with dancing feet or a desire to hear the strains of your favorite tunes, Poipu won't let you down. Many restaurants in the area feature piano music or small combos, often with a Hawaiian flair.

Keoki's, in the Poipu Shopping Village, gently sways with contemporary Hawaiian music Thurs.-Saturday. Come for dinner or a quiet beer and *pu pu,* and let your cares drift away.

SHOPPING

Shopping in Poipu is varied and reasonably extensive for such a small area. The Poipu Shopping Village has the largest concentration of shops, but don't forget Poipu Plaza, the hotel arcades, and the Spouting Horn flea market.

Food Stores

Poipu is home to the generally well-stocked **Kukuiula Store,** at Poipu Plaza, open Mon.-Fri. 8 a.m.-8:30 p.m. and Saturday and Sunday 8 a.m.-6:30 p.m., where you'll find groceries, produce, bakery goods, sundries, and liquor. **Whaler's General Store,** at Poipu Shopping Village, open daily 7:30 a.m.-10 p.m., is a well-stocked convenience store with a good selection of wines and liquors; and **Brennecke's Mini Mart,** heavily hurricane-damaged but coming back, is across from Poipu Beach County Park.

Note: If you're staying in a Poipu condo and are buying large quantities of food, you may save money by making the trip to a larger market in one of the nearby towns. See "Food Shopping" under "Koloa," earlier in this chapter.

Poipu Shopping Village

The Poipu Shopping Village offers unique one-stop shopping in a number of shops including **The Ship Store Gallery,** open daily 9 a.m.-9 p.m., tel. (808) 742-7123, for all things nautical including sea-inspired art, especially of the great sailing days of discovery. Some of the nautical artists on display include Raymond Massey and the internationally famous Anthony Cassay, along with Hashiotsuka, who renders colorful Japanese scenes, and sculptor Dale Joseph Evers, who brings dolphins and manta rays up from the deep. **The Black Pearl Collection** sells pearls and jewelry; **Traders of Kauai** features distinctive gifts, children's wear, and alohawear; **Tropical Shirts** puts original airbrush designs on shirts, Red Dirt T-shirts, and sweatshirts; **For Your Eyes Only** carries distinctive sunglasses. Next door to each other you'll find **Onboard,** for men's clothing, and **Overboard,** for women's clothing, both open Mon.-Sat. 9 a.m.-9 p.m. and Sunday until 6 p.m. Both feature casual to elegant alohawear. A freestanding shop named **Pineapples from Paradise,** open

Mon.-Sat. 10 a.m.-8 p.m. and Sunday 1-7 p.m., sells food items mostly made from pineapple—salsa, pepper sauce, and various jellies and jams. There's also mango chutney and guava syrup. Besides the food items, they have a wall filled with gold, silver, and crystal jewelry, many pieces fashioned into a pineapple motif. A pewter wine stopper or perhaps some bath lotions and gels make great souvenirs. Notice the juice cans lining the shop; they've been collected from around the world

Photo Needs

Poipu Fast Photo, tel. (808) 742-7322, in the Poipu Shopping Village, sells cameras and film and does processing.

SPORTS AND RECREATION

The Koloa/Poipu area has many surf and sailing shops that rent sports equipment and diving gear and sponsor boating excursions.

Outfitters Kauai, an ecology-minded sports shop offering kayaking and mountain biking, is owned and operated by Rick and Julie Havilend. Located in the Poipu Plaza, at 2827-A Poipu Rd., P.O. Box 1149, Poipu Beach, HI, 96756, tel. (808) 742-9667, Outfitters Kauai is open Mon.-Sat. 9 a.m.-5 p.m. and Sunday by arrangement. The shop's Poipu "interpretive bike course," self-guided with map and narrative information, is $20-33, $35 tandem, depending upon the grade of bicycle chosen. Outfitters Kauai's most thrilling adventure is the South Shore Sea Kayaking Tour, offered Thursday or by arrangement; $48 per person; check in at 12:15 p.m., return by 4:30 p.m. Single or double kayaks are available, and the adventure includes snacks and cold drinks. Also offered is the Na Pali Kayak Adventure and the River Kayak Adventure, which takes you up Kauai's navigable rivers; $45 for a double kayak, $30 for a single. Mountain-bike rentals, 9 a.m.-5 p.m., helmet and water bottles included, are $20 (multiday discounts). The company also offers mountain "bike and hike" ecotours to Koke'e 7:30 a.m.-1:30 p.m. on Wednesday or by special arrangement. The relaxed-pace 16-mile ride (with a few vigorous climbs) focuses on the natural history of the area and includes cold drinks and a full lunch; $78 per person. Outfitters Kauai retails biking and kayaking incidentals in its shop along with Patagonia clothing—shorts, sweatshirts, shirts, and even hats. Rick and Julie are excellent athletes who know the mountains and seas of Kauai intimately. Their tours are educational as well as highly adventuresome; you couldn't find a better outfit to travel with.

Sea Sports Kauai, at Poipu Plaza, 2827 Poipu Rd., tel. (808) 742-9303, (800) 685-5889, is a full service snorkel/scuba/surf shop. Rentals include snorkel masks, fins, and snorkels at $5 per hour, $15 per day (includes complimentary lesson), $30 for a reef tour; surfboards at $5-10 and $15-20, depending on quality (surfing lessons run $30); two-tank introductory scuba dives for $110; one-tank certified dives for $75, and three-day certification courses for $395 (dive video available for $39.95). Sea Sports Kauai is also a sports boutique with boogie boards, surfboards, underwater equipment, T-shirts, sandals, and unique bags in the form of sharks and colorful reef fish.

Brennecke's Ocean Sports, tel. (808) 742-6570, specializes in snorkel and scuba lessons and also rents surfboards, boogie boards, and windsurfers, and offers canoe rides and charter boats.

Fathom Five Divers in Koloa, about 100 yards after you make the left-hand turn to Poipu, tel. (808) 742-6991 or (800) 972-3078, open daily 9 a.m.-6 p.m., is owned and operated by Karen Long-Olsen, is a complete diving center offering lessons, certification, and rentals. Two-tank boat dives for certified divers, including gear, are $95—$79 if you have your own equipment. Introductory dives, including lesson and gear, are $129 each; a one-tank shore dive is $64. Certification courses take five days and average about $359 (group). Tank refills are also available. Fathom Five also does half-day snorkeling cruises that include lessons and gear for $64. Snorkel rental is $5 per day, $15 per week.

World surfing champion Margo Oberg, tel. (808) 742-9533, will teach you how to mount a board and ride gracefully over the shimmering sea.

In Poipu, **Sea Star,** tel. (808) 332-8189, rents windsurfing gear (rack included), but does not offer lessons.

Snorkel Bob's, just past Koloa Town along Poipu Rd., tel. (808) 742-2206, rents inexpensive snorkel gear that can be taken inter-island.

Blue Dolphin Charters, tel. (808) 742-6731, will take you sailing, snorkeling, and scuba diving aboard the *Tropic Bird,* a 56-foot trimaran that's fully licensed and certified. Departing from Kukui'ula Harbor, they give you a good deal for a reasonable price.

Captain Andy's Sailing Adventures runs a catamaran along the lovely, sculpted south coast during winter. Famous are the sunset trips with this jovial seaman; call (808) 822-7833 for information. He also sails the north shore during the summer. **Bass Guides of Kauai,** tel. (808) 822-1405, operates charter tours for two people in 17-foot aluminum boats on the reservoirs near Koloa. All equipment is provided.

If you're into horseback riding, try **CJM Country Stables** for any of their three scheduled rides. The one-hour, easy beach ride leaves at 12:30 p.m. and costs $20. Departing at 2:30 p.m., the two-hour ride ($40) is more extensive, wandering along the beach, into the ironwood trees and cane fields, and over sand dunes. Leaving at 8:30 a.m., the beach breakfast ride takes you to a secluded beach girdled by high mountains where you relax while breakfast is prepared for you; $55, three hours. CJM is located two miles past Poipu Kai Resort on the dirt road. For information and reservations, call (808) 742-6096 or 245-6666.

Designed by Robert Trent Jones Jr., the **Kiahuna Golf Course** is an 18-hole, par 70 course just up the road from Poipu Shopping Village. Open for play 7 a.m. until sunset, the pro shop hours are 6:30 a.m.-6:30 p.m., with a snack bar available throughout the day. Reservations are requested a week in advance if possible.

The Poipu Bay Resort Golf Course and Pro Shop, tel. (808) 742-8711, the site of the PGA Grand Slam, is a par-72 Scottish Links-style course also designed by Robert Trent Jones, Jr. With 6,845 magnificent yards rolling along the oceanside with the mountains as backdrop, it's noted for stunning views and is described as the Pebble Beach of the Pacific.

The **Koloa Tennis Courts,** in Koloa Town, are open to the public, free, lighted at night, and operate on a first-come, first-served basis.

SERVICES AND INFORMATION

Medical, Emergency, and Health

At the Koloa Clinic, the **Kauai Medical Group,** tel. (808) 742-1621 (245-6810 after hours), offers medical services Mon.-Fri. 8 a.m.-5 p.m., Saturday 8 a.m.-noon, and after hours by arrangement. This clinic is located by the stream next to the Koloa Sugar Mill chimney. **Garden Island Medical Group, Inc.,** tel. (808) 742-1677, has an office at 3176 Poipu Rd. in Koloa. Hours are the same as those for the Kauau Medical Groups; for after-hours appointments, call (808) 338-9431. The **South Shore Pharmacy,** tel. (808) 742-7511, is in downtown Koloa, open Mon.-Fri. 9 a.m.-5 p.m. It has not only a prescription service but also first-aid supplies and skin- and health-care products. The **Koloa Chiropractic Clinic,** at 3176 Poipu Rd., and the **HPI Pharmacy,** just next door, can also help with medical problems and prescriptions. (If they can't help, the Kauai Mortuary is right down the street.)

General Information

The **Poipu Beach Resort Assoc.,** P.O. Box 730, Koloa, HI 96756, tel. (808) 742-7444, is an excellent organization that can help you to plan your trip in the Poipu area. It can provide brochures and tips on everything from dining to accommodations.

MARY ANN ABEL

banyan tree

BOB RACE

SOUTHWEST KAUAI

The sometimes turbulent but forever enduring love affair between non-Polynesian travelers and the Hawaiian Islands began in southwest Kauai, when Captain Cook hove to off Waimea Bay and a longboat full of wide-eyed sailors made the beach. Immediately, journals were filled with glowing descriptions of the loveliness of the newly found island and its people, and the liaison has continued unabated ever since.

The Kaumualii (Royal Oven) Highway (Rt. 50) steps west from Lihue, with the Hoary Head Mountains adding a dash of beauty to the south and Queen Victoria's Profile winking down from the heights. Soon, Maluhia (Peaceful) Road branches to the south through an open lei of fragrant eucalyptus trees lining the route to Koloa and Poipu. Quickly come the towns of Omao, Lawai, and Kalaheo, way stations on the road west. Hereabouts, three separate botanical gardens create a living canvas of color in blooms.

After Kalaheo, the road (Rt. 540) dips south again and passes Port Allen, a still-active harbor, and Ele'ele, then goes on to Hanapepe, at the mouth of the Hanapepe River, whose basin has long been known as one of the best taro lands in the islands. You pass tiny "sugar towns" and hidden beaches until you enter Waimea, whose east flank was once dominated by a Russian fort, the last vestige of a dream of island dominance gone sour. Captain Cook landed at Waimea in the midafternoon of January 20, 1778; a small monument in the town center commemorates the great event. A secondary road leading north from Waimea and another from Kekaha farther west converge inland, then meander along Waimea Canyon, the Pacific's most superlative gorge. Kekaha, with its belching sugar stacks, marks the end of civilization, and the hard road gives out just past the Barking Sands Pacific Missile Range. A cane road picks up and carries you to the wide, sun-drenched beach of Polihale (Protected Breast), the end of the line, and the southernmost extremity of the Na Pali coast.

The **Koloa District** starts just west of the Hoary Head Mountains and ends on the east bank of the Hanapepe River. It mostly incorporates the ancient *ahuapua'a,* a land division shaped like a piece of pie with its pointed end deep in the Alakai Swamp and the broad end along the coast. *Koloa* means "duck"; the area was so named probably because of the preponderance of ponds throughout the district that attract these water-loving fowl. Its villages are strung along Route 50, except for Koloa and Poipu, which lie south of the main road.

The adjoining *ahuapua'a* is the **Waimea District,** whose broad end continues from Hanapepe until it terminates about midway up the Na Pali coast. *Waimea* means "Red Waters"; the area was named for the distinctive color of the Waimea River, which bleeds from Mt. Waialeale. It cuts through Waimea Canyon depositing the rich red soil at its mouth.

Kauai's southwest underbelly has the best beaches on the island. They're not only lovely to look at and lie in the island's sunbelt; at most of them, the surf is also inviting and cooperative. At come you can camp, at all you can picnic, and a barefoot stroll is easy to come by just about anywhere along these 30 sun-drenched miles.

Note: Accommodations, Dining, and Other Practicalities
Lodging in southwest Kauai mostly means staying in the Poipu area. Otherwise, avail yourself of facilities in the county beach parks (for permits and general information, see "Camping and Hiking" in the On the Road chapter), Classic Cottages, the Koke'e Lodge Cabins, the Waimea Plantation Cottages, and at Kahili Mountain Park, which sits at the foot of Mt. Kahili ("Tower of Silence") off Rt. 50. Since the following villages are quite small, practicalities, usually given under separate headings, are gathered in one section for each location or incorporated in the descriptive text.

Gasoline is a problem to find after 9 p.m. in this region. The nearest open service station is in Lihue. Make sure not to leave yourself short.

WEST TO HANAPEPE

PUHI

This village is technically in Lihue District, but since it's the first settlement you pass heading west, it's included here. Two road signs tip you off that you're in Puhi—one for **Kauai Community College** and the other for the **Queen Victoria's Profile** scenic overlook turnout. It's beneficial to keep abreast of what's happening at the college by reading the local newspaper and free tourist brochures. Oftentimes, workshops and seminars concerning Hawaiian culture, folk medicine, and various crafts are offered; most are open to the general public and free of charge. Queen Victoria's Profile isn't tremendously remarkable, but a definite resemblance to the double-chinned monarch has been fashioned by nature on the ridge of the Hoary Head Mountains to the south. More importantly, look for the **People's Market** across from the college. Here, you can pick up fruit and vegetables, and they offer excellent prices for freshly strung plumeria lei, an inexpensive way to brighten your day. Next door is the brown-wood **Puhi Store,** a small sundries shop (built in 1917) that has the feel of bygone days. Also in Puhi is the Grove Farms Co., Inc., office, **Lappert's Ice Cream** shop, **Kauai Sausage** shop, the **Sea Star** store for windsurfing and ocean gear supplies, and a **Shell station,** with gas slightly cheaper than in either Lihue or Koloa.

LAWAI

In times past, *ali'i* from throughout the kingdom came to Lawai (along Rt. 50 near the intersection of Rt. 530, which comes up from Koloa) to visit an ancient fishpond in the caldera of an extinct volcano. Legend says that this was the first attempt by Madame Pele to dig herself a fiery home. From more recent times, look into the valley below town to see an abandoned pineapple factory.

Pacific Tropical Botanical Garden
The 186 acres of the Pacific Tropical Botanical Garden—now part of the National Botanical Gardens—constitute the only tropical plant research facility in the country. Its primary aims are

TO HANAPEPE

to preserve, propagate, and dispense knowledge about tropical plants. This is becoming increasingly important as large areas of the world's tropical forests are being destroyed. Chartered by Congress in 1964, this nonprofit botanical and horticultural research and educational organization is supported by private contributions.

Currently, the garden's living collection has over 6,000 species of tropical plants, and about 1,000 individual plants are added to the collection each year. The staggering variety flourishing here ranges from common bamboo to romantic orchids. The gardens are separated into individual sections that include plants of nutritional value, medicinal value, herbs and spices, and rare and endangered species in need of conservation; other groups include plants of special ethnobotanical interest, plants of unexploited potential, tropical fruits, and ornamentals. This garden also maintains two satellite gardens, one in the wetter Limahuli Valley on the north coast of Kauai (1,000 acres), and another at Hana, Maui (120 acres), which contains Piilanihale Heiau, the largest *heiau* in the islands.

These gardens are so enchanting that many visitors regard them as one of the real treats of their trip. The visitors center (with a small museum and gift shop) is open Mon.-Fri. 7:30 a.m.-4 p.m., and from there you can take a self-guided walking tour of the lawn surrounding the center and its two dozen labeled plants. Organized tours run weekdays at 9 a.m. and 1 p.m., Saturdays at 9 a.m., and Sundays at 1 p.m. (come at least 15 minutes early); they take you by van into the gardens proper and include a two-mile walk. The tour, led by knowledgeable horticultural staff or a Na Lima Kokua ("Helping Hands") volunteer, lasts for about two and a half hours and costs $15. The weekday tours include a walk into the Allerton Estate, while the weekend tours include only a partial tour of the estate and more time in the gardens. Wear good walking shoes, carry an umbrella if it looks like showers, and bring mosquito repellent! Reservations are needed and should be made four to five days in advance—longer during the Christmas and Thanksgiving seasons. Call the visitors center at (808) 332-7361, or write well in advance to the reservations secretary at P.O. Box 340, Lawai, HI 96765. Annual membership, from $35 and up, entitles you to many benefits not given casual visitors—write to the membership chairman at the address above.

Adjoining these gardens is the 100-acre Allerton Garden, started by John Allerton, a member of the Mainland cattle-raising family that founded the First National Bank of Chicago. This garden dates from the 1870s, when Queen Emma made the first plantings here at one of her summer vacation homes. John Allerton (grandson of the original owner), assisting and carrying on the work of his father, Robert, scoured the islands of the South Pacinic to bring back their living treasures. Oftentimes, old *kama'aina* families would send cuttings of their rarest plants to be included in the collection. For 20 years, father and son, helped by a host of gardeners, cleared the jungle and planted. The Lawai River runs through the property, and pools and statuary help set the mood. To reach the gardens, go 2.8 miles north from Koloa (or turn onto Rt. 530 from Rt. 50 if coming from Lihue). Turn into Hailima Road (the third right if coming from Rt. 50) and follow the gravel driveway past the Dead End sign to the visitors center.

Practicalities

In town next to the **post office,** at mile marker 10, is **Matsuura's Store,** a reasonably well-stocked way station open Mon.-Sat. 6 a.m.-6:30 p.m. and Sunday 6 a.m.-5 p.m. Next door is the **Lawai Restaurant,** open daily 7 a.m.-9 p.m., a very local restaurant that serves American standard and a smattering of Filipino food at very reasonable prices.

At the intersection of Routes 50 and 530 is the **Hawaiian Trading Post** gift shop and **Mustard's Last Stand** snack shop. Mustard's features over a dozen varieties of hot dogs and sausages, sandwiches, and delicious scoops of island-flavored Lappert's ice cream. The place lives up to its name—the condiment/mustard table has Dijon, Poupon, horseradish, salsas, and all the other trimmings to flavor your dog. Picnic tables in a pleasant grove of coconut, breadfruit, orange African tulip, and purple Hong Kong orchid trees sit next to a miniature golf course ($1 to play as long as you like). Everything at Mustard's (except the food) is made out of old surfboards. Notice the bottles that have been embedded in the cement floor, and the wave to the rear, fashioned from plaster, where you can stand on a surfboard and have your picture taken. Mustard's is excellent for what they have to offer, and the service is friendly. It is a big hit with the kids and reminds parents of roadside joints of times past.

The Hawaiian Trading Post, referred to by locals as "the tourist trap," sells a mind-boggling variety of handcrafted items as well as a large selection of souvenirs, treasures, and tourist junk. Featured are goods made from eelskin and other exotic leathers (chicken feet, python, lizard . . .). Other selections include T-shirts, jewelry, carvings, and an excellent display of shells that should be featured but are stuck away on a back counter. For $10 or so, you can

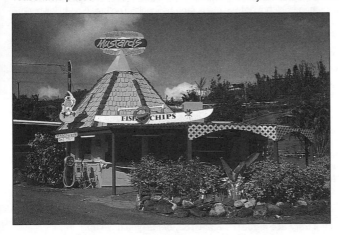

Mustard's Last Stand, featuring all the trimmings for your dog

treat a lot of people back home with purchases from here.

Lawai General Store, along Koloa Rd. just near Mustard's, sells sundries and groceries.

Maukalani, 4000 Koloa Rd., Lawai, HI 96756, tel. (808) 742-1700 or (800) 745-7414, is a deluxe, 650-square-foot cottage in a quiet residential area of Lawai. This one-bedroom unit offers a professionally decorated interior, complete kitchen, full bath, and total privacy. Prices are a very reasonable $55 d ($450 weekly). Maukalani is a perfect getaway for those who desire peace and quiet.

KALAHEO

The area around Kalaheo is springing up with many new housing subdivisions, and large tracts of coffee, tea, and macadamia nut trees are tinting the hillsides in new shades of green. In town are three gas stations, a liquor store, post office, a medical clinic, restaurants, a mini-mart, and a new office/shopping plaza, all along Rt. 50, making Kalaheo the first sizable town between Lihue and Hanapepe where you can pick up anything you may need before continuing west.

Kukui O Lono Park

Kukui O Lono Park is a personal gift from Walter D. McBryde, the well-known plantation owner who donated the land to the people of Kauai in 1919. Accept it! It's off the beaten track but definitely worth the trip. Turn left in Kalaheo at the Menehune Food Mart and go up Papalina Road for one mile until you come to the second Puu Road (the first skirts the hill below the park). A sharp right turn brings you through the large stone-and-metal-picket gate (open 6:30 a.m.-6:30 p.m. Inside the park is a golf course and Japanese-style garden. The entrance road leads through a tunnel of eucalyptus trees to a commemorative plaque to McBryde. A flock of green parrots that nest in the tall eucalyptus trees on the grounds can be heard in a symphony of sound in the early evening.

For the gardens and McBryde's memorial, head straight ahead to the parking lot; to get to the clubhouse, follow the road to your right for about a half mile. At the clubhouse are a pro shop and snack bar run by a very accommo-

dating man, Mr. Kajitani. He knows a lot about the park and the surrounding area and is willing to chat. A round of golf on the par-36 course is $5; carts and clubs are rented at a similarly reasonable rate. Lessons are $15 a half-hour and must be arranged with the pro.

As it's set on top of a hill, it's great fun, and the sweeping views in all directions are striking. Unfortunately, perfectly placed in the center of one of the nicest views is a microwave antenna and dish. Set amidst a grove of towering trees, the Japanese garden offers peace and tranquillity. A short stone bridge crosses a small pool, around which finely sculpted shrubs and small lanterns have been set; unusually, flowers line the adjoining walks. Many weddings are held here. The whole scene is conducive to Zen-like meditation. Enjoy it.

Olu Pua Gardens

Olu Pua Gardens are the former formal gardens of the Kauai Pineapple Plantation, which have been opened to the public. West of Kalaheo, just past the turnoff for Rt. 540, a sign on the right marks the private drive to this 12-acre garden and plantation estate. Olu Pua ("Floral Serenity") typifies the atmosphere of these grounds. There are basically four gardens: the *kau kau* garden, filled with fruit trees and other edible and exotic plants, a hibiscus garden, a palm garden that lives up to its name, and a jungle garden thick with tropical exotics like mahogany, vanilla orchids, and heliconia. The broad open lawn, dotted with flowering shade trees, leads up to the handsome house of the plantation manager.

Since the property is private, the garden manager wants to control the flow of visitors. The gardens open daily for guided tours (around $12) at 9:30 a.m., 11:30 a.m., and 1:30 p.m. Reservations are requested, so call ahead; drive-in guests are accommodated *only* if there is room. Soon (the manager says), the gardens will only be open to more expensive organized tour groups as part of a trip to Waimea Canyon or the shopping trips to Old Koloa Town and Kiahuna Shopping Village; call Kauai Island Tours for these arrangements, tel. (808) 245-9382. In regard to the present entrance situation, be sure to check with the Olu Pua Gardens office, P.O. Box 518, Kalaheo, HI 96741, tel. (808) 332-8182, *before* you drive up.

Practicalities

South Shore Vista B&B, in Kalaheo, tel. (808) 332-9339, offers a completely equipped one-bedroom apartment with an ocean view. The room, with its own private entrance, is almost 600 square feet of living space including a dining/living room, bath, kitchen, and deck. Fresh fruit from the garden, cereal, tea, and coffee are provided. At a rate of only $59 d, South Shore Vista is an excellent choice.

At the signal along Rt. 50 in Kalaheo, you'll find the **Menehune Food Mart** with **Steve's Mini Mart** across the street. Both can supply you with any sundries or light groceries that you may need.

Those in condos or with cooking facilities might even stop in at **Medeiro's Farm,** along Papalina Road toward Kukui O Lono Park, for fresh poultry and eggs. Along Papalina Road you will also find **Horner's Fish Corner,** in a distinctive blue building, where you can purchase fresh fish.

Local people out for an evening meal at reasonable prices give the nod to **Kalaheo Steak House,** at 4444 Papalina Rd., open daily 5:30-9:30 p.m., tel. (808) 332-9780, where you can get a well-prepared and hearty portion of steak, seafood, pork, or poultry. Make a left at the signal along Rt. 50 in Kalaheo and look for a green building on the left with an awning. The interior, very much in steak house motif, is completely knotty pine—simple, but tasteful, offering seating at a combination of black leatherette booths, and tables with wicker chairs. Hanging ferns, potted plants, and a mural of tropical fish complete the decor. Local lore has it that when you leave Kalaheo Steak house, the *doggie bag* contains more food than you're usually served at most restaurants.

If you're interested in a pizza or sandwich, stop in at **Brick Oven Pizza,** open Tues.-Sun. 11 a.m.-10 p.m. and Sunday noon-10 p.m., tel. (808) 332-8561 (if you're heading to Waimea or Polihale, call ahead to have a pizza ready for you), located mountain side in a brand-new building just as you enter Kalaheo. Pizzas range in price from a 10-inch cheese pizza for $7.35 to a large 15-inch deluxe with all the toppings for $22.85. Brick Oven also prepares vegetarian sandwiches and hot sausage sandwiches for around $5.75, along with pizza bread for $2.35

and a variety of salads $1.70-5.95. Wine, beer, and soft drinks are available. Brick Oven has a well-deserved excellent local reputation.

Grandma "Pomodoro," a native of Salerno, Italy, usually sits in the back room knitting while keeping an eye on the olive oil, garlic, and basil going into the dishes created by her son Tony, the former owner of Casa Italiana in Lihue. After Hurricane Iniki destroyed his restaurant, Tony opened **Pomodoro Restaurant,** along Rt. 50 on the right just before entering Kalaheo, tel. (808) 332-5945, open nightly 5:30-10 p.m. The menu opens with classics like antipasti, with mozzarella, prosciutto, or calamari, ranging in price from $6.50 to $8.50, a mixed green salad at $3.95, and a Caesar for $5.95. Pasta is spaghetti with meatballs or Italian sausage for $11.50, linguine shrimp marinara at $15.95, fettuccine Alfredo for $11.50, and an assortment of ravioli, cannelloni, manicotti, and lasagna in different sauces priced at $13.95. Specialties are veal Parmesan or picatta at $17.95, eggplant Parmesan at $15.95, and chicken cacciatore for $16.95. The wine list, by the bottle or glass, includes wines from California and Italy, with varietals like white zinfandel, merlot, chianti, and cabernet sauvignon. Top off your meal with an espresso and a choice of an Italian dessert made fresh daily. The dining room is small, intimate, and cheery, and the wait staff is professional.

Another option for food is the blue-and-white **Camp House Grill,** specializing in burgers, Hawaiian-style barbecued chicken, and box lunches, open for breakfast daily 6:30-10:30 a.m. and for lunch and dinner 11 a.m.-9 p.m., tel. (808) 332-9755. It's located across from the Menehune Food Mart along Rt. 50. Menu items are basic American standards with a Hawaiian twist and include their famous Camp House breakfasts, like a flour tortilla stuffed with scrambled eggs, sausage, and cheeses, topped with sauce and served with rice or Camp House hash browns at $4.95, a variety of omelettes for around $6.95, and early-bird specials for as little as $2.55. Lunches and dinners start with salad, soup, and chili, a deluxe garden salad at $4.95, chicken a la Eleele at $6.95, and a "quiche of the day" for $2.95. Camp House Grill is famous for its burgers, ranging $3.95-4.95 and topped with items like grilled pineapple and teriyaki sauce. Evening specialties are spaghetti at

$8.95, barbecued pork ribs at $9.95, and grilled breast of chicken at $6.95. For a snack, or to top off your meal, notice the pie case filled with luscious homemade beauties like macadamia nut pie, pineapple cream cheese pie, and sour cream apple pie. A nice homey touch is an ongoing childrens' place mat-coloring contest. When completed, the entries are pinned to the wall as permanent mementos, and prizes include free meals and coloring sets.

Classic Cottages, owned and operated by Wynnis and Richard Grow, at 2687 Onu Place, P.O. Box 901, Kalaheo, HI 96741, tel. (808) 332-9201, are six homey units where you can expect low daily rates while enjoying excellent access to nearby beaches, golf courses, and tennis courts. Rates are $55 for a garden studio and $60 for an oceanview; to include breakfast, add $5; for a third person, add $10; jacuzzi available.

PORT ALLEN AND VICINITY

As you roll along from Kalaheo to Port Allen, you're surrounded by sugarcane fields, and the traditional economy of the area is apparent. About halfway there, an HVB Warrior points to an overlook. Stop. **Hanapepe Valley Overlook** is no farther away than your car door, served up as easily as a fast-food snack at a drive-through window. For no effort, you get a remarkable panorama of a classic Hawaiian valley, much of it still planted in taro.

In a moment, you pass through **Ele'ele** (home of the famous Kauai Kookie Kompany—whose macadamia shortbread, Kona coffee, guava macadamia, and coconut krispies cookies, among others, are now available statewide) and **Port Allen,** separate communities on the east bank of the Hanapepe River, with Hanapepe on the west.

Practicalities

At the junction for Rt. 541, at mile marker 16, leading to Port Allen is the **Ele'ele Shopping Center,** marked by **McDonald's** golden arches. Here, along with various eateries, are a **post office,** a laundromat, a bank, a **Big Save Supermarket** (open Mon.-Sat 7 a.m.-10 p.m.), a service station, and **The Garden Isle Medical Group clinic,** tel. (808) 335-3107.

Toi's Thai Kitchen, in the shopping center and open weekdays 10:30 a.m.-2:30 p.m. and Saturday 11:30 a.m.-2:30 p.m. for lunch and daily 5:30-9:30 p.m. for dinner, is family operated and one of the best Thai restaurants on Kauai. Prepared by Mom and served by her lovely daughters, the menu offers spicy sour soup with lemongrass and ginger, priced $7.95-10.95 depending upon your choice of pork, beef, or seafood; jasmine rice soup with pork, shrimp, or chicken at $8.95-9.95; and tofu soup for $8.95-9.95. Entrees include stir-fried eggplant and tofu in a spicy sauce with your choice of meat, $8.95-10.95; savory sauté of beef, pork, chicken, shrimp, or tofu with sweet creamy peanut butter priced $7.95-10.95; and basil delight—your choice of meat stir-fried and then enhanced with fresh sweet basil leaves—$8.95-10.95.

What began as a slap from Mother Nature turned **Paradise Sportswear,** located in a large industrial building just before Port Allen Small Boat Harbor, tel. (808) 335-5670, from an obscure tiny company into one of the most famous in the state. After Hurricane Iniki ravaged Kauai in 1994, the staff returned to find the roof of the building completely torn off and the warehouse, containing shirts jobbed from other companies, inundated with red dirt and rendered unsellable—maybe! Amidst the devastation, the future seemed bleak, but as living legend would have it, one person said, in effect, "Ah, these shirts actually look pretty cool." Perhaps spurred by desperation, the forlorn faces, after rolling their eyes heavenward, slowly reconsidered and began to smile. *Voilà,* the **Red Dirt T-Shirt,** now on sale throughout Hawaii and moving onto the mainland, was born. Dedicated to the community, Paradise Sportswear is a true cottage industry, employing 16 local families who pick up ordinary white shirts, take them home, and repeatedly dip them in vats of Kauai's famous red dirt. After bringing them back, other local people working on the premises apply original silkscreen designs. Since absolutely no chemicals or dyes are used, no two shirts—which range in color from deep copper to burnt orange—are the same. Tour the factory (call for details) to watch the silkscreening process, and make sure to stop in at the retail shop, where you can choose from countless designs and styles, ranging from tiny tank tops for tots to XXXXXXLs for walking Sherman tanks, and take advantage of a 50% discount on factory seconds. Retail outlets featuring Red Dirt Ts are found on every island so far except the Big Island, with innumerable boutiques and shops carrying these very distinctive souvenirs. Mainlanders can even find them in Sedona, Arizona, and Moab, Utah.

HANAPEPE

Hanapepe ("Crushed Bay"), billing itself as "Kauai's Biggest Little Town," is divided into two sections. One section lies along Rt. 50, the other is Old Hanapepe, a "must-see" along Hanapepe Road, off to the right at the Y-intersection just near the Green Garden Restaurant.

Practicalities

The **Green Garden Restaurant,** an old standby, is marked by a tangle of vegetation that almost makes the building look overgrown. It's open daily 7 a.m.-2 p.m. for breakfast and lunch and daily except Tuesday 5-9 p.m. for dinner, tel. (808) 335-5422. This family-owned restaurant offers tourist-quality food in large portions, with *aloha* service. The new section of the restaurant is set up to hold busloads of tourists who arrive for lunch; go a little before or a little after noon. The old room has a few plants, but the name is really held up by the decor—green walls, chairs, tables, place mats, bathrooms. If you see anything on the menu that you might want to mix and match, just ask. Substitutions are made cheerfully. The full-meal selections, including beverage, are mostly under $10. The homemade pies are famous and always delicious.

Immediately past it, look for a tiny white building housing **Susie's Cafe,** tel. (808) 335-3989, an excellent downhome, health-conscious restaurant where you can have everything from a smoothie to Susie's beef stew and rice. Breakfast is particularly scrumptious, with farm-fresh eggs or pancakes made with rice and bananas and topped with macadamia nuts. Almost next door is a **Lappert's Ice Cream** stand. Then on your left is another island institution and oddity, the combination **Conrad's** and **Wong's** restaurants, open daily for breakfast, lunch, and dinner, but closed Monday after 2 p.m., tel. (808) 335-5066. Defying the adage "that two things can't occupy the same

space at the same time," the two different restaurants have two different menus in one giant dining room that's reminiscent of a small-town banquet hall that caters to local bowling leagues. Both are very reasonably priced, but they, too, are favorites of the tour buses and can be crowded. When you go into the cafeteria-style dining room, you're handed two separate menus. Feel free to order from either. Conrad's (formerly Mike's—his dad) has standard American fare with a Hawaiian twist. Most sandwiches are under $6, main-course dinners are under $8. Wong's specialties are Chinese and Japanese dishes, all under $10, with many around $7. The service is friendly, the portions large, but the cooking is mediocre—except for the pies. You won't complain, but you won't be impressed, either.

If that isn't enough, next door is **Omoide's Deli and Bakery,** and across the street, in a russet-colored building, is **Kauai Kitchens,** a local coffee shop. Both are open early in the morning for breakfast.

Even if you tried, you couldn't miss **Sinaloa Tacqueria,** open daily for lunch 11 a.m.-5 p.m. and for dinner 5-9 p.m., tel. (808) 335-0006, a huge piñata of a bright turquoise metal building trimmed in yellow and green. The inside is more colorful than a Kauai sunset, with pink, yellow, green, blue, and turquoise chairs and yellow and blue tiles. Dishes include spicy Mexican fare like burritos, *chile verde, carne asada, pollo poblano,* Mazatlan chiles rellenos, eggplant enchiladas, and seafood burritos, all served with extras like chips and salsa, guacamole, and sour cream. These dishes cost $7-12 for lunch, about $2 more for dinner. The bar serves imported beers like Bohemia, Tecate, and Pacifico, and they also have pitchers of Coors Lite and Fire Gold, a great microbrew from Kona. The house standard is Cuervo Gold Margaritas for $5.50, or by the pitcher for $19.50, with happy-hour prices from 4-6 p.m. daily.

In the center of town, along Rt. 50, keep a lookout for the **Soto Zen Temple Zenshuji** on your left. It's quite large and interesting to people who haven't visited a temple before. Also along the highway in town are the **Westside Pharmacy,** tel. (808) 335-5342; a library; **Bali Hai Helicopter** offices, tel. (808) 335-3166; **Mariko Mini-Mart; Inter-Island Helicopters,** tel. (808) 335-5009; and several gas stations.

As you leave town heading west along Rt. 50, a small gift shop called **The Station** sits on the right. A friendly young woman sells yarn, crochet material, and Hawaiian-style needlepoint designs.

On the western outskirts of town, just past The Station, a sign points *makai* down Rt. 543 to the Kauai Humane Society and Hanapepe Refuse Disposal. Follow the sign to a small Japanese cemetery (there are several others nearby), where an HVB Warrior points to **Salt Pond Beach County Park,** the best beach and windsurfing spot on this end of the island. This beach is at the west end of the runway for the Port Allen Airport, once the major airport for the island but now servicing only a few helicopters and the glider company. The local people from around Hanapepe enjoy this popular beach park with its pavilions, tables, toilets, showers, and camping (with county permit). The swimming and snorkeling are excellent, and a natural breakwater in front of the lifeguard makes a pool safe for tots. Surfers enjoy the breaks here, and a constant gentle breeze makes the area popular with windsurfers. Along the road to Salt Pond Beach, you pass the actual salt ponds, evaporative basins cut into the red earth that have been used for hundreds of years. The sea salt here is still harvested but isn't considered pure enough for commercial use. The local people know better; they make and harvest the salt in the spring and summer and, because of its so-called impurities (which actually add a special flavor), it is a sought-after commodity and an appreciated gift for family and friends. If you see salt in the basins, it belongs to someone, but there won't be any hassles if you take a *small* pinch. Don't scrape it up with your fingers because the sharp crystals can cut you—and you'll rub salt into your own wounds in the process.

OLD HANAPEPE

Much more interesting, Old Hanapepe's is a time-frozen still life of vintage false front buildings housing a palate of art studios, local dry-goods stores, a tavern, and an excellent restaurant/coffee shop that's a must-stop. Old Hanapepe, although tiny, is two sections on each side of "the bridge." Make sure to see it all. At the eastern approach to town, along Rt. 50 just at the Green Garden Restaurant, bear right at the Y-intersection and you'll soon be heading down the main drag. As you approach, look up to your right; if it's early winter, you'll see an entire hillside of bougainvilleas ablaze with a multicolored patchwork of blossoms.

Practicalities

As you come into town, the first shop, housed in a vintage plantation house, is **Uncle Eddie's Aloha Angels,** open Mon.-Sat. 9:30 a.m.-5 p.m. and Sunday from 10 until the mood strikes, tel. (808) 335-0713, featuring angels of all sorts and purposes. If you're unsure of what to expect after your visit from the Grim Reaper, try this tiny shop for a sneak preview of kingdom come.

Along the main street, make sure to stop in at the fine art studio of **Dawn M. Traina,** tel. (808) 335-3993, who, knowing she wanted to be an artist since childhood, pursued an education in art on both coasts, receiving a B.A. in Massachusetts, and an M.A. in California. Working in multimedia with acrylics, pastels, and pencils, Dawn specializes in portraiture ranging from the recognizable actor Tom Selleck to a "Hawaiian Madonna" with suckling babe. She not only captures the feeling of what's current today, working on portraits of passing tourists and celebrities, but somehow, since moving to Hawaii in 1979, has been able to tap into the lore of Hawaii and to visibly render the spirit of ancient chants, dances, legends, and the gentility of the Plantation Days. Dawn says, "It is my hope that the images in my artwork may help in some small way to increase not only the general public's awareness of, but also the respect and concern for, the native Hawaiian people and their rich cultural heritage."

The Village Gallery, on the left as you enter town, open Tues.-Sat. 9:30 a.m.-5 p.m. and Sunday 11 a.m.-4 p.m., tel. (808) 335-0343, offers a collection of art by local artists. Prices are reasonable. A little farther down the road is the **Lele Aka Studio and Gallery,** featuring art ranging from wild mythological creatures to portraits of the children of Kauai.

Another minute's stroll brings you to **Kauai Fine Arts,** at 3848 Hanapepe Rd., P.O. Box 1079, Hanapepe, HI 96716, tel. (808) 335-3778, open Mon.-Fri. 10 a.m.-5 p.m., Saturday and Sunday by appointment only (a monthly catalog costs $8 for a year's subscription). The building is all natural wood, floor to ceiling, and is like walking into a giant treasure chest. The floor is hardwood and the walls and ceiling are all pine imported from Florida. Owned and operated by Caribbean islander Mona Nicolaus, Kauai Fine Arts specializes in original engravings, antique prints mainly of the Pacific Islands, antique maps, and vintage natural science photos from as far afield as Australia and Egypt; it's also home to a collection of antique bottles. Other distinctive and easily transportable items include hand-painted, washable, Hawaiian-theme pillow covers at $18.50 designed by Mona and rendered in Bali, along with matching quilts (single, double, queen, and king) that vary from $90 to $260, all in 100% cotton. Kauai Fine Arts offers framing and worldwide shipping. If not buying, at least stop and browse in this museum-like atmosphere, where fine vintage items touch the face of old Hawaii and the Pacific at large.

Cane Field Clothing, open weekdays 10 a.m.-5 p.m., and until 3 p.m. Saturday, is mainly a ladies' boutique featuring Japanese and island-style print dresses made from either rayon or cotton. A small rack also holds fine aloha shirts for men. Although most dresses have a casual flair, they are quite elegant and perfect for an evening out. Bright with tropical prints, you'll feel as beautiful as a Hawaiian flower. A consignment shop in the rear of the store sells used clothing at bargain prices.

Hanapepe Bookstore Cafe and Espresso Bar, open Tues.-Sat. 8-11 a.m. for breakfast, 11 a.m.-2 p.m. for lunch, and Thurs.-Sat. 6-9 p.m. for dinner with live music, tel. (808) 335-5011, is a fantastic eclectic restaurant for mind and body operated by Chris and Larry, who are still working out the multiple hyphenation possibilities of their last names. Housed in the town's drugstore (circa 1939), the espresso bar/restaurant section is fashioned from the original soda fountain counter tastefully modernized with a black-and-white checkerboard motif. All the food served is health-conscious vegetarian with an attempt at organic and locally grown whenever possible, but always fresh and definitely savory and satisfying. Breakfast is terrific, with home-made pastries and pies washed down with steaming cups of espresso, hot chocolate, cappuccino, caffe latte, and an assortment of herbal teas all priced $1.75-2.75. Lunch brings a garden burger made from rolled oats, low-fat mozzarella cheese, cottage cheese, bulgur wheat, walnuts, the kitchen sink, and sautéed mushrooms for $5.95; Chris's Caesar salad for $3.50 or a large bowl of homemade minestrone soup, all served with fresh bread. Dinner is always vegetarian Italian a la Hawaii and could be baked lasagna al forno, linguine with pesto, or artichokes with cannelloni, all served with soup, salad, and bread for $15.95-17.95. Dinner music is usually provided by a solo local performer playing everything from slack-key to classical flute music. A new "Grazing Menu" is being prepared offering vegetarian *pu pu* that you can munch while enjoying the music. The original wide-board floor and simple shelves in the bookstore/boutique section are reminiscent of an old-time general store. The focus of these articles, including jewelry, handcrafted tiles, and T-shirts, is mostly on Hawaiiana. Magazines, postcards, and books on Hawaii can also be found. If you are craving a snack, quiet cup of coffee, a full meal, or just a good read, you can't beat the Hanapepe Bookstore Cafe and Espresso Bar.

A **farmers' market** operates in the big park right behind the fire station near the post office every Thursday 4-6 p.m. Those in the know are on time; the best pickings are gone in the first hour. The late bird gets the wormy apple! Also lining the main drag is the **Sandbox,** a bar about as local as you can get, the **Bank of Hawaii,** and a few small grocery stores.

For local food at moderate prices, try **Linda's Restaurant,** offering breakfast specials for $2.50 and inexpensive dinners; the **Da Imu Hut Cafe,** open Tues.-Fri. 7 a.m.-2:30 p.m., then from 4:30-9 p.m., offering a full assortment of local grinds; and **Uekoa Store** (notice the architecture), where you can buy sundries, Kauai coffee, and gifts; and, for a real treat, **Shimonishi Orchid Nursery.** There are hundreds of varieties of this tropical favorite and this is *the* place on the island to buy and ask about orchids.

Over the Bridge

After you meander the two or so blocks of Old Hanapepe, you bear left to rejoin Rt. 50, the main road to Waimea and points west. But before you do, make sure to bear right first and go "over the bridge," to the other half of the town.

In a moment, you'll pass **Kauai Fishing Company,** a great place to purchase fresh fish for an at-home meal or beach cookout.

In 1943, when the entire world was ugly with war, Matsuuki Shimonishi looked for simple beauty, which he found in the delicate blooms of orchids. Until his death in 1989, he worked daily with the flowers, hybridizing many, one of which he named *dandrobum tokiwa shimonishi* for his wife, Tokiwa. **Shimonishi Orchid Nursery,** just over the bridge on the right, open daily except Sunday and Wednesday 9 a.m. to noon and again from 1-4 p.m., tel. (808) 335-5562 or (800) 510-8684, is now in the care of his daughter. Born and raised on Kauai, Elsie and her husband, Tom Godbey, returned to the island in 1984 to help restore the nursery after it was ravaged by Hurricane Iwa. After Mr. Shimonishi passed away in 1989, the Godbeys took over the operation and have run the nursery full time since then. You are welcome to tour the nursery to find that perfect flower to take with you or have shipped back to the mainland. Many are unique hybrids from Mr. Shimonishi's experiments; the "Tokiwa," for instance is a lavender and white cluster orchid modified from a gangly flower that tipped over when put in a vase, to the present, smaller variety perfect as a centerpiece.

Next door, in a commercial space owned by the nursery, you will find the **James Hoyle Gallery,** tel. (808) 335-3582, open daily 9 a.m.- 6 p.m. and by appointment. James Hoyle has been able to capture the spirit of Hawaii through fantastic color and movement. The sense that permeates all of Hoyle's work is that in Hawaii, humanity cannot conquer nature but must learn to live in harmony with the *aina.* These fine works range in price from $800 to $40,000. If you can't afford an original, serigraphs finished and embellished in vivid color by the artist go for around $700. Hoyle also plans an artists' workshop that would be located on the main street as you pull into town.

Also in the commercial space you will find **All About Fabrics,** open daily 9 a.m.-5 p.m., featuring custom-sewn classics like aloha shirts and muumuu, made on the premises from aloha cotton, rayon, and 100% cotton Bali prints. They also offer mail-order sales.

The **Bay Town Loft,** a vacation rental owned by the Shimonishi Nursery and originally built as a small hotel in the '40s and closed in the '60s, tel. (808) 335-5562 or (800) 510-8684, has been completely refurbished and reopened as four condo suites renting for $60 nightly, $400 weekly, and $900 monthly. The cross-ventilated units, cooled by ceiling fans, are laid out with a combination dining room, kitchenette, and conversation nook along with a master bedroom and full tiled bath. Fully furnished, the units are appointed with microwaves, toasters, remote-control color TVs, coffee makers, and full refrigerators. Walls are painted in muted tans and pinks and highlighted with natural wood, and the furniture is rattan, made comfortable with puff pillows. The master bedrooms, trimmed in natural wood, feature king-size, double, or twin beds covered by flowered Hawaiian-style quilts; large closets; knotty-pine furniture; and wicker lounging chairs. The shuttered sash windows overlook the orchid nursery. The feeling is totally modern but at the same time homey, reminiscent of when Hanapepe was a sleepy plantation town.

PAST HANAPEPE TO POLIHALE

SUGAR TOWNS:
PAST HANAPEPE TO KEKAHA

The road hugs the coast after Hanapepe, by-passing a series of still-working sugar towns until you arrive in Waimea. **Kaumakani,** a small cluster of homes with a few dirt lanes, has a post office, mini-mart, and the **Niihau Helicopter** office, tel. (808) 335-3500. Put to use mostly for medical emergencies and airlifting supplies to Niihau, the helicopter is scheduled for occasional tours to the island, where the company has the exclusive landing rights and is the only way to get there without a special invitation.

Olokele is another sugar town; when you get here, take a fast drive through, drawing your own conclusions on the quality of life. You'll find small homes that are kept up with obvious pride. The road dips down to the sugar refinery, the focus of the town, while the main street is lined with quaint lampposts giving an air of the last century.

Next is **Pakala,** noted more for its surfing beach than for the town itself. At mile marker 21, a bunch of cars pulled off the road means the surf's up. Follow the pathway to try the waves yourself or just to watch the show. Popular with surfers, this beach is not an official park. Walk down past the bridge to a well-worn pathway leading through a field. In a few minutes is the beach, a 500-yard-long horseshoe of white sand. Off to the left is a rocky promontory popular with local fishermen. The swimming is fair, and the reef provides good snorkeling, but the real go is the surf—the beach is nicknamed "Infinity" because the waves last so long; they come rolling in in graceful arcs to spill upon the beach, then recede in a regular, hypnotic pattern, causing the next wave to break and roll perfectly. Sunset is a wonderful time to come here for a romantic evening picnic.

WAIMEA

The remains of the Russian fort still guard the eastern entrance to Waimea town. Turn left at the sign for **Russian Fort Elizabeth State Park;** the remains are right there. The fort, shaped like a six-pointed star, dates from 1817 when a German doctor, George Anton Scheffer, built it in the name of Czar Nicholas of Russia, naming it after the potentate's daughter. Scheffer, a self-styled adventurer and one-time Moscow policeman, saw great potential in the domination of Hawaii, and built other forts in Honolulu and along the Waioli River, which empties into Hanalei Bay on Kauai's north shore. Due to poli-

The sugar mill is the economy of west Kauai.

tical maneuverings with other European nations, Czar Nicholas never warmed to Scheffer's enterprises and withdrew official support. For a time, Kauai's King Kaumuali'i continued to fly the Russian flag, perhaps in a subtle attempt to play one foreign power against another. The fort fell into disrepair and was virtually dismantled in 1864, when 38 guns of various sizes were removed. The stout walls, once 30 feet thick, are now mere rubble, humbled by time-encircling, nondescript underbrush. However, if you climb onto the ramparts you'll still get a commanding view of Waimea Bay.

Just after you cross the Waimea River, signs point to **Lucy Wright Beach County Park,** a five-acre park popular with the local folk. There's a picnic area, restrooms, showers, playground, and tent camping (with county permit). Pick up supplies in Waimea. The park is situated around the mouth of the river, which makes the water a bit murky. The swimming is fair if the water is clear, and the surfing is decent around the rivermouth. A few hundred feet to the west of this park is a recreational pier good for fishing. Reach it by walking along the beach or down a back street behind the Waimea Library.

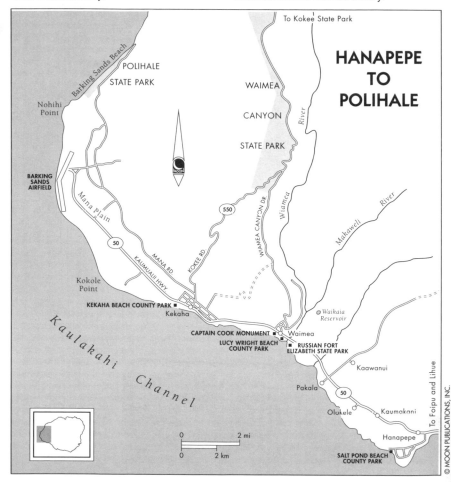

HANAPEPE TO POLIHALE

Captain Cook's achievements were surely deserving of more than the uninspiring commemorative markers around Waimea indicate. Whether you revere him as a great explorer or denigrate him as an opportunistic despoiler, his accomplishments in mapping the great Pacific were unparalleled, and changed the course of history. In his memory are **Captain Cook's Landing,** a modest marker near Lucy Wright Beach Park, commemorating his "discovery" of the Sandwich Islands at 3:30 p.m. on September 20, 1778, and **Captain Cook's Monument,** on a little median strip in downtown Waimea. If you're fascinated by Kauai's half-legendary little people, you might want to take a look at the **Menehune Ditch,** a stone wall encasing an aqueduct curiously built in a fashion unused and apparently unknown to the Polynesian settlers of Hawaii. The oral tradition states that the ditch was built by ordor of Ola, high chief of Waimea, and that he paid his little workers in *opae,* a tiny shrimp that was their staple. On payday, they supposedly sent up such a great cheer that they were heard on Oahu. Today, the site is greatly reduced, as many of the distinctively hand-hewn boulders have been removed for use in buildings around the island, especially in the Protestant church in Waimea. Some steadfastly maintain that the Menehune never existed, but a census taken in the 1820s at the request of capable King Kaumuali'i officially listed 65 persons living in Wainiha Valley as Menehune!

The town of Waimea is of little interest as far as sights go, but there is an unescorted walking tour that introduces you to the major historical sites in town. Ask at the library (tel. 808-338-1738) for the free map and description of each site. The walk should take about one and a half hours. Waimea does have some reasonably good restaurants and shopping.

Practicalities

The **Captain's Cargo Company,** tel. (808) 338-0333, 9984 Kaumuali'i Hwy. (Rt. 50), and office of **Liko Kauai Cruises,** is operated by Debra Hookano, wife of Captain Liko. The small but tasteful boutique, open daily 8 a.m.-5 p.m., offers jewelry, fashionable dresses, shorts, T-shirts, and even brocaded vests. The boutique also rents and sells surfboards, boogie boards,

and snorkel equipment. Rent boogie boards for $5 per hour and $15 per day, surfboards for $5 and $20, and snorkel gear for $2 and $5.

Along the main road, facing Captain Cook's statue, is **Ishihara's Market,** where you'll find all the necessities. Kitty-corner across the intersection is the police station; the street running inland from there goes to the Menehune Ditch. Across the street is a well-stocked **Big Save Supermarket.** Their lunch counter, believe it or not, features terrific local dishes at very reasonable prices. In town are three gas stations, **Da Booze Shop,** a laundromat, a photography supply shop, a bank, a discount clothing shop, **Kiyoki's Art Gallery,** and **West Side Sporting Goods.** A **Dairy Queen** is at the west end of town, along with the **Menehune Pharmacy,** and a half-mile up Waimea Canyon Road is **Kauai Veterans Memorial Hospital.**

Aside from a few private rental homes, **Waimea Plantation Cottages** is virtually the only place to stay along the south shore west of Poipu—and what a place it is. Owned by the Kikiaola Land Company, Ltd., and operated by Astin Resorts, this oceanfront property is set in a grove of over 750 coconut palms and a few huge banyan trees at the west end of Waimea. Not victimized by big bucks or modern resort development, workers' and supervisors' cottages and the manager's house from the former Waimea sugar plantation have been renovated and preserved, and the grounds maintained in an old-style way. Here you are treated to a touch from the past. While some modern amenities such as full kitchens, bathrooms, and color cable TVs have been added for comfort and convenience, an effort has been made to keep each unit as much in its original state (1920-30s period) as possible; period furniture and other furnishings add to the feel of that bygone era. Most buildings have bare wood floors and painted wood walls. Nearly all have ceiling fans and lanai. Weekly housekeeping and linen service are included. Complimentary washers and dryers are available on the premises. A swimming pool in the 1930s style has been constructed on the lawn, along with a court and the Grove Dining Room. In accordance with this philosophy of preservation, some long-time employees of the plantation (no longer a functioning entity) are still offered low- or no-rent cottages behind the company office rather than being turned out to make way for development of the land.

Presently, there are 48 units, including 11 cottages moved from the Kekaha Plantation. Rates for the cottages range from a one-bedroom for $160-190 to an oceanfront five-bedroom with four baths and a kitchen for $450; weekly discounts are available, and about a $20 increase applies during peak season. The Manager's House is available only at a weekly rate of $2,520. The average length of stay is a week to 10 days, with a 35% return rate; make your reservations several months in advance. Low-key and unpretentious, this institution aims to please and offers an opportunity for seclusion and serenity. What could be better than to relax and read a favorite book on your breezy lanai, watch the sunset through the coconut grove, or take a moonlight stroll along the gently lapping shore? Waimea Plantation Cottages also manages a six-bedroom house and a one-bedroom cottage on the beach in Hanalei. If you are going to the north coast and need a place to stay, check with the office here about these two accommodations. The manager, Mr. Fred Mayo, or either of the very helpful office workers can provide additional information at tel. (808) 338-1625 or (800) 992-4632 daily 7 a.m.-9 p.m., or write Waimea Plantation Cottages, P.O. Box 367, Waimea, HI 96796.

The Grove Dining Room, open Tues.-Sat. for dinner only, is adjacent to the new administrative center. The menu starts with appetizers like sautéed mushroom at $5.95, fresh fruit plate for $8.50, crisp nori-wrapped ahi sashimi tempura at $8.95, and chicken rolls with spicy Thai plum sauce for $6.75. Entrees include the fresh island catch at market price, prime rib for $15, or shrimp, scallops, fish, and penne pasta for $16.50. All entrees come with your choice of potato, white rice, or fries, and fresh-baked taro rolls. Desserts are Kikialoa Sand Pie at $3.95, or a fresh-baked mini-apple pie à la mode for $2.95. Beverages offered are wine by the glass, tropical drinks, and a full range of soft drinks. Weekends bring the soothing strains of live Hawaiian music.

It's easy to imagine a grizzled *paniolo* contentedly dangling his spurs over the banister of the distinctive veranda of **The Wrangler Steak House,** in downtown Waimea at 9852 Kamualii,

open Mon.-Sat. for lunch 11 a.m.-5 p.m. and for dinner 5-9 p.m., tel. (808) 338-1218. The interior is a large open beamed room with hardwood floors, cooled by ceiling fans. You can choose to dine inside at a private booth, at a table made comfortable with high-backed wicker chairs, or alfresco on the big veranda or in the red blaze—a ginger garden out back. The decor is pure cowboy, with a *paniolo* whistling his lariat through the air, cowhides and old lanterns for effect, and sculptures of riders and ranch life. A full-service bar stocked with a complete assortment of liquors, wines, and beers complements all meals. The lunch menu begins with Mexican fare such as deluxe nachos or enchiladas at $6.50, a big veggie burrito at $7.75, or an island-inspired crab burrito at $8.50. The sandwich board is loaded with items like breast of chicken, turkey club, or a New York steak sandwich on a French roll, all priced $6.50-7.95. Salads include seafood, taco, or a Caesar chicken, all in the $6.95-8.25 range. Heartier lunches include Japanese-style chicken *katsu,* Kailua cabbage with pork, or the *kau kau* tin lunch—a traditional plantation worker's special with soup, rice, beans, teriyaki beef, and shrimp tempura served in a three-tiered pot. From the broiler comes Korean-style *kalbi* chicken, pepper steak, or a variety of burgers priced $6.75-9.50. The dinner menu appetizers include steak *pu pu* at $7.25, escargot, or sautéed mushrooms for $6.95. More Mexican favorites are seafood enchiladas stuffed with sautéed shrimp, scallops, fresh fish, and calamari with cream sauce for $11.25, and a (faux crab) crab burrito sautéed with cheese, tomatoes, onions, sliced olives, and green chilies. House specialties are breast of chicken cordon bleu for $11.25, hamburger steak and onions for $10.50, baby back ribs for $14.95, fresh catch at market price, bouillabaisse, and pork Mexicana for $10.95. Steaks sizzling, garlicked, peppered, and capered start at one pound! Wrangler cut, for those tiny appetites, to a platter-filling 20-ounce macho cut complete the menu. The Wrangler Steak House is the only real restaurant in Waimea, but the good news is that it is excellent, friendly, and priced right for what you get.

Heading west out of Waimea, look left to see **Waimea Pizza and Deli,** tel. (808) 338-0009, open Mon.-Sat. 11 a.m.-9 p.m. and Sunday 11 a.m.-8 p.m., offering sandwiches, pizza, espresso, and ice cream, with free delivery throughout this area. Sandwiches like French dip, vegetarian, and tuna are under $5.50, while pizzas range from $8 for a small plain pie to $25 for the Tony Special. Refreshing drinks include Tropical Smoothies with pineapple, mango, or papaya, home-brewed ice tea, and coffee drinks from espresso to latte.

Nearby are **Subway** and **Two Scoops,** an ice-cream parlor featuring Jelly Belly jelly beans. Heading out of town toward Kekaha, look for **Waimea Tropical Tees,** featuring Kauai Red Dirt T-shirts, and **Aloha Oe,** a small shop with Hawaiian Island gifts and pottery made from the red dirt of Kauai.

WAIMEA CANYON AND KOKE'E STATE PARKS

The "Grand Canyon of the Pacific" is an unforgettable part of any trip to Kauai, and you shouldn't miss it for any reason. Waimea Canyon Drive (just near the Dairy Queen) begins in Waimea, heading inland past sugarcane fields for six miles, where it joins Koke'e Road (Rt. 550) coming up from Kekaha town. Either route is worthwhile, and you can catch both by going in on one leg and coming out on the other. In about a mile you enter **Waimea Canyon State Park,** a ridgetop park that flanks the road to

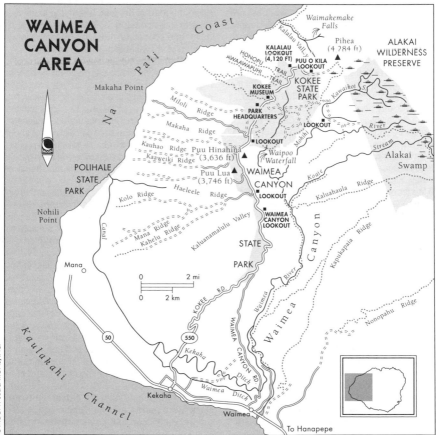

Koke'e. This serpentine route runs along a good but narrow road into Kauai's cool interior, with plenty of fascinating vistas and turnouts along the way. Going up, the passenger gets the better view. Behind you, the coastal towns and their tall refinery stacks fade into the pale blue sea, while the cultivated fields are a study of green on green.

Ever climbing, you feel as though you're entering a mountain fortress. The canyon yawns, devouring clouds washed down by draughts of sunlight. The colors are diffuse, blended strata of grays, royal purples, vibrant reds, russets, jet blacks, and schoolgirl pink. You reach the thrilling spine, where the trees on the red bare earth are gnarled and twisted. The road becomes a roller coaster whipping you past raw beauty, immense and powerful. Drink deeply, contemplate, and move on into the clouds at the 2,000-foot level, where the trees get larger again. As you climb, every lookout demands a photo. At **Waimea Canyon Overlook** (3,400 feet), you have the most expansive view of the canyon and across to valleys that slice down from the lofty peak. From here it's obvious why this canyon was given its nickname. Keep a watch out for soaring birds, mountain goats, and low-flying helicopters.

From **Pu'u Ka Pele Overlook,** Waipoo Waterfall is seen tumbling forcefully off the hanging valley across the canyon. A small rest area with a few picnic tables lies across the road. **Pu'u Hinahina Overlook** (3,500 feet) provides the best views down the canyon toward the ocean. Walk up a short trail behind the restrooms and you have a good view of Niihau adrift in the ocean to the west. A little farther along is a NASA space flight and tracking station, and at the same turnoff is a track that leads into the valley, from which several trails start. From here, Koke'e's trails come one after another.

After passing Pu'u Hinahina Overlook, you enter **Koke'e State Park** and soon reach park headquarters, then the **Koke'e Natural History Museum** and the **Koke'e Lodge.** At the headquarters, helpful staff (when duties allow them to be present) can provide you with a map of walking trails in the park and some information about the region's flora and fauna. Open 10 a.m.-4 p.m. daily, the museum is a better place for maps and additional information about the

mountain environment of Kauai. Inside are displays of native birds, descriptions of plants and animals found in the park, books on Kauai and Hawaii, detailed hiking maps of the park and the surrounding national forests, and a relief map of the island. The lodge is open Sun.-Thurs. 8:30 a.m.-5:30 p.m. and Friday and Saturday until 10 p.m. Its restaurant serves a full breakfast and lunch daily 8:30 a.m.-3:30 p.m., dinner on Friday and Saturday evenings only, 6-9 p.m. The cool weather calls especially for a slice of homemade pie and a steaming pot of coffee. Drinks can be bought at the lounge. Prices for food and drink are on the high side, but, after all, everything has to be trucked up the mountain. The next nearest restaurant or bar is 15 miles down the road at Kekaha. Also in the lodge is a shop that sells postcards, T-shirts, snacks, sundries, and souvenirs, most of which are island-themed and available nowhere else on Kauai.

Temperatures here are several degrees cooler than along the coast and can be positively chilly at night, so bring a sweater or jacket. Wild boar hunting and trout fishing are permitted within the park at certain times of the year, but check with the Department of Land and Natural Resources in Lihue (third floor of the state office building) about licenses, limits, season, etc., *before* coming up the mountain. To see wildlife anywhere in the park, it's best early in the morning or late in the afternoon when they are out to feed.

Two spectacular lookouts await you farther up the road. At **Kalalau Valley Overlook** (4,120 feet), walk a minute and pray that the clouds are cooperative, allowing lasers of sunlight to illuminate the humpbacked, green-cloaked mountains, silent and tortured, plummeting straight down to the roiling sea far, far below. **Pu'u O Kila Lookout** (4,176 feet) is the end of the road. From here you not only get a wonderful view into the Kalalau Valley—the widest and largest valley along the Na Pali coast—but also up across the Alakai Swamp to Mt. Waialeale—if the clouds permit. One trail starts here and runs along an abandoned road construction project to Pihea, from where others run out to Alealau Point, high above the ocean, and in to the Alakai Swamp.

Tent camping is allowed at **Koke'e State Park** with a permit, and the **Koke'e Lodge** also provides a dozen self-contained cabins, furnished with stoves, refrigerators, hot showers, cooking and eating utensils, and bedding; wood is available for woodstoves. The cabins cost $35 or $45 per night (five-night maximum; two-night minimum if one of the nights is Friday or Saturday) and vary from one large room (for three people) to two-bedroom units that sleep seven. The cabins are tough to get on holidays, in trout-fishing season (August to September), and during the wild plum harvest in June and July. For reservations, write well in advance to Koke'e Lodge, P.O. Box 819, Waimea, HI 96796, tel. (808) 335-6061. Please include a SASE, number of people, and dates requested. Full payment is required within two weeks of making reservations, with a refund possible (less a $15 service fee) if reservations are cancelled *at least one week* before arrival. Check-in is 2 p.m., check-out is 11 a.m.

KEKAHA

You enter Kekaha passing the homes of former plantation workers trimmed in neat green lawns and shaded from the baking sun by palm and mango trees. Japanese gardens peek from behind fences. Along the main street are two gas stations—your last chance if heading west or up Waimea Canyon—**Traveler's Den Restaurant,** and the post office. Until 1996, cane trucks, like worker bees returning to the hive, carried their burdens into the ever-hungry jaws of the **Kekaha Sugar Company,** whose smokestack owns the skyline but belches black soot no more. Still, a sweet molasses smell lingers in the air.

The turnoff for Rt. 550, leading to Waimea Canyon and Koke'e 15 miles away, branches off in the center of town. At this intersection you'll find a small mall with shops like the **Menehune Food Market,** your last chance for snacks and sundries; a **saimin stand** with burgers, *bento,* and plate lunches, open "until midnight unless we close at 10"; **Barbies** and **Emperors Emporium,** side-by-side places to buy postcards, cheap jewelry, outlet alohawear, and souvenirs; and **Lappert's Ice Cream** for a cone, hot dog, or bowl of chili. Every Saturday at noon there is a **farmers' market** where you can pick up fresh produce. As the location changes, ask around

for the current spot. Kekaha isn't large, so it shouldn't be hard to find.

Route 50 proceeds along the coast. When still in town, you pass **H.P. Faye Park.** Then the golden sands of **Kekaha Beach County Park** stretch for miles, widening as you head west, with pulloffs and shade-tree clusters now and again. The sun always shines, and the swimming and surfing are excellent. Pick your spot anywhere along the beach. The area is good for swimming and snorkeling during calm weather, and fair for surfing, although the reef can be quite shallow in spots. In town, across the road from H.P. Faye Park, are Kekaha Beach County Park's pavilion, tables, toilets, and grills. Since there's no tourist development in the area, it's generally quite empty.

The sea sparkles, and the land flattens wide and long, with green cane billowing all around. Dry gulches and red buttes form an impromptu inland wall. In six miles are the gates of **Barking Sands Airfield and Pacific Missile Range.** Here howl the dogs of war, leashed but on guard. You can use its beach and even arrange to camp for a few days if maneuvers are not in progress by calling (808) 335-4111. They're hot, shadeless, and pounded by unfriendly surf, but they afford the best view of Niihau, a purple Rorschach blot on the horizon—and the closest you're likely ever to get to the "Forbidden Island." The Barking Sands beach has the largest sand dunes on Kauai, due to the ocean's shallowness between the two islands. Supposedly, if you slide down the dunes, made from a mixture of sand and ground coral, the friction will cause a sound like a barking dog.

The Kauai Educational Association for the Study of Astronomy, a.k.a. **KEASA** welcomes islanders and visitors of all ages to peer through its 14 inch computerized telescope every month on the Saturday nearest the full moon. To get there, turn into the gate at Barking Sands Airfield outside Mana at mile marker 30 and inform the guard of your destination. For a schedule of events, write to KEASA , P.O. Box 161, Waimea, HI 96796.

In late 1996, NASA announced that one of the most advanced studies of the earth's atmosphere will be conducted at the Pacific Missile Range Facility. The research will feature "Pathfinder," an experimental remote-controlled light aircraft that is fueled entirely by solar power. NASA officials chose Kauai because its weather provides 360 clear days, offering perfect flying in virtually unobstructed air space. The program should bring $1 million into the local economy and provide hands-on experience for some lucky students at Kauai's community college.

POLIHALE STATE PARK

Route 50 curves to the right after you pass the missile range, and an HVB Warrior points left to Polihale State Park. You go in by five miles of well-graded dirt cane road. The earth is a definite buff color here, unlike the deep red that predominates throughout the rest of the island. At a stop sign at a crossroads, you're pointed to Polihale ("Home of the Spirits"). You can day-trip to soak up the sights and you'll find pavilions, showers, toilets, and grills. Both RV and tent camping are allowed with a state park permit. The camping area is on the top of the dune on the left before you get to the pavilions. There are generally no hassles, but the rangers do come around, and you should have a permit with you—it's a long way back to Lihue to get one.

From the parking area at the chain gate, walk over the dune and down to the beach. The swimming can be dangerous, but the hiking is grand. The powdery white sand beach stretches for nearly three miles, pushing up against the Na Pali cliffs to the north and meeting the Mana Plain to the east. Literally at the end of the road, this beach takes you away from the crowds, but you'll hardly ever be all by yourself. Here the cliffs come down to the sea, brawny and rugged with the Na Pali coast beginning around the far bend. Where the cliffs meet the sea is the ruin of **Polihale Heiau.** This is a powerful spot, where the souls of the dead made their leap from land into infinity. The priests of this temple chanted special prayers to speed them on their way, as the waters of life flowed from a sacred spring in the mountainside.

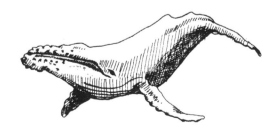

DIANA LASICH HARPER

BOB RACE

THE FORBIDDEN ISLAND

The only thing forbidding about Niihau is its nickname, "The Forbidden Island." Ironically, it's one of the last real havens of peace, tranquillity, and tradition left on the face of the earth. This privately owned island, operating as one large cattle and sheep ranch, is staffed by the last remaining pure Hawaiians in the state. To go there, you must have a personal invitation by the owners or one of the residents. Some people find this situation strange, but it would be no stranger than walking up to an Iowa farmhouse unannounced and expecting to be invited in to dinner. The islanders are free to come and go as they wish and are given the security of knowing that the last real Hawaiian place is not going to be engulfed by the modern world. Niihau is a reservation, but a *free-will* reservation—something you'll admire if you've ever felt that the world was too much with you.

Tours
Niihau Helicopters, P.O. Box 370, Makaweli, HI 96769, tel. (808) 335-3500, offers limited tours to the island. The primary purpose of Ni-

ihau Helicopters is to provide medical and emergency treatment for the residents of Niihau. However, to defray costs, they offer occasional nonscheduled tourist charters on their twin-engine Agusta 109A. Two of their flights last 90 and 110 minutes, each with a 30-minute stop on a secluded beach on Niihau; fares are $185 and $235, respectively. Two other options are an overflight of Niihau for $135 and a tour of the Na Pali coast with a Niihau overflight for $235. Let pilot Tom Mishler show you a bit of this forbidden island.

Hunting expeditions offered by **Niihau Safaris** offer another way to visit the island.

The Land and Climate
The 17-mile **Kaulakahi Channel** separates Niihau from the western tip of Kauai. The island's maximum dimensions are 18 miles long by six miles wide, with a total area of 73 square miles. The highest point on the island, Paniau (1,281 feet), lies on the east-central coast. There are no port facilities on the island, but the occasional boats put in at Kii and Lehua Landings, both on

the northern tip. Since Niihau is so low and lies in the rainshadow of Kauai, it receives only 30 inches of precipitation per year, making it rather arid. Oddly enough, low-lying basins, eroded from the single shield volcano that made the island, act as a catchment system. In them are the state's largest naturally occurring lakes, Halalii and the slightly larger, 182-acre Lake Halulu. Two uninhabited islets join Niihau as part of Kauai County: Lehua, just off the northern tip and exceptional for scuba diving, and Kaula, a few miles off the southern tip; each barely covers one-half square mile.

HISTORY

After the goddess Papa returned from Tahiti and discovered that her husband, Wakea, was playing around, she left him. The great Wakea did some squirming, and after these island-parents reconciled, Papa became pregnant and gave birth to Kauai. According to the creation chants found in the *Kumulipo,* Niihau popped out as the afterbirth, along with Lehua and Kaula, the last of the low reef islands.

Niihau was never a very populous island because of the relatively poor soil, so the islanders had to rely on trade with nearby Kauai for many necessities, including poi. Luckily, the fishing grounds off the island's coastal waters are the richest in the area, and Niihauans could always trade fish. The islanders became famous for Niihau mats, a good trade item, made from *makaloa,* a sedge plant that's plentiful on the island. Craftsmen also fashioned *ipu pawehe,* a geometrically designed gourd highly prized in the old days. When Captain Cook arrived and wished to provision his ships, he remarked that the Niihau natives were much more eager to trade than those on Kauai, and he secured potatoes and yams that seemed to be in abundant supply.

Kamehameha IV Sells
Along with Kauai, Niihau became part of the kingdom under Kamehameha. It passed down to his successors, and in the 1860s, Kamehameha IV sold it to the Robinson family for $10,000. This Scottish family, which came to Hawaii via New Zealand, has been the sole proprietor of the island ever since, although they now live on Kauai. They began a sheep and cattle ranch, hiring the island's natives as workers. No one can say exactly why, but it's evident that this family felt a great sense of responsibility and purpose. Tradition passed down over the years dictated that islanders could live on Niihau as long as they pleased, but that visitors were not welcome without a personal invitation. With the native Hawaiian population so devastated, the Robinsons felt that these proud people should have at least one place to call theirs and theirs alone. To keep the race pure, male visitors to the island were generally asked to leave by sundown.

Niihau Invaded
During WW II, Niihau was the only island of Hawaii to be occupied by the Japanese. A Zero pilot developed engine trouble after striking Pearl Harbor and had to ditch on Niihau. At first the islanders took him prisoner, but he somehow managed to escape and commandeer the machine guns from his plane. He terrorized the island, and the residents headed for the hills. One old woman who refused to leave was like a Hawaiian Barbara Fritchie. She told the Japanese prisoner to shoot her if he wished, but to

please stop making a nuisance of himself—it wasn't nice! He would have saved himself a lot of trouble if he had only listened. Fed up with hiding, one huge *kanaka*, Benehakaka Kanahele, decided to approach the pilot with *aloha*. He was convinced the intruder would see the error of his ways. This latter-day samurai shot Mr. Kanahele for his trouble. Ben persisted and was shot again. An expression of pain, disgust, and disbelief at the stranger's poor manners spread across Ben's face, but still he tried pleading with the prisoner, who shot him for the third time. Ben had had enough, and grabbed the astonished pilot and flung him headlong against a wall, cracking his skull and killing him instantly. This incident gave rise to a wartime maxim— "Don't shoot a Hawaiian three times or you'll make him mad"—and a song titled, "You Can't Conquer Niihau, Nohow." Mr. Kanahele lived out his life on Niihau and died in the 1960s.

LIFE TODAY

The only reliable connection that the islanders have with the outside world is a WW II-vintage landing craft, which they use to bring in supplies from Kauai, and a new Agusta helicopter used for medical emergencies, supplies, and aerial tours. Until recently, homing pigeons were used to send messages, but they have been replaced by two-way radios. There's no communal electricity on the island, but people do have generators to power refrigerators and TVs. Transistor radios are very popular, and most people get around either on horseback or in pickup trucks. The population numbers around 230 people, 95% of whom are Hawaiian, the other 5% Japanese. There is one elementary school, in which English is used, but most people speak Hawaiian at home. The children go off to Kauai for high school, but after they get a taste of what the world at large has to offer, a surprisingly large number return to Niihau.

After Hurricane Iwa battered the island a few years back and Hurricane Iniki followed suit in 1992, the state was very eager to offer aid. The people of Niihau thanked them for their concern but told them not to bother—that they would take care of things themselves. Niihau was the only island to reject statehood in the plebiscite of 1959. In November 1988, when a group of environmentally conscious Kauaians took a boat to Niihau to try to clear some of the beaches of the floating sea junk that had washed up on shore, the Niihauans felt that the island was being trespassed—they didn't want such help in any case—and a few shots were fired, a warning to back off. Still unsettled, the controversy focuses on the question of who owns the beach— all beaches in Hawaii are open to free access, yet the whole island of Niihau is privately owned.

Today, some people accuse the Robinson family of being greedy barons of a medieval fiefdom, holding the Niihauans as virtual slaves. This idea is utter nonsense. Besides the fact that the islanders have an open door, the Robinsons would make immeasurably more money selling the island off to resort developers than running it as a livestock ranch. As if the spirit of old Hawaii was trying to send a sign, it's interesting that Niihau's official lei is fashioned from the *pupu*, a rare shell found only on the island's beaches, and the island's official color is white, the universal symbol of purity.

Niihau Shellwork

The finest shellwork made in Hawaii comes from Niihau, in a tradition passed down over the generations. The shells themselves—tiny and very rare *kahelelani* and *kamoa*—are abundant only in the deep waters off the windward

Niihau shellwork

coast. Sometimes, the tides and winds are just right and they are deposited on Niihau's beaches, but rarely more than three times per year. When that does happen, islanders stop everything and head for the shore to painstakingly collect them. The shells are sorted according to size and color, and only the finest are kept: 80% are discarded. The most prized are so tiny that a dozen fit on a thumbnail. Colors are white, yellow, blue, and the very rare gold. The best-shells are free from chips or cracks. After being sorted, the shells are drilled. Various pieces of jewelry are fashioned, but the traditional pieces are necklaces and lei. These can be short, single-strand chokers, or the lovely *pikake* pattern—a heavy double strand. The rice motif is always popular; these are usually multistranded with the main shells clipped on the ends with various colored shells strung in as highlights.

A necklace takes long hours to create, with every shell connected by intricate and minute knots. Usually the women of Niihau do this work. Clasps are made from a type of cowrie shell found only on Niihau. No two necklaces are exactly alike. They sell by the inch, and the pure white and golden ones are very expensive—most are handed down as priceless heirlooms. Although Niihau shellwork is available in fine stores all over the state, Kauai, because it's closest, gets the largest selection. If you're after a once-in-a-lifetime purchase, consider Niihau shellwork.

BOOKLIST

ASTRONOMY

Bryan, E.H. *Stars over Hawaii*. Hilo, HI: Petroglyph Press, 1977. Charts featuring the stars that fill the night sky in Hawaii.

Rhoads, Samuel. *The Sky Tonight—A Guided Tour of the Stars over Hawaii*. Honolulu: Bishop Museum, 1993. Four pages per month of star charts—one each for the horizon in every cardinal direction. Exceptional!

COOKING

Alexander, Agnes. *How to Use Hawaiian Fruit*. Hilo, HI: Petroglyph Press, 1984. A full range of recipes using delicious and different Hawaiian fruits.

Beeman, Judy, and Martin Beeman. *Joys of Hawaiian Cooking*. Hilo, HI: Petroglyph Press, 1977. A collection of favorite recipes from Big Island chefs.

Choy, Sam. *Cooking From the Heart with Sam Choy*. Honolulu: Mutual Publishing, 1995. This beautiful handbound cookbook contains many color photos by Douglas Peebles.

Fukuda, Sachi. *Pupus, An Island Tradition*. Honolulu, HI: Bess Press, 1995.

Margah, Irish, and Elvira Monroe. *Hawaii, Cooking with Aloha*. San Carlos, CA: Wide World, 1984. Island recipes including *kalua* pig, *lomi* salmon, and hints on decor.

Rizzuto, Shirley. *Fish Dishes of the Pacific from the Fishwife*. Honolulu: Hawaii Fishing News, 1986. Features recipes using all the fish commonly caught in Hawaiian waters (husband Jim Rizzuto is the author of *Fishing, Hawaiian Style*).

CULTURE

Hartwell, Jay. *Na Mamo: Hawaiian People Today*. Honolulu: Ai Pohaku Press, 1996. Profiles 12 people practicing Hawaiian traditions in the modern world.

Heyerdahl, Thor. *American Indians in the Pacific*. London: Allen and Unwin Ltd., 1952. Theoretical and anthropological accounts of the influence on Polynesia of the Indians along the Pacific coast of North and South America. Though no longer in print, this book is fascinating reading, presenting unsubstantiated but intriguing theories.

Kirch, Patrick V. *Feathered Gods and Fishhooks: An Introduction to Hawaiian Archaeology and Prehistory*. Honolulu: University of Hawaii Press, 1985. This scholarly, lavishly illustrated, very readable book gives new insight into the development of pre-contact Hawaiian civilization. It focuses on the sites and major settlements of old Hawaii and chronicles the main cultural developments while weaving in the social climate that contributed to change. A very worthwhile read.

FAUNA

Boom, Robert. *Hawaiian Seashells*. Honolulu: Waikiki Aquarium, 1972. Photos by Jerry Kringle. A collection of 137 seashells found in Hawaiian waters, including many found nowhere else on earth. Broken into categories with accompanying text including common and scientific names, physical descriptions, and likely habitats. A must for shell collectors.

Carpenter, Blyth, and Russell Carpenter. *Fish Watching in Hawaii*. San Mateo, CA: Natural World Press, 1981. A color guide to many of the reef fish found in Hawaii and often spotted by snorkelers. If you're interested in the fish that you'll be looking at, this guide will be very helpful.

Fielding, Ann, and Ed Robinson. *An Underwater Guide to Hawaii*. Honolulu: University of Hawaii Press, 1987. If you've ever had a desire to snorkel or scuba the living reef waters of Hawaii and to be familiar with what you're seeing, get this small but fact-packed book. The amazing array of marinelife found througout the archipelago is captured in glossy photos with informative accompanying text. Both the scientific and common names of specimens are given. This book will enrich your underwater experience and serve as an easily understood reference guide for many years.

Goodson, Gar. *The Many-Splendored Fishes of Hawaii*. Stanford, CA: Stanford University Press, 1985. This small but thorough fishwatchers' book includes entries on some deep-sea fish.

Hobson, Edmund, and E.H. Chave. *Hawaiian Reef Animals*. Honolulu: University of Hawaii Press, 1987. Colorful photos and descriptions of the fish, invertabrates, turtles, and seals that call the reefs of Hawaii their home.

Hosaka, Edward. *Shore Fishing in Hawaii*. Hilo, HI: Petroglyph Press, 1984. Known as the best book on Hawaiian fishing since 1944, this book receives the highest praise because it has virtually created many Hawaiian fishermen.

Kay, Alison, and Olive Schoenberg-Dole. *Shells of Hawaii*. Honolulu: University of Hawaii Press, 1991. Color photos and tips on where to look for certain shells.

Mahaney, Casey. *Hawaiian Reef Fish, The Identification Book*. 1993. A spiral-bound reference work featuring many color photos and descriptions of common reef fish found in Hawaiian waters.

Nickerson, Roy. *Brother Whale, A Pacific Whalewatcher's Log*. San Francisco: Chronicle Books, 1977. Introduces the average person to the life of earth's greatest mammals. Provides historical accounts, photos, and tips on whalewatching. Well written and descriptive, it's the best first-time book on whales.

Pratt, H.D., P.L. Bruner, and D.G. Berrett. *The Birds of Hawaii and the Tropical Pacific*. Princeton, N.J.: Princeton University Press, 1987. Useful field guide for novice and expert birdwatchers, covering Hawaii, as well as other pacific island groups.

Van Riper, Charles, and Sandra van Riper. *A Field Guide to the Mammals of Hawaii*. Honolulu: Oriental Publishing, 1982. A guide to the surprising number of mammals introduced into Hawaii. Full-color pages document description, uses, tendencies, and habitat. Small and thin, this book makes a worthwhile addition to any serious trekker's backpack.

FLORA

Kepler, Angela. *Exotic Tropicals of Hawaii*. Honolulu: Mutual Publishing, 1989. This small-format book features many color photos of exotic tropical flowers.

Kuck, Lorraine, and Richard Togg. *Hawaiian Flowers and Flowering Trees*. Rutland, VT: Tuttle, 1960. A classic (though no longer in print) field guide to tropical and subtropical flora, illustrated in watercolor. To-the-point descriptions of Hawaiian plants and flowers with brief histories of their places of origin and introduction to Hawaii.

Merrill, Elmer. *Plant Life of the Pacific World*. Rutland, VT: Tuttle, 1983. The definitive book for anyone planning a botanical tour anywhere in the Pacific Basin. Originally published in the 1930s, it remains a tremendous work, worth tracking down through out-of-print-book services.

Miyano, Leland. *Hawaii, A Floral Paradise*. Honolulu, HI: Mutual Publising, 1995. Photographed by Douglas Peebles, this large format book is filled with informative text and beautiful color shots of tropical flowers commonly seen in Hawaii.

Sohmer, S. H., and R. Gustafson. *Plants and Flowers of Hawaii*. Honolulu: University of Hawaii Press, 1987. Sohmer and Gustafson cover the vegetation zones of Hawaii, from mountains to coast, introducing you to the wide and varied floral biology of the islands. They give a good introduction to the history and unique evolution of Hawaiian plantlife. Beautiful color plates are accompanied by clear and concise plant descriptions, with the scientific and common Hawaiian names listed.

Teho, Fortunato. *Plants of Hawaii—How to Grow Them*. Hilo, HI: Petroglyph Press, 1992. A small but useful book for those who want their backyards to bloom into a tropical paradise.

HEALTH

McBride, L.R. *Practical Folk Medicine of Hawaii*. Hilo, HI: Petroglyph Press, 1975. An illustrated guide to Hawaii's medicinal plants as used by the *kahuna lapa'au* (medical healers). Includes a thorough section on ailments—including diagnosis and proper folk remedy. Illustrated by the author, a renowned botanical researcher and former ranger at Volcanoes National Park.

Wilkerson, James A., M.D., ed. *Medicine for Mountaineering and Other Wilderness*. 4th ed. Seattle: The Mountaineers, 1992. Don't let the title fool you. Although the book focuses on specific health problems that may be encountered while mountaineering, it is the best first-aid and general health guide available today. Written by doctors for the layman to use until help arrives, it is jam-packed with easily understandable techniques and procedures. For those intending extended treks, it is a must.

HISTORY

Apple, Russell A. *Trails: From Steppingstones to Kerbstones*. Honolulu: Bishop Museum Press, 1965. This "Special Publication #53" is a special-interest archaeological survey focusing on the state's trails, roadways, footpaths, and highways and how they were designed and maintained throughout the years. Many "royal highways" from pre-contact Hawaii are cited.

Ashdown, Inez MacPhee. *Old Lahaina*. Honolulu: Hawaiian Service Inc., 1976. A small pamphlet-type book listing most of the historical attractions of Lahaina Town, past and present. Ashdown is a lifelong resident of Hawaii and gathered her information firsthand by listening to and recording stories told by ethnic Hawaiians and old *kama'aina* families.

Cameron, Roderick. *The Golden Haze*. New York: World Publishing, 1964. An account of Captain James Cook's voyages of discovery throughout the South Seas. Uses original diaries and journals for an on-the-spot reconstruction of this great seafaring adventure.

Daws, Gavan. *Shoal of Time, A History of the Hawaiian Islands*. Honolulu: University of Hawaii Press, 1974. A highly readable history of Hawaii from its "discovery" by the Western world to its acceptance as the 50th state. Good insight into the psychological makeup of influential characters who helped form Hawaii's past.

Finney, Ben, and James D. Houston. *Surfing, A History of the Ancient Hawaiian Sport*. Los Angeles: Pomegranate, 1996. Features many early etchings and old photos of Hawaiian surfers practicing their native sport.

Free, David. *Vignettes of Old Hawaii*. Honolulu: Crossroads Press,1994. A collection of short essays on a variety of subjects.

Fuchs, Lawrence. *Hawaii Pono*. New York: Harcourt, Brace and World, 1961. A detailed, scholarly work presenting an overview of Hawaii's history, based upon psychological and sociological interpretations. Encompasses most socio-ethnological groups from native Hawaiians to modern entrepreneurs. A must for social historical background.

Handy, E.S., and Elizabeth Handy. *Native Planters in Old Hawaii*. Honolulu: Bishop Museum Press, 1972. A superbly written, easily understandable scholarly work on the intimate relationship of pre-contact Hawaiians and the *aina*. Much more than its title implies, this book should be read by anyone seriously interested in Polynesian Hawaii.

Ii, John Papa. *Fragments of Hawaiian History.* Honolulu: Bishop Museum Press, 1959. Hawaii's history under Kamehameha I as told by a Hawaiian who actually experienced it.

Joesting, Edward. *Hawaii: An Uncommon History.* New York: W.W. Norton Co., 1978. A truly uncommon history told in a series of vignettes relating to the lives and personalities of the first white men in Hawaii, Hawaiian nobility, sea captains, writers, and adventurers. Brings history to life. Absolutely excellent!

Kurisu, Yasushi. *Sugar Town, Hawaiian Plantation Days Remembered.* Honolulu: Watermark Publishing, 1995. Reminiscences of life growing up on sugar plantations on the Hamakua coast of the Big Island. Features many old photos.

Liliuokalani. *Hawaii's Story by Hawaii's Queen.* 1964. Reprint, Rutland, VT: Tuttle, 1991. A moving personal account of Hawaii's inevitable move from monarchy to U.S. Territory by its last queen. The facts can be found in other histories, but none provides the emotion or point of view expressed by Hawaii's deposed monarch. A must-read to get the whole picture.

McBride, Likeke. *Petroglyphs of Hawaii.* Hilo, HI: Petroglyph Press, 1996. A revised and updated guide to petroglyphs found in the Hawaiian islands.

Nickerson, Roy. *Lahaina, Royal Capital of Hawaii.* Honolulu: Hawaiian Service, 1978. The story of Lahaina from whaling days to present, spiced with ample photographs.

INTRODUCTORY

Cohen, David, and Rick Smolan. *A Day in the Life of Hawaii.* New York: Workman, 1984.

On December 2, 1983, 50 of the world's top photojournalists were invited to Hawaii to photograph the variety of daily life on the islands. The photos are excellently reproduced, and accompanied by a minimum of text.

Day, A.G., and C. Stroven. *A Hawaiian Reader.* 1959. Reprint, New York: Appleton, Century, Crofts, 1985. A poignant compilation of essays, diary entries, and fictitious writings that takes you from the death of Captain Cook through the "statehood services."

Department of Geography, University of Hawaii. *Atlas of Hawaii.* 2nd ed. Honolulu: University of Hawaii Press, 1983. Much more than an atlas filled with reference maps, it also contains commentary on the natural environment, culture, and sociology; a gazetteer; and statistical tables. Actually a mini-encyclopedia.

Jones, James. *From Here to Eternity.* New York: Dell Publishing Co., 1991 (orig. 1951). Irresistibly romantic he-man soap opera of soldiers, military brass, prostitutes, and bored Army wives set at Oahu's Schofield Barracks just prior to the attack on Pearl Harbor. (Especially for island visitors, the highly atmospheric book is better than the Oscar-winning 1953 movie.)

Michener, James A. *Hawaii.* New York: Random House, 1959. Michener's historical novel has done more to inform—and *mis*inform readers about Hawaii than any other book ever written. A great tale with plenty of local color and information—but read it for pleasure, not facts.

Piercy, LaRue. *Hawaii This and That.* Honolulu, HI: Mutual Publishing, 1994. Illustrated by Scot Ebanez. A 60-page book filled with one-sentence facts and oddities about all manner of things Hawaiian. Informative, amazing, and fun to read.

LANGUAGE

Elbert, Samuel, and Mary Pukui. *Hawaiian Dictionary.* Honolulu: University of Hawaii, 1986. The best dictionary of the Hawaiian language available. The *Pocket Hawaiian Dictionary* is a less expensive, condensed version of this dictionary, and adequate for most travelers with a general interest in the language.

Elbert, Samuel. *Spoken Hawaiian*. Honolulu: University of Hawaii Press, 1970. Progressive conversational lessons.

MYTHOLOGY AND LEGENDS

Beckwith, Martha. *Hawaiian Mythology*. Honolulu: University of Hawaii Press, 1977. Forty-five years after its original printing, this work remains the definitive text on Hawaiian mythology. Beckwith compiled this book from many sources, giving exhaustive cross-references to genealogies and legends expressed in the oral tradition. If you are going to read one book on Hawaii's folklore, it should be this one.

Colum, Padraic. *Legends of Hawaii*. New Haven: Yale University Press, 1937. Selected legends of old Hawaii reinterpreted, but closely based upon the originals.

Elbert, S., comp. *Hawaiian Antiquities and Folklore*. Honolulu: Univerity of Hawaii Press, 1959. Illustrated by Jean Charlot. A selection of the main legends from Abraham Fornander's great work, *An Account of the Polynesian Race*.

Kalakaua, His Hawaiian Majesty, King David. *The Legends and Myths of Hawaii*. Edited by R.M. Daggett, with a foreword by Glen Grant. Honolulu: Mutual Publishing, 1990. Originally published in 1888, Hawaii's own King Kalakaua draws upon his scholarly and formidable knowledge of the classic oral tradition to bring alive ancient tales from pre-contact Hawaii. A powerful yet somewhat Victorian voice from Hawaii's past speaks clearly and boldly, especially about the intimate role of pre-Christian religion in the lives of the Hawaiian people.

Melville, Leinanai. *Children of the Rainbow*. Wheaton, Ill.: Theosophical Publishing, 1969.

A book on higher spiritual consciousness attuned to nature, which was the basic belief of pre-Christian Hawaii. The appendix contains illustrations of mystical symbols used by the *kahuna*. An enlightening book in many ways.

Thrum, Thomas. *Hawaiian Folk Tales*. Chicago, IL: McClurg and Co., 1950. A collection of Hawaiian tales from the oral tradition as told to the author from various sources.

Westervelt, W.D. *Hawaiian Legends of Volcanoes*. Boston: Ellis Press, 1991. A small book concerning the volcanic legends of Hawaii and how they related to the fledgling field of volcanism at the turn of the century. The vintage photos alone are worth a look.

NATURAL SCIENCES

Abbott, Agatin, Gordon MacDonald, and Frank Peterson. *Volcanoes in the Sea*. Honolulu: University of Hawaii Press, 1983. A simplified yet comprehensive text covering the geology and volcanism of the Hawaiian Islands. Focuses upon the forces of nature (wind, rain, and surf) that shape the islands.

Carlquist, Sherwin. *Hawaii: A Natural History*, 2nd ed. National Tropical Botany, 1980. Definitive account of Hawaii's natural history.

Hazlett, Richard, and Donald Hyndman. *Roadside Geology of Hawaii*. Missoula, MT: Mountain Press Publishing, 1996. Begins with a general discusion of the geology of the Hawaiian islands, followed by a road guide to the individual islands offering descriptions of features easily seen when traveling by road.

Hubbard, Douglass, and Gordon MacDonald. *Volcanoes of the National Parks of Hawaii*. Volcanoes, HI: Hawaii Natural History Association, 1989. The volcanology of Hawaii, documenting the major lava flows and their geological effects on the state.

Kay, E. Alison, comp. *A Natural History of the Hawaiian Islands*. Honolulu: University of Hawaii Press, 1994. A selection of concise articles by experts in the fields of volcanism, oceanography, meteorology, and biology. An excellent reference source.

PERIODICALS

Aloha, The Magazine of Hawaii and the Pacific. Davick Publications, P.O. Box 49035, Escondido, CA 92046. This excellent bimonthly magazine is much more than just slick and glossy photography. Special features may focus on sports, the arts, history, flora and fauna, or just pure island adventure. *Aloha* is equally useful as a "dream book" for those who wish that they could visit Hawaii and as a current resource for those actually going. One of the best for an overall view of Hawaii, and well worth the subscription price.

Hawaii Magazine. 1400 Kapiolani Blvd., Suite B, Honolulu, HI, 96814. This magazine covers the Hawaiian Islands like a tropical breeze. Feature articles deal with all aspects of life in the islands while special departments cover travel, events, exhibits, and restaurant reviews. Up-to-the-minute information, and a fine read.

Naturist Society Magazine. P.O. Box 132, Oshkosh, WI 54920. This excellent magazine not only uncovers bathing-suit-optional beaches throughout the islands—giving tips for au naturelists visiting Hawaii—but also reports on local politics, environment, and conservation measures from the health-conscious nudist point of view. A fine publication.

PICTORIALS

La Brucherie, Roger. *Hawaiian World, Hawaiian Heart.* Pine Valley, CA: Imagenes Press, 1989.

Grant, Glenn. *Hawaii The Big Island.* Honolulu: Mutual Publishing, 1988. Includes the historic, social, and nature photos of many photographers.

POLITICAL SCIENCE

Albertini, Jim, et al. *The Dark Side of Paradise, Hawaii in a Nuclear War.* Honolulu: cAtholic Action of Hawaii. Well-documented research outlining Hawaii's role and vulnerability in a nuclear world. This book presents the antinuclear and antimilitary side of the political issue in Hawaii.

Bell, Roger. *Last Among Equals: Hawaiian Statehood and American Politics.* Honolulu: University of Hawaii, 1984. Documents Hawaii's long and rocky road to statehood, tracing political partisanship, racism, and social change.

SPORTS

Ambrose, Greg. *Surfer's Guide to Hawaii.* Honolulu: Bess Press, 1991. Island-by-island guide to surfing spots.

Chisholm, Craig. *Hawaiian Hiking Trails: the Guide for All the Islands,* 8th ed. Lake Oswego, OR: Fernglen Press 1994.

Morey, Kathy. *Kauai Trails.* Berkeley, CA: Wilderness Press, 1993. Morey's books are specialized, detailed trekker's guides to Hawaii's outdoors. Complete with useful maps, historical references, official procedures, and plants and animals encountered along the way. If you're focused on hiking, these are the best to take along. *Maui Trails, Hawaii Trails,* and *Oahu Trails* are also available.

Rosenberg, Steve. *Diving Hawaii.* Locust Valley, NY: Aqua Quest, 1990. Gives descriptions of diving locations on the major islands and the marine life divers are likely to see. Includes many color photos.

Thorne, Chuck, and Lou Zitnik. *A Diver's Guide to Hawaii.* Kihei, HI: Hawaii's Diver's Guide, 1984. An expanded diver's and snorkeler's guide to the waters of the six main Hawaiian Islands. Complete list of maps with full descriptions, tips, and ability levels. A must for all levels of snorkelers and divers.

Valier, Kathy. *On the Na Pali Coast: a Guide for Hikers and Boaters.* Honolulu: University of Hawaii Press, 1988. Indispensable guide to the coast's natural history, plant and animal life, legends, tales, and archaeological sites.

Wallin, Doug. *Diving & Snorkeling Guide to the Hawaiian Islands,* 2nd ed. Houston, TX: Pisces Books (Gulf Publishing Co.), 1991. A guide offering brief descriptions of diving locations on the four major islands.

TRAVEL

Clark, John. *Beaches of the Big Island.* Honolulu: University of Hawaii Press, 1985. Do-

finitive guide to beaches, including many off the beaten path. Features maps and black & white photos.

Riegert, Ray. *Hidden Hawaii.* Berkeley, CA: And/Or Press, 1992. Ray offers a user-friendly guide to the islands.

Stanley, David. *South Pacific Handbook.* 6th ed. Chico, CA: Moon Publications, 1996. The model upon which all travel guides should be based. Simply the best book in the world for travel throughout the South Pacific.

Warner, Evie, and Al Davies. *Bed and Breakfast Goes Hawaiian.* Kapa'a, HI: Island Bed and Breakfast, 1990. A combination bed and breakfast directory and guide to sights, activities, events, and restaurants on the six major islands.

GLOSSARY

Words marked with an asterisk (*) are used commonly throughout the islands.

a'a*—rough clinker lava. *A'a* has become the correct geological term to describe this type of lava wherever it is found in the world.

ahupua'a—pie-shaped land divisions running from mountain to sea traditionally governed by *konohiki,* local *ali'i* who owed their allegiance to a reigning chief

aikane—friend; pal; buddy

aina—land; the binding spirit to all Hawaiians. Love of the land is paramount in traditional Hawaiian beliefs.

akamai—smart; clever; wise

akua—a god, or simply "divine"

ali'i*—a Hawaiian chief or noble

aloha*—the most common greeting in the islands; can mean both "hello" and "goodbye," "welcome" and "farewell." It can also mean romantic love, affection, or best wishes.

amakua—a personal or family spirit, usually an ancestral spirit. Favorites are the shark and the *pueo* (Hawaiian owl).

aole—no

auwe—alas; ouch! When a great chief or loved one died, it was a traditional wail of mourning.

ewa—crooked; place-name for west Honolulu, used as a directional term

halakahiki—pineapple

halau—originally a longhouse, now used mostly to describe hula halau, i.e., a hula school

hale*—house or building. Often combined with other words to name a specific place such as Haleakala ("House of the Sun") or Hale Pai ("Printing House").

hana*—work; combined with *pau* means end of work or quitting time

hanai—literally, "to feed." Part of the true *aloha* spirit, a *hanai* is a permanent guest, or an adopted family member—usually an old person or a child. This is an enduring cultural phenomenon in Hawaii, in which a child from one family (perhaps that of a brother or sister, and quite often one's grandchild) is raised as one's own without formal adoption.

haole*—a word that at one time meant "foreigner" but which now means a white person or Caucasian. Many etymological definitions have been put forth, but none satisfies everyone. Some feel that it signified a person without a background, because the first white men could not chant their genealogies as was common among Hawaiians.

hapa*—half—you may hear a mixed-blood person referred to as *hapa haole.*

hapai*—pregnant; used by all ethnic groups when a *keiki* is on the way

haupia*—a coconut custard dessert often served at *luau*

heiau*—a traditional Hawaiian temple—a platform made of skillfully fitted rocks, upon which structures were built and offerings made to the gods

holomuu*—an ankle-length dress much more fitted than a muumuu, often worn on formal occasions

hono—bay, as in Honolulu (Sheltered Bay)

ho'oilo—traditional Hawaiian winter, which began in November

hoolaulea—any happy event but especially a family outing or picnic

hoomalimali*—sweet talk; flattery

huhu*—angry; irritated

hui*—a group; meeting; society. Often used to refer to Chinese businesspeople or family members who pool their money to get businesses started.

hukilau—traditional shoreline fish-gathering, in which everyone lends a hand to *huki* (pull) the huge net. Anyone taking part shares in the *lau* (food). It is much more like a party than hard work, and if you're lucky you'll be able to take part in one.

hula*—a native Hawaiian dance in which the rhythm of the islands is captured by swaying hips and stories told by lyrically moving hands. A *halau* is a group or school of *hula.*

huli huli—barbecue, as in *huli huli* chicken

huna—the practice and philosophy of the mystical arts of ancient Hawaii.

i'a—fish in general (*I'a maka* is raw fish)

imu*—underground oven filled with hot rocks and used for baking. The main cooking feature at luau, used to steam-bake pork and other succulent dishes. The tending of the *imu* was traditionally for men only.

ipo—sweetheart; lover; girlfriend or boyfriend

kahili—a tall pole topped with feathers, resembling a huge feather duster. It was used by an *ali'i* to announce his or her presence.

kahuna*—priest; sorcerer; doctor; skillful person. *Kahuna* had tremendous power in old Hawaii, which they used for both good and evil. The *kahuna ana'ana* was a feared individual because he practiced black magic and could pray a person to death, while the *kahuna lapa'au* was a medical practitioner bringing aid and comfort to the people.

kai—the sea. Many businesses and hotels employ *kai* as part of their name.

kalua—roasted underground in an *imu*. One favorite island dish, for instance, is *kalua* pork.

kama'aina*—a child of the land; an old-timer; a longtime island resident of any ethnic background; a resident of Hawaii or native son or daughter. Hotels and airlines often offer discounts called *"kama'aina* rates" to anyone who can prove island residency.

kanaka—man or commoner; later used to distinguish a Hawaiian from other races. Tone of voice can make it a derisive expression.

kane*—means man, but actually used to signify a relationship such as husband or boyfriend. Written on a door it means "men's room."

kaola*—any food that has been broiled or barbecued

kapu*—forbidden; taboo; keep out; do not touch

kapuna—a grandparent or old-timer; usually means someone who has gained wisdom. The statewide school system now invites *kapuna* to talk to the children about the old ways and methods.

kaukau*—slang word meaning food or chow; grub. Some of the best food in Hawaii comes from the *"kaukau* wagons," trucks that sell plate lunches and other morsels.

kauwa—a landless, untouchable caste once confined to living on reservations. Members of this caste were often used as human sacrifices at *heiau*. Calling someone *kauwa* is still considered a grave insult.

kava—a mildly intoxicating traditional drink made from the juice of chewed *awa* root, spit into a bowl, and used in religious ceremonies

keiki*—child or children; used by all ethnic groups. "Have you hugged your *keiki* today?"

kiawe—an algaroba tree from South America commonly found in Hawaii along the shore. It grows a nasty long thorn that can easily puncture a tire. Legend has it that the trees were introduced to the islands by a misguided missionary who hoped the thorns would coerce natives into wearing shoes. Actually, they are good for fuel, as fodder for hogs and cattle, and for reforestation—none of which you'll appreciate if you step on one of their thorns or flatten a tire on your rental car!

koa—a hard, fine-grained native Hawaiian wood preferred as a material to fashion furniture and bowls

kokua—help. As in "Your *kokua* is needed to keep Hawaii free from litter."

kona wind*—a muggy subtropical wind that blows from the south and hits the leeward side of the islands. It usually brings sticky hot weather and is one of the few times when air-conditioning will be appreciated.

konane—a traditional Hawaiian game, similar to checkers, played with pebbles on a large flat stone used as a board

koolau—windward side of the island

kuhina nui—the highest regent in the days of the monarchy

kukui—a candlenut tree; the pods are polished and then strung together to make a beautiful lei. Traditionally, the oil-rich nuts were strung on the rib of a coconut leaf and used as a candle.

kuleana—homesite; the old homestead; small farm. Especially used to describe the small spreads on Hawaiian Homes Lands on Molokai.

kuma hula—a master dancer or teacher of hula.

Kumulipo*—ancient Hawaiian genealogical chant that records the pantheon of gods, creation, and the beginning of humankind

la—the sun. Often combined with other words to be more descriptive, such as *La*haina (Merciless Sun) or Haleaka*la* (House of the Sun).

lanai*—veranda or porch. You'll pay more for a hotel room if it has a lanai with an ocean view.

lani—sky or the heavens

lau hala*—traditional Hawaiian weaving of mats, hats, etc., from the prepared fronds of the pandanus (screw pine)

lei*—a traditional garland of flowers or vines. One of Hawaii's most beautiful customs. Given at any auspicious occasion but especially when arriving in and leaving Hawaii.

lele—the stone altar at a *heiau*

limu—edible seaweed of various types. Gathered from the shoreline, it makes an excellent salad. It's used to garnish many island dishes and is a favorite at luau.

loco-moco—A local dish consisting of hamburger, two fried eggs, brown gravy, and rice

lomi lomi—traditional Hawaiian massage; also, raw salmon made into a vinegared salad with chopped onion and spices

lua*—the toilet; the head; the bathroom

luakini—a human-sacrifice temple. Introduced to Hawaii in the 13th century at Wahaula Heiau on the Big Island.

luau*—a Hawaiian feast featuring poi, *imu*-baked pork, and other traditional foods. Good ones provide some of the best gastronomical delights in the world.

luna—foreman or overseer in the plantation fields. *Luna* were often mounted on horseback and were renowned for either their fairness or their cruelty. They represented the middle class and served as a buffer between plantation workers and white plantation owners.

mahalo*—thank you. *Mahalo nui* means "big thanks" or "thank you very much."

mahele—division. The "Great Mahele" of 1848 changed Hawaii forever when the traditional common lands were broken up into privately owned plots.

mahimahi*—a favorite eating fish. Often called a dolphin, but a mahimahi is a true fish, not a cetacean.

mahu—a homosexual; often used derisively like "fag" or "queer"

maile—a fragrant vine used in traditional lei. It looks ordinary but smells delightful.

maka'ainana—a commoner; a person "belonging" to the *aina,* who supported the *ali'i* by fishing and farming and as a warrior

makai*—toward the sea; used by most islanders when giving directions

make—dead; deceased

malihini*—newcomer; tenderfoot; recent arrival

malo—the native Hawaiian loincloth. Never worn anymore except at festivals or pageants.

mana*—power from the spirit world; innate energy of all things animate or inanimate; the grace of god. Mana could be passed on from one person to another, or even stolen. Great care was taken to protect the *ali'i* from having their mana defiled. Commoners were required to lie flat on the ground and cover their faces whenever a great *ali'i* approached. *Kahuna* were often enlisted to regain or transfer mana.

manauahi—free; gratis; extra

manini—stingy; tight. A Hawaiianized word taken from the name of Don Francisco *Marin,* who was instrumental in bringing many fruits and plants to Hawaii but who was known for never sharing any of the bounty from his substantial gardens on Vineyard Street in Honolulu.

mauka*—toward the mountains; used by most islanders when giving directions

mauna—mountain. Often combined with other words to be more descriptive, such as Mauna Kea (White Mountain).

mele—a song or chant in the Hawaiian oral tradition that records the history and genealogies of the *ali'i*

menehune—the legendary "little people" of Hawaii. Like leprechauns, they are said to have shunned humans and possessed magical powers. Stone walls said to have been completed in one night are often attributed to them. Some historians argue that they actually existed and were the aboriginals of Hawaii, inhabiting the islands before the coming of the Polynesians.

moa—chicken; fowl

moana*—the ocean; the sea. Many businesses, hotel, and place names have *moana* in their names.

moe—sleep

moolelo—ancient tales kept alive by oral tradition and recited only by day

muumuu*—a "Mother Hubbard," an ankle-length dress with a high neckline introduced by the missionaries to cover the nakedness of the Hawaiians. It has become fashionable attire for almost any occasion in Hawaii.

nani—beautiful

nui—big; great; large; as in *mahalo nui* (thank you very much)

ohana—a family; the fundamental social division; extended family. Now used to denote a social organization with grass-roots overtones, as in the "Protect Kahoolawe Ohana."

okolehau—literally, "iron bottom"; a traditional booze made from ti root. *Okole* means "rear end" and *hau* means "iron," which was descriptive of the huge blubber pots in which *okolehau* was made. Also, if you drink too much of it, it'll surely knock you on your *okole*.

ono*—delicious; delightful; the best. *Ono ono* means "extra" or "absolutely" "delicious."

opihi—a shellfish or limpet that clings to rocks and is gathered as one of the islands' favorite *pu pu*. Custom dictates that you never remove all of the *opihi* from a rock; some are always left to grow for future generations.

opu—belly; stomach

pahoa—a dagger, as used by ancient Hawaiians

pa'hoehoe*—smooth, ropey lava that looks like burnt pancake batter. *"Pa'hoehoe"* is now the correct geological term used to describe this type of lava found anywhere in the world.

pakalolo—marijuana; the state's most productive cash crop

pake—a Chinese person. Can be derisive, depending on tone in which it is used. It is a bastardization of the Chinese word meaning "uncle."

pali*—a cliff; precipice. Hawaii's geology makes them quite common. The most famous are those in Oahu, where a major battle was fought.

paniolo*—a Hawaiian cowboy. Derived from the Spanish *espaniola*. The first cowboys brought to Hawaii during the early 19th century were Mexicans from California.

papale—hat. Except for the feathered helmets of the *ali'i* warriors of old Hawaii, hats were generally not worn. However, once the islanders saw their practical uses and how fashionable they were, they began weaving them from various materials and quickly became experts at manufacture and design.

pau*—finished; done; completed. Often combined into *pau hana,* which means end of work or quitting time.

pa'u—long split skirt often worn by women when horseback riding. Last century, an island treat was *pa'u* riders in their beautiful dresses at Kapiolani Park in Honolulu. The tradition is carried on today at many of Hawaii's rodeos.

pilau—stink; bad smell; stench

pilikia—trouble of any kind, big or small; bad times

poi*—a glutinous paste made from the pounded corm of taro which ferments slightly and has a light sour taste. Purplish in color, it's a staple at luau, where it is called one-, two-, or three-finger poi, depending upon its thickness.

pono—righteous or excellent

pua—flower

puka*—a hole of any size. *Puka* is used by all island residents, whether talking about a pinhole in a rubber boat or a tunnel through a mountain.

punalua—the tradition of sharing mates in practice before the missionaries came. Western seamen took advantage of it, and this led to the spreading of contagious diseases and eventually to the ultimate demise of the Hawaiian people.

punee*—bed; narrow couch. Used by all ethnic groups. To recline on a *punee* on a breezy lanai is a true island treat.

pu pu*—an appetizer; snack; hors d'oeuvres; can be anything from cheese and crackers to sushi. Often, bars or nightclubs offer them free.

pupule—crazy; nuts; out of your mind

pu'u—hill, as in Pu'u Ulaula (Red Hill)

tapa*—a traditional paper cloth made from beaten bark. Intricate designs were stamped in using beaters, and natural dyes added color. The tradition was lost for many years but is now making a comeback and provides some of the most beautiful folk art in the islands.

taro*—the staple of old Hawaii. A plant with a distinctive broad leaf that produces a starchy root. It was brought by the first Polynesians and was grown on magnificently irrigated plantations. According to the oral tradition, the life-giving properties of taro hold mystical significance for Hawaiians, since it was created by the gods at about the same time humans were.

ti—a broad-leafed plant whose foliage served many purposes, from plates to hula skirts (never grass). Especially used to wrap religious offerings presented at the *heiau*.

tutu*—grandmother; granny; older woman. Used by all as a term of respect and endearment.

ukulele*—*uku* means "flea" and *lele* means "jumping," so, literally, the word means "jumping flea"—the analogy the Hawaiians came up with to describe the quick finger movements used on the banjolike Portuguese folk instrument called a *cavaquinho*. The ukulele quickly became synonymous with the islands.

wahine*—young woman; female; girl; wife. Used by all ethnic groups. When written on a door, it means "women's room."

wai—fresh water; drinking water

wela—hot. *Wela kahao* is "a hot time" or "making whoopee."

wiki*—quickly; fast; in a hurry. Often seen as *wiki wiki* (very fast), as in Wiki Wiki Messenger Service.

INDEXES

ACCOMMODATIONS INDEX

FOOD INDEX

INDEX

Page numbers in **boldface** indicate the primary reference; numbers in *italics* indicate information in captions, illustrations, special topics, charts, or maps.

ABOUT THE AUTHOR
J.D. BISIGNANI 1947-1997

Joe Bisignani was a fortunate man because he made his living doing the two things that he liked best: traveling and writing. He will be greatly missed.

A mainstay of Moon Publications since 1979, he was best known in the travel world for his wildly successful, five-volume Hawaii Handbook series, of which *Maui Handbook* won the Hawaii Visitors Bureau's Best Guidebook Award in 1991, while *Hawaii Handbook* earned Best Guidebook as well as the Grand Award for Excellence in 1988. His *Japan Handbook* won the Lowell Thomas Travel Journalism Gold Award in 1993. Together with founder Bill Dalton and other writers, "Joe Biz," profoundly influenced the company's success in the travel publishing world.

MOON TRAVEL HANDBOOKS
THE IDEAL TRAVELING COMPANIONS

Moon Travel Handbooks provide focused, comprehensive coverage of distinct destinations all over the world. Our goal is to give travelers all the background and practical information they'll need for an extraordinary travel experience.

Every Handbook begins with an in-depth essay about the land, the people, their history, art, politics, and social concerns—an entire bookcase of cultural insight and introductory information in one portable volume. We also provide accurate, up-to-date coverage of all the practicalities: language, currency, transportation, accommodations, food, and entertainment. And Moon's maps are legendary, covering not only cities and highways, but parks and trails that are often difficult to find in other sources.

Below are highlights of Moon's North America and Hawaii Travel Handbook series. Our complete list of Handbooks, covering North America and Hawaii, Mexico, Central America and the Caribbean, and Asia and the Pacific, is on the order form on the accompanying pages. To purchase Moon Travel Handbooks, please check your local bookstore or order by phone: (800) 345-5473 Monday-Friday 8 a.m.-5 p.m. PST.

MOON OVER NORTH AMERICA
THE NORTH AMERICA AND HAWAII TRAVEL HANDBOOK SERIES

> "Moon's greatest achievements may be the individual state books they offer. . . . Moon not only digs up little-discovered attractions, but also offers thumbnail sketches of the culture and state politics of regions that rarely make national headlines."
> —*The Millennium Whole Earth Catalog*

ALASKA-YUKON HANDBOOK
by Deke Castleman and Don Pitcher, 500 pages, **$17.95**
"Exceptionally rich in local culture, history, and reviews of natural attractions. . . . One of the most extensive pocket references. . . . An essential guide!" — *The Midwest Book Review*

ALBERTA AND THE NORTHWEST TERRITORIES
by Nadina Purdon and Andrew Hempstead, 466 pages, **$17.95**
"*Alberta and the Northwest Territories Handbook* provides strong coverage of the most rugged territories in Canada."
—*The Bookwatch*

ARIZONA TRAVELER'S HANDBOOK
by Bill Weir and Robert Blake, 486 pages, **$17.95**
"If you don't own this book already, buy it immediately"
—*Arizona Republic*

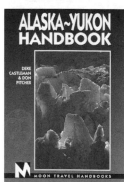

ATLANTIC CANADA HANDBOOK
by Nan Drosdick and Mark Morris, 436 pages, **$17.95**
New Brunswick, Nova Scotia, Prince Edward Island,
Newfoundland and Labrador.
"The new *Atlantic Canada* is the best I've seen on the region—
superior maps, travel tips, and cultural essays."
—Peter Aiken, *Providence Journal-Bulletin*

BIG ISLAND OF HAWAII HANDBOOK
by J.D. Bisignani, 349 pages, **$13.95**
"The best general guidebooks available." —*Hawaii Magazine*

BRITISH COLUMBIA HANDBOOK
by Jane King, 375 pages, **$15.95**
"Deftly balances the conventional and the unconventional, for both
city lovers and nature lovers."
—*Reference and Research Book News*

COLORADO HANDBOOK
by Stephen Metzger, 447 pages, **$18.95**
"Hotel rooms in the Aspen area, in the height of winter sports
season, for $20-$30? . . . who but a relentless researcher from
Moon could find it?" —The New York *Daily News*

GEORGIA HANDBOOK
by Kap Stann, 360 pages, **$17.95**
"[a] gold medal winner . . . Anyone who is interested in the South
should get this book." —*Eclectic Book Review*

HAWAII HANDBOOK
by J.D. Bisignani, 1004 pages, **$19.95**
Winner: Grand Excellence and Best Guidebook Awards, Hawaii
Visitors' Bureau
"No one since Michener has told us so much about our 50th
state." —*Playboy*

HONOLULU-WAIKIKI HANDBOOK
by J.D. Bisignani, 365 pages, **$14.95**
"The best general guidebooks available." —*Hawaii Magazine*

IDAHO HANDBOOK
by Don Root, 600 pages, **$18.95**
"It's doubtful that visitors to the Gem State will find a better, more
detailed explanation anywhere."
—*The Salt Lake Tribune*

KAUAI HANDBOOK
by J.D. Bisignani, 330 pages, **$15.95**
"This slender guide is tightly crammed. . . . The information
provided is staggering." —*Hawaii Magazine*

MAUI HANDBOOK
by J.D. Bisignani, 393 pages, **$14.95**
Winner: Best Guidebook Award, Hawaii Visitors' Bureau
"*Maui Handbook* should be in every couple's suitcase. It
intelligently discusses Maui's history and culture, and you can
trust the author's recommendations for best beaches, restaurants,
and excursions." —*Bride's Magazine*

MONTANA HANDBOOK
by W.C. McRae and Judy Jewell, 454 pages, **$17.95**
"Well-organized, engagingly written, tightly edited, and chock-full
of interesting facts about localities, backcountry destinations,
traveler accommodations, and cultural and natural history."
—*Sierra Magazine*

NEVADA HANDBOOK
by Deke Castleman, 473 pages, **$16.95**
"Veteran travel writer Deke Castleman says he covered more
than 10,000 miles in his research for this book and it shows."
—*Nevada Magazine*

NEW MEXICO HANDBOOK
by Stephen Metzger, 320 pages, **$15.95**
"The best current guide and travel book to all of New Mexico"
—New Mexico Book League

NEW YORK HANDBOOK
by Christiane Bird, 615 pages, **$19.95**
Contains voluminous coverage not only of New York City, but also
of myriad destinations along the Hudson River Valley, in the
Adirondack Mountains, around Leatherstocking Country, and
elsewhere throughout the state.

NORTHERN CALIFORNIA HANDBOOK
by Kim Weir, 779 pages, **$19.95**
"That rarest of travel books—both a practical guide to the region
and a map of its soul." —*San Francisco Chronicle*

OREGON HANDBOOK
by Stuart Warren
and Ted Long Ishikawa, 520 pages, **$16.95**
". . . the most definitive tourist guide to the state ever published."
—*The Oregonian*

TENNESSEE HANDBOOK
by Jeff Bradley, 500 pages, **$17.95**
Features nonpareil coverage of Nashville and Memphis, as well as the Appalachian Trail, Great Smoky Mountains National Park, Civil War battlefields, and a wide assortment of unusual amusements off the beaten path.

TEXAS HANDBOOK
by Joe Cummings, 598 pages, **$17.95**
"Reveals a Texas with a diversity of people and culture that is as breathtaking as that of the land itself."
—*Planet Newspaper,* Australia

"I've read a bunch of Texas guidebooks, and this is the best one."
—Joe Bob Briggs

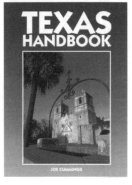

UTAH HANDBOOK
by Bill Weir and W.C. McRae, 500 pages, **$17.95**
" . . . a one-volume, easy to digest, up-to-date, practical, factual guide to all things Utahan. . . . This is the best handbook of its kind I've yet encountered." —*The Salt Lake Tribune*

WASHINGTON HANDBOOK
by Don Pitcher, 866 pages, **$19.95**
"Departs from the general guidebook format by offering information on how to cope with the rainy days and where to take the children. . . . This is a great book, informational, fun to read, and a good one to keep." —*Travel Publishing News*

WISCONSIN HANDBOOK
by Thomas Huhti, 400 pages, **$16.95**
Lake Michigan, Lake Superior, and Wisconsin's 65 state parks and national forests offer unrivaled outdoor recreational opportunities, from hiking, biking, and water sports to the myriad pleasures of Door County, the "crown jewel of the Midwest."

WYOMING HANDBOOK
by Don Pitcher, 570 pages, **$17.95**
"Wanna know the real dirt on Calamity Jane, white Indians, and the tacky Cheyenne gunslingers? All here. And all fun."
—The New York *Daily News*

Hit The Road With Moon Travel Handbooks

ROAD TRIP USA
Cross-Country Adventures on America's Two-Lane Highways
by Jamie Jensen, 800 pages, **$22.50**
This Handbook covers the entire United States with 11
intersecting routes, allowing travelers to create their own
cross-country driving adventures

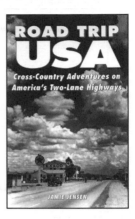

   Packed with both practical information and entertaining
sidebars, *Road Trip USA* celebrates the spontaneity and culture of
the American highway without sacrificing the essential comforts of
bed and bread.

   The World Wide Web edition of *Road Trip USA* features the
entire text plus links to local Internet sites. WWW explorers are
encouraged to participate in the exhibit by contributing their own
travel tips on small towns, roadside attractions, regional foods,
and interesting places to stay. Visit *Road Trip USA* online at:
http://www.moon.com/rdtrip.html

"Essential for travelers who are more interested in finding the real America than the fastest way
from points A to B. Highly recommended."   —*Library Journal*

"For budding myth collectors, I can't think of a better textbook than Moon Publications' cross-
country adventure guide."   —*Los Angeles Times*

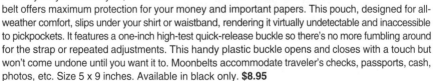

MOONBELT

A new concept in moneybelts. Made
of heavy-duty Cordura nylon, the Moon-
belt offers maximum protection for your money and important papers. This pouch, designed for all-
weather comfort, slips under your shirt or waistband, rendering it virtually undetectable and inaccessible
to pickpockets. It features a one-inch high-test quick-release buckle so there's no more fumbling around
for the strap or repeated adjustments. This handy plastic buckle opens and closes with a touch but
won't come undone until you want it to. Moonbelts accommodate traveler's checks, passports, cash,
photos, etc. Size 5 x 9 inches. Available in black only. **$8.95**

Travel Matters

Smart Reading for the Independent Traveler

Travel Matters is Moon Publications' free newsletter, loaded with specially commissioned travel articles and essays that get at the heart of the travel experience. Every issue includes:

Feature Stories covering a wide array of travel and cultural topics about destinations on and off the beaten path. Past feature stories in *Travel Matters* include Mexican professional wrestling, traveling to the Moon, and why Germans get six weeks vacation and Americans don't.

The Offbeat Path exploring unusual customs and practices from toothfiling ceremonies in Bali to the serving of deep fried bull testicles in a small Colorado bar.

Health Matters, by Dirk Schroeder, author of *Staying Healthy in Asia, Africa, and Latin America,* focusing on the most recent medical findings that affect travelers.

Reviews providing readers with assessments of the latest travel books, videos, multimedia, support materials, and Internet resources.

Travel Q&A, a reader question-and-answer column for travelers written by an international travel agent and world traveler.

To receive a free subscription to *Travel Matters,* call (800) 345-5473, e-mail us at travel@moon.com, or write to us at:

Moon Publications
P.O. Box 3040
Chico, CA 95927-3040

Current and back issues of *Travel Matters* can also be found on our web site at **http://www.moon.com**

Please note: Subscribers who live outside of the United States will be charged $7 per year for shipping and handling.

MOON TRAVEL HANDBOOKS

NORTH AMERICA AND HAWAII

Alaska-Yukon Handbook (0897) $17.95
Alberta and the Northwest Territories Handbook (0463) $17.95
Arizona Traveler's Handbook (0714). $17.95
Atlantic Canada Handbook (0072) $17.95
Big Island of Hawaii Handbook (1001). $15.95
British Columbia Handbook (0145). $15.95
California Handbook (0803) $21.95
Colorado Handbook (0447) $18.95
Georgia Handbook (0390) $17.95
Hawaii Handbook (0005). $19.95
Honolulu-Waikiki Handbook (0587) $14.95
Idaho Handbook (0889). $18.95
Kauai Handbook (0919) $15.95
Maui Handbook (0579) $14.95
Montana Handbook (0498). $17.95
Nevada Handbook (0641) $16.95
New Mexico Handbook (0862). $15.95
New York Handbook (0811) $19.95
Northern California Handbook (3840) $19.95
Oregon Handbook (0102) $16.95
Road Trip USA (0366). $22.50
Southern California Handbook (1028) $19.95
Tennessee Handbook (0439) $17.95
Texas Handbook (0633) $17.95
Utah Handbook (0870) $17.95
Washington Handbook (0455). $19.95
Wisconsin Handbook (0927) $16.95
Wyoming Handbook (0854) $17.95

ASIA AND THE PACIFIC

Australia Handbook (0722) $21.95
Bali Handbook (0730). $19.95
Bangkok Handbook (0595) $13.95
Fiji Islands Handbook (0382) $13.95
Hong Kong Handbook (0560) $15.95
Indonesia Handbook (0625). $25.00
Japan Handbook (3700) $22.50

Micronesia Handbook (0773) $14.95
Nepal Handbook (0412) $18.95
New Zealand Handbook (0331) $19.95
Outback Australia Handbook (0471) $18.95
Pakistan Handbook (0692) $22.50
Philippines Handbook (0048) $17.95
Singapore Handbook (0781) $15.95
Southeast Asia Handbook (0021) $21.95
South Korea Handbook (0749) $19.95
South Pacific Handbook (0404) $22.95
Tahiti-Polynesia Handbook (0374) $13.95
Thailand Handbook (0420) $19.95
Tibet Handbook (3905) $30.00
Vietnam, Cambodia & Laos Handbook (0293) $18.95

MEXICO

Baja Handbook (0528) $15.95
Cabo Handbook (0285) $14.95
Cancún Handbook (0501) $13.95
Central Mexico Handbook (0234) $15.95
Mexico Handbook (0315) $21.95
Northern Mexico Handbook (0226) $16.95
Pacific Mexico Handbook (0978) $17.95
Puerto Vallarta Handbook (0986) $14.95
Yucatán Peninsula Handbook (0242) $15.95

CENTRAL AMERICA AND THE CARIBBEAN

Belize Handbook (0307) $15.95
Caribbean Handbook (0277) $16.95
Costa Rica Handbook (0358) $19.95
Cuba Handbook (0951) $19.95
Dominican Republic Handbook (0900) $16.95
Honduras Handbook (0994) $15.95
Jamaica Handbook (0706) $15.95
Virgin Islands Handbook (0935) $13.95

INTERNATIONAL

Egypt Handbook (3891) $18.95
Moon Handbook (0668) $10.00
Moscow-St. Petersburg Handbook (3913) $13.95
Staying Healthy in Asia, Africa, and Latin America (0269) $11.95
The Practical Nomad (0765) $17.95

www.moon.com

MOON PUBLICATIONS

Welcome to <u>Moon Travel Handbooks</u>, publishers of comprehensive travel guides to <u>North America</u>, <u>Mexico</u>, <u>Central America and the Caribbean</u>, <u>Asia</u>, and the <u>Pacific Islands</u>. We're always on the lookout for new ideas, so please feel free to e-mail any comments and suggestions about these exhibits to <u>travel@moon.com</u>.

If you like Moon Travel Handbooks, you'll enjoy our travel information center on the World Wide Web (WWW), loaded with interactive exhibits designed especially for the Internet.

Our featured exhibit contains the complete text of *Road Trip USA*, a travel guide to the "blue highways" that crisscross America between the interstates, published in paperback in 1996. The WWW version contains a large, scrollable point-and-click imagemap with links to hundreds of original entries; a sophisticated network of links to other major U.S. Internet sites; and a running commentary from our online readers contributing their own travel tips on small towns, roadside attractions, regional foods, and interesting places to stay.

Other attractions on Moon's Web site include:

- Excerpted hypertext adaptations of Moon's bestselling *New Zealand Handbook, Costa Rica Handbook*, and *Big Island of Hawaii Handbook*

- The complete 75-page introduction to *Staying Healthy in Asia, Africa, and Latin America,* as well as the *Trans-Cultural Study Guide,* both coproduced with Volunteers in Asia

- The complete, annotated bibliographies from Moon's Handbooks to Japan, South Korea, Thailand, the Philippines, Indonesia, Australia, and New Zealand

- Current and back issues of Moon's free triannual newsletter, *Travel Matters*

- Updates on the latest titles and editions to join the Moon Travel Handbook series

Come visit us at: **http://www.moon.com**

WHERE TO BUY MOON TRAVEL HANDBOOKS

BOOKSTORES AND LIBRARIES: Moon Travel Handbooks are sold worldwide. Please contact our sales manager for a list of wholesalers and distributors in your area.

TRAVELERS: We would like to have Moon Travel Handbooks available throughout the world. Please ask your bookstore to write or call us for ordering information. If your bookstore will not order our guides for you, please contact us for a free catalog.

> **Moon Publications, Inc.**
> **P.O. Box 3040**
> **Chico, CA 95927-3040 U.S.A.**
> **tel.: (800) 345-5473**
> **fax: (916) 345-6751**
> **e-mail: travel@moon.com**

IMPORTANT ORDERING INFORMATION

PRICES: All prices are subject to change. We always ship the most current edition. We will let you know if there is a price increase on the book you order.

SHIPPING AND HANDLING OPTIONS: Domestic UPS or USPS first class (allow 10 working days for delivery): $3.50 for the first item, 50 cents for each additional item.

EXCEPTIONS: *Tibet Handbook, Mexico Handbook,* and *Indonesia Handbook* shipping $4.50; $1.00 for each additional *Tibet Handbook, Mexico Handbook,* or *Indonesia Handbook.*

Moonbelt shipping is $1.50 for one, 50 cents for each additional belt.

Add $2.00 for same-day handling.

UPS 2nd Day Air or Printed Airmail requires a special quote.

International Surface Bookrate 8-12 weeks delivery: $3.00 for the first item, $1.00 for each additional item. Note: Moon Publications cannot guarantee international surface bookrate shipping. Moon recommends sending international orders via air mail, which requires a special quote.

FOREIGN ORDERS: Orders that originate outside the U.S.A. must be paid for with an international money order, a check in U.S. currency drawn on a major U.S. bank based in the U.S.A., or Visa or MasterCard.

TELEPHONE ORDERS: We accept Visa or MasterCard payments. Minimum order is US$15. Call in your order: (800) 345-5473, 8 a.m.-5 p.m. Pacific standard time.